THE COLLECTED WORKS OF
G. K. CHESTERTON

VI

THE COLLECTED WORKS OF
G. K. CHESTERTON
VI

THE CLUB OF QUEER TRADES

THE NAPOLEON OF NOTTING HILL

THE BALL AND THE CROSS

THE MAN WHO WAS THURSDAY

Compiled and introduced by Denis J. Conlon

IGNATIUS PRESS   SAN FRANCISCO

© 1991 Ignatius Press, San Francisco
All rights reserved
ISBN 0-89870-364-6 (HB)
ISBN 0-89870-365-4 (SB)
Library of Congress catalogue number 85-81511
Printed in the United States of America

CONTENTS

General Editors' Introduction   9

A Note on the Texts   11

A Note on the Notes   13

Introduction   15

Acknowledgments   47

THE CLUB OF QUEER TRADES   49

       Note from the Editor   51
    I   The Tremendous Adventures of Major Brown   52
    II   The Painful Fall of a Great Reputation   84
    III   The Awful Reason of the Vicar's Visit   106
    IV   The Singular Speculation of the House Agent   130
    V   The Noticeable Conduct of Professor Chad   156
    VI   The Eccentric Seclusion of the Old Lady   180

THE NAPOLEON OF NOTTING HILL   215

       BOOK I
    I   Introductory Remarks on the Art of Prophecy   220
    II   The Man in Green   226
    III   The Hill of Humour   242

       BOOK II
    I   The Charter of the Cities   249
    II   The Council of the Provosts   260
    III   Enter a Lunatic   271

       BOOK III
    I   The Mental Condition of Adam Wayne   283
    II   The Remarkable Mr. Turnbull   295
    III   The Experiment of Mr. Buck   304

BOOK IV

   I The Battle of the Lamps   317
  II The Correspondent of the *Court Journal*   328
 III The Great Army of South Kensington   338

BOOK V

   I The Empire of Notting Hill   355
  II The Last Battle   367
 III Two Voices   373

THE BALL AND THE CROSS   381

    I A Discussion Somewhat in the Air   385
   II The Religion of the Stipendiary Magistrate   399
  III Some Old Curiosities   410
  IV A Discussion at Dawn   420
   V The Peacemaker   433
  VI The Other Philosopher   439
 VII The Other Philosopher (Continued)   447
VIII The Village of Grassley-in-the-Hole   451
  IX The Edge of England   460

THE MAN WHO WAS THURSDAY   467

     Foreword   469

   I The Two Poets of Saffron Park   475
  II The Secret of Gabriel Syme   487
 III The Man Who Was Thursday   495
 IV The Tale of a Detective   505
  V The Feast of Fear   515
 VI The Exposure   524
VII The Unaccountable Conduct of
     Professor de Worms   532

VIII	The Professor Explains	541
IX	The Man in Spectacles	552
X	The Duel	567
XI	The Criminals Chase the Police	582
XII	The Earth in Anarchy	590
XIII	The Pursuit of the President	605
XIV	The Six Philosophers	617
XV	The Accuser	628

GENERAL EDITORS' INTRODUCTION

The French critic Las Vargras described G. K. Chesterton the novelist as exuberant. He was not alone in his praise, for G. K. C.'s novels were admired by many of this century's leading men of letters, including J. R. R. Tolkien, C. S. Lewis, W. H. Auden, T. S. Eliot and Kingsley Amis. In *Other Inquisitions*, Jorge Luis Borges described the great storyteller with these words: "Chesterton restrained himself from being Edgar Allan Poe or Franz Kafka, but something in the make-up of his personality leaned toward the nightmarish, something secret and blind and central."

In this volume Dr. Denis J. Conlon introduces Chesterton's first three novels. We are very pleased to include the original illustrations for *The Club of Queer Trades* that appeared in *The Idler's* monthly episodes between June and December 1905. The drawings were etched by G. K. Chesterton and have never appeared in book form. Also, the text used for *The Ball and the Cross* is from the serialized version that appeared in *The Commonwealth, A Christian Social Magazine* from volume 10, number 3, of March 1905, to volume 11, number 11, of November 1906.

Dr. Conlon, a professor of English literature and culture at the University of Antwerp, is a noted Chestertonian. His publications include *G. K. Chesterton: The Critical Judgments, 1900–1937*; *G. K. Chesterton: A Half Century of Views*; and Volume XI of *The Collected Works of G. K. Chesterton*. Dr. Conlon is also editor and compiler of Chesterton's short stories for *The Collected Works*.

GEORGE J. MARLIN
RICHARD P. RABATIN
JOHN L. SWAN
  General Editors

JOSEPH SOBRAN
  Consulting Editor

PATRICIA AZAR
JOE MYSAK
REV. RANDALL PAINE, O.R.C.
  Associate Editors

BARBARA D. MARLIN
  Assistant

A NOTE ON THE TEXTS

The introduction for *The Club of Queer Trades* comes from the June 1904 edition of *The Idler*. It was written by the magazine's editor, Jerome K. Jerome. *The Club of Queer Trades* originally appeared in monthly episodes between June and December 1904 and included illustrations by G. K. Chesterton. The text used in this volume is from the 1960 bound edition published by the English publishing house Darwen Finlayson. The illustrations are not from that edition but are the original etchings by Chesterton that appeared in *The Idler*.

The Napoleon of Notting Hill was published in March 1904 by W. Graham Robertson of London and New York. In this volume the text is from the 1927 Methuen and Company's *Chesterton Omnibus*.

The text for *The Ball and the Cross* comes from the serialized version that appeared in *The Commonwealth, A Christian Social Magazine* from volume 10, number 3, of March 1905, to volume 11, number 11, of November 1906. The episodes appeared regularly every month until February 1906, then in April, June and finally November 1906, when the episode concluded as usual: (to be continued). However, no more episodes appeared. This early version varies slightly in detail from the 1909 version that was published by John Lane of New York.

The Man Who Was Thursday originally appeared in a 1907 pilot edition. In 1908 the same publishers, J. W. Arrowsmith (Bristol) and Simkin Marshall, Hamilton, Kent, and Company, Ltd. (London), brought out the principal first edition. The text used in this volume is from the *Chesterton Omnibus* published in 1927 by Methuen and Company.

A NOTE ON THE NOTES

Chesterton never used footnotes, and he would be surprised and amused that we are propping up some of his pages with these little annotations. We have decided, however, both in deference to G. K. C. and for the training of the reader, to let the vast majority of the pages stand on their own and leave a host of generally familiar names and references unannotated. As a rule, therefore, notes are furnished only for references clearly crucial to the context and of sufficient obscurity to send even the well-educated reader to the encyclopedia, lest the thread of narrative or argument be lost.

INTRODUCTION

By Denis J. Conlon

Gilbert Keith Chesterton was born on May 29, 1874, "of respectable but honest parents . . . on Campden Hill, Kensington; and baptized according to the formularies of the Church of England in the little church of St. George opposite the large Waterworks Tower that dominated that ridge".[1] His father was Edward Chesterton, an estate agent whose family firm still figures largely in the advertizements of the better daily and weekly newspapers; his mother, Marie Louise, née Grosjean, was of mixed French and Scottish ancestry.

The family seems to have had an aversion to funerals and other reminders of death; when Beatrice, the eldest child, died at the age of eight, Edward Chesterton moved his family to a new home at 11 Warwick Gardens on what was then a quiet road some three-quarters of a mile away from Sheffield Terrace, Campden Hill.

Warwick Gardens was to be the permanent family home. The house and the surrounding area always figured in a very warm light in Chesterton's memories, for it was here that he spent his childhood in the company of the neighbors' children and of his brother, Cecil, who was five years his junior: "What was wonderful about childhood is that anything in it was a wonder. It was not merely a world full of miracles; it was a miraculous world. What gives me this shock is almost anything I really recall; not the things I should think most worth recalling . . . this was my real life; the real beginning of what should have been a more real life; a lost experience in the land of the living. It seems to me that when I came out of the house and stood on that hill of houses, where the roads sank steeply towards Holland Park, and terraces of new red houses could look out across a vast hollow and see far away the sparkle of the Crystal Palace (and seeing it was a juvenile sport in those parts), I was subconsciously certain then, as I am consciously certain now, that there was the white and solid road and the worthy beginning of the life of man; and that it is man who afterwards darkens it with dreams or goes astray."

[1] Quotations are from *Collected Works of G. K. Chesterton*, Vol. XVI, *The Autobiography* (San Francisco: Ignatius Press, 1988), unless otherwise stated.

In some ways Gilbert Chesterton was a backward child, not talking until he was three years old and not learning to read until eight. But in the walled garden and numerous box-rooms and odd cubbyholes at 11 Warwick Gardens, Chesterton and his brother, a remarkably grubby boy who kept pet cockroaches, could play cops and robbers, play with their father's toy-theatre, and in the evenings listen to him reading countless stories: "To us he appeared to be indeed the Man with the Golden Key, a magician opening the gates of goblin castles or the sepulchres of dead heroes; and there was no incongruity in calling his lantern a magic-lantern."

Chesterton began school late at Bewsher's School, Colet Court on the Hammersmith Road, a preparatory school grooming boys for entry to St. Paul's. At nine years old he was still clad in a sailor-suit even though he was a lanky boy, towering over his fellows, among whom he seems to have made few friends. He gave the impression of showing little interest in his school-work and was judged to be lazy and somewhat given to day-dreaming. In January 1887, when he was twelve years old, he was transferred across the Hammersmith Road to St. Paul's School and found himself placed in the second form among boys who were two years his junior; even so, he had difficulty in keeping up with them in his work. By now he was six feet tall, incredibly untidy and ill-kempt, and gave all the appearance of being an absent-minded blunderer. In fact the sleepy look and general clumsiness hid the fact that his mind was elsewhere thinking over what he had read, for by now he was a voracious though solitary reader, devouring every book he could lay his hands on but carefully concealing his knowledge from any school-master: "I was being instructed by somebody I did not know, about something I did not want to know. . . . The idea that I had come to school to work was too grotesque to cloud my mind for an instant. . . . We were all hag-ridden with a horror of showing off, which was perhaps the only coherent moral principle we possessed. . . . I can remember running to school in sheer excitement, repeating militant lines of *Marmion* with passionate emphasis and exultation; and then going into class and repeating the same lines in the lifeless manner of a hurdy-gurdy, hoping that there was nothing in my intonation to indicate that I distinguished between the sense of one word and another."

It was his wide reading and unsuspected literary interests that sealed the bond of friendship established in a fight with a fellow pupil, E. C. Bentley, already the inventor of the clerihew and later to be the author of *Trent's Last Case* and a leader writer on the *Daily Telegraph*. Once Bentley had taken up the bumbling fool of the class, he was accepted by the others, and when twelve of them formed a Junior Debating Club, Chesterton, then sixteen years old, was acknowledged as the leader of the group and elected chairman, a position he took very seriously indeed. The J.D.C. held meetings to read papers on literary topics in the homes of the members, thus largely concealing their activities from the masters at St. Paul's. This mask of secrecy was lifted when the J.D.C. printed a magazine, *The Debater*, and hawked it around the school to achieve a circulation of between sixty and a hundred copies. The quality of the contributions was remarkably high when one considers that the magazine was produced by school-boys of fifteen to seventeen. Chesterton contributed either prose or verse to every issue, and he was urged by his friends to offer his poems to magazines outside the school; this he did, and his first success came at the age of seventeen when he had a poem published in *The Speaker*. At about the same time, Chesterton, to everyone's surprise, won the school's Milton Prize for a poem on St. Francis Xavier.

The friendships formed in the J.D.C. were to be life-long, as was the formative influence of the club itself. Together with his fierce arguments with his younger brother, Cecil, the J.D.C. helped Chesterton to develop the debating talents that were later to enable him to indulge in the thrust and parry of public debates with opponents such as George Bernard Shaw: "The man who had got used to arguing with Cecil Chesterton has never since had any reason to fear an argument with anybody."

About this time the High Master of St. Pauls, making a rapid reassessment, described Chesterton as "six foot of genius", but when his fellow pupils took scholarships to Oxford or Cambridge, they left Chesterton behind still undecided on his future career. Eventually, because he showed talent as an artist, he drifted to Calderon's Art

School in North London, transferring after a few months to the Slade School of Art, where he spent three years between 1892 and 1895; he also managed to attend lectures in English literature, some given by A. E. Housman, at University College. It has been said that at the Slade he always seemed to be writing and at University College he was always drawing. However, perhaps he himself gave the best description of what he was up to: "An art school is a place where about three people work with feverish energy and everybody else idles to a degree that I have conceived unattainable by human nature. Moreover, those who work are, I will not say the least intelligent, but, by the very nature of the case, for the moment the most narrow; those whose keen intelligence is for the time narrowed to a strictly technical problem. They do not want to be discursive and philosophical; because the trick they are trying to learn is at once incommunicable and practical; like playing the violin. Thus philosophy is generally left to the idle; and it is generally a very idle philosophy."

At this time Chesterton went through a crisis, perhaps of identity, perhaps of doubt, but certainly of confidence in reality or the appearance of reality. Except for the vacations and the occasional letter in between, he had lost contact with his friends of the J.D.C., and he was also faced with the problem of the physical changes of a very late puberty. His mind was in a turmoil, not helped by the current influences at the Slade, which seem to have been the remnants of art nouveau on the one hand and Impressionism, especially *pointilisme* with its suggestion of the deceptiveness of appearances, on the other. The result was that Chesterton developed an excessively morbid imagination:

> I had thought my way back to thought itself. It is a very dreadful thing to do; for it may lead to thinking that there is nothing but thought. At this time I did not clearly distinguish between dreaming and waking; not only as a mood, but as a metaphysical doubt, I felt as if everything might be a dream. It was as if I had myself projected the universe from within, with its trees and stars; and that is so near to the notion of being God that it is manifestly even nearer to going mad. Yet I was not mad, in any medical or physical sense; I was simply carrying the scepticism of my time as far as it would go. And I soon

found it would go a great deal further than most of the sceptics went. While dull atheists came and explained to me that there was nothing but matter, I listened with a sort of calm horror of detachment, suspecting that there was nothing but mind. . . .

And as with mental, so with moral extremes. There is something truly menacing in the thought of how quickly I could imagine the maddest, when I had never committed the mildest crime. Something may have been due to the atmosphere of the Decadents, and their perpetual hints of the luxurious horrors of paganism; but I am not disposed to dwell much on that defence; I suspect I manufactured most of my morbidities for myself. But anyhow, it is true that there was a time when I had reached that condition of moral anarchy within, in which a man says, in the words of Wilde, that "Atys with the blood-stained knife were better than the thing I am." I have never indeed felt the faintest temptation to the particular madness of Wilde; but I could at this time imagine the worst and wildest disproportions and distortions of more normal passion; the point is that the whole mood was overpowered and oppressed with a sort of congestion of imagination. As Bunyan, in his morbid period, described himself as prompted to utter blasphemies, I had an overpowering impulse to record or draw horrible ideas and images; plunging deeper and deeper as in a blind spiritual suicide. . . .

I think there was a spiritual significance in Impressionism, in connection with this age as the age of scepticism. I mean that it illustrated scepticism in the sense of subjectivism. Its principle was that if all that could be seen of a cow was a white line and a purple shadow, we should only render the line and the shadow; in a sense we should only believe in the line and the shadow, rather than in the cow. In one sense the Impressionist sceptic contradicted the poet who said he had never seen a purple cow. He tended rather to say that he had only seen a purple cow; or rather that he had not seen the cow but only the purple. Whatever may be the merits of this as a method of art; there is obviously something highly subjective and sceptical about it as a method of thought. It naturally lends itself to the metaphysical suggestion that things only exist as we perceive them, or that things do not exist at all. The philosophy of Impressionism is necessarily close to the philosophy of Illusion. And this atmosphere also tended to contribute, however indirectly, to a certain mood of unreality and sterile isolation that settled at this time upon me (pp. 94–96).

This mood may have been influenced by an interest in Spiritualism, and by the current vogue for Madame Blavatsky and various theosophical groups: "What I may call my period of madness coincided with a period of drifting and doing nothing; in which I could not settle down to any regular work. I dabbled in a number of things; and some of them may have had something to do with the psychology of the affair. I would not for a moment suggest it as a cause, far less as an excuse, but it is a contributory fact that among these dabblings in this dubious time, I dabbled in Spiritualism without having even the decision to be a Spiritualist. Indeed I was, in a rather unusual manner, not only detached but indifferent." By the long vacation of 1894 Chesterton seemed to have passed through his crisis and in a letter to E. C. Bently was able to declare:

> Inwardly speaking, I have had a funny time. A meaningless fit of depression, taking the form of certain absurd psychological worries, came upon me, and instead of dismissing it and talking to people, I had it out and went very far into the abysses, indeed. The result was that I found that things, when examined, necessarily *spelt* such a mystically satisfactory state of things, that without getting back to earth, I saw lots that made me certain it is all right. The vision is fading into common day now, and I am glad. The frame of mind was the reverse of gloomy, but it would not do for long.[2]

Chesterton was still a voracious reader and, as the dedicatory verses to *The Man Who Was Thursday* show, he was strongly influenced by Stevenson and Walt Whitman, although he never fully accepted the overwhelming optimism of the latter. Perhaps he kept too strong a memory of the reality of evil and of the devil. His growing acceptance of orthodox morality is attested in the notebooks he kept at the time, and confirmed in *Orthodoxy* and "The Diabolist":

> The man asked me abruptly why I was becoming orthodox. Until he said it, I really had not known that I was; but the moment he had said it I knew it to be literally true. And the process had been so long and full that I answered him at once, out of existing stores of explanation. "I am becoming orthodox", I said, "because I have come, rightly or

[2] Maisie Ward: *Gilbert Keith Chesterton*, chap. 4 (London and New York: Sheed and Ward, 1944).

wrongly, after stretching my brain till it bursts, to the old belief that heresy is worse even than sin. An error is more menacing than a crime, for an error begets crimes".[3]

In 1895, abandoning his hopes of an artistic career, Chesterton set new hopes on a literary one and, leaving the Slade, went to work as a reader for a Mr. Redway, a publisher of Spiritualist literature. At the very least he seems to have enjoyed himself: "The jolliest Spiritualist I ever met, at least until long afterwards, and the psychic enquirer for whom I felt the most immediate sympathy, was a man who firmly believed that he had once got a successful tip for the Derby out of some medium somewhere, and was still pursuing mediums for information of the same kind. I suggested to him that he should purchase *The Pink-'un* and turn it into a paper combining the two interests, and sold at every bookstall under the name of *The Sporting and Spiritual Times.*" This enjoyment extended to the type of work he was required to do: "Redway says, 'We've got too many MSS; read through them, will you, and send back those that are too bad at once.' I go slap through a room full of MSS, criticizing deuced conscientiously, with the result that I post back some years of MSS to addresses, which I should imagine, must be private asylums. . . . Redway says, 'I'm going to give you entire charge of the press department, sending copies to Reviews, etc.' Consequence is, one has to keep an elaborate book and make it tally with other elaborate books, and one has to remember all the magazines that exist and what sort of books they'd crack up. I used to think I hated responsibility: I am positively getting to enjoy it."

Nevertheless, within the year he had left Redway's and moved to Fisher Unwin's, where he was to stay for the next six years, busy reading manuscripts, editing, choosing illustrations, and ghosting other people's books. The young editor was already carrying a sword-stick and gaining a reputation for quaffing beer, but he was also reviewing books for *The Bookman* and soon placed one poem with *The Clarion* and three others with *The Speaker.* Every spare moment was being filled with his writing of a notebook and of first drafts of work that was to be published in later years.

[3] "The Diabolist", *Daily News*, November 9, 1907.

One day in 1896 Chesterton was taken by Lucien Oldershaw, an old friend from the J.D.C., to visit the Blogg family in Bedford Park, "a colony for artists who were almost aliens; a refuge for persecuted poets and painters hiding in their red-brick catacombs or dying behind their red-brick barricades". W. B. Yeats was among many distinguished residents in what was the first garden suburb, but the main attraction for Chesterton and Oldershaw was the three daughters of the Blogg family—Ethel, who had taken Oldershaw's fancy; Gertrude, who was Rudyard Kipling's secretary, and Frances. Chesterton was soon drawn into the debating clubs and literary societies that abounded in Bedford Park, and in return he saw to it that they very soon acquired a strong ex-J.D.C. membership. His philosophical position was growing steadily more orthodox as his means of defending it became more unorthodox, and he found a ready supporter in Frances Blogg, an odd fish in the society of Bedford Park, where her church-going was considered almost an eccentricity:

> She practised gardening; in that curious Cockney culture she would have been quite ready to practise farming; and on the same perverse principle, she actually practised a religion. This was something utterly unaccountable both to me and to the whole fussy culture in which she lived. Any number of people proclaimed religions, chiefly oriental religions, analysed or argued about them; but that anybody could regard religion as a practical thing like gardening was something quite new to me and, to her neighbours, new and incomprehensible (p. 149).

After what can only be called a romantic courtship, and after a great deal of dithering, Chesterton at last proposed marriage to Frances Blogg one day in 1898. At the time he was earning £1.25p. per week with little prospect of more to come, in no position to support a wife, let alone a family, and he could hold out no hopes of providing a house. Both families considered his prospects as being far from good and were understandably less than enthusiastic about the match. The only way by which he could contemplate turning his engagement into marriage was to earn what he could as a writer, and so he began to collect his poems, started to write a verse drama, and by later 1898 had begun a novel. His activity is revealed in the very frequent letters he wrote to his fiancée between December 1898 and September 1899:

The book for Nutt [later *Greybeards at Play*] has reached its worst stage, that of polishing up for the eye of Nutt, instead of merely rejoicing in the eye of God. Do you know this is the only one of the lot about which I am at all worried. . . . To publish a book of my nonsense verses seems to me exactly like summoning the whole of the people of Kensington to see me smoke cigarettes. . . . The collection of more serious poems . . . You shall have a hand in the selection of these when you get back. . . . *The Novel*—which though I have put it aside for the present, yet *has become too much a part of me not to be constantly having chapters written—or rather growing out of the others* . . . (July 11, 1899) *The novel*, after which you so kindly enquire, *is proceeding headlong*. . . . (Sept. 29, 1899) Work till six, take my hat and walking-stick and come home, *write the Novel till 11.*[4]

In fact Gilbert Chesterton was to marry Frances Blogg on June 28, 1901, long before *The Napoleon of Notting Hill* appeared in print on March 22, 1904, and so it is a matter of conjecture as to which novel was the work in progress in 1898–99. Chesterton had been drafting novels since his school-days and in the case of *The Napoleon of Notting Hill* we have his brother's assurance that "The cold fact is that Mr. Chesterton . . . has had the story by him in a more or less developed form since his school-days. . . . Its introductory chapter . . . is a dozen years younger than the book itself."[5] Cecil Chesterton's assertion is confirmed by members of the J.D.C. recalling a school-master at St. Paul's who had an appearance similar to that of Auberon Quin, and that masters at the school did tend to walk in pairs with their frock coat tails swinging in the wind like Barker's and Lambert's did as they were metamorphosed into a pair of dragons.

So was the novel that was being written with such eagerness in 1898–99 *The Napoleon of Notting Hill*? Hardly, if we are to believe that it existed "in a more or less developed form since his school-days", and unlikely, if it needed the Borough Councils Act (1902) and the South African War of 1899–1902 to bring Chesterton to revise what was gathering dust in his notebooks. And yet we do

---

[4] Maisie Ward, op. cit., chap. 6.
[5] Unsigned review by Cecil Chesterton, *Vanity Fair*, April 7, 1904.

know that all his life he was to rework and adapt material he had by him, *Manalive* making use of "The Pistol" story from the 1890s, *The Ball and the Cross* incorporating the theme of *Earthquake Esquire* and *The Flying Inn* including both earlier songs and the gist of the play of the same title. The work in progress could have been *The Ball and the Cross*, as the MacIan/Turnbull controversy reflects many facets of arguments in Bedford Park with Archie MacGregor, W. B. Yeats, and others, but what published evidence there is tends to suggest that Chesterton was in fact writing *The Man Who Was Thursday*, a novel published only in 1907 yet one which, as the dedicatory verses aver, "is a tale of those old fears", the fears that gripped Chesterton during his solipsist nightmare while he was a student at the Slade School of Art and that he partly reveals in his poem "The Mirror of Madmen".[6] In 1896 he had also published "A Picture of Tuesday" in the Slade magazine *The Quarto*, a story to which he refers in his letter to E. C. Bently: "There is that confounded 'Picture of Tuesday' which I have been scribbling at the whole evening, and have at last got it presentable." Presentable it certainly was insofar as one of the basic themes of *The Man Who Was Thursday* was at its center.

How many other draft versions of *The Man Who Was Thursday* sprang from Chesterton's pen we can never know, but one at least survives in fragmentary form in a single sheet which is page 11 of Chesterton's dramatized version, one which is fundamentally different from any episode of the published novel:

(NICKEL *sits down suddenly . . . [several words missing] and weeps.*)

NICKEL: Here snaps the last tie between me and humanity. What shall I do? What shall I do?

SMITH: Oh, if you have pity and a human heart, nothing.

GOGOL: I know you are very clever, Mr. Nickel. But I think you could best help us by — by — by a sort of passive strength. A silent pervasive influence, you know.

NICKEL: (*starting up suddenly*) I have it! I will consult the President. Where is the President?

GOGOL: (*in a hollow voice — pointing to the window*) There is the President.

---

[6] *Collected Poems* (London: Cecil Palmer, 1927), p. 344.

NICKEL: (*stands for a moment staring*) But why does he sit in the front of the window like that?

SMITH: He says that he won't be noticed.

NICKEL: In the front of the window!

SMITH: Well, have you noticed him up to now?

NICKEL: (*suddenly throwing his policeman's helmet on the ground*) No, by God, that's true! He must be a clever fellow. But why does he write up in his window "Charitable contributions received"?

SMITH: Oh, he says he does that so as not to be disturbed.

NICKEL: (*firmly*) He is a great man. I throw myself at his feet. I give in. Perhaps my own ideas were a little crude. (*He steps towards the window*) Mr. President. (*There is no answer*) Mr. President.

GOGOL: Has he gone to sleep?

SMITH: He doesn't seem to take any notice.

NICKEL: (*suddenly and very loud*) What the devil is the matter with his shoulders!

SMITH: (*sharply*) He's always laughing at us. Mr. President! Mr. President!

With one or more completed or very nearly completed novels under his belt, Chesterton then did what he was to do on several occasions during his lifetime:[7] he put them to one side and did something else. There was every reason to do so, for he was newly married, his work at the publishers Fisher Unwin not particularly well paid and he was beginning to make his mark as a poet and as a literary critic. He accepted work as a regular columnist on *The Speaker* and *The Daily News* and resigned from Fisher Unwin, but, finding it hard to make ends meet, he was to some extent at the mercy of the market and had to put aside his novels to concentrate on earning a regular income. In one of his articles[8] for *The Speaker*, he discussed popular literature and revealed an interest in detective

[7] Cf. *Time's Abstract and Brief Chronicle* and *The Return of Don Quixote*, both of which were abandoned in mid-narrative, the latter on two occasions.

[8] "The Value of Detective Stories", part 2 of "The Truth about Popular Literature", *The Speaker*, June 22, 1901.

stories. It must have been about that time that he made the discovery that was to ensure that he would write detective stories for the rest of his life: they could be sold to magazines to produce a source of cash in times of need. He now had the best of both worlds, as he could derive an income from tales of human frailty cast in the form of philosophical mysteries set against the background of those London streets on which he had grown up. He discusses why detective stories are popular in "The Value of Detective Stories" (*The Speaker*, June 22, 1901):

In attempting to reach the genuine psychological reason for the popularity of detective stories, it is necessary to rid ourselves of many mere phrases. It is not true, for example, that the populace prefer bad literature to good, and accept detective stories because they are bad literature. The mere absence of artistic subtlety does not make a book popular. Bradshaw's *Railway Guide* contains few gleams of psychological comedy, yet it is not read aloud uproariously on winter evenings. If detective stories are read with more exuberance than railway guides, it is certainly because they are more artistic. Many good books have fortunately been popular; many bad books, still more fortunately, have been unpopular. A good detective story would probably be even more popular than a bad one. The trouble in this matter is that many people do not realise that there is such a thing as a good detective story; it is to them like speaking of a good devil. To write a story about a burglary is, in their eyes a sort of spiritual manner of committing it. To persons of somewhat weak sensibility this is natural enough; it must be confessed that many detective stories are as full of sensational crime as one of Shakespeare's plays.

There is, however, between a good detective story and a bad detective story as much, or, rather more, difference than there is between a good epic and a bad one. Not only is a detective story a perfectly legitimate form of art, but it has certain definite and real advantages as an agent of the public weal.

The first essential value of the detective story lies in this, that it is the earliest and only form of popular literature in which is expressed some sense of the poetry of modern life. Men lived among mighty mountains and eternal forests for ages before they realised that they were poetical; it may reasonably be inferred that some of our descendants may see the chimney-pots as rich a purple as the mountain-peaks, and find the lamp-posts as old and natural as the trees. Of this realisation of a great city itself as something wild and obvious the detective story is certainly the *Iliad.* No one can have failed to notice that in these stories the hero or the investigator crosses London with something of the loneliness and liberty of a prince in a tale of elfland, that in the course of that incalculable journey the casual omnibus assumes the primal colours of a fairy ship. The lights of the city begin to glow like innumerable goblin eyes, since they are the guardians of some secret, however crude, which the writer knows and the reader does not. Every twist of the road is like a finger pointing to it; every fantastic skyline of chimney-pots seems wildly and derisively signalling the meaning of the mystery.

This realisation of the poetry of London is not a small thing. A city is, properly speaking, more poetic even than a contryside, for while nature is a chaos of unconscious forces, a city is a chaos of conscious ones. The crest of the flower or the pattern of the lichen may or may not be significant symbols. But there is no stone in the street and no brick in the wall that is not actually a deliberate symbol—a message from some man, as much as if it were a telegram or a post card. The narrowest street posseses, in every crook and twist of its intention, the soul of the man who built it, perhaps long in his grave. Every brick has as human a hieroglyph as if it were a graven brick of Babylon; every slate on the roof is as educational a document as if it were a slate covered with addition and subtraction sums. Anything which tends, even under the fantastic form of the minutiae of Sherlock Holmes, to assert this romance of detail in civilisation, to emphasise this unfathomably human character in flints and tiles, is a good thing. It is good that the average man should fall into the habit of looking imaginatively at ten men in the street even if it is only on the chance that the eleventh might be a notorious thief. We may dream, perhaps, that it might be possible to have another and higher romance of London, that men's souls have stranger adventures than their bodies, and that it would be harder and more exciting to hunt their virtues than to hunt their crimes. But since our great authors (with the admirable exception of Stevenson) decline to write of that thrilling mood and moment when the eyes of the great city, like the eyes of a cat, begin to flame in the dark, we must give fair credit to the popular literature which, amid a babble of pedantry and preciosity, declines to regard the present as prosaic or the common as commonplace. Popular art in all ages has been interested in contemporary manners and costume; it dressed the groups around the Crucifixion in the garb of Florentine gentlefolk or Flemish burghers. In the last century it was the custom for distinguished actors to present Macbeth in a powdered wig and ruffles. How far we are ourselves in this age from such conviction of the poetry of our own life and manners may easily be conceived by any one who chooses to imagine a picture of Alfred the Great toasting the cakes dressed in tourist's knickerbockers, or a performance of *Hamlet* in which the prince appeared in a frock-coat, with a crape band round his hat. But this instinct of the age to look back, like Lot's wife, could not go on for ever. A rude, popular literature of the romantic possibilities of the modern city was bound to arise. It has arisen in the popular detective stories, as rough and refreshing as the ballads of Robin Hood.

There is, however, another good work that is done by detective stories. While it is the constant tendency of the Old Adam to rebel against so universal and automatic a thing as civilisation, to preach departure and rebellion, the romance of police activity keeps in some sense before the mind the fact that civilisation itself is the most sensational of departures and the most romantic of rebellions. By dealing with the unsleeping sentinels who guard the outposts of society, it tends to remind us that we live in an armed camp, making war with a chaotic world, and that the criminals, the children of chaos, are nothing but the traitors within our gates. When the detective in a police romance stands alone, and somewhat fatuously fearless amid the knives and fists of a thieves' kitchen, it does certainly serve to make us remember that it is the agent of social justice who is the original and poetic figure, while the burglars and footpads are merely placid old cosmic conservatives, happy in the immemorial respectability of apes and wolves. The romance of the police force is thus the whole romance of man. It is based on the fact that morality is the most dark and daring of conspiracies. It reminds us that the whole noiseless and unnoticeable police management by which we are ruled and protected is only a successful knight-errantry.

Of the evil element in detective stories . . . I shall speak subsequently. For the present it is enough to point out that this form of art, like every form of art down to a comic song, has the whole truth of the universe behind it.

The Chestertonian detective story was always to stand a little apart from those of other writers, for he broke many of the unwritten rules by accepting philosophy and theology as normal ingredients of everyday life and then presenting humdrum normality in such a vivid upside-down way that it appeared to be nothing other than a series of fantastic topsy-turvy mysteries. He also managed to invert whatever influence, and there was some, he had derived from the Sherlock Holmes stories of Arthur Conan Doyle. Chesterton's first detective, Basil Grant, the retired High Court judge, is based more on Mycroft Holmes than on the younger brother, Sherlock, while the Club of Queer Trades is a mirror image of the Diogenes Club, with all the distortions that Alice also found through the looking-glass. Chesterton's narrator, the clubbable Gully Swinburne, and his all too gullible would-be detective, Rupert Grant, play the Watson and Lestrade parts by continually stumbling on mysteries that they misinterpret so grotesquely that Basil Grant is required to come to their rescue. The self-same situation was occasionally implied in the Sherlock Holmes stories but never fully developed; Chesterton takes it and develops it in the fantastic world he creates from everyday London where people are not always what they seem to be. Adventure has entered ordinary life to produce mysteries, and any investigation must be based not on deduction of the facts but on the meaning of the facts and indeed on a feeling for what those facts imply. The outcome is inevitably a clarification of the initial misunderstanding and the revelation that there is neither crime nor criminal, only the plying of his profession by one or other of the members of the Club of Queer Trades. The jovial middle-aged trio involved in running the various members to earth, and indeed the investigations themselves, do not stand too deep a scrutiny of their inconsistencies, but nor do James Bond, Hercule Poirot, and Holmes himself.

The formula was successful, and a quarter of a century later Chesterton was to return to it in *Tales of the Long Bow*, *The Paradoxes of Mr. Pond* and *The Poet and the Lunatics*. Its initial success came when the first of the philosophical detective stories published in 1903 caught the eye of Jerome K. Jerome, author of *Three Men in a Boat* and editor of *The Idler*, who immediately commissioned the

other stories that now make up *The Club of Queer Trades* together
with the forty-four drawings added by Chesterton to illustrate the
adventures. This was to be the last time he illustrated his own work
at such length, although he was employed subsequently as an illustrator by other writers, especially by Hilaire Belloc in the series of
novels now known as the *Chesterbelloc*. To all of them he brought his
not inconsiderable skill with a pencil, but, as was noted at the time,
his style was to be forever rooted in that of the toy-theatre.

By the time *The Club of Queer Trades* appeared in *The Idler*,
Chesterton had also published *Twelve Types* (1902), *Robert Browning*
(1903) and *G. F. Watts* (1904) and was contributing "Time's
Abstract and Brief Chronicle" to the *Fortnightly Review*. He was
overstretched and something had to give; he discontinued his work
for *The Speaker* in September 1904 and "Time's Abstract" ceased
somewhat abruptly in May 1905; in their place came versions of
work set aside in the 1890s but now revised to take some account of
the contemporary situation. The first, published on March 22, 1904,
was *The Napoleon of Notting Hill*. As Cecil Chesterton has revealed,
the outline story dated from the early 1890s, but now his brother
took into account the fight by the Boers in the South African War
of 1899–1902, a war that had earned Gilbert Chesterton the reputation of a "Little Englander", thanks to his support for the Boers. In
addition, he took note of the County Boroughs Act, which osten-
sibly gave new powers to the various locally elected authorities
throughout London, while taking real power away from them and
giving it to a centralized body.

It would seem that Book One of *The Napoleon of Notting Hill*,
consisting of chapters 1, 2 and most of chapter 3, might well have
been written in the early 1890s, but the rest of the book was revised
and adapted before John Lane published it at The Bodley Head in
1904. Chesterton marshalled material that drew on his school-days,
on his personal solipsist crisis while at the Slade School of Art and on
the political position he had taken up in opposition to the South
African War. As usual, Chesterton is quite explicit in his dedicatory
verses that he is really playing war-games in the streets of his
childhood:

I saw the dream; the streets I trod,
The lit straight streets shot out and met
The starry streets that point to God.
This legend of an epic hour
A child I dreamed, and dream it still,
Under the great grey water-tower
That strikes the stars on Campden Hill.

And so we return not just to the early 1890s but to the 1880s when the little boy from Sheffield Terrace looked up at the Campden Hill water-tower and walked nearly every one of the streets of Holland Park and Notting Hill, every one except Pump Street, for that he could walk only in his imagination.

The scenario of the action in *The Napoleon of Notting Hill* is the creation of a fool, perhaps a bloody fool, but in many ways a holy fool, someone completely irresponsible who becomes completely beyond all control when elected absolute monarch in a world eighty years after 1904 and, therefore, the world of 1984.[9] Chesterton takes no account of possible technological developments, leaving such things for H. G. Wells and his ilk, and so his 1984 is little different from 1904 except for one thing, King Auberon Quin's Charter of the Cities. King Auberon's joke, perhaps a sick joke, has created a ridiculous backdrop for his obsession of making all his acquaintances dress up in a monstrous game of charades, but, upon meeting a red-headed little boy in Notting Hill, he encourages the child to love and defend his insalubrious district. Without King Auberon either knowing or intending it, "I am King of the Castle" thereupon ceases to be the game of a child and becomes a mission, for Adam Wayne, with the total solemnity of a child, believes heart and soul and cap-a-pie in the task entrusted to him by the irresponsible King Auberon, and for ever and aye he will defend his Hill of Notting. Like most children, he believes that promises must be kept, and again like most children, he may have a sense of fun but lacks that very adult quality of a sense of humor. Chesterton has defined it:

[9] Cf. George Orwell's novel *1984*. Orwell was familiar with Chesterton's work.

If we take out of the mind of a man an essential human quality, it may often happen that what we leave behind is sometimes like inspiration. A prophet may sometimes be an ordinary man minus an ordinary quality. . . .[10]

For twenty years the boy without a sense of humor will grow to manhood, when he will emerge full of common sense but devoid of common nonsense as Auberon's time-bomb waiting to explode.

Auberon Quin may be a fool, may even be mad nor'-nor'-west, but his proposals that everyone should dress in a manner that reveals his trade, his derivations, and even his personality was one very close to Chesterton's heart. It may seem redolent of the imperial Chinese court, but it prefigures many of the ideas of existentialist thinkers such as Sartre and Camus—you are what you make of yourself and so it is logical that you accept that situation, in Chesterton's opinion, by not only wearing your heart upon your sleeve but also by declaring your identity in the way a medieval knight did by wearing his escutcheon on his tabard. Chesterton's own identity and his very roots on Campden Hill are paraded throughout *The Napoleon of Notting Hill* but so are those aspects of himself that so troubled him in his student years: was it all a dream? Did anything exist outside himself? Was it all a joke? This line of thought seems to have culminated in a split-personality crisis, a schizophrenic dream with which he eventually came to terms by recognizing and accepting it and then rebuilding the various parts of himself back into a single whole. Like Auberon Quin he had bordered on madness; like Adam Wayne he had been a fanatic; like them the logical and illogical spheres of his brain had come apart for a while. Now the situation could be acknowledged in the words of Adam Wayne to Auberon Quin:

We are mad, because we are two lobes of the same brain, and that brain has been cloven in two. And if you ask for the proof of it, it is not hard to find. It is not merely that you, the humorist, have been in these dark days stripped of the joy of gravity. It is not merely that I, the fanatic, have had to grope without humour. It is that though we seem to be opposite in everything, we have been opposite like man

10 "The Great Shawkspear Mystery", *Daily News*, April 15, 1905.

and woman aiming at the same moment at the same practical thing . . . in healthy people there is no war between us.

Oddly enough, Chesterton throughout the whole extent of his career found it difficult to convince many of his readers that when he was at his most serious he would illustrate his arguments with a joke, that solemn kind of hilarious joke akin to the "laughter on the secret face of God".[11] In *The Napoleon of Notting Hill* Chesterton is utterly serious in telling the story of a joke played on an almost cosmic scale, perhaps like the Creation, possibly like the fate of Job, but a joke that in the end man has no choice but to take seriously, for he must accept his lot and fight for justice. The underlying message is that Nicaragua is ridiculous, Notting Hill is ridiculous, and all the cities along with their charters are supremely ridiculous, but Adam Wayne, Buck, Barker, Lambert, et al., and even Auberon Quin, are not ridiculous, for the reason that they have given their lives meaning. Fools or fanatics they might well be, solemnity and levity personified, but they are the two sides of one problem, of the one conflict and ultimately of each human personality. The real adventure is to stand firm and balance the two halves so that they form an integrated whole, and that is in some measure what Gilbert Chesterton did in the 1890s and is in part the story he told in 1904.

Another aspect of that struggle was to be revealed within the year. It is generally forgotten that Chesterton was brought up in a largely freethinking family, that his first encounter with a human being who seriously practised a religion was when he met his future wife, and that, pace Father Brown, he became a convert to Roman Catholicism only in 1922 at the age of forty-eight, when he had only fourteen years to live. It must, therefore, have seemed somewhat odd that in 1905 in *The Commonwealth*, an Anglican magazine and organ of the Christian Social Union, he should begin to publish a serial in which one of the protagonists was a Highland Scottish Roman Catholic, Ewan MacIan, and the other the freethinking Lowland Scottish editor of *The Atheist*, John Turnbull. Once again Chesterton used a frame tale that probably predated the main narrative, this time that of Michael,

---

[11] "The Fish", *Collected Poems*, op. cit.

a Bulgarian monk and his conflict with (Professor) Lucifer, but his main concern was to present the story of two men who held sincere and diametrically opposed beliefs, which they were willing to uphold in all circumstances even unto death in a duel. Both have red hair, though MacIan's red is brighter than Turnbull's, a color code which in Chesterton's works always suggests that the personalities concerned are on the side of the angels; it was also the color of the hair of Archie MacGregor and of Bernard Shaw with both of whom Chesterton enjoyed arguing and debating and with both of whom he would have a life-long friendship based on a deep mutual respect for the beliefs and opinions of each other. This respect for other people's opinions went back to the debates of the J.D.C. at St. Paul's School and to the heated arguments of many a convivial evening in Bedford Park at houses such as the Blogg's and the Yeats', arguments which so often concerned belief and non-belief in many subjects, but which included the opposition of materialism and deism, in Christian terms of *The Ball and the Cross*. It is usually presumed that Chesterton was always an adherent of the Cross, but it is important to remember that his conversion to Anglicanism only came about quite gradually after his meeting Frances Blogg in 1896, and he might well have at times taken up the freethinking position in an argument. He was to think and argue himself into an entirely new philosophical position only then to make the final discovery that it was in fact the orthodoxy of which he was to write in 1908, but that process would take some years. Even then it was to remain Anglo-Catholic orthodoxy for many a long year, and Gilbert was not averse to poking sly fun at his brother Cecil, who had become a Roman Catholic. The secret of success in balancing the two sides of the quarrel between MacIan and Turnbull was that he supported or had supported both their arguments and had fought their battles inside himself. What emerges is an empathy and personal liking between two individuals who find that they have more common ground than they could possibly have imagined, and that stand together in opposition to a series of people who for various reasons of their own wish to bring their quarrel to an end or to pervert it for their own purposes. However, both MacIan and Turnbull are willing to fight for their ideals because they both believe in them and know what they involve, and so when those ideals are perverted each man can recognize that something has gone wrong with his dream and he wakes from what has become a nightmare. Turnbull will reject revolutionary brutality and MacIan will spurn Catholic fascism; Chesterton's description of the dome of St. Paul's Cathedral swathed to make it resemble a papal tiara and surrounded by knights akin to the Swiss and Palatine Guards is written very much by an Anglican with his tongue in his cheek and is a dreadful warning to those of ultramontane persuasion. The narrative of the novel would eventually show MacIan and Turnbull, like D'Artagnan and the Musketeers, putting aside their fight but not their quarrel to unite in a moral cause; as a result they are consigned to a lunatic asylum. However, long before the serial in *The Commonwealth* was to reach that point it was discontinued in mid-story in September 1906. Possibly the guillotine fell because the editorial board of the magazine had tired of the Roman Catholic/Freethinker flavor of the tale, but it seems more likely that once again Chesterton could not manage to fit in the writing or rewriting of the material; instead of appearing in each issue the episodes started to appear only intermittently before in the end no longer appearing at all despite the final one ending with the note: (to be continued). Indeed it was continued but only in the full novel published some years later in 1909–10 in a slightly different format.

Faced, like those creatures in Carroll's *Alice in Wonderland*, with the dilemma expressed in "Will you, won't you join the dance?" Chesterton would eventually opt for MacIan's doctrine but also for Turnbull's command of logic and reason. His sympathies for the other side of the argument are beautifully expressed in the couplet from "Lepanto":

> Men with no right to their right reason,
> Men with good reason to be wrong.[12]

What did the freethinkers think of it all? They loved it, suggesting that Chesterton must really have achieved some measure of impartiality:

[12] "Lepanto", *Collected Poems*, op. cit.

Attired in motley and banging a bladder, Mr. G. K. Chesterton has
for some years haunted the camp fires of the army of Liberty.
Although identified with the enemy, his personality is so jolly, his
quips and cranks so amusing, that he is always a welcome guest. In
return he often displays a quiet fondness for Freethought traditions,
and in his writings his flights of fancy are often barbed with icon-
oclastic points which are as disconcerting to his own side as they are
diverting to Freethinkers. In a recent work, *The Ball and the Cross*,
Mr. Chesterton has introduced an Atheist as one of the principal
characters. Of course, the author "wears his rue with a difference,"
and his Atheist is unlike the traditional iconoclast of orthodox
publications. He is Chestertonian; but we think we recognise some of
the lineaments as being borrowed from life . . . Mr. Chesterton simply cannot keep humanity out of his books. His big, breezy, jolly
nature, refuses to be cribb'd, cabin'd, and confined within the narrow
limits of ecclesiasticism. Let him write what he will, he is always sure
of an audience. He is a licensed jester.[13]

Those attempts at a novel in 1898–99, successful or otherwise we
shall never really know, came at last to fruition in 1907 with the
publication of *The Man Who Was Thursday*, in which Chesterton
takes us once more on a trip to a slightly disguised Bedford Park and
thence on a nightmare journey around his old stamping grounds,
most of which are described with great accuracy of detail, especially
at points where the author seems to be indulging in fantasy. The
party in Saffron (Bedford) Park could well have been held in the
Blogg's garden at 8 Bath Road or in that of the Yeats' at 3 Blenheim
Road, for the meeting and conflict of Syme, poet of order, and
Gregory, poet of anarchy, is yet another stage in the ongoing
dichotomy previously represented by Quin/Wayne, MacIan/Turn-
bull, but now with an added dimension in that they also represent
Gabriel (Syme) versus Lucifer (Lucien Gregory). General Booth said
that the devil should not be allowed to have all the best tunes, but
Chesterton reverses that sentiment by ensuring that Lucien Gregory
at least has a fair hearing; if he appears to be sidelined after his initial
impact, it is because Gabriel Syme, logical poet, philosophical detective

---

[13] "'Minermus': A Licensed Jester", *Freethinker*, October 16, 1910.

dedicated to the extinction of dynamiters and philosophical heretics, does have the advantage of his logical reasoning and can, therefore, appear to be a bigger and better anarchist than the real anarchist, and so is elected in his place to the General Anarchist Council under the code name Thursday. Equipped with the paraphernalia of Chesterton's daily life, Syme/Thursday goes forth to pursue his investigations among the Council of the Days headed by the dreaded Sunday.

It seems a truism to remark that seven days make a week just as it is to say that a week consists of seven days, but it is partly on such truisms that Chesterton based his novel. *The Man Who Was Thursday* is also a profoundly religious novel, in which Chesterton gives some account of how he discovered religion, so it is with some sense of excitement and not a little trepidation that he recounts a semi-autobiographical tale of how he first encountered the Bible and came to terms with the concept of God. To Chesterton, reading and thinking through the Bible story, all was fresh and marvelous and terrrible, be it the Genesis account of Creation over six days, Job's encounter with God in the whirlwind, or Exodus' account of Moses seeing God: "And the Lord said, 'Behold, there is a place by me where you shall stand upon the rock; and while my glory passes by I will put you in a cleft of the rock, and I will cover you with my hand until I have passed by; then I will take away my hand, and you shall see my back; but my face shall not be seen.' "[14] These images stuck hard and in 1904 in his *G. F. Watts* he took up this "most awful and mysterious thing in the universe, it is impossible to speak about it" and did the impossible:

> To walk behind anyone along a lane is a thing that, properly speaking, touches the oldest nerve of awe. Watts has realized this as no one in art or letters has realized it in the whole history of the world: it has made him great. There is one exception to his monopoly of this magnificent craze. Two thousand years before, in the dark scriptures of a nomad people, it had been said that their prophet saw the immense Creator of all things, but only saw Him from behind.

Perhaps it would be as well to begin at the beginning, as Dickens said. Saffron Park is not the start; the start is the dynamite outrage

[14] Exodus 33, 21–23.

that is followed by Syme's thinking of throwing himself from the Thames Embankment into the river and his subsequent recruitment as a detective by the philosophical policeman. Syme wishes to pursue the anarchist dynamiters, so he is all too willing to hunt down philosophical heretics on behalf of the Chief of Detectives, the man in the dark room at Scotland Yard. Is he qualified to do so? Yes, he is told, anyone can be a martyr to a cause. And so Gabriel Syme comes to Saffron Park, presumably to find heretical dynamiters. Find one he does in Lucien Gregory, who appears to be a paler parody of everything an anarchist should be to the extent that nobody can take his anarchism seriously. Stung by Syme's jibes, Gregory, out of hurt vanity, decides to reveal his credentials as a true anarchist to the one man from whom he should keep them concealed. Bound by mutual undertakings of secrecy, binding in 1907 but almost preposterous today, Gregory introduces the logical poet and philosophical detective into the local anarchist lodge, only to find himself outwitted by logic and reason to such a point that Syme is elected to the General Anarchist Council of the Days as Thursday; Syme accordingly goes forth to give battle in a six-day war, on his own in the face of his enemies:

> Make God recall the good days of his youth
> Ere saints had saddened Him,
> When he came back Conqueror of Chaos
> In a six day's war.
>   "The Wild Knight"[15]

Now *The Man Who Was Thursday* is an onion with a great many skins, some still unpeeled, a book that has puzzled many and infuriated some because they could not or would not plumb its depths, a book that both comments on the ideas and trends of its era and investigates problems of human identity. Syme undertakes that investigation first as he meets Monday, secretary of the Council of the Days, then as he leaves the normal human world to climb up to the balcony in Leicester Square, from which he can see Sunday's monstrous back as he addresses his fellow conspirators. He has entered a

[15] *Collected Poems*, op. cit.

nightmare world in becoming Thursday, his fellow poet and would-be Thursday left behind in Saffron Park like an alter ego, and now he must play out his lonely role as an undercover agent. It is at this point that the monstrous Sunday, with a face like the mask of Memnon in the British Museum, levels his accusation that there is a traitor among them. Syme grips his revolver but it is Tuesday, Gogol, who leaps to his feet to acknowledge defiantly that he is a Scotland Yard detective. Syme can breathe again, but is once more isolated; if only he had known that Gogol, that parody of a revolutionary, was really a friend among enemies! Impelled first to flee, he is tailed by Friday, the disgusting nihilist Professor Worms, and harried close to the point of desperation before that individual also reveals that he is a detective. From that moment on it is really no surprise to discover that most of the members of the Council of the Days were policemen, but Chesterton is everywhere strewing clues to more subtle intentions such as: only Syme can start the car; darkness falls as Monday is knocked to the ground. It must all mean something, but what? Syme eventually comes up with an answer when he realizes that six men are going to ask Sunday what they mean.

When Sunday is eventually run, or lets himself be run, to ground he reveals the secret of their identity by dressing them up as the six days of Creation: Monday is Light, so it follows that darkness falls when he is knocked down; Syme is Enlightenment and so he can start the car, and so on. But there is also a deeper parallel imagery in which Syme's nightmare and Chesterton's personal nightmare from the 1890s merge: Syme undergoes his nightmare because he is a fragmented multi-schizoid personality, perhaps blown to smithereens by the dynamiter's bomb or broken up like light in an Impressionist painting. Perhaps he did leave part of himself in Saffron Park, a part that will return only when he has gathered together and come to terms with other parts of himself, when he has put the days together to make a week. He has feared the other days for what they seemed to represent: Monday may be light, lucidity, and clarity, but he also represents seeing things in black and white, and his sardonic, twisted smile implies intellectual doubt; Tuesday may represent the limitless firmament, but he also stands for fanaticism and unreason;

Wednesday represents earth, but also earthy passions hard to control; Thursday, Syme himself, is Man's logical powers of reasoning as represented by the great lights that rule the day and night; Friday represents the monstrousness of the waters, which, like a cold shower can bring despair—a despair that can come from the self-disgust associated with personal appearance; Saturday is animal life, vibrant but often coldly inimical, rational but devoid of perception.

Syme (and Chesterton?) had feared them all, but once they are stripped of their masks, disguises, and dark glasses, they are revealed as friends, for indeed people are not always what they seem. So Gilbert Chesterton in his crisis learned to come to terms with his own doubts, fanaticism, sexuality, reason, despairs, and perception of good and evil, each of which in a fully integrated personality can be viewed as a friend struggling to prevent anarchy. For Syme and his fellow conspirator-detectives, there remains still one piece of the puzzle to slot into place. There is Sunday, arch-anarchist now revealed as that chief officer of law and order, the man in the dark room.

In "How I Found the Superman"[16] Chesterton depicts the Superman as living in a dark room, but he also describes the Superman as a grotesque being. Is Sunday a superman? Is he a sort of proto-Fu Manchu whose tentacles stretch far and wide to subvert politics, business, the police and the forces of anarchy? He is most certainly a larger-than-life figure, topsy-turvy, black and white, good and evil, Alpha and Omega, the beginning and the end, and when the conspirator-detectives go to ask him for an explanation, all he does is give them a good run for their money. That pursuit of Sunday is perplexing in being completely devoid of any point unless one is provided with the key or the clue to the wild goose chase. That is once again to be found in Chesterton's encounter with the Bible, especially what he called its darkest books, Job and Revelation. Job is maltreated, abused and tormented, apparently for no reason, and he demands an explanation and a chance to justify himself. Chesterton has discussed the Book of Job several times and it is there that we can seek some explanation:

[16] *Daily News*, December 5, 1908.

The one thing which would make our agony infamous would be the idea that it was deserved. On the other hand, the doctrine which makes it most endurable is exactly the opposite doctrine, that life is a battle in which the best put their bodies in the front, in which God sends only His holiest into the hail of the arrows of hell. In the book of Job is foreshadowed that better doctrine full of a dark chivalry that he that bore the worst that men can suffer was the best that bore the form of man.

There is one central conception of the book of Job, which literally makes it immortal, which will make it survive our modern time and our modern philosophies as it has survived many better times and many better philosophies. That is the conception that the universe, if it is to be admired, is to be admired for its strangeness and not for its rationality, for its splendid unreason and not for its reason. Job's friends attempt to comfort him with philosophical optimism, like the intellectuals of the eighteenth century. Job tries to comfort himself with philosophical pessimism like the intellectuals of the nineteenth century. But God comforts Job with indecipherable mystery, and for the first time Job is comforted. Eliphaz gives one answer, Job gives another answer, and the question still remains an open wound. God simply refuses to answer, and somehow the question is answered. Job flings at God one riddle, God flings back at Job a hundred riddles, and Job is at peace. He is comforted with conundrums. For the grand and enduring idea in the poem, as suggested above, is that if we are to be reconciled to this great cosmic experience it must be as something divinely strange and divinely violent, a quest, or a conspiracy, or some sacred joke. The last chapters of the colossal monologue of the Almighty are devoted in a style superficially queer enough to the detailed description of two monsters. Behemoth and Leviathan may, or may not be, the hippopotamus and the crocodile. But, whatever they are, they are evidently embodiments of the enormous absurdity of nature. They typify that cosmic trait which anyone may see in the Zoological Gardens, the folly of the Lord, which is wisdom. And in connection with one of them, God is made to utter a splendid satire upon the prim and orderly piety of the vulgar optimist. "Wilt thou play with him as with a bird? Wilt thou bind him for thy maidens?" That is the main message of the book of Job. Whatever this cosmic monster may be, a good animal or a bad animal, he is at least a wild animal and not a tame animal; it is a wild world and not a tame world. ("Leviathan and the Hook", *The Speaker*, September 9, 1905)

The Old Testament idea was . . . what may be called the common-sense idea, that strength is strength, that cunning is cunning, that worldly success is worldly success, and that Jehovah uses these things for His own ultimate purpose, just as He uses natural forces or physical elements. He uses the strength of a hero as He uses that of a Mammoth—without any particular respect for the Mammoth. . . .

. . . Everywhere . . . the Old Testament positively rejoices in the obliteration of man in comparison with the divine purpose. The Book of Job stands definitely alone because the Book of Job definitely asks, "But what is the purpose of God? Is it worth the sacrifice even of our miserable humanity? Of course it is easy enough to wipe out our own paltry wills for the sake of a will that is grander and kinder. But is it grander and kinder? Let God use His tools; let God break His tools. But what is He doing and what are they being broken for?" It is because of this question that we have to attack as a philosophical riddle the riddle of the Book of Job. . . .

When, at the end of the poem, God enters (somewhat abruptly), is struck the sudden and splendid note which makes the thing as great as it is. All the human beings through the story, and Job especially, have been asking questions of God. . . . By a touch truly to be called inspired, when God enters, it is to ask a number more questions on His own account. In this drama of scepticism God Himself takes up the rôle of sceptic. He does what all the great voices defending religion have always done. He does, for instance, what Socrates did. He turns rationalism against itself. He seems to say that if it comes to asking questions, He can ask some questions which will fling down and flatten out all conceivable human questioners. The poet by an exquisite intuition has made God ironically accept a kind of controversial equality with His accusers. He is willing to regard it as if it were a fair intellectual duel: "Gird up now thy loins like a man; for I will demand of thee, and answer thou me." The everlasting adopts an enormous and sardonic humility. He is quite willing to be prosecuted. He only asks for the right which every prosecuted person possesses; He asks to be allowed to cross-examine the witness for the prosecution. And He carries yet further the correctness of the legal parallel. For the first question, essentially speaking, which He asks of Job is the question that any criminal accused by Job would be most entitled to ask. He asks Job who he is. And Job, being a man of candid intellect, takes a little time to consider, and comes to the conclusion that he does not know.

God comes in at the end, not to answer riddles, but to propound them. The other great fact which, taken together with this one, makes the whole work religious instead of merely philosophical, is that other great surprise which makes Job suddenly satisfied with the mere presentation of something impenetrable. Verbally speaking the enigmas of Jehovah seem darker and more desolate than the enigmas of Job; yet Job was comfortless before the speech of Jehovah and is comforted after it. He has been told nothing, but he feels the terrible and tingling atmosphere of something which is too good to be told. The refusal of God to explain His design is itself a burning hint of His design. The riddles of God are more satisfying than the solutions of man.

. . . Of course, it is one of the splendid strokes that God rebukes alike the man who accused, and the men who defended Him; that He knocks down pessimists and optimists with the same hammer. And it is in connection with the mechanical and supercilious comforters of Job that there occurs the still deeper and finer inversion of which I have spoken. The mechanical optimist endeavours to justify the universe avowedly upon the ground that it is a rational and consecutive pattern. He points out that the fine thing about the world is that it can all be explained. That is the one point, if I may put it so, on which God, in return, is explicit to the point of violence. God says, in effect, that if there is one fine thing about the world, as far as men are concerned, it is that it cannot be explained. He insists on the inexplicableness of everything; "Hath the rain a father? . . . Out of whose womb came the ice?" He goes farther, and insists on the positive and palpable unreason of things; "Hast thou sent the rain upon the desert where no man is, and upon the wilderness wherein there is no man?" God will make man see things, if it is only against the black background of nonentity. God will make Job see a startling universe if He can only do it by making Job see an idiotic universe. To startle man God becomes for an instant a blasphemer; one might almost say that God becomes for an instant an atheist. He unrolls before Job a long panorama of created things; the horse, the eagle, the raven, the wild ass, the peacock, the ostrich, the crocodile. He so describes each of them that it sounds like a monster walking in the sun. The whole is a sort of psalm or rhapsody of the sense of wonder. The maker of all things is astonished at the things He has Himself made.

The Book of Job is chiefly remarkable, as I have insisted throughout, for the fact that it does not end in a way that is conventionally satisfactory. Job is not told that his misfortunes were due to his sins or a part of any plan for his improvement. But in the prologue we see Job tormented not because he was the worst of men, but because he was the best. It is the lesson of the whole work that man is most comforted by paradoxes. Here is the very darkest and strangest of the paradoxes; and it is by all human testimony the most reassuring. I need not suggest what a high and strange history awaited this paradox of the best man in the worst fortune. I need not say that in the freest and most philosophical sense there is one Old Testament figure who is truly a type; or say what is pre-figured in the wounds of Job. (Introduction to the Book of Job, 1907)

Sunday runs away and then poses conundrums to his pursuers while he is on the run. A cross between Job's riddling God in the whirlwind and the *Deus absconditus*, he shows off his modern Leviathans, the hansom cab, the omnibus, and the fire-engine, then tiring of riddles displays the oddities of Creation in Regent's Park Zoo before escaping once again on an elephant whose special etymology must have been *Behemoth>mammoth>elephant*, only to take refuge in a balloon that climbs higher than the Great Wheel that blocked out the wheel of stars in Chesterton's boyhood days. When his pursuers catch up with him and the balloon, they have been through thick and thin, rough and smooth, and have some idea of how Job must have felt when he came to ask for an explanation. Like Job, they will not receive one other than to have the mythology of the Days explained by the new clothes offered to replace those in which they have been put to the test, although they will also see Creation revealed when its parts all turn to show their faces instead of their backs at the fancy dress ball held in their honor. One might be forgiven for wondering whether Chesterton had any explanation to give, for he too seemed to find it a problem:

Bernard Shaw suggests that all the active figures in my idle fictions are made as fat as I am; though I cannot recall that any of them are fat at all, except a semi-supernatural monster in a nightmare called *The Man Who Was Thursday*. ("Ego et Shavius Meus", *The Uses of Diversity*)

I have often been asked what I meant by the monstrous pantomime ogre who was called Sunday . . . some have suggested, and in one sense not untruly, that he was meant for a blasphemous version of the Creator. . . . But the point of the whole story is a nightmare of things . . . and the ogre who appears brutal but is also cryptically benevolent is not so much God, in the sense of religion and irreligion, but rather nature as it appears to the pantheist.

The point is that it described . . . a pantomime ogre. This line of logic, or lunacy, led many to infer that this equivocal being was meant for a serious description of the Deity. (*Illustrated London News*, June 13, 1936) People have asked me whom I mean by Sunday. . . . I think you can take him to stand for Nature as distinguished from God. Huge, boisterous, full of vitality, dancing with a hundred legs, bright with the glare of the sun, and at first sight, somewhat regardless of us and our desires. There is a phrase used at the end, spoken by Sunday: "Can ye drink from the cup that I drink of," which seems to mean that Sunday is God. That is the only serious note in the book, the face of Sunday changes, you tear off the mask of Nature and you find God.

Possibly he is the God Chesterton found in the 1890s, far different from the One he worshipped at the time of his death. Perhaps Sunday is "the laughter on the secret face of God", but, if so, that is very close to identifying Sunday with that most flamboyant person of the Trinity, the Holy Ghost. It might be wondered what final part of the puzzle of days would then complete the Week: in a word—Inspiration.

Once that piece of the puzzle is in place, the nightmare is over and Syme returns at dawn to Saffron Park after "a very entertaining evening" to find himself again in the company of the poet Lucian Gregory, the one loose end in the tale. Gregory has been "the real anarchist", the Accuser of the Book of Job, and there is something of a whiff of brimstone about him. Nevertheless,[17] it is as well to recall Chesterton's interest in William Blake in whose *Marriage of Heaven and Hell* there is written: "In the *Book of Job* Milton's Messiah is call'd Satan". So exactly who is taking Gabriel Syme home to breakfast? In Chesterton's solipsist crisis he had been his own worst enemy by tormenting himself, accusing himself of transgressing Saint Michael's battle-cry: "Who is like to God?":

[17] Job 2:1–7.

I dreamed a dream of heaven, white as frost,
The splendid stillness of a living host;
Vast choirs of upturned faces, line o'er line,
Then my blood froze; for every face was mine.

* * *

I cowered like one that in a tower doth bide,
Shut in by mirrors upon every side;
Then I saw, islanded in skies alone
And silent, one that sat upon a throne.

* * *

But as I gazed, a silent worshipper,
Methought the cloud began to faintly stir;
Then I fell flat, and screamed with grovelling head,
"If thou hast any lightning, strike me dead!"

But spare a brow where the clean sunlight fell,
The crown of a new sin that sickens hell.
Let me not look aloft and see mine own
Feature and form upon the Judgment-throne.

Then my dream snapped. . . .

"The Mirror of Madmen"

Perhaps for Syme, as for Chesterton, the best remedy after what has been a nightmare night out is to take oneself home. Especially when, somewhere in Saffron (Bedford) Park, there is a pretty girl waiting.

ACKNOWLEDGMENTS

I should like to acknowledge the help of Mr. J. Ashby of Sealink Harbours; Mr. Tony Brown, senior public relations officer of British Gas (North Thames); Mr. V. Bryant, archivist of Earls Court Ltd.; the local history librarians of Chiswick Library and Ealing Central Library; Mr. R. Fish, librarian of the Zoological Society of London; Mr. John Fisher of the Guildhall Library, London; Mr. R. Gillis of the Archives Department of New Scotland Yard; the Greater London Photograph Library; Mr. R. J. Howes of Thames Water Utilities; Mr. J. D. Duggan, public relations officer of the Isle of Man Steam Packet Company Ltd.; the librarian of the London Gas Museum; the curator of the London Transport Museum; Miss Melanie Rolfe of the Post Office Archives, London; Mr. Brian Curle and Mr. John Hamp of the Royal Borough of Kensington and Chelsea Central Library; the Victorian Society; Mr. Graham Wootten of Telecom Technology Showcase; and the Victoria Library (Archives and Local Studies Department) of the City of Westminister.

I also wish to thank the staffs of the Universitaire Faculteiten Sint Ignatius te Antwerpen (Universiteit Antwerpen) and of the Kent County Library branch in Canterbury for their patience and good will as well as for their assistance. I am particularly indebted to Mr. George J. Marlin, whose happy accident in backing into and knocking over a box of papers apparently belonging to Mrs. Frances Chesterton brought to light the single sheet from Chesterton's dramatised version of *The Man Who Was Thursday*, and to Mr. Aidan Mackey, who informed me of the extra sketches included only in the original version of *The Club of Queer Trades* in *The Idler*, and who has kindly furnished me with copies of the illustrations from the 1905 version and from the first edition of *The Napoleon of Notting Hill.*

THE CLUB OF QUEER TRADES

1904

Illustrations by the Author

Max Beerbohm's "Mr. G. K. Chesterton" from The Idler, *June 1904*

NOTE FROM THE EDITOR

Just a year ago I read in manuscript "The Tremendous Adventures of Major Brown," by Mr. Chesterton, and I knew that if the author could write a series of tales even fifty per cent as good, and let me have them, I should be possessed of a literary gold mine. A year seems a long time to wait, but I have the consolation of knowing that such a series could not be written by anyone else in a century.

I have now five of the stories in hand. Incredible as it may seem, each appears more striking than the one that preceded it. They form the most remarkable set of stories that any magazine has ever been privileged to print since magazines were first published. Their humour is delicious; their ingenuity is marvellous; they are unique, and will always stand alone in the literature of short stories.

The Club of Queer Trades "is an eccentric and Bohemian Club, of which the absolute condition of membership lies in this, that the candidate must have invented the method by which he earns his living. It must be an entirely new trade. The exact definition of this requirement is given in the two principal rules. First, it must not be a mere application or variation of an existing trade. Thus, for instance, the Club would not admit an insurance agent simply because instead of insuring men's furniture against being burnt in a fire, he insured, let us say, their trousers against being torn by a mad dog."

THE EDITOR
[*Jerome K. Jerome*]
THE IDLER

I

THE TREMENDOUS ADVENTURES
OF MAJOR BROWN

Rabelais, or his wild illustrator Gustave Doré, must have had something to do with the designing of the things called flats in England and America. There is something entirely Gargantuan in the idea of economising space by piling houses on top of each other, front doors and all. And in the chaos and complexity of those perpendicular streets anything may dwell or happen, and it is in one of them, I believe, that the inquirer may find the offices of the Club of Queer Trades. It may be thought at the first glance that the name would attract and startle the passer-by, but nothing attracts or startles in these dim immense hives. The passer-by is only looking for his own melancholy destination, the Montenegro Shipping Agency or the London office of the *Rutland Sentinel*,[1] and passes through the twilight passages as one passes through the twilight corridors of a dream. If the Thugs[2] set up a Strangers' Assassination Company in one of the great buildings in Norfolk Street and sent in a mild man in spectacles to answer inquiries, no inquiries would be made. And the Club of Queer Trades reigns in a great edifice hidden like a fossil in a mighty cliff of fossils.

The nature of this society, such as we afterwards discovered it to be, is soon and simply told. It is an eccentric and Bohemian club, of which the absolute condition of membership lies in this, that the candidate must have invented the method by which he earns his living. It must be an entirely new trade. The exact definition of this requirement is given in the two principal rules. First, it must not be a

---

[1] *The Rutland Sentinel* was the county newspaper of what was then the smallest county in England, which was incorporated into the county of Leicestershire in the 1960s.

[2] Thugs were Indian assassins, devotees of the goddess Kali, who disguised themselves as traveling merchants in order to waylay other travelers, whom they strangled for their goods.

mere application or variation of an existing trade. Thus, for instance, the Club would not admit an insurance agent simply because instead of insuring men's furniture against being burnt in a fire, he insured, let us say, their trousers against being torn by a mad dog. The principle (as Sir Bradcock Burnaby-Bradcock, in the extraordinarily eloquent and soaring speech to the Club on the occasion of the question being raised in the Stormby Smith affair, said wittily and keenly) is the same. Secondly, the trade must be a genuine commercial source of income, the support of its inventor. Thus the Club would not receive a man simply because he chose to pass his days collecting broken sardine tins, unless he could drive a roaring trade in them. Professor Chick made that quite clear. And when one remembers what Professor Chick's own new trade was, one doesn't know whether to laugh or cry.

The discovery of this strange society was a curiously refreshing thing; to realise that there were ten new trades in the world was like looking at the first ship or the first plough. It made a man feel what he should feel, that he was still in the childhood of the world. That I should have come at last upon so singular a body was, I may say without vanity, not altogether singular, for I have a mania for belonging to as many societies as possible: I may be said to collect clubs, and I have accumulated a vast and fantastic variety of specimens ever since, in my audacious youth, I collected the Athenaeum.[3] At some future day, perhaps, I may tell tales of some of the other bodies to which I have belonged. I will recount the doings of the Dead Man's Shoes Society (that superficially immoral, but darkly justifiable communion); I will explain the curious origin of the Cat and Christian, the name of which has been so shamefully misinterpreted; and the world shall know at least why the Institute of Typewriters coalesced with the Red Tulip League. Of the Ten Teacups, of couse I dare not say a word. The first of my revelations, at any rate, shall be concerned with the Club of Queer Trades, which, as I have said, was one of this class, one which I was almost bound to come across sooner or later, because of my singular hobby.

[3] The Athenaeum is a gentleman's club on Pall Mall founded in 1824.

The wild youth of the metropolis call me facetiously "The King of Clubs." They also call me "The Cherub," in allusion to the roseate and youthful appearance I have presented in my declining years. I only hope the spirits in the better world have as good dinners as I have. But the finding of the Club of Queer Trades has one very curious thing about it. The most curious thing about it is that it was not discovered by me; it was discovered by my friend Basil Grant, a star-gazer, a mystic, and a man who scarcely stirred out of his attic.

Very few people knew anything of Basil; not because he was in the least unsociable, for if a man out of the street had walked into his rooms he would have kept him talking till morning. Few people knew him, because, like all poets, he could do without them; he welcomed a human face as he might welcome a sudden blend of colour in a sunset; but he no more felt the need of going out to parties than he felt the need of altering the sunset clouds. He lived in a queer and comfortable garret in the roofs of Lambeth. He was surrounded by a chaos of things that were in odd contrast to the slums around him; old fantastic books, swords, armour—the whole dust-hole of romanticism. But his face, amid all these quixotic relics, appeared curiously keen and modern—a powerful, legal face. And no one but I knew who he was.

Long ago as it is, everyone remembers the terrible and grotesque scene that occurred in——, when one of the most acute and forcible of the English judges suddenly went mad on the bench. I had my own view of that occurrence; but about the facts themselves there is no question at all. For some months, indeed for some years, people had detected something curious in the judge's conduct. He seemed to have lost interest in the law, in which he had been beyond expression brilliant and terrible as a K.C., and to be occupied in giving personal and moral advice to the people concerned. He talked more like a priest or a doctor, and a very outspoken one at that. The first thrill was probably given when he said to a man who had attempted a crime of passion: "I sentence you to three years' imprisonment, under the firm, and solemn, and God-given conviction, that what you require is three months at the seaside." He accused criminals from the bench, not so much of their obvious legal crimes, but of things that had never been heard of in a court of justice, monstrous egoism, lack of humour, and morbidity deliberately encouraged. Things came to a head in that celebrated diamond case in which the Prime Minister himself, that brilliant patrician, had to come forward, gracefully and reluctantly, to give evidence against his valet. After the detailed life of the household had been thoroughly exhibited, the judge requested the Premier again to step forward, which he did with quiet dignity. The judge then said, in a sudden, grating voice: "Get a new soul. That thing's not fit for a dog. Get a new soul." All this, of course, in the eyes of the sagacious, was premonitory of that melancholy and farcical day when his wits actually deserted him in open court. It was a libel case between two very eminent and powerful financiers, against both of whom charges of considerable defalcation were brought. The case was long and complex; the advocates were long and eloquent; but at last, after weeks of work and rhetoric, the time came for the great judge to give a summing up; and one of his celebrated masterpieces of lucidity and pulverising logic was eagerly looked for. He had spoken very little during the prolonged affair, and he looked sad and lowering at the end of it. He was silent for a few moments, and then burst into a stentorian song. His remarks (as reported) were as follows:

"O Rowty-owty tiddly-owty
Tiddly-owty tiddly-owty
Highty-ighty tiddly-ighty
Tiddly-ighty ow."

He then retired from public life and took the garret in Lambeth.

I was sitting there one evening, about six o'clock, over a glass of that gorgeous Burgundy which he kept behind a pile of black-letter folios; he was striding about the room, fingering, after a habit of his, one of the great swords in his collection; the red glare of the strong fire struck his square features and his fierce grey hair; his blue eyes were even unusually full of dreams, and he had opened his mouth to speak dreamily, when the door was flung open, and a pale, fiery man, with red hair and a huge furred overcoat, swung himself panting into the room.

"Sorry to bother you, Basil," he gasped. "I took a liberty—made an appointment here with a man—a client—in five minutes—I beg your pardon, sir," and he gave me a bow of apology.

Basil smiled at me. "You didn't know," he said, "that I had a practical brother. This is Rupert Grant, Esquire, who can and does all there is to be done. Just as I was a failure at one thing, he is a success at everything. I remember him as a journalist, a house-agent, a naturalist, an inventor, a publisher, a schoolmaster, a—what are you now, Rupert?"

"I am and have been for some time," said Rupert, with some dignity, "a private detective, and there's my client."

A loud rap at the door had cut him short, and, on permission being given, the door was thrown sharply open and a stout, dapper man walked swiftly into the room, set his silk hat with a clap on the table, and said, "Good evening, gentlemen," with a stress on the last syllable that somehow marked him out as a martinet, military, literary and social. He had a large head streaked with black and grey, and an abrupt black moustache, which gave him a look of fierceness which was contradicted by his sad sea-blue eyes.

Basil immediately said to me, "Let us come into the next room, Gully," and was moving towards the door, but the stranger said:

"Not at all. Friends remain. Assistance possibly."

The moment I heard him speak I remembered who he was, a certain Major Brown I had met years before in Basil's society. I had forgotten altogether the black dandified figure and the large solemn head, but I remembered the peculiar speech, which consisted of only saying about a quarter of each sentence, and that sharply, like the crack of a gun. I do not know, it may have come from giving orders to troops.

Major Brown was a V.C., and an able and distinguished soldier, but he was anything but a warlike person. Like many among the iron men who recovered British India, he was a man with the natural beliefs and tastes of an old maid. In his dress he was dapper and yet demure; in his habits he was precise to the point of the exact adjustment of a tea-cup. One enthusiasm he had, which was of the nature of a religion—the cultivation of pansies. And when he talked

about his collection, his blue eyes glittered like a child's at a new
toy, the eyes that had remained untroubled when the troops were
roaring victory round Roberts at Candahar.

"Well, Major," said Rupert Grant, with a lordly heartiness, flinging himself into a chair, "What is the matter with you?"

"Yellow pansies. Coal cellar. P. G. Northover," said the Major,
with righteous indignation.

We glanced at each other with inquisitiveness. Basil, who had his
eyes shut in his abstracted way, said simply:

"I beg your pardon."

"Fact is. Street, you know, man, pansies. On wall. Death to me.
Something. Preposterous."

We shook our heads gently. Bit by bit, and mainly by the seemingly sleepy assistance of Basil Grant, we pieced together the Major's
fragmentary, but excited narration. It would be infamous to submit
the reader to what we endured; therefore I will tell the story of Major Brown in my own words. But the reader must imagine the
scene. The eyes of Basil closed as in a trance, after his habit, and the
eyes of Rupert and myself getting rounder and rounder as we listened
to one of the most astounding stories in the world, from the lips of
the little man in black, sitting bolt upright in his chair and talking
like a telegram.

Major Brown was, I have said, a successful soldier, but by no
means an enthusiastic one. So far from regretting his retirement on
half-pay, it was with delight that he took a small neat villa, very like
a doll's house, and devoted the rest of his life to pansies and weak
tea. The thought that battles were over when he had once hung up
his sword in the little front hall (along with two patent stew-pots
and a bad water-colour), and betaken himself instead to wielding the
rake in his little sunlit garden, was to him like having come into a
harbour in heaven. He was Dutch-like and precise in his taste in
gardening, and had, perhaps, some tendency to drill his flowers like
soldiers. He was one of those men who are capable of putting four
umbrellas in the stand rather than three, so that two may lean one
way and two another; he saw life like a pattern in a freehand
drawing-book. And assuredly he would not have believed, or even

understood, anyone who had told him that within a few yards of his brick paradise he was destined to be caught in a whirlpool of incredible adventure, such as he had never seen or dreamed of in the horrible jungle, or the heat of battle.

One certain bright and windy afternoon, the Major, attired in his usual faultless manner, had set out for his usual constitutional. In crossing from one great residential thoroughfare to another, he happened to pass along one of those aimless-looking lanes which lie along the back-garden walls of a row of mansions, and which in their empty and discoloured appearance give one an odd sensation as of being behind the scenes of a theatre. But mean and sulky as the scene might be in the eyes of most of us, it was not altogether so in the Major's, for along the coarse gravel footway was coming a thing which was to him what the passing of a religious procession is to a devout person. A large, heavy man, with fish-blue eyes and a ring of irradiating red beard, was pushing before him a barrow, which was ablaze with incomparable flowers. There were splendid specimens of almost every order, but the Major's own favourite pansies predominated. The Major stopped and fell into conversation, and then into bargaining. He treated the man after the manner of collectors and other mad men, that is to say, he carefully and with a sort of anguish selected the best roots from the less excellent, praised some, disparaged others, made a subtle scale ranging from a thrilling worth and rarity to a degraded insignificance, and then bought them all. The man was just pushing off his barrow when he stopped and came close to the Major.

"I'll tell you what, sir," he said. "If you're interested in them things, you just get on to that wall."

"On the wall!" cried the scandalised Major, whose conventional soul quailed within him at the thought of such fantastic trespass.

"Finest show of yellow pansies in England in that there garden, sir," hissed the tempter. "I'll help you up, sir."

How it happened no one will ever know, but that positive enthusiasm of the Major's life triumphed over all its negative traditions, and with an easy leap and swing that showed that he was in no need of physical assistance, he stood on the wall at the end of the strange garden. The second after, the flapping of the frock-coat at his knees made him feel inexpressibly a fool. But the next instant all such trifling sentiments were swallowed up by the most appalling shock of surprise the old soldier had ever felt in all his bold and wandering existence. His eyes fell upon the garden, and there across a large bed in the centre of the lawn was a vast pattern of pansies; they were splendid flowers, but for once it was not their horticultural aspects that Major Brown beheld, for the pansies were arranged in gigantic capital letters so as to form the sentence:

"DEATH TO MAJOR BROWN"

A kindly looking old man, with white whiskers, was watering them.

Brown looked sharply back at the road behind him; the man with the barrow had suddenly vanished. Then he looked again at the lawn with its incredible inscription. Another man might have thought he had gone mad, but Brown did not. When romantic ladies gushed over his V.C. and his military exploits, he sometimes felt himself to be a painfully prosaic person, but by the same token he knew he was incurably sane. Another man, again, might have thought himself a victim of a passing practical joke, but Brown could not easily believe this. He knew from his own quaint learning that the garden arrangement was an elaborate and expensive one; he thought it extravagantly improbable that anyone would pour out money like water for a joke against him. Having no explanation whatever to offer, he admitted the fact to himself, like a clear-headed man, and waited as he would have done in the presence of a man with six legs.

At this moment the stout old man with white whiskers looked up, and the watering can fell from his hand shooting a swirl of water down the gravel path.

"Who on earth are you?" he gasped, trembling violently.

"I am Major Brown," said that individual, who was always cool in the hour of action.

The old man gaped helplessly like some monstrous fish. At last he stammered wildly, "Come down — come down here!"

"At your service," said the Major, and alighted at a bound on the grass beside him, without disarranging his silk hat.

The old man turned his broad back and set off at a sort of waddling run towards the house, followed with swift steps by the Major. His guide led him through the back passage of a gloomy, but gorgeously appointed house, until they reached the door of the front room. Then the old man turned with a face of apoplectic terror dimly showing in the twilight.

"For heaven's sake," he said, "don't mention jackals."

Then he threw open the door, releasing a burst of red lamplight, and ran downstairs with a clatter.

The Major stepped into a rich, glowing room, full of red copper, and peacock and purple hangings, hat in hand. He had the finest manners in the world, and, though mystified, was not in the least embarrassed to see that the only occupant was a lady, sitting by the window, looking out.

"Madam," he said, bowing simply, "I am Major Brown."

"Sit down," said the lady; but she did not turn her head.

She was a graceful, green-clad figure, with fiery red hair and a flavour of Bedford Park.[4] "You have come I suppose," she said mournfully, "To tax me about the hateful title-deeds."

"I have come, madam," he said, "to know what is the matter. To know why my name is written across your garden. Not amicably either."

He spoke grimly, for the thing had hit him. It is impossible to describe the effect produced on the mind by that quiet and sunny garden scene, the frame for a stunning and brutal personality. The evening air was still, and the grass was golden in the place where the little flowers he studied cried to heaven for his blood.

[4] Bedford Park was a so-called "garden suburb" built to the west of Kensington (where Chesterton was born and brought up) and to the north of Chiswick. The locality and houses were taken up by would-be avant-garde writers, such as the poet W. B. Yeats, a group that delighted in the buildings designed by Norman Shaw. At 6 Bath Road lived Frances Blogg (later to become Mrs. G. K. Chesterton), who may well have been the original "graceful green-clad figure with fiery red hair and a flavour of Bedford Park". Bedford Park also appeared in *The Man Who Was Thursday* under the guise of Saffron Park.

"For Heaven's sake don't mention jackals."

"You know I must not turn round," said the lady; "every afternoon till the stroke of six I must keep my face turned to the street."

Some queer and unusual inspiration made the prosaic soldier resolute to accept these outrageous riddles without surprise.

"It is almost six," he said; and even as he spoke the barbaric copper clock upon the wall clanged the first stroke of the hour. At the sixth the lady sprang up and turned on the Major one of the queerest and yet most attractive faces he had ever seen in his life; open, and yet tantalising, the face of an elf.

"That makes the third year I have waited," she cried. "This is an anniversary. The waiting almost makes one wish the frightful thing would happen once and for all."

And even as she spoke, a sudden rending cry broke the stillness. From low down on the pavement of the dim street (it was already twilight) a voice cried out with a raucous and merciless distinctness:

"Major Brown, Major Brown, where does the jackal dwell?"

Brown was decisive and silent in action. He strode to the front door and looked out. There was no sign of life in the blue gloaming of the street, where one or two lamps were beginning to light their lemon sparks. On returning, he found the lady in green trembling.

"It is the end," she cried, with shaking lips; "it may be death for both of us. Whenever — "

But even as she spoke her speech was cloven by another hoarse proclamation from the dark street, again horribly articulate.

"Major Brown, Major Brown, how did the jackal die?"

Brown dashed out of the door and down the steps, but again he was frustrated; there was no figure in sight, and the street was far too long and empty for the shouter to have run away. Even the rational Major was a little shaken as he returned in a certain time to the drawing-room. Scarcely had he done so than the terrific voice came:

"Major Brown, Major Brown, where did — "

Brown was in the street almost at a bound, and he was in time — in time to see something which at first glance froze the blood. The cries appeared to come from a decapitated head resting on the pavement.

The next moment the pale Major understood. It was the head of a

"*The cries appeared to come from a decapitated head resting on the pavement.*"

man thrust through the coal-hole in the street. The next moment, again, it had vanished, and Major Brown turned to the lady. "Where's your coal cellar?" he said, and stepped out into the passage.

She looked at him with wild grey eyes. "You will not go down," she cried, "alone, into the dark hole, with that beast?"

"Is this the way?" replied Brown, and descended the kitchen stairs three at a time. He flung open the door of a black cavity and stepped in, feeling in his pocket for matches. As his right hand was thus occupied, a pair of great slimy hands came out of the darkness, hands clearly belonging to a man of gigantic stature, and seized him by the back of the head. They forced him down, down in the suffocating darkness, a brutal image of destiny. But the Major's head, though upside down, was perfectly clear and intellectual. He gave quietly under the pressure until he had slid down almost to his hands and knees. Then finding the knees of the invisible monster within a foot of him, he simply put out one of his long, bony, and skilful hands, and gripping the leg by a muscle pulled it off the ground and laid the huge living man, with a crash, along the floor. He strove to rise, but Brown was on top like a cat. They rolled over and over. Big as the man was, he had evidently now no desire but to escape; he made sprawls hither and thither to get past the Major to the door, but that tenacious person had him hard by the coat collar and hung with the other hand to a beam. At length there came a strain in holding back this human bull, a strain under which Brown expected his hand to rend and part from the arm. But something else rent and parted; and the dim fat figure of the giant vanished out of the cellar, leaving the torn coat in the Major's hand; the only fruit of his adventure and the only clue to the mystery. For when he went up and out at the front door, the lady, the rich hangings, and the whole equipment of the house had disappeared. It had only bare boards and whitewashed walls.

"The lady was in the conspiracy, of course," said Rupert, nodding. Major Brown turned brick red. "I beg your pardon," he said, "I think not."

Rupert raised his eyebrows and looked at him for a moment, but said nothing. When next he spoke he asked:

"A pair of great slimy hands came out of the darkness and seized him by the back of the head."

"Was there anything in the pockets of the coat?"

"There was sevenpence halfpenny in coppers and a threepenny-bit," said the Major carefully; "there was a cigarette-holder, a piece of string, and this letter," and he laid it on the table.

It ran as follows:

Dear Mr. Plover,
*   I am annoyed to hear that some delay has occurred in the arrangements re Major Brown. Please see that he is attacked as per arrangement to-morrow. The coal-cellar, of course.*
                                    Yours faithfully,
                                        P. G. Northover.

Rupert Grant was leaning forward listening with hawk-like eyes. He cut in:

"Is it dated from anywhere?"

"No—oh, yes!" replied Brown, glancing upon the paper; "14 Tanner's Court, North——"

Rupert sprang up and struck his hands together.

"Then why are we hanging here? Let's get along. Basil, lend me your revolver."

Basil was staring into the embers like a man in a trance; and it was some time before he answered:

"I don't think you'll need it."

"Perhaps not," said Rupert, getting into his fur coat. "One never knows. But going down a dark court to see criminals——"

"Do you think they are criminals?" asked his brother.

Rupert laughed stoutly. "Giving orders to a subordinate to strangle a harmless stranger in a coal-cellar may strike you as a very blameless experiment, but——"

"Do you think they wanted to strangle the Major?" asked Basil, in the same distant and monotonous voice.

"My dear fellow, you've been asleep. Look at the letter."

"I am looking at the letter," said the mad judge calmly; though, as a matter of fact, he was looking at the fire. "I don't think it's the sort of letter one criminal would write to another."

"My dear boy, you are glorious," cried Rupert, turning round, with laughter in his blue bright eyes. "Your methods amaze me.

Why, there *is* the letter. It *is* written, and it does give orders for a crime. You might as well say that the Nelson Column was not at all the sort of thing that was likely to be set up in Trafalgar Square."

Basil Grant shook all over with a sort of silent laughter, but did not otherwise move.

"That's rather good," he said; "but, of course, logic like that's not what is really wanted. It's a question of spiritual atmosphere. It's not a criminal letter."

"It is. It's a matter of fact," cried the other in an agony of reasonableness.

"Facts," murmured Basil, like one mentioning some strange, far-off animals, "how facts obscure the truth. I may be silly — in fact, I'm off my head — but I never could believe in that man — what's his name, in those capital stories? — Sherlock Holmes. Every detail points to something, certainly; but generally to the wrong thing. Facts point in all directions, it seems to me, like the thousands of twigs on a tree. It's only the life of the tree that has unity and goes up — only the green blood that springs, like a fountain, at the stars."

"But what the deuce else can the letter be but criminal?"

"We have eternity to stretch our legs in," replied the mystic. "It can be an infinity of things. I haven't seen any of them — I've only seen the letter. I look at that, and say it's not criminal."

"Then what's the origin of it?"

"I haven't the vaguest idea."

"Then why don't you accept the ordinary explanation?"

Basil continued for a little to glare at the coals, and seemed collecting his thoughts in a humble and even painful way. Then he said:

"Suppose you went out into the moonlight. Suppose you passed through silent, silvery streets and squares until you came into an open and deserted space, set with a few monuments, and you beheld one dressed as a ballet girl dancing in the argent glimmer. And suppose you looked, and saw it was a man disguised. And suppose you looked again, and saw it was Lord Kitchener.[5] What would you think?"

[5] Horatio Herbert Lord Kitchener (1850–1916), 1st Earl of Khartoum and of Broome, was the British Commander in Chief who organized tactics against the Boers' guerrilla campaign (1900–1902) during the South African War. He was created a Field Marshall in 1909.

He paused a moment, and went on:

"You could not adopt the ordinary explanation. The ordinary explanation of putting on singular clothes is that you look nice in them; you would not think that Lord Kitchener dressed up like a ballet girl out of ordinary personal vanity. You would think it much more likely that he inherited a dancing madness from a great grandmother; or had been hypnotised at a séance; or threatened by a secret society with death if he refused the ordeal. With Baden-Powell,[6] say, it might be a bet—but not with Kitchener. I should know all that, because in my public days I knew him quite well. So I know that letter quite well, and criminals quite well. It's not a criminal's letter. It's all atmospheres." And he closed his eyes and passed his hand over his forehead.

Rupert and the Major were regarding him with a mixture of respect and pity. The former said:

"Well, I'm going, anyhow, and shall continue to think—until your spiritual mystery turns up—that a man who sends a note recommending a crime, that is, actually a crime that is actually carried out, at least tentatively, is, in all probability, a little casual in his moral tastes. Can I have that revolver?"

"Certainly," said Basil, getting up. "But I am coming with you." And he flung an old cape or cloak round him, and took a sword-stick from the corner.

"You!" said Rupert, with some surprise, "you scarcely ever leave your hole to look at anything on the face of the earth."

Basil fitted on a formidable old white hat.

"I scarcely ever," he said, with an unconscious and colossal arrogance, "hear of anything on the face of the earth that I do not understand at once, without going to see it."

And he led the way out into the purple night.

We four swung along the flaring Lambeth streets, across Westminster Bridge, and along the Embankment in the direction of that part of Fleet Street which contained Tanner's Court. The erect,

[6] Robert Stevenson Smyth (1857–1941), 1st Baron Baden-Powell, was a British general who held Mafeking during a siege of 217 days until relieved on May 17, 1900. He was later to be the founder of the Boy Scouts movement.

" 'You!' said Rupert . . . 'you scarcely ever leave your hole to look at anything'."

black figure of Major Brown, seen from behind, was a quaint contrast to the hound-like stoop and flapping mantle of young Rupert Grant, who adopted, with childlike delight, all the dramatic poses of the detective of fiction. The finest among his many fine qualities was his boyish appetite for the colour and poetry of London. Basil, who walked behind, with his face turned blindly to the stars, had the look of a somnambulist.

Rupert paused at the corner of Tanner's Court, with a quiver of delight at danger, and gripped Basil's revolver in his great-coat pocket.

"Shall we go in now?" he asked.

"Not get police?" asked Major Brown, glancing sharply up and down the street.

"I am not sure," answered Rupert, knitting his brows. "Of course, it's quite clear, the thing's all crooked. But there are four of us, and——"

"I shouldn't get the police," said Basil in a queer voice. Rupert glanced at him and stared hard.

"Basil," he cried, "you're trembling. What's the matter—are you afraid?"

"Cold, perhaps," said the Major, eyeing him. There was no doubt that he was shaking.

At last, after a few moments' scrutiny, Rupert broke into a curse.

"You're laughing," he cried. "I know that confounded, silent, shaky laugh of yours. What the deuce is the amusement, Basil? Here we are, all four of us, within a yard of a den of ruffians——"

"But I shouldn't call the police," said Basil. "We four heroes are quite equal to a host," and he continued to quake with his mysterious mirth.

Rupert turned with impatience and strode swiftly down the court, the rest of us following. When he reached the door of No. 14 he turned abruptly, the revolver glittering in his hand.

"Stand close," he said in the voice of a commander. "The scoundrel may be attempting an escape at this moment. We must fling open the door and rush in."

The four of us cowered instantly under the archway, rigid, except for the old judge and his convulsion of merriment.

" 'Stand close,' he said . . . 'we must fling open the door and rush in'."

"Now," hissed Rupert Grant, turning his pale face and burning eyes suddenly over his shoulder, "when I say 'Four,' follow me with a rush. If I say 'Hold him,' pin the fellows down, whoever they are. If I say 'Stop,' stop. I shall say that if there are more than three. If they attack us I shall empty my revolver on them. Basil, have your sword-stick ready. Now—one, two, three, four!"

With the sound of the word the door burst open, and we fell into the room like an invasion, only to stop dead.

The room, which was an ordinary and neatly-appointed office, appeared, at the first glance, to be empty. But on a second and more careful glance, we saw seated behind a very large desk with pigeon-holes and drawers of bewildering multiplicity, a small man with a black waxed moustache, and the air of a very average clerk, writing hard. He looked up as we came to a standstill.

"Did you knock?" he asked pleasantly. "I am sorry if I did not hear. What can I do for you?"

There was a doubtful pause, and then, by general consent, the Major himself, the victim of the outrage, stepped forward.

The letter was in his hand, and he looked unusally grim.

"Is your name P. G. Northover?" he asked.

"That is my name," replied the other, smiling.

"I think," said Major Brown, with an increase in the dark glow of his face, "that this letter was written by you." And with a loud clap he struck open the letter on the desk with his clenched fist. The man called Northover looked at it with unaffected interest and merely nodded.

"Well, sir," said the Major, breathing hard, "what about that?"

"What about it, precisely," said the man with the moustache.

"I am Major Brown," said that gentleman sternly.

Northover bowed. "Pleased to meet you, sir. What have you to say to me?"

"Say!" cried the Major, loosing a sudden tempest; "why, I want this confounded thing settled. I want——"

"Certainly, sir," said Northover, jumping up with a slight elevation of the eyebrows. "Will you take a chair for a moment." And he pressed an electric bell just above him, which thrilled and tinkled in a room beyond. The Major put his hand on the back of the chair offered him, but stood chafing and beating the floor with his polished boot.

The next moment an inner glass door was opened, and a fair, weedy, young man, in a frock-coat, entered from within.

"Mr. Hopson," said Northover, "this is Major Brown. Will you please finish that thing for him I gave you this morning and bring it in?"

"Yes, sir," said Mr. Hopson, and vanished like lightning.

"You will excuse me, gentlemen," said the egregious Northover, with his radiant smile, "if I continue to work until Mr. Hopson is ready. I have some books that must be cleared up before I get away on my holiday to-morrow. And we all like a whiff of the country, don't we? Ha! Ha!"

The criminal took up his pen with a childlike laugh, and a silence ensued; a placid and busy silence on the part of Mr. P. G. Northover; a raging silence on the part of everybody else.

At length the scratching of Northover's pen in the stillness was mingled with a knock at the door, almost simultaneous with the turning of the handle, and Mr. Hopson came in again with the same silent rapidity, placed a paper before his principal, and disappeared again.

The man at the desk pulled and twisted his spiky moustache for a few moment as he ran his eye up and down the paper presented to him. He took up his pen, with a slight, instantaneous frown, and altered something, muttering—"Careless." Then he read it again with the same impenetrable reflectiveness, and finally handed it to the frantic Brown, whose hand was beating the devil's tattoo on the back of the chair.

"I think you will find that all right, Major," he said briefly.

The Major looked at it; whether he found it all right or not will appear later, but he found it like this:

Major Brown to P. G. Northover.

	£	s.	d.
January 1, to account rendered	5	6	0
May 9, to potting and embedding of 200 pansies . . .	2	0	0
To cost of trolley with flowers	0	15	0
To hiring of man with trolley	0	5	0

To hire of house and garden for one day	1	0	0
To furnishing of room in peacock curtains,			
copper ornaments, etc.	3	0	0
To salary of Miss Jameson	1	0	0
To salary of Mr. Plover	1	0	0

Total   £14   6   0

A remittance will oblige.

"What," said Brown, after a dead pause, and with eyes that seemed slowly rising out of his head, "what in heaven's name is this?"

"What is it?" repeated Northover, cocking his eyebrow with amusement. "It's your account, of course."

"My account!" The Major's ideas appeared to be in a vague stampede. "My account! And what have I got to do with it?"

"Well," said Northover, laughing outright, "naturally I prefer you to pay it."

The Major's hand was still resting on the back of the chair as the words came. He scarcely stirred otherwise, but he lifted the chair bodily into the air with one hand and hurled it at Northover's head.

The legs crashed against the desk, so that Northover only got a blow on the elbow as he sprang up with clenched fists, only to be seized by the united rush of the rest of us. The chair had fallen clattering on the empty floor.

"Let me go, you scamps," he shouted. "Let me——"

"Stand still," cried Rupert authoritatively. "Major Brown's action is excusable. The abominable crime you have attempted——"

"A customer has a perfect right," said Northover hotly, "to question an alleged overcharge, but, confound it all, not to throw furniture."

"What, in God's name, do you mean by your customers and overcharges?" shrieked Major Brown, whose keen feminine nature, steady in pain or danger, became almost hysterical in the presence of a long and exasperating mystery. "Who are you? I've never seen you or your insolent tomfool bills. I know one of your cursed brutes tried to choke me——"

"Mad," said Northover, gazing blankly round; "all of them mad. I didn't know they travelled in quartettes."

" 'My account! And what have I got to do with it?' "

"Enough of this prevarication," said Rupert; "your crimes are discovered. A policeman is stationed at the corner of the court. Though only a private detective myself, I will take the responsibility of telling you that anything you say——"

"Mad," repeated Northover, with a weary air.

And at this moment, for the first time, there struck in among them the strange, sleepy voice of Basil Grant.

"Major Brown," he said, "may I ask you a question?"

The Major turned his head with an increased bewilderment.

"You?" he cried; "certainly, Mr. Grant."

"Can you tell me," said the mystic, with sunken head and lowering brow, as he traced a pattern in the dust with his sword-stick, "can you tell me what was the name of the man who lived in your house before you?"

The unhappy Major was only faintly more disturbed by this last and futile irrelevancy, and he answered vaguely:

"Yes, I think so; a man named Gurney something—a name with a hyphen—Gurney-Brown; that was it."

"And when did the house change hands?" said Basil, looking up sharply. His strange eyes were burning brilliantly.

"I came in last month," said the Major.

And at the mere word the criminal Northover suddenly fell into his great office chair and shouted with a volleying laughter.

"Oh! it's too perfect—it's too exquisite," he gasped, beating the arms with his fists. He was laughing deafeningly; Basil Grant was laughing voicelessly; and the rest of us only felt that our heads were like weathercocks in a whirlwind.

"Confound it, Basil," said Rupert, stamping. "If you don't want me to go mad and blow your metaphysical brains out, tell me what all this means."

Northover rose.

"Permit me, sir, to explain," he said. "And, first of all, permit me to apologise to you, Major Brown, for a most abominable and unpardonable blunder, which has caused you menace and inconvenience, in which, if you will allow me to say so, you have behaved with astonishing courage and dignity. Of course you need not trouble about the bill. We will stand the loss." And, tearing the paper across, he flung the halves into the waste-paper basket and bowed.

Poor Brown's face was still a picture of distraction. "But I don't even begin to understand," he cried. "What bill? what blunder? what loss?"

Mr. P. G. Northover advanced in the centre of the room, thoughtfully, and with a great deal of unconscious dignity. On closer consideration, there were apparent about him other things beside a screwed moustache, especially a lean, sallow face, hawk-like, and not without a careworn intelligence. Then he looked up abruptly.

"Do you know where you are, Major?" he said.

"God knows I don't" said the warrior, with fervour.

"You are standing," replied Northover, "in the office of the Adventure and Romance Agency, Limited."

"And what's that?" blankly inquired Brown.

The man of business leaned over the back of the chair, and fixed his dark eyes on the other's face.

"Major," said he, "did you ever, as you walked along the empty street upon some idle afternoon, feel the utter hunger for something to happen — something, in the splendid words of Walt Whitman: 'Something pernicious and dread; something far removed from a puny and pious life; something unproved; something in a trance; something loosed from its anchorage, and driving free.' Did you ever feel that?"

"Certainly not," said the Major shortly.

"Then I must explain with more elaboration," said Mr. Northover, with a sigh. "The Adventure and Romance Agency has been started to meet a great modern desire. On every side, in conversation and in literature, we hear of the desire for a larger theatre of events — for something to waylay us and lead us splendidly astray. Now the man who feels this desire for a varied life pays a yearly or a quarterly sum to the Adventure and Romance Agency; in return, the Adventure and Romance Agency undertakes to surround him with startling and weird events. As a man is leaving his front door, an excited sweep approaches him and assures him of a plot against his life; he gets into a cab, and is driven to an opium den; he receives

" 'Do you know where you are, Major?' "

a mysterious telegram or a dramatic visit, and is immediately in a vortex of incidents. A very picturesque and moving story is first written by one of the staff of distinguished novelists who are at present hard at work in the adjoining room. Yours, Major Brown (designed by our Mr. Grigsby), I consider peculiarly forcible and pointed; it is almost a pity you did not see the end of it. I need scarcely explain further the monstrous mistake. Your predecessor in your present house, Mr. Gurney-Brown, was a subscriber to our agency, and our foolish clerks, ignoring alike the dignity of the hyphen and the glory of military rank, positively imagined that Major Brown and Mr. Gurney-Brown were the same person. Thus you were suddenly hurled into the middle of another man's story."

"How on earth does the thing work?" asked Rupert Grant, with bright and fascinated eyes.

"We believe that we are doing a noble work," said Northover warmly. "It has continually struck us that there is no element in modern life that is more lamentable than the fact that the modern man has to seek all artistic existence in a sedentary state. If he wishes to float into fairyland, he reads a book; if he wishes to dash into the thick of battle, he reads a book; if he wishes to soar into heaven, he reads a book; if he wishes to slide down the banisters, he reads a book. We give him these visions, but we give him exercise at the same time, the necessity of leaping from wall to wall, of fighting strange gentlemen, of running down long streets from pursuers — all healthy and pleasant exercises. We give him a glimpse of that great morning world of Robin Hood or the Knights Errant, when one great game was played under the splendid sky. We give him back his childhood, that godlike time when we can act stories, be our own heroes, and at the same instant dance and dream."

Basil gazed at him curiously. The most singular psychological discovery had been reserved to the end, for as the little business man ceased speaking he had the blazing eyes of a fanatic.

Major Brown received the explanation with complete simplicity and good humour.

"Of course; awfully dense, sir," he said. "No doubt at all, the scheme excellent. But I don't think——" He paused a moment, and

" 'No doubt at all, the scheme excellent. But I don't think . . . I don't think you will find me in it.' "

looked dreamily out of the window. "I don't think you will find me in it. Somehow, when one's seen — seen the thing itself, you know — blood and men screaming, one feels about having a little house and a little hobby; in the Bible, you know, 'There remaineth a rest.'"

Northover bowed. Then after a pause he said:

"Gentlemen, may I offer you my card. If any of the rest of you desire, at any time, to communicate with me, despite Major Brown's view of the matter——"

"I should be obliged for your card, sir," said the Major, in his abrupt but courteous voice. "Pay for chair."

The agent of Romance and Adventure handed his card, laughing.

It ran, "P. G. Northover, B.A., C.Q.T. Adventure and Romance Agency, 14 Tanner's Court, Fleet Street."

"What on earth is 'C.Q.T.'?" asked Rupert Grant, looking over the Major's shoulder.

"Don't you know?" returned Northover. "Haven't you ever heard of the Club of Queer Trades?"

"There seems to be a confounded lot of funny things we haven't heard of," said the little Major reflectively. "What's this one?"

"The Club of Queer Trades is a society consisting exclusively of people who have invented some new and curious way of making money. I was one of the earliest members."

"You deserve to be," said Basil, taking up his great white hat, with a smile, and speaking for the last time that evening.

When they had passed out the Adventure and Romance agent wore a queer smile, as he trod down the fire and locked up his desk. "A fine chap, that Major; when one hasn't a touch of the poet one stands some chance of being a poem. But to think of such a clockwork little creature of all people getting into the nets of one of Grigsby's tales," and he laughed out aloud in the silence.

Just as the laugh echoed away, there came a sharp knock at the door. An owlish head, with dark moustaches, was thrust in, with deprecating and somewhat absurd inquiry.

"What! back again, Major?" cried Northover in surprise. "What can I do for you?"

The Major shuffled feverishly into the room.

"It's horribly absurd," he said. "Something must have got started in me that I never knew before. But upon my soul I feel the most desperate desire to know the end of it all."

"The end of it all?"

"Yes," said the Major. " 'Jackals,' and the title-deeds, and 'Death to Major Brown.' "

The agent's face grew grave, but his eyes were amused.

"I am terribly sorry, Major," said he, "but what you ask is impossible. I don't know anyone I would sooner oblige than you; but the rules of the agency are strict. The Adventures are confidential; you are an outsider; I am not allowed to let you know an inch more than I can help. I do hope you understand——"

"There is no one," said Brown, "who understands discipline better than I do. Thank you very much. Good-night."

And the little man withdrew for the last time.

He married Miss Jameson, the lady with the red hair and the green garments. She was an actress, employed (with many others) by the Romance Agency; and her marriage with the prim old veteran caused some stir in her languid and intellectualised set. She always replied very quietly that she had met scores of men who acted splendidly in the charades provided for them by Northover, but that she had only met one man who went down into a coal-cellar when he really thought it contained a murderer.

The Major and she are living as happily as birds, in an absurd villa, and the former has taken to smoking. Otherwise he is unchanged —except, perhaps, there are moments when, alert and full of feminine unselfishness as the Major is by nature, he falls into a trance of abstraction. Then his wife recognises with a concealed smile, by the blind look in his blue eyes, that he is wondering what were the title-deeds, and why he was not allowed to mention jackals. But, like so many old soldiers, Brown is religious, and believes that he will realise the rest of those purple adventures in a better world.

II

THE PAINFUL FALL OF A GREAT
REPUTATION

Basil Grant and I were talking one day in what is perhaps the most perfect place for talking on earth—the top of a tolerably deserted tramcar. To talk on the top of a hill is superb, but to talk on the top of a flying hill is a fairy tale.

The vast blank space of North London was flying by; the very pace gave us a sense of its immensity and its meanness. It was, as it were, a base infinitude, a squalid eternity, and we felt the real horror of the poor parts of London, the horror that is so totally missed and misrepresented by the sensational novelists who depict it as being a matter of narrow streets, filthy houses, criminals and maniacs, and dens of vice. In a narrow street, in a den of vice, you do not expect civilisation, you do not expect order. But the horror of this was the fact that there was civilisation, that there was order, but that civilisation only showed its morbidity, and order only its monotony. No one would say, in going through a criminal slum, "I see no statues. I notice no cathedrals." But here there were public buildings; only they were mostly lunatic asylums. Here there were statues; only they were mostly statues of railway engineers and philanthropists—two dingy classes of men united by their common contempt for the people. Here there were churches; only they were the churches of dim and erratic sects, Agapemonites or Irvingites. Here, above all, there were broad roads and vast crossings and tramway lines and hospitals and all the real marks of civilisation. But though one never knew, in one sense, what one would see next, there was one thing we knew we should not see—anything really great, central, of the first class, anything that humanity had adored. And with revulsion indescribable our emotions returned, I think, to those really close and crooked entries, to those really mean streets, to those genuine slums which lie round the Thames and the City, in which nevertheless a real possibility remains that at any chance corner

" 'There is the wickedest man in London.' "

the great cross of the great cathedral of Wren may strike down the street like a thunderbolt.

"But you must always remember also," said Grant to me, in his heavy abstracted way, when I had urged this view, "That the very vileness of the life of these ordered plebeian places bears witness to the victory of the human soul. I agree with you. I agree that they have to live in something worse than barbarism. They have to live in a fourth-rate civilisation. But yet I am practically certain that the majority of people here are good people. And being good is an adventure far more violent and daring than sailing round the world. Besides——"

"Go on," I said.

No answer came.

"Go on," I said, looking up.

The big blue eyes of Basil Grant were standing out of his head and he was paying no attention to me. He was staring over the side of the tram.

"What is the matter?" I asked, peering over also.

"It is very odd," said Grant at last, grimly, "that I should have been caught out like this at the very moment of my optimism. I said all these people were good, and there is the wickedest man in London."

"Where?" I asked, leaning over further, "where?"

"Oh, I was right enough," he went on, in that strange continuous and sleepy tone which always angered his hearers at acute moments. "I was right enough when I said all these people were good. They are heroes; they are saints. Now and then they may perhaps steal a spoon or two; they may beat a wife or two with the poker. But they are saints all the same; they are angels; they are robed in white; they are clad with wings and haloes—at any rate compared to that man."

"Which man?" I cried again, and then my eye caught the figure at which Basil's bull's eyes were glaring.

He was a slim, smooth person, passing very quickly among the quickly passing crowd, but though there was nothing about him sufficient to attract a startled notice, there was quite enough to demand a curious consideration when once that notice was attracted.

He wore a black top-hat, but there was enough in it of those strange curves whereby the decadent artist of the eighties tried to turn the top-hat into something as rhythmic as an Etruscan vase. His hair, which was largely grey, was curled with the instinct of one who appreciated the gradual beauty of grey and silver. The rest of his face was oval and, I thought, rather Oriental; he had two black tufts of moustache.

"What has he done?" I asked.

"I am not sure of the details," said Grant, "but his besetting sin is a desire to intrigue to the disadvantage of others. Probably he has adopted some imposture or other to effect his plan."

"What plan?" I asked. "If you know all about him, why don't you tell me why he is the wickedest man in England? What is his name?"

Basil Grant stared at me for some moments.

"I think you've made a mistake in my meaning," he said. "I don't know his name. I never saw him before in my life."

"Never saw him before!" I cried, with a kind of anger; "then what in heaven's name do you mean by saying that he is the wickedest man in England?"

"I meant what I said," said Basil Grant calmly. "The moment I saw that man, I saw all these people stricken with a sudden and splendid innocence. I saw that while all ordinary poor men in the streets were being themselves, he was not being himself. I saw that all the men in these slums, cadgers, pickpockets, hooligans, are all, in the deepest sense, trying to be good. And I saw that that man was trying to be evil."

"But if you never saw him before——" I began.

"In God's name, look at his face," cried out Basil in a voice that startled the driver. "Look at the eyebrows. They mean that infernal pride which made Satan so proud that he sneered even at heaven when he was one of the first angels in it. Look at his moustaches, they are so grown as to insult humanity. In the name of the sacred heavens look at his hair. In the name of God and the stars, look at his hat."

I stirred uncomfortably.

"But, after all," I said, "this is very fanciful—perfectly absurd.

" 'Why don't you tell me why he is the wickedest man in England?' "

Look at the mere facts. You have never seen the man before, you——"

"Oh, the mere facts," he cried out in a kind of despair. "The mere facts! Do you really admit—are you still so sunk in superstitions, so clinging to dim and prehistoric altars, that you believe in facts? Do you not trust an immediate impression?"

"Well, an immediate impression may be," I said, "a little less practical than facts."

"Bosh," he said. "On what else is the whole world run but immediate impressions? What is more practical? My friend, the philosophy of this world may be founded on facts, its business is run on spiritual impressions and atmospheres. Why do you refuse or accept a clerk? Do you measure his skull? Do you read up his physiological state in a handbook? Do you go upon facts at all? Not a scrap. You accept a clerk who may save your business—you refuse a clerk that may rob your till, entirely upon those immediate mystical impressions under the pressure of which I pronounce, with a perfect sense of certainty and sincerity, that that man walking in that street beside us is a humbug and a villain of some kind."

"You always put things well," I said, "but, of course, such things cannot immediately be put to the test."

Basil sprang up straight and swayed with the swaying car.

"Let us get off and follow him," he said. "I bet you five pounds it will turn out as I say."

And with a scuttle, a jump, and a run, we were off the car.

The man with the curved silver hair and the curved Eastern face walked along for some time, his long splendid frock-coat flying behind him. Then he swung sharply out of the great glaring road and disappeared down an ill-lit alley. We swung silently after him.

"This is an odd turning for a man of that kind to take," I said.

"A man of what kind?" asked my friend.

"Well," I said, "a man with that kind of expression and those boots. I thought it rather odd, to tell the truth, that he should be in this part of the world at all."

"Ah, yes," said Basil, and said no more.

We tramped on, looking steadily in front of us. The elegant

figure, like the figure of a black swan, was silhouetted suddenly against the glare of intermittent gas-light and then swallowed again in night. The intervals between the lights were long, and a fog was thickening the whole city. Our pace, therefore, had become swift and mechanical between the lamp-posts; but Basil came to a standstill suddenly like a reined horse; I stopped also. We had almost run into the man. A great part of the solid darkness in front of us was the darkness of his body.

At first I thought he had turned to face us. But though we were hardly a yard off he did not realise that we were there. He tapped four times on a very low and dirty door in the dark, crabbed street. A gleam of gas cut the darkness as it opened slowly. We listened intently, but the interview was short and simple and inexplicable as an interview could be. Our exquisite friend handed in what looked like a paper or a card and said:

"At once. Take a cab."

A heavy, deep voice from inside said:

"Right you are."

And with a click we were in the blackness again, and striding after the striding stranger through a labyrinth of London lanes, the lights just helping us. It was only five o'clock, but winter and the fog had made it like midnight.

"This is really an extraordinary walk for the patent-leather boots," I repeated.

"I don't know," said Basil humbly. "It leads to Berkeley Square."

As I tramped on I strained my eyes through the dusky atmosphere and tried to make out the direction described. For some ten minutes I wondered and doubted; at the end of that I saw that my friend was right. We were coming to the great dreary spaces of fashionable London—more dreary, one must admit, even than the dreary plebeian spaces.

"This is very extraordinary!" said Basil Grant, as we turned into Berkeley Square.

"What is extraordinary?" I asked. "I thought you said it was quite natural."

"I do not wonder," answered Basil, "at his walking through nasty

"Our exquisite friend handed in what looked like a paper."

streets; I do not wonder at his going to Berkeley Square. But I do wonder at his going to the house of a very good man."

"What very good man?" I asked with exasperation.

"The operation of time is a singular one," he said with his imperturbable irrelevancy. "It is not a true statement of the case to say that I have forgotten my career when I was a judge and a public man. I remember it all vividly, but it is like remembering some novel. But fifteen years ago I knew this square as well as Lord Rosebery[7] does, and a confounded long sight better than that man who is going up the steps of old Beaumont's house."

"Who is old Beaumont?" I asked irritably.

"A perfectly good fellow. Lord Beaumont of Foxwood—don't you know his name? He is a man of transparent sincerity, a nobleman who does more work than a navvy, a socialist, an anarchist, I don't know what; anyhow, he's a philosopher and philanthropist. I admit he has the slight disadvantage of being, beyond all question, off his head. He has that real disadvantage which has arisen out of the modern worship of progress and novelty; and he thinks anything odd and new must be an advance. If you went to him and proposed to eat your grandmother, he would agree with you, so long as you put it on hygienic and public grounds, as a cheap alternative to cremation. So long as you progress fast enough it seems a matter of indifference to him whether you are progressing to the stars or the devil. So his house is filled with an endless succession of literary and political fashions; men who wear long hair because it is romantic; men who wear short hair because it is medical; men who walk on their feet only to exercise their hands; and men who walk on their hands for fear of tiring their feet. But though the inhabitants of his *salons* are generally fools, like himself, they are almost always, like himself, good men. I am really surprised to see a criminal enter there."

"My good fellow," I said firmly, striking my foot on the pavement, "the truth of this affair is very simple. To use your own eloquent language, you have the 'slight disadvantage' of being off *your* head. You see a total stranger in a public street; you choose to

[7] Lord Rosebery, Archibald Phillip Primrose (1847–1929), was an English Liberal politician and author who resided in Berkeley Square.

start certain theories about his eyebrows. You then treat him as a burglar because he enters an honest man's door. The thing is too monstrous. Admit that it is, Basil, and come home with me. Though these people are still having tea, yet with the distance we have to go, we shall be late for dinner."

Basil's eyes were shining in the twilight like lamps.

"I thought," he said, "that I had outlived vanity."

"What do you want now?" I cried.

"I want," he cried out, "what a girl wants when she wears her new frock; I want what a boy wants when he goes in for a slanging match with a monitor—I want to show somebody what a fine fellow I am. I am as right about that man as I am about your having a hat on your head. You say it cannot be tested. I say it can. I will take you to see my old friend Beaumont. He is a delightful man to know."

"Do you really mean——?" I began.

"I will apologise," he said calmly, "for our not being dressed for a call," and walking across the vast misty square, he walked up the dark stone steps and rang at the bell.

A severe servant in black and white opened the door to us: on receiving my friend's name his manner passed in a flash from astonishment to respect. We were ushered into the house very quickly, but not so quickly but that our host, a white-haired man with a fiery face, came out quickly to meet us.

"My dear fellow," he cried, shaking Basil's hand again and again, "I have not seen you for years. Have you been—er——" he said, rather wildly, "have you been in the country?"

"Not for all that time," answered Basil, smiling. "I have long given up my official position, my dear Philip, and have been living in a deliberate retirement. I hope I do not come at an inopportune moment."

"An inopportune moment," cried the ardent gentleman. "You come at the most opportune moment I could imagine. Do you know who is here?"

"I do not," answered Grant, with gravity. Even as he spoke a roar of laughter came from the inner room.

"Basil," said Lord Beaumont solemnly, "I have Wimpole here."

" 'My dear fellow,' he cried, shaking Basil's hand again and again, 'I
have not seen you for years.' "

"And who is Wimpole?"

"Basil," cried the other, "you must have been in the country. You must have been in the antipodes. You must have been in the moon. Who is Wimpole? Who was Shakespeare?"

"As to who Shakespeare was," answered my friend placidly, "my views go no further than thinking that he was not Bacon. More probably he was Mary Queen of Scots. But as to who Wimpole is—" and his speech also was cloven with a roar of laughter from within.

"Wimpole!" cried Lord Beaumont, in an sort of ecstasy. "Haven't you heard of the great modern wit? My dear fellow, he has turned conversation, I do not say into an art—for that, perhaps, it always was—but into a great art, like the statuary of Michael Angelo—an art of masterpieces. His repartees, my good friend, startle one like a man shot dead. They are final; they are—"

Again there came the hilarious roar from the room, and almost with the very noise of it, a big, panting apoplectic old gentleman came out of the inner house into the hall where we were standing.

"Now, my dear chap," began Lord Beaumont hastily.

"I tell you, Beaumont, I won't stand it," exploded the large old gentleman. "I won't be made game of by a two-penny literary adventurer like that. I won't be made a guy, I won't—"

"Come, come," said Beaumont feverishly. "Let me introduce you. This is Mr. Justice Grant—that is, Mr. Grant. Basil, I am sure you have heard of Sir Walter Cholmondeliegh."

"Who has not?" asked Grant, and bowed to the worthy old baronet, eyeing him with some curiosity. He was hot and heavy in his momentary anger, but even that could not conceal the noble though opulent outline of his face and body, the florid white hair, the Roman nose, the body stalwart though corpulent, the chin aristocratic though double. He was a magnificent courtly gentleman; so much of a gentleman that he could show an unquestionable weakness of anger without altogether losing dignity; so much of a gentleman that even his *faux pas* were well-bred.

"I am distressed beyond expression, Beaumont," he said gruffly, "to fail in respect to these gentlemen, and even more especially to fail in it in your house. But it is not you or they that are in any way concerned, but that flashy half-caste jackanapes—"

"'Now, my dear chap,' began Lord Beaumont, hastily."

At this moment a young man with a twist of red moustache and a sombre air came out of the inner room. He also did not seem to be greatly enjoying the intellectual banquet within.

"I think you remember my friend and secretary, Mr. Drummond," said Lord Beaumont, turning to Grant, "even if you only remember him as a schoolboy."

"Perfectly," said the other. Mr. Drummond shook hands pleasantly and respectfully, but the cloud was still on his brow. Turning to Sir Walter Cholmondeliegh, he said:

"I was sent by Lady Beaumont to express her hope that you were not going yet, Sir Walter. She says she has scarcely seen anything of you."

The old gentleman, still red in the face, had a temporary internal struggle; then his good manners triumphed, and with a gesture of obeisance and a vague utterance of, "If Lady Beaumont . . . a lady, of course," he followed the young man back into the *salon*. He had scarcely been deposited there half a minute before another peal of laughter told that he had (in all probability) been scored off again.

"Of course, I can excuse dear old Cholmondeliegh," said Beaumont, as he helped us off with our coats. "He has not the modern mind."

"What is the modern mind?" asked Grant.

"Oh, it's enlightened, you know, and progressive—and faces the facts of life seriously." At this moment another roar of laughter came from within.

"I only ask," said Basil, "because of the last two friends of yours who had the modern mind; one thought it wrong to eat fishes and the other thought it right to eat men. I beg your pardon—this way, if I remember right."

"Do you know," said Lord Beaumont, with a sort of feverish entertainment, as he trotted after us towards the interior, "I can never quite make out which side you are on. Sometimes you seem so liberal and sometimes so reactionary. *Are* you a modern, Basil?"

"No," said Basil, loudly and cheerfully, as he entered the crowded drawing-room.

This caused a slight diversion, and some eyes were turned away from our slim friend with the Oriental face for the first time that afternoon. Two people, however, still looked at him. One was the daughter of the house, Muriel Beaumont, who gazed at him with great violet eyes and with the intense and awful thirst of the female upper class for verbal amusement and stimulus. The other was Sir Walter Cholmondeliegh, who looked at him with a still and sullen but unmistakable desire to throw him out of the window.

He sat there, coiled rather than seated on the easy chair; everything from the curves of his smooth limbs to the coils of his silvered hair suggesting the circles of a serpent more than the straight limbs of a man—the unmistakable, splendid serpentine gentleman we had seen walking in North London, his eyes shining with repeated victory.

"What I can't understand, Mr. Wimpole," said Muriel Beaumont eagerly, "is how you contrive to treat all this so easily. You say things quite philosophical and yet so wildly funny. If I thought of such things, I'm sure I should laugh outright when the thought first came."

"I agree with Miss Beaumont," said Sir Walter, suddenly exploding with indignation. "If I had thought of anything so futile, I should find it difficult to keep my countenance."

"Difficult to keep your countenance," cried Mr. Wimpole, with an air of alarm; "oh, do keep your countenance! Keep it in the British Museum."

Everyone laughed uproariously, as they always do at an already admitted readiness, and Sir Walter, turning suddenly purple, shouted out:

"Do you know who you are talking to, with your confounded tomfooleries?"

"I never talk tomfooleries," said the other, "without first knowing my audience."

Grant walked across the room and tapped the red-moustached secretary on the shoulder. That gentleman was leaning against the wall regarding the whole scene with a great deal of gloom; but, I fancied, with very particular gloom when his eyes fell on the young lady of the house rapturously listening to Wimpole.

"May I have a word with you outside, Drummond?" asked Grant. "It is about business. Lady Beaumont will excuse us."

I followed my friend, at his own request, greatly wondering, to this strange external interview. We passed abruptly into a kind of side room out of the hall.

"Drummond," said Basil sharply, "there are a great many good people, and a great many sane people here this afternoon. Unfortunately, by a kind of coincidence, all the good people are mad, and all the sane people are wicked. You are the only person I know of here who is honest and has also some common sense. What do you make of Wimpole?"

Mr. Secretary Drummond had a pale face and red hair; but at this his face became suddenly as red as his moustache.

"I am not a fair judge of him," he said.

"Why not?" asked Grant.

"Because I hate him like hell," said the other, after a long pause and violently.

Neither Grant nor I needed to ask the reason; his glances towards Miss Beaumont and the stranger were sufficiently illuminating. Grant said quietly:

"But before—before you came to hate him, what did you really think of him?"

"I am in a terrible difficulty," said the young man, and his voice told us, like a clear bell, that he was an honest man. "If I spoke about him as I feel about him now, I could not trust myself. And I should like to be able to say that when I first saw him I thought he was charming. But again, the fact is I didn't. I hate him, that is my private affair. But I also disapprove of him—really I do believe I disapprove of him quite apart from my private feelings. When first he came, I admit he was much quieter, but I did not like, so to speak, the moral swell of him. Then that jolly old Sir Walter Cholmondeliegh got introduced to us, and this fellow, with his cheap-jack wit, began to score off the old man in the way he does now. Then I felt that he must be a bad lot; it must be bad to fight the old and the kindly. And he fights the poor old chap savagely, unceasingly, as if he hated old age and kindliness. Take, if you want it, the evidence of a prejudiced witness. I admit that I hate the man because a certain person admires him. But I believe that apart from that I should hate the man because old Sir Walter hates him."

This speech affected me with a genuine sense of esteem and pity for the young man; that is, of pity for him because of his obviously hopeless worship of Miss Beaumont, and of esteem for him because of the direct realistic account of the history of Wimpole which he had given. Still, I was sorry that he seemed so steadily set against the man, and could not help referring it to an instinct of his personal relations, however nobly disguised from himself.

In the middle of these meditations, Grant whispered in my ear what was perhaps the most startling of all interruptions.

"In the name of God, let's get away."

I have never known exactly in how odd a way this odd old man affected me. I only know that for some reason or other he so affected me that I was, within a few minutes, in the street outside.

"This," he said, "is a beastly but amusing affair."

"What is?" I asked, baldly enough.

"This affair. Listen to me, my old friend. Lord and Lady Beaumont have just invited you and me to a grand dinner-party this very night, at which Mr. Wimpole will be in all his glory. Well, there is nothing very extraordinary about that. The extraordinary thing is that we are not going."

"Well, really," I said, "it is already six o'clock and I doubt if we could get home and dress. I see nothing extraordinary in the fact that we are not going."

"Don't you?" said Grant. "I'll bet you'll see something extraordinary in what we're doing instead."

I looked at him blankly.

"Doing instead?" I asked. "What are we doing instead?"

"Why," said he, "we are waiting for one or two hours outside this house on a winter evening. You must forgive me; it is all my vanity. It is only to show you that I am right. Can you, with the assistance of this cigar, wait until both Sir Walter Cholmondeliegh and the mystic Wimpole have left this house?"

"Certainly," I said. "But I do not know which is likely to leave first. Have you any notion?"

"No," he said. "Sir Walter may leave first in a glow of rage. Or again, Mr. Wimpole may leave first, feeling that his last epigram is a thing to be flung behind him like a firework. And Sir Walter may remain some time to analyse Mr. Wimpole's character. But they will both have to leave within reasonable time, for they will both have to get dressed and come back to dinner here to-night."

As he spoke the shrill double whistle from the porch of the great house drew a dark cab to the dark portal. And then a thing happened that we really had not expected. Mr. Wimpole and Sir Walter Cholmondeliegh came out at the same moment.

They paused for a second or two opposite each other in a natural doubt; then a certain geniality, fundamental perhaps in both of them, made Sir Walter smile and say: "The night is foggy. Pray take my cab."

Before I could count twenty the cab had gone rattling up the street with both of them. And before I could count twenty-three Grant had hissed in my ear:

"Run after the cab; run as if you were running from a mad dog —run."

We pelted on steadily, keeping the cab in sight, through dark mazy streets. God only, I thought, knows why we are running at all, but we are running hard. Fortunately we did not run far. The cab pulled up at the fork of two streets and Sir Walter paid the cabman, who drove away rejoicing, having just come in contact with the more generous among the rich. Then the two men talked together as men do talk together after giving and receiving great insults, the talk which leads either to forgiveness or a duel—at least so it seemed as we watched it from ten yards off. Then the two men shook hands heartily, and one went down one fork of the road and one down another.

Basil, with one of his rare gestures, flung his arms forward.

"Run after that scoundrel," he cried; "let us catch him now."

We dashed across the open space and reached the juncture of two paths.

"Stop!" I shouted wildly to Grant. "That's the wrong turning."

He ran on.

"Idiot!" I howled. "Sir Walter's gone down there. Wimpole has slipped us. He's half a mile down the other road. You're wrong. . . .

Are you deaf? You're wrong!"

"I don't think I am," he panted, and ran on.

"But I saw him!" I cried. "Look in front of you. Is that Wimpole? It's the old man. . . . What are you doing? What are we to do?"

"Keep running," said Grant.

Running soon brought us up to the broad back of the pompous old baronet, whose white whiskers shone silver in the fitful lamp-light. My brain was utterly bewildered. I grasped nothing.

"Charlie," said Basil hoarsely, "can you believe in my common sense for four minutes?"

"Of course," I said, panting.

"Then help me to catch that man in front and hold him down. Do it at once when I say 'Now.' Now!"

We sprang on Sir Walter Cholmondeliegh, and rolled that portly old gentleman on his back. He fought with a commendable valour, but we got him tight. I had not the romotest notion why. He had a splendid and full-blooded vigour; when he could not box he kicked, and we bound him; when he could not kick he shouted, and we gagged him. Then, by Basil's arrangement, we dragged him into a small court by the street side and waited. As I say, I had no notion why.

"I am sorry to incommode you," said Basil calmly out of the darkness; "but I have made an appointment here."

"An appointment!" I said blankly.

"Yes," he said, glancing calmly at the apoplectic old aristocrat gagged on the ground, whose eyes were starting impotently from his head. "I have made an appointment here with a thoroughly nice young fellow. An old friend. Jasper Drummond his name is — you may have met him this afternoon at the Beaumonts. He can scarcely come though till the Beaumonts' dinner is over."

For I do not know how many hours we stood there calmly in the darkness. By the time those hours were over I had thoroughly made up my mind that the same thing had happened which had happened long ago on the bench of a British Court of Justice. Basil Grant had gone mad. I could imagine no other explanation of the facts, with the portly, purple-faced old country gentleman flung there strangled on the floor like a bundle of wood.

"We sprang on Sir Walter Cholmondeliegh."

After about four hours a lean figure in evening dress rushed into the court. A glimpse of gaslight showed the red moustache and white face of Jasper Drummond.

"Mr. Grant," he said blankly, "the thing is incredible. You were right; but what did you mean? All through this dinner party, where dukes and duchesses and editors of Quarterlies had come especially to hear him, that extraordinary Wimpole kept perfectly silent. He didn't say a funny thing. He didn't say anything at all. What does it mean?"

Grant pointed to the portly old gentleman on the ground.

"That is what it means," he said.

Drummond, on observing a fat gentleman lying so calmly about the place, jumped back, as from a mouse.

"What?" he said weakly, ". . . what?"

Basil bent suddenly down and tore a paper out of Sir Walter's breast-pocket, a paper which the baronet, even in his hampered state, seemed to make some effort to retain.

It was a large loose piece of white wrapping paper, which Mr. Jasper Drummond read with a vacant eye and undisguised astonishment. As far as he could make out, it consisted of a series of questions and answers, or at least of remarks and replies, arranged in the manner of a catechism. The greater part of the document had been torn and obliterated in the struggle, but the termination remained. It ran as follows:

"*C*. Says——Keep countenance.

"*W*. Keep——British Museum.

"*C*. Know whom talk——absurdities.

"*W*. Never talk absurdities without——"

"What is it?" cried Drummond, flinging the paper down in a sort of final fury.

"What is it?" replied Grant, his voice rising into a kind of splendid chant. "What is it? It is a great new profession. A great new trade. A trifle immoral, I admit, but still great, like piracy."

"A new profession!" said the young man with the red moustache vaguely; "a new trade!"

"A new trade," repeated Grant, with a strange exultation, "a new profession! What a pity it is immoral."

"Tore a paper out of Sir Walter's breast-pocket."

"But what the deuce is it?" cried Drummond and I in a breath of blasphemy.

"It is," said Grant calmly, "the great new trade of the Organiser of Repartee. This fat old gentleman lying on the ground strikes you, as I have no doubt, as very stupid and very rich. Let me clear his character. He is, like ourselves, very clever and very poor. He is also not really at all fat; all that is stuffing. He is not particularly old, and his name is not Cholmondeliegh. He is a swindler, and a swindler of a perfectly delightful and novel kind. He hires himself out at dinner parties to lead up to other people's repartees. According to a pre-concerted scheme (which you may find on that piece of paper), he says the stupid things he has arranged for himself, and his client says the clever things arranged for him. In short, he allows himself to be scored off for a guinea a night."

"And this fellow Wimpole——" began Drummond with indignation.

"This fellow Wimpole," said Basil Grant, smiling, "will not be an intellectual rival in the future. He had some fine things, elegance and silvered hair, and so on. But the intellect is with our friend on the floor."

"That fellow," cried Drummond furiously, "that fellow ought to be in gaol."

"Not at all," said Basil indulgently; "he ought to be in the Club of Queer Trades."

III

THE AWFUL REASON OF THE
VICAR'S VISIT

The revolt of Matter against Man (which I believe to exist) has now been reduced to a singular condition. It is the small things rather than the large things which make war against us and, I may add, beat us. The bones of the last mammoth have long ago decayed, a mighty wreck; the tempests no longer devour our navies, nor the mountains with hearts of fire heap hell over our cities. But we are engaged in a bitter and eternal war with small things; chiefly with microbes and with collar studs. The stud with which I was engaged (on fierce and equal terms) as I made the above reflections, was one which I was trying to introduce into my shirt collar when a loud knock came at the door.

My first thought was as to whether Basil Grant had called to fetch me. He and I were to turn up at the same dinner-party (for which I was in the act of dressing), and it might be that he had taken it into his head to come my way, though we had arranged to go separately. It was a small and confidential affair at the table of a good but unconventional political lady, an old friend of his. She had asked us both to meet a third guest, a Captain Fraser, who had made something of a name and was an authority on chimpanzees. As Basil was an old friend of the hostess and I had never seen her, I felt that it was quite possible that he (with his usual social sagacity) might have decided to take me along in order to break the ice. The theory, like all my theories, was complete; but as a fact it was not Basil.

I was handed a visiting card inscribed: "Rev. Ellis Shorter," and underneath was written in pencil, but in a hand in which even hurry could not conceal a depressing and gentlemanly excellence, "Asking the favour of a few moments' conversation on a most urgent matter."

I had already subdued the stud, thereby proclaiming that the image of God has supremacy over all matters (a valuable truth), and throwing on my dress-coat and waist-coat, hurried into the drawing-room. He rose at my entrance, flapping like a seal; I can use no other description. He flapped a plaid shawl over his right arm; he flapped a pair of pathetic black gloves; he flapped his clothes; I may say, without exaggeration, that he flapped his eyelids, as he rose. He was a bald-browed, white-haired, white-whiskered old clergyman, of a flappy and floppy type. He said:

"I am so sorry. I am so very sorry. I am so extremely sorry. I come— I can only say—I can only say in my defence, that I come— upon an important matter. Pray forgive me."

I told him I forgave perfectly and waited.

"What I have to say," he said brokenly, "is so dreadful—it is so dreadful—I have lived a quiet life."

I was burning to get away, for it was already doubtful if I should be in time for dinner. But there was something about the old man's honest air of bitterness that seemed to open to me the possibilites of life larger and more tragic than my own.

I said gently: "Pray go on."

Nevertheless the old gentleman, being a gentleman as well as old, noticed my secret impatience and seemed still more unmanned.

"I'm so sorry," he said meekly; "I wouldn't have come—but for—your friend Major Brown recommended me to come here."

"Major Brown!" I said, with some interest.

"Yes," said the Reverend Mr. Shorter, feverishly flapping his plaid shawl about. "He told me you helped him in a great difficulty—and my difficulty! Oh, my dear sir, it's a matter of life and death."

I rose abruptly, in an acute perplexity. "Will it take long, Mr. Shorter?" I asked. "I have to go out to dinner almost at once."

He rose also, trembling from head to foot, and yet somehow, with all his moral palsy, he rose to the dignity of his age and his office.

"I have no right, Mr. Swinburne—I have no right at all," he said. "If you have to go out to dinner, you have of course—a perfect right—of course a perfect right. But when you come back—a man will be dead."

And he sat down, quaking like a jelly.

"He rose at my entrance, flapping like a seal."

The triviality of the dinner had been in those two minutes dwarfed and drowned in my mind. I did not want to go and see a political widow, and a captain who collected apes; I wanted to hear what had brought this dear, doddering old vicar into relation with immediate perils.

"Will you have a cigar?" I said.

"No, thank you," he said, with indescribable embarrassment, as if not smoking cigars was a social disgrace.

"A glass of wine?" I said.

"No, thank you, no, thank you; not just now," he repeated with that hysterical eagerness with which people who do not drink at all often try to convey that on any other night of the week they would sit up all night drinking rum-punch. "Not just now, thank you."

"Nothing else I can get for you?" I said, feeling genuinely sorry for the well-mannered old donkey. "A cup of tea?"

I saw a struggle in his eye and I conquered. When the cup of tea came he drank it like a dipsomaniac gulping brandy. Then he fell back and said:

"I have had such a time, Mr. Swinburne. I am not used to these excitements. As Vicar of Chuntsey, in Essex"—he threw this in with an indescribable airiness of vanity—"I have never known such things happen."

"What things happen?" I asked.

He straightened himself with sudden dignity.

"As Vicar of Chuntsey, in Essex," he said, "I have never been forcibly dressed up as an old woman and made to take part in a crime in the character of an old woman. Never once. My experience may be small. It may be insufficient. But it has never occurred to me before."

"I have never heard of it," I said, "as among the duties of a clergyman. But I am not well up in church matters. Excuse me if perhaps I failed to follow you correctly. Dressed up—as what?"

"As an old woman," said the vicar solemnly, "as an old woman."

I thought in my heart that it required no great transformation to make an old woman of him, but the thing was evidently more tragic than comic, and I said respectfully:

"May I ask how it occurred?"

"I will begin at the beginning," said Mr. Shorter, "and I will tell my story with the utmost possible precision. At seventeen minutes past eleven this morning I left the vicarage to keep certain appointments and pay certain visits in the village. My first visit was to Mr. Jervis, the treasurer of our League of Christian Amusements, with whom I concluded some business touching the claim made by Parkes the gardener in the matter of the rolling of our tennis lawn. I then visited Mrs. Arnett, a very earnest chruchwoman, but permanently bedridden. She is the author of several small works of devotion, and of a book of verse, entitled (unless my memory misleads me), 'Eglantine.' "

He uttered all this not only with deliberation, but with something that can only be called, by a contradictory phase, eager deliberation. He had, I think, a vague memory in his head of the detectives in the detective stories, who always sternly require that nothing should be kept back.

"I then proceeded," he went on, with the same maddening conscientiousness of manner, "to Mr. Carr (not Mr. James Carr,[8] of course; Mr. Robert Carr) who is temporarily assisting our organist, and having consulted with him (on the subject of a choir boy who is accused, I cannot as yet say whether justly or not, of cutting holes in the organ pipes), I finally dropped in upon a Dorcas meeting[9] at the house of Miss Brett. The Dorcas meetings are usually held at the vicarage, but my wife being unwell, Miss Brett, a newcomer in our village, but very active in church work, had very kindly consented to hold them. The Dorcas society is entirely under my wife's management as a rule, and except for Miss Brett, who, as I say, is very active, I scarcely know any members of it. I had, however, promised to drop in on them, and I did so.

"When I arrived there were only four other maiden ladies with Miss Brett, but they were sewing very busily. It is very difficult, of

[8] James Carr was probably the Reverend James Carr (1784–1874), Perpetual Curate of South Shields and Canon of Durham.

[9] A Dorcas meeting is that of a sewing or needlework guild devoted to making clothes for the poor.

"Temporarily assisting our organist."

course, for any person, however strongly impressed with the necessity in these matters of full and exact exposition of the facts, to remember and repeat the actual details of a conversation, particularly a conversation which (though inspired with a most worthy and admirable zeal for good work) was one which did not greatly impress the hearer's mind at the time and was, in fact—er—mostly about socks. I can, however, remember distinctly that one of the spinster ladies (she was a thin person with a woollen shawl, who appeared to feel the cold, and I am almost sure she was introduced to me as Miss James) remarked that the weather was very changeable. Miss Brett then offered me a cup of tea, which I accepted, I cannot recall in what words. Miss Brett is a short and stout lady with white hair. The only other figure in the group that caught my attention was a Miss Mowbray, a small and neat lady of aristocratic manners, silver hair, and a high voice and colour. She was the most emphatic member of the party; and her views on the subject of pinafores, though expressed with a natural deference to myself, were in themselves strong and advanced. Beside her (although all five ladies were dressed simply in black) it could not be denied that the others looked in some way what you men of the world would call dowdy.

"After about ten minutes' conversation I rose to go, and as I did so I heard something which—I cannot describe it—something which seemed to—but I really cannot describe it."

"What did you hear?" I asked, with some impatience.

"I heard," said the vicar solemnly, "I heard Miss Mowbray (the lady with the silver hair) say to Miss James (the lady with the woollen shawl), the following extraordinary words. I committed them to memory on the spot, and as soon as circumstances set me free to do so, I noted them down on a piece of paper. I believe I have it here." He fumbled in his breast-pocket, bringing out mild things, note-books, circulars and programmes of village concerts. "I heard Miss Mowbray say to Miss James, the following words: 'Now's your time, Bill.' "

He gazed at me for a few moments after making this announcement, gravely and unflinchingly, as if conscious that here he was unshaken about his facts. Then he resumed, turning his bald head more towards the fire.

"This appeared to me remarkable. I could not by any means understand it. It seemed to me first of all peculiar that one maiden lady should address another maiden lady as 'Bill.' My experience, as I have said, may be incomplete; maiden ladies may have among themselves and in exclusively spinster circles wilder customs than I am aware of. But it seemed to me odd, and I could almost have sworn (if you will not misunderstand the phrase), I should have been strongly impelled to maintain at the time that the words, 'Now's your time, Bill,' were by no means pronounced with that upper-class intonation which, as I have already said, had up to now characterised Miss Mowbray's conversation. In fact, the words, 'Now's your time, Bill,' would have been, I fancy, unsuitable if pronounced with that upper-class intonation.

"I was surprised, I repeat, then, at the remark. But I was still more surprised when, looking round me in bewilderment, my hat and umbrella in hand, I saw the lean lady with the woollen shawl leaning upright against the door out of which I was just about to make my exit. She was still knitting, and I supposed that this erect posture against the door was only an eccentricity of spinsterhood and an oblivion of my intended departure.

"I said genially, 'I am so sorry to disturb you, Miss James, but I must really be going. I have—er——' I stopped here, for the words she had uttered in reply, though singularly brief and in tone extremely businesslike, were such as to render that arrest of my remarks, I think, natural and excusable. I have these words also noted down. I have not the least idea of their meaning; so I have only been able to render them phonetically. But she said," and Mr. Shorter peered short-sightedly at his papers, "she said: 'Chuck it, fat 'ead,' and she added something that sounded like, 'It's a kop,' or (possibly) 'a kopt.' And then the last cord, either of my sanity or the sanity of the universe, snapped suddenly. My esteemed friend and helper, Miss Brett, standing by the mantel-piece, said: 'Put 'is old 'ead in a bag, Sam, and tie 'im up before you start jawin'. You'll be kopt yourselves some o' these days with this way of doin' things, har lar theater.'[10]

[10] Har lar theater is à la théâtre pronounced with a London Cockney accent somewhat like "after the scole of Stratford atte Bowe", as Chaucer's prioress said.

"My head went round and round. Was it really true, as I had suddenly fancied a moment before, that unmarried ladies had some dreadful riotous society of their own from which all others were excluded? I remembered dimly in my classical days (I was a scholar in a small way once, but now, alas! rusty), I remembered the mysteries of the Bona Dea[11] and their strange female freemasonry. I remembered the witches' Sabbaths. I was just, in my absurd light-headedness, trying to remember a line of verse about Diana's[12] nymphs, when Miss Mowbray threw her arm round me from behind. The moment it held me I knew it was not a woman's arm.

"Miss Brett—or what I had called Miss Brett—was standing in front of me with a big revolver in her hand and a broad grin on her face. Miss James was still leaning against the door, but had fallen into an attitude so totally new, and so totally unfeminine, that it gave one a shock. She was kicking her heels, with her hands in her pockets and her cap on one side. She was a man. I mean he was a wo—no, that is I saw that instead of being a woman she—he, I mean—that is, it was a man."

Mr. Shorter became indescribably flurried and flapping in endeavouring to arrange these genders and his plaid shawl at the same time. He resumed with a higher fever of nervousness:

"As for Miss Mowbray, she—he, held me in a ring of iron. He had her arm—that is she had his arm—round her neck—my neck I mean—and I could not cry out. Miss Brett—that is, Mr. Brett, at least Mr. something who was not Miss Brett—had the revolver pointed at me. The other two ladies—or er—gentlemen, were rummaging in some bag in the background. It was all clear at last: they were criminals dressed up as women, to kidnap me! To kidnap the Vicar of Chuntsey, in Essex. But why? Was it to be Nonconformists?

"The brute leaning against the door called out carelessly, ''Urry up, 'Arry. Show the old bloke what the game is, and let's get off.'

---

[11] Bona Dea is a Roman fertility goddess whose devotees were almost exclusively female. The term can also be used of her cult.

[12] Diana, also known as Artemis, is the daughter of Jupiter and Latona. Her cult worshipped her as goddess of hunting, virginity and chastity.

"A big revolver in her hand."

" 'Curse 'is eyes,' said Miss Brett—I mean the man with the revolver—'why should we show 'im the game?'

" 'If you take my advice you bloomin' well will,' said the man at the door, whom they called Bill. 'A man wot knows wot 'e's doin' is worth ten wot don't, even if 'e's a potty old parson.'

" 'Bill's right enough,' said the coarse voice of the man who held me (it had been Miss Mowbray's). 'Bring out the picture, 'Arry.'

"The man with the revolver walked across the room to where the other two women—I mean men—were turning over baggage, and asked them for something which they gave him. He came back with it across the room and held it out in front of me. And compared to the surprise of that display, all the previous surprises of this awful day shrank suddenly.

"It was a portrait of myself. That such a picture should be in the hands of these scoundrels might in any case have caused a mild surprise; but no more. It was no mild surprise that I felt. The likeness was an extremely good one, worked up with all the accessories of the conventional photographic studio. I was leaning my head on my hand and was relieved against a painted landscape of woodland. It was obvious that it was no snapshot; it was clear that I had sat for this photograph. And the truth was that I had never sat for such a photograph. It was a photograph that I had never had taken.

"I stared at it again and again. It seemed to me to be touched up a good deal; it was glazed as well as framed, and the glass blurred some of the details. But there unmistakably was my face, my eyes, my nose and mouth, my head and hand, posed for a professional photographer. And I had never posed so for any photographer.

" 'Be'old the bloomin' miracle,' said the man with the revolver, with ill-timed facetiousness. 'Parson, prepare to meet your God.' And with this he slid the glass out of the frame. As the glass moved, I saw that part of the picture was painted on it in Chinese white, notably a pair of white whiskers and a clerical collar. And underneath was a portrait of an old lady in a quiet black dress, leaning her head on her hand against the woodland landscape. The old lady was as like me as one pin is like another. It had required only the whiskers and the collar to make it me in every hair.

" 'Entertainin', ain't it?' said the man described as 'Arry, as he shot the glass back again. 'Remarkable resemblance, parson. Gratifyin' to the lady. Gratifyin' to you. And hi may hadd, particlery gratifyin' to us, as bein' the probable source of a very tolerable haul. You know Colonel Hawker, the man who's come to live in these parts, don't you?'

"I nodded.

" 'Well,' said the man 'Arry, pointing to the picture, 'that's 'is mother. 'Oo ran to catch 'im when 'e fell? She did,' and he flung his fingers in a general gesture towards the photograph of the old lady who was exactly like me.

" 'Tell the old gent wot 'e's got to do and be done with it,' broke out Bill from the door. 'Look 'ere, Reverend Shorter, we ain't goin' to do you no 'arm. We'll give you a sov. for your trouble if you like. And as for the old woman's clothes—why, you'll look lovely in 'em.'

" 'You ain't much of a 'and at a description, Bill,' said the man behind me. 'Mr. Shorter, it's like this. We've got to see this man Hawker to-night. Maybe 'e'll kiss us all and 'ave up the champagne when 'e sees us. Maybe on the other 'and—'e won't. Maybe 'e'll be dead when we goes away. Maybe not. But we've got to see 'im. Now as you know, 'e shuts 'isself up and never opens the door to a soul; only you don't know why and we does. The only one as can ever get at 'im is 'is mother. Well, it's a confounded funny coincidence,' he said, accenting the penultimate, 'it's a very unusual piece of good luck, but you're 'is mother.'

" 'When first I saw 'er picture,' said the man Bill, shaking his head in a ruminant manner, 'when I first saw it I said—old Shorter. Those were my exact words—old Shorter.'

" 'What do you mean, you wild creatures?' I gasped. 'What am I to do?'

" 'That's easy said, your 'oliness,' said the man with the revolver, good-humouredly; 'you've got to put on those clothes,' and he pointed to a poke-bonnet and a heap of female clothes in the corner of the room.

"I will not dwell, Mr. Swinburne, upon the details of what followed.

I had no choice. I could not fight five men, to say nothing of a loaded pistol. In five minuts, sir, the Vicar of Chuntsey was dressed as an old woman—as somebody else's mother, if you please, and was dragged out of the house to take part in a crime.

"It was already late in the afternoon, and the nights of winter were closing in fast. On a dark road, in a blowing wind, we set out towards the lonely house of Colonel Hawker, perhaps the queerest cortège that ever straggled up that or any other road. To every human eye, in every external, we were six very respectable old ladies of small means, in black dresses and refined but antiquated bonnets; and we were really five criminals and a clergyman.

"I will cut a long story short. My brain was whirling like a windmill as I walked, trying to think of some manner of escape. To cry out, so long as we were far from houses, would be suicidal, for it would be easy for the ruffians to knife me or to gag me and fling me into a ditch. On the other hand, to attempt to stop strangers and explain the situation was impossible, because of the frantic folly of the situation itself. Long before I had persuaded the chance postman or carrier of so absurd a story, my companions would certainly have got off themselves, and in all probability would have carried me off, as a friend of theirs who had the misfortune to be mad or drunk. The last thought, however, was an inspiration; though a very terrible one. Had it come to this, that the Vicar of Chuntsey must pretend to be mad or drunk? It had come to this.

"I walked along with the rest up the deserted road, imitating and keeping pace, as far as I could, with their rapid and yet lady-like step, until at length I saw a lamp-post and a policeman standing under it. I had made up my mind. Until we reached them we were all equally demure and silent and swift. When we reached them I suddenly flung myself against the railings and roared out: 'Hooray! Hooray! Hooray! Rule Britannia! Get your 'air cut. Hoop-la! Boo!' It was a condition of no little novelty for a man in my position.

"The constable instantly flashed his lantern on me, or the draggled, drunken old woman that was my travesty. 'Now then, mum,' he began gruffly.

" 'Come along quiet, or I'll eat your heart,' cried Sam in my ear hoarsely. 'Stop, or I'll flay you.' It was frightful to hear the words and see the neatly-shawled old spinster who whispered them.

"I yelled, and yelled—I was in for it now. I screamed comic refrains that vulgar young men had sung, to my regret, at our village concerts; I rolled to and fro like a ninepin about to fall.

" 'If you can't get your friend on quiet, ladies,' said the policeman, 'I shall have to take 'er up. Drunk and disorderly she is right enough.'

"I redoubled my efforts. I had not been brought up to this sort of thing; but I believe I eclipsed myself. Words that I did not know I had ever heard of seemed to come pouring out of my open mouth.

" 'When we get you past,' whispered Bill, 'you'll howl louder; you'll howl louder when we're burning your feet off.'

"I screamed in my terror those awful songs of joy. In all the nightmares that men have ever dreamed, there has never been anything so blighting and horrible as the faces of those five men, looking out of their poke-bonnets; the figures of district visitors with the faces of devils. I cannot think there is anything so heartbreaking in hell.

"For a sickening instant I thought that the bustle of my companions and the perfect respectability of all our dresses would overcome the policeman and induce him to let us pass. He wavered, so far as one can describe anything so solid as a policeman as wavering. I lurched suddenly forward and ran my head into his chest, calling out (if I remember correctly), 'Oh, crikey, blimey, Bill.' It was at that moment that I remembered most clearly that I was the Vicar of Chuntsey, in Essex.

"My desperate coup saved me. The policeman had me hard by the back of the neck.

" 'You come along with me,' he began, but Bill cut in with his perfect imitation of a lady's finnicking voice.

" 'Oh, pray, constable, don't make a disturbance with our poor friend. We will get her quietly home. She does drink too much, but she is quite a lady—only eccentric.'

" 'She butted me in the stomach,' said the policeman briefly.

" 'Eccentricities of genius,' said Sam earnestly.

" 'Pray let me take her home,' reiterated Bill, in the resumed character of Miss James, 'she wants looking after.'

" 'She does,' said the policeman, 'but I'll look after her.'

" 'That's no good,' cried Bill feverishly. 'She wants her friends. She wants a particular medicine we've got.'

" 'Yes,' assented Miss Mowbray, with excitement, 'no other medicine any good, constable. Complaint quite unique.'

" 'I'm all righ'. Cutchy, cutchy, coo!' remarked, to his eternal shame, the Vicar of Chuntsey.

" 'Look here, ladies,' said the constable sternly, 'I don't like the eccentricity of your friend, and I don't like 'er songs, or 'er 'ead in my stomach. And now I come to think of it, I don't like the looks of you. I've seen many as quiet dressed as you as was wrong 'uns. Who are you?'

" 'We've not our cards with us,' said Miss Mowbray, with indescribable dignity. 'Nor do we see why we should be insulted by any Jack-in-office who chooses to be rude to ladies, when he is paid to protect them. If you choose to take advantage of the weakness of our unfortunate friend, no doubt you are legally entitled to take her. But if you fancy you have any legal right to bully us, you will find yourself in the wrong box.'

"The truth and dignity of this staggered the policeman for a moment. Under cover of their advantage my five persecutors turned for an instant on me faces like faces of the damned and then swished off into the darkness. When the constable first turned his lantern and his suspicions on to them, I had seen the telegraphic look flash from face to face saying that only retreat was possible now.

"By this time I was sinking slowly to the pavement, in a state of acute reflection. So long as the ruffians were with me, I dared not quit the role of drunkard. For if I had begun to talk reasonably and explain the real case, the officer would merely have thought that I was slightly recovered and would have put me in charge of my friends. Now, however, if I liked I might safely undeceive him.

"But I confess I did not like. The chances of life are many, and it may doubtless sometimes lie in the narrow path of duty for a clergyman of the Church of England to pretend to be a drunken old woman; but such necessities are, I imagine, sufficiently rare to appear to many improbable. Suppose the story got about that I had pretended to be drunk. Suppose people did not all think it was pretence!

"I lurched up, the policeman half-lifting me. I went along weakly and quietly for about a hundred yards. The officer evidently thought that I was too sleepy and feeble to effect an escape, and so held me lightly and easily enough. Past one turning, two turnings, three turnings, four turnings, he trailed me with him, a limp and slow and reluctant figure. At the fourth turning, I suddenly broke from his hand and tore down the street like a maddened stag. He was unprepared, he was heavy, and it was dark. I ran and ran and ran, and in five minutes' running, found I was gaining. In half an hour I was out in the fields under the holy and blessed stars, where I tore off my accursed shawl and bonnet and buried them in clean earth."

The old gentleman had finished his story and leant back in his chair. Both the matter and the manner of his narration had, as time went on, impressed me favourably. He was an old duffer and pedant, but behind these things he was a country-bred man and gentleman, and had showed courage and a sporting instinct in the hour of desperation. He had told his story with many quaint formalities of diction, but also with a very convincing realism.

"And now——" I began.

"And now," said Shorter, leaning forward again with something like servile energy, "and now, Mr. Swinburne, what about that unhappy man Hawker. I cannot tell what those men meant, or how far what they said was real. But surely there is danger. I cannot go to the police, for reasons that you perceive. Among other things, they wouldn't believe me. What is to be done?"

I took out my watch. It was already half-past twelve.

"My friend Basil Grant," I said, "is the best man we can go to. He and I were to have gone to the same dinner to-night; but he will just have come back by now. Have you any objection to taking a cab?"

"Not at all," he replied, rising politely, and gathering up his absurd plaid shawl.

A rattle in a hansom brought us underneath the sombre pile of

" *I tore off my accursed shawl and bonnet*'."

workmen's flats in Lambeth which Grant inhabited; a climb up a wearisome wooden staircase brought us to his garret. When I entered that wooden and scrappy interior, the white gleam of Basil's shirt-front and the lustre of his fur coat flung on the wooden settle, struck me as a contrast. He was drinking a glass of wine before retiring. I was right; he had come back from the dinner-party.

He listened to the repetition of the story of the Rev. Ellis Shorter with the genuine simplicity and respect which he never failed to exhibit in dealing with any human being. When it was over he said simply:

"Do you know a man named Captain Fraser?"

I was so startled at this totally irrelevant reference to the worthy collector of chimpanzees with whom I ought to have dined that evening, that I glanced sharply at Grant. The result was that I did not look at Mr. Shorter. I only heard him answer, in his most nervous tone, "No."

Basil, however, seemed to find something very curious about his answer or his demeanour generally, for he kept his big blue eyes fixed on the old clergyman, and though the eyes were quite quiet they stood out more and more from his head.

"You are quite sure, Mr. Shorter," he repeated, "that you don't know Captain Fraser?"

"Quite," answered the vicar, and I was certainly puzzled to find him returning so much to the timidity, not to say the demoralisation, of his tone when he first entered my presence.

Basil sprang smartly to his feet.

"Then our course is clear," he said. "You have not even begun your investigation, my dear Mr. Shorter; the first thing for us to do is to go together to see Captain Fraser."

"When?" asked the clergyman, stammering.

"Now," said Basil, putting one arm in his fur coat.

The old clergyman rose to his feet, quaking all over.

"I really do not think that it is necessary," he said.

Basil took his arm out of the fur coat, threw it over the chair again, and put his hands in his pockets.

"Oh," he said, with emphasis. "Oh—you don't think it necessary;

then," and he added the words with great clearness and deliberation, "then, Mr. Ellis Shorter, I can only say that I would like to see you without your whiskers."

And at these words I also rose to my feet, for the great tragedy of my life had come. Splendid and exciting as life was in continual contact with an intellect like Basil's, I had always the feeling that that splendour and excitement were on the borderland of sanity. He lived perpetually near the vision of the reason of things which makes men lose their reason. And I felt of his insanity as men feel of the death of friends with heart disease. It might come anywhere, in a field, in a hansom cab, looking at a sunset, smoking a cigarette. It had come now. At the very moment of delivering a judgment for the salvation of a fellow creature, Basil Grant had gone mad.

"Your whiskers," he cried, advancing with blazing eyes. "Give me your whiskers. And your bald head."

The old vicar naturally retreated a step or two. I stepped between.

"Sit down, Basil," I implored, "you're a little excited. Finish your wine."

"Whiskers," he answered sternly, "whiskers."

And with that he made a dash at the old gentleman, who made a dash for the door, but was intercepted. And then, before I knew where I was the quiet room was turned into something between a pantomime and a pandemonium by those two. Chairs were flung over with a crash, tables were vaulted with a noise like thunder, screens were smashed, crockery scattered in smithereens, and still Basil Grant bounded and bellowed after the Rev. Ellis Shorter.

And now I began to perceive something else, which added the last half-witted touch to my mystification. The Rev. Ellis Shorter, of Chuntsey, in Essex, was by no means behaving as I had previously noticed him to behave, or as, considering his age and station, I should have expected him to behave. His power of dodging, leaping, and fighting would have been amazing in a lad of seventeen, and in this doddering old vicar looked like a sort of farcical fairy-tale. Moreover, he did not seem to be so much astonished as I had thought. There was even a look of something like enjoyment in his eyes; so there was in the eye of Basil. In fact, the unintelligible truth must be told. They were both laughing.

" 'Whiskers,' he answered sternly, 'whiskers'."

At length Shorter was cornered.

"Come, come, Mr. Grant," he panted, "you can't do anything to me. It's quite legal. And it doesn't do anyone the least harm. It's only a social fiction. A result of our complex society, Mr. Grant."

"I don't blame you, my man," said Basil coolly. "But I want your whiskers. And your bald head. Do they belong to Captain Fraser?"

"No, no," said Mr. Shorter, laughing, "we provide them ourselves. They don't belong to Captain Fraser."

"What the deuce does all this mean?" I almost screamed. "Are you all in an infernal nightmare? Why should Mr. Shorter's bald head belong to Captain Fraser? How could it? What the deuce has Captain Fraser to do with the affair? What is the matter with him? You dined with him, Basil."

"No," said Grant, "I didn't."

"Didn't you go to Mrs. Thornton's dinner-party?" I asked, staring. "Why not?"

"Well," said Basil, with a slow and singular smile, "the fact is I was detained by a visitor. I have him, as a point of fact, in my bedroom."

"In your bedroom?" I repeated; but my imagination had reached that point when he might have said in his coal scuttle or his waistcoat pocket.

Grant stepped to the door of an inner room, flung it open and walked in. Then he came out again with the last of the bodily wonders of that wild night. He introduced into the sitting-room, in an apologetic manner, and by the nape of the neck, a limp clergyman with a bald head, white whiskers and a plaid shawl.

"Sit down, gentlemen," cried Grant, striking his hands heartily. "Sit down all of you and have a glass of wine. As you say, there is no harm in it, and if Captain Fraser had simply dropped me a hint I could have saved him from dropping a good sum of money. Not that you would have liked that, eh?"

The two duplicate clergymen, who were sipping their Burgundy with two duplicate grins, laughed heartily at this, and one of them carelessly pulled off his whiskers and laid them on the table.

"Basil," I said, "if you are my friend, save me. What is all this?"

He laughed again.

"Only another addition, Cherub, to your collection of Queer Trades. These two gentlemen (whose health I have now the pleasure of drinking) are Professional Detainers."

"And what on earth's that?" I asked.

"It's really very simple, Mr. Swinburne," began he who had once been the Rev. Ellis Shorter, of Chuntsey, in Essex; and it gave me a shock indescribable to hear out of that pompous and familiar form come no longer its own pompous and familiar voice, but the brisk sharp tones of a young city man. "It is really nothing very important. We are paid by our clients to detain in conversation, on some harmless pretext, people whom they want out of the way for a few hours. And Captain Fraser——" and with that he hesitated and smiled.

Basil smiled also. He intervened.

"The fact is that Captain Fraser, who is one of my best friends, wanted us both out of the way very much. He is sailing to-night for East Africa, and the lady with whom we were all to have dined is—er—what is I believe described as 'the romance of his life.' He wanted that two hours with her, and employed these two reverend gentlemen to detain us at our houses so as to let him have the field to himself."

"And of course," said the late Mr. Shorter apologetically to me, "as I had to keep a gentleman at home from keeping an appointment with a lady, I had to come with something rather hot and strong— rather urgent. It wouldn't have done to have been tame."

"Oh," I said, "I acquit you of tameness."

"Thank you, sir," said the man respectfully, "always very grateful for any recommendation, sir."

The other man idly pushed back his artificial bald head, revealing close red hair, and spoke dreamily, perhaps under the influence of Basil's admirable Burgundy.

"It's wonderful how common it's getting, gentlemen. Our office is busy from morning till night. I've no doubt you've often knocked up against us before. You just take notice. When an old bachelor goes on boring you with hunting stories, when you're burning to be introduced to somebody, he's from our bureau. When a lady calls on parish work and stops hours, just when you wanted to go to the Robinsons', she's from our bureau. The Robinson hand, sir, may be darkly seen."

"There is one thing I don't understand," I said. "Why you are both vicars."

A shade crossed the brow of the temporary incumbent of Chuntsey, in Essex.

"That may have been a mistake, sir," he said. "But it was not our fault. It was all the munificence of Captain Fraser. He requested that the highest price and talent on our tariff should be employed to detain you gentlemen. Now the highest payment in our office goes to those who impersonate vicars, as being the most respectable and more of a strain. We are paid five guineas a visit. We have had the good fortune to satisfy the firm with our work; and we are now permanently vicars. Before that we had two years as colonels, the next in our scale. Colonels are four guineas."

" 'We are now permanently vicars'."

IV

THE SINGULAR SPECULATION OF
THE HOUSE AGENT

Lieutenant Drummond Keith was a man about whom conversation always burst like a thunderstorm the moment he left the room. This arose from many separate touches about him. He was a light, loose person, who wore light, loose clothes, generally white, as if he were in the tropics; he was lean and graceful, like a panther, and he had restless black eyes.

He was very impecunious. He had one of the habits of the poor, in a degree so exaggerated as immeasurably to eclipse the most miserable of the unemployed; I mean the habit of continual change of lodgings. There are inland tracts of London where, in the very heart of artificial civilisation, humanity has almost become nomadic once more. But in that restless interior there was no ragged tramp so restless as the elegant officer in the loose white clothes. He had shot a great many things in his time, to judge from his conversation, from partridges to elephants, but his slangier acquaintances were of opinion that "the moon" had been not unfrequently amid the victims of his victorious rifle.[13] The phrase is a fine one, and suggests a mystic, elvish, nocturnal hunting.

He carried from house to house and from parish to parish a kit which consisted practically of five articles. Two odd-looking, large-bladed spears, tied together, the weapons, I suppose, of some savage tribe, a green umbrella, a huge and tattered copy of the "Pickwick Papers," a big game rifle, and a large sealed jar of some unholy Oriental wine. These always went into every new lodging, even for one night; and they went in quite undisguised, tied up in wisps of string or straw, to the delight of the poetic gutter boys in the little grey streets.

I had forgotten to mention that he always carried also his old

[13] Shooting the moon had the same meaning as "a moonlight flit", moving out by night in order to avoid paying overdue rent.

"*They went in quite undisguised, tied up in wisps of string or straw, to the delight of the poetic gutter boys.*"

regimental sword. But this raised another odd question about him. Slim and active as he was, he was no longer very young. His hair, indeed, was quite grey, though his rather wild almost Italian moustache retained its blackness, and his face was careworn under its almost Italian gaiety. To find a middle-aged man who has left the Army at the primitive rank of Lieutenant is unusual and not necessarily encouraging. With the more cautious and solid this fact, like his endless flitting, did the mysterious gentleman no good.

Lastly, he was a man who told the kind of adventures which win a man admiration, but not respect. They came out of queer places, where a good man would scarcely find himself, out of opium dens and gambling halls; they had the heat of the thieves' kitchens or smelled of a strange smoke from cannibal incantations. These are the kind of stories which discredit a person almost equally whether they are believed or no. If Keith's tales were false he was a liar; if they were true he had had, at any rate, every opportunity of being a scamp.

He had just left the room in which I sat with Basil Grant and his brother Rupert, the voluble amateur detective. And as I say was invariably the case, we were all talking about him. Rupert Grant was a clever young fellow, but he had that tendency which youth and cleverness, when sharply combined, so often produce, a somewhat extravagant scepticism. He saw doubt and guilt everywhere, and it was meat and drink to him. I had often got irritated with this boyish incredulity of his, but on this particular occasion I am bound to say that I thought him so obviously right that I was astounded at Basil's opposing him, however banteringly.

I could swallow a good deal, being naturally of a simple turn, but I could not swallow Lieutenant Keith's autobiography.

"You don't seriously mean, Basil," I said, "that you think that that fellow really did go as a stowaway with Nansen and pretend to be the Mad Mullah and——"

"He has one fault," said Basil thoughtfully, "or virtue, as you may happen to regard it. He tells the truth in too exact and bald a style; he is too veracious."

"Oh! if you are going to be paradoxical," said Rupert contemptuously, "be a bit funnier than that. Say, for instance, that he has lived all his life in one ancestral manor."

"No, he's extremely fond of change of scene," replied Basil dispassionately, "and of living in odd places. That doesn't prevent his chief trait being verbal exactitude. What you people don't understand is that telling a thing crudely and coarsely as it happened makes it sound frightfully strange. The sort of things Keith recounts are not the sort of things that a man would make up to cover himself with honour; they are too absurd. But they are the sort of things that a man would do if he were sufficiently filled with the soul of skylarking."

"So far from paradox," said his brother, with something rather like a sneer, "you seem to be going in for journalese proverbs. Do you believe that truth is stranger than fiction?"

"Truth must of necessity be stranger than fiction," said Basil placidly. "For fiction is the creation of the human mind, and therefore is congenial to it."

"Well, your lieutenant's truth is stranger, if it is truth, than anything I ever heard of," said Rupert, relapsing into flippancy. "Do you, on your soul, believe in all that about the shark and the camera?"

"I believe Keith's words," answered the other. "He is an honest man."

"I should like to question a regiment of his landladies," said Rupert cynically.

"I must say, I think you can hardly regard him as unimpeachable merely in himself," I said mildly; "his mode of life——"

Before I could complete the sentence the door was flung open and Drummond Keith appeared again on the threshold, his white Panama on his head.

"I say, Grant," he said, knocking off his cigarette ash against the door, "I've got no money in the world till next April. Could you lend me a hundred pounds? There's a good chap."

Rupert and I looked at each other in an ironical silence. Basil, who was sitting by his desk, swung the chair round idly on its screw and picked up a quill-pen.

"Shall I cross it?" he asked, opening a cheque-book.

"Really," began Rupert, with a rather nervous loudness, "since Lieutenant Keith has seen fit to make this suggestion to Basil before his family, I——"

"Here you are, Ugly," said Basil, fluttering a cheque in the direction of the quite nonchalant officer. "Are you in a hurry?"

"Yes," replied Keith, in a rather abrupt way. "As a matter of fact I want it now. I want to see my—er—business man."

Rupert was eyeing him sarcastically, and I could see that it was on the tip of his tongue to say, inquiringly, "Receiver of stolen goods, perhaps." What he did say was:

"A business man? That's rather a general description, Lieutenant Keith."

Keith looked at him sharply, and then said, with something rather like ill-temper:

"He's a thingum-my-bob, a house-agent, say. I'm going to see him."

"Oh, you're going to see a house-agent, are you?" said Rupert Grant grimly. "Do you know, Mr. Keith, I think I should very much like to go with you."

Basil shook with his soundless laughter. Lieutenant Keith started a little; his brow blackened sharply.

"I beg your pardon," he said. "What did you say?"

Rupert's face had been growing from stage to stage of ferocious irony, and he answered:

"I was saying that I wondered whether you would mind our strolling along with you to this house-agent's."

The visitor swung his stick with a sudden whirling violence.

"Oh, in God's name, come to my house-agent's! Come to my bedroom. Look under my bed. Examine my dust-bin. Come along!" And with a furious energy which took away our breath he banged his way out of the room.

Rupert Grant, his restless blue eyes dancing with his detective excitement, soon shouldered alongside him, talking to him with that transparent camaraderie which he imagined to be appropriate from the disguised policeman to the disguised criminal. His interpretation was certainly corroborated by one particular detail, the unmistakable unrest, annoyance, and nervousness of the man with whom he walked. Basil and I tramped behind, and it was not necessary for us to tell each other that we had both noticed this.

Lieutenant Drummond Keith led us through very extraordinary and unpromising neighbourhoods in the search for his remarkable house-agent. Neither of the brothers Grant failed to notice this fact. As the streets grew closer and more crooked and the roofs lower and the gutters grosser with mud, a darker curiosity deepened on the brows of Basil, and the figure of Rupert seen from behind seemed to fill the street with a gigantic swagger of success. At length, at the end of the fourth or fifth lean grey street in that sterile district, we came suddenly to a halt, the mysterious lieutenant looking once more about him with a sort of sulky desperation. Above a row of shutters and a door, all indescribably dingy in appearance and in size scarce sufficient even for a penny toyshop, ran the inscription: "P. Montmorency, House-Agent."

"This is the office of which I spoke," said Keith, in a cutting voice. "Will you wait here a moment, or does your astonishing tenderness about my welfare lead you to wish to overhear everything I have to say to my business adviser?"

Rupert's face was white and shaking with excitement; nothing on earth would have induced him now to have abandoned his prey.

"If you will excuse me," he said, clenching his hands behind his back, "I think I should feel myself justified in——"

"Oh! Come along in," exploded the lieutenant. He made the same gesture of savage surrender. And he slammed into the office, the rest of us at his heels.

P. Montmorency, house-agent, was a solitary old gentleman sitting behind a bare brown counter. He had an egglike head, froglike jaws, and a grey hairy fringe of aureole round the lower part of his face; the whole combined with a reddish, aquiline nose. He wore a shabby black frock-coat, a sort of semi-clerical tie worn at a very unclerical angle, and looked, generally speaking, about as unlike a house-agent as anything could look, short of something like a sandwich man or a Scotch Highlander.

We stood inside the room for fully forty seconds, and the odd old gentleman did not look at us. Neither, to tell the truth, odd as he was, did we look at him. Our eyes were fixed, where his were fixed, upon something that was crawling about on the counter in front of him. It was a ferret.

"Our eyes were fixed where his eyes were fixed, upon something on the counter. It was a ferret."

The silence was broken by Rupert Grant. He spoke in that sweet and steely voice which he reserved for great occasions and practised for hours together in his bedroom. He said:

"Mr. Montmorency, I think?"

The old gentleman started, lifted his eyes with a bland bewilderment, picked up the ferret by the neck, stuffed it alive into his trousers pocket, smiled apologetically, and said: "Sir."

"You are a house-agent, are you not?" asked Rupert.

To the delight of that criminal investigator, Mr. Montmorency's eyes wandered unquietly towards Lieutenant Keith, the only man present that he knew.

"A house-agent," cried Rupert again, bringing out the word as if it were "burglar."

"Yes . . . oh, yes," said the man, with a quavering and almost coquettish smile. "I am a house-agent . . . oh, yes."

"Well, I think," said Rupert, with a sardonic sleekness, "that Lieutenant Keith wants to speak to you. We have come in by his request."

Lieutenant Keith was lowering gloomily, and now he spoke.

"I have come, Mr. Montmorency, about that house of mine."

"Yes, sir," said Montmorency, spreading his fingers on that flat counter. "It's all ready, sir. I've attended to all your suggestions—er—about the br——"

"Right," cried Keith, cutting the word short with the startling neatness of a gunshot. "We needn't bother about all that. If you've done what I told you, all right."

And he turned sharply towards the door.

Mr. Montmorency, house-agent, presented a picture of pathos. After stammering a moment he said: "Excuse me . . . Mr. Keith . . . there was another matter . . . about which I wasn't quite sure. I tried to get all the heating apparatus possible under the circumstances . . . but in winter . . . at that elevation . . ."

"Can't expect much, eh?" said the lieutenant, cutting in with the same sudden skill. "No, of course not. That's all right, Montmorency. There can't be any more difficulties," and he put his hand on the handle of the door.

"I think," said Rupert Grant, with a satanic suavity, "that Mr.

Montmorency has something further to say to you, Lieutenant."

"Only," said the house-agent, in desperation, "what about the birds?"

"I beg your pardon," said Rupert, in a general blank.

"What about the birds?" said the house-agent doggedly. Basil, who had remained throughout the proceedings in a state of Napoleonic calm, which might be more accurately described as a state of Napoleonic stupidity, suddenly lifted his leonine head.

"Before you go, Lieutenant Keith," he said. "Come now. Really, what about the birds?"

"I'll take care of them," said Lieutenant Keith, still with his long back turned to us; "they shan't suffer."

"Thank you, sir, thank you," cried the incomprehensible house-agent, with an air of ecstasy. "You'll excuse my concern, sir. You know I'm wild on wild animals. I'm as wild as any of them on that. Thank you, sir. But there's another thing . . ."

The lieutenant, with his back turned to us, exploded with an indescribable laugh and swung round to face us. It was a laugh, the purport of which was direct and essential, and yet which one cannot exactly express. As near as it said anything, verbally speaking, it said: "Well, if you must spoil it, you must. But you don't know what you're spoiling."

"There is another thing," continued Mr. Montmorency weakly. "Of course, if you don't want to be visited you'll paint the house green, but——"

"Green!" shouted Keith. "Green! Let it be green or nothing. I won't have a house of another colour. Green!" and before we could realise anything the door had banged between us and the street.

Rupert Grant seemed to take a little time to collect himself; but he spoke before the echoes of the door died away.

"Your client, Lieutenant Keith, appears somewhat excited," he said. "What is the matter with him? Is he unwell?"

"Oh, I should think not," said Mr. Montmorency, in some confusion. "The negotiations have been somewhat difficult—the house is rather——"

"Green," said Rupert calmly. "That appears to be a very important point. It must be rather green. May I ask you, Mr. Montmorency,

"The Lieutenant . . . swung round to face us."

before I rejoin my companion outside, whether, in your business, it is usual to ask for houses by their colour? Do clients write to a house-agent asking for a pink house or a blue house? Or, to take another instance, for a green house?"

"Only," said Montmorency, trembling, "only to be inconspicuous."

Rupert had his ruthless smile. "Can you tell me any place on earth in which a green house would be inconspicuous?"

The house-agent was fidgeting nervously in his pocket. Slowly drawing out a couple of lizards and leaving them to run on the counter, he said:

"No; I can't."

"You can't suggest an explanation?"

"No," said Mr. Montmorency, rising slowly and yet in such a way as to suggest a sudden situation, "I can't. And may I, as a busy man, be excused if I ask you, gentlemen, if you have any demand to make of me in connection with my business. What kind of house would you desire me to get for you, sir?"

He opened his blank blue eyes on Rupert, who seemed for the second staggered. Then he recovered himself with perfect common sense and answered:

"I am sorry, Mr. Montmorency. The fascination of your remarks has unduly delayed us from joining our friend outside. Pray excuse my apparent impertinence."

"Not at all, sir," said the house-agent, taking a South American spider idly from his waistcoat pocket and letting it climb up the slope of his desk. "Not at all, sir. I hope you will favour me again."

Rupert Grant dashed out of the office in a gust of anger, anxious to face Lieutenant Keith. He was gone. The dull, starlit street was deserted.

"What do you say now?" cried Rupert to his brother. His brother said nothing now.

We all three strode down the street in silence, Rupert ferverish, myself dazed, Basil, to all appearance, merely dull. We walked through grey street after grey street, turning corners, traversing squares, scarcely meeting anyone, except occasional drunken knots of two or three.

In one small street, however, the knots of two or three began abruptly to thicken into knots of five or six and then into great groups and then into a crowd. The crowd was stirring very slightly. But anyone with a knowledge of the eternal populace knows that if the outside rim of a crowd stirs ever so slightly it means that there is madness in the heart and core of the mob. It soon became evident that something really important had happened in the centre of this excitement. We wormed our way to the front, with the cunning which is known only to cockneys, and once there we soon learned the nature of the difficulty. There had been a brawl concerned with some six men, and one of them lay almost dead on the stones of the street. Of the other four, all interesting matters were, as far as we were concerned, swallowed up in one stupendous fact. One of the four survivors of the brutal and perhaps fatal scuffle was the immaculate Lieutenant Keith, his clothes torn to ribbons, his eyes blazing, blood on his knuckles. One other thing, however, pointed at him in a worse manner. A short sword, or very long knife, had been drawn out of his elegant walking-stick, and lay in front of him upon the stones. It did not, however, appear to be bloody.

The police had already pushed into the centre with their ponderous omnipotence, and even as they did so, Rupert Grant sprang forward with his incontrollable and intolerable secret.

"That is the man, constable," he shouted, pointing at the battered Lieutenant. "He is a suspicious character. He did the murder."

"There's been no murder done, sir," said the policeman, with his automatic civility. "The poor man's only hurt. I shall only be able to take the names and addresses of the men in the scuffle and have a good eye kept on them."

"Have a good eye kept on that one," said Rupert, pale to the lips, and pointing to the ragged Keith.

"All right, sir," said the policeman unemotionally, and went the round of the people present, collecting the addresses. When he had completed his task the dusk had fallen and most of the people not immediately connected with the examination had gone away. He still found, however, one eager-faced stranger lingering on the outskirts of the affair. It was Rupert Grant.

"Constable," he said, "I have a very particular reason for asking you a question. Would you mind telling me whether that military fellow who dropped his swordstick in the row gave you an address or not?"

"Yes, sir," said the policeman, after a reflective pause; "yes, he gave me his address."

"My name is Rupert Grant," said that individual, with some pomp. "I have assisted the police on more than one occasion. I wonder whether you would tell me, as a special favour, what address?"

The constable looked at him.

"Yes," he said slowly, "if you like. His address is: 'The Elms, Buxton Common, near Purley, Surrey.' "

"Thank you," said Rupert, and ran home through the gathering night as fast as his legs could carry him, repeating the address to himself.

*   *   *

Rupert Grant generally came down late in a rather lordly way to breakfast; he contrived, I don't know how, to achieve always the attitude of the indulged younger brother. Next morning, however, when Basil and I came down we found him ready and restless.

"Well," he said sharply to his brother almost before we sat down to the meal. "What do you think of your Drummond Keith now?"

"What do I think of him?" inquired Basil slowly. "I don't think anything of him."

"I'm glad to hear it," said Rupert, buttering his toast with an energy that was somewhat exultant. "I thought you'd come round to my view, but I own I was startled at your not seeing it from the beginning. The man is a translucent liar and knave."

"I think," said Basil, in the same heavy monotone as before, "that I did not make myself clear. When I said that I thought nothing of him I meant grammatically what I said. I meant that I did not think about him; that he did not occupy my mind. You, however, seem to me to think a lot of him, since you think him a knave. I should say he was glaringly good myself."

"I sometimes think you talk paradox for its own sake," said

Rupert, breaking an egg with unnecessary sharpness. "What the deuce is the sense of it? Here's a man whose original position was, by our common agreement, dubious. He's a wanderer, a teller of tall tales, a man who doesn't conceal his acquaintance with all the blackest and bloodiest scenes on earth. We take the trouble to follow him to one of his appointments, and if ever two human beings were plotting together and lying to everyone else, he and that impossible house-agent were doing it. We followed him home, and the very same night he is in the thick of a fatal, or nearly fatal, brawl, in which he is the only man armed. Really, if this is being glaringly good, I must confess that the glare does not dazzle me."

Basil was quite unmoved. "I admit his moral goodness is of a certain kind, a quaint, perhaps a casual kind. He is very fond of change and experiment. But all the points you so ingeniously make against him are mere coincidence or special pleading. It's true he didn't want to talk about his house business in front of us. No man would. It's true that he carries a swordstick. Any man might. It's true he drew it in the shock of a street fight. Any man would. But there's nothing really dubious in all this. There's nothing to confirm——"

As he spoke a knock came at the door.

"If you please, sir," said the landlady, with an alarmed air, "there's a policeman wants to see you."

"Show him in," said Basil, amid the blank silence.

The heavy, handsome constable who appeared at the door spoke almost as soon as he appeared there.

"I think one of you gentlemen," he said, curtly but respectfully, "was present at the affair in Copper Street last night, and drew my attention very strongly to a particular man."

Rupert half rose from his chair, with eyes like diamonds, but the constable went on calmly, referring to a paper.

"A young man with grey hair. Had light grey clothes, very good, but torn in the struggle. Gave his name as Drummond Keith."

"This is amusing," said Basil, laughing. "I was in the very act of clearing that poor officer's character of rather fanciful aspersions. What about him?"

"Well, sir," said the constable, "I took all the men's addresses and had them all watched. It wasn't serious enough to do more than that. All the other addresses are all right. But this man Keith gave a false address. The place doesn't exist."

The breakfast table was nearly flung over as Rupert sprang up, slapping both his thighs.

"Well, by all that's good," he cried. "This is a sign from heaven."

"It's certainly very extraordinary," said Basil quietly, with knitted brows. "It's odd the fellow should have given a false address, considering he was perfectly innocent in the——"

"Oh, you jolly old early Christian duffer," cried Rupert, in a sort of rapture, "I don't wonder you couldn't be a judge. You think everyone as good as yourself. Isn't the thing plain enough now? A doubtful acquaintance; rowdy stories, a most suspicious conversation, mean streets, a concealed knife, a man nearly killed, and, finally, a false address. That's what we call glaring goodness."

"It's certainly very extraordinary," repeated Basil. And he strolled moodily about the room. Then he said: "You are quite sure, constable, that there's no mistake? You got the address right, and the police have really gone to it and found it was a fraud?"

"It was very simple, sir," said the policeman, chuckling. "The place he named was a well-known common quite near London, and our people were down there this morning before any of you were awake. And there's no such house. In fact, there are hardly any houses at all. Though it is so near London, it's a blank moor with hardly five trees on it, to say nothing of Christians. Oh, no, sir, the address was a fraud right enough. He was a clever rascal, and chose one of those scraps of lost England that people know nothing about. Nobody could say off-hand that there was not a particular house dropped somewhere about the heath. But as a fact, there isn't."

Basil's face during this sensible speech had been growing darker and darker with a sort of desperate sagacity. He was cornered almost for the first time since I had known him; and to tell the truth I rather wondered at the almost childish obstinacy which kept him so close to his original prejudice in favour of the wildly questionable lieutenant. At length he said:

"You really searched the common? And the address was really not known in the district—by the way, what was the address?"

The constable selected one of his slips of paper and consulted it, but before he could speak Rupert Grant, who was leaning in the window in a perfect posture of the quiet and triumphant detective, struck in with the sharp and suave voice he loved so much to use.

"Why, I can tell you that, Basil," he said graciously as he idly plucked leaves from a plant in the window. "I took the precaution to get this man's address from the constable last night."

"And what was it?" asked his brother gruffly.

"The constable will correct me if I am wrong," said Rupert, looking sweetly at the ceiling. "It was 'The Elms, Buxton Common, near Purley, Surrey.' "

"Right, sir," said the policeman, laughing and folding up his papers.

There was a silence, and the blue eyes of Basil looked blindly for a few seconds into the void. Then his head fell back in his chair so suddenly that I started up, thinking him ill. But before I could move further his lips had flown apart (I can use no other phrase) and a peal of gigantic laughter struck and shook the ceiling—laughter that shook the laughter, laughter redoubled, laughter incurable, laughter that could not stop.

Two whole minutes afterwards it was still unended; Basil was ill with laughter; but still he laughed. The rest of us were by this time ill almost with terror.

"Excuse me," said the insane creature, getting at last to his feet. "I am awfully sorry. It is horribly rude. And stupid, too. And also unpractical, because we have not much time to lose if we're to get down to that place. The train service is confoundedly bad, as I happen to know. It's quite out of proportion to the comparatively small distance."

"Get down to that place?" I repeated blankly. "Get down to what place?"

"I have forgotten its name," said Basil vaguely, putting his hands in his pockets as he rose. "Something Common near Purley. Has any one got a time-table?"

"You don't seriously mean," cried Rupert, who had been staring in a sort of confusion of emotions. "You don't mean that you want to go to Buxton Common, do you? You can't mean that!"

"Why shouldn't I go to Buxton Common?" asked Basil, smiling.

"Why should you?" said his brother, catching hold again restlessly of the plant in the window and staring at the speaker.

"To find our friend, the lieutenant, of course," said Basil Grant. "I thought you wanted to find him?"

Rupert broke a branch brutally from the plant and flung it impatiently on the floor. "And in order to find him," he said, "you suggest the admirable expedient of going to the only place on the habitable earth where we know he can't be."

The constable and I could not avoid breaking into a kind of assenting laugh, and Rupert, who had family eloquence, was encouraged to go on with a reiterated gesture:

"He may be in Buckingham Palace; he may be sitting astride the cross of St. Paul's; he may be in jail (which I think most likely); he may be in the Great Wheel;[14] he may be in my pantry; he may be in your store cupboard; but out of all the innumerable points of space, there is only one where he has just been systematically looked for and where we know that he is not to be found—and that, if I understand you rightly, is where you want us to go."

"Exactly," said Basil calmly, getting into his great-coat; "I thought you might care to accompany me. If not, of course, make yourselves jolly here till I come back."

It is our nature always to follow vanishing things and value them

[14] The Great Wheel, or the Gigantic Wheel, was situated on the Earl's Court Exhibition site on Warwick Road; with a diameter of 284 feet and a total height of over 300 feet, it enabled passengers to see as far as Windsor and beyond. It must have been a prominent sight in the London sky. The wheel revolved on a fifty-ton axle and had forty carriages the size of railway cars. Built in 1893 to the designs of Lieutenant Walter B. Bassett, AMICE, USN (d. 1907), the Gigantic Wheel was larger than the Ferris Wheel built for the 1891 Chicago World's Columbian Exhibition and continued to be a popular attraction until it was demolished in 1906. Several other Bassett Wheels were built, one 240 foot example at Blackpool continuing until 1928, but the only surviving wheel is that in the Prater in Vienna, which was featured in Carol Reed's 1950 film of Graham Greene's *The Third Man*.

if they really show a resolution to depart. We all followed Basil, and I cannot say why, except that he was a vanishing thing, that he vanished decisively with his great-coat and his stick. Rupert ran after him with a considerable flurry of rationality.

"My dear chap," he cried, "do you really mean that you see any good in going down to this ridiculous scrub, where there is nothing but beaten tracks and a few twisted trees, simply because it was the first place that came into a rowdy lieutenant's head when he wanted to give a lying reference in a scrape?"

"Yes," said Basil, taking out his watch, "and what's worse, we've lost the train."

He paused a moment and then added: "As a matter of fact, I think we may just as well go down later in the day. I have some writing to do, and I think you told me, Rupert, that you thought of going to the Dulwich Gallery.[15] I was rather too impetuous. Very likely he wouldn't be in. But if we get down by the 5:15, which gets to Purley[16] about 6, I expect we shall just catch him."

"Catch him!" cried his brother, in a kind of final anger. "I wish we could. Where the deuce shall we catch him now?"

"I keep forgetting the name of the common," said Basil, as he buttoned up his coat. "The Elms—what is it? Buxton Common, near Purley. That's where we shall find him."

"But there is no such place," groaned Rupert; but he followed his brother downstairs.

We all followed him. We snatched our hats from the hat-stand and our sticks from the umbrella-stand; and why we followed him we did not and do not know. But we always followed him, whatever was the meaning of the fact, whatever was the nature of his mastery. And the strange thing was that we followed him the more completely the more nonsensical appeared the thing which he said. At bottom, I believe, if he had risen from our breakfast table

[15] Dulwich Gallery is a small art gallery attached to Dulwich College in south London and noted for its collection of old masters.

[16] Purley is a suburb some twelve miles south of central London. Although long since swallowed by the conurbation, it marked the beginning of open country at the time Chesterton was writing.

and said: "I am going to find the Holy Pig with Ten Tails," we should have followed him to the end of the world.

I don't know whether this mystical feeling of mine about Basil on this occasion has got any of the dark and cloudy colour, so to speak, of the strange journey that we made the same evening. It was already very dense twilight when we struck southward from Purley. Suburbs and things on the London border may be, in most cases, commonplace and comfortable. But if ever by any chance they really are empty solitudes they are to the human spirit more desolate and dehumanised than any Yorkshire moors or Highland hills, because the suddenness with which the traveller drops into that silence has something about it as of evil elf-land. It seems to be one of the ragged suburbs of the cosmos half-forgotten by God—such a place was Buxton Common, near Purley.

There was certainly a sort of grey futility in the landscape itself. But it was enormously increased by the sense of grey futility in our expedition. The tracts of grey turf looked useless, the occasional wind-stricken trees looked useless, but we, the human beings, more useless than the hopeless turf or the idle trees. We were maniacs akin to the foolish landscape, for we were come to chase the wild goose which has led men and left men in bogs from the beginning. We were three dazed men under the captaincy of a madman going to look for a man whom we knew was not there in a house that had no existence. A livid sunset seemed to look at us with a sort of sickly smile before it died.

Basil went on in front with his coat collar turned up, looking in the gloom rather like a grotesque Napoleon. We crossed swell after swell of the windy common in increasing darkness and entire silence. Suddenly Basil stopped and turned to us, his hands in his pockets. Through the dusk I could just detect that he wore a broad grin as of comfortable success.

"Well," he cried, taking his heavily gloved hands out of his pockets and slapping them together, "here we are at last."

The wind swirled sadly over the homeless heath; two desolate elms rocked above us in the sky like shapeless clouds of grey. There was not a sign of man or beast to the sullen circle of the horizon,

"*Suddenly Basil stopped and turned to us, his hands in his pockets.*"

and in the midst of that wilderness Basil Grant stood rubbing his hands with the air of an innkeeper standing at an open door.

"How jolly it is," he cried, "to get back to civilisation. That notion that civilisation isn't poetical is a civilised delusion. Wait till you've really lost yourself in nature, among the devilish woodlands and the cruel flowers. Then you'll know that there's no star like the red star of man that he lights on his hearthstone; no river like the red river of man, the good red wine, which you, Mr. Rupert Grant, if I have any knowledge of you, will be drinking in two or three minutes in enormous quantities."

Rupert and I exchanged glances of fear. Basil went on heartily, as the wind died in the dreary trees.

"You'll find our host a much more simple kind of fellow in his own house. I did when I visited him when he lived in the cabin at Yarmouth, and again in the loft at the city warehouse. He's really a very good fellow. But his greatest virtue remains what I said originally."

"What do you mean?" I asked, finding his speech straying towards a sort of sanity. "What is his greatest virtue?"

"His greatest virtue," replied Basil, "is that he always tells the literal truth."

"Well, really," cried Rupert, stamping about between cold and anger, and slapping himself like a cabman, "he doesn't seem to have been very literal or truthful in this case, nor you either. Why the deuce, may I ask, have you brought us out to this infernal place?"

"He was too truthful, I confess," said Basil, leaning against the tree; "too hardly veracious, too severely accurate. He should have indulged in a little more suggestiveness and legitimate romance. But come, it's time we went in. We shall be late for dinner."

Rupert whispered to me with a white face:

"Is it a hallucination, do you think? Does he really fancy he sees a house?"

"I supose so," I said. Then I added aloud, in what was meant to be a cheery and sensible voice, but which sounded in my ears almost as strange as the wind:

"Come, come, Basil, my dear fellow. Where do you want us to go?"

"Why, up here," cried Basil, and with a bound and a swing he was above our heads, swarming up the grey column of the collossal tree.

"Come up, all of you," he shouted out of the darkness, with the voice of a schoolboy. "Come up. You'll be late for dinner."

The two great elms stood so close together that there was scarcely a yard anywhere, and in some places not more than a foot between them. Thus occasional branches and even bosses and boles formed a series of footholds that almost amounted to a rude natural ladder. They must, I supposed, have been some sport of growth, Siamese twins of vegetation.

Why we did it I cannot think; perhaps, as I have said, the mystery of the waste and dark had brought out and made primary something wholly mystical in Basil's supremacy. But we only felt that there was a giant's staircase going somewhere, perhaps to the stars; and the victorious voice above called to us out of heaven. We hoisted ourselves up after him.

Half-way up some cold tongue of the night air struck and sobered me suddenly. The hypnotism of the madman above fell from me, and I saw the whole map of our silly actions as clearly as if it were printed. I saw three modern men in black coats who had begun with a perfectly sensible suspicion of a doubtful adventurer and who had ended, God knows how, half-way up a naked tree on a naked moorland, far from that adventurer and all his works, that adventurer who was at that moment, in all probability, laughing at us in some dirty Soho restaurant. He had plenty to laugh at us about, and no doubt he was laughing his loudest; but when I thought what his laughter would be if he knew where we were at that moment, I nearly let go of the tree and fell.

"Swinburne," said Rupert suddenly, from above, "what are we doing? Let's get down again," and by the mere sound of his voice I knew that he too felt the shock of wakening to reality.

"We can't leave poor Basil," I said. "Can't you call to him or get hold of him by the leg?"

"He's too far ahead," answered Rupert; "he's nearly at the top of the beastly thing. Looking for Lieutenant Keith in the rooks' nests, I suppose."

We were ourselves by this time far on our frantic vertical journey. The mighty trunks were beginning to sway and shake slightly in the wind. Then I looked down and saw something which made me feel that we were far from the world in a sense and to a degree that I cannot easily describe. I saw that the almost straight lines of the tall elm tree diminished a little in perspective as they fell. I was used to seeing parallel lines taper towards the sky. But to see them taper towards the earth made me feel lost in space, like a falling star.

"Can nothing be done to stop Basil?" I called out.

"No," answered my fellow climber. "He's too far up. He must get to the top, and when he finds nothing but wind and leaves he may go sane again. Hark at him above there; you can just hear him talking to himself."

"Perhaps he's talking to us," I said.

"No," said Rupert, "he'd shout if he was. I've never known him to talk to himself before; I'm afraid he really is bad to-night; it's a known sign of the brain going."

"Yes," I said sadly, and listened. Basil's voice certainly was sounding above us, and not by any means in the rich and riotous tones in which he had hailed us before. He was speaking quietly, and laughing every now and then, up there among the leaves and stars.

After a silence mingled with this murmur, Rupert Grant suddenly said, "My God!" with a violent voice.

"What's the matter—are you hurt?" I cried, alarmed.

"No. Listen to Basil," said the other in a very strange voice. "He's not talking to himself."

"Then he is talking to us," I cried.

"No," said Rupert simply, "he's talking to somebody else."

Great branches of the elm loaded with leaves swung about us in a sudden burst of wind, but when it died down I could still hear the conversational voice above. I could hear two voices.

Suddenly from aloft came Basil's boisterous hailing voice as before: "Come up, you fellows. Here's Lieutenant Keith."

And a second afterwards came the half-American voice we had heard in our chambers more than once. It called out:

"Happy to see you, gentlemen; pray come in."

"'Happy to see you, gentlemen; pray come in'."

Out of a hole in an enormous dark egg-shaped thing, pendent in the branches like a wasps' nest, was protruding the pale face and fierce moustache of the lieutenant, his teeth shining with that slightly Southern air that belonged to him.

Somehow or other, stunned and speechless, we lifted ourselves heavily into the opening. We fell into the full glow of a lamp-lit, cushioned, tiny room, with a circular wall lined with books, a circular table, and a circular seat around it. At this table sat three people. One was Basil, who, in the instant after alighting there, had fallen into an attitude of marmoreal ease as if he had been there from boyhood; he was smoking a cigar with a slow pleasure. The second was Lieutenant Drummond Keith, who looked happy also, but feverish and doubtful compared with his granite guest. The third was the little bald-headed house-agent with the wild whiskers, who called himself Montmorency. The spears, the green umbrella, and the cavalry sword hung in parallels on the wall. The sealed jar of strange wine was on the mantelpiece, the enormous rifle in the corner. In the middle of the table was a magnum of champagne. Glasses were already set for us.

The wind of the night roared far below us, like an ocean at the foot of a light house. The room stirred slightly, as a cabin might in a mild sea.

Our glasses were filled, and we still sat there dazed and dumb. Then Basil spoke.

"You seem still a little doubtful, Rupert. Surely there is no further question about the cold veracity of our injured host."

"I don't quite grasp it all," said Rupert, blinking still in the sudden glare. "Lieutenant Keith said his address was — "

"It's really quite right, sir," said Keith, with an open smile. "The bobby asked me where I lived. And I said, quite truthfully, that I lived in the elms on Buxton Common, near Purley. So I do. This gentleman, Mr. Montmorency, whom I think you have met before, is an agent for houses of this kind. He has a special line in arboreal villas. It's being kept rather quiet at present, because the people who want these houses don't want them to get too common. But it's just the sort of thing a fellow like myself, racketing about in all sorts of queer corners of London, naturally knocks up against."

"Are you really an agent for arboreal villas?" asked Rupert eagerly, recovering his ease with the romance of reality.

Mr. Montmorency, in his embarrassment, fingered one of his pockets and nervously pulled out a snake, which crawled about the table.

"W-well, yes, sir," he said. "The fact was—er—my people wanted me very much to go into the house-agency business. But I never cared myself for anything but natural history and botany and things like that. My poor parents have been dead some years now, but—naturally I like to respect their wishes. And I thought somehow that an arboreal villa agency was a sort of—of compromise between being a botanist and being a house-agent."

Rupert could not help laughing. "Do you have much custom?" he asked.

"N-not much," replied Mr. Montmorency, and then he glanced at Keith, who was (I am convinced) his only client. "But what there is—very select."

"My dear friends," said Basil, puffing his cigar, "always remember two facts. The first is that though when you are guessing about anyone who is sane, the sanest thing is the most likely; when you are guessing about anyone who is, like our host, insane, the maddest thing is the most likely. The second is to remember that very plain literal fact always seems fantastic. If Keith had taken a little brick box of a house in Clapham with nothing but railings in front of it and had written 'The Elms' over it, you wouldn't have thought there was anything fantastic about that. Simply because it was a great blaring, swaggering lie you would have believed it."

"Drink your wine, gentlemen," said Keith, laughing, "for this confounded wind will upset it."

We drank, and as we did so, although the hanging house, by a cunning mechanism, swung only slightly, we knew that the great head of the elm-tree swayed in the sky like a stricken thistle.

V

THE NOTICEABLE CONDUCT OF
PROFESSOR CHADD

Basil Grant had comparatively few friends besides myself; yet he was the reverse of an unsociable man. He would talk to anyone anywhere, and talk not only well but with perfectly genuine concern and enthusiasm for that person's affairs. He went through the world, as it were, as if he were always on the top of an omnibus or waiting for a train. Most of these chance acquaintances, of course, vanished into darkness out of his life. A few here and there got hooked on to him, so to speak, and became his lifelong intimates, but there was an accidental look about all of them as if they were windfalls, samples taken at random, goods fallen from a goods train or presents fished out of a bran-pie. One would be, let us say, a veterinary surgeon with the appearance of a jockey; another, a mild prebendary with a white beard and vague views; another, a young captain in the Lancers, seemingly exactly like other captains in the Lancers; another, a small dentist from Fulham, in all reasonable certainty precisely like every other dentist from Fulham. Major Brown, small, dry, and dapper, was one of these; Basil had made his acquaintance over a discussion in a hotel cloak-room about the right hat, a discussion which reduced the little major almost to a kind of masculine hysterics, the compound of the selfishness of an old bachelor and the scrupulosity of an old maid. They had gone home in a cab together and then dined with each other twice a week until they died. I myself was another. I had met Grant while he was still a judge, on the balcony of the National Liberal Club,[17] and exchanged a few words about the weather. Then we had talked for about an hour about politics and God; for men always talk about the most important things to total strangers. It is because in the total stranger

[17] The National Liberal Club is situated on Northumberland Avenue, which runs from Trafalgar Square down toward the Embankment.

we perceive man himself; the image of God is not disguised by re-
semblances to an uncle or doubts of the wisdom of a moustache.

One of the most interesting of Basil's motley group of acquaintances was Professor Chadd. He was known to the ethnological
world (which is a very interesting world, but a long way off this
one) as the second greatest, if not the greatest, authority on the relations of savages to language. He was known to the neighbourhood
of Hart Street, Bloomsbury,[18] as a bearded man with a bald head,
spectacles, and a patient face, the face of an unaccountable Nonconformist[19] who had forgotten how to be angry. He went to and fro
between the British Museum and a selection of blameless tea-shops,
with an armful of books and a poor but honest unbrella.[20] He was
never seen without the books and the umbrella, and was supposed
(by the lighter wits of the Persian MS. room) to go to bed with
them in his little brick villa in the neighbourhood of Shepherd's
Bush.[21] There he lived with three sisters, ladies of solid goodness,
but sinister demeanour. His life was happy, as are almost all the lives
of methodical students, but one would not have called it exhilarating.
His only hours of exhilaration occurred when his friend, Basil Grant,
came into the house, late at night, a tornado of conversation.

Basil, though close on sixty, had moods of boisterous babyishness,[22] and these seemed for some reason or other to descend upon
him particularly in the house of his studious and almost dingy friend.
I can remember vividly (for I was acquainted with both parties

[18] Bloomsbury is the area between Gray's Inn Road and Tottenham Court Road
where the British Museum, the British Library, and University College are situated.

[19] A nonconformist is someone not conforming to the position and beliefs of the
established Church of England, but invariably a Protestant and almost certainly a
nondrinker.

[20] This artifact, a poor but honest umbrella, together with the preceding description of Professor Chadd, seems to indicate that, with the sole exception of the beard,
the basic appearance of Father Brown was already running through Chesterton's
mind in 1904.

[21] Shepherd's Bush is the area to the north of Kensington and to the west of Notting Hill.

[22] Babyishness in the sense used by Chesterton in 1904 was what we would now
call boyishness or tomfoolery.

and often dined with them) the gaiety of Grant on that particular evening when the strange calamity fell upon the professor. Professor Chadd was, like most of his particular class and type (the class that is at once academic and middle-class), a Radical[23] of a solemn and old-fashioned type. Grant was a Radical himself, but he was that more discriminating and not uncommon type of Radical who passes most of his time in abusing the Radical party. Chadd had just contributed to a magazine an article called "Zulu Interests and the New Makango Frontier," in which a precise scientific report of his study of the customs of the people of T'Chaka[24] was reinforced by a severe protest against certain interferences with these customs both by the British and the Germans.[25] He was sitting with the magazine in front of him, the lamplight shining on his spectacles, a wrinkle in his forehead, not of anger, but of perplexity, as Basil Grant strode up and down the room, shaking it with his voice, with his high spirits and his heavy tread.

"It's not your opinions that I object to, my esteemed Chadd," he was saying, "it's you. You are quite right to champion the Zulus, but for all that you do not sympathise with them. No doubt you know the Zulu way of cooking tomatoes and the Zulu prayer before blowing one's nose; but for all that you don't understand them as well as I do, who don't know an assegai[26] from an alligator. You are more learned, Chadd, but I am more Zulu. Why is it that the jolly old barbarians of this earth are always championed by people who are their antithesis? Why is it? You are sagacious, you are benevolent, you are well informed, but, Chadd, you are not savage. Live no longer under that rosy illusion. Look in the glass. Ask your sisters. Consult the librarian of the British Museum. Look at this umbrella." And he held

[23] Radical was the term generally applied to the more extremely reformist members of the Liberal Party.

[24] T'Chaka was a Bantu-speaking chieftain who organized various tribes to form the Zulu nation between 1818 and 1822. He became king of the Zulus but was assassinated in 1828.

[25] Germans did have colonies in Southwest Africa and Tanganyika, but here Chesterton intends to refer to the Boers of South Africa, whose origins were more specifically Dutch.

[26] An *assegai* is a short wooden stabbing spear tipped with iron, which was adopted by T'Chaka's warriors.

up that sad but still respectable article. "Look at it. For ten mortal years to my certain knowledge you have carried that object under your arm, and I have no sort of doubt that you carried it at the age of eight months, and it never occurred to you to give one wild yell and hurl it like a javelin — thus — "

And he sent the umbrella whizzing past the professor's bald head, so that it knocked over a pile of books with a crash and left a vase rocking.

Professor Chadd appeared totally unmoved, with his face still lifted to the lamp and the wrinkle cut in his forehead.

"Your mental processes," he said, "always go a little too fast. And they are stated without method. There is no kind of inconsistency" — and no words can convey the time he took to get to the end of the word — "between valuing the right of the aborigines to adhere to their stage in the evolutionary process, so long as they find it congenial and requisite to do so. There is, I say, no inconsistency between this concession which I have just described to you and the view that the evolutionary stage in question is, nevertheless, so far as we can form any estimate of values in the variety of cosmic processes, definable in some degree as an inferior evolutionary stage."

Nothing but his lips had moved as he spoke, and his glasses still shone like two pallid moons.

Grant was shaking with laughter as he watched him.

"True," he said, "there is no inconsistency, my son of the red spear. But there is a great deal of incompatibility of temper. I am very far from being certain that the Zulu is on an inferior evolutionary stage, whatever the blazes that may mean. I do not think there is anything stupid or ignorant about howling at the moon or being afraid of devils in the dark. It seems to me perfectly philosophical. Why should a man be thought a sort of idiot because he feels the mystery and peril of existence itself? Suppose, my dear Chadd, suppose it is we who are the idiots because we are not afraid of devils in the dark?"

Professor Chadd slit open a page of the magazine[27] with a bone paper-knife and the intent reverence of the bibliophile.

[27] The pages would have been uncut, as is still the custom in many parts of Europe. The practice is now almost unknown in Britain and North America.

"Beyond all question," he said, "it is a tenable hypothesis.[28] I allude to the hypothesis which I understand you to entertain, that our civilisation is not or may not be an advance upon, and indeed (if I apprehend you), is or may be a retrogression from states identical with or analogous to the state of the Zulus. Moreover, I shall be inclined to concede that such a proposition is of the nature, in some degree at least, of a primary proposition, and cannot adequately be argued, in the same sense, I mean, that the primary proposition of pessimism, or the primary proposition of the non-existence of matter, cannot adequately be argued. But I do not conceive you to be under the impression that you have demonstrated anything more concerning this proposition than that it is tenable, which, after all, amounts to little more than the statement that it is not a contradiction in terms."

Basil threw a book at his head and took out a cigar.

"You don't understand," he said, "but, on the other hand, as a compensation, you don't mind smoking. Why you don't object to that disgustingly barbaric rite I can't think. I can only say that I began it when I began to be a Zulu, about the age of ten. What I maintained was that although you knew more about Zulus in the sense that you are a scientist, I know more about them in the sense that I am a savage. For instance, your theory of the origin of language, something about its having come from the formulated secret language of some individual creature, though you knocked me silly with facts and scholarship in its favour, still does not convince me, because I have a feeling that that is not the way that things happen. If you ask me why I think so I can only answer that I am a Zulu; and if you ask me (as you most certainly will) what is my definition of a Zulu, I can answer that also. He is one who has climbed a Sussex apple-tree at seven and been afraid of a ghost in an English lane."

"Your process of thought——" began the immovable Chadd, but his speech was interrupted. His sister, with that masculinity which always in such families concentrates in sisters, flung open the door with a rigid arm and said:

"James, Mr. Bingham of the British Museum wants to see you again."

[28] Professor Chadd speaks in a dry academic style no doubt adopted by many with whom Chesterton debated.

The philosopher rose with a dazed look, which always indicates in such men the fact that they regard philosophy as a familiar thing, but practical life as a weird and unnerving vision, and walked dubiously out of the room.

"I hope you do not mind my being aware of it, Miss Chadd," said Basil Grant, "but I hear that the British Museum has recognised one of the men who have deserved well of their commonwealth. It is true, is it not, that Professor Chadd is likely to be made keeper of Asiatic manuscripts?"

The grim face of the spinster betrayed a great deal of pleasure and a great deal of pathos also. "I believe it's true," she said. "If it is, it will not only be great glory which women, I assure you, feel a great deal, but great relief, which they feel more; relief from worry from a lot of things. James' health has never been good, and while we are as poor as we are he had to do journalism and coaching, in addition to his own dreadful grinding notions and discoveries, which he loves more than man, woman, or child. I have often been afraid that unless something of this kind occurred we should really have to be careful of his brain. But I believe it is practically settled."

"I am delighted," began Basil, but with a worried face, "but these red-tape negotiations are so terribly chancy that I really can't advise you to build on hope, only to be hurled down into bitterness. I've known men, and good men like your brother, come nearer than this and be disappointed. Of course, if it is true——"

"If it is true," said the woman fiercely, "it means that people who have never lived may make an attempt at living."

Even as she spoke the professor came into the room still with the mazed look in his eyes.

"Is it true?" asked Basil, with burning eyes.

"Not a bit true," answered Chadd after a moment's bewilderment. "Your argument was in three points fallacious."

"What do you mean?" demanded Grant.

"Well," said the professor slowly, "in saying that you could possess a knowledge of the essence of Zulu life distinct from——"

"Oh! confound Zulu life," cried Grant, with a burst of laughter. "I mean, have you got the post?"

"You mean the post of keeper of the Asiatic manuscripts," he said, opening his eyes with childlike wonder. "Oh, yes, I got that. But the real objection to your argument, which has only, I admit, occurred to me since I have been out of the room, is that it does not merely presuppose a Zulu truth apart from the facts, but infers that the discovery of it is absolutely impeded by the facts."

"I am crushed," said Basil, and sat down to laugh, while the professor's sister retired to her room, possibly to laugh, possibly not.

*   *   *

It was extremely late when we left the Chadds, and it is an extremely long and tiresome journey from Shepherd's Bush to Lambeth. This may be our excuse for the fact that we (for I was stopping the night with Grant) got down to breakfast next day at a time inexpressibly criminal, a time, in point of fact, close upon noon. Even to that belated meal we came in a very lounging and leisurely fashion. Grant, in particular, seemed so dreamy at table that he scarcely saw the pile of letters by his plate, and I doubt if he would have opened any of them if there had not lain on the top that one thing which has succeeded amid modern carelessness in being really urgent and coercive—a telegram. This he opened with the same heavy distraction with which he broke his egg and drank his tea. When he read it he did not stir a hair or say a word, but something, I know not what, made me feel that the motionless figure had been pulled together suddenly as strings are tightened on a slack guitar. Though he said nothing and did not move, I knew that he had been for an instant cleared and sharpened with a shock of cold water. It was scarcely any surprise to me when a man who had drifted sullenly to his seat and fallen into it, kicked it away like a cur from under him and came round to me in two strides.

"What do you make of that?" he said, and flattened out the wire in front of me.

It ran: "Please come at once. James' mental state dangerous. Chadd."

"What does the woman mean?" I said after a pause, irritably.

" 'What do you make of that?' "

"Those women have been saying that the poor old professor was mad ever since he was born."

"You are mistaken," said Grant composedly. "It is true that all sensible women think all studious men mad. It is true, for the matter of that, all women of any kind think all men of any kind mad. But they don't put it in telegrams, any more than they wire to you that grass is green or God all-merciful. These things are truisms, and often private ones at that. If Miss Chadd has written down under the eye of a strange woman in a post-office that her brother is off his head you may be perfectly certain that she did it because it was a matter of life and death, and she can think of no other way of forcing us to come promptly."

"It will force us of course," I said, smiling.

"Oh, yes," he replied; "there is a cab-rank near."

Basil scarcely said a word as we drove across Westminster Bridge, through Trafalgar Square, along Piccadilly, and up the Uxbridge Road. Only as he was opening the gate he spoke.

"I think you will take my word for it, my friend," he said; "this is one of the most queer and complicated and astounding incidents that ever happened in London or, for that matter, in any high civilisation."

"I confess with the greatest sympathy and reverence that I don't quite see it," I said. "Is it so very extraordinary or complicated that a dreamy somnambulant old invalid who has always walked on the borders of the inconceivable should go mad under the shock of great joy? Is it so very extraordinary that a man with a head like a turnip and a soul like a spider's web should not find his strength equal to a confounding change of fortunes? Is it, in short, so very extraordinary that James Chadd should lose his wits from excitement?"

"It would not be extraordinary in the least," answered Basil, with placidity. "It would not be extraordinary in the least," he repeated, "if the professor had gone mad. That was not the extraordinary circumstance to which I referred."

"What," I asked, stamping my foot, "was the extraordinary thing?"

"The extraordinary thing," said Basil, ringing the bell, "is that he has not gone mad from excitement."

The tall and angular figure of the eldest Miss Chadd blocked the doorway as the door opened. Two other Miss Chadds seemed in the same way to be blocking the narrow passage and the little parlour. There was a general sense of their keeping something from view. They seemed like three black-clad ladies in some strange play of Maeterlinck,[29] veiling the catastrophe from the audience in the manner of the Greek chorus.

"Sit down, won't you?" said one of them, in a voice that was somewhat rigid with pain. "I think you had better be told first what has happened."

Then, with her bleak face looking unmeaningly out of the window, she continued, in an even and mechanical voice:

"I had better state everything that occurred just as it occurred. This morning I was clearing away the breakfast things, my sisters were both somewhat unwell, and had not come down. My brother had just gone out of the room, I believe, to fetch a book. He came back again, however, without it, and stood for some time staring at the empty grate. I said, 'Were you looking for anything I could get?' He did not answer, but this constantly happens, as he is often very abstracted. I repeated my question, and still he did not answer. Sometimes he is so wrapped up in his studies that nothing but a touch on the shoulder would make him aware of one's presence, so I came round the table towards him. I really do not know how to describe the sensation which I then had. It seems simply silly, but at the moment it seemed something enormous, upsetting one's brain. The fact is, James was standing on one leg."

Grant smiled slowly and rubbed his hands with a kind of care.

"Standing on one leg?" I repeated.

"Yes," replied the dead voice of the woman without an inflection to suggest that she felt the fantasticality of her statement. "He was standing on the left leg and the right drawn up at a sharp angle, the toe pointing downwards. I asked him if his leg hurt him. His only answer was to shoot the leg straight at right angles to the other, as if pointing to the other with his toe to the wall. He was still looking quite gravely at the fireplace.

[29] Maurice Materlinck (1862–1949) was a Belgian symbolist poet and dramatist, best known for *The Blue Bird*.

"James was standing on one leg."

" 'James, what is the matter?' I cried, for I was thoroughly frightened. James gave three kicks in the air with the right leg, flung up the other, gave three kicks in the air with it also and spun round like a teetotum the other way. 'Are you mad?' I cried. 'Why don't you answer me?' He had come to a standstill facing me, and was looking at me as he always does, with his lifted eyebrows and great spectacled eyes. When I had spoken he remained a second or two motionless, and then his only reply was to lift his left foot slowly from the floor and describe circles with it in the air. I rushed to the door and shouted for Christina. I will not dwell on the dreadful hours that followed. All three of us talked to him, implored him to speak to us with appeals that might have brought back the dead, but he has done nothing but hop and dance and kick with a solemn silent face. It looks as if his legs belonged to someone else or were possessed by devils. He has never spoken to us from that time to this."[30]

"Where is he now?" I said, getting up in some agitation. "We ought not to leave him alone."

"Doctor Colman is with him," said Miss Chadd calmly. "They are in the garden. Doctor Colman thought the air would do him good. And he can scarcely go into the street."

Basil and I walked rapidly to the window which looked out on the garden. It was a small and somewhat smug suburban gaden; the flower beds a little too neat and like the pattern of a coloured carpet; but on this shining and opulent summer day even they had the exuberance of something natural, I had almost said tropical. In the middle of a bright and verdant but painfully circular lawn stood two figures. One of them was a small, sharp-looking man with black whiskers and a very polished hat (I presume Dr. Colman), who was talking very quietly and clearly, yet with a nervous twitch, as it were, in his face. The other was our old friend, listening with his old forbearing expression and owlish eyes, the strong sunlight gleaming on his glasses as the lamplight had gleamed the night before, when the boisterous Basil had rallied him on his studious decorum.

[30] Chesterton's interest in semaphore codes was to continue, and he would subsequently use the theme several times. Compare the finger code used by Syme (Thursday) and the pseudo-Professor Worms in *The Man Who Was Thursday*.

But for one thing the figure of this morning might have been the identical figure of last night. That one thing was that while the face listened reposefully the legs were industriously dancing like the legs of a marionette. The neat flowers and the sunny glitter of the garden lent an indescribable sharpness and incredulity to the prodigy — the prodigy of the head of a hermit and the legs of a harlequin. For miracles should always happen in broad daylight. The night makes them credible and therefore commonplace.

The second sister had by this time entered the room and came somewhat drearily to the window.

"You know, Adelaide," she said, "that Mr. Bingham from the Museum is coming again at three."

"I know," said Adelaide Chadd bitterly. "I suppose we shall have to tell him about this. I thought that no good fortune would ever come easily to us."

Grant suddenly turned round. "What do you mean?" he said. "What will you have to tell Mr. Bingham?"

"You know what I shall have to tell him," said the professor's sister, almost fiercely. "I don't know that we need give it its wretched name. Do you think that the keeper of Asiatic manuscripts will be allowed to go on like that?" And she pointed for an instant at the figure in the garden, the shining, listening face and the unresting feet.

Basil Grant took out his watch with an abrupt movement. "When did you say the British Museum man was coming?" he said.

"Three o'clock," said Miss Chadd briefly.

"Then I have an hour before me," said Grant, and without another word threw up the window and jumped out into the garden. He did not walk straight up to the doctor and lunatic, but strolling round the garden path drew near them cautiously and yet apparently carelessly. He stood a couple of feet off them, seemingly counting halfpence out of his trousers pocket, but, as I could see, looking up steadily under the broad brim of his hat.

Suddenly he stepped up to Professor Chadd's elbow, and said, in a loud familiar voice, "Well, my boy, do you still think the Zulus our inferiors?"

The doctor knitted his brows and looked anxious, seeming to be about to speak. The professor turned his bald and placid head towards Grant in a friendly manner, but made no answer, idly flinging his left leg about.

"Have you converted Dr. Colman to your views?" Basil continued, still in the same loud and lucid tone.

Chadd only shuffled his feet and kicked a little with the other leg, his expression still benevolent and inquiring. The doctor cut in rather sharply. "Shall we go inside, professor?" he said. "Now you have shown me the garden. A beautiful garden. A most beautiful garden. Let us go in," and he tried to draw the kicking ethnologist by the elbow, at the same time whispering to Grant: "I must ask you not to trouble him with questions. Most risky. He must be soothed."

Basil answered in the same tone, with great coolness;

"Of course your directions must be followed out, doctor. I will endeavour to do so, but I hope it will not be inconsistent with them if you will leave me alone with my poor friend in this garden for an hour. I want to watch him. I assure you, Dr. Colman, that I shall say very little to him, and that little shall be as soothing as—as syrup."

The doctor wiped his eyeglass thoughtfully.

"It is rather dangerous for him," he said, "to be long in the strong sun without his hat. With his bald head, too."

"That is soon settled," said Basil composedly, and took off his own big hat and clapped it on the egglike skull of the professor. The latter did not turn round but danced away with his eyes on the horizon.

The doctor put on his glasses again, looked severely at the two for some seconds, with his head on one side like a bird's, and then saying, shortly, "All right," strutted away into the house, where the three Misses Chadd were all looking out from the parlour window on to the garden. They looked out on it with hungry eyes for a full hour without moving, and they saw a sight which was more extraordinary than madness itself.

Basil Grant addressed a few questions to the madman, without succeeding in making him do anything but continue to caper, and when he had done this slowly took a red note-book out of one pocket and a large pencil out of another.

He began hurriedly to scribble notes. When the lunatic skipped away from him he would walk a few yards in pursuit, stop, and make notes again. Thus they followed each other round and round the foolish circle of turf, the one writing in pencil with the face of a man working out a problem, the other leaping and playing like a child.

After about three-quarters of an hour of this imbecile scene, Grant put the pencil in his pocket, but kept the note-book open in his hand, and walking round the mad professor, planted himself directly in front of him.

Then occurred something that even those already used to that wild morning had not anticipated or dreamed. The professor, on finding Basil in front of him, stared with a blank benignity for a few seconds, and then drew up his left leg and hung it bent in the attitude that his sister had described as being the first of all his antics. And the moment he had done it Basil Grant lifted his own leg and held it out rigid before him, confronting Chadd with the flat sole of his boot. The professor dropped his bent leg, and swinging his weight on to it kicked out the other behind, like a man swimming. Basil crossed his feet like a saltire cross, and then flung them apart again, giving a leap into the air. Then before any of the spectators could say a word or even entertain a thought about the matter, both of them were dancing a sort of jig or hornpipe opposite each other; and the sun shone down on two madmen instead of one.

They were so stricken with the deafness and blindness of monomania that they did not see the eldest Miss Chadd come out feverishly into the garden with gestures of entreaty, a gentleman following her. Professor Chadd was in the wildest posture of a *pas-de-quatre*, Basil Grant seemed about to turn a cart-wheel, when they were frozen in their follies by the steely voice of Adelaide Chadd saying, "Mr. Bingham of the British Museum."

Mr. Bingham was a slim well-clad gentleman with a pointed and slightly effeminate grey beard, unimpeachable gloves, and formal but agreeable manners. He was the type of the over-civilised, as Professor Chadd was of the uncivilised pedant. His formality and agreeableness

"They followed each other round and round . . . one writing in pencil with the face of a man working out a problem, the other leaping and playing like a child."

did him some credit under the circumstances. He had a vast experience of books and a considerable experience of the more dilettante fashionable salons. But neither branch of knowledge had accustomed him to the spectacle of two grey-haired middle-class gentlemen in modern costume throwing themselves about like acrobats as a substitute for an after-dinner nap.

The professor continued his antics with perfect placidity, but Grant stopped abruptly. The doctor had reappeared on the scene, and his shiny black eyes, under his shiny black hat, moved restlessly from one of them to the other.

"Dr. Colman," said Basil, turning to him, "will you entertain Professor Chadd again for a little while? I am sure that he needs you. Mr. Bingham, might I have the pleasure of a few moments private conversation? My name is Grant."

Mr. Bingham, of the British Museum, bowed in a manner that was respectful but a trifle bewildered.

"Miss Chadd will excuse me," continued Basil easily, "if I know my way about the house." And he led the dazed librarian rapidly through the back door into the parlour.

"Mr. Bingham," said Basil, setting a chair for him, "I imagine that Miss Chadd has told you of this distressing occurrence."

"She has, Mr. Grant," said Bingham, looking at the table with a sort of compassionate nervousness. "I am more pained than I can say by this dreadful calamity. It seems quite heart-rending that the thing should have happened just as we have decided to give your eminent friend a position which falls far short of his merits. As it is, of course — really, I don't know what to say. Professor Chadd may, of course, retain — I sincerely trust he will — his extraordinarily valuable intellect. But I am afraid — I am really afraid — that it would not do to have the curator of the Asiatic manuscripts — er — dancing about."

"I have a suggestion to make," said Basil, and sat down abruptly in his chair, drawing it up to the table.

"I am delighted, of course," said the gentleman from the British Museum, coughing and drawing up his chair also.

The clock on the mantelpiece ticked for just the moments required for Basil to clear his throat and collect his words, and then he said:

"My proposal is this. I do not know that in the strict use of words you could altogether call it a compromise, still it has something of that character. My proposal is that the Government (acting, as I presume, through your Museum) should pay Professor Chadd £800 a year until he stops dancing."

"Eight hundred a year!" said Mr. Bingham, and for the first time lifted his mild blue eyes to those of his interlocutor — and he raised them with a mild blue stare. "I think I have not quite understood you. Did I understand you to say that Professor Chadd ought to be employed, in his present state, in the Asiatic manuscript department at eight hundred a year?"

Grant shook his head resolutely.

"No," he said firmly. "No. Chadd is a friend of mine, and I would say anything for him I could. But I do not say, I cannot say, that he ought to take on the Asiatic manuscripts. I do not go so far as that. I merely say that until he stops dancing you ought to pay him £800. Surely you have some general fund for the endowment of research."

Mr. Bingham looked bewildered.

"I really don't know," he said, blinking his eyes, "what you are talking about. Do you ask us to give this obvious lunatic nearly a thousand a year for life?"

"Not at all," cried Basil, keenly and triumphantly. "I never said for life. Not at all."

"What for, then?" asked the meek Bingham, suppressing an instinct meekly to tear his hair. "How long is this endowment to run? Not till his death? Till the Judgment day?"

"No," said Basil, beaming, "but just what I said. Till he has stopped dancing." And he lay back with satisfaction and his hands in his pockets.

Bingham had by this time fastened his eyes keenly on Basil Grant and kept them there.

"Come, Mr. Grant," he said. "Do I seriously understand you to suggest that the Government pay Professor Chadd an extraordinarily high salary simply on the ground that he has (pardon the phrase) gone mad? That he should be paid more than four good clerks solely on the ground that he is flinging his boots about in the back yard?"

" 'My proposal is that the government should pay Professor Chadd £800 a year until he stops dancing'."

"Precisely," said Grant composedly.

"That this absurd payment is not only to run on with the absurd dancing, but actually to stop with the absurd dancing?"

"One must stop somewhere," said Grant. "Of course."

Bingham rose and took up his perfect stick and gloves.

"There is really nothing more to be said, Mr. Grant," he said coldly. "What you are trying to explain to me may be a joke—a slightly unfeeling joke. It may be your sincere view, in which case I ask your pardon for the former suggestion. But, in any case, it appears quite irrelevant to my duties. The mental morbidity, the mental downfall, of Professor Chadd, is a thing so painful to me that I cannot easily endure to speak of it. But it is clear there is a limit to everything. And if the Archangel Gabriel went mad it would sever his connection, I am sorry to say, with the British Museum Library."

He was stepping towards the door, but Grant's hand, flung out in dramatic warning, arrested him.

"Stop!" said Basil sternly, "Stop while there is yet time. Do you want to take part in a great work, Mr. Bingham? Do you want to help in the glory of Europe—in the glory of science? Do you want to carry your head in the air when it is bald or white because of the part that you bore in a great discovery? Do you want——"

Bingham cut in sharply:

"And if I do want this, Mr. Grant——"

"Then," said Basil lightly, "your task is easy. Get Chadd £800 a year till he stops dancing."

With a fierce flap of his swinging gloves Bingham turned impatiently to the door, but in passing out of it found it blocked. Dr. Colman was coming in.

"Forgive me, gentlemen," he said, in a nervous, confidential voice, "the fact is, Mr. Grant, I—er—have made a most disturbing discovery about Mr. Chadd."

Bingham looked at him with grave eyes.

"I was afraid so," he said. "Drink, I imagine."

"Drink!" echoed Colman, as if that were a much milder affair. "Oh, no, it's not drink."

Mr. Bingham became somewhat agitated, and his voice grew hurried and vague. "Homicidal mania——" he began.

"No, no," said the medical man impatiently.

"Thinks he's made of glass," said Bingham feverishly, "or says he's God—or——"

"No," said Dr. Colman sharply; "the fact is, Mr. Grant, my discovery is of a different character. The awful thing about him is——"

"Oh, go on, sir," cried Bingham, in agony.

"The awful thing about him is," repeated Colman, with deliberation, "that he isn't mad."

"Not mad!"

"There are quite well-known physical tests of lunacy," said the doctor shortly; "he hasn't got any of them."

"But why does he dance?" cried the despairing Bingham. "Why doesn't he answer us? Why hasn't he spoken to his family?"

"The devil knows," said Dr. Colman coolly. "I'm paid to judge of lunatics, but not of fools. The man's not mad."

"What on earth can it mean? Can't we make him listen?" said Mr. Bingham. "Can none get into any kind of communication with him?"

Grant's voice struck in sudden and clear, like a steel bell:

"I shall be very happy," he said, "to give him any message you like to send."

Both men stared at him.

"Give him a message?" they cried simultaneously. "How will you give him a message?"

Basil smiled in his slow way.

"If you really want to know how I shall give him your message," he began, but Bingham cried:

"Of course, of course," with a sort of frenzy.

"Well," said Basil, "like this." And he suddenly sprang a foot into the air, coming down with crashing boots, and then stood on one leg.

His face was stern, though this effect was slightly spoiled by the fact that one of his feet was making wild circles in the air.

" 'The awful thing about him is that he isn't mad'."

"You drive me to it," he said. "You drive me to betray my friend. And I will, for his own sake, betray him."

The sensitive face of Bingham took on an extra expression of distress as of one anticipating some disgraceful disclosure. "Anything painful, of course——" he began.

Basil let his loose foot fall on the carpet with a crash that struck them all rigid in their feeble attitudes.

"Idiots!" he cried. "Have you seen the man? Have you looked at James Chadd going dismally to and fro from his dingy house to your miserable library, with his futile books and his confounded umbrella, and never seen that he has the eyes of a fanatic? Have you never noticed, struck casually behind his spectacles and above his seedy old collar, the face of a man who might have burned heretics, or died for the philosopher's stone? It is all my fault, in a way: I lit the dynamite of his deadly faith. I argued against him on the score of his famous theory about language — the theory that language was complete in certain individuals and was picked up by others simply by watching them. I also chaffed him about not understanding things in rough and ready practice. What has this glorious bigot done? He has answered me. He has worked out a system of language of his own (it would take too long to explain); he has made up, I say, a language of his own. And he has sworn that till people understand it, till he can speak to us in this language, he will not speak in any other. And he shall not. I have understood, by taking careful notice; and, by heaven, so shall the others. This shall not be blown upon. He shall finish his experiment. He shall have £800 a year from somewhere till he has stopped dancing. To stop him now is an infamous war on a great idea. It is religious persecution."

Mr. Bingham held out his hand cordially.

"I thank you, Mr. Grant," he said. "I hope I shall be able to answer for the source of the £800, and I fancy that I shall. Will you come in my cab?"

"No, thank you very much, Mr. Bingham," said Grant heartily. "I think I will go and have a chat with the professor in the garden."

The conversation between Chadd and Grant appeared to be personal and friendly. They were still dancing when I left.

"They were still dancing when I left."

VI

THE ECCENTRIC SECLUSION OF
THE OLD LADY

The conversation of Rupert Grant had two great elements of interest — first, the long fantasias of detective deduction in which he was engaged, and, second, his genuine romantic interest in the life of London. His brother Basil said of him: "His reasoning is particularly cold and clear, and invariably leads him wrong. But his poetry comes in abruptly and leads him right." Whether this was true of Rupert as a whole, or no, it was certainly curiously supported by one story about him which I think worth telling.

We were walking along a lonely terrace in Brompton[31] together. The street was full of that bright blue twilight which comes about half-past eight in summer, and which seems for the moment to be not so much a coming of darkness as the turning on of a new azure illuminator, as if the earth were lit suddenly by a sapphire sun. In the cool blue the lemon tint of the lamps had already begun to flame, and as Rupert and I passed them, Rupert talking excitedly, one after another the pale sparks sprang out of the dusk. Rupert was talking excitedly because he was trying to prove to me the nine hundred and ninety-ninth of his amateur detective theories. He would go about London, with this mad logic in his brain, seeing a conspiracy in a cab accident, and a special providence in a falling fusee.[32] His suspicions at the moment were fixed upon an unhappy milkman who walked in front of us. So arresting were the incidents which afterwards overtook us that I am really afraid that I have forgotten what were the main outlines of the milkman's crime. I think it had something to do with the fact that he had only one small can of milk to carry, and that of that he had left the lid loose and walked so

[31] Brompton is the area of London north of Chelsea and between Harrod's department store and the South Kensington museums.

[32] A falling *fusée* is a spent firework of the rocket type.

quickly that he spilled milk on the pavement. This showed that he was not thinking of his small burden, and this again showed that he anticipated some other than lacteal business at the end of his walk, and this (taken in conjunction with something about muddy boots) showed something else that I have entirely forgotten. I am afraid that I derided this detailed revelation unmercifully; and I am afraid that Rupert Grant, who, though the best of fellows, had a good deal of the sensitiveness of the artistic temperament, slightly resented my derision. He endeavoured to take a whiff of his cigar, with the placidity which he associated with his profession, but the cigar, I think, was nearly bitten through.

"My dear fellow," he said acidly, "I'll bet you half a crown[33] that wherever that milkman comes to a real stop I'll find out something curious."

"My resources are equal to that risk," I said, laughing. "Done."

We walked on for about a quarter of an hour in silence in the trail of the mysterious milkman. He walked quicker and quicker, and we had some ado to keep up with him: and every now and then he left a splash of milk, silver in the lamplight. Suddenly, almost before we could note it, he disappeared down the area steps[34] of a house. I believe Rupert really believed that the milkman was a fairy; for a second he seemed to accept him as having vanished. Then calling something to me which somehow took no hold on my mind, he darted after the mystic milkman, and disappeared himself into the area.

I waited for at least five minutes, leaning against a lamp-post in the lonely street. Then the milkman came swinging up the steps without his can and hurried off clattering down the road. Two or three minutes more elapsed, and then Rupert came bounding up also, his face pale but yet laughing; a not uncommon contradiction in him, denoting excitement.

"My friend," he said, rubbing his hands, "so much for all your

[33] Half a crown was a silver coin worth one eighth of a pound sterling. At the time Chesterton was writing, half a crown was the equivalent of fifty cents when fifty cents was half a silver dollar.

[34] The area steps were a stone stairway leading down from the street to a small yard, which gave access to the basement of a large town house.

scepticism. So much for your philistine ignorance of the possibilities of a romantic city. Two and sixpence[35] my boy, is the form in which your prosaic good nature will have to express itself."

"What?" I said incredulously, "do you mean to say that you really did find anything the matter with the poor milkman?"

His face fell.

"Oh, the milkman," he said, with a miserable affectation at having misunderstood me. "No, I—I—didn't exactly bring anything home to the milkman himself, I——"

"What did the milkman say and do?" I said, with inexorable sternness.

"Well, to tell the truth," said Rupert, shifting restlessly from one foot to another, "the milkman himself, as far as merely physical appearances went, just said, 'Milk, Miss,' and handed in the can. That is not to say, of course, that he did not make some secret sign or some——"

I broke into a violent laugh. "You idiot," I said, "why don't you own yourself wrong and have done with it? Why should he have made a secret sign any more than anyone else? You own he said nothing and did nothing worth mentioning. You own that, don't you?"

His face grew grave.

"Well, since you ask me, I must admit that I do. It is possible that the milkman did not betray himself. It is even possible that I was wrong about him."

"Then come along with you," I said, with a certain amicable anger, "and remember that you owe me half a crown."

"As to that, I differ from you," said Rupert coolly. "The milkman's remarks may have been quite innocent. Even the milkman may have been. But I do not owe you half a crown. For the terms of the bet were, I think, as follows, as I propounded them, that wherever that milkman came to a real stop I should find out something curious."

"Well?" I said.

[35] Two and sixpence was two shillings and sixpence, equivalent to half a crown. See note 33.

"Well," he answered, "I jolly well have. You just come with me," and before I could speak he had turned tail once more and whisked through the blue dark into the moat or basement of the house. I followed almost before I made any decision.

When we got down into the area I felt indescribably foolish —literally, as the saying is, in a hole. There was nothing but a closed door, shuttered windows, the steps down which we had come, the ridiculous well in which I found myself, and the ridiculous man who had brought me there, and who stood there with dancing eyes. I was just about to turn back when Rupert caught me by the elbow.

"Just listen to that," he said, and keeping my coat gripped in his right hand, he rapped with the knuckles of his left on the shutters of the basement window. His air was so definite that I paused and even inclined my head for a moment towards it. From inside was coming the murmur of an unmistakable human voice.

"Have you been talking to somebody inside?" I asked suddenly, turning to Rupert.

"No, I haven't," he replied, with a grim smile, "but I should very much like to. Do you know what somebody is saying in there?"

"No, of course not," I replied.

"Then I recommend you to listen," said Rupert sharply.

In the dead silence of the aristocratic street at evening, I stood a moment and listened. From behind the wooden partition, in which there was a long lean crack, was coming a continuous and moaning sound which took the form of the words: "When shall I get out? When shall I get out? Will they ever let me out?" or words to that effect.

"Do you know anything about this?" I said, turning upon Rupert very abruptly.

"Perhaps you think I am the criminal," he said sardonically, "instead of being in some small sense the detective. I came into this area two or three minutes ago, having told you that I knew there was something funny going on, and this woman behind the shutters (for it evidently is a woman) was moaning like mad. No, my dear friend, beyond that I do not know anything about her. She is not, startling as it may seem, my disinherited daughter, or a member of my secret

"'Just listen to that,' he said."

seraglio.[36] But when I hear a human being wailing that she can't get out, and talking to herself like a mad woman and beating on the shutters with her fists, as she was doing two or three minutes ago, I think it worth mentioning, that is all."

"My dear fellow," I said, "I apologise; this is no time for arguing. What is to be done?"

Rupert Grant had a long clasp-knife naked and brilliant in his hand.

"First of all," he said, "house-breaking." And he forced the blade into the crevice of the wood and broke away a huge splinter, leaving a gap and glimpse of the dark window-pane inside. The room within was entirely unlighted, so that for the first few seconds the window seemed a dead and opaque surface, as dark as a strip of slate. Then came a realisation which, though in a sense gradual, made us step back and catch our breath. Two large dim human eyes were so close to us that the window itself seemed suddenly to be a mask. A pale human face was pressed against the glass within, and with increased distinctness, with the increase of the opening came the words:

"When shall I get out?"

"What can all this be?" I said.

Rupert made no answer, but lifting his walking-stick and pointing the ferrule like a fencing sword at the glass, punched a hole in it, smaller and more accurate than I should have supposed possible. The moment he had done so the voice spouted out of the hole, so to speak, piercing and querulous and clear, making the same demand for liberty.

"Can't you get out, madam?" I said, drawing near the hole in some perturbation.

"Get out? Of course I can't," moaned the unknown female bitterly. "They won't let me. I told them I would be let out. I told them I'd call the police. But it's no good. Nobody knows, nobody comes. They could keep me as long as they liked only — "

I was in the very act of breaking the window finally with my

---

[36] A seraglio is a harem.

stick, incensed with this very sinister mystery, when Rupert held my arm hard, held it with a curious, still and secret rigidity as if he desired to stop me, but did not desire to be observed to do so. I paused a moment, and in the act swung slightly round, so that I was facing the supporting wall of the front door steps. The act froze me into a sudden stillness like that of Rupert, for a figure almost as motionless as the pillars of the portico, but unmistakably human, had put his head out from between the doorposts and was gazing down into the area. One of the lighted lamps of the street was just behind his head, throwing it into abrupt darkness. Consequently, nothing whatever could be seen of his face beyond one fact, that he was unquestionably staring at us. I must say I thought Rupert's calmness magnificent. He rang the area bell quite idly, and went on talking to me with the easy end of a conversation which had never had any beginning. The black glaring figure in the portico did not stir. I almost thought it was really a statue. In another moment the grey area was golden with gaslight as the basement door was opened suddenly and a small and decorous housemaid stood in it.

"Pray excuse me," said Rupert, in a voice which he contrived to make somehow or other at once affable and underbred, "but we thought perhaps that you might do something for the Waifs and Strays. We don't expect——"

"Not here," said the small servant, with the incomparable severity of the menial of the non-philanthropic, and slammed the door in our faces.

"Very sad, very sad—the indifference of these people," said the philanthropist with gravity, as we went together up the steps. As we did so the motionless figure in the portico suddenly disappeared.

"Well, what do you make of that?" asked Rupert, slapping his golves together when we got into the street.

I do not mind admitting that I was seriously upset. Under such conditions I had but one thought.

"Don't you think," I said a trifle timidly, "that we had better tell your brother?"

"Oh, if you like," said Rupert, in a lordly way. "He is quite near, as I promised to meet him at Gloucester Road Station.[37] Shall we take a cab? Perhaps, as you say, it might amuse him."

---

[37] Gloucester Road Station was and is on the underground railway.

Gloucester Road Station had, as if by accident, a somewhat deserted look. After a little looking about we discovered Basil Grant with his great head and his great white hat blocking the ticket-office window. I thought at first that he was taking a ticket for somewhere and being an astonishingly long time about it. As a matter of fact, he was discussing religion with the booking-office clerk, and had almost got his head through the hole in his excitement. When we dragged him away it was some time before he would talk of anything but the growth of an Oriental fatalism in modern thought, which had been well typified by some of the official's ingenious but perverse fallacies. At last we managed to get him to understand that we had made an astounding discovery. When he did listen, he listened attentively, walking between us up and down the lamp-lit street, while we told him in a rather feverish duet of the great house in South Kensington, of the equivocal milkman, of the lady imprisoned in the basement, and the man staring from the porch. At length he said:

"If you're thinking of going back to look the thing up, you must be careful what you do. It's no good you two going there. To go twice on the same pretext would look dubious. To go on a different pretext would look worse. You may be quite certain that the inquisitive gentleman who looked at you looked thoroughly, and will wear, so to speak, your portraits next to his heart. If you want to find out if there is anything in this without a police raid I fancy you had better wait outside. I'll go in and see them."

His slow and reflective walk brought us at length within sight of the house. It stood up ponderous and purple against the last pallor of twilight. It looked like an ogre's castle. And so apparently it was.

"Do you think it's safe, Basil," said his brother, pausing, a little pale, under the lamp, "to go into that place alone? Of course we shall be near enough to hear if you yell, but these devils might do something—something sudden—or odd. I can't feel it's safe."

"I know of nothing that is safe," said Basil composedly, "except, possibly—death," and he went up the steps and rang at the bell. When the massive respectable door opened for an instant, cutting a square of gaslight in the gathering dark, and then closed with a

"Discussing religion with the booking-office clerk."

bang, burying our friend inside, we could not repress a shudder. It had been like the heavy gaping and closing of the dim lips of some evil leviathan. A freshening night breeze began to blow up the street, and we turned up the collars of our coats. At the end of twenty minutes, in which we had scarcely moved or spoken, we were as cold as icebergs, but more, I think, from apprehension than the atmosphere. Suddenly Rupert made an abrupt movement towards the house.

"I can't stand this," he began, but almost as he spoke sprang back into the shadow, for the panel of gold was again cut out of the black house front, and the burly figure of Basil was silhouetted against it coming out. He was roaring with laughter and talking so loudly that you could have heard every syllable across the street. Another voice, or, possibly, two voices, were laughing and talking back at him from within.

"No, no, no," Basil was calling out, with a sort of hilarious hostility. "That's quite wrong. That's the most ghastly heresy of all. It's the soul, my dear chap, the soul that's the arbiter of cosmic forces. When you see a cosmic force you don't like, trick it, my boy. But I must really be off."

"Come and pitch into us again," came the laughing voice from out of the house. "We still have some bones unbroken."

"Thanks very much, I will—good-night," shouted Grant, who had by this time reached the street.

"Good-night," came the friendly call in reply, before the door closed.

"Basil," said Rupert Grant, in a hoarse whisper, "what are we to do?"

The elder brother looked thoughtfully from one of us to the other.

"What is to be done, Basil?" I repeated in uncontrollable excitement.

"I'm not sure," said Basil doubtfully. "What do you say to getting some dinner somewhere and going to the Court Theatre[38] tonight? I tried to get those fellows to come, but they couldn't."

[38] The Court Theatre is situated in Holland Park in Kensington, but there is also the Royal Court Theatre situated in Sloane Square about a mile away in Chelsea. Chesterton seems to confuse them.

We stared blankly.

"Go to the Court Theatre?" repeated Rupert. "What would be the good of that?"

"Good? What do you mean?" answered Basil, staring also. "Have you turned Puritan or Passive Resister,[39] or something? For fun, of course."

"But, great God in Heaven! What are we going to do, I mean!" cried Rupert. "What about the poor woman locked up in that house? Shall I go for the police?"

Basil's face cleared with immediate comprehension, and he laughed.

"Oh, that," he said. "I'd forgotten that. That's all right. Some mistake, possibly. Or some quite trifling private affair. But I'm sorry those fellows couldn't come with us. Shall we take one of these green omnibuses? There is a restaurant in Sloane Square."

"I sometimes think you play the fool to frighten us," I said irritably. "How can we leave that woman locked up? How can it be a mere private affair? How can crime and kidnapping and murder, for all I know, be private affairs? If you found a corpse in a man's dressing-room, would you think it bad taste to talk about it just as if it was a confounded dado or an infernal etching?"

Basil laughed heartily.

"That's very forcible," he said. "As a matter of fact, though, I know it's all right in this case. And there comes the green omnibus."

"How do you know it's all right in this case?" persisted his brother angrily.

"My dear chap, the thing's obvious," answered Basil, holding a return ticket between his teeth while he fumbled in his waistcoat pocket. "Those two fellows never committed a crime in their lives. They're not the kind. Have either of you chaps got a halfpenny? I want to get a paper before the omnibus comes."

"Oh, curse the paper!" cried Rupert, in a fury. "Do you mean to tell me, Basil Grant, that you are going to leave a fellow creature in pitch darkness in a private dungeon, because you've had ten minutes' talk with the keepers of it and thought them rather good men?"

---

[39] A passive resister is a conscientious objector.

"Good men do commit crimes sometimes," said Basil, taking the ticket out of his mouth. "But this kind of good man doesn't commit that kind of crime. Well, shall we get on this omnibus?"

The great green vehicle was indeed plunging and lumbering along the dim wide street towards us. Basil had stepped from the curb, and for an instant it was touch and go whether we should all have leaped on to it and been borne away to the restaurant and the theatre.

"Basil," I said, taking him firmly by the shoulder, "I simply won't leave this street and this house."

"Nor will I," said Rupert, glaring at it and biting his fingers. "There's some black work going on there. If I left it I should never sleep again."

Basil Grant looked at us both seriously.

"Of course if you feel like that," he said, "we'll investigate further. You'll find it's all right, though. They're only two young Oxford fellows. Extremely nice, too, though rather infected with this pseudo-Darwinian business. Ethics of evolution and all that."

"I think," said Rupert darkly, ringing the bell, "that we shall enlighten you further about their ethics."

"And may I ask," said Basil gloomily, "what it is that you propose to do?"

"I propose, first of all," said Rupert, "to get into this house; secondly, to have a look at these nice young Oxford men; thirdly, to knock them down, bind them, gag them, and search the house."

Basil stared indignantly for a few minutes. Then he was shaken for an instant with one of his sudden laughs.

"Poor little boys," he said. "But it almost serves them right for holding such silly views, after all," and he quaked again with amusement; "there's something confoundedly Darwinian about it."

"I suppose you mean to help us?" said Rupert.

"Oh, yes, I'll be in it," answered Basil, "if it's only to prevent your doing the poor chaps any harm."

He was standing in the rear of our little procession, looking indifferent and sometimes even sulky, but somehow the instant the door opened he stepped first into the hall, glowing with urbanity.

"So sorry to haunt you like this," he said. "I met two friends outside who very much want to know you. May I bring them in?"

"Delighted, of course," said a young voice, the unmistakable voice of the Isis,[40] and I realised that the door had been opened, not by the decorous little servant girl, but by one of our hosts in person. He was a short, but shapely young gentleman, with curly dark hair and a square, snub-nosed face. He wore slippers and a sort of blazer of some incredible college purple.

"This way," he said; "mind the steps by the staircase. This house is more crooked and old-fashioned than you would think from its snobbish exterior. There are quite a lot of odd corners in the place really."

"That," said Rupert, with a savage smile, "I can quite believe."

We were by this time in the study or back parlour, used by the young inhabitants as a sitting-room, an apartment littered with magazines and books ranging from Dante to detective stories. The other youth, who stood with his back to the fire smoking a corncob, was big and burly, with dead brown hair brushed forward and a Norfolk jacket. He was that particular type of man whose every feature and action is heavy and clumsy, and yet who is, you would say, rather exceptionally a gentleman.

"Any more arguments?" he said, when introductions had been effected. "I must say, Mr. Grant, you were rather severe upon eminent men of science such as we. I've half a mind to chuck my D. Sc. and turn minor poet."

"Bosh," answered Grant. "I never said a word against eminent men of science. What I complain of is a vague popular philosophy which supposes itself to be scientific when it is really nothing but a sort of new religion and an uncommonly nasty one. When people talked about the fall of man they knew they were talking about a mystery, a thing they didn't understand. Now that they talk about the survival of the fittest they think they do understand it, whereas they have not merely no notion, they have an elaborately false notion of what the words mean. The Darwinian movement has made no difference to mankind, except that, instead of talking unphilosophically about philosophy, they now talk unscientifically about science."

[40] The unmistakable voice of the Isis refers to the accents heard at Oxford University. The part of the River Thames running through the city of Oxford is always called the Isis.

"Smoking a corn-cob."

"That is all very well," said the big young man, whose name appered to be Burrows. "Of course, in a sense, science, like mathematics or the violin, can only be perfectly understood by specialists. Still, the rudiments may be of public use. Greenwood here," indicating the little man in the blazer, "doesn't know one note of music from another. Still, he knows something. He knows enough to take off his hat when they play 'God save the King.' He doesn't take it off by mistake when they play 'Oh, dem Golden Slippers.' Just in the same way science——"

Here Mr. Burrows stopped abruptly. He was interrupted by an argument uncommon in philosophical controversy and perhaps not wholly legitimate. Rupert Grant had bounded on him from behind, flung an arm round his throat, and bent the giant backwards.

"Knock the other fellow down, Swinburne," he called out, and before I knew where I was I was locked in a grapple with the man in the purple blazer. He was a wiry fighter, who bent and sprang like a whalebone, but I was heavier and had taken him utterly by surprise. I twitched one of his feet from under him; he swung for a moment on the single foot, and then we fell with a crash amid the litter of newspapers, myself on top.

My attention for a moment released by victory, I could hear Basil's voice finishing some long sentence of which I had not heard the beginning.

". . . wholly, I must confess, unintelligible to me, my dear sir, and I need not say unpleasant. Still one must side with one's old friends against the most fascinating new ones. Permit me, therefore, in tying you up in this antimacassar, to make it as commodious as handcuffs can reasonably be while . . ."

I had staggered to my feet. The gigantic Burrows was toiling in the garrotte of Rupert, while Basil was striving to master his mighty hands. Rupert and Basil were both particularly strong, but so was Mr. Burrows; how strong, we knew a second afterwards. His head was held back by Rupert's arm, but a convulsive heave went over his whole frame. An instant after his head plunged forward like a bull's, and Rupert Grant was slung head over heels, a catherine wheel of legs, on the floor in front of him. Simultaneously the bull's head butted Basil in the chest, bringing him also to the ground with a crash, and the monster, with a Berserker[41] roar, leaped at me and knocked me into the corner of the room, smashing the waste-paper basket. The bewildered Greenwood sprang furiously to his feet. Basil did the same. But they had the best of it now.

Greenwood dashed to the bell and pulled it violently, sending peals through the great house. Before I could get panting to my feet, and before Rupert, who had been literally stunned for a few moments, could even lift his head from the floor, two footmen were in the room. Defeated even when we were in a majority, we were now outnumbered. Greenwood and one of the footmen flung themselves upon me, crushing me back into the corner upon the wreck of the paper basket. The other two flew at Basil, and pinned him against the wall. Rupert lifted himself on his elbow, but he was still dazed.

In the strained silence of our helplessness I heard the voice of Basil come with a loud incongruous cheerfulness.

"Now this," he said, "is what I call enjoying oneself."

I caught a glimpse of his face, flushed and forced against the bookcase, from between the swaying limbs of my captors and his. To my astonishment his eyes were really brilliant with pleasure, like those of a child heated by a favourite game.

I made several apoplectic efforts to rise, but the servant was on top of me so heavily that Greenwood could afford to leave me to him. He turned quickly to come to reinforce the two who were mastering Basil. The latter's head was already sinking lower and lower, like a leaking ship, as his enemies pressed him down. He flung up one hand just as I thought him falling and hung on to a huge tome in the bookcase, a volume, I afterwards discovered, of St. Chrysostom's theology. Just as Greenwood bounded across the room towards the group, Basil plucked the ponderous tome bodily out of the shelf, swung it, and sent it spinning through the air, so that it struck Greenwood flat in the face and knocked him over like a rolling ninepin. At the same instant Basil's stiffness broke, and he sank, his enemies closing over him.

---

[41] Berserker was a Norse warrior given to being gripped by violent rages.

Rupert's head was clear, but his body shaken; he was hanging as best he could on to the half-prostrate Greenwood. They were rolling over each other on the floor, both somewhat enfeebled by their falls, but Rupert certainly the more so. I was still successfully held down. The floor was a sea of torn and trampled papers and magazines, like an immense waste-paper basket. Burrows and his companion were almost up to the knees in them, as in a drift of dead leaves. And Greenwood had his leg struck right through a sheet of the *Pall Mall Gazette*,[42] which clung to it ludicrously, like some fantastic trouser frill.

Basil, shut from me in a human prison, a prison of powerful bodies, might be dead for all I knew. I fancied, however, that the broad back of Mr. Burrows, which was turned towards me, had a certain bend of effort in it as if my friend still needed some holding down. Suddenly that broad back swayed hither and thither. It was swaying on one leg; Basil, somehow, had hold of the other. Burrows' huge fists and those of the footmen were battering Basil's sunken head like an anvil, but nothing could get the giant's ankle out of his sudden and savage grip. While his own head was forced slowly down in darkness and great pain, the right leg of his captor was being forced in the air. Burrows swung to and fro with a purple face. Then suddenly the floor and the walls and the ceiling shook together, as the colossus fell, all his length seeming to fill the floor. Basil sprang up with dancing eyes, and with three blows like battering-rams knocked the footman into a cocked hat. Then he sprang on top of Burrows, with one antimacassar in his hand and another in his teeth, and bound him hand and foot almost before he knew clearly that his head had struck the floor. Then Basil sprang at Greenwood whom Rupert was struggling to hold down, and between them they secured him easily. The man who had hold of me let go and turned to his rescue, but I leaped up like a spring released, and, to my infinite satisfaction, knocked the fellow down. The other footman, bleeding at the mouth and quite demoralised, was stumbling out of the room. My late captor, without a word, slunk after him, seeing that the battle was won. Rupert was sitting

[42] The *Pall Mall Gazette* was a literary newspaper of radical persuasion founded in 1865 by Frederick Greenwood (1830–1909).

astride the pinioned Mr. Greenwood, Basil astride the pinioned Mr. Burrows.

To my surprise the latter gentleman, lying bound on his back, spoke in a perfectly calm voice to the man who sat on top of him.

"And now, gentlemen," he said, "since you have got your own way, perhaps you wouldn't mind telling us what the deuce all this is?"

"This," said Basil, with a radiant face, looking down at his captive, "this is what we call the survival of the fittest."

Rupert, who had been steadily collecting himself throughout the latter phases of the fight, was intellectually altogether himself again at the end of it. Springing up from the prostrate Greenwood, and knotting a handkerchief round his left hand, which was bleeding from a blow, he sang out quite coolly:

"Basil, will you mount guard over the captive of your bow and spear and antimacassar? Swinburne and I will clear out the prison downstairs."

"All right," said Basil, rising also and seating himself in a leisured way in an armchair. "Don't hurry for us," he said, glancing round at the litter of the room, "we have all the illustrated papers."

Rupert lurched thoughtfully out of the room, and I followed him even more slowly; in fact, I lingered long enough to hear, as I passed through the room, the passages and the kitchen stairs, Basil's voice continuing conversationally:

"And now, Mr. Burrows," he said, settling himself sociably in the chair, "there's no reason why we shouldn't go on with that amusing argument. I'm sorry that you have to express yourself lying on your back on the floor, and, as I told you before, I've no more notion why you are there than the man in the moon. A conversationalist like yourself, however, can scarcely be seriously handicapped by any bodily posture. You were saying, if I remember right, when this incidental fracas occurred, that the rudiments of science might with advantage be made public."

"Precisely," said the large man on the floor in an easy tone. "I hold that nothing more than a rough sketch of the universe as seen by science can be . . ."

And here the voices died away as we descended into the basement. I noticed that Mr. Greenwood did not join in the amicable controversy. Strange as it may appear, I think he looked back upon our proceedings with a slight degree of resentment. Mr. Burrows, however, was all philosophy and chattiness. We left them, as I say, together, and sank deeper and deeper into the under-world of that mysterious house, which, perhaps, appeared to us somewhat more Tartarean[43] than it really was, owing to our knowledge of its semi-criminal mystery and of the human secret locked below.

The basement floor had several doors, as is usual in such a house; doors that would naturally lead to the kitchen, the scullery, the pantry, the servants' hall, and so on. Rupert flung open all the doors with indescribable rapidity. Four out of the five opened on entirely empty apartments. The fifth was locked. Rupert broke the door in like a bandbox, and we fell into the sudden blackness of the sealed, unlighted room.

Rupert stood on the threshold, and called out like a man calling into an abyss:

"Whoever you are, come out. You are free. The people who held you captive are captives themselves. We heard you crying and we came to deliver you. We have bound your enemies upstairs hand and foot. You are free."

For some seconds after he had spoken into the darkness there was a dead silence in it. Then there came a kind of muttering and moaning. We might easily have taken it for the wind or rats if we had not happened to have heard it before. It was unmistakably the voice of the imprisoned woman, drearily demanding liberty, just as we had heard her demand it.

"Has anybody got a match?" said Rupert grimly. "I fancy we have come pretty near the end of this business."

I struck a match and held it up. It revealed a large, bare, yellow-papered apartment with a dark clad figure at the other end of it near the window. An instant after it burned my fingers and dropped, leaving darkness. It had, however, revealed something more practical—

[43] Tartarean means hellish, referring to Tartarus, the underworld in Greek mythology.

an iron gas bracket just above my head. I struck another match and lit the gas. And we found ourselves suddenly and seriously in the presence of the captive.

At a sort of workbox in the window of this subterranean breakfast-room sat an elderly lady with a singularly high colour and almost startling silver hair. She had, as if designedly to relieve these effects, a pair of Mephistophelian black eyebrows and a very neat black dress. The glare of the gas lit up her piquant hair and face perfectly against the brown background of the shutters. The background was blue and not brown in one place; at the place where Rupert's knife had torn a great opening in the wood about an hour before.

"Madam," said he, advancing with a gesture of the hat, "permit me to have the pleasure of announcing to you that you are free. Your complaints happened to strike our ears as we passed down the street, and we have therefore ventured to come to your rescue."

The old lady with the red face and the black eyebrows looked at us for a moment with something of the apoplectic stare of a parrot. Then she said, with a sudden gust or breathing of relief:

"Rescue? Where is Mr. Greenwood? Where is Mr. Burrows? Did you say you had rescued me?"

"Yes, madam," said Rupert, with a beaming condescension. "We have very satisfactorily dealt with Mr. Greenwood and Mr. Burrows. We have settled affairs with them very satisfactorily."

The old lady rose from her chair and came very quickly towards us.

"What did you say to them? How did you persuade them?" she cried.

"We persuaded them, my dear madam," said Rupert, laughing, "by knocking them down and tying them up. But what is the matter?"

To the surprise of everyone the old lady walked slowly back to her seat by the window.

"Do I understand," she said, with the air of a person about to begin knitting, "that you have knocked down Mr. Burrows and tied him up?"

"We have," said Rupert proudly; "we have resisted their oppression and conquered it."

"Oh, thanks," answered the old lady, and sat down by the window.

A considerable pause followed.

"The road is quite clear for you, madam," said Rupert pleasantly.

The old lady rose, cocking her black eyebrows and her silver crest at us for an instant.

"But what about Greenwood and Burrows?" she said. "What did I understand you to say had become of them?"

"They are lying on the floor upstairs," said Rupert, chuckling. "Tied hand and foot."

"Well, that settles it," said the old lady, coming with a kind of bang into her seat again, "I must stop where I am."

Rupert looked bewildered.

"Stop where you are?" he said. "Why should you stop any longer where you are? What power can force you now to stop in this miserable cell?"

"The question rather is," said the old lady, with composure, "what power can force me to go anywhere else?"

We both stared wildly at her and she stared tranquilly at us both.

At last I said, "Do you really mean to say that we are to leave you here?"

"I suppose you don't intend to tie me up," she said, "and carry me off? I certainly shall not go otherwise."

"But, my dear madam," cried out Rupert, in a radiant exasperation, "we heard you with our own ears crying because you could not get out."

"Eavesdroppers often hear rather misleading things," replied the captive grimly. "I suppose I did break down a bit and lose my temper and talk to myself. But I have some sense of honour for all that."

"Some sense of honour?" repeated Rupert, and the last light of intelligence died out of his face, leaving it the face of an idiot with rolling eyes.

He moved vaguely towards the door and I followed. But I turned yet once more in the toils of my conscience and curiosity. "Can we do nothing for you, madam?" I said forlornly.

"Why," said the lady, "if you are particularly anxious to do me a little favour you might untie the gentlemen upstairs."

Rupert plunged heavily up the kitchen staircase, shaking it with his vague violence. With mouth open to speak he stumbled to the door of the sitting-room and scene of battle.

"Theoretically speaking, that is no doubt true," Mr. Burrows was saying, lying on his back and arguing easily with Basil; "but we must consider the matter as it appears to our sense. The origin of morality . . ."

"Basil," cried Rupert, gasping, "she won't come out."

"Who won't come out?" asked Basil, a little cross at being interrupted in an argument.

"The lady downstairs," replied Rupert. "The lady who was locked up. She won't come out. And she says that all she wants is for us to let these fellows loose."

"And a jolly sensible suggestion," cried Basil, and with a bound he was on top of the prostrate Burrows once more and was unknotting his bonds with hands and teeth.

"A brilliant idea. Swinburne, just undo Mr. Greenwood."

In a dazed and automatic way I released the little gentleman in the purple jacket, who did not seem to regard any of the proceedings as particularly sensible or brilliant. The gigantic Burrows, on the other hand, was heaving with herculean laughter.

"Well," said Basil, in his cheeriest way, "I think we must be getting away. We've so much enjoyed our evening. Far too much regard for you to stand on ceremony. If I may so express myself, we've made ourselves at home. Good-night. Thanks so much. Come along, Rupert."

"Basil," said Rupert desperately, "for God's sake come and see what you can make of the woman downstairs. I can't get the discomfort out of my mind. I admit that things look as if we had made a mistake. But these gentlemen won't mind perhaps . . ."

"No, no," cried Burrows, with a sort of Rabelaisian uproariousness. "No, no, look in the pantry, gentlemen. Examine the coalhole. Make a tour of the chimneys. There are corpses all over the house, I assure you."

This adventure of ours was destined to differ in one respect from others which I have narrated. I had been through many wild days

with Basil Grant, days for the first half of which the sun and the
moon seemed to have gone mad. But it had almost invariably happened that towards the end of the day and its adventure things had
cleared themselves like the sky after rain, and a luminous and quiet
meaning had gradually dawned upon me. But this day's work was
destined to end in confusion worse confounded. Before we left that
house, ten minutes afterwards, one half-witted touch was added
which rolled all our minds in cloud. If Rupert's head had suddenly
fallen off on the floor, if wings had begun to sprout out of Greenwood's shoulders, we could scarcely have been more suddenly
stricken. And yet of this we had no explanation. We had to go to
bed that night with the prodigy and get up next morning with it
and let it stand in our memories for weeks and months. As will be
seen, it was not until months afterwards that by another accident
and in another way it was explained. For the present I only state
what happened.

When all five of us went down the kitchen stairs again, Rupert
leading, the two hosts bringing up the rear, we found the door of
the prison again closed. Throwing it open we found the place again as
black as pitch. The old lady, if she was still there, had turned out the
gas: she seemed to have a weird preference for sitting in the dark.

Without another word Rupert lit the gas again. The little old
lady turned her bird-like head as we all stumbled forward in the
strong gaslight. Then, with a quickness that almost made me jump,
she sprang up and swept a sort of old-fashioned curtsey or reverence.
I looked quickly at Greenwood and Burrows, to whom it was natural to suppose this subservience had been offered. I felt irritated at
what was implied in this subservience, and desired to see the faces of
the tyrants as they received it. To my surprise they did not seem to
have seen it at all: Burrows was paring his nails with a small
penknife. Greenwood was at the back of the group and had hardly
entered the room. And then an amazing fact became apparent. It
was Basil Grant who stood foremost of the group, the golden gaslight lighting up his strong face and figure. His face wore an expression indescribably conscious, with the suspicion of a very grave
smile. His head was slightly bent with a restrained bow. It was he

who had acknowledged the lady's obeisance. And it was he, beyond any shadow of reasonable doubt, to whom it had really been directed.

"So I hear," he said, in a kindly yet somehow formal voice, "I hear, madam, that my friends have been trying to rescue you. But without success."

"No one, naturally, knows my faults better than you," answered the lady with a high colour. "But you have not found me guilty of treachery."

"I willingly attest it, madam," replied Basil, in the same level tones, "and the fact is that I am so much gratified with your exhibition of loyalty that I permit myself the pleasure of exercising some very large discretionary powers. You would not leave this room at the request of these gentlemen. But you know that you can safely leave it at mine."

The captive made another reverence. "I have never complained of your injustice," she said. "I need scarcely say what I think of your generosity."

And before our staring eyes could blink she had passed out of the room, Basil holding the door open for her.

He turned to Greenwood with a relapse into joviality. "This will be a relief to you," he said.

"Yes, it will," replied that immovable young gentleman with a face like a sphinx.

We found ourselves outside in the dark blue night, shaken and dazed as if we had fallen into it from some high tower.

"Basil," said Rupert at last, in a weak voice, "I always thought you were my brother. But are you a man? I mean—are you only a man?"

"At present," replied Basil, "my mere humanity is proved by one of the most unmistakable symbols—hunger. We are too late for the theatre in Sloane Square. But we are not too late for the restaurant. Here comes the green omnibus!" and he had leaped on it before we could speak.

*　　*　　*

" 'Basil,' said Rupert, 'I always thought you were my brother. But are you a man? I mean — are you only a man?' "

" 'Here comes the green omnibus!' "

As I said, it was months after that Rupert Grant suddenly entered my room, swinging a satchel in his hand and with a general air of having jumped over the garden wall, and implored me to go with him upon the latest and wildest of his expeditions. He proposed to himself no less a thing than the discovery of the actual origin, whereabouts, and headquarters of the source of all our joys and sorrows—the Club of Queer Trades. I should expand this story for ever if I explained how ultimately we ran this strange entity to its lair. The process meant a hundred interesting things. The tracking of a member, the bribing of a cabman, the fighting of roughs, the lifting of a paving stone, the finding of a cellar, the finding of a cellar below the cellar, the finding of the subterranean passage, the finding of the Club of Queer Trades.

I have had many strange experiences in my life, but never a stranger one than that I felt when I came out of those rambling, sightless, and seemingly hopeless passages into the sudden splendour of a sumptuous and hospitable dining-room, surrounded upon almost every side by faces that I knew. There was Mr. Montmorency, the Arboreal House-Agent, seated between the two brisk young men who were occasionally vicars, and always Professional Detainers. There was Mr. P. G. Northover, founder of the Adventure and Romance Agency. There was Professor Chadd, who invented the dancing Language.

As we entered, all the members seemed to sink suddenly into their chairs, and with the very action the vacancy of the presidential seat gaped at us like a missing tooth.

"The president's not here," said Mr. P. G. Northover, turning suddenly to Professor Chadd.

"N—no," said the philosopher, with more than his ordinary vagueness. "I can't imagine where he is."

"Good heavens," said Mr. Montmorency, jumping up, "I really feel a little nervous. I'll go and see." And he ran out of the room.

An instant after he ran back again, twittering with a timid ecstasy.

"He's there, gentlemen—he's there all right—he's coming in now," he cried, and sat down. Rupert and I could hardly help feeling

"Swinging a satchel."

"Mr. Montmorency, the arboreal house agent."

" 'The President's not here.' "

the beginnings of a sort of wonder as to who this person might be who was the first member of this insane brotherhood. Who, we thought indistinctly, could be maddest in this world of madmen: what fantastic was it whose shadow filled all these fantastics with so loyal an expectation?

Suddenly we were answered. The door flew open and the room was filled and shaken with a shout, in the midst of which Basil Grant, smiling and in evening dress, took his seat at the head of the table.

How we ate that dinner I have no idea. In the common way I am a person particularly prone to enjoy the long luxuriance of the club dinner. But on this occasion it seemed a hopeless and endless string of courses. *Hors-d'oeuvre* sardines seemed as big as herrings, soup seemed a sort of ocean, larks were ducks, ducks were ostriches until that dinner was over. The cheese course was maddening. I had often heard of the moon being made of green cheese. That night I thought the green cheese was made of the moon. And all the time Basil Grant went on laughing and eating and drinking, and never threw one glance at us to tell us why he was there, the king of these capering idiots.

At last came the moment which I knew must in some way enlighten us, the time of the club speeches and the club toasts. Basil Grant rose to his feet amid a surge of songs and cheers.

"Gentlemen," he said, "it is a custom in this society that the president for the year opens the proceedings not by any general toast of sentiment, but by calling upon each member to give a brief account of his trade. We then drink to that calling and to all who follow it. It is my business, as the senior member, to open by stating my claim to membership of this club. Years ago, gentlemen, I was a judge; I did my best in that capacity to do justice and to administer the law. But it gradually dawned on me that in my work, as it was, I was not touching even the fringe of justice. I was seated in the seat of the mighty, I was robed in scarlet and ermine; nevertheless, I held a small and lowly and futile post. I had to go by a mean rule as much as a postman, and my red and gold[44] was worth no more than his. Daily there passed before me taut and passionate problems, the

[44] Red and gold were the colors of the uniform of both judges and, at that time, postmen.

"*Basil Grant rose to his feet amid a surge of song and cheers.*"

stringency of which I had to pretend to relieve by silly im-
prisonments or silly damages, while I knew all the time, by the light
of my living common sense, that they would have been far better
relieved by a kiss or a thrashing, or a few word of explanation, or a
duel, or a tour in the West Highlands. Then, as this grew on me,
there grew on me continuously the sense of a mountainous frivolity.
Every word said in the court, a whisper or an oath, seemed more
connected with life than the words I had to say. Then came the time
when I publicly blasphemed the whole bosh, was classed as a madman and melted from public life."

Something in the atmosphere told me that it was not only Rupert
and I who were listening with intensity to this statement.

"Well, I discovered that I could be of no real use. I offered myself
privately as a purely moral judge to settle purely moral differences.
Before very long these unofficial courts of honour (kept strictly
secret) had spread over the whole of society. People were tried before
me not for the practical trifles for which nobody cares, such as committing a murder, or keeping a dog without a licence. My criminals
were tried for the faults which really make social life impossible.
They were tried before me for selfishness, or for an impossible vanity, or for scandal-mongering, or for stinginess to guests or depen-
dents. Of course these courts had no sort of real coercive powers.
The fulfilment of their punishments rested entirely on the honour of
the ladies and gentlement involved, including the honour of the
culprits. But you would be amazed to know how completely our
orders were always obeyed. Only lately I had a most pleasing example. A maiden lady in South Kensington whom I had condemned to
solitary confinement for being the means of breaking off an engagement through backbiting, absolutely refused to leave her prison,
although some well-meaning persons had been inopportune enough
to rescue her."

Rupert Grant was staring at his brother, his mouth fallen agape.
So, for the matter of that, I expect, was I. This, then, was the explanation of the old lady's strange discontent and her still stranger
content with her lot. She was one of the culprits of his Voluntary
Criminal Court. She was one of the clients of his Queer Trade.

We were still dazed when we drank, amid a crash of glasses, the health of Basil's new judiciary. We had only a confused sense of everything having been put right, the sense men will have when they come into the presence of God. We dimly heard Basil say:

"Mr. P. G. Northover will now explain the Adventure and Romance Agency."

And we heard equally dimly Northover beginning the statement he had made long ago to Major Brown. Thus our epic ended where it had begun, like a true cycle.

THE END

THE NAPOLEON OF
NOTTING HILL

1904

Illustrations by W. Graham Robertson

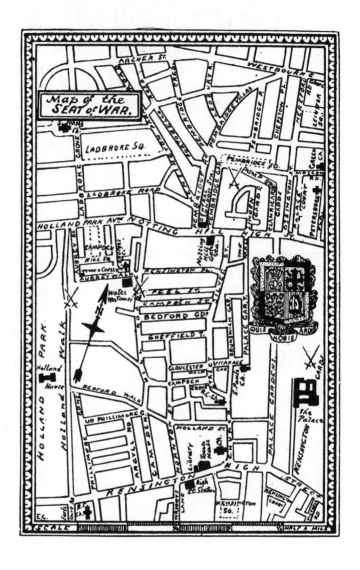

Map of the seat of war

TO HILAIRE BELLOC[1]

For every tiny town or place
God made the stars especially;
Babies look up with owlish face
And see them tangled in a tree:
You saw a moon from Sussex Downs.
A Sussex moon, untravelled still,
I saw a moon that was the town's,
The largest lamp on Campden Hill.[2]

Yea; Heaven is everywhere at home
The big blue cap that always fits,
And so it is (be calm; they come
To goal at last, my wandering wits),
So is it with the heroic thing;
This shall not end for the world's end
And though the sullen engines swing,
Be you not much afraid, my friend.

This did not end by Nelson's[3] urn
Where an immortal England sits—
Nor where your tall young men in turn
Drank death like wine at Austerlitz.[4]
And when the pedants bade us mark
What cold mechanic happenings

[1] Hilaire Belloc (1870–1953) was an English poet, historian, essayist, and politician. Born at La Celle, St. Cloud near Paris, he was educated in England but nevertheless undertook military service in the French artillery. He married an American, Elodie Hogan, in 1896, and he took British nationality in 1902, about which time he became a close friend of Chesterton's.

[2] Campden Hill Road runs from Kensington into Notting Hill. A side street called Sheffield Terrace is where Chesterton was born.

[3] Horatio Nelson (1758–1805), an English admiral, was the victor at the Battle of Trafalgar in which he died. He was the lover of Lady Hamilton.

[4] Austerlitz was a town in Austria where Napoleon Bonaparte won a battle against the Austrians in December 1805.

Must come; our souls said in the dark,
'Belike; but there are likelier things.'

Likelier across these flats afar
These sulky levels smooth and free
The drums shall crash a waltz of war
And Death shall dance with Liberty;
Likelier the barricades shall blare
Slaughter below and smoke above,
And death and hate and hell declare
That men have found a thing to love.

Far from your sunny uplands[5] set
I saw the dream; the streets I trod
The lit straight streets shot out and met
The starry streets that point to God.
This legend of an epic hour
A child I dreamed, and dream it still,
Under the great grey water-tower
That strikes the stars on Campden Hill.

                                        G. K. C.

[5] "Your sunny uplands" refers to the Sussex Downs, part of a chain of chalk hills running along the south coast of England. Belloc lived in Sussex.

VIEW OF THE NEW WORKS,
OF THE
GRAND JUNCTION WATER WORKS COMPANY, CAMPDEN HILL, KENSINGTON
1857.

JOSEPH CÖCK

The Royal Borough of Kensington and Chelsea Libraries and Arts Service

The Grand Junction Company's Water Works and Water Tower, Campden Hill. Lithograph by Alexander Fraser, 1857.

BOOK I

I

INTRODUCTORY REMARKS ON THE
ART OF PROPHECY

The human race, to which so many of my readers belong, has been
playing at children's games from the beginning, and will probably
do it till the end, which is a nuisance for the few people who grow
up. And one of the games to which it is most attached is called,
'Keep to-morrow dark', and which is also named (by the rustics in
Shropshire, I have no doubt) 'Cheat the Prophet'. The players listen
very carefully and respectfully to all that the clever men have to say
about what is to happen in the next generation. The players then
wait until all the clever men are dead, and bury them nicely. They
then go and do something else. That is all. For a race of simple tastes,
however, it is great fun.

For human beings, being children, have the childish wilfulness and
the childish secrecy. And they never have from the beginning of the
world done what the wise men have seen to be inevitable. They
stoned the false prophets, it is said; but they could have stoned true
prophets with a greater and juster enjoyment. Individually, men may
present a more or less rational appearance, eating, sleeping, and
scheming. But humanity as a whole is changeful, mystical, fickle, delightful. Men are men, but Man is a woman.[6]

But in the beginning of the twentieth century the game of Cheat
the Prophet was made far more difficult than it had ever been before.
The reason was, that there were so many prophets and so many
prophecies, that it was difficult to elude all their ingenuities. When a
man did something free and frantic and entirely his own, a horrible
thought struck him afterwards; it might have been predicted.
Whenever a duke climbed a lamp-post, when a dean got drunk, he

---

[6] Chesterton is re-echoing Verdi's "La donna e mobile".

could not be really happy, he could not be certain that he was not fulfilling some prophecy. In the beginning of the twentieth century you could not see the ground for clever men. They were so common that a stupid man was quite exceptional, and when they found him, they followed him in crowds down the street and treasured him up and gave him some high post in the State. And all these clever men were at work giving accounts of what would happen in the next age, all quite clear, all quite keen-sighted and ruthless, and all quite different. And it seemed that the good old game of hoodwinking your ancestors could not really be managed this time, because the ancestors neglected meat and sleep and practical politics, so that they might meditate day and night on what their descendants would be likely to do.

But the way the prophets of the twentieth century went to work was this. They took something or other that was certainly going on in their time, and then said that it would go on more and more until something extraordinary happened. And very often they added that in some odd place that extraordinary thing had happened, and that it showed the signs of the times.

Thus, for instance, there were Mr. H. G. Wells and others, who thought that science would take charge of the future; and just as the motor-car was quicker than the coach, so some lovely thing would be quicker than the motor-car; and so on for ever. And there arose from their ashes Dr. Quilp,[7] who said that a man could be sent on his machine so fast round the world that he could keep up a long chatty conversation in some old-world village by saying a word of a sentence each time he came round. And it was said that the experiment had been tried on an apoplectic old major, who was sent round the world so fast that there seemed to be (to the inhabitants of some other star) a continuous band round the earth of white whiskers, red complexion and tweeds — a thing like the ring of Saturn.

Then there was the opposite school. There was Mr. Edward Carpenter,[8]

[7] Dr. Quilp was probably Jocelyn Quilp, author of the romance *Baron Verdigris* (1894).

[8] Edward Carpenter (1844–1929) was a clergyman who gave up holy orders to preach socialism on street corners. He also lectured on science, music and sandal-making in towns in northern England as part of university extension courses.

who thought we should in a very short time return to Nature, and live simply and slowly as the animals do. And Edward Carpenter was followed by James Pickie, D.D. (of Pocahontas College), who said that men were immensely improved by grazing, or taking their food slowly and continuously, after the manner of cows. And he said that he had, with the most encouraging results, turned city men out on all fours in a field covered with veal cutlets. Then Tolstoy and the Humanitarians said that the world was growing more merciful, and therefore no one would ever desire to kill. And Mr. Mick not only became a vegetarian, but at length declared vegetarianism doomed ('shedding', as he called it finely, 'the green blood of the silent animals'), and predicted that men in a better age would live on nothing but salt. And then came the pamphlet from Oregon (where the thing was tried), the pamphlet called *Why should Salt Suffer?* and there was more trouble.

And on the other hand, some people were predicting that the lines of kinship would become narrower and sterner. There was Mr. Cecil Rhodes,[9] who thought that the one thing of the future was the British Empire, and that there would be a gulf between those who were of the Empire and those who were not, between the Chinaman in Hong Kong and the Chinaman outside, between the Spaniard on the Rock of Gibraltar and the Spaniard off it, similar to the gulf between man and the lower animals. And in the same way his impetuous friend, Dr. Zoppi ('the Paul of Anglo-Saxonism'), carried it yet further, and held that, as a result of this view, cannibalism shoud be held to mean eating a member of the Empire, not eating one of the subject peoples, who should, he said, be killed without needless pain. His horror at the idea of eating a man in British Guiana showed how they misunderstood his stoicism who thought him devoid of feeling. He was, however, in a hard position; as it was said that he had attempted the experiment, and, living in London, had to subsist entirely on Italian organ-grinders. And his end was terrible, for just when he had begun, Sir Paul Swiller read his great paper at the Royal Society,[10] proving that the savages

[9] Cecil Rhodes (1853–1902) was an English statesman who colonized southern Africa. He was the founder of the Rhodes fellowships.

[10] The Royal Society for Improving Natural Knowledge was founded in 1645 but incorporated under royal charter in the 1660s. In effect it is an academy of sciences whose members are among the most distinguished figures in their various fields.

"City men out on all fours in a field covered with veal cutlets."

were not only quite right in eating their enemies, but right on moral and hygienic grounds, since it was true that the qualities of the enemy, when eaten, passed into the eater. The notion that the nature of an Italian organ-man was irrevocably growing and burgeoning inside him was almost more than the kindly old professor could bear.

There was Mr. Benjamin Kidd,[11] who said that the growing note of our race would be the care for and knowledge of the future. His idea was developed more powerfully by William Borker, who wrote that passage which every schoolboy knows by heart, about men in future ages weeping by the graves of their descendants, and tourists being shown over the scene of the historic battle which was to take place some centuries afterwards.

And Mr. Stead,[12] too, was prominent, who thought that England would in the twentieth century be united to America; and his young lieutenant, Graham Podge, who included the states of France, Germany, and Russia in the American Union, the State of Russia being abbreviated to Ra.

There was Mr. Sidney Webb,[13] also, who said that the future would see a continuously increasing order and neatness in the life of the people, and his poor friend Fipps, who went mad and ran about the country with an axe, hacking branches off the trees whenever there were not the same number on both sides.

All these clever men were prophesying with every variety of ingenuity what would happen soon, and they all did it in the same way, by taking something they saw 'going strong', as the saying is, and carrying it as far as ever their imagination could stretch. This,

[11] Benjamin Kidd (1858–1916) was a sociologist and author of *Social Evolution* (1894), *Principles of Western Civilization* (1902) and *The Science of Power* (1918).

[12] Mr. Stead was probably Thomas William Stead (1849–1912), then editor of the *Pall Mall Gazette*, who as creator of the "new journalism" took responsibility for the dispatch in 1884 of General Gordon to Khartoum (where he was assassinated) and for the Criminal Law Amendment Act of 1885. Stead drowned in the S.S. *Titanic* disaster in 1912.

[13] Sidney Webb (1859–1947), Baron Passfield, was an English social reformer and historian who dominated the thinking of the socialist Fabian Society for many years. He was one of Chesterton's favorite targets.

they said, was the true and simple way of anticipating the future. 'Just as,' said Dr. Pellkins, in a fine passage, — 'just as when we see a pig in a litter larger than the other pigs, we know that by an unalterable law of the Inscrutable it will some day be larger than an elephant, — just as we know, when we see weeds and dandelions growing more and more thickly in a garden, that they must, in spite of all our efforts, grow taller than the chimney-pots and swallow the house from sight, so we know and reverently acknowledge, that when any power in human politics has shown for any period of time any considerable activity, it will go on until it reaches to the sky.'

And it did certainly appear that the prophets had put the people (engaged in the old game of Cheat the Prophet), in a quite unprecedented difficulty. It seemed really hard to do anything without fulfilling some of their prophecies.

But there was, nevertheless, in the eyes of labourers in the streets, of peasants in the fields, of sailors and children, and especially women, a strange look that kept the wise men in a perfect fever of doubt. They could not fathom the motionless mirth in their eyes. They still had something up their sleeve; they were still playing the game of Cheat the Prophet.

Then the wise men grew like wild things and swayed hither and thither, crying, 'What can it be? What can it be? What will London be like a century hence? Is there anything we have not thought of? Houses upside down — more hygienic, perhaps? Men walking on hands — make feet flexible, don't you know? Moon . . . motorcars . . . no heads . . .' And so they swayed and wondered until they died and were buried nicely.

Then the people went and did what they liked. Let me no longer conceal the painful truth. The people had cheated the prophets of the twentieth century. When the curtain goes up on this story, eighty years after the present date,[14] London is almost exactly like what it is now.

[14] As Chesterton was writing in 1904, his novel is set in 1984.

II

THE MAN IN GREEN

Very few words are needed to explain why London, a hundred years hence, will be very like it is now, or rather, since I must slip into a prophetic past, why London, when my story opens, was very like it was in those enviable days when I was still alive.

The reason can be stated in one sentence. The people had absolutely lost faith in revolutions. All revolutions are doctrinal — such as the French one, or the one that introduced Christianity. For it stands to common sense that you cannot upset all existing things, customs, and compromises, unless you believe in something outside them, something positive and divine. Now, England, during this century, lost all belief in this. It believed in a thing called Evolution. And it said, 'All theoretic changes have ended in blood and ennui. If we change, we must change slowly and safely, as the animals do. Nature's revolutions are the only successful ones. There has been no conservative reaction in favour of tails.'

And some things did change. Things that were not much thought of dropped out of sight. Things that had not often happened did not happen at all. Thus, for instance, the actual physical force ruling the country, the soldiers and police, grew smaller and smaller, and at last vanished almost to a point. The people combined could have swept the few policemen away in ten minutes; they did not, because they did not believe it would do them the least good. They had lost faith in revolutions.

Democracy was dead; for no one minded the governing class governing. England was now practically a despotism, but not an hereditary one. Some one in the official class was made King. No one cared how: no one cared who. He was merely a universal secretary.

In this manner it happened that everything in London was very quiet. That vague and somewhat depressed reliance upon things happening as they have always happened, which is with all Londoners a mood, had become an assumed condition. There was really no reason for any man doing anything but the thing he had done the day before.

There was therefore no reason whatever why the three young men who had always walked up to their Government office together should not walk up to it together on this particular wintry and cloudy morning. Everything in that age had become mechanical, and Government clerks especially. All those clerks assembled regularly at their posts. Three of those clerks always walked into town together. All the neighbourhood knew them: two of them were tall and one short. And on this particular morning the short clerk was only a few seconds late to join the other two as they passed his gate: he could have overtaken them in three strides; he could have called after them easily. But he did not.

For some reason that will never be understood until all souls are judged (if they are ever judged; the idea was at this time classed with fetish worship) he did not join his two companions, but walked steadily behind them. The day was dull, their dress was dull, everything was dull; but in some odd impulse he walked through street after street, through district after district, looking at the backs of the two men, who would have swung round at the sound of his voice. Now, there is a law written in the darkest of the Books of Life, and it is this: If you look at a thing nine hundred and ninety-nine times, you are perfectly safe; if you look at it the thousandth time, you are in frightful danger of seeing it for the first time.

So the short Government official looked at the coat-tails of the tall Government officials, and through street after street, and round corner after corner, saw only coat-tails, coat-tails, and again coat-tails—when, he did not in the least know why, something happened to his eyes.

Two black dragons were walking backwards in front of him. Two black dragons were looking at him with evil eyes. The dragons were walking backwards it was true. But they kept their eyes fixed on him none the less. The eyes which he saw were, in truth, only the two buttons at the back of a frock-coat: perhaps some traditional memory of their meaningless character gave this half-witted prominence to their gaze. The slit between the tails was the nose-line of the monster: whenever the tails flapped in the winter wind the dragons licked their lips. It was only a momentary fancy, but the small clerk found it imbedded in his soul ever afterwards. He never could again think of men in frock-coats except as dragons walking backwards. He explained afterwards, quite tactfully and nicely, to his two official friends, that while feeling an inexpressible regard for each of them he could not seriously regard the face of either of them as anything but a kind of tail. It was, he admitted, a handsome tail—a tail elevated in the air. But if, he said, any true friend of theirs wished to see their faces, to look into the eyes of their soul, that friend must be allowed to walk reverently round behind them, so as to see them from the rear.[15] There he would see the two black dragons with the blind eyes.

But when first the two black dragons sprang out of the fog upon the small clerk, they had merely the effect of all miracles—they changed the universe. He discovered the fact that all romantics know—that adventures happen on dull days, and not on sunny ones. When the chord of monotony is stretched most tight, then it breaks with a sound like song. He had scarcely noticed the weather before, but with the four dead eyes glaring at him he looked round and realized the strange dead day.

The morning was wintry and dim, not misty, but darkened with that shadow of cloud or snow which steeps everything in a green or copper twilight. The light there is on such a day seems not so much to come from the clear heavens as to be a phosphorescence clinging to the shapes themselves. The load of heaven and the clouds is like a load of waters, and the men move like fishes, feeling that they are on the floor of a sea. Everything in a London street completes the fantasy; the carriages and cabs themselves resemble deep-sea creatures with eyes of flame. He had been startled at first to meet two dragons. Now he found he was among deep-sea dragons possessing the deep sea.

The two young men in front were like the small young man himself, well-dressed. The lines of their frock-coats and silk hats had

[15] Compare Syme's (Thursday's) view of Sunday in *The Man Who Was Thursday* and Moses' view of God in Exodus.

that luxuriant severity which makes the modern fop, hideous as he is, a favourite exercise of the modern draughtsman; that element which Mr. Max Beerbohm[16] has admirably expressed in speaking of 'certain congruities of dark cloth and the rigid perfection of linen'.

They walked with the gait of an affected snail, and they spoke at the longest intervals, dropping a sentence at about every sixth lamp-post.

They crawled on past the lamp-posts; their mien was so immovable that a fanciful description might almost say that the lamp-posts crawled past the men, as in a dream. Then the small man suddenly ran after them and said:

'I want to get my hair cut. I say, do you know a little shop anywhere where they cut your hair properly? I keep on having my hair cut, but it keeps on growing again.'

One of the tall men looked at him with the air of a pained naturalist.

'Why, here is a little place,' cried the small man, with a sort of imbecile cheerfulness, as the bright bulging window of a fashionable toilet-saloon glowed abruptly out of the foggy twilight. 'Do you know, I often find hairdressers when I walk about London. I'll lunch with you at Cicconani's.[17] You know, I'm awfully fond of hairdressers' shops. They're miles better than those nasty butchers'.'
And he disappeared into the doorway.

The man called James continued to gaze after him, a monocle screwed into his eye.

'What the devil do you make of that fellow?' he asked his companion, a pale young man with a high nose.

The pale young man reflected conscientiously for some minutes, and then said:

[16] Max Beerbohm (1872–1956) was an English essayist, short story writer and cartoonist, perhaps best known for his only novel, *Zuleika Dobson*.

[17] Cicconani's does not appear in either the London telephone directory or in *Kelly's London Directory* for the period 1900–1904. However, Chesterton's references are usually very accurate, and so it should be remembered that at that time a telephone was a rarity and many businesses did not subscribe to trade directories. On the other hand, there was a Cicerelli's restaurant at 4 Sloane Square, a name which may have been corrupted in the telling.

'Had a knock on his head when he was a kid, I should think.'

'No, I don't think it's that,' replied the Honourable James Barker. 'I've sometimes fancied he was a sort of artist, Lambert.'

'Bosh!' cried Mr. Lambert, briefly.

'I admit I can't make him out,' resumed Barker, abstractedly; 'he never opens his mouth without saying something so indescribably half-witted that to call him a fool seems the very feeblest attempt at characterization. But there's another thing about him that's rather funny. Do you know that he has the one collection of Japanese lacquer in Europe? Have you ever seen his books? All Greek poets and medieval French and that sort of thing. Have you ever been in his rooms? It's like being inside an amethyst. And he moves about in all that and talks like—like a turnip.'

'Well, damn all books. Your blue books[18] as well,' said the ingenuous Mr. Lambert, with a friendly simplicity. 'You ought to understand such things. What do you make of him?'

'He's beyond me,' returned Barker. 'But if you asked me for my opinion, I should say he was a man with a taste for nonsense, as they call it—artistic fooling, and all that kind of thing. And I seriously believe that he has talked nonsense so much that he has half bewildered his own mind and doesn't know the difference between sanity and insanity. He has gone round the mental world, so to speak, and found the place where the East and the West are one, and extreme idiocy is as good as sense. But I can't explain these psychological games.'

'You can't explain them to me,' replied Mr. Wilfrid Lambert, with candour.

As they passed up the long streets towards their restaurant the copper twilight cleared slowly to a pale yellow, and by the time they reached it they stood discernible in a tolerable winter daylight. The Honourable James Barker, one of the most powerful officials in the English Government (by this time a rigidly official one), was a lean and elegant young man, with a blank handsome face and bleak blue eyes. He had a great amount of intellectual capacity, of that peculiar

[18] A blue book is a Parliamentary report published in blue paper covers, but also a far-fetched romance also published in blue covers.

kind which raises a man from throne to throne and lets him die loaded
with honours without having either amused or enlightened the
mind of a single man. Wilfrid Lambert, the youth with the nose
which appeared to impoverish the rest of his face, had also contributed little to the enlargement of the human spirit, but he had the
honourable excuse of being a fool.

Lambert would have been called a silly man; Barker, with all his
cleverness, might have been called a stupid man. But mere silliness
and stupidity sank into insignificance in the presence of the awful
and mysterious treasures of foolishness apparently stored up in the
small figure that stood waiting for them outside Cicconani's. The
little man, whose name was Auberon Quin, had an appearance compounded of a baby and an owl. His round head, round eyes, seemed
to have been designed by nature playfully with a pair of compasses.
His flat dark hair and preposterously long frock-coat gave him
something of the look of a child's 'Noah'. When he entered a room
of strangers they mistook him for a small boy, and wanted to take
him on their knees, until he spoke, when they preceived that a boy
would have been more intelligent.

'I have been waiting quite a long time,' said Quin, mildly. 'It's
awfully funny I should see you coming up the street at last.'

'Why?' asked Lambert, staring. 'You told us to come here
yourself.'

'My mother used to tell people to come to places,' said the sage.

They were about to turn into the restaurant with a resigned air,
when their eyes were caught by something in the street. The
weather, though cold and blank, was now quite clear and across the
dull brown of the wood pavement and between the dull grey terraces was moving something not to be seen for miles around—not to
be seen perhaps at that time in England—a man dressed in bright
colours. A small crowd hung on the man's heels.

He was a tall stately man, clad in a military uniform of brilliant
green, splashed with great silver facings. From the shoulder swung a
short green furred cloak, somewhat like that of a Hussar, the lining
of which gleamed every now and then with a kind of tawny crimson.
His breast glittered with medals; round his neck was the red ribbon

and star of some foreign order; and a long straight sword, with a blazing hilt, trailed and clattered along the pavement. At this time the pacific and utilitarian development of Europe had relegated all such customs to the Museums. The only remaining force, the small but well-organized police, were attired in a sombre and hygienic manner. But even those who remembered the last Life Guards and Lancers who disappeared in 1912[19] must have known at a glance that this was not, and never had been, an English uniform; and this conviction would have been heightened by the yellow aquiline face, like Dante carved in bronze, which rose, crowned with white hair, out of the green military collar, a keen and distinguished, but not an English face.

The magnificence with which the green-clad gentleman walked down the centre of the road would be something difficult to express in human language. For it was an ingrained simplicity and arrogance, something in the mere carriage of the head and body, which made ordinary moderns in the street stare after him; but it had comparatively little to do with actual conscious gestures or expression. In the matter of these merely temporary movements, the man appeared to be rather worried and inquisitive, but he was inquisitive with the inquisitiveness of a despot and worried as with the responsibilities of a god. The men who lounged and wondered behind him followed partly with an astonishment at his brilliant uniform, that is to say, partly because of that instinct which makes us all follow one who looks like a madman, but far more because of that instinct which makes all men follow (and worship) any one who chooses to behave like a king. He had to so sublime an extent that great quality of royalty—an almost imbecile unconsciousness of everybody, that people went after him as they do after kings—to see what would be the first thing or person he would take notice of. And all the time, as we have said, in spite of his quiet splendour, there was an air about him as if he were looking for somebody; an expression of inquiry.

Suddenly that expression of inquiry vanished, none could tell why,

[19] This is yet another instance of "cheat the prophet", for this did not happen in 1912.

and was replaced by an expression of contentment. Amid the rapt attention of the mob of idlers, the magnificent green gentleman deflected himself from his direct course down the centre of the road and walked to one side of it. He came to a halt opposite to a large poster of Colman's Mustard[20] erected on a wooden hoarding. His spectators almost held their breath.

He took from a small pocket in his uniform a little penknife; with this he made a slash at the stretched paper. Completing the rest of the operation with his fingers, he tore off a strip or rag of paper, yellow in colour and wholly irregular in outline. Then for the first time the great being addressed his adoring onlookers:

'Can any one,' he said, with a pleasing foreign accent, 'lend me a pin?'

Mr. Lambert, who happened to be nearest, and who carried innumerable pins for the purpose of attaching innumerable buttonholes, lent him one, which was received with extravagant but dignified bows, and hyperboles of thanks.

The gentleman in green, then, with every appearance of being gratified, and even puffed up, pinned the piece of yellow paper to the green silk and silver-lace adornments of his breast. Then he turned his eyes round again, searching and unsatisfied.

'Anything else I can do, sir?' asked Lambert, with the absurd politeness of the Englishman when once embarrassed.

'Red,' said the stranger, vaguely, 'red.'

'I beg your pardon?'

'I beg yours also, Señor,' said the stranger, bowing. 'I was wondering whether any of you had any red about you.'

'Any red about us? — well really — no, I don't think I have — I used to carry a red bandanna once, but — '

'Barker,' asked Auberon Quin, suddenly, 'where's your red cockatoo? Where's your red cockatoo?'

'What do you mean?' asked Barker, desperately. 'What cockatoo? You've never seen me with any cockatoo.'

'I know,' said Auberon, vaguely mollified. 'Where's it been all the time?'

[20] Colman's mustard is a brand of mustard sold in bright yellow tins and then advertised with bright yellow posters.

Barker swung round, not without resentment.

'I am sorry, sir,' he said, shortly but civilly, 'none of us seem to have anything red to lend you. But why, if one may ask —'

'I thank you, Señor, it is nothing. I can, since there is nothing else, fulfil my own requirements.'

And standing for a second of thought with the penknife in his hand, he stabbed his left palm. The blood fell with so full a stream that it struck the stones without dripping. The foreigner pulled out his handkerchief and tore a piece from it with his teeth. The rag was immediately soaked in scarlet.

'Since you are so generous, Señor,' he said, 'another pin, perhaps.'

Lambert held one out, with eyes protruding like a frog's.

The red linen was pinned beside the yellow paper, and the foreigner took off his hat.

'I have to thank you all, gentlemen,' he said; and wrapping the remainder of the handerchief round his bleeding hand, he resumed his walk with an overwhelming stateliness.

While all the rest paused, in some disorder, little Mr. Auberon Quin ran after the stranger and stopped him, with hat in hand. Considerably to everybody's astonishment, he addressed him in the purest Spanish.

'Señor,' he said in that language, 'pardon a hospitality, perhaps indiscreet, towards one who appears to be a distinguished, but a solitary guest in London. Will you do me and my friends, with whom you have held some conversation, the honour of lunching with us at the adjoining restaurant?'

The man in the green uniform had turned a fiery colour of pleasure at the mere sound of his own language, and he accepted the invitation with that profusion of bows which so often shows, in the case of the Southern races, the falsehood of the notion that ceremony has nothing to do with feeling.

'Señor,' he said, 'your language is my own; but all my love for my people shall not lead me to deny to yours the possession of so chivalrous an entertainer. Let me say that the tongue is Spanish but the heart English.' And he passed with the rest into Cicconani's.

'Now, perhaps,' said Barker, over the fish and sherry, intensely polite, but burning with curiosity, 'perhaps it would be rude of me to ask why you did that?'

'Did what, Señor?' asked the guest, who spoke English quite well, though in a manner indefinably American.

'Well,' said the Englishman, in some confusion, 'I mean tore a strip off a hoarding and . . . er . . . cut yourself . . . and . . .'

'To tell you that, Señor,' answered the other, with a certain sad pride, 'involves merely telling you who I am. I am Juan del Fuego, President of Nicaragua.'

The manner with which the President of Nicaragua leant back and drank his sherry showed that to him this explanation covered all the facts observed and a great deal more. Barker's brow, however, was still a little clouded.

'And the yellow paper,' he began, with anxious friendliness, 'and the red rag . . .'

'The yellow paper and the red rag,' said Fuego, with indescribable grandeur, 'are the colours of Nicaragua.'

'But Nicaragua . . .' began Barker, with great hesitation, 'Nicaragua is no longer a . . .'

'Nicaragua has been conquered like Athens. Nicaragua has been annexed like Jerusalem,' cried the old man, with amazing fire. 'The Yankee and the German and the brute powers of modernity have trampled it with the hoofs of oxen.[21] But Nicaragua is not dead. Nicaragua is an idea.'

Auberon Quin suggested timidly, 'A brilliant idea.'

'Yes,' said the foreigner, snatching at the word. 'You are right, generous Englishman. An idea *brilliant*, a burning thought. Señor, you asked me why, in my desire to see the colours of my country, I snatched at paper and blood. Can you not understand the ancient sanctity of colours? The Church has her symbolic colours. And think of what colours mean to us — think of the position of one like myself, who can see nothing but those two colours, nothing but the red and the yellow.[22] To me all shapes are equal, all common and

---

[21] After the destruction of Jerusalem by the Romans under Titus, it is alleged that the area was ploughed by teams of oxen.

[22] Adam Wayne's colors will also be red and yellow, pp. 285ff. below.

noble things are in a democracy of combination. Wherever there is a field of marigolds and the red cloak of an old woman, there is Nicaragua. Wherever there is a field of poppies and a yellow patch of sand, there is Nicaragua. Wherever there is a lemon and a red sunset, there is my country. Wherever I see a red pillar-box and a yellow sunset, there my heart beats. Blood and a splash of mustard can be my heraldry. If there be yellow mud and red mud in the same ditch, it is better to me than white stars.'

'And if,' said Quin, with equal enthusiasm, 'there should happen to be yellow wine and red wine at the same lunch, you could not confine yourself to sherry. Let me order some Burgundy, and complete, as it were, a sort of Nicaraguan heraldry in your inside.'

Barker was fiddling with his knife, and was evidently making up his mind to say something, with the intense nervousness of the amiable Englishman.

'I am to understand, then,' he said at last, with a cough, 'that you, ahem, were the President of Nicaragua when it made its—er—one must, of course, agree—its quite heroic resistance to—er—'

The ex-President of Nicaragua waved his hand.

'You need not hesitate in speaking to me,' he said. 'I am quite fully aware that the whole tendency of the world of to-day is against Nicaragua and against me. I shall not consider it any diminution of your evident courtesy if you say what you think of the misfortunes that have laid my republic in ruins.'

Barker looked immeasurably relieved and gratified.

'You are most generous, President,' he said, with some hesitation over the title, 'and I will take advantage of your generosity to express the doubts which, I must confess, we moderns have about such things as—er—the Nicaraguan independence.'

'So your sympathies are,' said Del Fuego, quite calmly, 'with the big nation which—'

'Pardon me, pardon me, President,' said Barker, warmly; 'my sympathies are with no nation. You misunderstand, I think, the modern intellect. We do not disapprove of the fire and extravagance of such commonwealths as yours only to become more extravagant on a larger scale. We do not condemn Nicaragua because we think

Britain ought to be more Nicaraguan. We do not discourage small nationalities because we wish large nationalities to have all their smallness, all their uniformity of outlook, all their exaggeration of spirit. If I differ with the greatest respect from your Nicaraguan enthusiasm, it is not because a nation or ten nations were against you; it is because civilization was against you. We moderns believe in a great cosmopolitan civilization, one which shall include all the talents of all the absorbed peoples——'

'The Señor will forgive me,' said the President. 'May I ask the Señor how, under ordinary circumstances, he catches a wild horse?'

'I never catch a wild horse,' replied Barker, with dignity.

'Precisely,' said the other; 'and there ends your absorption of the talents. That is what I complain of your cosmopolitanism. When you say you want all peoples to unite, you really mean that you want all peoples to unite to learn the tricks of your people. If the Bedouin Arab does not know how to read, some English missionary or schoolmaster must be sent to teach him to read, but no one ever says, "This schoolmaster does not know how to ride on a camel; let us pay a Bedouin to teach him." You say your civilization will include all talents. Will it? Do you really mean to say that at the moment when the Eskimo has learnt to vote for a County Council, you will have learnt to spear a walrus? I recur to the example I gave. In Nicaragua we had a way of catching wild horses—by lassoing the fore feet—which was supposed to be the best in South America. If you are going to include all the talents, go and do it. If not, permit me to say, what I have always said, that something went from the world when Nicaragua was civilized.'

'Something, perhaps,' replied Barker, 'but that something a mere barbarian dexterity. I do not know that I could chip flints as well as a primeval man, but I know that civilization can make these knives, which are better, and I trust to civilization.'

'You have good authority,' answered the Nicaraguan. 'Many clever men like you have trusted to civilization. Many clever Babylonians, many clever Egyptians, many clever men at the end of Rome. Can you tell me, in a world that is flagrant with the failures of civilization, what there is particularly immortal about yours?'

'I think you do not quite understand, President, what ours is,' answered Barker. 'You judge it rather as if England was still a poor and pugnacious island; you have been long out of Europe. Many things have happened.'

'And what,' asked the other, 'would you call the summary of those things?'

'The summary of those things,' answered Barker, with great animation, 'is that we are rid of the superstitions, and in becoming so we have not merely become rid of the superstitions which have been most frequently and most enthusiastically so described. The superstition of big nationalities is bad, but the superstition of small nationalities is worse. The superstition of reverencing our own country is bad, but the superstition of reverencing other people's countries is worse. It is so everywhere, and in a hundred ways. The superstition of monarchy is bad, and the superstition of aristocracy is bad, but the superstition of democracy is the worst of all.'

The old gentleman opened his eyes with some surprise.

'Are you, then,' he said, 'no longer a democracy in England?'

Barker laughed.

'The situation invites paradox,' he said. 'We are, in a sense, the purest democracy. We have become a despotism. Have you not noticed how continually in history democracy becomes despotism? People call it the decay of democracy. It is simply its fulfilment. Why take the trouble to number and register and enfranchise all the innumerable John Robinsons, when you can take one John Robinson with the same intellect or lack of intellect as all the rest, and have done with it? The old idealistic republicans used to found democracy on the idea that all men were equally intelligent. Believe me, the sane and enduring democracy is founded on the fact that all men are equally idiotic. Why should we not choose out of them one as much as another? All that we want for Government is a man not criminal and insane, who can rapidly look over some petitions and sign some proclamations. To think what time was wasted in arguing about the House of Lords, Tories saying it ought to be preserved because it was clever, and Radicals saying it ought to be destroyed because it was stupid, and all the time no one saw that it was right because it was stupid, because that chance mob of ordinary men thrown there by accident of blood were a great democratic protest against the Lower House, against the eternal insolence of the aristocracy of talents. We have established now in England the thing towards which all systems have dimly groped, the dull popular despotism without illusions. We want one man at the head of our State, not because he is brilliant or virtuous, but because he is one man and not a chattering crowd. To avoid the possible chance of hereditary diseases or such things, we have abandoned hereditary monarchy. The King of England is chosen like a juryman upon an official rotation list. Beyond that the whole system is quietly despotic, and we have not found it raise a murmur.'

'Do you really mean,' asked the President, incredulously, 'that you choose any ordinary man that comes to hand and make him despot—that you trust to the chance of some alphabetical list. . . .'

'And why not?' cried Barker. 'Did not half the historical nations trust to the chance of the eldest sons of eldest sons, and did not half of them get on tolerably well? To have a perfect system is impossible; to have a system is indispensable. All hereditary monarchies were a matter of luck: so are alphabetical monarchies. Can you find a deep philosophical meaning in the difference between the Stuarts and the Hanoverians? Believe me, I will undertake to find a deep philosophical meaning in the contrast between the dark tragedy of the A's, and the solid success of the B's.'

'And you risk it?' asked the other. 'Though the man may be a tyrant or a cynic or a criminal?'

'We risk it,' answered Barker, with a perfect placidity. 'Suppose he is a tyrant—he is still a check on a hundred tyrants. Suppose he is a cynic, it is to his interest to govern well. Suppose he is a criminal—by removing poverty and substituting power, we put a check on his criminality. In short, by substituting despotism we have put a total check on one criminal and a partial check on all the rest.'

The Nicaraguan old gentleman leaned over with a queer expression in his eyes.

'My Church, sir,' he said, 'has taught me to respect faith. I do not wish to speak with any disrespect of yours, however fantastic. But do you really mean that you will trust to the ordinary man, the man who may happen to come next, as a good despot?'

'I do,' said Barker, simply. 'He may not be a good man. But he will be a good despot. For when he comes to a mere business routine of government he will endeavour to do ordinary justice. Do we not assume the same thing in a jury?'

The old President smiled.

'I don't know,' he said, 'that I have any particular objection in detail to your excellent scheme of government. My only objection is a quite personal one. It is, that if I were asked whether I would belong to it, I should ask first of all, if I was not permitted, as an alternative, to be a toad in a ditch. That is all. You cannot argue with the choice of the soul.'

'Of the soul,' said Barker, knitting his brows, 'I cannot pretend to say anything, but speaking in the interests of the public——'

Mr. Auberon Quin rose suddenly to his feet.

'If you'll excuse me, gentlemen,' he said, 'I will step out for a moment into the air.'

'I'm so sorry, Auberon,' said Lambert, good-naturedly; 'do you feel bad?'

'Not bad exactly,' said Auberon, with self-restraint; 'rather good, if anything. Strangely and richly good. The fact is I want to reflect a little on those beautiful words that have just been uttered. "Speaking," yes, that was the phrase, "speaking in the interests of the public." One cannot get the honey from such things without being alone for a little.'

'Is he really off his chump, do you think?" asked Lambert.

The old President looked after him with queerly vigilant eyes.

'He is a man, I think,' he said, 'who cares for nothing but a joke. He is a dangerous man.'

Lambert laughed in the act of lifting some macaroni to his mouth.

'Dangerous!' he said. 'You don't know little Quin, sir!'

'Every man is dangerous,' said the old man without moving, 'who cares only for one thing. I was once dangerous myself.'

And with a pleasant smile he finished his coffee and rose, bowing profoundly, passed out into the fog, which had again grown dense and sombre. Three days afterwards they heard that he had died quietly in lodgings in Soho.[23]

*   *   *

Drowned somewhere else in the dark sea of fog was a little figure shaking and quaking, with what might at first sight have seemed terror or ague: but which was really that strange malady, a lonely laughter. He was repeating over and over to himself with a rich accent: 'But speaking in the interests of the public. . . .'

[23] Soho was then a cosmopolitan district of good restaurants and excellent shops bounded by Shaftesbury Avenue and Oxford Street rather than the sleazy area it has become in recent years.

III

THE HILL OF HUMOUR

'In a little square garden of yellow roses, beside the sea,' said Auberon Quin, 'there was a Nonconformist minister who had never been to Wimbledon. His family did not understand his sorrow or the strange look in his eyes. But one day they repented their neglect, for they heard that a body had been found on the shore, battered, but wearing patent leather boots. As it happened, it turned out not to be the minister at all. But in the dead man's pocket there was a return ticket to Maidstone.'

There was a short pause as Quin and his friends Barker and Lambert went swinging on through the slushy grass of Kensington Gardens. Then Auberon resumed.

'That story,' he said reverently, 'is the test of humour.'

They walked on farther and faster, wading through higher grass as they began to climb a slope.

'I perceive,' continued Auberon, 'that you have passed the test, and consider the anecdote excruciatingly funny; since you say nothing. Only coarse humour is received with pot-house applause. The great anecdote is received in silence, like a benediction. You felt pretty benedicted, didn't you, Barker?'

'I saw the point,' said Barker, somewhat loftily.

'Do you know,' said Quin, with a sort of idiot gaiety, 'I have lots of stories as good as that. Listen to this one.'

And he slightly cleared his throat.

'Dr. Polycarp was, as you all know, an unusually sallow bimetallist. "There," people of wide experience would say, "there goes the sallowest bimetallist in Cheshire." Once this was said so that he overheard it: it was said by an actuary, under a sunset of mauve and grey. Polycarp turned upon him. "Sallow!" he cried fiercely, "sallow! *Quis tulerit Gracchos de seditione querentes*."[24] It was said that no actuary ever made game of Dr. Polycarp again.'

[24] This is translated as "Who can stand the Gracchi complaining of treachery" from Juvenal, *Satires* II, 24.

Barker nodded with a simple sagacity. Lambert only grunted.

'Here is another,' continued the insatiable Quin.

'In a hollow of the grey-green hills of rainy Ireland, lived an old, old woman, whose uncle was always Cambridge at the Boat Race.[25] But in her grey-green hollows, she knew nothing of this: she didn't know that there was a Boat Race. Also she did not know that she had an uncle. She had heard of nobody at all, except of George the First, of whom she had heard (I know not why), and in whose historical memory she put her simple trust. And by and by, in God's good time, it was discovered that this uncle of hers was not really her uncle, and they came and told her so. She smiled through her tears, and said only, "Virtue is its own reward." '

Again there was a silence, and then Lambert said: 'It seems a bit mysterious.'

'Mysterious!' cried the other. 'The true humour is mysterious. Do you not realize the chief incident of the nineteenth and twentieth centuries?'

'And what's that?' asked Lambert, shortly.

'It is very simple,' replied the other. 'Hitherto it was the ruin of a joke that people did not see it. Now it is the sublime victory of a joke that people do not see it. Humour, my friends, is the one sanctity remaining to mankind. It is the one thing you are thoroughly afraid of. Look at that tree.'

His interlocutors looked vaguely towards a beech that leant out towards them from the ridge of the hill.

'If,' said Mr. Quin, 'I were to say that you did not see the great truths of science exhibited by that tree, though they stared any man of intellect in the face, what would you think or say? You would merely regard me as a pedant with some unimportant theory about vegetable cells. If I were to say that you did not see in that tree the vile mismanagement of local politics, you would dismiss me as a Socialist crank with some particular fad about public parks. If I were to say that you were guilty of the supreme blasphemy of looking at

[25] He supported Cambridge in the annual University Boat Race between Oxford and Cambridge, which is rowed over a course from Putney to Mortlake on the River Thames in London.

that tree and not seeing in it a new religion, a special revelation of God, you would simply say I was a mystic, and think no more about me. But if'—and he lifted a pontifical hand—'if I say that you cannot see the humour of that tree, and that I see the humour of it—my God! you will roll about at my feet.'

He paused a moment, and then resumed.

'Yes; a sense of humour, a weird and delicate sense of humour, is the new religion of mankind! It is towards that men will strain themselves with the ascetism of saints. Exercises, spiritual exercises, will be set in it. It will be asked, "Can you see the humour of this iron railing?" or "Can you see the humour of this field of corn? Can you see the humour of the stars? Can you see the humour of the sunsets?" How often I have laughed myself to sleep over a violet sunset.'

'Quite so,' said Mr. Barker, with an intelligent embarrassment.

'Let me tell you another story. How often it happens that the M.P.s for Essex are less punctual than one would suppose. The least punctual Essex M.P., perhaps, was James Wilson, who said, in the very act of plucking a poppy——'

Lambert suddenly faced round and struck his stick into the ground in a defiant attitude.

'Auberon,' he said, 'chuck it. I won't stand it. It's all bosh.'

Both men stared at him, for there was something very explosive about the words, as if they had ben corked up painfully for a long time.

'You have,' began Quin, 'no——'

'I don't care a curse,' said Lambert, violently, 'whether I have "a delicate sense of humour" or not. I won't stand it. It's all a confounded fraud. There's no joke in those infernal tales at all. You know there isn't as well as I do.'

'Well,' replied Quin, slowly, 'it is true that I, with my rather gradual mental processes, did not see any joke in them. But the finer sense of Barker perceived it.'

Barker turned a fierce red, but continued to stare at the horizon.

'You ass,' said Lambert; 'why can't you be like other people? Why can't you say something really funny, or hold your tongue? The man who sits on his hat in a pantomime is a long sight funnier than you are.'

Quin regarded him steadily. They had reached the top of the ridge and the wind struck their faces.

'Lambert,' said Auberon, 'you are a great and good man, though I'm hanged if you look it. You are more. You are a great revolutionist or deliverer of the world, and I look forward to seeing you carved in marble between Luther and Danton, if possible in your present attitude, the hat slightly on one side. I said as I came up the hill that the new humour was the last of the religions. You have made it the last of the superstitions. But let me give you a very serious warning. Be careful how you ask me to do anything *outré*, to imitate the man in the pantomime, and to sit on my hat. Because I am a man whose soul has been emptied of all pleasures but folly. And for twopence I'd do it.'

'Do it then,' said Lambert, swinging his stick impatiently. 'It would be funnier than the bosh you and Barker talk.'

Quin, standing on the top of the hill, stretched his hand out towards the main avenue of Kensington Gardens.

'Two hundred yards away,' he said, 'are all your fashionable acquaintances with nothing on earth to do but to stare at each other and at us. We are standing upon an elevation under the open sky, a peak as it were of fantasy, a Sinai of humour. We are in a great pulpit or platform, lit up with sunlight, and half London can see us. Be careful how you suggest things to me. For there is in me a madness which goes beyond martyrdom, the madness of an utterly idle man.'

'I don't know what you are talking about,' said Lambert, contemptuously. 'I only know I'd rather you stood on your silly head, than talked so much.'

'Auberon! for goodness' sake . . .' cried Barker, springing forward; but he was too late. Faces from all the benches and avenues were turned in their direction. Groups stopped and small crowds collected; and the sharp sunlight picked out the whole scene in blue, green, and black, like a picture in a child's toy-book. And on the top of the small hill Mr. Auberon Quin stood with considerable athletic neatness upon his head, and waved his patent-leather boots in the air.

'For God's sake, Quin, get up, and don't be an idiot,' cried Barker, wringing his hands; 'we shall have the whole town here.'

'Yes, get up, get up, man,' said Lambert, amused and annoyed. 'I was only fooling; get up.'

Auberon did so with a bound, and flinging his hat higher than the trees, proceeded to hop about on one leg with a serious expression. Barker stamped wildly.

'Oh, let's get home, Barker, and leave him,' said Lambert; 'some of your proper and correct police will look after him. Here they come!'

Two grave-looking men in quiet uniforms came up the hill towards them. One held a paper in his hand.

'There he is, officer,' said Lambert, cheerfully; 'we ain't responsible for him.'

The officer looked at the capering Mr. Quin with a quiet eye.

'We have not come, gentlemen,' he said, 'about what I think you are alluding to. We have come from headquarters to announce the selection of His Majesty the King. It is the rule, inherited from the old régime, that the news should be brought to the new Sovereign immediately, wherever he is; so we have followed you across Kensington Gardens.'

Barker's eyes were blazing in his pale face. He was consumed with ambition throughout his life. With a certain dull magnanimity of the intellect he had really believed in the chance method of selecting despots. But this sudden suggestion, that the selection might have fallen upon him, unnerved him with pleasure.

'Which of us,' he began, and the respectful official interrupted him.

'Not you, sir, I am sorry to say. If I may be permitted to say so, we know your services to the Government, and should be very thankful if it were. The choice has fallen . . .'

'God bless my soul!' said Lambert, jumping back two paces. 'Not me. Don't say I'm autocrat of All the Russias.'

'No, sir,' said the officer, with a slight cough and a glance towards Auberon, who was at that moment putting his head between his legs and making a noise like a cow; 'the gentleman whom we have to congratulate seems at the moment—er—er—occupied.'

'Not Quin!' shrieked Barker, rushing up to him; 'it can't be. Auberon, for God's sake pull yourself together. You've been made King!'

With his head still upside down between his legs, Mr. Quin answered modestly:

'I am not worthy. I cannot reasonably claim to equal the great men who have previously swayed the sceptre of Britain. Perhaps the only peculiarity that I can claim is that I am probably the first monarch that ever spoke out his soul to the people of England with his head and body in this position. This may in some sense give me, to quote a poem that I wrote in my youth:

> A nobler office on the earth
> Than valour, power of brain, or birth
> Could give the warrior kings of old.

The intellect clarified by this posture——'

Lambert and Barker made a kind of rush at him.

'Don't you understand?' cried Lambert. 'It's not a joke. They've really made you King. By gosh! They must have rum taste.'

'The great Bishops of the Middle Ages,' said Quin, kicking his legs in the air, as he was dragged up more or less upside down, 'were in the habit of refusing the honour of election three times and then accepting it. A mere matter of detail separates me from those great men. I will accept the post three times and refuse it afterwards. Oh! I will toil for you, my faithful people! You shall have a banquet of humour.'

By this time he had been landed the right way up, and the two men were still trying in vain to impress him with the gravity of the situation.

'Did you not tell me, Wilfrid Lambert,' he said, 'that I should be of more public value if I adopted a more popular form of humour? And when should a popular form of humour be more firmly riveted upon me than now, when I have become the darling of a whole people? Officer,' he continued, addressing the startled messenger, 'are there no ceremonies to celebrate my entry into the city?'

'Ceremonies,' began the official, with embarrassment, 'have been more or less neglected for some little time, and——'

Auberon Quin began gradually to take off his coat.

'All ceremony,' he said, 'consists in the reversal of the obvious.

Thus men, when they wish to be priests or judges, dress up like women. Kindly help me on with this coat.' And he held it out.

'But, your Majesty,' said the officer, after a moment's bewilderment and manipulation, 'you're putting it on with the tails in front.'

'The reversal of the obvious,' said the King, calmly, 'is as near as we can come to ritual with our imperfect apparatus. Lead on.'

The rest of that afternoon and evening was to Barker and Lambert a nightmare, which they could not properly realize or recall. The King, with his coat on the wrong way, went towards the streets that were awaiting him, and the old Kensington Palace which was the Royal residence. As he passed small groups of men, the groups turned into crowds, and gave forth sounds which seemed strange in welcoming an autocrat. Barker walked behind, his brain reeling, and, as the crowds grew thicker and thicker, the sounds became more and more unusual. And when he had reached the great market-place opposite the church, Barker knew that he had reached it, though he was rods[26] behind, because a cry went up such as had never before greeted any of the kings of the earth.

[26] A rod is a measure of length of five and a half yards.

BOOK II

I

THE CHARTER OF THE CITIES

Lambert was standing bewildered outside the door of the King's apartments amid the scurry of astonishment and ridicule. He was just passing out into the street, in a dazed manner, when James Barker dashed by him.

'Where are you going?' he asked.

'To stop all this foolery, of course,' replied Barker; and he disappeared into the room.

He entered it headlong, slamming the door, and slapping his incomparable silk hat on the table. His mouth opened, but before he could speak, the King said:

'Your hat, if you please,'

Fidgeting with his fingers, and scarcely knowing what he was doing, the young politician held it out.

The King placed it on his own chair, and sat on it.

'A quaint old custom,' he explained, smiling above the ruins. 'When the King receives the representatives of the House of Barker, the hat of the latter is immediately destroyed in this manner. It represents the absolute finality of the act of homage expressed in the removal of it. It declares that never until that hat shall once more appear upon your head (a contingency which I firmly believe to be remote) shall the House of Barker rebel against the Crown of England.'

Barker stood with clenched fist, and shaking lip.

'Your jokes,' he began, 'and my property —' and then exploded with an oath, and stopped again.

'Continue, continue,' said the King, waving his hands.

'What does it all mean?' cried the other, with a gesture of passionate rationality. 'Are you mad?'

'Not in the least,' replied the King, pleasantly. 'Madmen are always serious; they go mad from lack of humour. You are looking serious yourself, James.'

'Why can't you keep it to your own private life?' expostulated the other. 'You've got plenty of money, and plenty of houses now to play the fool in, but in the interests of the public——'

'Epigrammatic,' said the King, shaking his finger sadly at him. 'None of your daring scintillations here. As to why I don't do it in private, I rather fail to understand your question. The answer is of comparative limpidity. I don't do it in private, because it is funnier to do it in public. You appear to think that it would be amusing to be dignified in the banquet-hall and in the street, and at my own fireside (I could procure a fireside) to keep the company in a roar. But that is what every one does. Every one is grave in public, and funny in private. My sense of humour suggests the reversal of this; it suggests that one should be funny in public, and solemn in private. I desire to make the State functions, parliaments, coronations, and so on, one roaring old-fashioned pantomime. But, on the other hand, I shut myself up alone in a small store-room for two hours a day, where I am so dignified that I come out quite ill.'

By this time Barker was walking up and down the room, his frock-coat flapping like the black wings of a bird.

'Well, you will ruin the country, that's all,' he said shortly.

'It seems to me,' said Auberon, 'that the tradition of ten centuries is being broken, and the House of Barker is rebelling against the Crown of England. It would be with regret (for I admire your appearance) that I should be obliged forcibly to decorate your head with the remains of this hat, but——'

'What I can't understand,' said Barker, flinging up his fingers with a feverish American movement, 'is why you don't care about anything else but your games.'

The King stopped sharply in the act of lifting the silken remnants, dropped them, and walked up to Barker, looking at him steadily.

'I made a kind of vow,' he said, 'that I would not talk seriously, which always means answering silly questions. But the strong man will always be gentle with politicians.

> 'The shape my scornful looks deride
> Required a God to form';

if I may so theologically express myself. And for some reason I cannot in the least understand, I feel impelled to answer that question of yours, and to answer it as if there were really such a thing in the world as a serious subject. You ask me why I don't care for anything else. Can you tell me, in the name of all the gods you don't believe in, why I should care for anything else?'

'Don't you realize common public necessities?' cried Barker. 'Is it possible that a man of your intelligence does not know that it is every one's interest—'

'Don't you believe in Zoroaster?[27] Is it possible that you neglect Mumbo-Jumbo?'[28] returned the King, with startling animation. 'Does a man of your intelligence come to me with these damned early Victorian ethics? If, on studying my features and manner, you detect any particular resemblance to the Prince Consort,[29] I assure you you are mistaken. Did Herbert Spencer ever convince you—did he ever convince anybody—did he ever for one mad moment convince himself—that it must be to the interest of the individual to feel a public spirit? Do you believe that, if you rule your department badly, you stand any more chance, or one-half of the chance, of being guillotined, that an angler stands, of being pulled into the river by a strong pike? Herbert Spencer refrained from theft for the same reason that he refrained from wearing feathers in his hair, because he was an English gentleman with different tastes. I am an English gentleman with different tastes. He likes philosophy. I like art. He liked writing ten books on the nature of human society. I like to see the Lord Chamberlain[30] walking in front of me with a piece of paper pinned to his coat-tails. It is my humour. Are you answered? At any

[27] Zoroaster, or Zarathustra, is the founder of the old Persian religion of Zoroastrianism, based on an ethical dualism in which a good god and an evil god are at war. It was the religion of the Magi and survives in modified form among the Parsees of India.

[28] Mumbo-jumbo is an object of superstitious reverence; also a deity worshipped by animists in West Africa.

[29] Prince Albert (1819–61), Duke of Saxony and Prince of Saxe-Cobourg and Gotha, was the consort of Queen Victoria, whom he married in 1840.

[30] The Lord Chamberlain is the superintendent of the royal household, an official who until the end of the 1960s also exercised the duty of censorship of plays for the theater.

rate, I have said my last serious word to-day, and my last serious word I trust for the remainder of my life in this Paradise of Fools. The remainder of my conversation with you to-day, which I trust will be long and stimulating, I propose to conduct in a new language[31] of my own by means of rapid and symbolic movements of the left leg.' And he began to pirouette slowly round the room with a preoccupied expression.

Barker ran round the room after him, bombarding him with demands and entreaties. But he received no response except in the new language. He came out banging the door again, and sick like a man coming on shore. As he strode along the streets he found himself suddenly opposite Cicconani's restaurant, and for some reason there rose up before him the green, fantastic figure of the Spanish General, standing, as he had seen him last, at the door with the words on his lips, 'You cannot argue with the choice of the soul.'

The King came out from his dancing with the air of a man of business legitimately tired. He put on an overcoat, lit a cigar, and went out into the purple night.

'I will go,' he said, 'and mingle with the people.'

He passed swiftly up a street in the neighbourhood of Notting Hill, when suddenly he felt a hard object driven into his waistcoat. He paused, put up a single eye-glass, and beheld a boy with a wooden sword and a paper cocked hat, wearing that expression of awed satisfaction with which a child contemplates his work when he has hit some one very hard. The King gazed thoughtfully for some time at his assailant, and slowly took a note-book from his breast-pocket.

'I have a few notes,' he said, 'for my dying speech'; and he turned over the leaves. 'Dying speech for political assassination; ditto, if by former friend—h'm, h'm. Dying speech for death at hands of injured husband (repentant). Dying speech for same (cynical). I am not quite sure which meets the present. . . .'

'I'm the King of the Castle,'[32] said the boy, truculently, and very pleased with nothing in particular.

---

[31] See note 30 p. 167, of *The Club of Queer Trades*.

[32] King of the Castle was a popular boys' game. In the London version a group of boys runs towards any convenient hillock, rock or wall. The first boy to reach the top then defends it by pushing down his companions while reciting "I am King of the Castle, get down, you dirty rascals" until he is toppled off by another, whereupon the pattern is repeated.

"I'm King of the Castle."

The King was a kind-hearted man, and very fond of children, like all people who are fond of the ridiculous.

'Infant,' he said, 'I'm glad you are so stalwart a defender of your old inviolate Notting Hill. Look up nightly to that peak, my child, where it lifts itself among the stars so ancient, so lonely, so unutterably Notting. So long as you are ready to die for the sacred mountain, even if it were ringed with all the armies of Bayswater——'

The King stopped suddenly, and his eyes shone.

'Perhaps,' he said, 'perhaps the noblest of all my conceptions. A revival of the arrogance of the old medieval cities applied to our glorious suburbs. Clapham with a city guard. Wimbledon with a city wall. Surbiton tolling a bell to raise its citizens. West Hampstead going into battle with its own banner. It shall be done. I, the King, have said it.' And hastily presenting the boy with half a crown,[33] remarking, 'For the war-chest of Notting Hill', he ran violently home at such a rate of speed that crowds followed him for miles. On reaching his study, he ordered a cup of coffee, and plunged into profound meditation upon the project. At length he called his favourite Equerry, Captain Bowler, for whom he had a deep affection, founded principally upon the shape of his whiskers.

'Bowler,' he said, 'isn't there some society of historical research, or something of which I am an honorary member?'

'Yes, sir,' said Captain Bowler, rubbing his nose, 'you are a member of "The Encouragers of Egyptian Renaissance", and "The Teutonic Tombs Club", and "The Society for the Recovery of London Antiquities", and——'

'That is admirable,' said the King. 'The London Antiquities does my trick. Go to the Society for the Recovery of London Antiquities and speak to their secretary, and their sub-secretary, and their president, and their vice-president, saying, "The King of England is proud, but the honorary member of the Society for the Recovery of London Antiquities is prouder than kings. I should like to tell you of

[33] Half a crown is a silver coin worth one eighth of a pound sterling (the equivalent of half a silver dollar). It was an immense sum to give to a child in 1904, when it was about one eighth of an average working man's income, but we must remember that Chesterton's novel is set in 1984 and he may have intended to shock his readers by the rate of inflation.

certain discoveries I have made touching the neglected traditions of the London boroughs. The revelations may cause some excitement, stirring burning memories and touching old wounds in Shepherd's Bush and Bayswater, in Pimlico and South Kensington. The King hesitates, but the honorary member is firm. I approach you invoking the vows of my initiation, the Sacred Seven Cats, the Poker of Perfection, and the Ordeal of the Indescribable Instant (forgive me if I mix you up with the Clan-na-Gael[34] or some other club I belong to), and ask you to permit me to read a paper at your next meeting on the 'Wars of the London Boroughs'." Say all this to the Society, Bowler. Remember it very carefully, for it is most important, and I have forgotten it altogether, and send me another cup of coffee and some of the cigars that we keep for vulgar and successful people. I am going to write my paper.'

The Society for the Recovery of London Antiquities met a month after in a corrugated iron hall on the outskirts of one of the southern suburbs of London. A large number of people had collected there under the coarse and flaring gas-jets when the King arrived, perspiring and genial. On taking off his great-coat, he was perceived to be in evening dress, wearing the Garter.[35] His appearance at the small table, adorned only with a glass of water, was received with respectful cheering.

The chairman (Mr. Huggins) said that he was sure that they had all been pleased to listen to such distinguished lectures as they had heard for some time past (hear, hear). Mr. Burton[36] (hear, hear), Mr. Cambridge,[37] Professor King[38] (loud and continued cheers),

[34] Clan-na-Gael in English means Brotherhood of Gaels, an Irish secret society founded around 1870 within the Fenian movement, the party of extreme violence in the fight for Irish independence.

[35] The Garter is the insignia of the Order of the Garter, the highest order of chivalry in Britain.

[36] Mr. Burton was probably Sir Richard Francis Burton (1820–90), explorer, traveller and translator of the *Arabian Nights* (1885–88), who disguised himself to make the pilgrimage to Mecca. The reference could equally well have been to Montague Burton, the multiple tailor, or Decimus Burton.

[37] Mr. Cambridge was possibly Frederick Octavius Cambridge (1860–1905), an expert on spiders.

[38] Professor King was probably Albert Freeman Africanus King (1841–1914), a physician and obstetrician who also did pioneering work in linking the mosquito to the spread of malaria.

our old friend Peter Jessop,[39] Sir William White[40] (loud laughter), and other eminent men, had done honour to their little venture (cheers). But there were other circumstances which lend a certain unique quality to the present occasion (hear, hear). So far as his recollection went, and in connexion with the Society for the Recovery of London Antiquities it went very far (loud cheers), he did not remember that any of their lecturers had borne the title of King. He would therefore call upon King Auberon briefly to address the meeting.

The King began by saying that this speech might be regarded as the first declaration of his new policy for the nation. 'At this supreme hour of my life I feel that to no one but the members of the Society for the Recovery of London Antiquities can I open my heart (cheers). If the world turns upon my policy, and the storms of popular hostility begin to rise (no, no), I feel that it is here, with my brave Recoverers around me, that I can best meet them, sword in hand' (loud cheers).

His Majesty then went on to explain that, now old age was creeping upon him, he proposed to devote his remaining strength to bringing about a keener sense of local patriotism in the various municipalities of London. How few of them knew the legends of their own boroughs? How many there were who had never heard of the true origin of the Wink of Wandsworth! What a large proportion of the younger generation in Chelsea neglected to perform the old Chelsea Chuff! Pimlico no longer pumped the Pimlies. Battersea had forgotten the name of Blick.

There was a short silence, and then a voice said, 'Shame.'

The King continued: 'Being called, however unworthily, to this high estate, I have resolved that, so far as possible, this neglect shall cease. I desire no military glory. I lay claim to no constitutional equality with Justinian[41] or Alfred. If I can go down to history as the

---

[39] Peter Jessop would appear to have been a real person known to Chesterton. Unfortunately, his biographical details have not been recorded in any work of reference.

[40] Sir William White (1831–1913), assistant director of contracts at the admiralty, wrote under the pseudonym Mark Rutherford as well as his own name on the subject of spiritual self-revelation.

[41] Justinian (A.D. 527–65), 1st emperor of the Byzantine empire, married Theodora, a former courtesan. His reputation is that of a law-giver.

man who saved from extinction a few old English customs, if our descendants can say it was through this man, humble as he was, that the Ten Turnips are still eaten in Fulham, and the Putney parish councillor still shaves one half of his head, I shall look my great fathers reverently but not fearfully in the face when I go down to the last house of Kings.'

The King paused, visibly affected, but collecting himself, resumed once more.

'I trust that to very few of you, at least, I need dwell on the sublime origins of these legends. The very names of your boroughs bear witness to them. So long as Hammersmith is called Hammersmith, its people will live in the shadow of that primal hero, the Blacksmith, who led the democracy of the Broadway into battle till he drove the chivalry of Kensington before him and overthrew them at that place which in honour of the best blood of the defeated aristocracy is still called Kensington Gore.[42] Men of Hammersmith will not fail to remember that the very name of Kensington originated from the lips of their hero. For at the great banquet of reconciliation held after the war, when the disdainful oligarchs declined to join in the songs of the men of the Broadway (which are to this day of a rude and popular character), the great Republican leader, with his rough humour, said the words which are written in gold upon his monument, "Little birds that can sing and won't sing, must be made to sing." So that the Eastern Knights were called Cansings or Kensings ever afterwards. But you also have great memories, O men of Kensington! You showed that you could sing, and sing great war-songs. Even after the dark day of Kensington Gore, history will not forget those three Knights who guarded your disordered retreat from Hyde Park (so called from your hiding there), those three Knights after whom Knightsbridge is named. Nor will it forget the day of your re-emergence, purged in the fire of calamity, cleansed of your oligarchic corruptions, when, sword in hand, you drove the Empire of Hammersmith back mile by mile, swept it past its own Broadway, and broke it at last in a battle so

[42] Kensington Gore is the stretch of road between the Royal Albert Hall and the Albert Memorial in Kensington.

long and bloody that the birds of prey have left their name upon it. Men have called it, with austere irony, the Ravenscourt. I shall not, I trust, wound the patriotism of Bayswater, or the lonelier pride of Brompton, or that of any other historic township, by taking these two special examples. I select them, not because they are more glorious than the rest, but partly from personal association (I am myself descended from one of the three heroes of Knightsbridge), and partly from the consciousness that I am an amateur antiquarian, and cannot presume to deal with times and places more remote and more mysterious. It is not for me to settle the question between two such men as Professor Hugg[43] and Sir William Whisky as to whether Notting Hill means Nutting Hill (in allusion to the rich woods which no longer cover it), or whether it is a corruption of Nothing-ill, referring to its reputation among the ancients as an Earthly Paradise. When a Podkins[44] and a Jossy[45] confess themselves doubtful about the boundaries of West Kensington (said to have been traced in the blood of Oxen), I need not be ashamed to confess a similar doubt. I will ask you to excuse me from further history, and to assist me with your encouragement in dealing with the problem which faces us to-day. Is this ancient spirit of the London townships to die out? Are our omnibus conductors and policemen to lose altogether that light which we see so often in their eyes, the dreamy light of

> 'Old unhappy far-off things
> And battles long ago'[46]

— to quote the words of a little-known poet who was a friend of my youth? I have resolved, as I have said, so far as possible, to preserve the eyes of policemen and omnibus conductors in their present

[43] Professor Hugg was possibly George Hugg, composer of "Father Time's best loved grandchild — a cantata for Christmas".

[44] Podkins was probably Peter Podkins, Jr., the pseudonym of the unknown author of *Betty Podkins' Letter Ted Queen on Cleopatra's Needle written ed Wardle* [*Weardale*] *dylect*, London 1877.

[45] Jossy is just possibly a reference to a character in *Love's the best doctor*, an English translation of Moliere's *L'Amour médecin*, in which Monsieur Jesse looks after his own interests.

[46] These lines are from William Wordsworth's "The Solitary Reaper", vv. 19-20.

dreamy state. For what is a state without dreams. And the remedy I propose is as follows:

'To-morrow morning at twenty-five minutes past ten, if Heaven spares my life, I purpose to issue a Proclamation. It has been the work of my life, and is about half-finished. With the assistance of a whisky and soda, I shall conclude the other half to-night, and my people will receive it to-morrow. All these boroughs where you were born, and hope to lay your bones, shall be reinstated in their ancient magnificence—Hammersmith, Kensington, Bayswater, Chelsea, Battersea, Clapham, Balham, and a hundred others. Each shall immediately build a city wall with gates to be closed at sunset. Each shall have a city guard, armed to the teeth. Each shall have a banner, a coat of arms, and, if convenient, a gathering cry. I will not enter into the details now, my heart is too full. They will be found in the proclamation itself. You will all, however, be subject to enrolment in the local city guards, to be summoned together by a thing called the Tocsin,[47] the meaning of which I am studying in my researches into history. Personally, I believe a tocsin to be some kind of highly paid official. If, therefore, any of you happen to have such a thing as a halberd in the house, I should advise you to practise with it in the garden.'

Here the King buried his face in his handkerchief and hurriedly left the platform, overcome by emotions.

The members of the Society for the Recovery of London Antiquities rose in an indescribable state of vagueness. Some were purple with indignation; an intellectual few were purple with laughter; the great majority found their minds a blank. There remains a tradition that one pale face with burning blue eyes remained fixed upon the lecturer, and after the lecture a red-haired boy ran out of the room.

[47] A tocsin is an alarm bell.

II

THE COUNCIL OF THE PROVOSTS

The King got up early next morning and came down three steps at a time like a schoolboy. Having eaten his breakfast hurriedly, but with an appetite, he summoned one of the highest officials of the Palace, and presented him with a shilling. 'Go and buy me,' he said, 'a shilling paint-box,[48] which you will get, unless the mists of time mislead me, in a shop at the corner of the second and dirtier street that leads out of Rochester Row. I have already requested the Master of the Buckhounds to provide me with cardboard. It seemed to me (I know not why) that it fell within his department.'

The King was happy all that morning with his cardboard and his paint-box. He was engaged in designing the uniforms and coats of arms for the various municipalities of London. They gave him deep and no inconsiderable thought. He felt the responsibility.

'I cannot think,' he said, 'why people should think the names of places in the country more poetical than those in London. Shallow romanticists go away in trains and stop in places called Hugmy-in-the-Hole, or Bumps-on-the-Puddle. And all the time they could, if they liked, go and live at a place with the dim, divine name of St. John's Wood. I have never been to St. John's Wood. I dare not. I should be afraid of the innumerable night of fir-trees, afraid to come upon a blood-red cup[49] and the beating of the wings of the Eagle. But all these things can be imagined by remaining reverently in the Harrow train.'

And he thoughtfully retouched his design for the head-dress of the halberdier of St. John's Wood, a design in black and red, compounded of a pine-tree and the plumage of an eagle. Then he turned to another card. 'Let us think of milder matters,' he said. 'Lavender

[48] A shilling paint-box refers to a box of cheap watercolors such as one might give to a child. A shilling was one twentieth of a pound sterling, now worth five pence in decimalized currency, but in 1904 a shilling was worth twenty cents.

[49] A blood-red cup is a reference to the Holy Grail of Arthurian legend.

Hill! Could any of your glebes[50] and combes[51] and all the rest of it produce so fragrant an idea? Think of a mountain of lavender lifting itself in purple poignancy into the silver skies and filling men's nostrils with a new breath of life — a purple hill of incense. It is true that upon my few excursions of discovery on a halfpenny tram I have failed to hit the precise spot. But it must be there; some poet called it by its name. There is at least warrant enough for the solemn purple plumes (following the botanical formation of lavender) which I have required people to wear in the neighbourhood of Clapham Junction. It is so everywhere, after all. I have never been actually to Southfields, but I suppose a scheme of lemons and olives represent their austral instincts. I have never visited Parson's Green, or seen either the Green or the Parson, but surely the pale-green shovel-hats I have designed must be more or less in the spirit. I must work in the dark and let my instincts guide me. The great love I bear to my people will certainly save me from distressing their noble spirit or violating their great traditions.'

As he was reflecting in this vein, the door was flung open, and an official announced Mr. Barker and Mr. Lambert.

Mr. Barker and Mr. Lambert were not particularly surprised to find the King sitting on the floor amid a litter of water-colour sketches. They were not particularly suprised because the last time they had called on him they had found him sitting on the floor, surrounded by a litter of children's bricks, and the time before surrounded by a litter of wholly unsuccessful attempts to make paper darts. But the trend of the royal infant's remarks, uttered from amid this infantile chaos, was not quite the same affair. For some time they let him babble on, conscious that his remarks meant nothing. And then a horrible thought began to steal over the mind of James Barker. He began to think that the King's remarks did not mean nothing.

'In God's name, Auberon,' he suddenly volleyed out, startling the quiet hall, 'you don't mean that you are really going to have these city guards and city walls and things?'

'I am, indeed,' said the infant, in a quiet voice. 'Why shouldn't

[50] Glebes are areas of land attached to parish churches for the use of the incumbent clergymen.
[51] Combes are narrow valleys.

I have them? I have modelled them precisely on your political principles. Do you know what I've done, Barker? I've behaved like a
true Barkerian. I've . . . but perhaps it won't interest you, the account of my Barkerian conduct.'

'Oh, go on, go on,' cried Barker.

'The account of my Barkerian conduct,' said Auberon, calmly,
'seems not only to interest, but to alarm you. Yet it is very simple. It
merely consists in choosing all the provosts under any new scheme
by the same principle by which you have caused the central despot to
be appointed. Each provost, of each city, under my charter, is to be
appointed by rotation. Sleep, therefore, my Barker, a rosy sleep.'

Barker's wild eyes flared.

'But, in God's name, don't you see, Quin, that the thing is quite
different? In the centre it doesn't matter so much, just because the
whole object of despotism is to get some sort of unity. But if any
damned parish can go to any damned man——'

'I see your difficulty,' said King Auberon, calmly. 'You feel that
your talents may be neglected. Listen!' And he rose with immense
magnificence. 'I solemnly give to my liege subject, James Barker, my
special and splendid favour, the right to override the obvious text of
the Charter of the Cities, and to be, in his own right, Lord High Provost of South Kensington. And now, my dear James, you are all
right. Good day.'

'But——' began Barker.

'The audience is at an end, Provost,' said the King, smiling.

How far his confidence was justified, it would require a somewhat
complicated description to explain. 'The Great Proclamation of the
Charter of the Free Cities' appeared in due course that morning, and
was posted by bill-stickers all over the front of the Palace, the King assisting them with animated directions, and standing in the middle of
the road, with his head on one side, contemplating the result. It was also
carried up and down the main thoroughfares by sandwichmen, and the
King was, with difficulty, restrained from going out in that capacity
himself, being, in fact, found by the Groom of the Stole[52] and Captain

[52] The Groom of the Stole, or Stool, is an honorary position much sought after by
senior noblemen, but basically the duties are those of a rather superior lavatory or
bathroom attendant.

Bowler, struggling between two boards. His excitement had positively to be quieted like that of a child.

The reception which the Charter of the Cities meant at the hands of the public may mildly be described as mixed. In one sense it was popular enough. In many happy homes that remarkable legal document was read aloud on winter evenings amid uproarious appreciation, when everything had been learnt by heart from that quaint but immortal old classic, Mr. W. W. Jacobs.[53] But when it was discovered that the King had every intention of seriously requiring the provisions to be carried out, of insisting that the grotesque cities, with their tocsins and city guards, should really come into existence, things were thrown into a far angrier confusion. Londoners had no particular objection to the King making a fool of himself, but they became indignant when it became evident that he wished to make fools of them; and protests began to come in.

The Lord High Provost of the Good and Valiant City of West Kensington wrote a respectful letter to the King, explaining that upon State occasions it would, of course, be his duty to observe what formalities the King thought proper, but that it was really awkward for a decent householder not to be allowed to go out and put a post card in a pillarbox without being escorted by five heralds, who announced, with formal cries and blasts of a trumpet, that the Lord High Provost desired to catch the post.

Lord High Provost of North Kensington, who was a prosperous draper, wrote a curt business note, like a man complaining of a railway company, stating that definite inconvenience had been caused him by the presence of the halberdiers, whom he had to take with him everywhere. When attempting to catch an omnibus to the City, he had found that while room could have been found for himself, the halberdiers had a difficulty in getting into the vehicle—believe him, theirs faithfully.

The Lord High Provost of Shepherd's Bush said his wife did not like men hanging round the kitchen.

The King was always delighted to listen to these grievances, delivering lenient and kingly answers, but as he always insisted, as

[53] W. W. Jacobs (1863–1943) was an English author best known for his stories such as "The Monkey's Paw".

the absolute *sine qua non*, that verbal complaints should be presented to him with the fullest pomp of trumpets, plumes, and halberds, only a few resolute spirits were prepared to run the gauntlet of the little boys in the street.

Among these, however, was prominent the abrupt and business-like gentleman who ruled North Kensington. And he had, before long, occasion to interview the King about a matter wider and even more urgent than the problem of the halberdiers and the omnibus. This was the greatest question which then and for long afterwards brought a stir to the blood and a flush to the cheek of all the specula-tive builders and house agents from Shepherd's Bush to the Marble Arch, and from Westbourne Grove to High Street, Kensington. I refer to the great affair of the improvements in Notting Hill. The scheme was conducted chiefly by Mr. Buck, the abrupt North Ken-sington magnate, and by Mr. Wilson, the Provost of Bayswater. A great thoroughfare was to be driven through three boroughs, through West Kensington, North Kensington, and Notting Hill, opening at one end into Hammersmith Broadway, and at the other into Westbourne Grove. The negotiations, buyings, sellings, bullying and bribing took ten years, and by the end of it Buck, who had con-ducted them almost single-handed, had proved himself a man of the strongest type of material energy and material diplomacy. And just as his splendid patience and more splendid impatience had finally brought him victory, when workmen were already demolishing houses and walls along the great line from Hammersmith, a sudden obstacle appeared that had neither been reckoned with nor dreamed of, a small and strange obstacle, which, like a speck of grit in a great machine, jarred the whole vast scheme and brought it to a standstill, and Mr. Buck, the draper, getting with great impatience into his robes of office and summoning with indescribable disgust his halber-diers, hurried over to speak to the King.

Ten years had not tired the King of his joke. There were still new faces to be seen looking out from the symbolic head-gears he had de-signed, gazing at him from amid the pastoral ribbons of Shepherd's Bush or from under the sombre hoods of the Blackfriars Road. And the interview which was promised him with the Provost of North

Kensington he anticipated with a particular pleasure, for 'he never really enjoyed', he said, 'the full richness of the medieval garments unless the people compelled to wear them were very angry and business-like.'

Mr. Buck was both. At the King's command the door of the audience-chamber was thrown open and a herald appeared in the purple colours of Mr. Buck's commonwealth emblazoned with the Great Eagle which the King had attributed to North Kensington, in vague reminiscence of Russia, for he always insisted on regarding North Kensington as some kind of semi-arctic neighbourhood. The herald announced that the Provost of that city desired audience of the King.

'From North Kensington?' said the King, rising graciously. 'What news does he bring from that land of high hills and fair women? He is welcome.'

The herald advanced into the room, and was immediately followed by twelve guards clad in purple, who were followed by an attendant bearing the banner of the Eagle, who was followed by another attendant bearing the keys of the city upon a cushion, who was followed by Mr. Buck in a great hurry. When the King saw his strong animal face and steady eyes, he knew that he was in the presence of a great man of business, and consciously braced himself.

'Well, well,' he said, cheerily coming down two or three steps from a dais, and striking his hands lightly together, 'I am glad to see you. Never mind, never mind. Ceremony is not everything.'

'I don't understand your Majesty,' said the Provost, stolidly.

'Never mind, never mind,' said the King, gaily. 'A knowledge of Courts is by no means an unmixed merit; you will do it next time, no doubt.'

The man of business looked at him sulkily from under his black brows and said again without show of civility:

'I don't follow you.'

'Well, well,' replied the King, good-naturedly, 'if you ask me I don't mind telling you, not because I myself attach any importance to these forms in comparison with the Honest Heart. But it is usual—it is usual—that is all, for a man when entering the presence of Royalty to lie down on his back on the floor and elevating his feet towards heaven (as the source of Royal power) to say three times "Monarchical institutions improve the manners". But there, there—such pomp is far less truly dignified than your simple kindliness.'

The Provost's face was red with anger, and he maintained silence.

'And now,' said the King, lightly, and with the exasperating air of a man softening a snub; 'what delightful weather we are having! You must find your official robes warm, my Lord. I designed them for your own snow-bound land.'

'They're as hot as hell,' said Buck, briefly. 'I came here on business.'

'Right,' said the King, nodding a great number of times with quite unmeaning solemnity; 'right, right, right. Business, as the sad glad old Persian[54] said, is business. Be punctual. Rise early. Point the pen to the shoulder. Point the pen to the shoulder, for you know not whence you come nor why. Point the pen to the shoulder, for you know not when you go nor where.'

The Provost pulled a number of papers from his pocket and savagely flapped them open.

'Your Majesty may have heard,' he began, sarcastically, 'of Hammersmith and a thing called a road. We have been at work ten years buying property and getting compulsory powers and fixing compensation and squaring vested interests, and now at the very end, the thing is stopped by a fool. Old Prout, who was Provost of Notting Hill, was a business man, and we dealt with him quite satisfactorily. But he's dead, and the cursed lot has fallen to a young man named Wayne, who's up to some game that's perfectly incomprehensible to me. We offer him a better price than any one ever dreamt of, but he won't let the road go through. And his Council seem to be backing him up. It's midsummer madness.'

The King, who was rather inattentively engaged in drawing the Provost's nose with his finger on the window-pane, heard the last two words.

'What a perfect phrase that is,' he said. ' "Midsummer madness!" '

'The chief point is,' continued Buck, doggedly, 'that the only part that is really in question is one dirty little street—Pump Street[55]—a

---

[54] The sad glad old Persian is Omar Khayyam (c. 1048–1122), the Persian poet translated and adapted by Edward Fitzgerald (1809–83) in 1859.

[55] Pump Street is the only fictitious location in the book.

street with nothing in it but a public-house and a penny toyshop, and that sort of thing. All the respectable people of Notting Hill have accepted our compensation. But the ineffable Wayne sticks out over Pump Street. Says he's Provost of Notting Hill. He's only Provost of Pump Street.'

'A good thought,' replied Auberon. 'I like the idea of a Provost of Pump Street. Why not let him alone?'

'And drop the whole scheme!' cried out Buck, with a burst of brutal spirit. 'I'll be damned if we do. No. I'm for sending in workmen to pull down without more ado.'

'Strike for the purple Eagle,' cried the King, hot with historical associations.

'I'll tell you what it is,' said Buck losing his temper altogether. 'If your Majesty would spend less time in insulting respectable people with your silly coats of arms, and more time over the business of the nation —'

The King's brow wrinkled thoughtfully.

'The situation is not bad,' he said; 'the haughty burgher defying the King in his own Palace. The burgher's head should be thrown back and the right arm extended; the left may be lifted towards Heaven, but that I leave to your private religious sentiment. I have sunk back in this chair stricken with baffled fury. Now again, please.'

Buck's mouth opened like a dog's, but before he could speak another herald appeared at the door.

'The Lord High Provost of Bayswater,' he said, 'desires an audience.'

'Admit him,' said Auberon. 'This *is* a jolly day.'

The halberdiers of Bayswater wore a prevailing uniform of green, and the banner which was borne after them was emblazoned with a green bay-wreath on a sliver ground, which the King, in the course of his researches into a bottle of champagne had discovered to be the quaint old punning cognizance of the city of Bayswater.

'It is a fit symbol,' said the King, 'your immortal bay-wreath. Fulham may seek for wealth, and Kensington for art, but when did the men of Bayswater care for anything but glory?'

Immediately behind the banner, and almost completely hidden by it, came the Provost of the city, clad in splendid robes of green and silver with white fur and crowned with bay. He was an anxious little man with red whiskers, originally the owner of a small sweetstuff shop.

'Our cousin of Bayswater,' said the King, with delight; 'what can we get for you?' The King was heard also distinctly to mutter, 'Cold beef, cold 'am, cold chicken', his voice dying into silence.

'I came to see your Majesty,' said the Provost of Bayswater, whose name was Wilson, 'about that Pump Street affair.'

'I have just been explaining the situation to his Majesty,' said Buck, curtly, but recovering his civility. 'I am not sure, however, whether his Majesty knows how much the matter affects you also.'

'It affects both of us, yer see, yer Majesty, as this scheme was started for the benefit of the 'ole neighbourhood. So Mr. Buck and me we put our 'eads together——'

The King clasped his hands.

'Perfect,' he cried in ecstasy. 'Your heads together! I can see it! Can't you do it now? Oh, do do it now.'

A smothered sound of amusement appeared to come from the halberdiers, but Mr. Wilson looked merely bewildered, and Mr. Buck merely diabolical.

'I suppose,' he began, bitterly, but the King stopped him with a gesture of listening.

'Hush,' he said, 'I think I hear some one else coming. I seem to hear another herald, a herald whose boots creak.'

As he spoke another voice cried from the doorway:

'The Lord High Provost of South Kensington desires an audience.'

'The Lord High Provost of South Kensington!' cried the King. 'Why, that is my old friend James Barker! What does he want, I wonder? If the tender memories of friendship have not grown misty, I fancy he wants something for himself, probably money. How are you, James?'

Mr. James Barker, whose guard was attired in a splendid blue, and whose blue banner bore three gold birds singing, rushed, in his blue and gold robes into the room. Despite the absurdity of all the dresses, it was worth noticing that he carried his better than the rest, though he loathed it as much as any of them. He was a gentleman, and a very handsome man, and could not help unconsciously wearing even his preposterous robe as it should be worn. He spoke quickly, but with the slight initial hesitation he always showed in addressing the King, due to suppressing an impulse to address his old acquaintance in the old way.

'Your Majesty—pray forgive my intrusion. It is about this man at Pump Street. I see you have Buck here, so you have probably heard what is necessary. I—'

The King swept his eyes anxiously round the room, which now blazed with the trappings of three cities.

'There is one thing necessary,' he said.

'Yes, your Majesty,' said Mr. Wilson of Bayswater, a little eagerly. 'What does yer Majesty think necessary?'

'A little yellow,' said the King, firmly. 'Send for the Provost of West Kensington.'

Amid some materialistic protests he was sent for and arrived with his yellow halberdiers in his saffron robes, wiping his forehead with a handkerchief. After all, placed as he was, he had a good deal to say on the matter.

'Welcome, West Kensington,' said the King. 'I have long wished to see you, touching that matter of the Hammersmith land to the south of the Rowton House.[56] Will you hold it feudally from the Provost of Hammersmith? You have only to do him homage by putting his left arm in his overcoat and then marching home in state.'

'No, your Majesty; I'd rather not,' said the Provost of West Kensington, who was a pale young man with a fair moustache and whiskers, who kept a successful dairy.

The King struck him heartily on the shoulder.

'The fierce old West Kensington blood,' he said; 'they are not wise who ask it to do homage.'

Then he glanced again round the room. It was full of a roaring sunset of colour, and he enjoyed the sight, possible to so few artists—the sight of his own dreams moving and blazing before him. In the foreground the yellow of the West Kensington liveries outlined itself against the dark blue draperies of South Kensington. The

---

[56] The Rowton House was a poor man's hostel opened in 1892 by Montague William Lowry-Corry, Baron Rowton (1838–1903).

crests of these again brightened suddenly into green as the almost woodland colours of Bayswater rose behind them. And over and behind all, the great purple plumes of North Kensington showed almost funereal and black.

'There is something lacking,' said the King, 'something lacking. What can — ah, there it is! — there it is!'

In the doorway had appeared a new figure, a herald in flaming red. He cried in a loud but unemotional voice:

'The Lord High Provost of Notting Hill desires an audience.'

III

ENTER A LUNATIC

The King of the Fairies,[57] who was, it is to be presumed, the god-father of King Auberon, must have been very favourable on this particular day to his fantastic godchild, for with the entrance of the guard of the Provost of Notting Hill there was a certain more or less inexplicable addition to his delight. The wretched navvies and sandwich-men who carried the colours of Bayswater or South Kensington, engaged merely for the day to satisfy the Royal hobby, slouched into the room with a comparatively hang-dog air, and a great part of the King's intellectual pleasure consisted in the contrast between the arrogance of their swords and feathers and the meek misery of their faces. But these Notting Hill halberdiers in their red tunics belted with gold had the air rather of an absurd gravity. They seemed, so to speak, to be taking part in the joke. They marched and wheeled into position with an almost startling dignity and discipline.

They carried a yellow banner with a great red lion, named by the King as the Notting Hill emblem, after a small public-house in the neighbourhood which he once frequented.

Between the two lines of his followers there advanced towards the king a tall, red-haired young man, with high features, and bold blue eyes. He would have been called handsome, but that a certain indefinable air of his nose being too big for his face, and his feet for his legs, gave him a look of awkwardness and extreme youth. His robes were red, according to the King's heraldry, and alone among the Provosts, he was girt with a great sword. This was Adam Wayne, the intractable Provost of Notting Hill.

The King flung himself back in his chair, and rubbed his hands.

'What a day, what a day!' he said to himself. 'Now there'll be a row. I'd no idea it would be such fun as it is. These Provosts are so very indignant, so very reasonable, so very right. This fellow, by the

---

[57] The King of the Fairies was, of course, called Oberon or Auberon.

look in his eyes, is even more indignant than the rest. No sign in those
large blue eyes, at any rate, of ever having heard of a joke. He'll remonstrate with the others, and they'll remonstrate with him, and they'll all
make themselves sumptuously happy remonstrating with me.'

'Welcome, my Lord,' he said aloud. 'What news from the Hill of
a Hundred Legends? What have you for the ear of your King? I
know that troubles have arisen between you and these others, our
cousins, but these troubles it shall be our pride to compose. And I
doubt not, and cannot doubt, that your love for me is not less
tender, no less ardent than theirs.'

Mr. Buck made a bitter face, and James Barker's nostrils curled;
Wilson began to giggle faintly, and the Provost of West Kensington
followed in a smothered way. But the big blue eyes of Adam Wayne
never changed, and he called out in an odd, boyish voice down the hall:

'I bring homage to my King. I bring him the only thing I
have—my sword.'

And with a great gesture he flung it down on the ground, and
knelt on one knee behind it.

There was a dead silence.

'I beg your pardon,' said the King, blankly.

'You speak well, sire,' said Adam Wayne, 'as you ever speak,
when you say that my love is not less than the love of these. Small
would it be if it were not more. For I am the heir of your
scheme—the child of the great Charter. I stand here for the rights
the Charter gave me, and I swear, by your sacred crown, that where
I stand, I stand fast.'

The eyes of all five men stood out of their heads.

Then Buck said, in his jolly, jarring voice: 'Is the whole world mad?'

The King sprang to his feet, and his eyes blazed.

'Yes,' he cried, in a voice of exultation, 'the whole world is mad,
but Adam Wayne and me. It is true as death what I told you long
ago, James Barker, seriousness sends men mad. You are mad, because you care for politics, as mad as a man who collects tram
tickets. Buck is mad, because he cares for money, as mad as a man
who lives on opium. Wilson is mad, because he thinks himself right,
as mad as a man who thinks himself God Almighty. The Provost of
West Kensington is mad, because he thinks he is respectable, as mad

"I bring homage to my king."

as a man who thinks he is a chicken. All men are mad, but the humorist, who cares for nothing and possesses everything. I thought that there was only one humorist in England. Fools! — dolts! — open your cows' eyes; there are two! In Notting Hill — in that unpromising elevation — there has been born an artist! You thought to spoil my joke, and bully me out of it, by becoming more and more modern, more and more practical, more and more bustling and rational. Oh, what a feast it was to answer you by becoming more and more august, more and more gracious, more and more ancient and mellow! But this lad has seen how to bowl me out. He has answered me back, vaunt for vaunt, rhetoric for rhetoric. He has lifted the only shield I cannot break, the shield of an impenetrable pomposity. Listen to him. You have come, my Lord, about Pump Street?'

'About the city of Notting Hill,' answered Wayne, proudly. 'Of which Pump Street is a living and rejoicing part.'

'Not a very large part,' said Barker, contemptuously.

'That which is large enough for the rich to covet,' said Wayne, drawing up his head, 'is large enough for the poor to defend.'

The King slapped both his legs, and waved his feet for a second in the air.

'Every respectable person in Notting Hill,' cut in Buck, with his cold, coarse voice, 'is for us and against you. I have plenty of friends in Notting Hill.'

'Your friends are those who have taken your gold for other men's hearthstones, my Lord Buck,' said Provost Wayne. 'I can well believe they are your friends.'

'They've never sold dirty toys, anyhow,' said Buck, laughing shortly.

'They've sold dirtier things,' said Wayne, calmly; 'they have sold themselves.'

'It's no good, my Buckling,' said the King, rolling about on his chair. 'You can't cope with this chivalrous eloquence. You can't cope with an artist. You can't cope with the humorist of Notting Hill. O, *Nunc dimittis* — that I have lived to see this day! Provost Wayne, you stand firm?'

'Let them wait and see,' said Wayne. 'If I stood firm before, do you think I shall weaken now that I have seen the face of the King? For I fight for something greater, if greater there can be than the hearth-stones of my people and the Lordship of the Lion. I fight for your royal vision, for the great dream you dreamt of the League of the Free Cities. You have given me this liberty. If I had been a beggar and you had flung me a coin, if I had been a peasant in a dance and you had flung me a favour, do you think I would have let it be taken by any ruffians on the road? This leadership and liberty of Notting Hill is a gift from your Majesty. And if it is taken from me, by God! it shall be taken in battle, and the noise of that battle shall be heard in the flats of Chelsea and in the studios of St. John's Wood.'

'It is too much — it is too much,' said the King. 'Nature is weak. I must speak to you, brother artist, without further disguise. Let me ask you a solomn question. Adam Wayne, Lord High Provost of Notting Hill, don't you think it splendid?'

'Splendid!' cried Adam Wayne. 'It has the splendour of God.'

'Bowled out again,' said the King. 'You will keep up the pose. Funnily, of course, it is serious. But seriously, isn't it funny?'

'What?' asked Wayne, with the eyes of a baby.

'Hang it all, don't play any more. The whole business — the Charter of the Cities. Isn't it immense?'

'Immense is no unworthy word for that glorious design.'

'Oh, hang you — but, of course, I see. You want me to clear the room of these reasonable sows. You want the two humorists alone together. Leave us, gentlemen.'

Buck threw a sour look at Barker, and at a sullen signal the whole pageant of blue and green, of red, gold, and purple rolled out of the room, leaving only two in the great hall, the King sitting in his seat on the dais, and the red-clad figure still kneeling on the floor before his fallen sword.

The King bounded down the steps and smacked Provost Wayne on the back.

'Before the stars were made,' he cried, 'we were made for each other. It is too beautiful. Think of the valiant independence of Pump Street. That is the real thing. It is the deification of the ludicrous.'

The kneeling figure sprang to his feet with a fierce stagger.

'Ludicrous!' he cried, with a fiery face.

'Oh, come, come,' said the King, impatiently. 'You needn't keep it up with me. The augurs must wink sometimes from sheer fatigue of the eyelids. Let us enjoy this for half an hour, not as actors, but as dramatic critics. Isn't it a joke?'

Adam Wayne looked down like a boy, and answered in a constrained voice:

'I do not understand your Majesty. I cannot believe that while I fight for your royal charter your Majesty deserts me for these dogs of the gold hunt.'

'Oh, damn your — But what's this? What the devil's this?'

The King stared into the young Provost's face, and in the twilight of the room began to see that his face was quite white and his lip shaking.

'What in God's name is the matter?' cried Auberon holding his wrist.

Wayne flung back his face, and the tears were shining on it.

'I am only a boy,' he said, 'but it's true. I would paint the Red Lion on my shield if I had only my blood.'

King Auberon dropped the hand and stood without stirring, thunderstruck.

'My God in Heaven!' he said; 'is it possible that there is within the four seas of Britain a man who takes Notting Hill seriously? — '

'And my God in Heaven!' said Wayne passionately; 'is it possible that there is within the four seas of Britain a man who does not take it seriously?'

The King said nothing, but merely went back up the steps of the dais, like a man dazed. He fell back in his chair again and kicked his heels.

'If this sort of thing is to go on,' he said weakly, 'I shall begin to doubt the superiority of art to life. In Heaven's name, do not play with me. Do you really mean that you are — God help me! — a Notting Hill patriot — that you are — '

Wayne made a violent gesture, and the King soothed him wildly.

'All right — all right — I see you are; but let me take it in. You do really propose to fight these modern improvers with their boards and inspectors and surveyors and all the rest of it——'

'Are they so terrible?' asked Wayne, scornfully.

The King continued to stare at him as if he were a human curiosity.

'And I suppose,' he said, 'that you think that the dentists and small tradesmen and maiden ladies who inhabit Notting Hill, will rally with war-hymns to your standard?'

'If they have blood they will,' said the Provost.

'And I suppose,' said the King, with his head back among the cushions, 'that it never crossed your mind that'—his voice seemed to lose itself luxuriantly—'never crossed your mind that any one ever thought that the idea of a Notting Hill idealism was—er—slightly—slightly ridiculous.'

'Of course they think so,' said Wayne. 'What was the meaning of mocking the prophets?'

'Where?' asked the King, leaning forward. 'Where in Heaven's name did you get this miraculously inane idea?'

'You have been my tutor, sire,' said the Provost, 'in all that is high and honourable.'

'Eh?' said the King.

'It was your Majesty who first stirred my dim patriotism into flame. Ten years ago, when I was a boy (I am only nineteen), I was playing on the slope of Pump Street, with a wooden sword and a paper helmet, dreaming of great wars. In an angry trance I struck out with my sword and stood petrified, for I saw that I had struck you, sire, my King, as you wandered in a noble secrecy, watching over your people's welfare. But I need have had no fear. Then was I taught to understand Kingliness. You neither shrank nor frowned. You summoned no guards. You invoked no punishments. But in august and burning words, which are written in my soul, never to be erased, you told me ever to turn my sword against the enemies of my inviolate city. Like a priest pointing to the altar, you pointed to the hill of Notting. "So long," you said, "as you are ready to die for the sacred mountain, even if it were ringed with all the armies of Bayswater." I have not forgotten the words, and I have reason now to remember them, for the hour is come and the crown of your prophecy.

The sacred hill is ringed with the armies of Bayswater, and I am ready to die.'

The King was lying back in his chair, a kind of wreck.

'O Lord, Lord, Lord,' he murmured, 'what a life! what a life! All my work! I seem to have done it all. So you're the red-haired boy that hit me in the waistcoat. What have I done? God, what have I done? I thought I would have a joke, and I have created a passion. I tried to compose a burlesque, and it seems to be turning half-way through into an epic. What is to be done with such a world? In the Lord's name wasn't the joke broad and bold enough? I abandoned my subtle humour to amuse you, and I seem to have brought tears to your eyes. What's to be done with people when you write a pantomime for them — call the sausages classic festoons, and the policeman cut in two a tragedy of public duty? But why am I talking? Why am I asking questions of a nice young gentleman who is totally mad? What is the good of it? What is the good of anything? O Lord, O Lord!'

Suddenly he pulled himself upright.

'Don't you really think the sacred Notting Hill at all absurd?'

'Absurd?' asked Wayne, blankly. 'Why should I?'

The King stared back equally blankly.

'I beg your pardon?' he said.

'Notting Hill,' said the Provost, simply, 'is a rise or high ground of the common earth, on which men have built houses to live, in which they are born, fall in love, pray, marry, and die. Why should I think it absurd?'

The King smiled.

'Because, my Leonidas[58] — ' he began, then suddenly, he knew not how, found his mind was a total blank. After all, why was it absurd? Why was it absurd? He felt as if the floor of his mind had given way. He felt as all men feel when their first principles are hit hard with a question. Barker always felt so when the King said, 'Why trouble about politics?'

The King's thoughts were in a kind of rout; he could not collect them.

[58] Leonidas (490? – 480 B.C.) was King of Sparta, the hero of Thermopylae, which he defended to the death against the Persians.

'It is generally felt to be a little funny,' he said, vaguely.

'I suppose,' said Adam, turning on him with a fierce suddenness, 'I suppose you fancy crucifixion was a serious affair?'

'Well, I——' began Auberon, 'I admit I have generally thought it had its graver side.'

'Then you are wrong,' said Wayne, with incredible violence. 'Crucifixion is comic. It is exquisitely diverting. It was an absurd and obscene kind of impaling reserved for people who were made to be laughed at—for slaves and provincials—for dentists and small tradesmen, as you would say. I have seen the grotesque gallows-shape, which the little Roman gutter-boys scribbled on walls as a vulgar joke, blazing on the pinnacles of the temples of the world. And shall I turn back?'

The King made no answer.

Adam went on, his voice ringing in the roof.

'This laughter with which men tyrannize is not the great power you think it. Peter was crucified, and crucified head downwards. What could be funnier than the idea of a respectable old Apostle upside down? What could be more in the style of your modern humour? But what was the good of it? Upside down or right side up, Peter was Peter to mankind. Upside down he still hangs over Europe, and millions move and breathe only in the life of his church.'

King Auberon got up absently.

'There is something in what you say,' he said. 'You seem to have been thinking, young man.'

'Only feeling, sire,' answered the Provost. 'I was born, like other men, in a spot of the earth which I loved because I had played boys' games there, and fallen in love, and talked with my friends through nights that were nights of the gods. And I feel the riddle. These little gardens where we told our loves. These streets where we brought out our dead. Why should they be commonplace? Why should they be absurd? Why should it be grotesque to say that a pillar-box is poetic when for a year I could not see a red pillar-box against the yellow evening in a certain street without being wracked with something of which God keeps the secret, but which is stronger than sorrow or joy? Why should any one be able to raise a laugh by saying "the Cause of Notting Hill"?—Notting Hill, where thousands of immortal spirits blaze with alternate hope and fear.'

Auberon was flicking dust off his sleeve with quite a new serious-ness on his face, distinct from the owlish solemnity which was the pose of his humour.

'It is very difficult,' he said at last. 'It is a damned difficult thing. I see what you mean—I agree with you even up to a point—or I should like to agree with you, if I were young enough to be a prophet and poet. I feel a truth in everything you say until you come to the words "Notting Hill". And then I regret to say that the old Adam awakes roaring with laughter and makes short work of the new Adam, whose name is Wayne.'

For the first time Provost Wayne was silent, and stood gazing dream-ily at the floor. Evening was closing in, and the room had grown darker.

'I know,' he said, in a strange, almost sleepy voice, 'there is truth in what you say, too. It is hard not to laugh at the common names—I only say we should not. I have thought of a remedy; but such thoughts are rather terrible.'

'What thoughts?' asked Auberon.

The Provost of Notting Hill seemed to have fallen into a kind of trance; in his eyes was an elvish light.

'I know of a magic wand, but it is a wand that only one or two may rightly use, and only seldom. It is a fairy wand of great fear, stronger than those who use it—often frightful, often wicked to use. But whatever is touched with it is never again wholly common. Whatever is touched with it takes a magic from outside the world. If I touch, with this fairy wand, the railways and the roads of Not-ting Hill, men will love them, and be afraid of them for ever.'

'What the devil are you talking about?' asked the King.

'It has made mean landscapes magnificent, and hovels outlast ca-thedrals,' went on the madman. 'Why should it not make lamp-posts fairer than Greek lamps, and an omnibus ride like a painted ship? The touch of it is the finger of a strange perfection.'

'What is your wand?' cried the King, impatiently.

'There it is,' said Wayne; and pointed to the floor, where his sword lay flat and shining.

'The sword!' cried the King; and sprang up straight on the dais.

'Yes, yes,' cried Wayne, hoarsely. 'The things touched by that are not vulgar. The things touched by that——'

King Auberon made a gesture of horror.

'You will shed blood for that!' he cried. 'For a cursed point of view——'

'Oh, you king, you kings,' cried out Adam, in a burst of scorn. 'How humane you are, how tender, how considerate. You will make war for a frontier, or the imports of a foreign harbour; you will shed blood for the precise duty on lace, or the salute to an admiral. But for the things that make life itself worthy or miserable—how humane you are. I say here, and I know well what I speak of, there were never any necessary wars but the religious wars. There were never any just wars but the religious wars. There were never any humane wars but the religious wars. For these men were fighting for something that claimed, at least, to be the happiness of a man, the virtue of a man. A Crusader thought, at least, that Islam hurt the soul of every man, king or tinker, that it could really capture. I think Buck and Barker and these rich vultures hurt the soul of every man, hurt every inch of the ground, hurt every brick of the houses, that they can really capture. Do you think I have no right to fight for Notting Hill, you whose English Government has so often fought for tomfooleries? If, as your rich friends say, there are no gods, and the skies are dark above us, what should a man fight for, but the place where he had the Eden of childhood and the short heaven of first love? If no temples and no scriptures are sacred, what is sacred if a man's own youth is not sacred?'

The King walked a little restlessly up and down the dais.

'It is hard,' he said, biting his lips, 'to assent to a view so desperate—so responsible . . .'

As he spoke, the door of the audience chamber fell ajar, and through the aperture came, like the sudden chatter of a bird, the high, nasal, but well-bred voice of Barker.

'I said to him quite plainly—the public interests——'

Auberon turned on Wayne with violence.

'What the devil is all this? What am I saying? What are you saying?

Have you hypnotized me? Curse your uncanny blue eyes! Let me go. Give me back my sense of humour. Give it me back. Give it me back, I say!'

'I solemnly assure you,' said Wayne, uneasily, with a gesture, as if feeling all over himself, 'that I haven't got it.'

The King fell back in his chair, and went into a roar of Rabelaisian laughter.

'I don't think you have,' he cried.

BOOK III

I

THE MENTAL CONDITION OF ADAM WAYNE

A little while after the King's accession a small book of poems appeared, called *Hymns on the Hill*. They were not good poems, nor was the book successful, but it attracted a certain amount of attention from one particular school of critics. The King himself, who was a member of the school, reviewed it in his capacity of literary critic to *Straight from the Stables*, a sporting journal. They were known as the Hammock School, because it had been calculated malignantly by an enemy that no less than thirteen of their delicate criticisms had begun with the words, 'I read this book in a hammock: half asleep in the sleepy sunlight, I . . .'; after that there were important differences. Under these conditions they liked everything, but especially everything silly. 'Next to authentic goodness in a book,' they said—'next to authentic goodness in a book (and that, alas! we never find) we desire a rich badness.' Thus it happened that their praise (as indicating the presence of a rich badness) was not universally sought after, and authors became a little disquieted when they found the eye of the Hammock School fixed upon them with peculiar favour.

The peculiarity of *Hymns on the Hill* was the celebration of the poetry of London as distinct from the poetry of the country. This sentiment or affectation was, of course, not uncommon in the twentieth century, nor was it, although sometimes exaggerated, and sometimes artificial, by any means without a great truth at its root, for there is one respect in which a town must be more poetical than the country, since it is closer to the spirit of man; for London, if it be not one of the masterpieces of man, is at least one of his sins. A street is really more poetical than a meadow, because a street has a secret. A street is going somewhere, and a meadow nowhere. But, in the case of the book called *Hymns on the Hill*, there was another peculiarity, which the King pointed out with great acumen in his review. He was naturally interested in the matter, for he had himself published a volume of lyrics about London under his pseudonym of Daisy Daydream'.

This difference, as the King pointed out, consisted in the fact that, while mere artificers like 'Daisy Daydream' (on whose elaborate style the King, over his signature of 'Thunderbolt', was perhaps somewhat too severe) thought to praise London by comparing it to the country—using nature, that is, as a background from which all poetical images had to be drawn—the more robust author of *Hymns on the Hill* praised the country, or nature, by comparing it to the town, and used the town itself as a background. 'Take', said the critic, 'the typically feminine lines, "To the Inventor of The Hansom Cab":

> 'Poet, whose cunning carved this amorous shell,
>   Where twain may dwell.'

'Surely,' wrote the King, 'no one but a woman could have written those lines. A woman has always a weakness for nature; with her, art is only beautiful as an echo or shadow of it. She is praising the hansom cab by theme and theory, but her soul is still a child by the sea, picking up shells. She can never be utterly of the town, as a man can; indeed, do we not speak (with sacred propriety) of "a man about town"? Who ever spoke of a woman about town? However much, physically, "about town" a woman may be, she still models herself on nature; she tries to carry nature with her; she bids grasses to grow on her head, and furry beasts to bite her about the throat. In the heart of a dim city, she models her hat on a flaring cottage garden of flowers. We, with our nobler civic sentiment, model ours on a chimney-pot; the ensign of civilization. And rather than be without birds, she will commit massacre, that she may turn her head into a tree, with dead birds to sing on it.'

This kind of thing went on for several pages, and then the critic remembered his subject, and returned to it.

> 'Poet, whose cunning carved this amorous shell,
>   Where twain may dwell.'

'The peculiarity of these fine though feminine lines', continued 'Thunderbolt', 'is, as we have said, that they praise the hansom cab by comparing it to the shell, to a natural thing. Now, hear the author of *Hymns on the Hill*, and how he deals with the same subject.

In his fine nocturne, entitled "The Last Omnibus", he relieves the rich and poignant melancholy of the theme by a sudden sense of rushing at the end:

> 'The wind round the old street corner
> Swung sudden and quick as a cab.'

'Here the distinction is obvious. "Daisy Daydream" thinks it a great compliment to a hansom cab to be compared to one of the spiral chambers of the sea. And the author of *Hymns on the Hill* thinks it a great compliment to the immortal whirlwind to be compared to a hackney coach. He surely is the real admirer of London. We have no space to speak of all his perfect applications of the idea; of the poem in which, for instance, a lady's eyes are compared, not to stars, but to two perfect street-lamps guiding the wanderer. We have no space to speak of the fine lyric, recalling the Elizabethan spirit, in which the poet, instead of saying that the rose and the lily contend in her complexion, says, with a purer modernism, that the red omnibus of Hammersmith and the white omnibus of Fulham fight there for the mastery. How perfect the image of two contending omnibuses!'

Here, somewhat abruptly, the review concluded, probably because the King had to send off his copy at that moment, as he was in some want of money. But the King was a very good critic, whatever he may have been as King, and he had, to a considerable extent, hit the right nail on the head. *Hymns on the Hill* was not at all like the poems originally published in praise of the poetry of London. And the reason was that it was really written by a man who had seen nothing else but London, and who regarded it, therefore, as the universe. It was written by a raw, red-headed lad of seventeen, named Adam Wayne, who had been born in Notting Hill. An accident in his seventh year prevented his being taken away to the seaside, and thus his whole life had been passed in his own Pump Street, and in its neighbourhood. And the consequence was, that he saw the street-lamps as things quite as eternal as the stars; the two fires were mingled. He saw the houses as things enduring, like the mountains, and so he wrote about them as one would write about mountains. Nature puts on a disguise when she speaks to every man; to this man she put on the disguise of Notting Hill. Nature would mean to a poet born in the Cumberlands hills, a stormy skyline and sudden rocks. Nature would mean to a poet born in the Essex flats, a waste of splendid waters and splendid sunsets. So nature meant to this man Wayne a line of violet roofs and lemon lamps, the chiaroscuro of the town. He did not think it clever or funny to praise the shadows and colours of the town; he had seen no other shadows or colours, and so he praised them—because they were shadows and colours. He saw all this because he was poet, though in practice a bad poet. It is too often forgotten that just as a bad man is nevertheless a man, so a bad poet is nevertheless a poet.

Mr. Wayne's little volume of verse was a complete failure; and he submitted to the decision of fate with a quite rational humility, went back to his work, which was that of a draper's assistant, and wrote no more. He still retained his feeling about the town of Notting Hill, because he could not possibly have any other feeling, because it was the back and base of his brain. But he does not seem to have made any particular attempt to express it or insist upon it.

He was a genuine natural mystic, one of those who live on the border of fairyland. But he was perhaps the first to realize how often the boundary of fairyland runs through a crowded city. Twenty feet from him (for he was very short-sighted) the red and white and yellow suns of the gas-lights thronged and melted into each other like an orchard of fiery trees, the beginning of the woods of elf-land.

But, oddly enough, it was because he was a small poet that he came to his strange and isolated triumph. It was because he was a failure in literature that he became a portent in English history. He was one of those to whom nature has given the desire without the power of artistic expression. He had been a dumb poet from his cradle. He might have been so to his grave, and carried unuttered into the darkness a treasure of new and sensational song. But he was born under the lucky star of a single coincidence. He happened to be at the head of his dingy municipality at the time of the King's jest, at the time when all municipalities were suddenly commanded to break out into banners and flowers. Out of the long procession of the silent poets who have been passing since the beginning of the world, this one man found himself in the midst of an heraldic vision, in which he could act and speak and live lyrically. While the author and the victims alike treated the whole matter as a silly public charade, this one man, by taking it seriously, sprang suddenly into a throne of artistic omnipotence. Armour, music, standards, watch-fires, the noise of drums, all the theatrical properties were thrown before him. This one poor rhymster, having burnt his own rhymes, began to live that life of open air and acted poetry of which all the poets of the earth have dreamed in vain; the life for which the Iliad is only a cheap substitute.

Upwards from his abstracted childhood, Adam Wayne had grown strongly and silently in a certain quality or capacity which is in modern cities almost entirely artificial, but which can be natural, and was primarily almost brutally natural in him, the quality or capacity of patriotism. It exists, like other virtues and vices, in a certain undiluted reality. It is not confused with all kinds of other things. A child speaking of his country or his village may make every mistake in Mandeville[59] or tell every lie in Munchausen,[60] but in his statement there will be no psychological lies any more than there can be in a good song. Adam Wayne, as a boy, had for his dull streets in Notting Hill the ultimate and ancient sentiment that went out to Athens or Jerusalem. He knew the secret of the passion, those secrets which make real old national songs sound so strange to our civilization. He knew that real patriotism tends to sing about sorrows and forlorn hopes much more than about victory. He knew that in proper names themselves is half the poetry of all national poems. Above all, he knew the supreme psychological fact about patriotism, as certain in connexion with it as that fine shame comes to all lovers,

[59] Sir John Mandeville was the author, possibly under a pseudonym, of a far-fetched book of travels in Latin, French and English, published in that order.

[60] Baron Munchausen (1720-97), a German officer who was born and died in Hanover, was known for the fantastic stories attributed to him and collected in compilations such as Rudolph Erich Ruspe's *Baron Munchausen's Narrative of his Marvellous Travels* (1785).

the fact that the patriot never under any circumstances boasts of the largeness of his country, but always, and of necessity, boasts of the smallness of it.

All this he knew, not because he was a philosopher or a genius, but because he was a child. Any one who cares to walk up a side slum like Pump Street, can see a little Adam claiming to be king of a paving-stone. And he will always be proudest if the stone is almost too narrow for him to keep his feet inside it.

It was while he was in such a dream of defensive battle, marking out some strip of street or fortress of steps as the limit of his haughty claim, that the King had met him, and, with a few words flung in mockery, ratified for ever the strange boundaries of his soul. Thenceforward the fanciful idea of the defence of Notting Hill in war became to him a thing as solid as eating or drinking or lighting a pipe. He disposed his meals for it, altered his plans for it, lay awake in the night and went over it again. Two or three shops were to him an arsenal; an area was to him a moat; corners of balconies and turns of stone steps were points for the location of a culverin or an archer. It is almost impossible to convey to any ordinary imagination the degree to which he had transmitted the leaden London landscape to a romantic gold. The process began almost in babyhood, and became habitual like a literal madness. It was felt most keenly at night, when London is really herself, when her lights shine in the dark like the eyes of innumerable cats, and the outline of the dark houses has the bold simplicity of blue hills. But for him the night revealed instead of concealing, and he read all the blank hours of morning and afternoon, by a contradictory phrase, in the light of that darkness. To this man, at any rate, the inconceivable had happened. The artificial city had become to him nature, and he felt the kerbstones and gas-lamps as things as ancient as the sky.

One instance may suffice. Walking along Pump Street with a friend, he said, as he gazed dreamily at the iron fence of a little front garden. 'How those railings stir one's blood.'

His friend, who was also a great intellectual admirer, looked at them painfully, but without any particular emotion. He was so troubled about it that he went back quite a large number of times on quiet evenings and stared at the railings, waiting for something to happen to his blood, but without success. At last he took refuge in asking Wayne himself. He discovered that the ecstasy lay in the one point he had never noticed about the railings even after his six visits, the fact that they were like the great majority of others in London, shaped at the top after the manner of a spear. As a child, Wayne had half unconsciously compared them with the spears in pictures of Lancelot and St. George, and had grown up under the shadow of the graphic association. Now, whenever he looked at them, they were simply the serried weapons that made a hedge of steel round the sacred homes of Notting Hill. He could not have cleansed his mind of that meaning even if he tried. It was not a fanciful comparison, or anything like it. It would not have been true to say that the familiar railings reminded him of spears; it would have been far truer to say that the familiar spears occasionaly remined him of railings.

A couple of days after his interview with the King, Adam Wayne was pacing like a caged lion in front of five shops that occupied the upper end of the disputed street. They were a grocer's, a chemist's, a barber's, an old curiosity shop, and a toyshop that sold also newspapers. It was these five shops which his childish fastidiousness had first selected as the essentials of the Notting Hill campaign, the citadel of the city. If Notting Hill was the heart of the universe, and Pump Street was the heart of Notting Hill, this was the heart of Pump Street. The fact that they were all small and side by side realized that feeling for a formidable comfort and compactness which, as we have said, was the heart of his patriotism and of all patriotism. The grocer (who had a wine and spirit licence) was included because he could provision the garrison; the old curiosity shop because it contained enough swords, pistols, partisans, cross-bows, and blunderbusses to arm a whole irregular regiment; the toy-and-paper shop because Wayne thought a free Press an essential centre for the soul of Pump Street; the chemist's to cope with outbreaks of disease among the besieged; and the barber's because it was in the middle of all the rest, and the barber's son was an intimate friend and spiritual affinity.

It was a cloudless October evening settling down through the purple into pure silver around the roofs and chimneys of the steep little street, which looked black and sharp and dramatic. In the deep shadows the gas-lit shop-fronts gleamed like five fires in a row, and before them, darkly outlined like a ghost against some purgatorial furnaces, passed to and fro the tall bird-like figure and eagle nose of Adam Wayne.

He swung his stick restlessly, and seemed fitfully talking to himself.

'There are, after all, enigmas,' he said, 'even to the man who has faith. There are doubts that remain even after the true philosophy is completed in every rung and rivet. And here is one of them. Is the normal human need, the normal human condition, higher or lower than those special states of the soul which call out a doubtful and dangerous glory? those special powers of knowledge or sacrifice which are made possible only by the existence of evil? Which should come first to our affections, the enduring sanities of peace or the half-maniacal virtues of battle? Which should come first, the man great in the daily round or the man great in emergency? Which should come first, to return to the enigma before me, the grocer or the chemist? Which is more certainly the stay of the city, the swift chivalrous chemist or the benignant all-providing grocer? In such ultimate spiritual doubts it is only possible to choose a side by the higher instincts and abide the issue. In any case, I have made my choice. May I be pardoned if I choose wrongly, but I choose the grocer.'

'Good morning, sir,' said the grocer, who was a middle-aged man, partially bald, with harsh red whiskers and beard, and forehead lined with all the cares of the small tradesman. 'What can I do for you, sir?'

Wayne removed his hat on entering the shop, with a ceremonious gesture, which, slight as it was, made the tradesman eye him with the beginnings of wonder.

'I come, sir,' he said soberly, 'to appeal to your patriotism.'

'Why, sir,' said the grocer, 'that sounds like the times when I was a boy and we used to have elections.'

'You will have them again,' said Wayne, firmly, 'and far greater things. Listen, Mr. Mead. I know the temptations which a grocer has to a too cosmopolitan philosophy. I can imagine what it must be to sit all day as you do surrounded with wares from all the ends of the earth, from strange seas that we have never sailed and strange forests that we could not even picture. No Eastern king ever had such argosies or such cargoes coming from the sunrise and the sunset, and Solomon in all his glory was not enriched like one of you. India is at your elbow,' he cried, lifting his voice and pointing his stick at a drawer of rice, the grocer making a movement of some alarm, 'China is before you, Demerara is behind you, America is above your head, and at this very moment, like some old Spanish admiral, you hold Tunis in your hands.'

Mr. Mead dropped the box of dates which he was just lifting, and then picked it up again vaguely.

Wayne went on with a heightened colour, but in a lowered voice:

'I know, I say, the temptations of so international, so universal a vision of wealth. I know that it must be your danger not to fall like many tradesmen into too dusty and mechanical a narrowness, but rather to be too broad, to be too general, too liberal. If a narrow nationalism be the danger of the pastrycook, who makes his own wares under his own heavens, no less is cosmopolitanism the danger of the grocer. But I come to you in the name of that patriotism which no wanderings or enlightenments should ever wholly extinguish, and I ask you to remember Notting Hill. For, after all, in this cosmopolitan magnificence, she has played no small part. Your dates may come from the tall palms of Barbary, your sugar from the strange islands of the tropics, your tea from the secret villages of the Empire of the Dragon. That this room might be furnished, forests may have been spoiled under the Southern Cross, and leviathans speared under the Polar Star. But you yourself—surely no inconsiderable treasure—you yourself, the brain that wields these vast interests—you yourself, at least, have grown to strength and wisdom between these grey houses and under this rainy sky. This city which made you, and thus made your fortunes, is threatened with war. Come forth and tell to the ends of the earth this lesson. Oil is from the North and fruits from the South; rices are from India and spices from Ceylon; sheep are from New Zealand and men from Notting Hill.'

The grocer sat for some little while, with dim eyes and his mouth open, looking rather like a fish. Then he scratched the back of his head, and said nothing. Then he said:

'Anything out of the shop, sir?'

Wayne looked round in a dazed way. Seeing a pile of tins of pineapple chunks, he waved his stick generally towards them.

'Yes,' he said, 'I'll take those.'

'All those, sir?' said the grocer, with greatly increased interest.

'Yes, yes; all those,' replied Wayne, still a little bewildered, like a man splashed with cold water.

'Very good, sir; thank you, sir,' said the grocer with animation. 'You may count upon my patriotism, sir.'

'I count upon it already,' said Wayne, and passed out into the gathering night.

The grocer put the box of dates back in its place.

'What a nice fellow he is,' he said. 'It's odd how often they are nice. Much nicer than those as are all right.'

Meanwhile Adam Wayne stood outside the glowing chemist's shop, unmistakably wavering.

'What a weakness it is,' he muttered. 'I have never got rid of it from childhood. The fear of this magic shop. The grocer is rich, he is romantic, he is poetical in the truest sense, but he is not—no, he is not supernatural. But the chemist! All the other shops stand in Notting Hill, but this stands in Elf-land. Look at those great burning bowls of colour. It must be from them that God paints the sunsets. It is superhuman, and the superhuman is all the more uncanny when it is beneficent. That is the root of the fear of God. I am afraid. But I must be a man and enter.'

He was a man, and entered. A short, dark young man was behind the counter with spectacles, and greeted him with a bright but entirely business-like smile.

'A fine evening, sir,' he said.

'Fine, indeed, strange Father,' said Adam, stretching his hands somewhat forward. 'It is on such clear and mellow nights that your shop is most itself. Then they appear most perfect, those moons of green and gold and crimson, which from afar, oft guide the pilgrim of pain and sickness to this house of merciful witchcraft.'

'Can I get you anything?' asked the chemist.

'Let me see,' said Wayne, in a friendly but vague manner. 'Let me have some sal volatile.'[61]

'Eightpence, tenpence, or one and sixpence[62] a bottle?' said the young man genially.

'One and six—one and six,' replied Wayne, with a wild submissiveness. 'I come to ask you, Mr. Bowles, a terrible question.'

He paused and collected himself.

'It is necessary,' he muttered—'it is necessary to be tactful, and to suit the appeal to each profession in turn.

'I come,' he resumed aloud, 'to ask you a question which goes to the roots of your miraculous toils. Mr. Bowles, shall all this witchery cease?' And he waved his stick around the shop.

Meeting with no answer, he continued with animation:

'In Notting Hill we have felt to its core the elfish mystery of your profession. And now Notting Hill itself is threatened.'

'Anything more, sir?' asked the chemist.

'Oh,' said Wayne, somewhat disturbed—'oh, what is it chemists sell? Quinine, I think. Thank you. Shall it be destroyed? I have met these men of Bayswater and North Kensington—Mr. Bowles, they are materialists. They see no witchery in your work, even when it is brought within their own borders. They think the chemist is commonplace. They think him human.'

The chemist appeared to pause, only a moment, to take in the insult, and immediately said:

'And the next article, please?'

'Alum,' said the Provost, wildly. 'I resume. It is in this sacred town alone that your priesthood is reverenced. Therefore, when you fight for us you fight not only for yourself, but for everything you typify. You fight not only for Notting Hill, but for Fairyland, for as surely as Buck and Barker and such men hold sway, the sense of Fairyland in some strange manner diminishes.'

[61] Sal volatile is a solution of carbonate of ammonia sold as a refeshing drink or, in stronger solutions, as a reviver for those who have fainted; smelling salts.

[62] One and sixpence was one shilling and sixpence, the equivalent of thirty cents in a silver dollar, or of seven and a half pence in decimalized currency.

'Anything more, sir?' asked Mr. Bowles, with unbroken cheerfulness.

'Oh, yes, jujubes[63] — Gregory powder[64] — magnesia. The danger is imminent. In all this matter I have felt that I fought not merely for my own city (though to that I owe all my blood), but for all places in which these great ideas could prevail. I am fighting not merely for Notting Hill, but for Bayswater itself; for North Kensington itself. For if the gold-hunters prevail, these also will lose all their ancient sentiments and all the mystery of their national soul. I know I can count upon you.'

'Oh, yes, sir,' said the chemist, with great animation, 'we are always glad to oblige a good customer.'

Adam Wayne went out of the shop with a deep sense of fulfilment of soul.

'It is so fortunate,' he said, 'to have tact, to be able to play upon the peculiar talents and specialities, the cosmopolitanism of the grocer and the world-old necromancy of the chemist. Where should I be without tact?'

[63] Jujubes are jellylike candies made of sugar and gum.

[64] Gregory powder was made from rhubarb, magnesia and ginger as an antacid and laxative.

THE REMARKABLE MR. TURNBULL

After two more interviews with shopmen, however, the patriot's confidence in his own psychological diplomacy began vaguely to wane. Despite the care with which he considered the peculiar rationale and the peculiar glory of each separate shop, there seemed to be something unresponsive about the shopmen. Whether it was a dark resentment against the uninitiate for peeping into their masonic magnificence, he could not quite conjecture.

His conversation with the man who kept the shop of curiosities had begun encouragingly. The man who kept the shop of curiosities had indeed enchanted him with a phrase. He was standing drearily at the door of his shop, a wrinkled man with a grey pointed beard, evidently a gentleman who had come down in the world.

'And how does your commerce go, you strange guardian of the past?' said Wayne, affably.

'Well, sir, not very well,' replied the man, with that patient voice of his class which is one of the most heart-breaking things in the world. 'Things are terribly quiet.'

Wayne's eyes shone suddenly.

'A great saying,' he said, 'worthy of a man whose merchandise is human history. Terribly quiet; that is in two words the spirit of this age, as I have felt it from my cradle. I sometimes wondered how many other people felt the oppression of this union between quietude and terror. I see blank well-ordered streets and men in black moving about inoffensively, sullenly. It goes on day after day, day after day, and nothing happens; but to me it is like a dream from which I might wake screaming. To me the straightness of our life is the straightness of a thin cord stretched tight. Its stillness is terrible. It might snap with a noise like thunder. And you who sit, amid the *débris* of the great wars, you who sit, as it were, upon a battle-field, you know that war was less terrible than this evil peace; you know that the idle lads who carried those swords under Francis or

Elizabeth, the rude Squire or Baron who swung that mace about in Picardy or Northumberland battles, may have been terribly noisy, but were not like us, terribly quiet.'

Whether it was a faint embarrassment of conscience as to the original source and date of the weapons referred to, or merely an engrained depression, the guardian of the past looked, if anything, a little more worried.

'But I do not think,' continued Wayne, 'that this horrible silence of modernity will last, though I think for the present it will increase. What a farce is this modern liberality. Freedom of speech means practically in our modern civilization that we must only talk about unimportant things. We must not talk about religion, for that is illiberal; we must not talk about bread and cheese, for that is talking shop; we must not talk about death, for that is depressing; we must not talk about birth, for that is indelicate. It cannot last. Something must break this strange indifference, this strange dreamy egoism, this strange loneliness of millions in a crowd. Something must break it. Why should it not be you and I? Can you do nothing else but guard relics?'

The shopman wore a gradually clearing expression, which would have led those unsympathetic with the cause of the Red Lion to think that the last sentence was the only one to which he had attached any meaning.

'I am rather old to go into a new business,' he said, 'and I don't quite know what to be either.'

'Why not,' said Wayne, gently, having reached the crisis of his delicate persuasion—'why not be a Colonel?'

It was at this point, in all probability, that the interview began to yield more disappointing results. The man appeared inclined at first to regard the suggestion of becoming a Colonel as outside the sphere of immediate and relevant discussion. A long exposition of the inevitable war of independence, coupled with the purchase of a doubtful sixteenth-century sword for an exaggerated price, seemed to resettle matters. Wayne left the shop, however, somewhat infected with the melancholy of its owner.

That melancholy was completed at the barber's.

'Shaving, sir?' inquired that artist from inside his shop.

'War!' replied Wayne, standing on the threshold.

'I beg your pardon,' said the other, sharply.

'War!' said Wayne, warmly. 'But not for anything inconsistent with the beautiful and the civilized arts. War for beauty. War for society. War for peace. A great chance is offered you of repelling that slander which, in defiance of the lives of so many artists, attributes poltroonery to those who beautify and polish the surface of our lives. Why should not hairdressers be heroes? Why should not—'

'Now, you get out,' said the barber, irascibly. 'We don't want any of your sort here. You get out.'

And he came forward with the desperate annoyance of a mild person when enraged.

Adam Wayne laid his hand for a moment on the sword, then dropped it.

'Notting Hill,' he said, 'will need her bolder sons'; and he turned gloomily to the toyshop.

It was one of those queer little shops so constantly seen in the side-streets of London, which must be called toyshops only because toys upon the whole predominate; for the remainder of goods seem to consist of almost everything else in the world—tobacco, exercise-books, sweetstuff, novelettes, halfpenny paper clips, halfpenny pencil sharpeners, bootlaces, and cheap fireworks. It also sold newspapers, and a row of dirty-looking posters hung along the front of it.

'I am afraid,' said Wayne, as he entered, 'that I am not getting on with these tradesmen as I should. Is it that I have neglected to rise to the full meaning of their work? Is there some secret buried in each of these shops which no mere poet can discover?'

He stepped to the counter with a depression which he rapidly conquered as he addressed the man on the other side of it—a man of short stature, and hair prematurely white, and the look of a large baby.

'Sir,' said Wayne, 'I am going from house to house in this street of ours, seeking to stir up some sense of the danger which now threatens our city. Nowhere have I felt my duty so difficult as here. For the toyshop keeper has to do with all that remains to us of Eden before the first wars began. You sit here meditating continually upon the wants of that wonderful time when every staircase leads to the stars, and every garden-path to the other end of nowhere. Is it thoughtlessly, do you think, that I strike the dark old drum of peril in the paradise of children? But consider a moment; do not condemn me hastily. Even that paradise itself contains the rumour or beginning of that danger, just as the Eden that was made for perfection contained the terrible tree. For judge childhood, even by your own arsenal of its pleasures. You keep bricks; you make yourself thus, doubtless, the witness of the constructive instinct older than the destructive. You keep dolls; you make yourself the priest of that divine idolatry. You keep Noah's Arks; you perpetuate the memory of the salvation of all life as a precious, an irreplaceable thing. But do you keep only, sir, the symbols of this prehistoric sanity, this childish rationality of the earth? Do you not keep more terrible things? What are those boxes, seemingly of lead soldiers, that I see in that glass case? Are they not witnesses to that terror and beauty, that desire for a lovely death, which could not be excluded even from the immortality of Eden? Do not despise the lead soldiers, Mr. Turnbull.'

'I don't,' said Mr. Turnbull, of the toyshop, shortly, but with great emphasis.

'I am glad to hear it,' replied Wayne. 'I confess that I feared for my military schemes the awful innocence of your profession. How, I thought to myself, will this man, used only to the wooden swords that give pleasure, think of the steel swords that give pain? But I am at least partly reassured. Your tone suggests to me that I have at least the entry of a gate of your fairyland—the gate through which the soldiers enter, for it cannot be denied—I ought, sir, no longer to deny, that it is of soldiers that I come to speak. Let your gentle employment make you merciful towards the troubles of the world. Let your own silvery experience tone down our sanguine sorrows. For there is war in Notting Hill.'

The little toyshop keeper sprang up suddenly, slapping his fat hands like two fans on the counter.

'War?' he cried. 'Not really, sir? Is it true? Oh, what a joke! Oh, what a sight for sore eyes!'

Wayne was almost taken aback by this outburst.

'I am delighted,' he stammered. 'I had no notion——'

He sprang out of the way just in time to avoid Mr. Turnbull, who took a flying leap over the counter and dashed to the front of the shop.

'You look here, sir,' he said; 'you just look here.'

He came back with two of the torn posters in his hand which were flapping outside his shop.

'Look at those, sir,' he said, and flung them down on the counter. Wayne bent over them, and read on one:

> 'LAST FIGHTING.
> REDUCTION OF THE CENTRAL DERVISH CITY.
> REMARKABLE, ETC.'

On the other he read:

> 'LAST SMALL REPUBLIC ANNEXED.
> NICARAGUAN CAPITAL SURRENDERS AFTER A
> MONTH'S FIGHTING.
> GREAT SLAUGHTER.'

Wayne bent over them again, evidently puzzled; then he looked at the dates. They were both dated in August fifteen years before.

'Why do you keep these old things?' he said, startled entirely out of his absurd tact of mysticism. 'Why do you hang them outside your shop?'

'Because,' said the other, simply, 'they are the records of the last war. You mentioned war just now. It happens to be my hobby.'

Wayne lifted his large blue eyes with an infantile wonder.

'Come with me,' said Turnbull, shortly, and led him into a parlour at the back of the shop.

In the centre of the parlour stood a large deal table. On it were set rows and rows of the tin and lead soldiers which were part of the shopkeeper's stock. The visitor would have thought nothing of it if it had not been for a certain odd grouping of them, which did not seem either entirely commercial or entirely haphazard.

'You are acquainted, no doubt,' said Turnbull, turning his big eyes upon Wayne — 'you are acquainted, no doubt, with the arrangement of the American and Nicaraguan troops in the last battle.' And he waved his hand towards the table.

'I am afraid not,' said Wayne. 'I—'

'Ah, you were at that time occupied too much, perhaps, with the Dervish affair. You will find it in this corner.' And he pointed to a part of the floor where there was another arrangement of children's soldiers grouped here and there.

'You seem,' said Wayne, 'to be interested in military matters.'

'I am interested in nothing else,' answered the toyshop keeper, simply.

Wayne appeared convulsed with a singular suppressed excitement.

'In that case,' he said, 'I may approach you with an unusual degree of confidence. Touching the matter of the defence of Notting Hill, I—'

'Defence of Notting Hill? Yes, sir. This way, sir,' said Turnbull, with great pertubation. 'Just step into this side room'; and he led Wayne into another apartment, in which the table was entirely covered with an arrangement of children's bricks. A second glance at it told Wayne that the bricks were arranged in the form of a precise and perfect plan of Notting Hill. 'Sir,' said Turnbull, impressively, 'you have, by a kind of accident, hit upon the whole secret of my life. As a boy, I grew up among the last wars of the world, when Nicaragua was taken and the dervishes wiped out. And I adopted it as a hobby, sir, as you might adopt astronomy or bird-stuffing. I had no ill-will to any one, but I was interested in war as a science, as a game. And suddenly I was bowled out. The big Powers of the world, having swallowed up all the small ones, came to that confounded agreement, and there was no more war. There was nothing more for me to do but to do what I do now—to read the old campaigns in dirty old newspapers, and to work them out with tin soldiers. One other thing had occurred to me. I thought it an amusing fancy to make a plan of how this district of ours ought to be defended if it were ever attacked. It seems to interest you, too.'

'If it were ever attacked,' repeated Wayne, awed into almost mechanical enunciation. 'Mr. Turnbull, it is attacked. Thank heaven, I am bringing to at least one human being the news that is at bottom the only good news to any son of Adam. Your life has not been useless. Your work has not been play. Now, when the hair is already grey on your head, Turnbull, you shall have your youth. God has not destroyed it, He has only deferred it. Let us sit down here, and you shall explain to me this military map of Notting Hill. For you and I have to defend Notting Hill together.'

Mr. Turnbull looked at the other for a moment, then hesitated, and then sat down beside the bricks and the stranger. He did not rise again for seven hours, when the dawn broke.

*   *   *

The headquarters of Provost Adam Wayne and his Commander-in Chief consisted of a small and somewhat unsuccessful milk-shop at the corner of Pump Street. The blank white morning had only just begun to break over the blank London buildings when Wayne and Turnbull were to be found seated in the cheerless and unswept shop. Wayne had something feminine in his character; he belonged to that class of persons who forget their meals when anything interesting is in hand. He had had nothing for sixteen hours but hurried glasses of milk, and, with a glass standing empty beside him, he was writing and sketching and dotting and crossing out with inconceivable rapidity with a pencil and a piece of paper. Turnbull was of that more masculine type in which a sense of responsibility increases the appetite and with his sketch-map beside him he was dealing strenuously with a pile of sand-wiches in a paper packet, and a tankard of ale from the tavern oppo-site, whose shutters had just been taken down. Neither of them spoke, and there was no sound in the living stillness except the scratching of Wayne's pencil and the squealing of an aimless-looking cat. At length Wayne broke the silence by saying:

"Seventeen pounds, eight shillings and ninepence.'

Turnbull nodded and put his head in the tankard.

'That,' said Wayne, 'is not counting the five pounds you took yes-terday. What did you do with it?'

'Ah, that is rather interesting!' replied Turnbull, with his mouth full. 'I used that five pounds in a kindly and philanthropic act.'

Wayne was gazing with mystification in his queer and innocent eyes.

'I used that five pounds,' continued the other, 'in giving no less than forty little London boys rides in hansom cabs.'

'Are you insane?' asked the Provost.

'It is only my light touch,' returned Turnbull. 'These hansom-cab rides will raise the tone—raise the tone, my dear fellow—of our London youths, widen their horizon, brace their nervous system, make them acquainted with the various public monuments of our great city. Education, Wayne, education. How many excellent thinkers have pointed out that political reform is useless until we produce a cultured populace. So that twenty years hence, when these boys are grown up—'

'Mad!' said Wayne, laying down his pencil; 'and five pounds gone!'

'You are in error,' explained Turnbull. 'You grave creatures can never be brought to understand how much quicker work really goes with the assistance of nonsense and good meals. Stripped of its decorative beauties, my statement was stricly accurate. Last night I gave forty half-crowns to forty little boys, and sent them all over London to take hansom cabs. I told them in every case to tell the cabman to bring them to this spot. In half an hour from now the declaration of war will be posted up. At the same time the cabs will have begun to come in, you will have ordered out the guard, the little boys will drive up in state, we shall commandeer the horses for cavalry, use the cabs for barricade, and give the men the choice between serving in our ranks and detention in our basements and cellars. The little boys we can use as scouts. The main thing is that we start the war with an advantage unknown in all the other armies—horses. And now,' he said, finishing his beer, 'I will go and drill the troops.'

And he walked out of the milk-shop, leaving the Provost staring.

A minute or two afterwards, the Provost laughed. He only laughed once or twice in his life,[65] and then he did it in a queer way as if it were an art he had not mastered. Even he saw something funny in the preposterous coup of the half-crowns and the little boys. He did not see the monstrous absurdity of the whole policy and the whole war. He enjoyed it seriously as a crusade, that is, he enjoyed it far more than any joke can be enjoyed. Turnbull enjoyed it partly as a joke, even more perhaps as a reversion from the things he hated—modernity and

---

[65] This is a reference to the wizard Merlin.

monotony and civilization. To break up the vast machinery of modern life and use the fragments as engines of war, to make the barricade of omnibuses and points of vantage of chimney-pots, was to him a game worth infinite risk and trouble. He had that rational and deliberate preference which will always to the end trouble the peace of the world, the rational and deliberate preference for a short life and a merry one.

III

THE EXPERIMENT OF MR. BUCK

An earnest and eloquent petition was sent up to the King signed with the names of Wilson, Barker, Buck, Swindon, and others. It urged that at the forthcoming conference to be held in his Majesty's presence touching the final disposition of the property in Pump Street, it might be held not inconsistent with political decorum and with the unutterable respect they entertained for his Majesty if they appeared in ordinary morning-dress, without the costume decreed for them as Provosts. So it happened that the company appeared at that council in frock-coats and that the King himself limited his love of ceremony to appearing (after his not unusual manner), in evening dress with one order—in this case not the Garter, but the button of the Club of Old Clipper's Best Pals, a decoration obtained (with difficulty) from a halfpenny boy's paper. Thus also it happened that the only spot of colour in the room was Adam Wayne, who entered in great dignity with the great red robes and the great sword.

'We have met,' said Auberon, 'to decide the most arduous of modern problems. May we be successsful.' And he sat down gravely.

Buck turned his chair a little and flung one leg over the other.

'Your Majesty,' he said, quite good-humouredly, 'there is only one thing I can't understand, and that is why this affair is not settled in five minutes. Here's a small property which is worth a thousand to us and is not worth a hundred to any one else. We offer the thousand. It's not business-like, I know, for we ought to get it for less, and it's not reasonable and it's not fair on us, but I'm damned if I can see why it's difficult.'

'The difficulty may be very simply stated,' said Wayne. 'You may offer a million and it will be very difficult for you to get Pump Street.'

'But, look here, Mr. Wayne,' cried Barker, striking in with a kind of cold excitement. 'Just look here. You've no right to take up a position like that. You've a right to stand out for a bigger price, but you aren't doing that. You're refusing what you and every sane man knows to be a splendid offer simply from malice or spite—it must be malice or spite. And that kind of thing is really criminal; it's against the public good. The King's Government would be justified in forcing you.'

With his lean fingers spread on the table he stared anxiously at Wayne's face, which did not move.

'In forcing you . . . it would,' he repeated.

'It shall,' said Buck, shortly, turning to the table with a jerk. 'We have done our best to be decent.'

Wayne lifted his large eyes slowly.

'Was it my Lord Buck,' he inquired, 'who said that the King of England "shall" do something?'

Buck flushed and said testily:

'I mean it must—it ought to, as I say we've done our best to be generous. I defy any one to deny it. As it is Mr. Wayne, I don't want to say a word that's uncivil. I hope it's not uncivil to say that you can be, and ought to be, in jail. It is criminal to stop public works for a whim. A man might as well burn ten thousand onions in his front garden or bring up his children to run naked in the street, as do what you say you have a right to do. People have been compelled to sell before now. The King could compel you, and I hope he will.'

'Until he does,' said Wayne, calmly, 'the power and Government of this great nation is on my side and not yours, and I defy you to defy it.'

'In what sense,' cried Barker, with his feverish eyes and hands, 'is the Government on your side?'

With one ringing movement Wayne unrolled a great parchment on the table. It was decorated down the sides with wild water-colour sketches of vestrymen in crowns and wreaths.

'The Charter of the Cities,' he began.

Buck exploded in a brutal oath and laughed.

'That tomfool's joke. Haven't we had enough—'

'And there you sit,' cried Wayne, springing erect and with a voice like a trumpet, 'with no argument but to insult the King before his face.'

Buck rose also with blazing eyes.

'I am hard to bully,' he began — and the slow tones of the King struck in with incomparable gravity:

'My Lord Buck, I must ask you to remember that your King is present. It is not often that he needs to protect himself among his subjects.'

Barker turned to him with frantic gestures.

'For God's sake don't back up the madman now,' he implored. 'Have your joke another time. Oh, for Heaven's sake — '

'My Lord Provost of South Kensington,' said King Auberon, steadily. 'I do not follow your remarks which are uttered with a rapidity unusual at Court. Nor do your well-meant efforts to convey the rest with your fingers materially assist me. I say that my Lord Provost of North Kensington, to whom I spoke, ought not in the presence of his Sovereign to speak disrespectfully of his Sovereign's ordinances. Do you disagree?'

Barker turned restlessly in his chair, and Buck cursed without speaking. The King went on in a comfortable voice:

'My Lord Provost of Notting Hill, proceed.'

Wayne turned his blue eyes on the King, and to every one's surprise there was a look in them not of triumph, but of a certain childish distress.

'I am sorry, your Majesty,' he said; 'I fear I was more than equally to blame with the Lord Provost of North Kensington. We were debating somewhat eagerly, and we both rose to our feet. I did so first, I am ashamed to say. The Provost of North Kensington is, therefore, comparatively innocent. I beseech your Majesty to address your rebuke chiefly, at least, to me. Mr. Buck is not innocent, for he did no doubt, in the heat of the moment, speak disrespectfully. But the rest of the discussion he seems to me to have conducted with great good temper.'

Buck looked genuinely pleased, for business men are all simple-minded, and have therefore that degree of communion with fanatics. The King, for some reason, looked, for the first time in his life, ashamed.

'This very kind speech of the Provost of Notting Hill,' began Buck, pleasantly, 'seems to me to show that we have at last got on to a friendly footing. Now come, Mr. Wayne. Five hundred pounds have been offered to you for a property you admit not to be worth a hundred. Well, I am a rich man and I won't be outdone in generosity. Let us say fifteen hundred pounds, and have done with it. And let us shake hands.' And he rose, glowing and laughing.

'Fifteen hundred pounds,' whispered Mr. Wilson of Bayswater; 'can we do fifteen hundred pounds?'

'I'll stand the racket,' said Buck heartily. 'Mr. Wayne is a gentleman and has spoken up for me. So I suppose the negotiations are at an end.'

Wayne bowed.

'They are indeed at an end. I am sorry I cannot sell you the property.'

'What?' cried Mr. Barker, starting to his feet.

'Mr. Buck has spoken correctly,' said the King.

'I have, I have,' cried Buck, springing up also; 'I said — '

'Mr. Buck has spoken correctly,' said the King; 'the negotiations are at an end.'

All the men at the table rose to their feet; Wayne alone rose without excitement.

'Have I, then,' he said, 'your Majesty's permission to depart? I have given my last answer.'

'You have it,' said Auberon, smiling, but not lifting his eyes from the table. And amid a dead silence the Provost of Notting Hill passed out of the room.

'Well?' said Wilson, turning round to Barker, 'Well?'

Barker shook his head desperately.

'The man ought to be in an asylum,' he said. 'But one thing is clear, we need not bother further about him. The man can be treated as mad.'

'Of course,' said Buck, turning to him with sombre decisiveness. 'You're perfectly right, Barker. He is a good enough fellow, but he can be treated as mad. Let's put it in simple form. Go and tell any twelve men in any town, go and tell any doctor in any town, that there is a man offered fifteen hundred pounds for a thing he could sell commonly for four hundred, and that when asked for a reason for not accepting it he pleads the inviolate sanctity of Notting Hill and calls it the Holy Mountain. What would they say? What more can we have on our side than the common sense of everybody? On what else do all laws rest? I'll tell you, Barker, what's better than any further discussion. Let's send in workmen on the spot to pull down Pump Street. And if old Wayne says a word, arrest him as a lunatic. That's all.'

Barker's eyes kindled.

'I always regarded you, Buck, if you don't mind my saying so, as a very strong man. I'll follow you.'

'So, of course, will I,' said Wilson.

Buck rose again impulsively.

'Your Majesty,' he said, glowing with popularity, 'I beseech your Majesty to consider favourably the proposal to which we have committed ourselves. Your Majesty's leniency, our own offers, have fallen in vain on that extraordinary man. He may be right. He may be God. He may be the devil. But we think it, for practical purposes, more probable that he is off his head. Unless that assumption were acted on, all human affairs would go to pieces. We act on it, and we propose to start operations in Notting Hill at once.'

The King leaned back in his chair.

'The Charter of the Cities . . .' he said with a rich intonation.

But Buck, being finally serious, was also cautious, and did not again make the mistake of disrespect.

'Your Majesty,' he said, bowing, 'I am not here to say a word against anything your Majesty has said or done. You are a far better educated man than I, and no doubt there were reasons, upon intellectual grounds, for those proceedings. But may I ask you and appeal to your common good-nature for a sincere answer? When you drew up the Charter of the Cities did you contemplate the rise of a man like Adam Wayne? Did you expect that the Charter — whether it was an experiment, or a scheme of decoration, or a joke — could ever really come to this — to stopping a vast scheme of ordinary business, to shutting up a road, to spoiling the chances of cabs, omnibuses, railway stations, to disorganizing half a city, to risking a kind of civil war? Whatever were your objects, were they that?'

Barker and Wilson looked at him admiringly; the King more admiringly still.

"Provost Buck," said Auberon, 'you speak in public uncommonly well. I give you your point with the magnanimity of an artist. My scheme did not include the appearance of Mr. Wayne. Alas! would that my poetic power had been great enough.'

'I thank your Majesty,' said Buck, courteously but quickly. 'Your Majesty's statements are always clear and studied: therefore I may draw a deduction. As the scheme, whatever it was, on which you set your heart did not include the appearance of Mr. Wayne, it will survive his removal. Why not let us clear away this particular Pump Street, which does interfere with our plans, and which does not, by your Majesty's own statement, interfere with yours.'

'Caught out!' said the King, enthusiastically and quite impersonally, as if he were watching a cricket match.

'This man Wayne,' continued Buck, 'would be shut up by any doctors in England. But we only ask to have it put before them. Meanwhile no one's interests, not even in all probability his own, can be really damaged by going on with the improvements in Notting Hill. Not our interests, of course, for it has been the hard and quiet work of ten years. Not the interests of Notting Hill, for nearly all its educated inhabitants desire the change. Not the interests of your Majesty, for you say, with characteristic sense, that you never contemplated the rise of the lunatic at all. Not, as I say, his own interests, for the man has a kind heart and many talents, and a couple of good doctors would probably put him righter than all the free cities and sacred mountains in creation. I therefore assume, if I may use so bold a word, that your Majesty will not offer any obstacle to our proceeding with the improvements.'

And Mr. Buck sat down amid subdued but excited applause among the allies.

'Mr. Buck,' said the King, 'I beg your pardon, for a number of beautiful and sacred thoughts, in which you were generally classified as a fool. But there is another thing to be considered. Suppose you send in your workmen, and Mr. Wayne does a thing regrettable indeed, but of which, I am sorry to say, I think him quite capable —knocks their teeth out.'

'I have thought of that, your Majesty,' said Mr. Buck, easily, 'and

I think it can simply be guarded against. Let us send in a strong
guard of say a hundred men — a hundred of the North Kensington
Halberdiers' (he smiled grimly), 'of whom your Majesty is so fond.
Or say — a hundred and fifty. The whole population of Pump Street,
I fancy, is only about a hundred.'

'Still they might stand together and lick you,' said the King,
dubiously.

'Then say two hundred,' said Buck, gaily.

'It might happen,' said the King, restlessly, 'that one Notting
Hiller fought better than two North Kensingtons.'

'It might,' said Buck, coolly; 'then say two hundred and fifty.'

The King bit his lip.

'And if they are beaten, too,' he said viciously.

'Your Majesty,' said Buck, and leaned back easily in his chair,
'suppose they are. If anything be clear, it is clear that all fighting
matters are mere matters of arithmetic. Here we have a hundred and
fifty say of Notting Hill soldiers. Or say two hundred. If one of
them can fight two of us — we can send in, not four hundred, but six
hundred, and smash him. That is all. It is out of all immediate probability that one of them could fight four of us. So what I say is this.
Run no risks. Finish it at once. Send in eight hundred men and
smash him — smash him almost without seeing him. And go on with
the improvements.'

And Mr. Buck pulled out a bandanna and blew his nose.

'Do you know, Mr. Buck,' said the King, staring gloomily at the
table, 'the admirable clearness of your reason prouduces in my mind
a sentiment which I trust I shall not offend you by describing as an
aspiration to punch your head. You irritate me sublimely. What can
it be in me? Is it the relic of a moral sense?'

'But your Majesty,' said Barker, eagerly and suavely, 'does not refuse our proposals?'

'My dear Barker, your proposals are as damnable as your manners.
I want to have nothing to do with them. Suppose I stopped them altogether. What would happen?'

Barker answered in a very low voice:

'Revolution.'

The King glanced quickly at the men around the table. They were all looking down silently: their brows were red.

He rose with a startling suddenness, and an unusual pallor.

'Gentlemen,' he said, 'you have overruled me. Therefore I can speak plainly. I think Adam Wayne, who is as mad as a hatter, worth more than a million of you. But you have the force, and, I admit, the common sense, and he is lost. Take your eight hundred halberdiers and smash him. It would be more sportsmanlike to take two hundred.'

'More sportsmanlike,' said Buck, grimly, 'but a great deal less humane. We are not artists, and streets purple with gore do not catch our eye in the right way.'

'It is pitiful,' said Auberon. 'With five or six times their number there will be no fight at all."

'I hope not,' said Buck, rising and adjusting his gloves. 'We desire no fight, your Majesty. We are peaceable business men.'

'Well,' said the King, wearily, 'the conference is at an end at last.'

And he went out of the room before any one else could stir.

*   *   *

Forty workmen, a hundred Bayswater halberdiers, two hundred from South, and three from North Kensington, assembled at the foot of Holland Walk and marched up it, under the general direction of Barker, who looked flushed and happy in full dress. At the end of the procession a small and sulky figure lingered like an urchin. It was the King.

'Barker,' he said at length, appealingly, 'you are an old friend of mine—you understand my hobbies as I understand yours. Why can't you let it alone? I hoped that such fun might come out of this Wayne business. Why can't you let it alone? It doesn't really so much matter to you—what's a road or so? For me it's the one joke that may save me from pessimism. Take fewer men and give me an hour's fun. Really and truly, James, if you collected coins or hummingbirds, and I could buy one with the price of your road, I would buy it. I collect incidents—those rare, those precious things. Let me have one. Pay a few pounds for it. Give these Notting Hillers a chance. Let them alone.'

'Auberon,' said Barker, kindly, forgetting all royal titles in a rare moment of sincerity, 'I do feel what you mean. I have had moments when these hobbies have hit me. I have had moments when I have sympathized with your humours. I have had moments, though you may not easily believe it, when I have sympathized with the madness of Adam Wayne. But the world, Auberon, the real world, is not run on these hobbies. It goes on great brutal wheels of facts — wheels on which you are the butterfly. And Wayne is the fly on the wheel.'

Auberon's eyes looked frankly at the other's.

'Thank you, James; what you say is true. It is only a parenthetical consolation to me to compare the intelligence of flies somewhat favourably with the intelligence of wheels. But it is the nature of flies to die soon, and the nature of wheels to go on for ever. Go on with the wheel. Good-bye, old man.'

And James Barker went on, laughing, with a high colour, slapping his bamboo on his leg.

The King watched the tail of the retreating regiment with a look of genuine depression, which made him seem more like a baby than ever. Then he swung round and struck his hands together.

'In a world without humour,' he said, 'the only thing to do is to eat. And how perfect an exception! How can these people strike dignified attitudes, and pretend that things matter, when the total ludicrousness of life is proved by the very method by which it is supported? A man strikes the lyre, and says, "Life is real, life is earnest", and then goes into a room and stuffs alien substances into a hole in his head. I think Nature was indeed a little broad in her humour in these matters. But we all fall back on the pantomime, as I have in this municipal affair. Nature has her farces, like the act of eating or the shape of the kangaroo, for the more brutal appetite. She keeps her stars and mountains for those who can appreciate something more subtly ridiculous.' He turned to his equerry. 'But as I said "eating", let us have a picnic like two nice little children. Just run and bring me a table and a dozen courses or so, and plenty of champagne, and under these swinging boughs, Bowler, we will return to Nature.'

It took about an hour to erect in Holland Lane the monarch's simple repast, during which time he walked up and down and whistled, but still with an unaffected air of gloom. He had really been done out of a pleasure he had promised himself, and had that empty and sickened feeling which a child has when disappointed of a pantomime. When he and the equerry had sat down, however, and consumed a fair amount of dry champagne, his spirits began mildly to revive.

'Things take too long in this world,' he said. 'I detest all this Barkerian business about evolution and the gradual modification of things. I wish the world had been made in six days, and knocked to pieces again in six more. And I wish I had done it. The joke's good enough in a broad way, sun and moon and the image of God, and all that, but they keep it up so damnably long. Did you ever long for a miracle, Bowler?'

'No, sir,' said Bowler, who was an evolutionist, and had been carefully brought up.

'Then I have,' answered the King. 'I have walked along a street with the best cigar in the cosmos in my mouth, and more Burgundy inside me than you ever saw in your life, and longed that the lamp-post would turn into an elephant to save me from the hell of blank existence. Take my word for it, my evolutionary Bowler, don't you believe people when they tell you that people sought for a sign, and believed in miracles because they were ignorant. They did it because they were wise, filthily, vilely wise — too wise to eat or sleep or put on their boots with patience. This seems delightfully like a new theory of the origin of Christianity, which would itself be a thing of no mean absurdity. Take some more wine.'

The wind blew round them as they sat at their little table, with its white cloth and bright wine-cups, and flung the tree-tops of Holland Park against each other, but the sun was in that strong temper which turns green into gold. The King pushed away his plate, lit a cigar slowly, and went on:

'Yesterday I thought that something next door to a really entertaining miracle might happen to me before I went to amuse the worms. To see that red-haired maniac waving a great sword, and making speeches to his incomparable followers would have been a glimpse of that Land of Youth from which the Fates shut us out. I had planned some quite delightful things. A Congress of Knightsbridge with a treaty, and myself in the chair, and perhaps a Roman triumph, with jolly old Barker led in chains. And now these wretched prigs have gone and stamped out the exquisite Mr. Wayne altogether, and I suppose they will put him in a private asylum somewhere in their damned humane way. Think of the treasures daily poured out to his unappreciative keeper! I wonder whether they would let me be his keeper. But life is a vale. Never forget at any moment of your existence to regard it in the light of a vale. This graceful habit, if not acquired in youth——'

The King stopped, with his cigar lifted, for there had slid into his eyes the startled look of a man listening. He did not move for a few moments; then he turned his head sharply towards the high, thin, and lath-like paling which fenced certain long gardens and similar spaces from the lane. From behind it there was coming a curious scrambling and scraping noise, as of a desperate thing imprisoned in this box of thin wood. The King threw away his cigar, and jumped on to the table. From this position he saw a pair of hands hanging with a hungry clutch on the top of the fence. Then the hands quivered with a convulsive effort, and a head shot up between them — the head of one of the Bayswater Town Council, his eyes and whiskers wild with fear. He swung himself over, and fell on the other side on his face, and groaned openly and without ceasing. The next moment the thin, taut wood of the fence was struck as by a bullet, so that it reverberated like a drum, and over it came, tearing and cursing, with torn clothes and broken nails and bleeding faces, twenty men at one rush. The King sprang five feet clear off the table on to the ground. The moment after the table was flung over, sending bottles and glasses flying, and the *débris* was literally swept along the ground by that stream of men pouring past, and Bowler was borne along with them, as the King said in his famous newspaper article, 'like a captured bride'. The great fence swung and split under the load of climbers that still scaled and cleared it. Tremendous gaps were torn in it by this living artillery; and through them the King could see more and more frantic faces, as in a dream, and more and more men running. They were as miscellaneous as if some one had taken the lid off a human dustbin. Some were untouched, some were slashed and battered and bloody, some were splendidly dressed, some tattered and half-naked, some were in the fantastic garb of the burlesque cities, some in the dullest modern dress. The King stared at all of them, but none of them looked at the King. Suddenly he stepped forward.

'Barker,' he said, 'what is all this?'

'Beaten,' said the politician, 'beaten all to hell!' And he plunged past with nostrils shaking like a horse's, and more and more men plunged after him.

Almost as he spoke, the last standing strip of fence bowed and snapped, flinging, as from a catapult, a new figure upon the road. He wore the flaming red of the halberdiers of Notting Hill, and on his weapon there was blood, and in his face victory. In another moment masses of red glowed though the gaps of the fence, and the pursuers, with their halberds, came pouring down the lane. Pursued and pursuers alike swept by the little figure with the owlish eyes, who had not taken his hand out of his pockets.

The King had still little beyond the confused sense of a man caught in a torrent—the feeling of men eddying by. Then something happened which he was never able afterwards to describe, and which we cannot describe for him. Suddenly in the dark entrance, between the broken gates of a garden, there appeared framed a flaming figure.

Adam Wayne, the conqueror, with his face flung back, and his mane like a lion's, stood with his great sword point upwards, the red raiment of his office flapping round him like the red wings of an archangel. And the King saw, he knew not how, something new and overwhelming. The great green trees and the great red robes swung together in the wind. The sword seemed made for the sunlight. The preposterous masquerade, born of his own mockery, towered over him and embraced the world. This was the normal, this was sanity, this was nature; and he himself, with his rationality and his detachment and his black frock-coat, he was the exception and the accident—a blot of black upon a word of crimson and gold.

"In the dark passage there appeared a flaming figure."

BOOK IV

I

THE BATTLE OF THE LAMPS

Mr. Buck, who, though retired, frequently went down to his big drapery stores in Kensington High Street, was locking up those premises, being the last to leave. It was a wonderful evening of green and gold, but that did not trouble him very much. If you had pointed it out, he would have agreed seriously, for the rich always desire to be artistic.

He stepped out into the cool air, buttoning up his light coat, and blowing great clouds from his cigar, when a figure dashed up to him in another yellow overcoat, but unbuttoned and flying behind him.

'Hullo, Barker!' said the draper. 'Any of our summer articles? You're too late. Factory Acts,[66] Barker. Humanity and progress, my boy.'

'Oh, don't chatter,' cried Barker, stamping. 'We've been beaten.'

'Beaten—by what?' asked Buck, mystified.

'By Wayne.'

Buck looked at Barker's fierce white face for the first time, as it gleamed in the lamplight.

'Come and have a drink,' he said.

They adjourned to a cushioned and glaring buffet, and Buck established himself slowly and lazily in a seat, and pulled out his cigar-case.

'Have a smoke,' he said.

Barker was still standing, and on the fret, but after a moment's hesitation, he sat down, as if he might spring up again the next minute. They ordered drinks in silence.

'How did it happen?' asked Buck, turning his big bold eyes on him.

'How the devil do I know?' cried Barker. 'It happened like—like a dream. How can two hundred men beat six hundred? How can they?'

'Well,' said Buck, coolly. 'How did they? You ought to know.'

'I don't know. I can't describe,' said the other, drumming on the

[66] Factory Acts were legislation designed to regulate conditions of employment and limit working hours.

table. 'It seemed like this. We were six hundred and marched with those damned poleaxes of Auberon's—the only weapons we've got. We marched two abreast. We went up to Holland Walk, between the high palings which seemed to me to go straight as an arrow for Pump Street. I was near the tail of the line and it was a long one. When the end of it was still between the high palings, the head of the line was already crossing Holland Park Avenue. Then the head plunged into the network of narrow streets on the other side, and the tail and myself came out on the great crossing. When we also had reached the northern side and turned up a small street that points, crookedly as it were, towards Pump Street, the whole thing felt different. The streets dodged and bent so much that the head of our line seemed lost altogether: it might as well have been in North America. And all this time we hadn't seen a soul.'

Buck, who was idly dabbing the ash of his cigar on the ash-tray, began to move it deliberately over the table, making feathery grey lines, a kind of map.

'But though the little streets were all deserted (which got a trifle on my nerves), as we got deeper and deeper into them, a thing began to happen that I couldn't understand. Sometimes a long way ahead—three turns or corners ahead, as it were—there broke suddenly a sort of noise, clattering, and confused cries, and then stopped. Then, when it happened, something, I can't describe it—a kind of shake or stagger went down the line, as if the line were a live thing, whose head had been struck, or had been an electric cord. None of us knew why we were moving, but we moved and jostled. Then we recovered, and went on through the little dirty streets, round corners, and up twisted ways. The little crooked streets began to give me a feeling I can't explain—as if it were a dream. I felt as if things had lost their reason, and we should never get out of the maze. Odd to hear me talk like that, isn't it? The streets were quite well-known streets, all down on the map. But the fact remains. I wasn't afraid of something happening. I was afraid of nothing ever happening—nothing ever happening for all God's eternity.'

He drained his glass and called for more whisky. He drank it and went on.

'And then something did happen. Buck, it's the solemn truth, that nothing has ever happened to you in your life. Nothing had ever happened to me in my life.'

'Nothing ever happened!' said Buck, staring. 'What do you mean?'

'Nothing has ever happened,' repeated Barker, with a morbid obstinacy. 'You don't know what a thing happening means? You sit in your office expecting customers, and customers come; you walk in the street expecting friends, and friends meet you; you want a drink and get it; you feel inclined for a bet and make it. You expect either to win or lose, and you do either one or the other. But things are happening!' and he shuddered ungovernably.

'Go on,' said Buck, shortly. 'Get on.'

'As we walked wearily round the corners, something happened. When something happens, it happens first, and you see it afterwards. It happens of itself, and you have nothing to do with it. It proves a dreadful thing—that there are other things besides one's self. I can only put it in this way. We went round one turning, two turnings, three turnings, four turnings, five. Then I lifted myself slowly up from the gutter where I had been shot half senseless, and was beaten down again by living men crashing on top of me, and the world was full of roaring, and big men rolling about like ninepins.'

Buck looked at his map with knitted brows.

'Was that Portobello Road?'[67] he asked.

'Yes,' said Barker. 'Yes; Portobello Road—I saw it afterwards; but, my God—what a place it was! Buck, have you ever stood and let a six foot of a man lash and lash at your head with six feet of pole with six pounds of steel at the end? Because, when you have had that experience, as Walt Whitman says, "you re-examine philosophies and religions".'

'I have no doubt,' said Buck. 'If that was Portobello Road, don't you see what happened?'

'I know what happened exceedingly well. I was knocked down four times; an experience which, as I say, has an effect on the mental attitude. And another thing happened, too. I knocked down two

---

[67] Portobello Road was then and still is famous for its street market.

men. After the fourth fall (there was not much bloodshed — more brutal rushing and throwing — for nobody could use their weapons), after the fourth fall, I say, I got up like a devil, and I tore a poleaxe out of a man's hand and struck where I saw the scarlet of Wayne's fellows, struck again and again. Two of them went over, bleeding on the stones, thank God — and I laughed and found myself sprawling in the gutter again, and got up again, and struck again, and broke my halberd to pieces. I hurt a man's head, though.'

Buck set down his glass with a bang, and spat out curses through his thick moustache.

'What is the matter?' asked Barker, stopping, for the man had been calm up to now, and now his agitation was far more violent than his own.

'The matter?' said Buck, bitterly; 'don't you see how these maniacs have got us? Why should two idiots, one a clown and the other a screaming lunatic, make sane men so different from themselves? Look here, Barker; I will give you a picture. A very well-bred young man of this century is dancing about in frock-coat. He has in his hands a nonsensical seventeenth-century halberd with which he is trying to kill men in a street in Notting Hill. Damn it! don't you see how they've got us? Never mind how you felt — that is how you looked. The King would put his cursed head on one side and call it exquisite. The Provost of Notting Hill would put his cursed nose in the air and call it heroic. But in Heaven's name what would you have called it — two days before?'

Barker bit his lip.

'You haven't been through it, Buck,' he said. 'You don't understand fighting — the atmosphere.'

'I don't deny the atmosphere,' said Buck, striking the table. 'I only say it's their atmosphere. It's Adam Wayne's atmosphere. It's the atmosphere which you and I thought had vanished from an educated world for ever.'

'Well, it hasn't,' said Barker; 'and if you have any lingering doubts, lend me a poleaxe and I'll show you.'

There was a long silence, and then Buck turned to his neighbour and spoke in that good-tempered tone that comes of a power of looking facts in the face; the tone in which he concluded great bargains.

'Barker,' he said, 'you are right. This old thing—this fighting, has come back. It has come back suddenly and taken us by surprise. So it is first blood to Adam Wayne. But, unless reason and arithmetic and everything else have gone crazy, it must be next and last blood to us. But when an issue has really arisen, there is only one thing to do—to study that issue as such and win in it. Barker, since it is fighting, we must understand fighting. I must understand fighting as coolly and completely as I understand drapery; you must understand fighting as coolly and completely as you understand politics. Now, look at the facts. I stick without hesitation to my original formula. Fighting, when we have the stronger force, is only a matter of arithmetic. It must be. You asked me just now how two hundred men could defeat six hundred. I can tell you. Two hundred men can defeat six hundred when the six hundred behave like fools. When they forget the very conditions they are fighting in; when they fight in a swamp as if it were a mountain; when they fight in a forest as if it were a plain; when they fight in streets without remembering the object of streets.'

'What is the object of streets?' asked Barker.

'What is the object of supper?' cried Buck, furiously. 'Isn't it obvious? This military science is mere common sense. The object of a street is to lead from one place to another; therefore all streets join; therefore street fighting is quite a peculiar thing. You advanced into that hive of streets as if you were advancing into an open plain where you could see everything. Instead of that you were advancing into the bowels of a fortress, with streets pointing at you, streets turning on you, streets jumping out at you, and all in the hands of the enemy. Do you know what Portobello Road is? It is the only point on your journey where two side-streets run up opposite each other. Wayne massed his men on the two sides, and when he had let enough of your line go past, cut it in two like a worm. Don't you see what would have saved you?'

Barker shook his head.

'Can't your "atmosphere" help you?' asked Buck, bitterly. 'Must

I attempt explanations in the romantic manner? Suppose that, as you were fighting blindly with the red Notting Hillers who imprisoned you on both sides, you had heard a shout from behind them. Suppose, oh, romantic Barker! that behind the red tunics you had seen the blue and gold of South Kensington taking them in the rear, surrounding them in their turn and hurling them on to your halberds.'

'If the thing had been possible,' began Barker, cursing.

'The thing would have been as possible,' said Buck, simply; 'as simple as arithmetic. There are a certain number of street entries that lead to Pump Street. There are not nine hundred; there are not nine million. They do not grow in the night. They do not increase like mushrooms. It must be possible with such an overwhelming force as we have to advance by all of them at once. In every one of the arteries, or approaches, we can put almost as many men as Wayne can put into the field altogether. Once do that and we have him to demonstration. It is like a proposition in Euclid.'

'You think that is certain,' said Barker, anxious but dominated delightfully.

'I'll tell you what I think,' said Buck, getting up jovially. 'I think Adam Wayne made an uncommonly spirited little fight. And I think I am confoundedly sorry for him.'

'Buck, you are a great man,' cried Barker, rising also. 'You've knocked me sensible again. I am ashamed to say it, but I was getting romantic. Of course, what you say is adamantine sense. Fighting, being physical, must be mathematical. We were beaten because we were neither mathematical nor physical nor anything else—because we deserved to be beaten. Hold all the approaches, and with our force we must have him. When shall we open the next campaign?'

'Now,' said Buck, and walked out of the bar.

'Now!' cried Barker, following him eagerly. 'Do you mean now? It is so late.'

Buck turned on him, stamping.

'Do you think fighting is under the Factory Acts?' he said, and he called a cab. 'Notting Hill Gate Station,'[68] he said, and the two drove off.

[68] Notting Hill Gate Station was and is an underground railway station on the Circle Line.

*   *   *

A genuine reputation can sometimes be made in an hour. Buck, in the next sixty or eighty minutes showed himself a really great man of action. His cab carried him like a thunderbolt from the King to Wilson, from Wilson to Swindon, from Swindon to Barker again; if his course was jagged, it had the jaggedness of the lightning. Only two things he carried with him, his inevitable cigar and the map of North Kensington and Notting Hill. There were, as he again and again pointed out, with every variety of persuasion and violence, only nine possible ways of approaching Pump Street within a quarter of a mile around it; three out of Westbourne Grove, two out of Ladbroke Grove, and four out of Notting Hill High Street. And he had detachments of two hundred each, stationed at every one of the entrances before the last green of that strange sunset had sunk out of the black sky.

The sky was particularly black, and on this alone was one false protest raised against the triumphant optimism of the Provost of North Kensington. He overruled it with his infectious common sense.

'There is no such thing,' he said, 'as night in London. You have only to follow the line of street lamps. Look, here is the map. Two hundred purple North Kensington soldiers under myself march up Ossington Street, two hundred more under Captain Bruce, of the North Kensington Guard, up Clanricarde Gardens.* Two hundred yellow West Kensingtons under Provost Swindon attack from Pembridge Road. Two hundred more of my men from the eastern streets, leading away from Queen's Road. Two detachments of yellows enter by two roads from Westbourne Grove. Lastly, two hundred green Bayswaters come down from the North through Chepstow Place, and two hundred more under Provost Wilson himself, through the upper part of Pembridge Road. Gentlemen, it is mate in two moves. The enemy must either mass in Pump Street and be cut

---

* Clanricarde Gardens at this time was no longer a cul-de-sac, but was connected by Pump Street to Pembridge Square. See map, p. 216.

to pieces—or they must retreat past the Gaslight & Coke Co.[69]—and rush on my four hundred—or they must retreat past St. Luke's Church, and rush on the six hundred from the West. Unless we are all mad, it's plain. Come on. To your quarters and await Captain Bruce's signal to advance. Then you have only to walk up a line of gas-lamps and smash this nonsense by pure mathematics. To-morrow we shall be all civilians again.'

His optimism glowed like a great fire in the night, and ran round the terrible ring in which Wayne was now held helpless. The fight was already over. One man's energy for one hour had saved the city from war.

For the next ten minutes Buck walked up and down silently beside the the motionless clump of his two hundred. He had not changed his appearance in any way, except to sling across his yellow overcoat a case with a revolver in it. So that his light-clad modern figure showed up oddly beside the pompous purple uniform of his halberdiers which darkly but richly coloured the black night.

At length a shrill trumpet rang from some way up the street; it was the signal of advance. Buck briefly gave the word, and the whole purple line, with its dimly shining steel, moved up the side alley. Before it was a slope of street, long, straight, and shining in the dark. It was a sword pointed at Pump Street, the heart at which nine other swords were pointed that night.

A quarter of an hour's silent marching brought them almost within earshot of any tumult in the doomed citadel. But still there was no sound and no sign of the enemy. This time, at any rate, they knew that they were closing in on it mechanically, and they marched on under the lamplight and the dark without any of that eerie sense of ignorance which Barker had felt when entering the hostile country by one avenue alone.

'Halt—point arms!' cried Buck, suddenly, and as he spoke there came a clatter of feet tumbling along the stones. But the halberds were levelled in vain. The figure that rushed up was a messenger from the contingent of the North.

[69] The Gaslight & Coke Co. premises on Pump Street did not exist for the simple reason that Pump Street did not exist. The nearest Gaslight & Coke depot was in Kensal Green, but here Chesterton is exercising author's license.

'Victory, Mr. Buck!' he cried, panting, 'they are ousted. Provost Wilson of Bayswater has taken Pump Street.'

Buck ran forward in his excitement.

'Then, which way are they retreating? It must be either by St. Luke's to meet Swindon or by the Gas Company to meet us. Run like mad to Swindon and see that the yellows are holding the St. Luke's Road. We will hold this, never fear. We have them in an iron trap. Run!'

As the messenger dashed away into the darkness, the great guard of North Kensington swung on with the certainty of a machine. Yet scarcely a hundred yards farther their halberd points again fell in line gleaming in the gas-light. For again a clatter of feet was heard on the stones, and again it proved to be only the messenger.

'Mr. Provost,' he said, 'the yellow West Kensingtons have been holding the road by St. Luke's for twenty minutes since the capture of Pump Street. Pump Street is not two hundred yards away, they cannot be retreating down that road.'

'Then they are retreating down this!' said Provost Buck, with a final cheerfulness, 'and by good fortune down a well-lighted road, though it twists about. Forward!'

As they moved along the last three hundred yards of their journey, Buck fell, for the first time in his life, perhaps, into a kind of philosophical reverie, for men of his type are always made kindly, and as it were melancholy, by success.

'I am sorry for poor old Wayne, I really am,' he thought. 'He spoke up splendidly for me at that Council. And he blacked old Barker's eye with considerable spirit. But I don't see what a man can expect when he fights against arithmetic, to say nothing of civilization. And what a wonderful hoax all this military genius is. I suspect I've just discovered what Cromwell discovered, that a sensible tradesman is the best general, and that a man who can buy men and sell men can lead and kill them. The thing's simply like adding up a column in a ledger. If Wayne has two hundred men, he can't put two hundred men in nine places at once. If they're ousted from Pump Street they're flying somewhere. If they're not flying past the church they're flying past the Works. And so we have them. We business men should have no chance at all except that cleverer people than we get bees in their bonnets that prevent them from reasoning properly—so we reason alone. And so I, who am comparatively stupid, see things as God sees them, as a vast machine. My God, what's this?' And he clapped his hands to his eyes and staggered back.

Then through the darkness he cried in a dreadful voice:

'Did I blaspheme God?—I am struck blind.'

'What?' wailed another voice behind him, the voice of a certain Wilfred Jarvis of North Kensington.

'Blind!' cried Buck; 'blind!'

'I'm blind, too!' cried Jarvis, in an agony.

'Fools, all of you,' said a gross voice behind them; 'we're all blind. The lamps have gone out.'

'The lamps—but why? where?' cried Buck, turning furiously in the darkness. 'How are we to get on? How are we to chase the enemy? Where have they gone?'

'The enemy went——' said the rough voice behind, and then stopped, doubtfully.

'Where?' shouted Buck, stamping like a madman.

'They went,' said the gruff voice, 'past the Gas Works, and they've used their chance.'

'Great God!' thundered Buck, and snatched at his revolver; 'do you mean they've turned out——'

But almost before he had spoken the words, he was hurled like a stone from a catapult into the midst of his own men.

'Notting Hill! Notting Hill!' cried frightful voices out of the darkness, and they seemed to come from all sides, for the men of North Kensington, unacquainted with the road, had lost all their bearings in the black world of blindness.

'Notting Hill! Notting Hill!' cried the invisible people, and the invaders were hewn down horribly with black steel, with steel that gave no glint against any light.

*   *   *

Buck, though badly maimed with the blow of a halberd, kept an angry but splendid sanity. He groped madly for the wall and found it. Struggling with crawling fingers along it, he found a side opening and retreated into it with the remnants of his men. Their adventures during that prodigious night are not to be described. They did not know whether they were going towards or away from the enemy. Not knowing where they themselves were, or where their opponents were, it was mere irony to ask where was the rest of their army. For a thing had descended upon them which London does not know—darkness, which was before the stars were made, and they were as much lost in it as if they had been made before the stars. Every now and then, as those frightful hours wore on, they buffeted in the darkness against living men, who struck at them and at whom they struck, with an idiot fury. When at last the grey dawn came, they found they had wandered back to the edge of the Uxbridge Road. They found that in those horrible eyeless encounters, the North Kensingtons and the Bayswaters and the West Kensingtons had again and again met and butchered each other, and they heard that Adam Wayne was barricaded in Pump Street.

II

THE CORRESPONDENT OF THE
COURT JOURNAL

Journalism had become like most other such things in England, under the cautious government and philosophy represented by James Barker, somewhat sleepy and much diminished in importance. This was partly due to the disappearance of party government and public speaking, partly to the compromise or deadlock which had made foreign wars impossible, but mostly, of course, to the temper of the whole nation, which was that of a people in a kind of back-water. Perhaps the most well known of the remaining newspapers was the *Court Journal*, which was published in a dusty but genteel-looking office just out of Kensington High Street. For when all the papers of a people have been for years growing more and more dim and decorous and optimistic, the dimmest and most decorous and most optimistic is very likely to win. In the journalistic competition which was still going on at the beginning of the twentieth century, the final victor was the *Court Journal*.

For some mysterious reason the King had a great affection for hanging about in the *Court Journal* office, smoking a morning cigarette and looking over files. Like all ingrainedly idle men, he was very fond of lounging and chatting in places where other people were doing work. But one would have thought that, even in the prosaic England of his day, he might have found a more bustling centre.

On this particular morning, however, he came out of Kensington Palace with a more alert step and a busier air than usual. He wore an extravagantly long frock-coat, a pale-green waistcoat, a very full and *dégagé* black tie, and curious yellow gloves. This was his uniform as Colonel of a regiment of his own creation, the 1st Decadents Green.[70] It

---

[70] The 1st Decadents Green was a nice conceit, for the decadents of the 1890s adopted as their badge a green carnation, as green flowers did not attract the insects necessary for their fertilization. When Chesterton refers to Quin drilling the 1st Decadents Green, he is probably poking fun at Oscar Wilde and his group.

was a beautiful sight to see him drilling them. He walked quickly across the Park and the High Street, lighting his cigarette as he went, and flung open the door of the *Court Journal* office.

'You've heard the news, Pally—you've heard the news?' he said.

The Editor's name was Hoskins, but the King called him Pally, which was an abbreviation of Palladium of our Liberties.

'Well, your Majesty,' said Hoskins, slowly (he was a worried, gentlemanly-looking person, with a wandering brown beard)— 'well, your Majesty, I have heard rather curious things, but I——'

'You'll hear more of them,' said the King, dancing a few steps of a kind of negro shuffle. 'You'll hear more of them, my blood-and-thunder tribune. Do you know what I am going to do for you?'

'No, your Majesty,' replied the Palladium, vaguely.

'I'm going to put your paper on strong, dashing, enterprising lines,' said the King. 'Now, where are your posters of last night's defeat?'

'I did not propose your, Majesty,' said the Editor, 'to have any posters exactly——'

'Paper, paper!' cried the King, wildly; 'bring me paper as big as a house. I'll do you posters. Stop, I must take my coat off.' He began removing that garment with an air of set intensity, flung it playfully at Mr. Hoskins' head, entirely enveloping him, and looked at himself in the glass. 'The coat off,' he said, 'and hat on. That looks like a sub-editor. It is indeed the very essence of sub-editing. Well,' he continued, turning round abruptly, 'come along with that paper.'

The Palladium had only just extricated himself reverently from the folds of the King's frock-coat, and said bewildered:

'I am afraid, your Majesty——'

'Oh, you've got no enterprise,' said Auberon. 'What's that roll in the corner? Wall-paper? Decorations for your private residence? Art in the home, Pally? Fling it over here, and I'll paint such posters on the back of it that when you put it up in your drawing-room you'll paste the original pattern against the wall.' And the King unrolled the wall-paper, spreading it over the whole floor. 'Now give me the scissors,' he cried, and took them himself before the other could stir.

He slit the paper into about five pieces each nearly as big as a door. Then he took a big blue pencil and went down on his knees on the dusty oil-cloth, and began to write on them in huge letters:

'FROM THE FRONT.
GENERAL BUCK DEFEATED.
DARKNESS, DANGER, AND DEATH.
WAYNE SAID TO BE IN PUMP STREET.
FEELING IN THE CITY.'

He contemplated it for some time, with his head on one side, and got up, with a sigh.

'Not quite intense enough,' he said—'not alarming. I want the *Court Journal* to be feared as well as loved. Let's try something more hard-hitting.' And he went down on his knees again. After sucking the blue pencil for some time, he began writing again busily. 'How will this do?' he said:

'WAYNE'S WONDERFUL VICTORY.'

'I suppose,' he said, looking up appealingly, and sucking the pencil—'I suppose we couldn't say "wictory"—"Wayne's wonderful wictory"? No, no. Refinement, Pally, refinement. I have it':

'WAYNE WINS.
ASTOUNDING FIGHT IN THE DARK.

The gas-lamps in their courses fought against Buck.'

'(Nothing like our fine old English translation.) What else can we say? Well, anything to annoy old Buck" and he added, thoughtfully, in smaller letters:

'Rumoured Court-martial on General Buck.'

'Those will do for the present,' he said, and turned them both face downwards. 'Paste, please.'

The Palladium, with an air of great terror, brought the paste out of an inner room.

The King slabbed it on with the enjoyment of a child messing with treacle. Then, taking one of his huge compositions fluttering in each hand, he ran outside, and began pasting them up in prominent positions over the front of the office.

'And now,' said Auberon, entering again with undiminished vivacity—'now for the leading article.'

He picked up another of the large strips of wall-paper, and, laying it across a desk, pulled out a fountain-pen and began writing with feverish intensity, reading clauses and fragments aloud to himself, and rolling them on his tongue like wine, to see if they had the pure journalistic flavour.

'The news of the disaster to our forces in Notting Hill, awful as it is, awful as it is—(no, distressing as it is), may do some good if it draws attention to the what's-his-name inefficiency (scandalous inefficiency, of course) of the Government's preparations. In our present state of information, it would be premature (what a jolly word!)—it would be premature to cast any reflections upon the conduct of General Buck, whose services upon so many stricken fields (ha, ha!), and whose honourable scars and laurels, give him a right to have judgment upon him at least suspended. But there is one matter on which we must speak plainly. We have been silent on it too long, from feelings, perhaps of mistaken caution, perhaps of mistaken loyalty. This situation would never have arisen but for what we can only call the indefensible conduct of the King. It pains us to say such things, but, speaking as we do in the public interest (I plagiarize from Barker's famous epigram), we shall not shrink because of the distress we may cause to any individual, even the most exalted. At this crucial moment of our country, the voice of the People demands with a single tongue, "Where is the King?" What is he doing while his subjects tear each other in pieces in the streets of a great city? Are his amusements and his dissipations (of which we cannot pretend to be ignorant) so engrossing that he can spare no thought for a perishing nation? It is with a deep sense of our responsibility that we warn that exalted person that neither his great position nor his incomparable talents will save him in the hour of delirium from the fate of all those who, in the madness of luxury or tryanny, have met the English people in the rare day of its wrath.'

'I am now,' said the King, 'going to write an account of the battle by an eye-witness.' And he picked up a fourth sheet of wall-paper. Almost at the same moment Buck strode quickly into the office. He had a bandage round his head.

'I was told,' he said with his usual gruff civility, 'that your Majesty was here.'

'And of all things on earth,' cried the King, with delight, 'here is an eye-witness! An eye-witness who, I regret to observe, has at present only one eye to witness with. Can you write us the special article Buck? Have you a rich style?'

Buck, with a self-restraint which almost approached politeness, took no notice whatever of the King's maddening geniality.

'I took the liberty, your Majesty,' he said shortly, 'of asking Mr. Barker to come here also.'

As he spoke, indeed, Barker came swinging into the office, with his usual air of hurry.

'What is happening now?' asked Buck, turning to him with a kind of relief.

'Fighting still going on,' said Barker. 'The four hundred from West Kensington were hardly touched last night. They hardly got near the place. Poor Wilson's Bayswater men got cut about, though. They fought confoundedly well. They took Pump Street once. What mad things do happen in the world. To think that of all of us it should be little Wilson with the red whiskers who came out best.'

The King made a note on his paper:

'Romantic conduct of Mr. Wilson.'

'Yes,' said Buck, 'it makes one a bit less proud of one's *h*'s.'

The King suddenly folded or crumpled up the paper, and put it in his pocket.

'I have an idea,' he said. 'I will be an eye-witness. I will write you such letters from the Front as will be more gorgeous than the real things. Give me my coat, Palladium. I entered this room a mere King of England. I leave it, Special War Correspondent of the *Court Journal*. It is useless to stop me, Pally; it is vain to cling to my knees, Buck; it is hopeless, Barker, to weep upon my neck. "When duty calls"—the remainder of the sentiment escapes me. You will receive my first article this evening by the eight o'clock post.'

And, running out of the office, he jumped upon a blue Bayswater omnibus that went swinging by.

'Well,' said Barker, gloomily, 'well.'

'Barker,' said Buck, 'business may be lower than politics, but war is, as I discovered last night, a long sight more like business. You politicians are such ingrained demagogues that even when you have a despotism you think of nothing but public opinion. So you learn to tack and run, and are afraid of the first breeze. Now we stick to a thing and get it. And our mistakes help us. Look here! at this moment we've beaten Wayne.'

'Beaten Wayne,' repeated Barker.

'Why the dickens not?' cried the other, flinging out his hands. 'Look here. I said last night that we had them by holding the nine entrances. Well, I was wrong. We should have had them but for a singular event—the lamps went out. But for that it was certain. Has it occurred to you, my brilliant Barker, that another singular event has happened since that singular event of the lamps going out?'

'What event?' asked Barker.

'By an astounding coincidence, the sun has risen,' cried out Buck, with a savage air of patience. 'Why the hell aren't we holding all those approaches now, and pressing in on them again? It should have been done at sunrise. The confounded doctor wouldn't let me go out. You were in command.'

Barker smiled grimly.

'It is a gratification to me, my dear Buck, to be able to say that we anticipated your suggestions precisely. We went as early as possible to reconnoitre the nine entrances. Unfortunately, while we were fighting each other in the dark, like a lot of drunken navvies, Mr. Wayne's friends were working very hard indeed. Three hundred yards from Pump Street, at every one of those entrances, there is a barricade nearly as high as the houses. They were finishing the last, in Pembridge Road, when we arrived. Our mistakes.' He cried bitterly, and flung his cigarette on the ground. 'It is not we who learn from them.'

There was a silence for a few moments, and Barker lay back wearily in a chair. The office clock ticked exactly in the stillness.

At length Barker said suddenly:

'Buck, does it ever cross your mind what this is all about? The Hammersmith to Maida Vale thoroughfare was an uncommonly good speculation. You and I hoped a great deal from it. But is it worth it? It will cost us thousands to crush this ridiculous riot. Suppose we let it alone?'

'And be thrashed in public by a red-haired madman whom any two doctors would lock up?' cried out Buck, starting to his feet. 'What do you propose to do, Mr. Barker? To apologize to the admirable Mr. Wayne? To kneel to the Charter of the Cities? To clasp to your bosom the flag of the Red Lion? To kiss in succession every sacred lamp-post that saved Notting Hill? No, by God! My men fought jolly well—they were beaten by a trick. And they'll fight again.'

'Buck,' said Barker, 'I always admired you. And you were quite right in what you said the other day.'

'In what?'

'In saying,' said Barker, rising quietly, 'that we had all got into Adam Wayne's atmosphere and out of our own. My friend, the whole territorial kingdom of Adam Wayne extends to about nine streets, with barricades at the end of them. But the spiritual kingdom of Adam Wayne extends, God knows where—it extends to this office at any rate. The red-haired madman whom any two doctors would lock up is filling this room with his roaring, unreasonable soul. And it was the red-haired madman who said the last word you spoke.'

Buck walked to the window without replying.

'You understand, of course,' he said at last, 'I do not dream of giving in.'

*　　*　　*

The King, meanwhile, was rattling along on the top of his blue omnibus. The traffic of London as a whole had not, of course, been greatly disturbed by these events, for the affair was treated as a Notting Hill riot, and that area was marked off as if it had been in the hands of a gang of recognized rioters. The blue omnibuses simply went round as they would have done if a road were being mended, and the omnibus on which the correspondent of the *Court Journal* was sitting swept round the corner of Queen's Road, Bayswater.

The King was alone on the top of the vehicle, and was enjoying the speed at which it was going.

'Forward, my beauty, my Arab,' he said, patting the omnibus encouragingly, 'fleetest of all thy bounding tribe. Are thy relations with thy driver, I wonder, those of the Bedouin and his steed? Does he sleep side by side with thee——'

His meditations were broken by a sudden and jarring stoppage. Looking over the edge, he saw that the heads of the horses were being held by men in the uniform of Wayne's army, and heard the voice of an officer calling out orders.

King Auberon descended from the omnibus with dignity. The guard or picket of red halberdiers who had stopped the vehicle did not number more than twenty, and they were under the command of a short, dark, clever-looking young man, conspicuous among the rest as being clad in an ordinary frock-coat, but girt round the waist with a red sash and a long seventeenth-century sword. A shiny silk hat and spectacles completed the outfit in a pleasing manner.

'To whom have I the honour of speaking?' said the King, endeavouring to look like Charles I, in spite of personal difficulties.

The dark man in spectacles lifted his hat with equal gravity.

'My name is Bowles,' he said. 'I am a chemist. I am also a captain of O Company of the army of Notting Hill. I am distressed at having to incommode you by stopping the omnibus, but this area is covered by our proclamation, and we intercept all traffic. May I ask to whom I have the honour—— Why, good gracious, I beg your Majesty's pardon. I am quite overwhelmed at finding myself concerned with the King.'

Auberon put up his hands with indescribable grandeur.

'Not with the King,' he said; 'with the special war correspondent for the *Court Journal*.'

'I beg your Majesty's pardon,' began Mr. Bowles, doubtfully.

'Do you call me Majesty? I repeat,' said Auberon firmly, 'I am a representative of the Press. I have chosen, with a deep sense of responsibility, the name of Pinker. I should desire a veil to be drawn over the past.'

'Very well, sir,' said Mr. Bowles, with an air of submission, 'in our eyes the sanctity of the Press is at least as great as that of the

"King Auberon descended from the omnibus with dignity."

throne. We desire nothing better than that our wrongs and our glories should be widely known. May I ask, Mr. Pinker, if you have any objection to being presented to the Provost and to General Turnbull?'

'The Provost I have had the honour of meeting,' said Auberon, easily. 'We old journalists, you know, meet everybody. I should be most delighted to have the same honour again. General Turnbull, also, it would be a gratification to know. The younger men are so interesting. We of the old Fleet Street gang lose touch with them.'

'Will you be so good as to step this way?' said the leader of O Company.

'I am always good,' said Mr. Pinker. 'Lead on.'

III

THE GREAT ARMY OF SOUTH KENSINGTON

The article from the special correspondent of the *Court Journal* arrived in due course, written on very coarse copy-paper in the King's arabesque of handwriting, in which three words filled a page, and yet were illegible. Moreover, the contribution was the more perplexing at first as it opened with a succession of erased paragraphs. The writer appeared to have attempted the article once or twice in several journalistic styles. At the side of one experiment was written, 'Try American style', and the fragment began:

'The King must go. We want gritty men. Flapdoodle is all very . . .'; and then broke off, followed by the note, 'Good sound journalism safer. Try it.'

The experiment in good sound journalism appeared to begin:

'The greatest of English poets has said that a rose by any . . .'

This also stopped abruptly. The next annotation at the side was almost indecipherable, but seemed to be something like:

'How about old Steevens[71] and the *mot juste*? E.g. . . .'

'Morning winked a little wearily at me over the curt edge of Campden Hill and its houses with their sharp shadows. Under the abrupt black cardboard of the outline, it took some little time to detect colours; but at length I saw a brownish yellow shifting in the obscurity, and I knew that it was the guard of Swindon's West Kensington army. They are being held as a reserve, and lining the whole ridge above the Bayswater Road. Their camp and their main force is under the great waterworks tower on Campden Hill.[72] I forgot to say that the waterworks tower looked swart.

'As I passed them and came over the curve of Silver Street, I saw the blue cloudy masses of Barker's men blocking the entrance to the

[71] Chesteron was referring to George Warrington (1869–1900), journalist and author.

[72] The great waterworks tower on Campden Hill was built, together with its pumping station, to the designs of Alexander Fraser (1823–95) by John Aird (1800–1876) for the Grand Junction Water Works Company. The tower was 160 feet tall.

high-road like a sapphire smoke (good). The disposition of the allied troops, under the general management of Mr. Wilson, appears to be as follows; The Yellow Army (if I may so describe the West Kensingtonians) lies, as I have said, in a strip along the ridge; its farthest point westward being the west side of Campden Hill Road, its farthest point eastward the beginning of Kensington Gardens. The Green Army of Wilson lines the Notting Hill High Road itself from Queen's Road to the corner of Pembridge Road, curving round the latter, and extending some three hundred yards up towards Westbourne Grove. Westbourne Grove itself is occupied by Barker of South Kensington. The fourth side of this rough square, the Queen's Road side, is held by some of Buck's Purple warriors.

'The whole resembles some ancient and dainty Dutch flower-bed. Along the crest of Campden Hill lie the golden crocuses of West Kensington. They are, as it were, the first fiery fringe of the whole. Northward lies our hyacinth Barker, with all his blue hyacinths. Round to the south-west run the green rushes of Wilson of Bayswater, and a line of violet irises (aptly symbolized by Mr. Buck) complete the whole. The argent exterior . . . (I am losing the style. I should have said "Curving with a whisk" instead of merely "Curving". Also I should have called the hyacinths "sudden". I cannot keep this up. War is too rapid for this style of writing. Please ask the office-boy to insert *mots justes*.)

'The truth is that there is nothing to report. That commonplace element which is always ready to devour all beautiful things (as the Black Pig in the Irish Mythology will finally devour the stars and gods); that commonplace element, as I say, has in its Black Piggish way devoured finally the chances of any romance in this affair; that which once consisted of absurd but thrilling combats in the streets, has degenerated into something which is the very prose of warfare—it has degenerated into a siege. A siege may be defined as a peace plus the inconvenience of war. Of course Wayne cannot hold out. There is no more chance of help from anywhere else than of ships from the moon. And if old Wayne had stocked his street with tinned meats till all his garrison had to sit on them, he couldn't hold out for more than a month or two. As matter of melancholy fact he has done something rather like this. He has stocked his street with food until there must be uncommonly little room to turn round. But what is the good? To hold out for all that time and then to give in of necessity, what does it mean? It means waiting until your victories are forgotten and then taking the trouble to be defeated. I cannot understand how Wayne can be so inartistic.

'And how odd it is that one views a thing quite differently when one knows it is defeated. I always thought Wayne was rather fine. But now, when I know that he is done for, there seems to be nothing else but Wayne. All the streets seem to point at him, all the chimneys seem to lean towards him. I suppose it is a morbid feeling; but Pump Street seems to be the only part of London that I feel physically. I suppose, I say, that it is morbid. I suppose it is exactly how a man feels about his heart when his heart is weak. "Pump Street" — the heart is a pump. And I am drivelling.

'Our finest leader at the front is beyond all question General Wilson. He has adopted alone among the other Provosts the uniform of his own halberdiers, although that fine old sixteenth-century garb was not originally intended to go with red side-whiskers. It was he who, against a most admirable and desperate defence, broke last night into Pump Street and held it for at least half an hour. He was afterwards expelled from it by General Turnbull, of Notting Hill, but only after desperate fighting and the sudden descent of that terrible darkness which proved so much more fatal to the forces of General Buck and General Swindon.

'Provost Wayne himself, with whom I had, with great good fortune, a most interesting interview, bore the most eloquent testimony to the conduct of General Wilson and his men. His precise words are as follows: "I have bought sweets at his funny little shop when I was four years old, and ever since. I never noticed anything, I am ashamed to say, except that he talked through his nose, and didn't wash himself particularly. And he came over our barricade like a devil from hell." I repeated this speech to General Wilson himself, with some delicate improvements, and he seemed pleased with it. He does not, however, seem pleased with anything so much just now as he is with the wearing of a sword. I have it from the front on the best authority that General Wilson was not completely shaved yesterday. It is believed in military circles that he is growing a moustache. . . .

'As I have said, there is nothing to report. I walk wearily to the pillar-box at the corner of Pembridge Road to post my copy. Nothing whatever has happened, except the preparations for a particularly long and feeble siege, during which I trust I shall not be required to be at the Front. As I glance up Pembridge Road in the growing dusk, the aspect of that road reminds me that there is one note worth adding. General Buck has suggested, with characteristic acumen, to General Wilson, that in order to obviate the possibility of such a catastrophe as overwhelmed the allied forces in the last advance on Notting Hill (the catastrophe, I mean, of the extinguished lamps), that each soldier should have a lighted lantern round his neck. This is one of the things which I really admire about General Buck. He possesses what people used to mean by "the humility of the man of science", that is he learns steadily from his mistakes. Wayne may score off him in some other way, but not in that way. The lanterns look like fairy lights as they curve round the end of Pembridge Road.

'*Later.* — I write with some difficulty, because the blood will run down my face and make patterns on the paper. Blood is a very beautiful thing; that is why it is concealed. If you ask me why blood runs down my face, I can only reply that I was kicked by a horse. If you ask me what horse, I can reply with some pride that it was a war-horse. If you ask me how a war-horse came on the scene in our simple pedestrian warfare, I am reduced to the necessity, so painful to a special correspondent, of recounting my experiences.

'I was, as I have said, in the very act of posting my copy at the pillar-box, and of glancing as I did so up the glittering curve of Pembridge Road, studded with the lights of Wilson's men. I don't know what made me pause to examine the matter, but I had a fancy that the line of lights, where it melted into the indistinct brown twilight, was more indistinct than usual. I was almost certain that in a certain stretch of the road where there had been five lights there were now only four. I strained my eyes; I counted them again, and there were only three. A moment after there were only two; an instant after only one; and an instant after that the lanterns near to me swung like jangled bells, as if struck suddenly. They flared and fell; and for the moment the fall of them was like the fall of the sun and stars out of heaven. It left everything in a primal blindness. As a matter of fact, the road was not yet legitimately dark. There were still red rays of a sunset in the sky, and the brown gloaming was still warmed, as it were, with a feeling as of firelight. But for three seconds after the lanterns swung and sank, I saw in front of me a blackness blocking the sky. And with the fourth second I knew that this blackness which blocked the sky was a man on a great horse; and I was trampled and tossed aside as a swirl of horsemen swept round the corner. As they turned I saw that they were not black but scarlet; they were a sortie of the beseiged, Wayne riding ahead.

'I lifted myself from the gutter, blinded with blood from a very slight skin-wound, and, queerly enough, not caring either for the blindness or for the slightness of the wound. For one mortal minute after that amazing cavalcade had spun past, there was dead stillness on the empty road. And then came Barker and all his halberdiers running like devils in the track of them. It had been their business to guard the gate by which the sortie had broken out; but they had not reckoned, and small blame to them, on cavalry. As it was, Barker and his men made a perfectly splendid run after them, almost catching Wayne's horses by the tails.

'Nobody can understand the sortie. It consists only of a small number of Wayne's garrison. Turnbull himself, with the vast mass of it, is undoubtedly still barricaded in Pump Street. Sorties of this kind are natural enough in the majority of historical sieges, such as the siege of Paris in 1870, because in such cases the besieged are certain of some support outside. But what can be the object of it in this case? Wayne knows (or if he is too mad to know anything, at least Turnbull knows) that there is not, and never has been, the smallest chance of support for him outside; that the mass of the sane modern inhabitants of London regard his farcical patriotism with as much contempt as they do the original idiocy that gave it birth—the folly

of our miserable King. What Wayne and his horsemen are doing nobody can even conjecture. The general theory round here is that he
is simply a traitor, and has abandoned the besieged. But all such
larger but yet more soluble riddles are as nothing compared to the
one small but unanswerable riddle: Where did they get the horses?

'*Later.* — I have heard a most extraordinary account of the origin
of the appearance of the horses. It appears that that amazing person,
General Turnbull, who is now ruling Pump Street in the absence of
Wayne, sent out, on the morning of the declaration of war, a vast
number of little boys (or cherubs of the gutter, as we pressmen say),
with half-crowns in their pockets, to take cabs all over London. No
less than a hundred and sixty cabs met at Pump Street; were com-
mandeered by the garrison. The men were set free, the cabs used to
make barricades, and the horses kept in Pump Street, where they
were fed and exercised for several days, until they were sufficiently
rapid and efficient to be used for this wild ride out of the town. If
this is so, and I have it on the best possible authority, the method of
the sortie is explained. But we have no explanation of its object. Just
as Barker's Blues were swinging round the corner after them, they
were stopped, but not by an enemy; only by the voice of one man,
and he a friend. Red Wilson of Bayswater ran alone along the main
road like a madman, waving them back with a halberd snatched
from a sentinel. He was in supreme command, and Barker stopped
at the corner, staring and bewildered. We could hear Wilson's voice
loud and distinct out of the dusk, so that it seemed strange that the
great voice should come out of the little body. "Halt, South
Kensington! Guard this entry, and prevent them returning. I will
pursue. Forward, the Green Guards!"

'A wall of dark blue uniforms and a wood of poleaxes were between me and Wilson, for Barker's men blocked the mouth of the
road in two rigid lines. But through them and through the dusk I
could hear the clear orders and the clank of arms, and see the Green
Army of Wilson marching by towards the west. They were our
great fighting-men. Wilson had filled them with his own fire; in a
few days they had become veterans. Each of them wore a silver medal

of a pump, to boast that they alone of all the allied armies had stood victorious in Pump Street.

'I managed to slip past the detachment of Barker's Blues, who are guarding the end of Pembridge Road, and a sharp spell of running brought me to the tail of Wilson's Green Army as it swung down the road in pursuit of the flying Wayne. The dusk had deepened into almost total darkness; for some time I only heard the throb of the marching pace. Then suddenly there was a cry, and the tall fighting men were flung back on me, almost crushing me, and again the lanterns swung and jingled, and the cold nozzles of great horses pushed into the press of us. They had turned and charged us.

' "You fools!" came the voice of Wilson, cleaving our panic with a splendid cold anger. "Don't you see? The horses have no riders!"

'It was true. We were being plunged at by a stampede of horses with empty saddles. What could it mean? Had Wayne met some of our men and been defeated? Or had he flung these horses at us as some kind of ruse or mad new mode of warfare, such as he seemed bent on inventing? Or did he and his men want to get away in disguise? Or did they want to hide in houses somewhere?

'Never did I admire any man's intellect (even my own) so much as I did Wilson's at that moment. Without a word, he simply pointed the halberd (which he still grasped) to the southern side of the road. As you know, the streets running up to the ridge of Campden Hill from the main road are peculiarly steep, they are more like sudden flights of stairs. We were just opposite Aubrey Road, the steepest of all; up that it would have been far more difficult to urge halftrained horses than to run up on one's feet.

' "Left wheel!" hallooed Wilson. "They have gone up here," he added to me, who happened to be at his elbow.

' "Why?" I ventured to ask.

' "Can't say for certain," replied the Bayswater General. "They've gone up here in a great hurry anyhow. They've simply turned their horses loose, because they couldn't take them up. I fancy I know. I fancy they're trying to get over the ridge to Kensington or Hammersmith, or somewhere, and are striking up here because it's just beyond the end of our line. Damned fools, not to have gone farther along the road, though. They've only just shaved our last outpost. Lambert is hardly four hundred yards from here. And I've sent him word."

' "Lambert!" I said. "Not young Wilfrid Lambert—my old friend."

' "Wilfrid Lambert's his name," said the General; "used to be a 'man about town'; silly fellow with a big nose. That kind of man always volunteers for some war or other. And what's funnier, he generally isn't half bad at it. Lambert is distinctly good. The yellow West Kensingtons I always reckoned the weakest part of the army; but he has pulled them together uncommonly well, though he's subordinate to Swindon, who's a donkey. In the attack from Pembridge Road the other night he showed great pluck."

' "He has shown greater pluck than that," I said. "He has criticized my sense of humour. That was his first engagement."

'This remark was, I am sorry to say, lost on the admirable commander of the allied forces. We were in the act of climbing the last half of Aubrey Road, which is so abrupt a slope that it looked like an old-fashioned map leaning up against the wall. There are lines of little trees, one above the other, as in the old-fashioned map.

'We reached the top of it, panting somewhat, and were just about to turn the corner by a place called (in chivalrous anticipation of our wars of sword and axe) Tower Crecy, when we were suddenly knocked in the stomach (I can use no other term) by a horde of men hurled back upon us. They wore the red uniform of Wayne; their halberds were broken; their foreheads bleeding; but the mere impetus of their retreat staggered us as we stood at the last ridge of the slope.

' "Good old Lambert!" yelled out, suddenly, the stolid Mr. Wilson of Bayswater, in an uncontrollable excitement. "Damned jolly old Lambert! He's got there already! He's driving them back on us! Hurrah! hurrah! Forward the Green Guards!"

'We swung round the corner eastwards, Wilson running first, brandishing the halberd.

'Will you pardon a little egotism? Every one likes a little egotism, when it takes the form, as mine does in this case, of a disgraceful confession. The thing is really a little interesting, because it shows how the merely artistic habit has bitten into men like me. It was the most intensely exciting occurrence that had ever come to me in my life; and I was really intensely excited about it. And yet, as we turned that corner, the first impression I had was of something that had nothing to do with the fight at all. I was stricken from the sky as by a thunderbolt, by the height of the Waterworks Tower on Campden Hill. I don't know whether Londoners generally realize how high it looks when one comes out, in this way, almost immediately under it. For the second it seemed to me that at the foot of it even human war was a triviality. For the second I felt as if I had been drunk with some trivial orgy, and that I had been sobered by the shock of that shadow. A moment afterwards, I realized that under it was going on something more enduring than stone, and something wilder than the dizziest height — the agony of man. And I knew that compared to that, this overwhelming tower was itself a triviality; it was a mere stalk of stone which humanity could snap like a stick.

'I don't know why I have talked so much about this silly old Waterworks Tower, which at the very best was only a tremendous background. It was that, certainly, a sombre and awful landscape, against which our figures were relieved. But I think the real reason was, that there was in my own mind so sharp a transition from the tower of stone to the man of flesh. For what I saw first when I had shaken off, as it were, the shadow of the towers, was a man, and a man I knew.

'Lambert stood at the farther corner of the street that curved round the tower, his figure outlined in some degree by the beginning of moonrise. He looked magnificent, a hero; but he looked something much more interesting than that. He was, as it happened, in almost precisely the same swaggering attitude in which he had stood nearly fifteen years ago, when he swung his walking-stick and struck it into the ground, and told me that all my subtlety was drivel. And, upon my soul, I think he required more courage to say that than to fight as he does now. For then he was fighting against something that was in the ascendant, fashionable, and victorious. And now he is fighting (at the risk of his life, no doubt) merely against something which is already dead, which is impossible, futile; of which nothing has been more impossible and futile than this very sortie which has brought him into contact with it. People nowadays allow infinitely too little for the psychological sense of victory as a factor in affairs. Then he was attacking the degraded but undoubtedly victorious Quin; now he is attacking the interesting but totally extinguished Wayne.

'His name recalls me to the details of the scene. The facts were these. A line of red halberdiers, headed by Wayne, were marching up the street, close under the northern wall, which is, in fact, the bottom of a sort of dyke or fortification of the Waterworks. Lambert and his yellow West Kensingtons had that instant swept round the corner and had shaken the Waynites heavily, hurling back a few of the more timid, as I have just described, into our very arms. When our force struck the tail of Wayne's, every one knew that all was up with him. His favourite military barber was struck down. His grocer was stunned. He himself was hurt in the thigh, and reeled back against the wall. We had him in a trap with two jaws. "Is that you?" shouted Lambert, genially, to Wilson, across the hemmed-in host of Notting Hill. "That's about the ticket," replied General Wilson; "keep them under the wall."

'The men of Notting Hill were falling fast. Adam Wayne threw up his long arms to the wall above him, and with a spring stood upon it, a gigantic figure against the moon. He tore the banner out of the hands of the standard-bearer below him, and shook it out suddenly above our heads, so that it was like thunder in the heavens.

' "Round the Red Lion!" he cried. "Swords round the Red Lion! Halberds round the Red Lion! They are the thorns round the rose."

'His voice and the crack of the banner made a momentary rally, and Lambert, whose idiotic face was almost beautiful with battle, felt it as by an instinct, and cried:

' "Drop your public-house flag, you footler! Drop it!"

' "The banner of the Red Lion seldom stoops," said Wayne, proudly, letting it out luxuriantly on the night wind.

'The next moment I knew that poor Adam's sentimental theatricality had cost him much. Lambert was on the wall at a bound, his sword in his teeth, and had slashed at Wayne's head before he had time to draw his sword, his hands being busy with the enormous flag. He stepped back only just in time to avoid the first cut, and let the flagstaff fall, so that the spear-blade at the end of it pointed to Lambert.

' "The banner stoops," cried Wayne, in a voice that must have startled streets. "The banner of Notting Hill stoops to a hero." And with the words he drove the spear-point and half the flagstaff through Lambert's body and dropped him dead upon the road below, a stone upon the stones of the street.

' "Notting Hill! Notting Hill!" cried Wayne in a sort of divine rage. "Her banner is all the holier for the blood of a brave enemy! Up on the wall, patriots! Up on the wall! Notting Hill!"

'With his long strong arm he actually dragged a man up on to the wall to be silhouetted against the moon, and more and more men climbed up there, pulled themselves and were pulled, till clusters and crowds of the half-massacred men of Pump Street massed upon the wall above us.

' "Notting Hill! Notting Hill!" cried Wayne, unceasingly.

' "Well, what about Bayswater?" said a worthy working-man in Wilson's army, irritably. "Bayswater for ever!"

' "We have won!" cried Wayne, striking his flagstaff in the ground. "Bayswater for ever! We have taught our enemies patriotism!"

' "Oh, cut these fellows up and have done with it!" cried one of Lambert's lieutenants, who was reduced to something bordering on madness by the responsibility of succeeding to the command.

' "Let us by all means try," said Wilson, grimly; and the two armies closed round the third.

*　　*　　*

'I simply cannot describe what followed. I am sorry, but there is such a thing as physical fatigue, as physical nausea, and, I may add, as physical terror. Suffice it to say that the above paragraph was written about 11 p.m., and that it is now about 2 a.m., and that the battle is not finished, and is not likely to be. Suffice it further to say that down the steep streets which lead from the Waterworks Tower to the Notting Hill High Road, blood has been running, and is running, in great red serpents, that curl out into the main thoroughfare and shine in the moon.

'*Later.* — The final touch has been given to all this terrible futility. Hours have passed; morning has broken; men are still swaying and fighting at the foot of the tower and round the corner of Aubrey Road; the fight has not finished. But I know it is a farce.

'News has just come to show that Wayne's amazing sortie, followed by the amazing resistance through a whole night on the wall of the Waterworks, is as if it had not been. What was the object of that strange exodus we shall probably never know, for the simple reason that every one who knew will probably be cut to pieces in the course of the next two or three hours.

'I have heard, about three minutes ago, that Buck and Buck's methods have won after all. He was perfectly right, of course, when one comes to think of it, in holding that it was physically impossible for a street to defeat a city. While we thought he was patrolling the eastern gates with his Purple Army; while we were rushing about the streets and waving halberds and lanterns; while poor old Wilson was scheming like Moltke and fighting like Achilles to entrap the wild Provost of Notting Hill — Mr. Buck, retired draper, has simply driven down in a hansom cab and done something about as plain as butter and about as useful and nasty. He has gone down to South Kensington, Brompton, and Fulham, and by spending about four thousand pounds of his private means, has raised an army of nearly as many men; that is to say, an army big enough to beat, not only Wayne, but Wayne and all his present enemies put together. The army, I understand, is encamped along High Street, Kensington, and fills it from the Church to Addison Road Bridge. It is to advance by ten different roads uphill to the north.

'I cannot endure to remain here. Everything makes it worse than it need be. The dawn, for instance, has broken round Campden Hill; splendid spaces of silver, edged with gold, are torn out of the sky. Worse still, Wayne and his men feel the dawn; their faces, though bloody and pale, are strangely hopeful . . . insupportably pathetic. Worst of all, for the moment they are winning. If it were not for Buck and the new army they might just, and only just, win.

'I repeat, I cannot stand it. It is like watching that wonderful play of old Maeterlinck's[73] (you know my partiality for the healthy, jolly old authors of the nineteenth century), in which one has to watch the quiet conduct of people inside a parlour, while knowing that the very men are outside the door whose word can blast it all with tragedy. And this is worse, for the men are not talking, but writhing and bleeding and dropping dead for a thing that is already settled — and settled against them. The great grey masses of men still toil and tug and sway hither and thither around the great grey tower; and the tower is still motionless, as it will always be motionless. These men will be crushed before the sun is set; and new men will arise and be crushed, and new wrongs done, and tyranny will always rise again like the sun, and injustice will always be as fresh as the flowers of spring. And the stone tower will always look down on it. Matter, in its brutal beauty, will always look down on those who are mad enough to consent to die, and yet more mad, since they consent to live.'

Thus ended abruptly the first and last contribution of the Special Correspondent of the *Court Journal* to that valued periodical.

The Correspondent himself, as has been said, was simply sick and gloomy at the last news of the triumph of Buck. He slouched sadly down the steep Aubrey road, up which he had the night before run in so unusual an excitement, and strolled out into the empty dawn-lit main road, looking vaguely for a cab. He saw nothing in the vacant space except a blue-and-gold glittering thing, running very fast, which looked at first like a very tall beetle, but turned out to his great astonishment, to be Barker.

'Have you heard the good news?' asked that gentleman.

'Yes,' said Quin, with a measured voice. 'I have heard the glad tidings of great joy. Shall we take a hansom down to Kensington? I see one over there.'

They took the cab, and, were, in four minutes, fronting the ranks of the multitudinous and invincible army. Quin had not spoken a word all the way, and something about him had prevented the essentially impressionable Barker from speaking either.

[73] Chesterton is probably referring to *Le Trésor des humbles*.

The great army, as it moved up Kensington High Street, calling many heads to the numberless windows, for it was long indeed—longer than the lives of most of the tolerably young—since such an army had been seen in London. Compared with the vast organization which was now swallowing up the miles, with Buck at its head as leader, and the King hanging at its tail as journalist, the whole story of our problem was insignificant. In the presence of that army the red Notting Hills and the green Bayswaters were alike tiny and straggling groups. In its presence the whole struggle round Pump Street was like an ant-hill under the hoof of an ox. Every man who felt or looked at that infinity of men knew that it was the triumph of Buck's brutal arithmetic. Whether Wayne was right or wrong, wise or foolish, was quite a fair matter for discussion. But it was a matter of history. At the foot of Church Street, opposite Kensington Church, they paused in their glowing good humour.

'Let us send some kind of messenger or herald up to them,' said Buck, turning to Barker and the King. 'Let us send and ask them to cave in without more muddle.'

'What shall we say to them?' said Barker, doubtfully.

'The facts of the case are quite sufficient,' rejoined Buck. 'It is the facts of the case that make an enemy surrender. Let us simply say that our army that is fighting their army, and their army that is fighting our army, amount altogether to about a thousand men. Say that we have four thousand. It is very simple. Of the thousand fighting, they have at the very most, three hundred, so that, with those three hundred, they have now to fight four thousand seven hundred men. Let them do it if it amuses them.'

And the Provost of North Kensington laughed.

The herald who was dispatched up Church Street in all the pomp of the South Kensington blue and gold, with the Three Birds on his tabard, was attended by two trumpeters.

'What will they do when they consent?' asked Barker, for the sake of saying something in the sudden stillness of that immense army.

'I know my Wayne very well,' said Buck, laughing. 'When he submits he will send a red herald flaming with the Lion of Notting Hill. Even defeat will be delightful to him, since it is formal and romantic.'

The King, who had strolled up to the head of the line, broke silence for the first time.

'I shouldn't wonder,' he said, 'if he defied you, and didn't send the herald after all. I don't think you do know your Wayne quite so well as you think.'

'All right, your Majesty,' said Buck, easily; 'If it isn't disrespectful, I'll put my political calculations in a very simple form. I'll lay you ten pounds to a shilling the herald comes with the surrender.'

'All right,' said Auberon. 'I may be wrong, but it's my notion of Adam Wayne that he'll die in his city, and that, till he is dead, it will not be a safe property.'

'The bet's made, your Majesty,' said Buck.

Another long silence ensued, in the course of which Barker alone, amid the motionless army, strolled and stamped in his restless way.

Then Buck suddenly leant forward.

'It's taking your money, your Majesty,' he said. 'I knew it was. There comes the herald from Adam Wayne.'

'It's not,' cried the King, peering forward also. 'You brute, it's a red omnibus.'

'It's not,' said Buck, calmly; and the King did not answer, for down the center of the spacious and silent Church street was walking, beyond question, the herald of the Red Lion, with two trumpeters.

Buck had something in him which taught him how to be magnanimous. In his hour of success he felt magnanimous towards Wayne, whom he really admired; magnanimous towards the King, off whom he had scored so publicly; and, above all, magnanimous towards Barker, who was the titular leader of this vast South Kensington army, which his own talent had evoked.

'General Barker,' he said, bowing, 'do you propose now to receive the message from the besieged?'

Barker bowed also, and advanced towards the herald.

'Has your master, Mr. Adam Wayne, received our request for surrender?' he asked.

The herald conveyed a solemn and respectful affirmative.

Barker resumed, coughing slightly, but encouraged.

'What answer does your master send?'

The herald again inclined himself submissively, and answered in a kind of monotone.

'My message is this. Adam Wayne, Lord High Provost of Notting Hill, under the charter of King Auberon and the laws of God and all mankind, free and of a free city, greets James Barker, Lord High Provost of South Kensington, by the same rights free and honourable, leader of the army of the South. With all friendly reverence, and with all constitutional consideration, he desires James Barker to lay down his arms, and the whole army under his command to lay down their arms also.'

Before the words were ended the King had run forward into the open space with shining eyes. The rest of the staff and the forefront of the army were literally struck breathless. When they recovered they began to laugh beyond restraint; the revulsion was too sudden.

'The Lord High Provost of Notting Hill,' continued the herald, 'does not propose, in the event of your surrender, to use his victory for any of those repressive purposes which others have entertained against him. He will leave you your free laws and your free cities, your flags and your governments. He will not destroy the religion of South Kensington, or crush the old customs of Bayswater.'

An irrepressible explosion of laughter went up from the forefront of the great army.

'The King must have had something to do with this humour,' said Buck, slapping his thigh. 'It's too deliciously insolent. Barker, have a glass of wine.'

And in his conviviality he actually sent a soldier across to the restaurant opposite the church and brought out two glasses for a toast.

When the laughter had died down, the herald continued quite monotonously:

'In the event of your surrendering your arms and dispersing under the superintendence of our forces, these local rights of yours shall be carefully observed. In the event of your not doing so, the Lord High Provost of Notting Hill desires to announce that he has just captured the Waterworks Tower, just above you, on Campden Hill, and that within ten minutes from now, that is, on the reception through me of your refusal, he will open the great reservoir and flood the whole valley where you stand in thirty feet of water. God save King Auberon!'

Buck had dropped his glass and sent a great splash of wine over the road.

'But—but——' he said; and then by a last and splendid effort of his great sanity, looked the facts in the face.

'We must surrender,' he said. 'You could do nothing against fifty thousand tons of water coming down a steep hill, ten minutes hence. We must surrender. Our four thousand men might as well be four. *Vicisti Galilaea!*[74] Perkins, you may as well get me another glass of wine.'

In this way the vast army of South Kensington surrendered and the Empire of Notting Hill began. One further fact in this connexion is perhaps worth mentioning—the fact that, after his victory, Adam Wayne caused the great tower on Campden Hill to be plated with gold and inscribed with a great epitaph, saying that it was the monument of Wilfrid Lambert, the heroic defender of the place and surmounted with a statue, in which his large nose was done something less than justice to.

[74] "You have conquered, O Galilean!", supposedly the last words of the Roman emperor Julian the Apostate (A.D. 331–63).

BOOK V

I

THE EMPIRE OF NOTTING HILL

On the evening of the third of October, twenty years after the great victory of Notting Hill, which gave it the dominion of London, King Auberon, came, as of old, out of Kensington Palace.

He had changed little, save for a streak or two of grey in his hair, for his face had always been old, and his step slow, and, as it were, decrepit.

If he looked old, it was not because of anything physical or mental. It was because he still wore, with a quaint conservatism, the frock-coat and high hat of the days before the great war. 'I have survived the Deluge,' he said. 'I am a pyramid, and must behave as such.'

As he passed up the street the Kensingtonians, in their pictur-esque blue smocks, saluted him as a King, and then looked after him as a curiosity. It seemed odd to them that men had once worn so elvish an attire.

The King, cultivating the walk attributed to the oldest inhabitant ('Gaffer Auberon' his friends were now confidentially desired to call him), went toddling northward. He paused, with reminiscence in his eye, at the Southern Gate of Notting Hill, one of those nine great gates of bronze and steel, wrought with reliefs of the old bat-tles, by the hand of Chiffy himself.

'Ah!' he said, shaking his head and assuming an unnecessary air of age, and a provincialism of accent, 'Ah! I mind when there warn't none of this here.'

He passed through the Ossington Gate, surmounted by a great lion, wrought in red copper on yellow brass, with the motto, 'Nothing Ill'. The guard in red and gold saluted him with his halberd.

It was about sunset, and the lamps were being lit. Auberon paused to look at them, for they were Chiffy's finest work, and his artistic eye never failed to feast on them. In memory of the Great Battle of the Lamps, each great iron lamp was surmounted by a veiled figure,

355

sword in hand, holding over the flame an iron hood or extinguisher, as if ready to let it fall if the armies of the South and West should again show their flags in the city. Thus no child in Notting Hill could play about the streets without the very lamp-posts reminding him of the salvation of his country in the dreadful year.

'Old Wayne was right in a way,' commented the King. 'The sword does make things beautiful. It has made the whole world romantic by now. And to think people once thought me a buffoon for suggesting a romantic Notting Hill. Deary me, deary me (I think that is the expression). It seems like a previous existence.'

Turning a corner he found himself in Pump Street, opposite the four shops which Adam Wayne had studied twenty years before. He entered idly the shop of Mr. Mead, the grocer. Mr. Mead was somewhat older, like the rest of the world, and his red beard, which he now wore with a moustache, and long and full, was partly blanched and discoloured. He was dressed in a long and richly embroidered robe of blue, brown, and crimson, interwoven with an Eastern complexity of pattern, and covered with obscure symbols and pictures, representing his wares passing from hand to hand and from nation to nation. Round his neck was the chain with the Blue Argosy cut in turquoise, which he wore as Grand Master of the Grocers. The whole shop had the sombre and sumptuous look of its owner. The wares were displayed as prominently as in the old days but they were now blended and arranged with a sense of tint and grouping, too often neglected by the dim grocers of those forgotten days. The wares were shown plainly, but shown not so much as an old grocer would have shown his stock, but rather as an educated virtuoso would have shown his treasures. The tea was stored in great blue and green vases inscribed with the nine indispensable sayings of the wise men of China. Other vases of a confused orange and purple, less rigid and dominant, more humble and dreamy, stored symbolically the tea of India. A row of caskets of a simple silvery metal contained tinned meats. Each was wrought with some rude but rhythmic form, as a shell, a horn, a fish, or an apple to indicate what material had been canned in it.

'Your Majesty,' said Mr. Mead sweeping an Oriental reverence. 'This is an honour to me, but yet more an honour to the city.'

Auberon took off his hat.

'Mr. Mead,' he said, 'Notting Hill, whether in giving or taking, can deal in nothing but honour. Do you happen to sell liquorice?'

'Liquorice, sire,' said Mr. Mead, 'is not the least important of our benefits out of the dark heart of Arabia.[75]

And going reverently towards a green and silver canister, made in the form of an Arabian mosque, he proceeded to serve his customer.

'I was just thinking, Mr. Mead,' said the King reflectively, 'I don't know why I should think about it just now, but I was just thinking of twenty years ago. Do you remember the times before the war?'

The grocer, having wrapped up the liquorice sticks in a piece of paper (inscribed with some appropriate sentiment), lifted his large grey eyes dreamily, and looked at the darkening sky outside.

'Oh, yes, your Majesty,' he said. 'I remember these streets before the Lord Provost began to rule us. I can't remember how we felt very well. All the great songs and the fighting change one so; and I don't think we can really estimate all we owe to the Provost; but I can remember his coming into this very shop twenty-two years ago, and I remember the things he said. The singular thing is that as far as I remember I thought the things he said odd at that time. Now it's the things that I said, as far as I can recall them, that seem to me odd—as odd as a madman's antics.'

'Ah!' said the King; and looked at him with an unfathomable quietness.

'I thought nothing of being a grocer then,' he said. 'Isn't that odd enough for anybody? I thought nothing of all the wonderful places that my goods come from, and wonderful ways that they are made. I did not know that I was for all practical purposes a king with slaves spearing fishes near the secret pool, and gathering fruits in the islands under the world. My mind was a blank on the thing. I was as mad as a hatter.'

The King turned also, and stared out into the dark, where the great lamps that commemorated the battle were already flaming.

'And is this the end of poor old Wayne?' he said, half to himself.

[75] Liquorice was much more likely to have come from Pontefract in Yorkshire. Perhaps Chesterton is confusing it with sherbet.

'To inflame every one so much that he is lost himself in the blaze. Is this his victory, that he, my incomparable Wayne, is now only one in a world of Waynes? Has he conquered and become by conquest commonplace? Must Mr. Mead, the grocer, talk as high as he? Lord! what a strange world in which a man cannot remain unique even by taking the trouble to go mad.'

And he went dreamily out of the shop.

He paused outside the next one almost precisely as the Provost had done two decades before.

'How uncommonly creepy this shop looks,' he said. 'But yet somehow encouragingly creepy, invitingly creepy. It looks like something in a jolly old nursery story in which you are frightened out of your skin, and yet know that things always end well. The way those low sharp gables are carved like great black bat's wings folded down, and the way those queer-coloured bowls underneath are made to shine like giant's eyeballs. It looks like a benevolent warlock's hut. It is apparently a chemist's.'

Almost as he spoke, Mr. Bowles, the chemist, came to his shop door in a long black velvet gown and hood, monastic as it were, but yet with a touch of the diabolic. His hair was still quite black, and his face even paler than of old. The only spot of colour he carried was a red star cut in some precious stone of strong tint, hung on his breast. He belonged to the Society of the Red Star of Charity, founded on the lamps displayed by doctors and chemists.

'A fine evening, sir,' said the chemist. 'Why, I can scarcely be mistaken in supposing it to be your Majesty. Pray step inside and share a bottle of sal volatile, or anything that may take your fancy. As it happens there is an old acquaintance of your Majesty's in my shop carousing (if I may be permitted the term) upon that beverage at this moment.'

The King entered the shop, which was an Aladdin's garden of shades and hues, for as the chemist's scheme of colour was more brilliant than the grocer's scheme, so it was arranged with even more delicacy and fancy. Never, if the phrase may be employed, had such a nosegay of medicines been presented to the artistic eye.

But even the solemn rainbow of that evening interior was rivalled

" 'A fine evening, Sir,' said the chemist."

or even eclipsed by the figure standing in the centre of the shop. His form, which was a large and stately one, was clad in a brilliant blue velvet, cut in the richest Renaissance fashion, and slashed so as to show gleams and gaps of a wonderful lemon or pale yellow. He had several chains round his neck and his plumes, which were of several tints of bronze and gold, hung down to the great gold hilt of his long sword. He was drinking a dose of sal volatile, and admiring its opal tint. The King advanced with a slight mystification towards the tall figure, whose face was in shadow, then he said:

'By the Great Lord of Luck, Barker!'

The figure removed his plumed cap, showing the same dark head and long, almost equine, face which the King had so often seen rising out of the high collar of Bond Street. Except for a grey patch on each temple, it was totally unchanged.

'Your Majesty,' said Barker, 'this is a meeting nobly retrospective, a meeting that has about it a certain October gold. I drink to old days'; and he finished his sal volatile with simple feeling.

'I am delighted to see you again, Barker,' said the King. 'It is, indeed, long since we met. What with my travels in Asia Minor, and my book having to be written (you have read my *Life of Prince Albert for Children,* of course), we have scarcely met twice since the great war. That is twenty years ago.'

'I wonder,' said Barker, thoughtfully, 'if I might speak freely to your Majesty.'

'Well,' said Auberon, 'it's rather late in the day to start speaking respectfully. Flap away, my bird of freedom.'

'Well, your Majesty,' replied Barker, lowering his voice, 'I don't think it will be so long to the next war.'

'What do you mean?' asked Auberon.

'We will stand this insolence no longer,' burst out Barker, fiercely. 'We are not slaves because Adam Wayne twenty years ago cheated us with a water-pipe. Notting Hill is Notting Hill; it is not the world. We in South Kensington, we also have memories—aye, and hopes. If they fought for these trumpery shops and a few lamp-posts, shall we not fight for the great High Street and the sacred Natural History Museum?'[76]

[76] The sacred Natural History Museum is the one in Cromwell Road, South Kensington.

'Great Heavens!' said the astounded Auberon. 'Will wonders never cease? Have the two greatest marvels been achieved? Have you turned altruistic, and has Wayne turned selfish? Are you the patriot, and he the tyrant?'

'It is not from Wayne himself altogether that the evil comes,' answered Barker. 'He, indeed, is now mostly wrapped in dreams, and sits with his old sword beside the fire. But Notting Hill is the tyrant, your Majesty. Its Council and its crowds have been so intoxicated by the spreading over the whole city of Wayne's old ways and visions, that they try to meddle with every one, and rule every one and civilize every one, and tell every one what is good for him. I do not deny the great impulse which his old war, wild as it seemed, gave to the civic life of our time. It came when I was still a young man, and I admit it enlarged my career. But we are not going to see our own cities flouted and thwarted from day to day because of something Wayne did for us all nearly a quarter of a century ago. I am just waiting here for news upon this very matter. It is rumoured that Notting Hill has vetoed the statue of General Wilson they are putting up opposite Chepstow Place. If that is so, it is a black and white shameless breach of the terms on which we surrendered to Turnbull after the battle of the Tower. We were to keep our own customs and self-government. If that is so——'

'It is so,' said a deep voice; and both men turned round.

A burly figure in purple robes, with a silver eagle hung round his neck and moustaches almost as florid as his plumes stood in the doorway.

'Yes,' he said, acknowledging the King's start, 'I am Provost Buck, and the news is true. These men of the Hill have forgotten that we fought round the Tower as well as they did, and that it is sometimes foolish, as well as base, to despise the conquered.'

'Let us step outside,' said Barker, with a grim composure.

Buck did so, and stood rolling his eyes up and down the lamp-lit street.

'I would like to have a go at smashing all this,' he muttered, 'though I am over sixty. I would like——'

His voice ended in a cry, and he reeled back a step, with his hands to his eyes, as he had done in those streets twenty years before.

'Darkness!' he cried—'darkness again! What does it mean?'

For in truth every lamp in the street had gone out, so that they could not see even each other's outline, except faintly. The voice of the chemist came with startling cheerfulness out of the density.

'Oh, don't you know?' he said. 'Did they never tell you this is the Feast of the Lamps, the anniversary of the great battle that almost lost and just saved Notting Hill? Don't you know, your Majesty, that on this night twenty-one years ago we saw Wilson's green uniforms charging down this street, and driving Wayne and Turnbull back upon the gas-works, fighting with their handful of men like fiends from hell? And that then, in that great hour, Wayne sprang through a window of the gas-works, with one blow of his hand brought darkness on the whole city, and then with a cry like a lion's, that was heard through four streets, flew at Wilson's men, sword in hand, and swept them, bewildered as they were, and ignorant of the map, clear out of the sacred street again? And don't you know that upon that night every year all lights are turned out for half an hour while we sing the Notting Hill anthem in the darkness? Hark! there it begins.'

Through the night came a crash of drums, and then a strong swell of human voices:

'When the world was in the balance, there was night on Notting Hill,
(There was night on Notting Hill): it was nobler than the day;
On the cities where the lights are and the firesides glow,
From the seas and from the deserts came the thing we did not know,
Came the darkness, came the darkness, came the darkness on the foe.
        And the old guard of God turned to bay.
For the old guard of God turns to bay, turns to bay,
And the stars fall down before it ere its banners fall to-day.
For when armies were around us as a howling and a horde.
When falling was the citadel and broken was the sword,
The darkness came upon them like the Dragon of the Lord,
        When the old guard of God turned to bay.'

The voices were just uplifting themselves in a second verse, when they were stopped by a scurry and a yell. Barker had bounded into the street with a cry of 'South Kensington!' and a drawn dagger. In

less time than man could blink, the whole packed street was full of
curses and struggling. Barker was flung back against the shop-front,
but used the second only to draw his sword as well as his dagger,
and calling out, 'This is not the first time I've come through the
thick of you', flung himself again into the press. It was evident that
he had drawn blood at last, for a more violent outcry arose, and
many other knives and swords were discernible in the faint light.
Barker, after having wounded more than one man, seemed on the
point of being flung back again, when Buck suddenly stepped out
into the street. He had no weapon, for he affected rather the peaceful
magnificence of the great burgher, than the pugnacious dandyism
which had replaced the old sombre dandyism in Barker. But with a
blow of his clenched fist he broke the pane of the next shop, which
was the old curiosity shop, and, plunging in his hand, snatched a
kind of Japanese scimitar, and calling out, 'Kensington! Kensington!'
rushed to Barker's assistance.

Barker's sword was broken, but he was laying about him with his
dagger. Just as Buck ran up, a man of Notting Hill struck Barker
down, but Buck struck the man down on top of him, and Barker
sprang up again, the blood running down his face.

Suddenly all these cries were cloven by a great voice, that seemed
to fall out of heaven. It was terrible to Buck and Barker and the
King from its seeming to come out the empty skies; but it was more
terrible because it was a familiar voice, and one which at the same
time they had not heard for so long.

'Turn up the lights,' said the voice from above them, and for a
moment there was no reply, but only a tumult.

'In the name of Notting Hill, and of the great Council of the City,
turn up the lights.'

There was again a tumult and a vagueness for a moment, then the
whole street and every object in it sprang suddenly out of the darkness, as every lamp sprang into life. And looking up they saw, standing upon a balcony near the roof of one of the highest houses, the
figure and the face of Adam Wayne his red hair blowing behind
him, a little streaked with grey.

'What is this, my people?' he said. 'Is it altogether impossible to make a thing good without it immediately insisting on being wicked? The glory of Notting Hill in having achieved its independence, has been enough for me to dream of for many years, as I sat beside the fire. Is it really not enough for you, who have had so many other affairs to excite and distract you? Notting Hill is a nation. Why should it condescend to be a mere Empire? You wish to pull down the statue of General Wilson, which the men of Bayswater have so rightly erected in Westbourne Grove. Fools! Who erected that statue? Did Bayswater erect it? No. Notting Hill erected it. Do you not see that it is the glory of our achievement that we have infected the other cities with the idealism of Notting Hill? It is we who have created not only our own side, but both sides of this controversy. O too humble fools—why should you wish to destroy your enemies? You have done something more to them. You have created your enemies. You wish to pull down that gigantic silver hammer, which stands, like an obelisk, in the centre of the Broadway of Hammersmith. Fools! Before Notting Hill arose, did any person passing through Hammersmith Broadway expect to see there a gigantic silver hammer? You wish to abolish the great bronze figure of a knight standing upon the artificial bridge at Knightsbridge. Fools! Who would have thought of it before Notting Hill arose? I have even heard, and with deep pain I have heard it, that the evil eye of our imperial envy has been cast towards the remote horizon of the west, and that we have objected to the great black monument of a crowned raven, which commemorates the skirmish of Ravenscourt Park. Who created all these things? Were they there before we came? Cannot you be content with the destiny which was enough for Athens, which was enough for Nazareth? the destiny, the humble purpose of creating a new world. Is Athens angry because Romans and Florentines have adopted her phraseology for expressing their own patriotism? Is Nazareth angry because as a little village it has become the type of all little villages out of which, as the Snobs say, no good can come? Has Athens asked every one to wear the chlamys?[77] Are all the followers of the Nazarene compelled to wear

[77] A chlamys is a short mantle or cloak.

turbans? No! but the soul of Athens went forth and made men drink hemlock and the soul of Nazareth went forth and made men consent to be crucified. So has the soul of Notting Hill gone forth and made men realize what it is to live in a city. Just as we inaugurated our symbols and ceremonies, so they have inaugurated theirs; and are you so mad as to contend against them? Notting Hill is right; it has always been right. It has moulded itself on its own necessities, its own *sine qua non*, it has accepted its own ultimatum. Because it is a nation it has created itself. And because it is a nation it can destroy itself. Notting Hill shall always be the judge. If it is your will because of this matter of General Wilson's statue to make war upon Bayswater——'

A roar of cheers broke in upon his words and further speech was impossible. Pale to the lips, the great patriot tried again and again to speak; but even his authority could not keep down the dark and roaring masses in the street below him. He said something further, but it was not audible. He descended at last sadly from the garret in which he lived, and mingled with the crowd at the foot of the houses. Finding General Turnbull, he put his hand on his shoulder with a queer affection and gravity, and said:

'To-morrow, old man, we shall have a new experience, as fresh as the flowers of spring. We shall be defeated. You and I have been through three battles together, and have somehow or other missed this peculiar delight. It is unfortunate that we shall not probably be able to exchange our experiences, because, as it most annoyingly happens, we shall probably both be dead.'

Turnbull looked dimly surprised.

'I don't mind so much about being dead,' he said, 'but why should you say that we shall be defeated?'

'The answer is very simple,' replied Wayne calmly. 'It is because we ought to be defeated. We have been in the most horrible holes before now; but in all those I was perfectly certain that the stars were on our side, and that we ought to get out. Now, I know that we ought not to get out; and that takes away from me everything with which I won.'

As Wayne spoke he started a little, for both men became aware that a third figure was listening to them — a small figure with wondering eyes.

'Is it really true, my dear Wayne,' said the King, interrupting, 'that you think you will be beaten tomorrow?'

'There can be no doubt about it whatever,' replied Adam Wayne; 'the real reason is the one of which I have just spoken. But as a concession to your materialism, I will add that they have an organized army of a hundred allied cities against our one. That in itself, however, would be unimportant.'

Quin, with his round eyes, seemed strangely insistent.

'You are quite sure,' he said,' that you must be beaten?'

'I am afraid,' said Turnbull, gloomily, 'that there can be no doubt about it.'

'Then,' cried the King, flinging out his arms, 'give me a halberd! Give me a halberd, somebody! I desire all men to witness that I, Auberon, King of England, do here and now abdicate and implore the Provost of Notting Hill to permit me to enlist in his army. Give me a halberd!'

He seized one from some passing guard, and, shouldering it, stamped solemnly after the shouting columns of halberdiers which were, by this time, parading the streets. He had, however, nothing to do with the wrecking of the statue of General Wilson, which took place before morning.

II

THE LAST BATTLE

The day was cloudy when Wayne went down to die with all his army in Kensington Gardens; it was cloudy again when that army had been swallowed up by the vast armies of a new world. There had been an almost uncanny interval of sunshine, in which the Provost of Notting Hill, with all the placidity of an onlooker, had gazed across to the hostile armies on the great spaces of verdure opposite; the long strips of green and blue and gold lay across the park in squares and oblongs like a proposition in Euclid wrought in a rich embroidery. But the sunlight was a weak and, as it were, a wet sunlight, and was soon swallowed up. Wayne spoke to the King, with a queer sort of coldness and languor, as to the military operations. It was as he had said the night before, that being deprived of his sense of an impracticable rectitude he was, in effect, being deprived of everything. He was out of date, and at sea in a mere world of compromise and competition, of Empire against Empire, of the tolerably right and the tolerably wrong. When his eye fell on the King, however, who was marching very gravely with a top hat and a halberd, it brightened slightly.

'Well, your Majesty,' he said, 'you at least ought to be proud today. If your children are fighting each other, at least those who win are your children. Other kings have distributed justice, you have distributed life. Other kings have ruled a nation, you have created nations. Others have made kingdoms, you have begotten them. Look at your children, father.' And he stretched his hand out towards the enemy.

Auberon did not raise his eyes.

'See how splendidly,' cried Wayne, 'the new cities come on — the new cities from across the river. See where Battersea advances over there — under the flag of the Lost Dog;[78] and Putney — don't you

---

[78] This is a reference to Battersea Dogs' Home, a refuge for stray animals.

see the Man on the White Boar shining on their standard as the sun catches it? It is the coming of a new age, your Majesty. Notting Hill is not a common empire; it is a thing like Athens, the mother of a mode of life, of a manner of living, which shall renew the youth of the world—a thing like Nazareth. When I was young I remember, in the old dreary days, wiseacres used to write books about how trains would get faster, and all the world would be one empire, and tram-cars go to the moon. And even as a child I used to say to myself, "Far more likely that we shall go on the crusades again, or worship the gods of the city." And so it has been. And I am glad, though this is my last battle.'

Even as he spoke there came a crash of steel from the left, and he turned his head.

'Wilson!' he cried, with a kind of joy. 'Red Wilson has charged our left. No one can hold him in; he eats swords. He is as keen a soldier as Turnbull, but less patient—less really great. Ha! and Barker is moving. How Barker has improved; how handsome he looks. It is not all having plumes; it is also having a soul in one's daily life. Ha!'

And another crash of steel on the right showed that Barker had closed with Notting Hill on the other side.

'Turnbull is there!' cried Wayne. 'See him hurl them back! Barker is checked! Turnbull charges—wins! But our left is broken. Wilson has smashed Bowles and Mead, and may turn our flank. Forward, the Provost's Guard!'

And the whole centre moved forward, Wayne's face and hair and sword flaming in the van.

The King ran suddenly forward.

The next instant a great jar that went through it told that it had met the enemy. And right over against them through the wood of their own weapons Auberon saw the Purple Eagle of Buck of North Kensington.

On the left Red Wilson was storming the broken ranks, his little green figure conspicuous even in the tangle of men and weapons, with the flaming red moustaches and the crown of laurel. Bowles slashed at his head and tore away some of the wreath, leaving the rest bloody, and, with a roar like a bull's Wilson sprang at him, and, after a rattle of fencing, plunged his point into the chemist, who fell, crying 'Notting Hill!' Then the Notting Hillers wavered, and Bayswater swept them back in confusion. Wilson had carried everything before him.

On the right, however, Turnbull had carried the Red Lion banner with a rush against Barker's men, and the banner of the Golden Birds bore up with difficulty against it. Barker's men fell fast. In the centre Wayne and Buck were engaged, stubborn and confused. So far as the fighting went, it was precisely equal. But the fighting was a farce. For behind the three small armies with which Wayne's small army was engaged lay the great sea of the allied armies, which looked on as yet as scornful spectators, but could have broken all four armies by moving a finger.

Suddenly they did move. Some of the front contingents, the pastoral chiefs from Shepherd's Bush, with their spears and fleeces, were seen advancing, and the rude clans from Paddington Green. They were advancing for a very good reason. Buck, of North Kensington, was signalling wildly; he was surrounded, and totally cut off. His regiments were a struggling mass of people, islanded in a red sea of Notting Hill.

The allies had been too careless and confident. They had allowed Barker's force to be broken to pieces by Turnbull, and the moment that was done, the astute old leader of Notting Hill swung his men round and attacked Buck behind and on both sides. At the same moment Wayne cried 'Charge!' and struck him in front like a thunderbolt.

Two-thirds of Buck's men were cut to pieces before their allies could reach them. Then the sea of cities came on with their banners like breakers, and swallowed Notting Hill for ever. The battle was not over, for not one of Wayne's men would surrender, and it lasted till sundown, and long after. But it was decided; the story of Notting Hill was ended.

When Turnbull saw it, he ceased a moment from fighting, and looked round him. The evening sunlight struck his face; it looked like a child's.

'I have had my youth,' he said. Then snatching an axe from a man, he dashed into the thick of the spears of Shepherd's Bush, and died somewhere far in the depths of their reeling ranks. Then the battle roared on; every man of Notting Hill was slain before night.

Wayne was standing by a tree alone after the battle. Several men approached him with axes. One struck at him. His foot seemed partly to slip; but he flung his hand out, and steadied himself against the tree.

Barker sprang after him, sword in hand, and shaking with excitement.

'How large now, my Lord,' he cried, 'is the Empire of Notting Hill?'

Wayne smiled in the gathering dark.

'Always as large as this,' he said, and swept his sword round in a semicircle of silver.

Barker dropped, wounded in the neck; and Wilson sprang over his body like a tiger-cat, rushing at Wayne. At the same moment there came behind the Lord of the Red Lion a cry and a flare of yellow, and a mass of the West Kensington halberdiers ploughed up the slope, knee-deep in grass, bearing the yellow banner of the city before them, and shouting aloud.

At the same second Wilson went down under Wayne's sword, seemingly smashed like a fly. The great sword rose again like a bird, but Wilson seemed to rise with it, and, his sword being broken, sprang at Wayne's throat like a dog. The foremost of the yellow halberdiers had reached the tree and swung his axe above the struggling Wayne. With a curse the King whirled up his own halberd and dashed the blade in the man's face. He reeled, and rolled down the slope, just as the furious Wilson was flung on his back again. And again he was on his feet, and again at Wayne's throat. Then he was flung again, but this time laughing triumphantly. Grasped in his hand was the red and yellow favour that Wayne wore as Provost of Notting Hill. He had torn it from the place where it had been carried for twenty-five years.

With a shout the West Kensington men closed round Wayne, the great yellow banner flapping over his head.

'Where is your favour now, Provost?' cried the West Kensington leader.

And a laugh went up.

Adam struck at the standard-bearer and brought him reeling forward. As the banner stooped, he grasped the yellow folds and tore off a shred. A halberdier struck him on the shoulder, wounding bloodily.

'Here is one colour!' he cried, pushing the yellow into his belt; 'and here!' he cried, pointing to his own blood, 'Here is the other.'

At the same instant the shock of a sudden and heavy halberd laid the King stunned or dead. In the wild visions of vanishing consciousness, he saw again something that belonged to an utterly forgotten time, something that he had seen somewhere long ago in a restaurant. He saw, with his swimming eyes, red and yellow, the colours of Nicaragua.

Quin did not see the end. Wilson, wild with joy, sprang again at Adam Wayne, and the great sword of Notting Hill was whirled above once more. Then men ducked instinctively at the rushing noise of the sword coming down out of the sky, and Wilson of Bayswater was smashed and wiped down upon the floor like a fly. Nothing was left of him but a wreck; but the blade that had broken him was broken. In dying he had snapped the great sword and the spell of it; the sword of Wayne was broken at the hilt. One rush of the enemy carried Wayne by force against the tree. They were too close to use halberd or even sword; they were breast to breast, even nostrils to nostrils. But Buck got his dagger free.

'Kill him!' he cried, in a strange stifled voice. 'Kill him! Good or bad, he is none of us! Do not be blinded by the face! . . . God! have we not been blinded all along!' and he drew his arm back for a stab and seemed to close his eyes.

Wayne did not drop the hand that hung on to the tree-branch. But a mighty heave went over his breast and his whole huge figure, like an earthquake over great hills. And with that convulsion of effort he rent the branch out of the tree, with tongues of torn wood. And swaying it once only, he let the splintered club fall on Buck, breaking his neck. The planner of the Great Road fell face foremost dead, with his dagger in a grip of steel.

'For you and me, and for all brave men, my brother,' said Wayne, in his strange chant, 'there is good wine poured in the inn at the end of the world.'

The packed men made another lurch or heave towards him; it was almost too dark to fight clearly. He caught hold of the oak again, this time getting his hand into a wide crevice and grasping, as it were, the bowels of the tree. The whole crowd, numbering some thirty men, made a rush to tear him away from it; they hung on with all their weight and numbers, and nothing stirred. A solitude could not have been stiller than that group of straining men. Then there was a faint sound.

'His hand is slipping,' cried two men in exultation.

'You don't know much of him,' said another, grimly (a man of the old war). 'More likely his bone cracks.'

'It is neither—by God, it is neither!' said one of the first two.

'What is it, then?' asked the second.

'The tree is falling,' he replied.

'As the tree falleth, so shall it lie,' said Wayne's voice out of the darkness, and it had the same sweet and yet horrible air that it had had throughout, of coming from a great distance, from before or after the event. Even when he was struggling like an eel or battering like a madman, he spoke like a spectator. 'As the tree falleth, so shall it lie,' he said. 'Men have called that a gloomy text. It is the essence of all exultation. I am doing now what I have done all my life, what is the only happiness, what is the only universality. I am clinging to something. Let it fall, and there let it lie. Fools, you go about and see the kingdoms of the earth, and are liberal, and wise, and cosmopolitan, which is all that the devil can give you—all that he could offer to Christ only to be spurned away. I am doing what the truly wise do. When a child goes out into the garden and takes hold of a tree, saying, "Let this tree be all I have", that moment its roots take hold on hell and its branches on the stars. The joy I have is what the lover knows when a woman is everything. It is what a savage knows when his idol is everything. It is what I know when Notting Hill is everything. I have a city. Let it stand or fall.'

As he spoke the turf lifted itself like a living thing, and out of it rose slowly, like crested serpents the roots of the oak. Then the great head of the tree, that seemed a green cloud among grey ones, swept the sky suddenly like a broom and the whole tree heeled over like a ship, smashing every one in its fall.

III

TWO VOICES

In a place in which there was total darkness for hours, there was also for hours total silence. Then a voice spoke out of the darkness, no one could have told from where, and said aloud:

'So ends the Empire of Notting Hill. As it began in blood, so it ended in blood, and all things are always the same.'

And there was silence again, and then again there was a voice, but it had not the same tone; it seemed that it was not the same voice.

'If all things are always the same, it is because they are always heroic. If all things are always the same, it is because they are always new. To each man one soul only is given; to each soul only is given a little power—the power at some moments to outgrow and swallow up the stars. If age after age that power comes upon men, whatever gives it to them is great. Whatever makes men feel old is mean—an empire or a skinflint shop.[79] Whatever makes men feel young is great—a great war or a love-story. And in the darkest of the books of God there is written a truth that is also a riddle. It is of the new things that men tire—of fashions and proposals and improvements and change. It is the old things that startle and intoxicate. It is the old things that are young. There is no sceptic who does not feel that many have doubted before. There is no rich and fickle man who does not feel that all his novelties are ancient. There is no worshipper of change who does not feel upon his neck the vast weight of the weariness of the universe. But we who do the old things are fed by nature with a perpetual infancy. No man who is in love thinks that any one has been in love before. No woman who has a child thinks that there have been such things as children. No people that fight for their own city are haunted with the burden of the broken empires. Yes, oh, dark voice, the world is always the same, for it is always unexpected.'

A little gust of wind blew through the night, and then the first voice answered:

[79] A skinflint shop is a small factory or workshop out to maximize its profits at the expense of both its workers and its customers.

'But in this world there are some, be they wise or foolish, whom nothing intoxicates. There are some who see all your disturbances like a cloud of flies. They know that while men will laugh at your Notting Hill, and will study and rehearse and sing of Athens and Jerusalem, Athens and Jerusalem were silly suburbs like your Notting Hill. They know that the earth itself is a suburb, and can feel only drearily and respectably amused as they move upon it.'

'They are philosophers or they are fools,' said the other voice. 'They are not men. Men live, as I say, rejoicing from age to age in something fresher than progress — in the fact that with every baby a new sun and a new moon are made. If our ancient humanity were a single man, it might perhaps be that he would break down under the memory of so many loyalties, under the burden of so many diverse heroisms, under the load and terror of all the goodness of men. But it has pleased God so to isolate the individual soul that it can only learn of all other souls by hearsay, and to each one goodness and happiness come with the youth and violence of lightning, as momentary and as pure. And the doom of failure that lies on all human systems does not in real fact affect them any more than the worms of the inevitable grave affect a children's game in a meadow. Notting Hill has fallen; Notting Hill has died. But that is not the tremendous issue. Notting Hill has lived.'

'But if,' answered the other voice, 'if what is achieved by all these efforts be only the common contentment of humanity, why do men so extravagantly toil and die in them? Has nothing been done by Notting Hill that any chance clump of farmers or clan of savages would not have done without it? What might have been done to Notting Hill if the world had been different may be a deep question; but there is a deeper. What could have happened to the world if Notting Hill had never been?'

The other voice replied:

'The same that would have happened to the world and all the starry systems if an apple-tree grew six apples instead of seven; something would have been eternally lost. There has never been anything in the world absolutely like Notting Hill. There will never be anything quite like it to the crack of doom. I cannot believe anything but that God loved it as He must surely love anything that is itself and unreplaceable. But even for that I do not care. If God, with all His thunders, hated it, I loved it.'

And with the voice a tall, strange figure lifted itself out of the *débris* in the half-darkness.

The other voice came after a long pause, and as it were hoarsely.

'But suppose the whole matter were really a hocus-pocus. Suppose that whatever meaning you may choose in your fancy to give to it, the real meaning of the whole was mockery. Suppose it was all folly. Suppose——'

'I have been in it,' answered the voice from the tall and strange figure, 'and I know it was not.'

A smaller figure seemed half to rise in the dark.

'Suppose I am God,' said the voice, 'and suppose I made the world in idleness. Suppose the stars, that you think eternal, are only the idiot fireworks of an everlasting schoolboy. Suppose the sun and the moon, to which you sing alternately, are only the two eyes of one vast and sneering giant, opened alternately in a never-ending wink. Suppose the trees, in my eyes, are as foolish as enormous toad-stools. Suppose Socrates and Charlemagne are to me only beasts, made funnier by walking on their hind legs. Suppose I am God, and having made things, laugh at them.'

'And suppose I am man,' answered the other. 'And suppose that I give the answer that shatters even a laugh. Suppose I do not laugh back at you, do not blaspheme you, do not curse you. But suppose standing up straight under the sky, with every power of my being, I thank you for the fool's paradise you have made. Suppose I praise you, with a literal pain of ecstasy, for the jest that has brought me so terrible a joy. If we have taken the child's games, and given them the seriousness of a Crusade, if we have drenched your grotesque Dutch garden with the blood of martyrs, we have turned a nursery into a temple. I ask you, in the name of Heaven, who wins?'

The sky close about the crest of the hills and trees was beginning to turn from black to grey, with a random suggestion of the morning. The slight figure seemed to crawl towards the larger one, and the voice was more human.

'But suppose, friend,' it said, 'suppose that, in a bitterer and more real sense it was all a mockery. Suppose that there had been, from the beginning of these great wars, one who watched them with a sense that is beyond expression, a sense of detachment, of responsibility, of irony, of agony. Suppose that there were one who knew it was all a joke.'

The tall figure answered:

'He could not know it. For it was not all a joke.'

And a gust of wind blew away some clouds that sealed the skyline, and showed a strip of silver behind his great dark legs. Then the other voice came, having crept nearer still.

'Adam Wayne,' it said, 'there are men who confess only in *articulo moritis*;[80] there are people who blame themselves only when they can no longer help others. I am one of them. Here, upon the field of the bloody end of it all, I come to tell you plainly what you would never understand before. Do you know who I am?'

'I know you, Auberon Quin,' answered the tall figure, 'and I shall be glad to unburden your spirit of anything that lies upon it.'

'Adam Wayne,' said the other voice, 'of what I have to say you cannot in common reason be glad to unburden me. Wayne, it was all a joke. When I made these cities, I cared no more for them than I care for a centaur, or a merman, or a fish with legs, or a pig with feathers, or any other absurdity. When I spoke to you solemnly and encouragingly about the flag of your freedom and the peace of your city, I was playing a vulgar practical joke on an honest gentleman, a vulgar practical joke that has lasted for twenty years. Though no one could believe it of me perhaps, it is the truth that I am a man both timid and tender-hearted. I never dared in the early days of your hope, or the central days of your supremacy, to tell you this; I never dared to break the colossal calm of your face. God knows why I should do it now, when my farce has ended in tragedy and the ruin of all your people! But I say it now. Wayne, it was done as a joke.'

There was silence, and the freshening breeze blew the sky clearer and clearer, leaving great spaces of the white dawn.

At last Wayne said, very slowly:

[80] This is Latin for "at the moment of death" or "when in danger of death".

"Wayne, it was all a joke."

'You did it all only as a joke?'

'Yes,' said Quin.

'When you conceived the idea,' went on Wayne, dreamily, 'of an army for Bayswater and a flag for Notting Hill, there was no gleam, no suggestion in your mind that such things might be real and passionate?'

'No,' answered Auberon, turning his round, white face to the morning with a dull and splendid sincerity; 'I had none at all.'

Wayne sprang down from the height above him and held out his hand.

'I will not stop to thank you,' he said, with a curious joy in his voice, 'for the great good for the world you have actually wrought. All that I think of that I have said to you a moment ago, even when I thought that your voice was the voice of a derisive omnipotence, its laughter older than the winds of heaven. But let me say what is immediate and true. You and I, Auberon Quin, have both of us throughout our lives been again and again called mad. And we are mad. We are mad, because we are not two men but one man. We are mad, because we are two lobes of the same brain, and that brain has been cloven in two. And if you ask for the proof of it, it is not hard to find. It is not merely that you, the humorist, have been in these dark days stripped of the joy of gravity. It is not merely that I, the fanatic, have had to grope without humour. It is that though we seem to be opposite in everything, we have been opposite like man and woman aiming at the same moment at the same practical thing. We are the father and the mother of the Charter of the Cities.'

Quin looked down at the *débris* of leaves and timber, the relics of the battle and stampede, now glistening in the glowing daylight, and finally said:

'Yet nothing can alter the antagonism—the fact that I laughed at these things and you adored them.'

Wayne's wild face flamed with something god-like, as he turned it to be struck by the sunrise.

'I know of something that will alter that antagonism, something that is outside us, something that you and I have all our lives perhaps taken too little account of. The equal and eternal human being will alter that antagonism, for the human being sees no real antagonism between laughter and respect, the human being, the common man, whom mere geniuses like you and me can only worship like a god. When dark and dreary days come, you and I are necessary, the pure fanatic, the pure satirist. We have between us remedied a great wrong. We have lifted the modern cities into that poetry which every one who knows mankind knows to be immeasurably more common than the commonplace. But in healthy people there is no war between us. We are but the two lobes of the brain of a ploughman. Laughter and love are everywhere. The cathedrals, built in the ages that loved God, are full of blasphemous grotesques. The mother laughs continually at the child, the lover laughs continually at the lover, the wife at the husband, the friend at the friend. Auberon Quin, we have been too long separated; let us go out together. You have a halberd and I a sword, let us start our wanderings over the world. For we are its two essentials. Come, it is already day.'

In the blank white light Auberon hesitated a moment. Then he made the formal salute with his halberd, and they went away together into the unknown world.

THE BALL AND THE CROSS

1905

In 1905 Gilbert Chesterton took two or more stories he had written some time earlier and began to adapt them as a serial for *The Commonwealth*, the magazine of the Christian Social Union. What emerged was *The Ball and the Cross*, a study in quarrelling based on the arguments and debates Chesterton had had with a variety of opponents during various soirées held in Bedford Park.

For some unknown reason Chesterton abandoned several successfully launched projects during 1905 and 1906 including *The Ball and the Cross*, but in its case he returned to it some time later when he revised parts of the narrative and rearranged the chapter divisions before completing the novel for publication in the U.S.A. in 1909. We now print the incomplete 1905 version of *The Ball and the Cross* in its chronological place among Chesterton's novels; the full, completed version of 1909 will appear later in Volume VII of *The Collected Works of G. K. Chesterton*.

George J. Marlin

THE BALL AND THE CROSS

I

A DISCUSSION SOMEWHAT IN THE AIR

The flying ship of Professor Lucifer sang through the skies like a silver arrow; the bleak white steel of it, gleaming in the bleak blue emptiness of the evening. That it was far above the earth was no expression of it; to the two men in it, it seemed to be far above the stars. The Professor had himself invented the flying machine, and had also invented nearly everything in it. Every sort of tool or apparatus had, in consequence, to the full, that fantastic and distorted look which belongs to the miracles of science. For the world of science and evolution is far more nameless and elusive and like a dream than the world of poetry or religion; since in these images and ideas remain themselves eternally, while it is the whole idea of evolution that identities melt into each other as they do in a nightmare.

All the tools of Professor Lucifer were the ancient human tools gone mad, grown into unrecognisable shapes, forgetful of their origin, forgetful of their names. That thing which looked like an enormous key with three wheels was really a patent and very deadly revolver. That object which seemed to be created by the entanglement of two corkscrews was really the key. The thing which might have been mistaken for a tricycle turned upside down was the inexpressibly important instrument which the corkscrew was the key to. All these things, as I say, the Professor had invented; he had invented everything in the flying ship, with the exception, perhaps, of himself. This he had been born too late actually to inaugurate, but he believed, at least, that he had considerably improved it.

There was however another man on board, so to speak, at the time. Him, also, by a curious coincidence, the Professor had not invented and him he had not even very greatly improved, though he had fished him up with a lasso out of his own back garden, in Western Bulgaria,

385

with the pure object of improving him. He was an exceedingly holy man, almost entirely covered with white hair. You could see nothing but his eyes, and he seemed to talk with them. A Monk of immense learning and acute intellect he had made himself happy in a little stone hut and a little stony garden in the Balkans, chiefly by writing the most crushing refutations and exposures of certain heresies, the last professors of which had been burnt generally by each other precisely 1,119 years previously. They were really very plausible and thoughtful heresies, and it was really a creditable or even glorious circumstance, that the old Monk had been intellectual enough to detect their fallacy; the only misfortune was that nobody in the modern world was intellectual enough even to understand their argument. The old Monk, one of whose names was Michael, and the other a name quite impossible to remember or repeat in our Western civilisation, had, however, as I have said, made himself quite happy while he was in a mountain hermitage in the society of wild animals. And now that his luck had lifted him above all the mountains in the society of a wild physicist, he made himself happy still.

"I have no intention, my good Michael," said Professor Lucifer, "of endeavouring to convert you by argument. The imbecility of your traditions can be quite finally exhibited to anybody by mere ordinary knowledge of the world, the same kind of knowledge which teaches us not to sit in draughts or not to encourage friendliness in impecunious people. It is folly to talk of this or that demonstrating the rationalist philosophy. Everything demonstrates it. Rubbing shoulders with men of all kinds——"

"You will forgive me," said the Monk, meekly from under loads of white beard, "but I fear I do not understand, was it in order that I might rub my shoulder against men of all kinds that you put me inside this thing?"

"An entertaining retort, in the narrow and deductive manner of the middle ages," replied the Professor, calmly, "but even upon your own basis I will illustrate my point. We are up in the sky. In your religion and all the religions, as far as I know (and I know everything), the sky is made the symbol of everything that is sacred and merciful. Well, now you are in the sky, you know better. Phrase it how you like, twist it how you like, you know that you know better. You know what are a man's real feelings about the heavens, when he finds himself alone in the heavens, surrounded by the heavens. You know the truth, and the truth is this. The heavens are evil, the sky is evil, the stars are evil. This mere space, this mere quantity, terrifies a man more than tigers or the terrible plague. You know that since our science has spoken, the bottom has fallen out of the Universe. Now, heaven is the hopeless thing, more hopeless than any hell. Now, if there be any comfort for all your miserable progeny of morbid apes, it must be in the earth, underneath you, under the roots of the grass, in the place where hell was of old. The fiery crypts, the lurid cellars of the under-world, to which you once condemned the wicked, are hideous enough, but at least they are more homely than the heaven in which we ride. And the time will come when you will all hide in them, to escape the horror of the stars."

"I hope you will excuse my interrupting you," said Michael, with a slight cough, "but I have always noticed——"

"Go on, pray go on," said Professor Lucifer, radiantly, "I really like to draw out your simple ideas."

"Well, the fact is," said the other, "that much as I admire your rhetoric and the rhetoric of your school, from a purely verbal point of view, such little study of you and your school in human history as I have been enabled to make has led me to—er—rather singular conclusion, which I find great difficulty in expressing, especially in a foreign language."

"Come, come," said the Professor, encouragingly, "I'll help you out. How did my view strike you?"

"Well, the truth is, I know I don't express it properly, but somehow it seemed to me that you always convey ideas of that kind with most eloquence, when—er—when——"

"Oh! get on," cried Lucifer, boisterously.

"Well, in point of fact when your flying ship is just going to run into something. I thought you wouldn't mind my mentioning it, but it's running into something now."

Lucifer exploded with an oath and leapt erect, leaning hard upon the handle that acted as a helm to the vessel. For the last 10 minutes they had been shooting downwards into great cracks and caverns of cloud. Now, through a sort of purple haze, could be seen comparatively near to them what seemed to be the upper part of a huge dark orb or sphere, islanded in a sea of cloud. The Professor's eyes were blazing like a maniac's.

"It is a new world," he cried, with a dreadful mirth. "It is a new planet and it shall bear my name. This star and not that other vulgar one[1] shall be 'Lucifer, sun of the morning.' Here we will have no chartered lunacies, here we will have no gods. Here man shall be as innocent as the daisies, as innocent and as cruel—here the intellect——"

"There seems," said Michael, timidly, "to be something sticking up in the middle of it."

"So there is," said the Professor, leaning over the side of the ship, his spectacles shining with intellectual excitement. "What can it be? It might of course be merely a——"

Then a shriek indescribable broke out of him of a sudden, and he flung up his arms like a lost spirit. The Monk took the helm in a tired way; he did not seem much astonished for he came from an igorant part of the world in which it is not uncommon for lost spirits to shriek when they see the curious shape which the Professor had just seen on the top of the mysterious ball, but he took the helm only just in time, and by driving it hard to the left he prevented the flying ship from smashing into St. Paul's Cathedral.

A plain of sad-coloured cloud lay along the level of the top of the Cathedral dome, so that the ball and cross looked like a buoy riding on a leaden sea. As the flying ship swept towards it, this plain of cloud looked as dry and definite and rocky as any grey desert. Hence it gave to the mind and body a sharp and unearthly sensation when the ship cut and sank into the cloud as into any common mist, a thing without resistance. There was, as it were, a deadly shock in the fact that there was no shock. It was as if they had cloven into ancient cliffs like so much butter. But sensations awaited them which were much stranger than those of sinking through the solid earth.

[1] He is referring to the planet Venus when it appears as a morning star.

For a moment their eyes and nostrils were stopped with darkness and opaque cloud; then the darkness warmed into a kind of brown fog. And far, far below them the brown fog fell until it warmed into fire. Through the dense London atmosphere they could see below them the flaming London lights; lights which lay beneath them in squares and oblongs of fire. The fog and fire were mixed in a passionate vapour; you might say that the fog was drowning the flames; or you might say that the flames had set the fog on fire. Beside the ship and beneath it (for it swung just under the ball), the immeasurable dome itself shot out and down into the dark like a combination of voiceless cataracts. Or it was like some cyclopean sea-beast sitting above London and letting down its tentacles bewilderingly on every side, a monstrosity in that starless heaven. For the clouds that belonged to London had closed over the heads of the voyagers sealing up the entrance of the upper air. They had broken through a roof and come into a temple of twilight.

They were so near to the ball that Lucifer leaned his hand against it, holding the vessel away, as men push a boat off from a bank. Above it the cross already draped in the dark mists of the borderland was shadowy and more awful in shape and size.

Professor Lucifer slapped his hand twice upon the surface of the great orb as if he were caressing some enormous animal. "This is the fellow," he said, "this is the one for my money."

"May I with all respect inquire," asked the old Monk, "what on earth you are talking about?"

"Why this," cried Lucifer, smiting the ball again, "here is the only symbol, my boy. So fat. So satisfied. Not like that scraggy individual, stretching his arms in stark weariness." And he pointed up to the cross, his face dark with a grin. "I was telling you just now, Michael, that I can prove the best part of the rationalist case and the Christian humbug from any symbol you like to give me, from any instance I came across. Here is an instance with a vengeance. What could possibly express your philosophy and my philosophy better than the shape of that cross and the shape of this ball? This globe is reasonable; that cross is unreasonable. It is a four-legged animal, with one leg longer than the others. The globe is inevitable. The cross is arbitrary. Above all the globe is at unity with itself; the cross is primarily and above all things at enmity with itself. The cross is the conflict of two hostile lines, of irreconcilable direction. That silent thing up there is essentially a collision, a crash, a struggle in stone. Pah! that sacred symbol of yours has actually given its name to a description of desperation and muddle. When we speak of men at once ignorant of each other and frustrated by each other, we say they are at cross purposes. Away with the thing. The very shape of it is a contradiction in terms."

"What you say is perfectly true," said Michael, with serenity. "But we like contradictions in terms. Man is a contradiction in terms; he is a beast whose superiority to other beasts consists in having fallen. That cross is, as you say, an eternal collision; so am I. That is a struggle in stone. Every form of life is a struggle in flesh. The shape of the cross is irrational, just as the shape of the human animal is irrational. You say the cross is a quadruped with one limb longer than the rest. I say man is a quadruped who only uses two of his legs.

The Professor frowned thoughtfully for an instant, and said: "Of course everything is relative, and I would not deny that the element of struggle and self contradiction, represented by that cross, has a necessary place at a certain evolutionary stage. But surely the cross is the lower development and the sphere the higher. After all it is easy enough to see what is really wrong with Wren's architectural arrangement."

"And what is that, pray?" inquired Michael, meekly.

"The cross is on top of the ball," said Professor Lucifer, simply. "That is surely wrong. The ball should be on top of the cross. The cross is a mere barbaric prop; the ball is perfection. The cross at its best is but the bitter tree of man's history; the ball is the rounded, the ripe and final fruit. And the fruit should be at the top of the tree, not at the bottom of it."

"Oh!" said the Monk, a wrinkle coming into his forehead. "So you think that in a rationalistic scheme of symbolism the ball should be on top of the cross?"

"It sums up my whole allegory," said the Professor.

"Well, that is really very interesting," resumed Michael, slowly, "because I think in that case you would see a most singular effect, an effect that has generally been achieved by all those able and powerful systems which rationalism, or the religion of the ball, has produced to lead or teach mankind. You would see, I think, that thing happen which is always the ultimate embodiment and logical outcome of your logical scheme."

"What are you talking about?" asked Lucifer. "What would happen?"

"I mean it would fall down," said the Monk, looking wistfully into the void.

Lucifer made an angry movement and opened his mouth to speak, but Michael, with all his air of deliberation, was proceeding before he could bring a word out.

"I once knew a man like you, Lucifer," he said, with a maddening monotony and slowness of articulation. "He took this—

"There is no man like me," cried Lucifer, with a violence that shook the ship.

"As I was observing," continued Michael, "this man also took the view that the symbol of Christianity was a symbol of savagery and all unreason. His history is rather amusing. It is also a perfect allegory of what happens to rationalists like yourself. He began, of course, by refusing to allow a crucifix in his house, or round his wife's neck, or even in a picture. He said, as you say, that it was an arbitrary and fantastic shape, that it was a monstrosity, loved because it was paradoxical. Then he began to grow fiercer and more eccentric; he would batter the crosses by the roadside; for he lived in a Roman Catholic country. Finally in a height of frenzy he climbed the steeple of the Parish Church, and tore down the cross, waving it in the air, and uttering wild soliloquies up there under the stars. Then one still summer evening as he was wending his way homewards, along a lane, the devil of his madness came upon him with a violence and transfiguration which changes the world. He was standing smoking, for a moment, in the front of an interminable line of palings, when his eyes were opened. Not a light shifted, not a leaf stirred, but he saw as if by a sudden change in the eyesight that this paling was an army of innumerable crosses linked together over hill and dale. And he whirled up his heavy stick and went at it as if at an army. Mile after mile along his homeward path he broke it down and tore it up. For he hated the cross and every paling is a wall of crosses. When he returned to his house he was a literal madman. He sat upon a chair and then started up from it for the cross bars of the carpentry repeated the intolerable image. He flung himself upon a bed only to remember that this, too, like all workmanlike things, was constructed on the accursed plan. He broke his furniture because it was made of crosses. He burnt his house because it was made of crosses. He was found in the river."

Lucifer was looking at him with a bitten lip.

"Is that story really true?" he asked.

"Oh, no," said Michael, airily. "It is a parable. It is a parable of you and all your rationalists. You begin by breaking up the cross; but you end by breaking up the habitable world. We leave you saying that nobody ought to join the Church against his will. When we meet you again you are saying that no one has any will to join it with. We leave you saying that there is no such place as Eden. We find you saying that there is no such place as Ireland. You start by hating the irrational and you come to hate everything, for everything is irrational and so——"

Lucifer leapt upon him with a cry like a wild beast's. "Ah," he screamed, "to every man his madness. You are mad on the cross. Let it save you."

And with a herculean energy he forced the Monk backwards out of the reeling car on to the upper part of the stone ball. Michael, with as abrupt an agility, caught one of the beams of the cross and saved himself from falling. At the same instant Lucifer drove down a lever and the ship shot up with him in it alone.

"Ha! ha!" he yelled, "what sort of a support do you find it, old fellow?"

"For practical purposes of support," replied Michael, grimly, "it is at any rate a great deal better than the ball. May I ask if you are going to leave me here?"

"Yes, yes. I mount! I mount!" cried the Professor, in ungovernable excitement "Altiora peto.[2] My path is upward."

"How often have you told me, Professor, that there is really no up or down in space?" said the Monk. "I shall mount up as much as you will."

"Indeed," said Lucifer, leering over the side of the flying ship. "May I ask what you are going to do?"

The Monk pointed downward at Ludgate Hill. "I am going," he said, "to climb up into a star."

---

[2] This is Latin for "I burst out to the heights".

Those who look at the matter most superficially regard paradox as something which belongs to jesting and light journalism. Paradox of this kind is to be found in the saying of the dandy, in the decadent comedy,[3] "Life is much too important to be taken seriously." Those who look at the matter a little more deeply or delicately see that paradox is a thing which especially belongs to all religions. Paradox of this kind is to be found in such a saying as "The meek shall inherit the earth." But those who see and feel the fundamental fact of the matter know that paradox is a thing that belongs not to religion only, but to all vivid and violent practical crises of human living. Paradox of this kind may be clearly perceived by anybody who happens to be hanging in mid space, clinging to one arm of the cross of St. Paul's.

Father Michael, in spite of his years, and in spite of his asceticism (or because of it, for all I know) was a very healthy and happy old gentleman. And as he swung on a bar above the sickening emptiness of air, he realised, with that sort of dead detachment which belongs to the brains of those in peril, the deathless and hopeless contradiction which is involved in the mere idea of courage. He was a happy and healthy old gentleman and therefore he was quite careless with it. And he felt as every man feels in the taut moment of such terror that his chief danger was terror itself; his only possible strength would be a coolness amounting to carelessness, a carelessness amounting almost to a suicidal swagger. His one wild chance of coming out safely would be in not too desperately desiring to be safe. There might be footholds down that awful facade, if only he could not care whether they were footholds or no. If he were foolhardy he might escape; if he were wise he would stop where he was till he dropped from the cross like a stone. And this antinomy kept on repeating itself in his mind, a contradiction as large and staring as the immense contradiction of the Cross; he remembered having often heard the words, "Whosoever shall lose his life the same shall save it." He remembered with a sort of strange pity that this had always been made to mean that whoever lost his physical life should save his spiritual life. Now he knew the truth that is known to all fighters, and hunters, and climbers of

[3] This is a reference to Oscar Wilde's *The Importance of being Earnest* (1895).

cliffs. He knew that even his animal life could only be saved by a considerable readiness to lose it.

Some will think it improbable that a human soul swinging desperately in mid air should think about philosophical inconsistencies. But such extreme states are dangerous things to dogmatise about. Frequently they produce a certain useless and joyless activity of the mere intellect, thought not only divorced from hope but even from desire. And if it is impossible to dogmatise about such states, it is still more impossible to describe them. To this spasm of sanity and clarity in Michael's mind succeeded a spasm of the elemental terror; the terror of the animal in us which regards the whole universe as its enemy; which, when it is victorious, has no pity, and so, when it is defeated has no imaginable hope. Of that ten minutes of terror it is not possible to speak in human words. But then again in that damnable darkness there began to grow a strange dawn as of grey and pale silver. And of this ultimate resignation or certainty it is even less possible to write; it is something stranger than hell itself; it is perhaps the last of the secrets of God. At the highest crisis of some incurable anguish there will suddenly fall upon the man the stillness of an insane contentment. It is not hope, for hope is broken and romantic and concerned with the future; this is complete and of the present. It is not faith, for faith by its very nature is fierce, and as it were at once doubtful and defiant; but this is simply a satisfaction. It is not knowledge, for the intellect seems to have no particular part in it. Nor is it (as the modern idiots would certainly say it is) a mere numbness or negative paralysis of the powers of grief. It is not negative in the least; it is as positive as good news. In some sense, indeed, it is good news. It seems almost as if there were some equality among things, some balance in all possible contingencies which we are not permitted to know lest we should learn indifference to good and evil, but which is sometimes shown to us for an instant as a last aid in our last agony.

Michael certainly could not have given any sort of rational account of this vast unmeaning satisfaction which soaked through him and filled him to the brim. He felt with sort of half-witted lucidity that the cross was there, and the ball was there and the dome was there, that he was going to climb down from them, and that he did not mind in the least whether he was killed or not. This mysterious mood lasted long enough to start him on his dreadful descent and to force him to continue it. But six times before he reached the highest of the outer galleries terror had returned on him like a flying storm of darkness and thunder. By the time he had reached that place of safety he almost felt (as in some impossible fit of drunkenness) that he had two heads; one was calm, careless and efficient; the other saw the danger like a deadly map, was wise, careful and useless. He had fancied that he would have to let himself vertically down the face of the whole building. When he dropped into the upper gallery he still felt as far from the terrestrial globe as if he had only dropped from the sun to the moon. He paused a little, panting in the gallery under the ball, and idly kicked his heels, moving a few yards along it. And as he did so a thunderbolt struck his soul. A man, a heavy ordinary man, with a composed indifferent face, and a prosaic sort of uniform; with a row of buttons, blocked his way. Michael had no mind to wonder whether this solid astonished man, with the brown moustache and the nickel buttons had also come on a flying ship. He merely let his mind float in an endless felicity about the man. He thought how nice it would be if he had to live up in that gallery with that one man for ever. He thought how he would luxuriate in the nameless shades of this man's soul and then hear with an endless excitement about the nameless shades of the souls of all his aunts and uncles. A moment before he had been dying alone. Now he was living in the same world with a man; an inexhaustible ecstacy. In the gallery below the ball Father Michael had found that man who is the noblest and most divine and most lovable of all men, better than all the saints, greater than all the heroes — man Friday.[4]

In the confused colour and music of his new paradise, Michael heard only in a faint and distant fashion some remarks that this beautiful solid man seemed to be making to him; remarks about some thing or other being after hours and against orders. He also seemed to

[4] Friday was the first human encountered by Crusoe after many years of isolation on his island in *Robinson Crusoe* (1719) by Daniel Defoe (1660–1731).

be asking how Michael "got up" there. This beautiful man evidently felt as Michael did that the earth was a star and was set in heaven.

At length Michael sated himself with the mere sensual music of the voice of the man in buttons. He began to listen to what he said, and even to make some attempt at answering a question which appeared to have been put several times and was now put with some excess of emphasis. Michael realised that the image of God in nickel buttons was asking him how he had come there. He said that he had come in Lucifer's ship. On his giving this answer the demeanour of the image of God underwent a remarkable change. From addressing Michael gruffly, as if he were a malefactor, he began suddenly to speak to him with a sort of eager and feverish amiability as if he were a child. He seemed particularly anxious to coax him away from the balustrade. He led him by the arm towards a door leading into the building itself, soothing him all the time. He gave what even Michael (slight as was his knowledge of the world) felt to be an improbable account of the sumptuous pleasures and varied advantages awaiting him downstairs. Michael followed him, however, if only out of politeness, down an apparently interminable spiral of staircase. At once point a door opened. Michael stepped through it, and the unaccountable man in buttons leapt after him and pinioned him where he stood. But he only wished to stand; to stand and stare. He had stepped as it were into another infinity, out under the dome of another heaven. But this was a dome of heaven made by man. The gold, and green, and crimson of its sunset were not in the shapeless clouds but in shapes of cherubim and seraphim, awful human shapes with a passionate plumage. Its stars were not above but far below, like fallen stars still in unbroken constellations; the dome itself was full of darkness. And far below, lower even than the lights, could be seen creeping or motionless, great black masses of men. The tongue of a terrible organ seemed to shake the very air in the whole void; and through it there came up to Michael the sound of a tongue more terrible; the dreadful everlasting voice of man, calling to his gods from the beginning to the end of the world. Michael felt almost as if he were a god, and all the voices were hurled at him.

"No, the pretty things aren't here," said the demi-god, in buttons, caressingly. "The pretty things are down stairs. You come along with me. There's something that will surprise you down stairs; something you want very much to see."

Evidently the man in buttons did not feel like a god, so Michael made no attempt to explain his feelings to him, but followed him meekly enough down the trail of the serpentine staircase. He had no notion where or at what level he was. He was still full of the cold splendour of space, and of what a French writer has brilliantly named the "vertigo of the infinite," when another door opened, and with a shock indescribable he found himself on the familiar level, in a street full of faces, with the houses and even the lamp-posts above his head. He felt suddenly happy and suddenly indescribably small. He fancied he had been changed into a child again; his eyes sought the pavement seriously as children's do as if it were a thing with which something satisfactory could be done. He felt the full warmth of that pleasure from which the proud shut themselves out; the pleasure which not only goes with humiliation, but which almost is humiliation. Men who have escaped death by a hair have it, and men whose love is returned by a woman unexpectedly, and men whose sins are forgiven them. Everything his eye fell on it feasted on, not aesthetically, but with a plain, jolly appetite as of a boy eating buns. He relished the squareness of the houses; he liked their clean angles as if he had just cut them with a knife. The lit squares of the shop windows excited him as the young are excited by the lit stage of some promising pantomime. He happened to see in one shop which projected with a bulging bravery on to the pavement some square tins of potted meat, and it seemed like a hint of a hundred hilarious high teas in a hundred streets of the world. He was, perhaps, the happiest of all the children of men. For in that unendurable instant when he hung, half slipping, to the ball of St. Paul's, the whole universe had been destroyed and re-created.

Suddenly through all the din of the dark streets came a crash of glass. With that mysterious suddenness of the Cockney mob, a rush was made in the right direction, a dingy office, next to the shop of the potted meat. The pane of glass was lying in splinters about the pavement. And the police already had their hands on a very tall young man, with dark lank hair and dark dazed eyes, with a grey plaid over his shoulder, who had just smashed the shop window with a single blow of his stick.

"I'd do it again," said the young man, with a furious white face. "Anybody would have done it. Did you see what it said? I swear I'd do it again." Then his eyes encountered the monkish habit of Michael and he pulled off his grey tam o'shanter with the gesture of a Catholic.

"Father, did you see what they said?" he cried trembling. "Did you see what they dared to say? I didn't understand it at first. I read it half through before I broke the window."

Michael felt he knew not how. The whole peace of the world was pentup painfully in his heart. The new and child-like world which he had seen so suddenly, men had not seen at all. Here they were still at their old bewildering, pardonable, useless quarrels, with so much to be said on both sides, and so little that need be said at all. A fierce inspiration fell on him suddenly; he would strike them where they stood with the love of God. They should not move till they saw their own sweet and startling existence. They should not go from that place till they went home embracing like brothers and shouting like men delivered. From the cross from which he had fallen fell the shadow of its fantastic mercy; and the first three words he spoke in a voice like a silver trumpet, held men as still as stones. Perhaps if he had spoken there for an hour in his illumination he might have founded a religion on Ludgate Hill. But the heavy hand of his guide fell suddenly on his shoulder.

"This poor fellow is dotty," he said good humouredly to the crowd. "I found him wandering in the Cathedral. Says he came in a flying ship. Is there a constable to spare to take care of him?"

There was a constable to spare. Two other constables attended to the tall, young man in grey; a fourth concerned himself with the owner of the shop who showed some tendency to be turbulent. They took the tall, young man away to a magistrate, whither we shall follow him in an ensuing chapter. And they took the happiest man in the world away to an Asylum.

THE RELIGION OF THE
STIPENDIARY MAGISTRATE

The editorial office of "The Atheist" had for some years past become less and less prominently interesting as a feature of Ludgate Hill. The paper was unsuited to the atmosphere. It showed an interest in the Bible unknown in the district, and a knowledge of that volume to which nobody else on Ludgate Hill could make any conspicuous claim. It was in vain that the editor of "The Atheist"[5] filled his front window with fierce and final demands as to what Noah in the Ark did with the neck of the Giraffe. It was in vain that he asked violently, as for the last time, how the statement "God is Spirit" could be reconciled with the statement "The earth is His footstool." It was in vain that he cried with an accusing energy that the Bishop of London was paid £12,000 a year for pretending to believe that the whale swallowed Jonah. It was in vain that he hung in conspicuous places the most thrilling scientific calculations about the width of the throat of a whale. Was it nothing to them all they that passed by? Did this sudden, and splendid, and truly sincere indignation never stir any of the people pouring down Ludgate Hill? Never. The little man who edited "The Atheist" would rush from his shop on starlit evenings and shake his fist at St. Paul's in the passion of his holy war upon the holy place. He might have spared his emotion. The cross at the top of St. Paul's and "The Atheist" shop at the foot of it were alike remote from the world. The shop and the Cross were equally uplifted and alone in the empty heavens.

To the little man who edited "The Atheist," a fiery little Scotchman, with fiery red hair and beard,[6] going by the name of Turnbull, all this decline in public importance seemed not so much sad or

---

[5] *The Atheist* is fictitious but seems to reflect the tone of *The Freethinker*, edited by George William Foote (1850–1915).

[6] The figure of Turnbull is probably based on Archie MacGregor, a denizen of Bedford Park and a friend of Yeats'. Chesterton described him "a fighting atheist . . . defending against the new ethic of Nietzsche the old ethic of Naboth."

even mad but merely bewildering and unaccountable. He had said
the worst thing that could be said; and it seemed accepted and ignored like the ordinary second best of the politicians. Every day his
blasphemies looked more glaring, and every day the dust lay thicker
upon them. It made him feel as if he were moving in a world of
idiots. He seemed among a race of men who smiled when told of
their own death, or looked vacantly at the day of judgment. Year
after year went by, and year after year the death of God in a shop in
Ludgate became a less and less important occurrence. All the forward men of his age discouraged Turnbull. The socialists said he was
cursing priests when he should be cursing capitalists. The artists said
that the soul was most spiritual, not when freed from religion, but
when freed from morality. Year after year went by and at last a man
came by who treated Mr. Turnbull's secularist shop with a real respect and seriousness. He was a young man, in a grey plaid, and he
smashed the window.

He was a young man, born in the Bay of Arishaig, opposite Rum
and the Isle of Skye. His high hawk-like features and snakey black
hair bore the mark of that unknown historic thing which is crudely
called Celtic, but which is probably far older than the Celts,
whoever they were. He was in name and stock a Highlander of the
Macdonalds; but his family took as was common in such cases, the
name of a subordinate sept as a surname, and for all the purposes
which could be answered in London, he called himself Evan MacIan.
He had been brought up in some loneliness and seclusion as a strict
Roman Catholic, in the midst of that little wedge of Roman Catholics which is driven into the Western Highlands. And he had found
his way as far as Fleet Street, seeking some half-promised employment, without having properly realised that there were in the world
any people who were not Roman Catholics. He had uncovered himself for a few moments before the statue of Queen Anne, in front of
St. Paul's Cathedral, under the firm impression that it was a figure
of the Virgin Mary. He was somewhat surprised at the lack of
deference shown to the figure by the people bustling by. He did not
understand that their one essential historical principle, the one law
truly graven on their hearts was the great and comforting statement

that Queen Anne is dead.[7] This faith was as fundamental as his faith, that Our Lady was alive. Any persons he had talked to since he had touched the fringe of our fashion or civilisation had been by a coincidence sympathetic or hypocritical. Or if they had spoken some established blasphemies, he had been unable to understand them merely owing to the pre-occupied satisfaction of his mind.

On that fantastic fringe of the Gaelic land where he walked as a boy, the cliffs were as fantastic as the clouds. Heaven seemed to humble itself and come closer to the earth. The common paths of his little village began to climb quite suddenly and seemed resolved to go to heaven. The sky seemed to fall down towards the hills; the hills took hold upon the sky. In the sumptuous sunset of gold and purple and peacock green cloudlets and islets were the same. Evan lived like a man walking on a borderland, the borderland between this world and another. Like so many men and nations who grow up with nature and the common things, he understood the supernatural before he understood the natural. He had looked at dim angels standing knee deep in the grass before he had looked at the grass. He knew that Our Lady's robes were blue before he knew the wild roses round her feet were red. The deeper his memory plunged into the dark house of childhood the nearer and nearer he came to the things that cannot be named. All through his life he thought of the daylight world as a sort of divine debris, the broken remainder of his first vision. The skies and mountains were the splendid off scourings of another place. The stars were lost jewels of the Queen. Our Lady had gone and left the stars by accident.

His private tradition was equally wild and unworldly. His great grandfather had been cut down at Culloden,[8] certain in his last instant, that God would restore the King.[9] His grandfather, then a

---

[7] "Queen Anne is dead" is a semi-proverbial riposte to stale news with the meaning of "tell me something new". Queen Anne (1702–14) was the last of the Stuart line and died without live issue, and the succession passed to the House of Hanover or of Brunswick.

[8] Culloden was the final decisive battle of the Jacobite rebellion when in 1746, on a moor near Inverness, the highlanders of Bonnie Prince Charlie (Prince Charles Edward Stuart, grandson of James II and known as the young pretender) were defeated by the forces of the Duke of Cumberland.

[9] The King referred to is James III, the Old Pretender (1688–1766), father of Bonnie Prince Charlie (1720–88).

boy of 10, had taken the terrible claymore from the hand of the dead and hung it up in his house, burnishing it and sharpening it for 60 years, to be ready for the next rebellion. His father, the youngest son and the last left alive, had refused to attend on Queen Victoria in Scotland.[10] And Evan himself had been of one piece with his progenitors; and was not dead with them, but alive in the twentieth century. He was not in the least the pathetic Jacobite of whom we read, left behind by a final advance of all things. He was, in his own fancy, a conspirator, fierce and up to date. In the long, dark afternoons of the Highland winter, he plotted and fumed in the dark. He drew plans of the capture of London on the desolate sand of Arishaig.

When he came up to capture London, it was not with an army of white Cockades,[11] but with a stick and a satchel. London overawed him a little, not because he thought it grand or even terrible, but because it bewildered him; it was not the Golden City or even hell; it was Limbo. He had one shock of sentiment, when he turned that wonderful corner of Fleet Street and saw St. Paul's sitting in the sky.

"Ah," he said, after a long pause, "that sort of thing was built under the Stuarts." Then with a sour grin he asked himself what was the corresponding monument of the Brunswicks[12] and the Protestant Constitution.[13] After some warning, he selected a sky-sign of some pill.

Half-an-hour afterwards his emotions left him with an emptied

[10] Scotland and things Scottish were rediscovered when George IV visited Edinburgh to be greeted by chieftains organized for the occasion by Sir Walter Scott. Even George IV wore a kilt. However, some Scottish nationalists refused to take part because they did not recognize the Hanoverian monarchs, and so, when Queen Victoria and Prince Albert became the hub of a Scottish cult at Balmoral, many Scots refused to join in.

[11] White Cockades referred to the badge that the Highlanders and later the Jacobites wore in their hats.

[12] The Brunswicks were the Royal House of Hanover, which in the person of George I acceded to the English throne in 1714, and by the Act of Union of 1707 to the Scottish throne.

[13] The Protestant Constitution was basically the Bill of Rights of 1689, assented to by William III and Mary II when they accepted the throne, taken together with the Act of Settlement of 1701. Both documents laid down the succession and debarred Roman Catholics from the throne.

mind on the same spot. And it was in a mood of mere idle investigation that he happened to come to a standstill opposite the office of "The Atheist." He did not see the word "atheist," or if he did, it is quite possible that he did not know the meaning of the word. Even as it was, the document would not have shocked even the innocent Highlander, but for the troublesome and quite unforeseen fact that the innocent Highlander read it stolidly to the end; a thing unknown among the most enthusiastic subscribers to the paper, and calculated in any case to create a new situation.

With a smart journalistic instinct characteristic of all his school, the editor of "The Atheist" had put first in his paper and most prominently in his window, an article called "The Mesopotamian Mythology and its effects on the Syriac Folk Lore." Mr. Evan Mac-Ian began to read this quite idly as he would have read a public statement beginning with a young girl dying in Brighton and ending with Bile Beans.[14] He received the very considerable amount of information accumulated by the author with that tired clearness of the mind which children have on heavy summer afternoons—that tired clearness which leads them to go on asking questions long after they have lost interest in the subject and are as bored as their nurse. The streets were full of people and empty of adventures. He might as well know about the Gods of Mesopotamia as not; so he flattened his long, lean face against the dim bleak pane of the window and read all there was to read about the Mesopotamian Gods. He read how the Mesopotamians had a God named Sho (sometimes pronounced Ji), and that he was described as being very powerful, a striking similarity to some expressions about Jahveh, who is also described as having power. Evan had never heard of Jahveh, in his life, and imagining him to be some other Mesopotamian idol, read on with a dull curiosity. He learnt that the name Sho, under its third form of Psa, occurs in an early legend which describes how the deity, after the manner of Jupiter on so many occasions, seduced a Virgin and begat a hero. This hero, whose name is not essential to our existence, was, it was said, the chief hero and Saviour of the Mesopotamian ethical scheme. Then

[14] Bile beans were a proprietary pick-me-up and general panacea.

followed a paragraph giving other examples of such heroes and
Saviours being born of some profligate intercourse between God and
mortal. Then followed a paragraph—but Evan did not understand
it. He read it again and then again. Then he did understand it. The
glass fell in ringing fragments on to the pavements, and Evan sprang
over the barrier into the shop, brandishing his stick.

"What is this," cried little Mr. Turnbull, starting up with hair
aflame. "How dare you break my window?"

"Because it was the quickest cut to you," cried Evan, stamping.
"Stand up and fight, you crapulous coward. You dirty lunatic, stand
up, will you! Have you any weapons here?"

"Are you mad?" asked Turnbull, glaring.

"Are you?" cried Evan. "Can you be anything else when you
plaster your own house with that God-defying filth. Stand up and
fight, I say."

A great light like dawn came into Mr. Turnbull's face. Behind his
red hair and beard he turned deadly pale with pleasure. Here, after
20 lone years of useless toil, he had his reward. Someone was angry
with the paper. He bounded to his feet like a boy; he saw a new
youth opening before him. And as not unfrequently happens to middle aged gentlemen when they see a new youth opening before
them, he found himself in the presence of the police.

The policemen, after some ponderous questionings, collared both
the two enthusiasts. They were more respectful, however, to the
young man who had smashed the window, than to the miscreant
who had had his window smashed. There was an air of refined
mystery about Evan MacIan, which did not exist in the irate little
shopkeeper, an air of refined mystery which appealed to the
policemen, for policemen, like most other English types, are at once
snobs and poets. MacIan might possibly be a gentleman, they felt,
the Editor manifestly was not. And the Editor's fine rational
republican appeals to his respect for law, and his ardour to be tried
by his fellow citizens, seemed to the police quite as much gibberish
as Evan's mysticism could have done. The police were not used to
hearing principles, even the principles of their own existence.

The police magistrate, before whom they were hurried and tried,

was a Mr. Cumberland Vane, a cheerful, middle-aged gentleman, hon-
ourably celebrated for the lightness of his sentences and the lightness of
his conversation. He occasionally worked himself up into a sort of theoretic rage about certain particular offenders, such as the men who took
pokers to their wives, talked in a loose, sentimental way about the de-
sirability of flogging them, and was hopelessly bewildered by the fact
that the wives seemed even more angry with him than with their hus-
bands. He was a tall, spruce man, with a twist of black moustache and
incomparable morning dress. He looked like a gentleman, and yet,
somehow, like a stage gentleman.

He had often treated serious crimes against mere order or property
with a humane flippancy. Hence, about the mere breaking of an
Editor's window, he was almost uproarious.

"Come, Mr. MacIan, come," he said, leaning back in his chair,
"do you generally enter your friends' houses by walking through the
glass?" (Laughter.)

"He is not my friend," said Evan, with the stolidity of a dull child.

"Not your friend, eh?" said the magistrate, sparkling. "Is he your
brother-in-law?" (Loud and prolonged laughter.)

"He is my enemy," said Evan, simply; "he is the enemy of God."

Mr. Vane shifted sharply in his seat, dropping the eye-glass out of
his eye in a momentary and not unmanly embarrassment.

"You mustn't talk like that here," he said, roughly, and in a kind
of hurry, "that has nothing to do with us."

Evan opened his great, blue eyes; "God," he began.

"Be quiet," said the magistrate, angrily, "it is most undesirable
that things of that sort should be spoken about—a—in public, and
in an ordinary Court of Justice. Religion is—a—too personal a matter to be mentioned in such a place."

"Is it?" answered the Highlander, "then what did those policemen swear by just now?"

"That is no parallel," answered Vane, rather irritably; "of course
there is a form of oath—to be taken reverently—reverently, and there's
an end of it. But to talk in a public place about one's most sacred and
private sentiments—well, I call it bad taste. (Slight applause.) I call it irreverent. I call it irreverent, and I'm not specially orthodox either."

"I see you are not," said Evan, "but I am."

"We are wandering from the point," said the police magistrate, pulling himself together.

"May I ask why you smashed this worthy citizen's window?"

Evan turned a little pale at the mere memory, but he answered with the same cold and deadly literalism that he showed throughout.

"Because he blasphemed Our Lady."

"I tell you once and for all," cried Mr. Cumberland Vane, rapping his knuckles angrily on the table, "I tell you, once for all, my man, that I will not have you turning on any religious rant or cant here. Don't imagine that it will impress me. The most religious people are not those who talk about it. (Applause.) You answer the questions and do nothing else."

"I did nothing else," said Evan, with a slight smile.

"Eh," cried Vane, glaring through his eyeglass.

"You asked me why I broke his window," said MacIan, with a face of wood. "I answered. 'Because he blasphemed Our Lady.' I had no other reason. So I have no other answer." Vane continued to gaze at him with a sternness not habitual to him.

"You are not going the right way to work, Sir," he said, with severity. "You are not going the right way to work to—a—have your case treated with special consideration. If you had simply expressed regret for what you had done, I should have been strongly inclined to dismiss the matter as an outbreak of temper. Even now, if you say that you are sorry I shall only—"

"But I am not in the least sorry," said Evan, "I am very pleased."

"I really believe you are insane," said the stipendiary, indignantly, for he had really been doing his best as a good-natured man, to compose the dispute. "What conceivable right have you to break other people's windows because their opinions do not agree with yours? This man only gave expression to his sincere belief."

"So did I," said the Highlander.

"And who are you?" exploded Vane. "Are your views necessarily the right ones? Are you necessarily in possession of the truth?"

"Yes," said MacIan.

The magistrate broke into a contemptuous laugh.

"Oh, you want a nurse to look after you," he said. "You must pay £10."

Evan MacIan plunged his hands into his loose grey garments and drew out a queer looking leather purse. It contained exactly 12 sovereigns. He paid down the 10, coin by coin, in silence, and equally silently returned the remaining two to the receptacle. Then he said, "May I say a word, your worship."

Cumberland Vane seemed half hypnotised with the silence and automatic movements of the stranger; he made a movement with his head, which might have been either "yes" or "no." "I only wished to say, your worship," said MacIan, putting back the purse in his trouser pocket, "that smashing that shop window was, I confess a useless and rather irregular business. It may be excused, however, as a mere preliminary to further proceedings, a sort of preface. Wherever and whenever I meet that man," and he pointed to the Editor of *The Atheist*, "whether it be outside this door in 10 minutes from now, or 20 years hence in some distant country, wherever and whenever I meet that man, I will fight him. Do not be afraid, I will not rush at him like a bully, or bear him down with any brute superiority. I will fight him like a gentleman; I will fight him as our fathers fought. He shall choose how, sword or pistol, horse or foot. But if he refuses, I will write his cowardice on every wall in the world. If he had said of my mother what he said of the Mother of God, there is not a club of clean men in Europe that would deny my right to call him out. If he had said it of my wife, you English would yourselves have pardoned me for beating him like a dog in the market place. Your worship, I have no mother; I have no wife. I have only that which the poor have equally with the rich; which the lonely have equally with the man of many friends. To me this whole strange world is homely because in the heart of it there is a home; to me this cruel world is kindly, because higher than the heavens there is something more human than humanity. If a man must not fight for this, may he fight for anything? I would fight for my friend, but if I lost my friend, I should still be there. I would fight for my country, but if I lost my country, I should still exist. But if what that devil dreams were true, I should not be—I should burst like a bubble and be gone. I could not live in that imbecile universe. Shall I not fight for my own existence?"

The magistrate recovered his voice and his presence of mind. The first part of the speech, the bombastic and brutally practical challenge, stunned him with surprise; but the rest of Evan's remarks branching off as they did into theoretic phrases, gave his vague and very English mind (full of memories of the hedging and compromise in English public speaking), an indistinct sensation of relief, as if the man, though mad, were not so dangerous as he had thought. He went into a sort of weary laughter.

"For Heaven's sake, man," he said, "don't talk so much. Let other people have a chance (laughter). I trust all that you said about asking Mr. Turnbull to fight, may be regarded as rubbish. In case of accidents, however, I must bind you over to keep the peace."

"To keep the peace," repeated Evan, "with whom?"

"With Turnbull," said Vane.

"Certainly not," answered MacIan. "What has he to do with peace?"

"Do you mean to say," began the magistrate, "that you refuse to . . ." The voice of Turnbull himself clove in for the first time.

"Might I suggest," he said, "that I, your worship, can settle to some extent this absurd matter myself. This rather wild gentleman promises that he will not attack me with any ordinary assault — and if he does, you may be sure the police shall hear of it. But he says he will not. He says he will challenge me to a duel; and I cannot say anything stronger about his mental state than to say that I think that it is highly probable that he will. (Laughter.) But it takes two to make a duel, your worship (renewed laughter). I do not in the least mind being described on every wall in the world as the coward who would not fight a man in Fleet Street, about whether the Virgin Mary had a parallel in Mesopotamian mythology. No, your worship. You need not trouble to bind him over to keep the peace. I bind myself over to keep the peace, and you may rest quite satisfied that there will be no duel with me in it."

Mr. Cumberland Vane rolled about, laughing in a sort of relief.

"You're like a breath of April air, sir," he cried. "You're ozone after that fellow. You're perfectly right. Perhaps I have taken the thing too seriously. I should love to see him sending you challenges and to see you smiling. Well, well."

Evan went out of the Court of Justice free, but strangely shaken, like a sick man. Any punishment or suppression he would have felt as natural; but the sudden juncture between the laughter of his judge and the laughter of the man he had wronged, made him feel suddenly small, or at least, defeated. It was really true that the whole modern world regarded his world as a bubble. No cruelty could have shown it, but their kindness showed it with a ghastly clearness. As he was brooding, he suddenly became conscious of a small, stern figure, fronting him in silence. Its eyes were grey and awful, and its beard red. It was Turnbull.

"Well, sir," said the Editor of *The Atheist*, "where is the fight to be. Name the field, sir."

Evan stood thunderstruck. He stammered out something, he knew not what; he only guessed it by the answer of the other.

"Do I want to fight? Do I want to fight?" cried the furious Freethinker. "Why, you moonstruck scarecrow of superstition, do you think your dirty saints are the only people who can die? Haven't you hung atheists and burned them, and boiled them, and did they ever deny their faith? Do you think we don't want to fight? Night and day I have prayed—I have longed—for an atheist revolution—I have longed to see your blood and ours in the streets. Let it be yours or mine?"

"But you said . . ." began MacIan.

"I know," said Turnbull, scornfully. "And what did you say? You damned fool, you said things that might have got us locked up for a year, and shadowed by the coppers for half a decade. If you wanted to fight, why did you tell that ass you wanted to? I got you out, to fight if you want to. Now, fight if you dare."

"I swear to you, then," said MacIan, after a pause. "I swear to you that nothing shall come between us. I swear to you that nothing shall be in my heart or in my head till our swords clash together. I swear it by the God you have denied, by the Blessed Lady you have blasphemed; I swear it by the seven swords in her heart. I swear it by the Holy Island where my fathers are,[15] by the honour of my mother, by the secret of my people, and by the chalice of the blood of God."

The atheist drew up his head. "And I," he said, "give my word."

[15] "The Holy Island where my fathers are" is probably Iona.

III

SOME OLD CURIOSITIES

The evening sky, a dome of solid gold, unflaked even by a single sunset cloud, steeped the meanest sights of London in a strange and mellow light. It made a little greasy street off St. Martin's Lane look as if it were paved with gold. It made the Pawnbroker's half way down it shine as if it were really that Mountain of Piety[16] that the French poetic instinct has named it; it made the mean pseudo-French bookshop, next but one to it, a shop packed with dreary indecency, show for a moment a kind of Parisian Colours. And the shop that stood between the pawnshop and the shop of dreary indecency, showed with quite a blaze of old world beauty, for it was, by accident, a shop not unbeautiful in itself. The front window had a glimmer of bronze and blue steel, lit, as by a few stars, by the sparks of what were alleged to be jewels; for it was in brief, a shop of bric-a-brac and Old Curiosities. A row of half burnished Seventeenth Century swords ran like an ornate railing along the front of the window; behind was a darker glimmer of old oak and old armour; and higher up hung the most extraordinary looking South Sea tools or utensils, whether designed for killing enemies or merely for cooking them, no mere white man could possibly conjecture. But the romance of the eye, which really on this rich evening, clung about the shop, had its main source in the accident of two doors standing open, the front door that opened on the street and a back door that opened on an odd green square of garden, that the sun turned to a square of gold. There is nothing more beautiful than thus to look as it were through the archway of a house; as if the open sky were an interior chamber, and the sun a secret lamp of the place.

I have suggested that the sunset light made everything lovely. To say that it made the Keeper of the Curiosity Shop lovely would be a tribute to it perhaps too extreme. It would easily have made him beautiful if he had been merely squalid; if he had been a Jew of the Fagin

[16] "Mountain of Piety" is from the French *Mont de piété*, which in turn is derived from the Italian *Monte di pietà*, meaning bank of charity.

type. But he was a Jew of another and much less admirable type; a Jew with a very well sounding name. For though there are no hard tests for separating the tares and wheat of any people; one rude but efficient guide is that the nice Jew is called Moses Solomon, and the nasty Jew is called Thornton Percy. The Keeper of the Curiosity Shop was of the Thornton Percy branch of the Chosen People; he belonged to those Lost Ten Tribes[17] whose industrious object is to lose themselves. He was a man still young, but already corpulent, with sleek dark hair, heavy handsome clothes, and a full, fat, permanent smile which looked at the first glance kindly, and at the second cowardly. The name over his shop was Henry Gordon, but two Scotchmen who were in his shop that evening could come upon no trace of a Scotch accent.

These two Scotchmen in this shop were careful purchasers, but free-handed payers. One of them who seemed to be the principal and the authority (whom, indeed, Mr. Henry Gordon fancied he had seen somewhere before), was a small, sturdy fellow, with fine grey eyes, a square red tie and a square red beard, that he carried aggressively forward as if he defied anyone to pull it. The other kept so much in the background in comparison that he looked almost ghostly in his grey cloak or plaid, a tall, sallow, silent young man.

The two Scotchmen were interested in Seventeenth Century swords. They were fastidious about them. They had a whole armory of these weapons brought out and rolled clattering about the counter, until they found two of precisely the same length. Presumably they desired the exact symmetry for some decorative trophy. Even then they felt the points, poised the swords for balance and bent them in a circle to see that they sprang straight again; which, for decorative purposes, seems carrying realism rather far.

"These will do," said the strange person with the red beard. "And perhaps I had better pay for them at once. And as you are the challenger, Mr. MacIan, perhaps you had better explain the situation."

[17] The Lost Ten Tribes of Israel were the ten tribes forming the Kingdom of Israel, as opposed to the kingdom of Judah, which was made up of the other two tribes after the death of Solomon (c. 930 B.C.). After defeat by the Chaldeans, they were transported to captivity in Babylon, but when Cyrus granted freedom to the Jews only the two tribes of Judah returned. The fate of the ten tribes is unknown, but they were no doubt assimilated.

The tall Scotchman and grey took a step forward and spoke in a voice quite clear and bold, and yet somehow lifeless, like a man going through an ancient formality.

"The fact is, Mr. Gordon, we have to place our honour in your hands. Words have passed between Mr. Turnbull and myself on a grave and invaluable matter, which can only be atoned for by fighting. Unfortunately, as the police are in some sense pursuing us we are hurried, and must fight now and without seconds. But if you will be so kind as to take us into your little garden and see fair play, we shall feel how——"

The shopman recovered himself from a stunning surprise and burst out—

"Gentlemen, are you drunk? A duel! A duel in my garden. Go home, gentlemen, go home. Why, what did you quarrel about?"

"We quarrelled," said Evan, in the same dead voice, "about religion." The fat shopkeeper rolled about in his chair with enjoyment.

"Well, this is a funny game," he said. "So you want to commit murder on behalf of religion. Well, well, my religion has a little respect for humanity, and——"

"Excuse me," cut in Turnbull, suddenly and fiercely, pointing towards the Pawnbroker's next door. "Don't you own that shop?"

"Why—er—yes," said Gordon.

"And don't you own that shop?" repeated the Secularist, pointing backward to the pornographic bookseller.

"What if I do?"

"Why, then" cried Turnbull, with grating contempt. "I will leave the religion of humanity confidently in your hands; but I am sorry I troubled you about such a thing as honour. Look here, my man. I do believe in humanity. I do believe in liberty. My father died for it under the swords of the Yeomanry.[18] I am going to die for it, if need be, under that sword on your counter. But if there is one sight that makes me doubt it it is your foul fat face. It is hard to believe you were not meant to be ruled like a dog or killed like a cockroach. Don't try

[18] The Yeomanry was a parttime mounted militia first raised in the eighteenth century from those who owned their own horses. On occasion it was called to arms in support of the civil authorities.

your slave's philosophy on me. We are going to fight, and we are going to fight in your garden, with your swords. Be still! Raise your voice above a whisper, and I run you through the body."

Turnbull put the bright point of the sword against the gay waistcoat of the dealer, who stood choking with rage and fear, and an astonishment so crushing as to be greater than either.

"MacIan," said Turnbull, falling almost into the familiar tone of a business partner, "MacIan, tie up this fellow and put a gag in his mouth. Be still, I say, or I kill you where you stand."

The man was too frightened to scream, but he struggled wildly, while Evan MacIan, whose long, lean hands were unusually powerful, tightened some old curtain cords round him, strapped a rope gag in his mouth and rolled him on his back on the floor.

"There's nothing very strong here," said Evan, looking about him. "I'm afraid he'll work through that gag in half-an-hour or so."

"Yes," said Turnbull, "but one of us will be killed by that time."

"Well, let's hope so," said the Highlander, glancing doubtfully at the squirming thing on the floor.

"And now," said Turnbull, twirling his fiery moustache and fingering his sword, "let us go into the garden. What an exquisite summer evening!"

MacIan said nothing, but lifting his sword from the counter went out into the sun.

The brilliant light ran along the blades, filling the channels of them with white fire; the combatants stuck their swords in the turf and took off their hats, coats, waistcoats and boots. Evan said a short Latin prayer to himself, during which Turnbull made something of a parade of lighting a cigarette which he flung away the instant after, when he saw MacIan apparently standing ready. Yet MacIan was not exactly ready. He stood staring like a man stricken with a trance.

"What are you staring at?" asked Turnbull. "Do you see the bobbies?"

"I see Jerusalem," said Evan, "all covered with the shields and standards of the Saracens."

"Jerusalem!" said Turnbull, laughing. "Well, we've taken the only inhabitant into Captivity."

And he picked up his sword and made it whistle like a boy's wand.
"I beg your pardon," said MacIan, drily. "Let us begin."

MacIan made a military salute with his weapon, which Turnbull
copied or parodied with an impatient contempt; and in the stillness
of the garden the swords came together with a clear sound like a
bell. The instant the blades touched, each felt them tingle to their
very points with a personal vitality as if they were two naked nerves
of steel. Evan had worn throughout an air of apathy, which might
have been the stale apathy of one who wants nothing. But it was indeed the more dreadful apathy of one who wants something and will
care for nothing else. And this was seen suddenly; for the instant
Evan engaged he disengaged and lunged with an infernal violence. His
opponent with a desperate promptitude parried and riposted; the parry
only just succeeded, the riposte failed. Something big and unbearable
seemed to have broken finally out of Evan in that first murderous lunge,
leaving him lighter and cooler and quicker upon his feet. He fell to
again, fiercely still, but now with a fierce caution. The next moment
Turnbull lunged; MacIan seemed to catch the point and throw it away
from him, and was thrusting back like a thunderbolt, when a sound
paralysed him; another sound beside their ringing weapons. Turnbull,
perhaps from an equal astonishment, perhaps from chivalry, stopped
also and forbore to send his sword through his exposed enemy.

"What's that?" asked Evan, hoarsely.

A heavy scraping sound, as of a trunk being dragged along a littered floor, came from the dark shop behind them.

"The old Jew has broken one of his strings, and he's crawling about,"
said Turnbull. "Be quick! We must finish before he gets his gag out."

"Yes, yes, quick! On guard!" cried the Highlander. The blades
crossed again with the same sound like song, and the men went to
work again with the same white and watchful faces. Evan, in his impatience, went back a little to his wildness. He made windmills, as
the French duellists say, and though he was probably a shade the
better fencer of the two, he found the other's point pass his face
twice so close as almost to graze his cheek. The second time he
realised the actual possiblity of defeat and pulled himself together

under a shock of the sanity of anger. He narrowed, and, so to speak, tightened his operations: he fenced (as the swordman's boast goes), in a wedding ring; he turned Turnbull's thrusts with a maddening and almost mechanical click, like that of a machine. Whenever Turnbull's sword sought to go over that other mere white streak it seemed to be caught in a complex network of steel. He turned one thrust, turned another, turned another. Then suddenly he went forward at the lunge with his whole living weight. Turnbull leaped back, but Evan lunged and lunged and lunged again like a devilish piston rod or battering ram. And high above all the sound of the struggle there broke into the silent evening a bellowing human voice, nasal, raucous, at the highest pitch of pain. "Help! Help! Police! Police! Murder!" The gag was broken; and the tongue of terror was loose.

"Keep on!" gasped Turnbull. "One may be killed before they come."

The voice of the screaming shopkeeper was loud enough to drown not only the noise of the swords but all other noises around it, but even through its rending din there seemed to be some other stir or scurry. And Evan, in the very act of thrusting at Turnbull, saw something in his eyes that made him drop his sword. The atheist, with his grey eyes at their widest and wildest, was staring straight over his shoulder at the little archway of shop that opened on the street beyond. And he saw the archway blocked and blackened with strange figures.

"We must bolt, MacIan," he said abruptly. "And there isn't a damned second to lose either. Do as I do."

With a bound he was beside the little cluster of his clothes and boots that lay on the lawn; he snatched them up, without waiting to put any of them on; and tucking his sword under his other arm, went wildly at the wall at the bottom of the garden and swung himself over it. Three seconds after he had alighted in his socks on the other side, MacIan alighted beside him, also in his socks and also carrying clothes and sword in a desperate bundle.

They were in a bye-street, very lean and lonely itself, but so close to a crowded thoroughfare that they could see the vague masses of vehicles going by, and could even see an individual hansom cab passing the corner at the instant. Turnbull put his fingers to his mouth like a gutter-snipe and whistled twice. Even as he did so he could hear the loud voices of the neighbours and the police coming down the garden.

The hansom swung sharply and came tearing down the little lane at his call. When the cabman saw his fares, however, two wild-haired men in their shirts and socks with naked swords under their arms, he not unnaturally brought his readiness to a rigid stop and stared suspiciously.

"You talk to him a minute," whispered Turnbull, and stepped back into the shadow of the wall.

"We want you," said MacIan to the cabman, with a superb Scotch drawl of indifference and assurance, "to drive us to St. Pancras Station—verra quick."

"Very sorry, sir," said the cabman, "but I'd like know it was all right. Might I arst where you come from, Sir?"

A second after he spoke MacIan heard a heavy voice on the other side of the wall, saying: "I suppose I'd better get over and look for them give me a back."

"Cabby," said MacIan, again assuming the most deliberate and lingering lowland Scotch intonation, "if ye're really verra anxious to ken whar a' come fra', I'll tell ye as a verra great secret. A' come from Scotland. And a'm gaein' to St. Pancras Station. Open the doors, cabby."

The cabman stared, but laughed. The heavy voice behind the wall said: "Now then, a better back this time, Mr. Price." And from the shadow of the wall Turnbull crept out. He had struggled wildly into his coat (leaving his waistcoat on the pavement) and he was with a fierce pale face climbing up the cab behind the cabman. MacIan had no glimmering notion of what he was up to, but an instinct of discipline, inherited from a hundred men of war, made him stick to his own part and trust the other man's.

"Open the doors, cabby," he repeated, with something of the obstinate solemnity of a drunkard, "open the doors. Did ye no hear me say St. Pancras Station?"

The top of a policeman's helmet appeared above the garden wall. The cabman did not see it, but he was still suspicious and began—

"Very sorry, Sir, but . . ." and with that the cat-like Turnbull tore him out of his seat and hurled him into the street below where he lay suddenly stunned.

"Give me his hat," said Turnbull in a silver voice, that the other obeyed like a bugle. "And get inside with the swords."

And just as the red and raging face of a policeman appeared above the wall, Turnbull tore the horse with a terrible cut of the whip and the two went whirling away like a boomerang.

They had spun through seven streets and three or four squares before anything further happened. Then, in the neighbourhood of the Maida Vale, the driver opened the trap and talked through it in a manner not wholly common in conversations through that aperture.

"Mr. MacIan," he said shortly and civilly.

"Mr. Turnbull," replied his motionless fare.

"Under circumstances such as those in which we were both recently placed there was no time for anything but very abrupt action. I trust therefore that you have no cause to complain of me if I have deferred until this moment a consultation with you on our present position or future action. Our present position, Mr. MacIan, I imagine that I am under no special necessity of describing. We have broken the law and we are fleeing from its officers. Our future action is a thing about which I myself entertain sufficiently strong views; but I have no right to assume or to anticipate yours, though I may have formed a decided conception of your character and a decided notion of what they will probably be. Still, by every principle of intellectual justice, I am bound to ask you now and seriously whether you wish to continue our interrupted relations."

MacIan leant his white and rather weary face back upon the cushions in order to speak up through the open door.

"Mr. Turnbull," he said, "I have nothing to add to what I have said before. It is strongly borne in upon me that you and I, the sole occupants of this run-a-way cab, are at this moment the two most important people in London, possibly in Europe. I have been looking at all the streets as we went past, I have been looking at all the shops as we went past, I have been looking at all the churches as we went past. At first, I felt a little dazed with the vastness of it all. I could not understand what it all meant. But now I know exactly what it all means. It means us. This whole civilization is only a dream. You and I are the realities."

"Religious symbolism," said Mr. Turnbull, through the trap, "does not, as you are probably aware, appeal ordinarily to thinkers of the school to which I belong. But in symbolism as you use it in this instance, I must, I think, concede a certain truth. We *must* fight this thing out somewhere; because, as you truly say, we have found each other's reality. We *must* kill each other — or convert each other. I used to think all Christians were hypocrites and I felt quite mildly towards them really. But I know you are sincere — and my soul is mad against you. In the same way you used, I suppose, to think that all atheists thought atheism would leave them free for immorality — and yet in your heart you tolerated them entirely. Now you *know* that I am an honest man, and you are mad against me, as I am against you. Yes, that's it. You can't be angry with bad men. But a good man in the wrong — why one thirsts for his blood. Yes, you open for me a vista of thought."

"Don't run into anything," said Evan, immovably.

"There's something in that view of yours too," said Turnbull, and shut down the trap.

They sped on through shining streets that shot by them like arrows. Mr. Turnbull had evidently a great deal of unused practical talent which was unrolling itself in this ridiculous adventure. They had got away with such stunning promptitude that the police chase had in all probability not even properly begun. But in case it had, the amateur cabman chose his dizzy course through London with a strange dexterity. He did not do what would have first occurred to any ordinary outsider desiring to destroy his tracks. He did not cut into bye-ways or twist his way through mean streets. His amateur common sense told him that it was precisely the poor street, the side street, that would be likely to remember and report the passing of a hansom cab, like the passing of a royal procession. He kept chiefly to the great roads so full of hansoms that a wilder pair than they might easily have passed in the press. In one of the quieter streets Evan put on his boots.

Towards the top of Albany Street the singular cabman again opened the trap.

"Mr. MacIan," he said, "I understand that we have now definitely settled that in the conventional language honour is not satisfied. Our action must at least go further than it has gone under recent interrupted conditions. That, I believe, is understood."

"Perfectly," replied the other with his bootlace in his teeth.

"Under those conditions," continued Turnbull, his voice coming through the hole with a slight note of trepidation very unusual with him, "I have a suggestion to make, if that can be called a suggestion, which has probably occurred to you as readily as to me. Until the actual event comes off we are practically in the position if not of comrades, at least of business partners. Until the event comes off, therefore, I should suggest that quarrelling would be inconvenient and rather inartistic; while the ordinary exchange of politeness between man and man would be not only elegant but uncommonly practical."

"You are perfectly right," answered MacIan with his melancholy voice, "in saying that all this has occurred to me. All duellists should behave like gentlemen to each other. But we, by the queerness of our position, are something much more than either duellists or gentlemen. We are, in the oddest and most exact sense of the term, brothers—in arms."

"Mr. MacIan," replied Turnbull calmly, "no more need be said." And he closed the trap once more.

They had reached Finchley Road before he opened it again.

Then he said, "Mr. MacIan, may I offer you a cigar. It will be a touch of realism."

"Thank you," answered Evan—"You are very kind." And he began to smoke in the cab.

IV

A DISCUSSION AT DAWN

The duellists had from their own point of view escaped or conquered the chief powers of the modern world. They had satisfied the magistrate, they had tied the tradesman neck and heels, and they had left the police behind. As far as their own feelings went they had melted into a monstrous sea; they were but the fare and driver of one of the million hansoms that fill London streets. But they had forgotten something; they had forgotten journalism. They had forgotten that there exists in the modern world, perhaps for the first time in history, a class of people whose interest is not that things should happen well or happen badly, should happen successfully or happen unsuccessfully, should happen to the advantage of this party or the advantage of that party, but whose interest simply is that things should happen.

It is the one great weakness of journalism as a picture of our modern existence, that it must be a picture made up entirely of exceptions. We announce on flaring posters that a man has fallen off a scaffolding. We do not announce on flaring posters that a man has not fallen off a scaffolding. Yet this latter fact is fundamentally more exciting, as indicating that that moving tower of terror and mystery, a man, is still abroad upon the earth. That the man has not fallen off a scaffolding is really more sensational; and it is also some thousand times more common. But journalism cannot reasonably be expected thus to insist upon the permanent miracles. Busy editors cannot be expected to put on their posters, "Mr. Wilkinson Still Safe," or "Mr. Jones, of Worthing, Not Dead Yet." They cannot announce the happiness of mankind at all. They cannot describe all the forks that are not stolen, or all the marriages that are not judicially dissolved. Hence the complete picture they give of life is of necessity fallacious; they can only represent what is unusual. However democratic they may be, they are only concerned with the minority.

The incident of the religious fanatic who broke a window on

Ludgate Hill was alone enough to set them up in good copy for the night. But when the same man was brought before a magistrate and defied his enemy to mortal combat in the open court, then the columns would hardly hold the excruciating information, and the headlines were so large that there was hardly room for any of the text. The *Daily Telegraph* headed a column, "A Duel on Divinity," and there was a correspondence afterwards which lasted for months, about whether police magistrates ought to mention religion. The *Daily Mail*, in its dull, sensible way, headed the events, "Wanted to fight for the Virgin." Mr. James Douglas,[19] in *The Star*, presuming on his knowledge of philosophical and theological terms, described the Christian's outbreak under the title of "Dualist and Duellist." The *Daily News* inserted a colourless account of the matter, but was pursued and eaten up for some weeks, with letters from outlying ministers, headed "Murder and Mariolatry." But the journalistic temperature was steadily and consistently heated by all these influences: the journalists had tasted blood, prospectively, and were in the mood for more; everything in the matter prepared them for further outbursts of moral indignation. And when a gasping reporter rushed in in the last hours of the evening with the announcement that the two heroes of the Police Court had literally been found fighting in a London back garden, with a shopkeeper bound and gagged in the front of the house, the Editors and Sub-Editors were stricken still as men are by great beatitudes.

The next morning, five or six of the great London dailies burst out simultaneously into great blossoms of eloquent leader-writing. Towards the end all the leaders tended to be the same, but they all began differently. The *Daily Telegraph*, for instance began, "There will be little difference among our readers or among all truly English and law-abiding men, touching the &c., &c." The *Daily Mail* said, "People must learn, in the modern world, to keep their theological differences to themselves. The fracas, &c., &c." The *Daily News* started, "Nothing could be more inimical to the cause of true

[19] James Douglas (1867–1940) was the literary critic and later editor of *The Star* and afterward editor of *The Sunday Express*. He was well known to Chesterton, whose *The Wild Knight* he had reviewed in 1900.

religion than &c., &c." The *Times* began with something about
Celtic disturbances of the equilibrium of Empire, and the *Daily Express* distinguished itself splendidly by omitting altogether so controversial a matter and substituting a leader about goloshes.

And the morning after that, the Editors and the newspapers were in
such a state, that, as the phrase is, there was no holding them. Whatever secret and elvish thing it is that broods over Editors and suddenly
turns their brains, that thing had seized on the story of the broken
glass and the duel in the garden. It became monstrous and omni-
present, as do in our time the unimportant doings of the sect of the
Agapemone,[20] or as did at an earlier time the dreary dishonesties
of the Rhodesian financiers.[21] Questions were asked about it, and
even answered, in the House of Commons. The Government were
solemnly denounced in the papers for not having done something,
nobody knew what, to prevent the window being broken. An enormous subscription was started to reimburse Mr. Gordon, the man
who had been gagged in the shop. Mr. MacIan, one of the combatants, became for some mysterious reason, singly and hugely popular as a comic figure in the comic papers and on the stage of the
music halls. He was always represented (in defiance of fact), with red
whiskers, and a very red nose, and in full Highland costume. And a
song, consisting of an unimaginable number of verses, in which his
name was rhymed with flat iron, the British Lion, sly'un, dandelion,
Spion (with Kop[22] in the next line), was sung to crowded houses

[20] The sect of the Agapemone had no connection with early Christians but was an institution called The Abode of Love, founded in 1848 by Henry James Prince at Charlwich
near Bridgewater in Somerset. Here he and his followers lived on a communal basis, pro-
fessing spiritual doctrines and sharing everything, including their wives. In 1859 the group
seems to have moved to a new Abode of Love at Spaxton, which had 15-foot-high walls
and an increased number (two hundred) of "spiritual wives".

[21] The dreary dishonesties of the Rhodesian financiers is not so much a reference to
Rhodesia as to the Transvaal and in particular to Johannesburg, where the maltreatment
of certain financiers claiming British nationality was a contributory factor, along with
friction between the British Colonies of Cape Colony and Natal and the Dutch (Boer) re-
publics of Orange Free State and Transvaal, to the Boer War of 1899–1902.

[22] Spion Kop is a hill in South Africa, scene of a battle in the Boer War.

every night. The papers developed a devouring thirst for the capture of the fugitives; and when they had not been caught for 48 hours, they suddenly turned the whole matter into a detective mystery. Letters under the heading, "Where are They," poured in to every paper, with every conceivable kind of explanation, running them to earth in the Monument,[23] the Twopenny Tube,[24] Epping Forest,[25] Westminster Abbey, rolled up in carpets at Shoolbreds,[26] locked up in safes in Chancery Lane.[27] Yes, the papers were very interesting, and Mr. Turnbull unrolled a whole bundle of them for the amusement of Mr. MacIan as they sat on a high common to the north of London, in the coming of the white dawn.

The darkness in the East had been broken with a bar of grey; the bar of grey was split with a sword of silver and morning lifted itself laboriously over London. From the spot where Turnbull and MacIan were sitting on one of the barren steeps behind Hampstead, they could see the whole of London shaping itself vaguely and largely in the grey and growing light, until the white sun stood over it and it lay at their feet, the splendid monstrosity that it is. Its bewildering squares and parallelograms were compact and perfect as a Chinese puzzle; an enormous hieroglyphic which man must decipher or die. There fell upon both of them, but upon Turnbull more than the other, because he knew more what the scene signified, that quite indescribable sense as of a sublime and passionate and heart-moving futility, which is never evoked by deserts or dead men or men neglected and barbarous, which can only be invoked by the sight of the enormous genius of man applied to anything other

[23] The Monument is a memorial to the Great Fire of London of 1666 and is situated on the site of the outbreak of the fire in Pudding Lane near London Bridge. The Monument was constructed by Christopher Wren in 1671–77.

[24] The Twopenny Tube is the London Underground Railway, more particularly the Circle Line, where there was a flat-rate fare of twopence.

[25] Epping Forest is an area of woodland and heathland to the northeast of London much of which is open to the public.

[26] Shoolbreds was James Shoolbred & Co., a grocer's and general emporium situated at 156 Tottenham Court Road.

[27] Chancery Lane is where the Public Records Office used to be situated.

than the best. Turnbull, the old idealistic democrat, had so often reviled the democracy and reviled them justly for their supineness, their snobbishness, their evil reverence for idle things. He was right enough; for our democracy has only one great fault; it is not democratic. And after denouncing so justly average modern men for so many years as sophists and as slaves he looked down from an empty slope in Hampstead and saw what gods they are. Their achievement seemed all the more heroic and divine, because it seemed doubtful whether it was worth doing at all. There seemed to be something greater than mere accuracy in making such a mistake as London. And what was to be the end of it all? what was to be the ultimate transformation of this common and incredible London man, this workman on a tram in Battersea, this clerk on an omnibus in Cheapside? Turnbull, as he stared drearily, murmured to himself the words of the old atheistic and revolutionary Swinburne who had intoxicated his youth—

> "And still we ask if God or man
> Can loosen thee Lazarus;
> Bid thee rise up republican,
> And save thyself and all of us.
> But no disciple's tongue can say
> If thou can'st take our sins away."

Turnbull shivered slightly as if behind the earthly morning he felt the evening of the world, the sunset of so many hopes. Those words were from "Songs before Sunrise." But Turnbull's songs at their best were songs after sunrise, and sunrise had been no such great thing after all. Turnbull shivered again in the sharp morning air. MacIan was also gazing with his face towards the city, but there was that about his blind and mystical stare that told one, so to speak, that his eyes were turned inwards. When Turnbull said something to him about London, they seemed to move as at a summons and come out like two householders coming out into their doorways.

"Yes," he said, with a sort of stupidity. "It's a very big place."

There was a somewhat unmeaning silence, and then MacIan said again: —

"It's a very big place. When I first came into it I was frightened of it. Frightened exactly as one would be frightened at the sight of a man 40 feet high. I am used to big things where I come from, big mountains that seem to fill God's infinity, and the big sea that goes to the end of the world. But then these things are all shapeless and confused things, not made in any familiar form. But to see the plain, square human things so large as that, houses so large and streets so large, and the town itself so large, was like having screwed some devil's magnifying glass into one's eye. It was like seeing a porridge bowl as big as a house, or a mouse trap made to catch elephants."

"Like the land of the Brobdingnagians," said Turnbull, smiling.

"Oh? Where is that?" said MacIan.

Turnbull said bitterly, "In a book," and the silence fell suddenly between them again.

They were sitting in a sort of litter on the hill side; all the things they had hurriedly collected, in various places, for their flight, were strewn indiscriminately round them. The two swords with which they had lately sought each other's lives were flung down on the grass at random, like two idle walking sticks. Some provisions they had bought last night, at a low public house, in case of undefined contingencies, were tossed about like the materials of an ordinary picnic, here a packet of chocolate, and there a bottle of wine. And to add to the disorder finally, there were strewn on top of everything, the most disorderly of modern things, newspapers, and more newspapers, and yet again newspapers, the ministers of the modern anarchy. Turnbull picked up one of them drearily, and took out a pipe.

"There's a lot about us," he said. "Do you mind if I light up?"

"Why should I mind?" asked MacIan.

Turnbull eyed with a certain studious interest, the man who did not understand any of the verbal courtesies; he lit his pipe and blew great clouds out of it.

"Yes," he resumed. "The matter on which you and I are engaged is at this moment really the best copy in England. I am a journalist and I know. For the first time, perhaps, for many generations, the English are really more angry about a wrong thing done in England than they are about a wrong thing done in France."

"It is not a wrong thing," said MacIan.

Turnbull laughed. "You seem unable to understand the ordinary use of the human language. If I did not suspect that you were a genius, I should certainly know you were a blockhead. I fancy we had better be getting along and collecting our baggage."

And he jumped up and began shoving the luggage into his pockets, or strapping it on to his back. As he thrust a tin of canned meat anyhow into his bursting side pocket, he said, casually: —

"I only meant that you and I are the most prominent people in the English papers."

"Well, what did you expect?" asked MacIan, opening his great grave blue eyes.

"The papers are full of us," said Turnbull, stooping to pick up one of the swords.

MacIan stooped and picked up the other.

"Yes," he said, in his simple way. "I have read what they have to say. But they don't seem to understand the point."

"The point of what?" asked Turnbull.

"The point of the sword," said MacIan, violently, and planted the steel point in the soil like a man planting a tree.

"That is a point," said Turnbull, grimly, "that we will discuss later. Come along."

Turnbull tied the last tin of biscuits desperately to himself with string; and then spoke, like a diver girt for plunging, short and sharp.

"Now, Mr. MacIan, you must listen to me. You must listen to me, not merely because I know the Country, which you might learn by looking at maps, but because I know the people of the Country, whom you could not know by living here 30 years. That infernal city down there is awake; and it is awake against us. All those endless rows of windows and windows are all eyes staring at us. All those forests of chimneys are fingers pointing at us, as we stand here on the hill side. This thing has caught on. For the next six mortal months they will think of nothing but us, as for six mortal months they thought of nothing but the Dreyfus Case.[28] Oh, I know it's funny. They let starving children, who don't want to die, drop by the score without looking round. But because two gentlemen, from private feelings of delicacy, do want to die, they will mobilise the army and navy to prevent them. For half a year or more, you and I, Mr. MacIan, will be an obstacle to every reform in the British Empire. We shall prevent the Chinese being sent out of the Transvaal and the blocks being stopped in the Strand. We shall be the conversational substitute when anyone recommends Home Rule, or complains of sky signs. Therefore, do not imagine, in your innocence, that we have only to melt away among those English hills as a Highland Cateran[29] might into your God-forsaken Highland Mountains. We must be eternally on our guard; we must live the hunted life of two distinguished criminals. We must expect to be recognised as much as if we were Napoleon escaping from Elba. We must be prepared for our descriptions being sent to every tiny village, and for our faces being recognised by every ambitious policeman. We must often sleep under the stars as if we were in Africa. Last and most important we must not dream of effecting our — our final settlement, which will be a thing as famous as the Phoenix Park murders,[30] unless we have made real and precise arrangements for our isolation — I will not say our safety. We must not, in short, fight; until we have thrown them off our scent, if only for a moment. For, take my word for it, Mr. MacIan, if the British Public once catches us up the British Public will prevent the duel, if it is only by locking us both up in asylums for the rest of our days."

[28] The Dreyfus Case was the case of a French officer of Jewish background condemned to Devil's Island in 1894 for allegedly selling secrets to the Germans. The flimsiness of the evidence against him caused Emile Zola to write *J'Accuse!* The Court of Appeal quashed the sentence in 1906, but in 1905 when Chesterton was writing, the affair was still a matter for debate and dispute.

[29] A Highland Cateran can be either a Highland band of men or a Highland brigand.

[30] The Phoenix Park murders involved the assassination in 1882 of two British officials on the grounds of Phoenix Park in Dublin.

MacIan was looking at the horizon with rather misty look.

"I am not at all surprised," he said, "at the world being against us. It makes me feel I was right to. . . ."

"Yes?" said Turnbull.

"To smash your window," said MacIan. "I have woken up the world."

"Very well, then," said Turnbull, stolidly. "Let us look at a few final facts. Beyond that hill there is comparatively clear country. Fortunately, I know the part well, and if you will follow me exactly, and, when necessary, on your stomach, we may be able to get 10 miles out of London, literally without meeting anyone at all, which will be the best possible beginning, at any rate. We have provisions for at least two days and two nights, three days if we do it carefully. We may be able to get 50 or 60 miles away without even walking into an inn door. I have the biscuits and the tinned meat, and the milk. You have the chocolate, I think? And the brandy?"

"Yes," said MacIan, like a soldier taking orders.

"Very well, then, come on. March. We turn under that third bush and so down into the Valley." And he set off ahead at a swinging walk.

Then he stopped suddenly; for he realised that the other was not following. Evan MacIan was leaning on his sword with a lowering face, like a man suddenly smitten still with doubt.

"What on earth is the matter?" asked Turnbull, staring in some anger.

Evan made no reply.

"What the deuce is the matter with you?" demanded the leader, again, his face slowly growing as red as his beard; then he said, suddenly, and in a more human voice, "Are you in pain, MacIan?"

"Yes," replied the Highlander, without lifting his face.

"Take some brandy," cried Turnbull, walking forward hurriedly towards him. "You've got it."

"It's not in the body," said MacIan, in his dull, strange way. "The pain has come into my mind. A very dreadful thing has just come into my thoughts."

"What the devil are you talking about?" asked Turnbull.

MacIan broke out with a queer and living voice.

"We must fight now, Turnbull. We must fight now. A frightful thing has come upon me, and I know it must be now and here. I must kill you here," he cried, with a sort of tearful rage impossible to describe. "Here, here, upon this blessed grass."

"Why, you idiot," began Turnbull.

"The hour has come—the black hour God meant for it. Quick, it will soon by gone. Quick!"

And he flung the scabbard from him furiously, and stood with the sunlight sparkling along his sword.

"You confounded fool," repeated Turnbull. Put that thing up again, you ass, people will come out of that house at the first clash of the steel."

"One of us will be dead before they come," said the other, hoarsely, "for this is the hour God meant."

"Well, I never thought much of God," said the Editor of *The Atheist*, losing all patience. "And I think less now. Never mind what God meant. Kindly enlighten my pagan darkness as to what the devil you mean."

"The hour will soon be gone. In a moment it will be gone," said the madman. "It is now, now, now that I must nail your blaspheming body to the earth—now, now that I must avenge our Lady on her vile slanderer. Now or never. For the dreadful thought is in my mind."

"And what thought," asked Turnbull, with frantic composure, "occupies what you call your mind?"

"I must kill you now," said the fanatic, "because. . . ."

"Well, because," said Turnbull, patiently.

"Because I have begun to like you."

Turnbull's face had a sudden spasm in the sunlight, a change so instantaneous that it left no trace behind it; and his features seemed still carved into a cold stare. But when he spoke again he seemed like a man who was placidly pretending to misunderstand something that he understood perfectly well.

"Your affection expresses itself in an abrupt form," he began, but MacIan broke the brittle and frivolous speech to pieces with a violent voice. "Do not trouble to talk like that," he said. "You know what I mean as well as I know it. Come on and fight, I say. Perhaps you are feeling just as I do."

Turnbull's face flinched again in the fierce sunlight, but his attitude kept its contemptuous ease.

"Your Celtic mind really goes too fast for me," he said, "let me be permitted in my heavy Lowland way to understand this new development. My dear Mr. MacIan, what do you really mean?"

MacIan still kept the shining sword-point towards the other's breast.

"You know what I mean. You mean the same yourself. We must fight now or else. . . ."

"Or else?" repeated Turnbull, staring at him with an almost blinding gravity.

"Or else we may not want to fight at all," answered Evan, and the end of his speech was like a despairing cry.

Turnbull took out his own sword suddenly as if to engage; then planting it point downwards for a moment, he said, "Before we begin, may I ask you a question?"

MacIan bowed patiently, but with burning eyes.

"You said, just now," continued Turnbull, presently, "that if we did not fight now, we might not want to fight at all. How would you feel about the matter if we came not to want to fight at all?"

"I should feel," answered the other, "just as I should feel if you had drawn your sword, and I had run away from it. I should feel that because I had been weak, justice had not been done."

"Justice," answered Turnbull, with a thoughtful smile, "but we are talking about your feelings. And what do you mean by justice, apart from your feelings?"

MacIan made a gesture of weary recognition. "Oh, Nominalism," he said, with a sort of sigh, "we had all that out in the 12th Century." "I wish we could have it out now," replied the other firmly. "Do you really mean that if you came to think me right, you would be certainly wrong?"

"If I had a blow on the back of my head, I might come to think you a green elephant," answered MacIan, "but have I not the right to say now, that if I thought that I should think wrong?"

"Then you are quite certain that it would be wrong to like me?" asked Turnbull, with a slight smile.

"No," said Evan, thoughtfully, "I do not say that. It may not be the devil, it may be some part of God I am not meant to know. But I had a work to do, and it is making the work difficult."

"And I suppose," said the atheist, quite gently, "that you and I know all about which part of God we ought to know."

MacIan burst out like a man driven back and explaining everything.

"The Church is not a thing like the Athenaeum Club,"[31] he cried. If the Athenaeum Club lost all its members, the Athenaeum Club would dissolve and cease to exist. But when we belong to the Church we belong to something which is outside all of us; which is outside everything you talk about, outside the Cardinals and the Pope. They belong to it, but it does not belong to them. If we all fell dead suddenly, the Church would still somehow exist in God. Confound it all, don't you see that I am more sure of its existence than I am of my own existence? And yet you ask me to trust my temperament; my own temperament which can be turned upside down by two bottles of claret or an attack of the jaundice. You ask me to trust that when it softens towards you and not to trust the thing which I believe to be outside myself and more real than the blood in my body."

"Stop a moment," said Turnbull, in the same easy tone, "even in the very act of saying that you believe this or that, you imply that there is a part of yourself that you trust even if there are many parts which you mistrust. If it is only you that like me, surely, also, it is only you that believe in the Catholic Church."

Evan remained in an unmoved and grave attitude.

"There is a part of me which is divine," he answered, "a part that can be trusted, but there are also affections which are entirely animal and idle."

"And you are quite certain, I suppose," continued Turnbull, "that if even you esteem me the esteem would be wholly animal and idle?" For the first time MacIan started as if he had not expected the thing that was said to him. At last he said.

"Whatever in earth or heaven it is that has joined us two together,

---

[31] The Athenaeum Club is a gentlemen's club in Pall Mall.

it seems to be something which makes it impossible to lie. No, I do not think that the movement in me towards you was . . . was that surface sort of thing. It may have been something deeper . . . something strange. I cannot understand the thing at all. But understand this and understand it thoroughly, if I loved you my love might be divine. But in that I hate you, my hatred most certainly is divine. No, it is not some trifle that we are fighting about. It is not some superstition or some symbol. When you wrote those words about Our Lady, you were in that act a wicked man doing a wicked thing. If I hate you it is because you have hated goodness. And if I like you . . . it is because you are good."

Turnbull's face wore an indecipherable expression.

"Well, shall we fight now?" he said.

"Yes," said MacIan, with a sudden contraction of his black brows, "yes, it must be now."

The bright swords crossed, and the first touch of them, travelling down blade and arm, told each combatant that the heart of the other was awakened. It was not in that way that the swords rang together when they had rushed on each other in the little garden behind the dealer's shop.

There was a pause, and then MacIan made a movement as if to thrust, and almost at the same moment Turnbull suddenly and calmly dropped his sword. Evan stared round in an unusual bewilderment, and then realised that a large man in pale clothes and a panama hat was strolling serenely towards them.

V

THE PEACEMAKER

When the combatants, with crossed swords, became suddenly conscious of a third party, they each made the same movement. It was as quick as the snap of a pistol, and they altered it instantaneously and recovered their original pose, but they had both made it, they had both seen it and they both knew what it was. It was not a movement of anger at being interrupted. Say or think what they would it was a movement of relief. A force within them, and yet quite beyond them, seemed slowly and pitilessly washing away the adamant of their oath. As mistaken lovers might watch the inevitable sunset of first love; these men watched the sunset of their first hatred.

Their hearts were growing weaker and weaker against each other. When their weapons rang and reposted in the little London garden, they could have been very certain that if a third party had interrupted them something at least would have happened. They would have killed each other or they would have killed him. But now nothing could undo or deny that flash or fact, that for a second they had been glad to be interrupted. Some new and strange thing was rising higher and higher in their hearts like a high sea at night. It was something that seemed all the more merciless, because it might turn out an enormous mercy. Was there, perhaps, some such fatalism in friendship as all lovers talk about in love? Did God make men love each other against their will?

"I'm sure you'll excuse my speaking to you," said the stranger, in a voice at once eager and deprecating.

The voice was too polite for good manners. It was incongruous with the eccentric spectacle of the duellists which ought to have startled a sane and free man. It was also incongruous with the full and healthy, though rather loose, physique of the man who spoke. At the first glance he looked a fine animal, with curling gold beard and hair and blue eyes, unusually bright. It was only at the second glance that the mind felt a sudden and perhaps unmeaning irritation

433

at the way in which the gold beard retreated backwards into the waistcoat, and the way in which the finely shaped nose went forward as if smelling its way. And it was only, perhaps, at the hundredth glance that the bright, blue eyes which normally before and afterwards seemed brilliant with intelligence, seemed as it were for one instant to be brilliant with idiocy. He was a heavy, healthy working man, who looked all the larger because of the loose, light coloured clothes that he wore, and that had in their extreme lightness and looseness, almost a touch of the tropics. But a closer examination of his attire would have shown that even in the tropics it would have been unique; but it was all woven according to some hygienic texture[32] which no human being had ever heard of before, and which was absolutely necessary even for a day's health. He wore a huge broad brimmed hat, equally hygienic, very much at the back of his head, and his voice coming out of so heavy and hearty a type of man was, as I have said, startlingly shrill and deferential.

"I'm sure you'll excuse my speaking to you," he said. "Now, I wonder if you are in some little difficulty which, after all, we could settle very comfortably together? Now, you don't mind my saying this, do you?"

The faces of both combatants remained somewhat stolid under this appeal. But the stranger, probably taking their silence for a gathering shame, continued with a kind of gaiety:

"So you are the young men I have read about in the papers. Well, of course, when one is young, one is rather romantic. Do you know what I always say to young people?"

A blank silence followed this gay enquiry. Then Turnbull said in a colourless voice:

"As I was 47 last birthday, I probably came into the world too soon for the experience."

"Very good, very good," said the friendly person, "Dry Scotch humour. Dry Scotch humour. Well now. I understand that you two people want to fight a duel. I suppose you aren't much up in the modern world. We've quite outgrown duelling, you know. In fact,

---

[32] There was a tendency among certain groups to wear only fabrics such as mohair or camel hair fashioned in designs such as those of Dr. Jaegar. Bernard Shaw bought his knickerbocker suits from Jaegar.

Tolstoy tells us that we shall soon outgrow war, which he says is simply a duel between nations. A duel between nations. But there is no doubt about one having outgrown duelling."

Waiting for some effect upon his wooden auditors, the stranger stood beaming for a moment and then resumed:

"Now, they tell me in the newspapers that you are really wanting to fight about something connected with Roman Catholicism. Now, do you know what I always say to Roman Catholics?"

"No," said Turnbull, heavily. "Do they?" It seemed to be a characteristic of the hearty hygienic gentleman that he always forgot the speech he had made the moment before. Without enlarging further on the fixed form of his appeal to the Church of Rome he laughed cordially at Turnbull's answer; then his wandering blue eyes caught the sunlight on the swords, and he assumed a good humoured gravity.

"But you know this is a serious matter," he said, eyeing Turnbull and MacIan, as if they had just been keeping the table in a roar with their frivolities. "I am sure that if I appealed to your higher natures . . . your higher natures. Every man has a higher nature and a lower nature. Now, let us put the matter very plainly, and without any romantic nonsense about honour or anything of that sort. Is not bloodshed a great sin?"

"No," said MacIan, speaking for the first time.

"Well, really, really!" said the peacemaker.

"Murder is a sin," said the immovable Highlander. "There is no sin of bloodshed."

"Well, we won't quarrel about a word," said the other, pleasantly.

"Why on earth not?" said MacIan, with a sudden asperity. "Why shouldn't we quarrel about a word? What is the good of words if they aren't important enough to quarrel over? Why do we choose one word more than another if there isn't any difference between them? If you called a woman a Chimpanzee instead of an angel, wouldn't there be a quarrel about a word? If you're not going to argue about words, what are you going to argue about? Are you going to convey your meaning to me by moving your ears?[33] The

---

[33] See footnote 30 in *The Club of Queer Trades*.

Church and the heresies always used to fight about words, because they are the only things worth fighting about. I say that murder is a sin, and bloodshed is not, and that there is as much difference between those words as there is between and word 'yes,' and the word 'no'; or rather more difference, for 'yes' and 'no,' at least, belong to the same category. Murder is a spiritual incident. Bloodshed is a physical incident. A surgeon commits bloodshed."

"Ah, you're a casuist," said the large man, wagging his head. "Now, do you know what I always say to casuists? . . ."

MacIan made a violent gesture; and Turnbull broke into open laughter. The peacemaker did not seem to be in the least annoyed, but continued in unabated enjoyment.

"Well, well," he said, "let us get back to the point. Now Tolstoy has shown that force is no remedy; so you see the position in which I am placed. I am doing my best to stop what I'm sure you won't mind my calling this really useless violence, this really quite wrong violence of yours. But it's against my principles to call in the police against you, because the police are still in a lower moral place so to speak, because, in short, the police undoubtedly sometimes employ force. Tolstoy has shown that violence merely breeds violence in the person towards whom it is used, whereas, Love, on the other hand, breeds Love. So you see how I am placed. I am reduced to use Love in order to stop you. I am obliged to use Love."

He gave to the word an indescribable sound of something hard and heavy; as if he were saying "boots." Turnbull suddenly gripped his sword and said, shortly, "I see how you are placed quite well, sir. You will not call the police. Mr. MacIan, shall we engage." MacIan plucked his sword out of the grass.

"I must, and will stop this shocking crime," cried the Tolstoyan, crimson in the face. "It is against all modern ideas. It is against the principle of Love. How you, sir, who pretend to be a Christian. . ."

MacIan turned upon him with a white face and bitter lip. "Sir," he said, "talk about the principle of Love as much as you like. You seem to me colder than a lump of stone; but I am willing to believe that you may at some time have loved a cat, or a dog, or a child. When you were a baby, I suppose you loved your mother.

Talk about Love, then, till the world is sick of the word. But don't you talk about Christianity. Don't you dare to say one word, white or black, about it. Christianity is, as far as you are concerned, a horrible mystery. Keep clear of it, keep silent upon it, as you would upon an abomination. It is a thing that has made men slay and torture each other; and you will never know why. It is a thing that has made men do evil that good might come; and you will never understand the evil, let alone the good. Christianity is a thing that could only make you vomit, till you are other than you are. I would not justify it to you even if I could. Hate it, in God's name, as Turnbull does, who is a man. It is a monstrous thing, for which men die. And if you will stand here and talk about Love for another 10 minutes it is very probable that you will see a man die for it."

And he fell on guard. Turnbull was busy settling something loose in his elaborate hilt, and the pause was broken by the stranger.

"Suppose I call the police," he said, with a heated face.

"And deny your most sacred dogma," said MacIan.

"Dogma!" cried the man in a sort of dismay. "Oh, we have no *dogmas*, you know."

There was another silence, and he said again, airily.

"You know, I think, there's something in what Shaw teaches about no moral principles being quite fixed. Have you ever read 'The Quintessence of Ibsenism?' Of course he went very wrong over the war."[34]

Turnbull, with a bent, flushed face, was tying up the loose piece of the pommel with string. With the string in his teeth, he said, "Oh, make up your damned mind and clear out."

"It's a serious thing," said the philosopher, shaking his head. "I must be alone and consider which is the higher point of view. I rather feel that in a case so extreme as this . . ." and he went slowly away. As he disappeared among the trees, they heard him murmuring in a sing-song voice, "New occasions teach new duties," out of a poem by James Russell Lowell.

"Ah," said MacIan, drawing a deep breath. "Don't you believe in prayer now? I prayed for an angel."

[34] Shaw was very much in favor of the British side in the Boer War. Chesterton was not.

"I am afraid I don't understand," answered Turnbull.

"An hour ago," said the Highlander in his heavy meditative voice, "I felt the devil weakening my heart and my oath against you, and I prayed that God would send an angel to my aid."

"Well," enquired the other, finishing his mending and wrapping the rest of the string round his hand to get a firmer grip.

"Well?"

"Well, that man was an angel," said MacIan.

"I didn't know they were as bad as that," answered Turnbull.

"We know that devils sometimes quote Scripture and counterfeit good," replied the mystic. "Why should not angels sometimes come to show us the black abyss of evil on whose brink we stand. If that man had not tried to stop us . . . I might . . . I might have stopped."

"I know what you mean," said Turnbull, grimly.

"But then he came," broke out MacIan, "and my soul said to me: give up fighting, and you will become like That. Give up vows and dogmas and fixed things, and you may grow like That. You may learn, also, that fog of false philosophy. You may grow fond of that mire of crawling, cowardly morals. You may come to think a blow bad, because it hurts, and not because it humiliates. You may come to think murder wrong, because it is violent and not because it is unjust. Oh, you blasphemer of the good, an hour ago I almost loved you. But do not fear for me now. I have heard the word Love pronounced in *his* intonation; and I know exactly what it means. On guard."

The swords caught on each other with a dreadful clang and jar, full of the old energy and hate; and at once plunged and replunged. Once more each man's heart had become the magnet of a mad sword. Suddenly, furious as they were, they were frozen for a moment motionless.

"What noise is that?" asked the Highlander, hoarsely.

"I think I know," replied Turnbull.

"What? . . . What?" cried the other.

"The student of Shaw and Tolstoy had made up his remarkable mind," said Turnbull, quietly. "The police are coming up the hill."

VI

THE OTHER PHILOSOPHER

Between high hedges in Hertfordshire, hedges so high as to create a kind of grove, two men were running. They did not run in a scampering or feverish manner; but in the steady swing of the pendulum. Across the great plains and uplands to the right and left of the lane, a long tide of sun-set light rolled like a sea of ruby, lighting up the long terraces of the hills and picking out the few windows of the scattered hamlets in startling bloodred sparks. But the lane was cut deep in the hill and remained in an abrupt shadow. The two men running in it had an impression not uncommonly experienced between those wild green English walls; a sense of being led between the walls of a maze.

Though their pace was steady it was vigorous: their faces were heated and their eyes fixed and bright. There was, indeed, something a little mad in the contrast between the evening's stillness over the empty country-side, and these two figures fleeing wildly from nothing. They had the look of two lunatics, possibly they were.

"Are you all right?" said Turnbull, with civility. "Can you keep this up?"

"Quite easily, thank you," replied MacIan, "I run very well."

"Is that a qualification in a family of warriors?" asked Turnbull.

"Undoubtedly. Rapid movement is essential," answered MacIan, who never saw a joke in his life.

Turnbull broke out into a short laugh, and silence fell between them, the panting silence of runners.

Then MacIan said, "We run better than any of those policemen. They are too fat. Why do you make your policemen so fat?"

"I didn't do much towards making them fat myself," replied Turnbull, genially, "but I flatter myself that I am now doing something towards making them thin. You'll see they will be as lean as rakes by the time they catch us. They will look like your friend Cardinal Manning."[35]

[35] Cardinal Henry Edward Manning (1808–92) was the Archdeacon of Chichester (1840) who converted to Roman Catholicism in 1851 and became Archbishop of Westminster in 1865. He was given a cardinal's hat in 1875.

"But they won't catch us," said MacIan, in his literal way.

"No, we beat them in the great military art of running away," returned the other. "They won't catch us unless—

MacIan turned his long equine face enquiringly: "Unless what?" he said, for Turnbull had gone silent suddenly, and seemed to be listening intently as he ran as a horse does with his ears turned back.

"Unless what?" repeated the Highlander.

"Unless they do—what they have done. Listen." MacIan slackened his trot, and turned his head to the trail they had left behind them. Across two or three billows of the up and down lane came along the ground the unmistakable throbbing of horses' hoofs.

"They have put the mounted police on us," said Thurnbull shortly. "Good Lord, one would think we were a Revolution."

"So we are,' said MacIan calmly, "what shall we do? Shall we turn on them with our points?"

"It may come to that," answered Turnbull, "though if it does, I reckon that will be the last act. We must put it off if we can."

And he stared and peered about him between the bushes. "If we could hide somewhere the beasts might go by us," he said. "The police have their faults but thank God they're inefficient. Why here's the very thing. Be quick and quiet. Follow me."

He suddenly swung himself up the high bank on one side of the lane. It was almost as high and smooth as a wall, and on the top of it the black hedge stood out over them at an angle, almost like a thatched roof of the lane. And the burning evening sky looked down at them through the tangle with red eyes as of an army of goblins.

Turnbull hoisted himself up and broke the hedge with his body. As his head and shoulders rose above it they turned to flame in the full glow as if lit up by an immense fire-light. His red hair and beard looked almost scarlet, and his pale face as bright as a boy's. Something violent, something that was at once love and hatred, surged in the strange heart of the Gael below him. He had an unutterable sense of epic importance as if he were somehow lifting all humanity into a prouder and more passionate region of the air. As he swung himself up also into the evening light he felt as if he were rising on enormous wings.

Legends of the morning of the world which he had heard in childhood or read in youth came back upon him in a cloudy splendour. Purple tales of wrath and friendship, like Roland and Oliver,[36] or Balin and Balan,[37] reminding him of emotional entanglements. Men who had loved each other and then fought each other; men who had fought each other and then loved each other, together made a mixed but monstrous sense of momentousness. The crimson seas of the sunset seemed to him like a bursting out of some sacred blood, as if the heart of the world had broken.

Turnbull was wholy unaffected by any written or spoken poetry; his was a powerful and prosaic mind. But even upon him there came for the moment something out of the earth and the passionate ends of the sky. The only evidence was in his voice which was still practical but a shade more quiet.

"Do you see that summer-house-looking thing over there?" he asked shortly. "That will do for us very well."

Keeping himself free from the tangle of the hedge he strolled across a triangle of obscure kitchen garden, and approached a dismal shed or lodge a yard or two beyond it. It was a weather-stained hut of grey wood, which with all its desolation retained a tag or two of trivial ornament, which suggested that the thing had once been a sort of summer house, and the place probably a sort of garden.

"That is quite invisible from the road," said Turnbull, as he entered it, "and it will cover us up for the night."

MacIan looked at him gravely for a few moments. "Sir," he said, "I ought to say something to you. I ought to say—"

"Hush," said Turnbull, suddenly lifting his hand, "be still, man."

In the sudden silence, the drumming of the distant horses grew louder and louder with inconceivable rapidity, and the cavalcade of police rushed by below them in the lane, almost with the roar and rattle of an express train.

"I ought to tell you," continued MacIan, still staring stolidly at

[36] Roland and Oliver were the two heroes of *The Song of Roland* and several other medieval epics.

[37] Balin and Balan were two brothers, both knights, whose deeds and death at each other's hands are recounted in a medieval French *chanson de geste*, in Sir Thomas Malory's *Morte d' Arthur* and in Swinburne's *Tale of Balen* (1896).

at the other, "that you are a great chief, and it is good to go to war, behind you."

Turnbull said nothing, but turned and looked out of the foolish lattice of the little windows, then he said, "We must have food and sleep first."

When the last echo of their eluded pursuers had died in the distant uplands, Turnbull began to unpack the provisions with the easy air of a man at a picnic. He had just laid out the last items, put a bottle of wine on the floor, and a tin of salmon on the window-ledge, when the bottomless silence of that forgotten place was broken. And it was broken by three heavy blows of a stick delivered upon the door.

Turnbull looked up in the act of opening a tin and stared silently at his companion. MacIan's long lean mouth had shut hard.

"Who the devil can that be?" said Turnbull.

"God knows," said the other. "It might be God."

Again the sound of the wooden stick reverberated on the wooden door. It was a curious sound, and on consideration did not resemble the ordinary effects of knocking on a door for admittance. It was rather as if the point of a stick were plunged again and again at the panels in an absurd attempt to make a hole in them.

A wild look sprang into MacIan's eyes and he got up half stupidly, with a kind of stagger, put his hand out and caught one of the swords. "Let us fight at once," he cried, "it is the end of the world."

"You're overdone, MacIan," said Turnbull, putting him on one side. "It's only someone playing the goat. Let me open the door."

But he also picked up a sword as he stepped to open it.

He paused one moment with his hand on the handle and then flung the door open. Almost as he did so the ferule of an ordinary bamboo cane came at his eyes, so that he had actually to parry it with the naked weapon in his hands. As the two touched, the point of the stick was dropped very abruptly, and the man with the stick stepped hurriedly back.

Against the heraldic background of sprawling crimson and gold offered him by the expiring sunset, the figure of the man with the stick showed at first merely black and fantastic. He was a small man with two whisps of long hair that curled up on each side, and seen in silhouette, looked like horns. He had a bow tie so big that the two ends showed on each side of his neck like unnatural stunted wings. He had his long black cane still tilted in his hand like a fencing foil and half presented at the opened door. His large straw hat had fallen behind him as he leapt backwards.

"With reference to your suggestion, MacIan," said Turnbull, placidly, "I think it looks more like the Devil."

"Who on earth are you?" cried the stranger in a high shrill voice, brandishing his cane defensively.

"Let me see," said Turnbull, looking round to MacIan with the same blandness, "Who are we?"

"Come out," screamed the little man with the stick.

"Certainly," said Turnbull, and went outside with the sword; MacIan following.

Seen more fully, with the evening daylight on his face, the strange man looked a little less like a goblin. He wore a square pale-grey jacket suit, on which the grey butterfly tie was the only indisputable touch of affectation. Against the great sunset his figure had looked merely small: seen in a more equal light it looked tolerably compact and shapely. His reddish brown hair combed into two great curls, looked like the long slow curling hair of the women in some pre-Raphaelite pictures. But within this feminine frame of hair his face was unexpectedly impudent, like a monkey's.

"What are you doing here?" he said in a sharp small voice.

"Well," said MacIan, in his grave childish way, "what are you doing here?"

"I," said the man indignantly, "I'm in my own garden."

"Oh," said MacIan simply, "I apologise." Turnbull was coolly curling his red moustache: and the stranger stared from one to the other temporarily stunned by their innocent assurance.

"But, may I ask," he said at last, "what the devil you are doing in my summer house?"

"Certainly," said MacIan, "we were just going to fight."

"To fight!" repeated the man.

"We had better tell this gentleman the whole business," broke in

Turnbull. Then turning to the stranger he said firmly, "I am sorry, sir, but we have something to do that must be done. And I may as well tell you at the beginning and to avoid waste of time or language, that we cannot admit any interference."

"We were just going to take some slight refreshment when you interrupted us. . . ."

The little man had a dawning expression of understanding and stooped and picked up the unused bottle of wine, eying it curiously.

Turnbull continued—

"But that refeshment was preparatory to something which I fear you will find less comprehensible, but on which our minds are entirely fixed, sir. We are forced to fight a duel. We are forced by honour and an internal intellectual need. Do not, for your own sake, attempt to stop us. I know all the excellent and ethical things that you will want to say to us. I know all about the essential requirements of civil order: I have written leading articles about them all my life. I know all about the sacredness of human life; I have bored all my friends with it. Try and understand our position. This man and I are alone in the modern world in that we think that God is essentially important. I think He does not exist; that is where the importance comes in for me. But this man thinks that He does exist, and thinking that very properly thinks him more important than anything else. Now we wish to make a great demonstration and assertion—something that will set the world on fire like the first Christian persecutions. If you like, we are attempting a mutual martyrdom. The papers have posted up every town against us. Scotland Yard has fortified every police station with our enemies; we are driven therefore to the edge of a lonely lane, and indirectly to taking liberties with your summer house in order to arrange our. . . ."

"Stop," roared the little man in the butterfly necktie, "Put me out of my intellectual misery. Are you really the two tomfools I have read of in all the papers? Are you the two people who wanted to spit at each other in the Police Court? Are you? Are you?"

"Yes," said MacIan, "it began in a police court."

The little man slung the bottle of wine twenty yards away like a stone.

"Come up to my place," he said. "I've got better stuff than that. I've got the best Beaune within fifty miles of here. Come up. You're the very men I wanted to see."

Even Turnbull, with his typical invulnerability, was a little taken aback by this boisterous and almost brutal hospitality.

"Why. . . . sir. . . ." he began.

"Come up! Come in!" howled the little man, dancing with delight. "I'll give you a dinner. I'll give you a bed! I'll give you a green smooth lawn and your choice of swords and pistols. Why, you fools, I adore fighting! It's the only good thing in God's world! I've walked about these damned fields and longed to see somebody cut up and killed and the blood running. Ha! Ha!"

And he made sudden lunges with his stick at the trunk of a neighbouring tree so that the ferule made fierce prints and punctures in the bark.

"Excuse me," said MacIan suddenly with the wide-eyed curiosity of a child, "Excuse me, but. . . ."

"Well?" said the small fighter, brandishing his wooden weapon.

"Excuse me," repeated MacIan, "But was that what you were doing at the door?"

The little man stared an instant and then said: "Yes," and Turnbull broke into a guffaw.

"Come on!" cried the little man, tucking his stick under his arm and taking quite suddenly to his heels. "Come on! Confound me, I'll see both of you eat and then I'll see one of you die. Lord bless me, the gods must exist after all—they have sent me one of my daydreams! Lord! A duel!"

He had gone flying along a winding path between the borders of the kitchen garden; and in the increasing twilight he was as hard to follow as a flying hare. But at length the path after many twists betrayed its purpose and led abruptly up two or three steps to the door of a tiny but very clean cottage. There was nothing about the outside to distinguish it from other cottages, except indeed its ominous cleanliness and one thing that was out of all the custom and tradition of all the cottages under the sun. In the middle of the little garden among the stocks and the marigolds there surged up in shapeless stone a South Sea Island idol. There was something gross and even evil in that eyeless and alien God among the most innocent of the English Flowers.

"Come in," cried the creature again, "Come in! it's better inside!"

Whether or no it was better inside it was at least a surprise. The moment the two duellists had pushed open the door of that inoffensive white-washed cottage they found that its interior was lined with fiery Gold. It was like stepping into a chamber in the Arabian Nights.[38] The door that closed behind them shut out England and all the energies of the West. The ornaments that shone and shimmered on every side of them were subtly mixed from many periods and lands, but were all oriental. Cruel Assyrian bas reliefs ran along the sides of the passage; cruel Turkish swords and daggers glinted above and below them; the two were separated by ages and fallen civilizations. Yet they seemed to sympathise since they were both harmonious and both merciless. The house seemed to consist of chamber within chamber and created that impression as of a dream which belongs also to the Arabian Nights themselves. The innermost room of all was like the inside of a jewel. The little man who owned it all threw himself on a heap of scarlet and golden cushions and struck his hands together. A negro in a white robe and turban appeared suddenly and silently behind them.

"Selim," said the host, "these two gentlemen are staying with me to-night. Send up the very best wine and dinner at once. And Selim. One of these gentlemen will probably die to-morrow. Make arrangements please."

The negro bowed and withdrew.

[38] Compare Ivywood House in Chesterton's *The Flying Inn.*

VII

THE OTHER PHILOSOPHER

(Continued)

Evan MacIan came out into the little garden in a fresh silver morning, his long face looking more austere than ever in that cold light, his eyelids a little heavy. He carried one of the swords. Turnbull was in the little house behind him, demolishing the end of an early breakfast and humming a tune to himself, which could be heard through the open window. A moment or two later he leapt to his feet and came out into the sunlight, still munching toast, his own sword stuck under his arm like a walking stick.

Their eccentric host had vanished from sight, with a polite gesture, some twenty minutes before. They imagined him to be occupied on some concerns in the interior of the house, and they waited for his emergence, stamping the garden in silence, the garden of tall fresh country flowers, in the midst of which the monstrous South Sea idol lifted itself as abruptly as the prow of a ship, riding on a sea of red and white and gold.

It was with a start, therefore, that they came upon the man himself already in the garden. They were all the more startled because of the still posture in which they found him. He was on his knees in front of the stone idol, rigid and motionless, like a Saint in a trance or ecstacy. Yet when Turnbull's tread broke a twig he was on his feet in a flash.

"Excuse me," he said with an irradiation of smiles, but yet with a kind of bewilderment. "So sorry . . . family prayers . . . old-fashioned . . . mother's knee. Let us go on to the lawn behind."

And he ducked rapidly round the statue to an open space of grass on the other side of it.

"This will do us best, Mr. MacIan," said he. Then he made a gesture towards the heavy stone figure on the pedestal, which had now its blank and shapeless back turned towards them. "Don't you be afraid," he added. "He can still see us."

MacIan turned his blue blinking eyes, which seemed still misty with sleep (or sleeplessness), towards the idol, but his brows drew together.

The little man with the long hair also had his eyes on the back view of the god. His eyes were at once liquid and burning; and he rubbed his hands slowly against each other.

"Do you know," he said, "I think he can see us better this way. I often think that this blank thing is his real face, watching, though it cannot be watched. He, he! Yes, I think he looks nice from behind. He looks more cruel from behind, don't you think?"

"What the devil is the thing?" asked Turnbull, gruffly.

"It is the only Thing there is," answered the other. "It is Force."

"Oh!" said Turnbull shortly.

"Yes, my friends," said the the little man with an animated countenance, fluttering his fingers in the air, "it was no chance that led you to this garden; surely it was the caprice of some old god, some happy, pitiless god. Perhaps it was his will—for he loves blood, and on that stone in front of him men have been butchered by hundreds, in the fierce, feasting islands of the South. In this cursed craven place I have not been permitted to kill men on his altar. Only rabbits; and cats sometimes."

In the stillness MacIan made a sudden movement, unmeaning apparently, and then remained rigid.

"But to-day, to-day," continued the small man in a shrill voice, "to-day his hour is come. To-day, his will is done on earth as it is in heaven. Men, men, men will bleed before him to-day." And he bit his forefinger in a kind of fever.

Still the two duellists stood with their swords as heavily as statues and the silence seemed to cool the eccentric and call him back to more rational speech.

"Perhaps I express myself a little too lyrically," he said, with an amicable abruptness. "My philosophy has its higher ecstacies, but perhaps you are hardly worked up to them yet. Let us confine ourselves to the unquestioned. You have found your way, gentlemen, by a beautiful accident, to the house of the only man in England (probably) who will favour and encourage your most reasonable project. From Cornwall to Cape Wrath this is one horrible solid block of humanitarianism. You will find men who will defend this or that war in a distant Continent. They will defend it on the contemptible ground of commerce or the more contemptible ground of social good. But do not fancy that you will find one other person who will comprehend a strong man taking the sword in his hand and wiping out his enemy. My name is Wimpey, Morrice Wimpey: I had a fellowship at Magdalen. But I assure you I had to drop it, owing to my having said something in a public lecture, infringing the popular prejudice against those great gentlemen, the assassins of the Italian Renascence. They let me say it at dinner and so on; and seemed to like it. But in a public lecture . . . so inconsistent. Well, as I say, here is your only refuge, a temple of honour. Here you can fall back on that naked and awful arbitration which is the only thing that balances the stars — a still continuous violence. *Vie Victis!*[39] Down, down, down with the defeated! Victory is the only ultimate fact. Carthage *was* destroyed: the Red Indians are being exterminated: that is the single certainty. In an hour from now that sun will still be shining and that grass growing; and one of you will be conquered: one of you will be the conqueror. When it has been done nothing will alter it. Heroes, I give you the hospitality fit for heroes. And I salute the survivor. Fall on."

The two men took their swords. Then MacIan said steadily, "Mr. Turnbull, lend me your sword a moment."

Turnbull, with a questioning glance, handed him the weapon. MacIan took the second sword in his left hand and with a violent gesture hurled it at the feet of little Mr. Wimpey.

"Fight!" he said in a loud harsh voice, "Fight me now!"

Wimpey took a step backward and bewildered words bubbled on his lips.

"Pick up that sword and fight me," repeated MacIan, with brows as black as thunder.

The little man turned to Turnbull with a gesture demanding judgment or protection.

"Really, Sir," he began, "this gentleman confuses. . . ."

"You stinking little coward," roared Turnbull, suddenly releasing his wrath, "Fight, if you're so fond of fighting. Fight if you're so fond of all that filthy philosophy. If winning is everything, go in

---

[39] This is Latin for "Cursed be the defeated!", Brennus' words as he threw his sword into the scales weighing gold intended to buy off the Gauls and secure their departure. See *Titus Livius*, V, 48.

and win. If the weak must go to the wall, go to the wall! Fight, you rat. Fight, or if you won't fight—run."

And he ran at Wimpey with blazing eyes.

Wimpey staggered back a few paces like a man struggling with his own limbs. Then he felt the furious Scotchman coming at him like an express train, doubling his size every second, with eyes as big as windows and a sword as bright as the sun. Something broke inside him and he found himself running away, tumbling over his own feet in terror and crying out as he ran.

"Chase him," shouted Turnbull, as MacIan snatched up the sword and joined in the scamper. "Chase him over a county! Chase him into the sea. Shoo! Shoo! Shoo!"

The little man plunged like a rabbit among the tall flowers, the two duellists after him. Turnbull kept at his tail with savage ecstacy, still shoo-ing him like a cat. But MacIan, as he ran past the South Sea idol, paused an instant to spring upon its pedestal. For five seconds he strained against the inert mass. Then it stirred; and he sent it over with a great crash among the flowers, that engulfed it altogether. Then he went bounding after the runaway.

In the energy of his alarm the ex-fellow of Magdalen managed to leap the paling of his garden. The two pursuers went over it after him like flying birds. He fled frantically down a long lane with his two terrors in his trail, till he came to a gap in the hedge and went across a steep meadow like the wind. The two Scotchmen as they ran kept up a cheery bellowing and waved their swords. Up three slanting meadows, down four slanting meadows on the other side, across another road, across a heath of snapping bracken, through a wood, across another road and to the brink of a big pool, they pursued the flying philosopher. But when he came to the pool, his pace was so precipitate that he could not stop it, and with a kind of lurching stagger he fell splash into the greasy water. Getting dripping to his feet, with the water up to his knees, the worshipper of force and victory waded disconsolately to the other side and drew himself on to the bank. And Turnbull sat down on the grass and went off into reverberations of laughter. A second afterwards the most extraordinary grimaces were seen to distort the stiff face of MacIan and unholy sounds came from within. He had never practiced laughing and it hurt him very much.

VIII

THE VILLAGE OF GRASSLEY-IN-THE-HOLE

At about half-past one, under a strong blue sky, Turnbull got up out of the grass and fern in which he had been lying, and his still intermittent laughter ended in a kind of yawn.

"I'm hungry," he said shortly. "Are you?"

"I have not noticed," answered MacIan. "What are you going to do?"

"There's a village down the road, past the pool," answered Turnbull. "I can see it from here. I can see the white-washed walls of some cottages and a kind of corner of the church. How jolly it all looks. It looks so — I don't know what the word is — so sensible. Don't fancy I'm under any illusions about Arcadian virtue and the innocent villagers. Men make beasts of themselves there with drink; but they don't deliberately make devils of themselves with mere talking. They kill wild animals in the wild woods, but they don't kill cats to the God of Victory. They don't" — he broke off and suddenly spat on the ground.

Excuse me," he said, "it was ceremonial. One has to get the taste out of one's mouth."

"The taste of what?" asked MacIan.

"I don't know the exact name for it," replied Turnbull. "Perhaps it is the South Sea Islands, or it may be Magdalen College."

There was a long pause and MacIan also lifted his large limbs off the ground; his eyes particularly dreamy.

"I know what you mean, Turnbull," he said, "but . . . I always thought you people agreed with all that."

"Agreed with all what?" asked the other.

"With all that about doing as one likes and the individual — and nature loving the stongest and all the things which that cockroach talked about."

Turnbull's big blue-grey eyes stood open with a grave astonishment.

"Do you really mean to say, MacIan," he said, "that you fancied

451

that we, the Free-Thinkers, that Bradlaugh,[40] or Holyoake,[41] or Ingersoll[42] believe all that dirty immoral mysticism about nature? Damn nature!"

"I supposed you did," said MacIan calmly. "It seems to me your most conclusive position."

"And you mean to tell me," rejoined the other, "that you broke my window and challenged me to mortal combat, and tied a tradesman up with ropes, and chased an Oxford Fellow across five meadows, all under the impression that I am such an illiterate idiot as to believe in nature!"

"I supposed you did," repeated MacIan with his usual mildness, "but I admit I know little of the details of your belief—or disbelief."

Turnbull swung round quite suddenly and set off towards the village.

"Come along," he cried, "come down to the village. Come down to the nearest decent inhabitable pub. This is a case for beer."

"I do not quite follow you," said the Highlander.

"Yes you do," answered Turnbull, "you follow me slap into the inn-parlour. I repeat, this is a case for beer. We must have the whole of this matter out thoroughly before we go a step further. Do you know that an idea has just struck me of great simplicity and of some cogency. Do not by any means let us drop our intentions of settling our difference with two steel swords. But do you not think that with two pewter pots we might do what we have never really thought of doing yet—discover what our difference is?"

"It never occurred to me before," answered MacIan with tranquility. "It is a good suggestion."

And they set out at an easy swing down the steep road to the village of Grassley-in-the-Hole.

[40] Charles Bradlaugh (1833–91) was an English politician and free thinker and M.P. for Northampton (1880–91).

[41] George Jacob Holyoake (1817–1906) was an English cooperator and secularist. He was a tinsmith who became a Chartist in 1832, a rationalist in 1841, and was imprisoned for blasphemy in 1842. Editor of *The Reasoner* (1846) and *Leader* (1850), he also wrote lives of *Tom Paine* (1851), *Robert Owen* (1859) and *John Stuart Mill* (1873), as well as the autobiographical *Sixty Years of an Agitator's Life* (1892) and *Bygones with Remembering* (1905).

[42] Robert Green Ingersoll, (1833–99) was a lawyer, lecturer and professional agnostic.

Grassley-in-the-Hole was a rude parallelogram of buildings, with two thoroughfares, which might have been called two high-streets if it had been possible to call them streets. One of these ways was higher on the slope than the other, the whole parallelogram lying aslant, so to speak, on the side of the hill. The upper of these two roads was decorated with a big public house, a butcher's shop, a small public house, a sweetstuff shop, a very small public house, and an illegible sign-post. The lower of the two roads boasted a horse-pond, a post office, a gentleman's garden with very high hedges, a microscopically small public house and two cottages. Where all the people lived who supported all the public houses was in this, as in many other English villages, a silent and smiling mystery. The Church lay a little above and beyond the village, with a square grey tower, dominating it decisively.

But even the Church was scarcely so central and solemn an institution as the large public house, the Valencourt Arms. It was named after some splendid family that had long gone bankrupt and whose seat was occupied by a man who had invented a hygienic bootjack; but the unfathomable sentimentalism of the English people insisted on regarding the Inn, the seat and the sitter in it as alike parts of a pure and marmoreal antiquity. And in the Valencourt Arms festivity itself had some solemnity and decorum; and beer was drunk with reverence, as it ought to be. Into the principal parlour of this place entered two strangers, who found themselves, as is always the case in such hostels, the object, not of fluttered curiosity or pert enquiry, but of steady, ceaseless, devouring ocular study. They had long coats down to their heels and carried under each coat something that looked like a stick. One was tall and dark, the other short and red-haired. They ordered a pot of ale each.

"MacIan," said Turnbull, lifting his tankard, "the fool who wanted us to be friends made us want to go on fighting. It is only natural that the fool who wanted us to fight should make us friendly. MacIan, your health."

Dusk was already dropping, the rustics in the tavern were already lurching and lumbering out of it by twos and threes, crying clamourous good-nights to a solitary old toper that remained, before

MacIan and Turnbull had reached the really important part of their discussion.

MacIan wore an expression of sad bewilderment not uncommon with him. "I am to understand then," he said, " that you don't believe in nature."

"You may say so in a very special and emphatic sense," said Turnbull. "I do not believe in nature just as I do not believe in Odin. She is a myth. It is not merely that I do not believe that nature can guide us. It is that I do not believe that nature exists."

"Exists," said MacIan in his monotonous way, settling his pewterpot on the table.

"Yes, in a real sense nature does not exist. I mean that nobody can discover what the original nature of things would have been if things had not interfered with it. The first blade of grass began to tear up the earth and eat it; it was interfering with nature, if there is any nature. The first wild ox began to tear up the grass and eat it; he was interfering with nature, if there is any nature. In the same way," continued Turnbull, "the human, when it asserts its dominance over nature, is just as natural as the thing which it destroys."

"And in the same way," said MacIan, almost dreamily, "the superhuman, the supernatural is just as natural as the nature which it destroys."

Turnbull took his head out of his pewterpot in some anger.

"The supernatural of course," he said, "is quite another thing, the case of the supernatural is simple. The supernatural does not exist."

"Quite so," said MacIan in a rather dull voice, "you said the same about the natural. If the natural does not exist the supernatural obviously can't." And he yawned a little over his ale.

Turnbull turned, for some reason, a little bit red, and remarked quickly, "That may be jolly clever, for all I know. But everyone does know that there is a division between the things that as a matter of fact do commonly happen and the things that don't. Things that break the evident laws of nature. . . ."

"Which does not exist," put in MacIan sleepily.

Turnbull struck the table with a sudden hand.

"Good Lord in Heaven," he cried—

"Who does not exist," murmured MacIan.

"Good Lord in Heaven," thundered Turnbull, without regarding the interruption, "Do you really mean to sit there and say that you, like anybody else, would not recognise the difference between a natural occurrence and a supernatural one—if there could be such a thing. If I flew up to the ceiling. . . ."

"You would bump your head badly," cried MacIan, suddenly starting up. "One can't talk of this kind of thing under a ceiling at all. Come outside. Come outside and ascend into heaven."

He burst the door open on a blue abyss of evening and they stepped out into it: it was suddenly and strangely cool.

"Turnbull," said MacIan, "you have said some things so true and some so false that I want to talk; and I will try to talk so that you understand. For at present you do not understand at all. We don't seem to mean the same things by the same words."

He stood silent for a second or two and then resumed.

"A minute or two ago I caught you out in a real contradiction. At that moment, logically I was right. And at that moment I knew I was wrong. Yes, there is a real difference between the natural and the supernatural: if you flew up into that blue sky this instant, I should think that you were moved by God—or the devil. But if you want to know what I really think. . . . I must explain."

He stopped again, abstractedly boring the point of his sword into the earth, and went on.

"I was born and bred and taught in a complete universe. The supernatural was not natural, but it was perfectly reasonable. Nay, the supernatural to me is more reasonable than the natural: for the supernatural is a direct message from God, who is reason. I was taught that some things are natural and some things divine. I mean that some things are mechanical and some things divine. But there is a great difficulty, Turnbull. The great difficulty is that, according to my teaching, you are divine."

"Me! Divine?" said Turnbull, truculently, "what do you mean?"

"That is just the difficulty," continued MacIan, thoughtfully. "I was told that there was a difference between the grass and a man's will: and the difference was that a man's will was special and divine. A man's free will, I heard, was supernatural."

"Rubbish," said Turnbull.

"Oh!" said MacIan patiently, "then if a man's free will isn't supernatural, why do your materialists deny that it exists?"

Turnbull was silent for a moment. Then he began to speak, but MacIan continued with the same steady voice and sad eyes.

"So what I feel is this. Here is this great divine creation I was taught to believe in. I can understand your disbelieving in it, but why disbelieve in a part of it? It was all one thing to me. God had authority because he was God. Man had authority because he was man. You cannot prove that God is better than a man: nor can you prove that a man is better than a horse. Why permit any ordinary thing? Why do you let a horse be saddled?"

"Some modern thinkers disapprove of it," said Turnbull, a little doubtfully.

"I know," said MacIan grimly, "that man who talked about Love, for instance."

Turnbull made a humourous grimace: then he said, "We seem to be talking in a kind of shorthand; but I won't pretend not to understand you. What you mean is this; that you learnt about all your saints and angels at the same time as you learnt about common morality, from the same people, in the same way. And you mean to say that if one may be disputed, so may the other. Well, let that pass for the moment. But let me ask you a question in turn. Did not this system of yours, which you swallowed whole, contain all sorts of things that were merely local, the respect for the chief of your clan, or such things, the village ghost, the family feud, or what not. Did you not take in those things too along with your theology?"

MacIan stared along the dim village road, down which the last straggler from the Inn was trailing his way.

"What you say is not unreasonable," he said. "But it is not quite true. The distinction between the chief and us did exist; but it was never anything like the distinction between the human and the divine or the human and the animal. It was more like the distinction between one animal and another. But. . . ."

"Well," said Turnbull.

MacIan was silent.

"Go on," repeated Turnbull, "what's the matter with you? What are you staring at?"

"I am staring," said MacIan, at last, "at that which shall judge us both."

"Oh yes," said Turnbull, in a tired way, "I suppose you mean God."

"No, I don't," said MacIan, shaking his head. "I mean him."

And he pointed to the half-tipsy yokel who was ploughing down the road.

"What do you mean?" asked the atheist.

"I mean him," repeated MacIan, with emphasis. "He goes out in the early dawn, he digs or he ploughs a field. Then he comes back and drinks ale and then he sings a song. All your philosophies and political systems are young compared to him. All your hoary Cathedrals, yes even the eternal Church, on earth, is new compared to him. The most mouldering gods in the British Museum are new facts beside him. It is he who in the end shall judge us all."

And MacIan rose to his feet, with a vague excitement.

"What are you going to do?"

"I am going to ask him," cried MacIan, "which of us is right."

Turnbull broke into a kind of laugh. "Ask that intoxicated turnip-eater . . ." he began.

"Yes—which of us is right," cried MacIan, violently. "Oh, you have long words and I have long words; and I talk of every man being the image of God; and you talk of every man being a citizen and enlightened enough to govern. But if every man typifies God, there is God. If every man is an enlightened citizen, there is your enlightened citizen. The first man one meets is always Man. Let us catch him up."

And in gigantic strides the long lean Highlander whirled away into the grey twilight, Turnbull following with a good humoured oath.

The track of the rustic was easy to follow, even in the faltering dark; for he was enlivening his wavering walk with song. It was an interminable poem, beginning with some unspecified King William,[43] who (it appeared) lived in London town, and who, after the second rise, vanished rather abruptly from the train of thought. The rest was almost entirely about beer, and was thick with local

[43] King William . . . lived in London town seems to be a reminiscence of an old folksong that appears in widely differing versions from all over the British Isles.

topography of a quite unrecognisable kind. The singer's step was neither very rapid, nor indeed exceptionally secure; so the song grew louder and louder and the two men soon overtook him.

He was a man elderly, or rather of any age, with lean grey hair and a lean red face; but with that remarkable rustic physiognomy in which it seems that all the features stand out independently from the face; the rugged red nose going out like a limb; the bleared blue eyes standing out like signals.

He gave them greeting with the elaborate urbanity of the slightly intoxicated. MacIan, who was vibrating with one of his silent violent decisions, opened the question without delay. He explained the philosophic position in words as short and simple as possible. But the singular old man with the lank red face seemed to think uncommonly little of the short words. He fixed with a fierce affection upon one or two of the long ones.

"Atheists," he repeated with luxurious scorn, "Atheists! I know their sort, master. Atheists! Don't talk to me about 'un. Atheists."

The grounds of his disdain seemed a little dark and confused; but they were evidently sufficient. MacIan resumed in some encouragement.

"You think as I do, I hope: you think that a man should be connected with the Church; with the common Christian . . ."

The old man extended a quivering stick in the direction of a distant hill.

"There's the Church," he said, thickly, "Grassley old church that is. Pulled down it was, in the old squire's time, and . . ."

"I mean," explained MacIan elaborately, "that you think that there should be someone typifying religion, a priest."

"Priests," said the old man, with sudden passion, "Priests. I know 'un. What they want in England? That's what I say. What they want in England?"

"They want you," said MacIan.

"Quite so," said Turnbull, "and me: but they won't get us. MacIan, your attempt on the primitive innocence does not seem very successful. Let me try. What you want, my friend, is your rights. You don't want any priests or churches. A vote, a right to speak is what you. . . ."

"Who says I ant got a right to speak," said the old man, facing round in an irrational frenzy, "I got a right to speak. I'm a man, I am. I don't want no votin' nor priests, I say a man's a man; that's what I say; if a man ant a man, what is he? That's what I say, if a man ant a man, what is he? When I sees a man, I sez'es a man."

"Quite so," said Turnbull, "a citizen."

"I say he's a man," said the rustic furiously, stopping and striking his stick on the ground, "not a city or owt else. He's a man."

"You're perfectly right," said the sudden voice of MacIan, falling like a sword. "And you have kept close to something the whole world of to-day tries to forget."

"Goodnight."

And the old man went on wildly singing into the night.

"A jolly old creature," said Turnbull, "he didn't seem able to get much beyond the fact that a man is a man."

"Has anyone got beyond it?" asked MacIan.

Turnbull looked at him curiously, "are you turning an Agnostic?" he asked.

"Oh! you do not understand," cried out MacIan, "we Catholics are all agnostics. We Catholics have only in that sense got as far as realising that a man is a man. But your Ibsen's, and your Zola's, and your Shaw's, and your Tolstoy's, have not even got so far."

IX

THE EDGE OF ENGLAND

Morning broke in bitter silver along the grey and level sea; and almost as it did so Turnbull and MacIan came out of a low scrubby wood on to the empty and desolate sea shore. They had walked all night.

They had walked all night and talked all night also, and if the subject had been capable of being exhausted they would have exhausted it. Their long and changing argument had taken them through districts and landscapes equally changing. They had discussed Haeckel[44] upon hills so high and steep that in spite of the coldness of the night it seemed as if the stars might burn them. They had explained and re-explained the massacre of St. Bartholomew[45] in little white lanes walled in with standing corn as with walls of gold. They had talked about Mr. Kensit[46] in dim and twinkling pine woods amid the bewildering monotony of the pines. And it was with the end of a long speech from MacIan, passionately defending the practical achievements and the solid prosperity of the Catholic tradition, that they came out upon the edge of the sea.

MacIan had learnt much and thought more since he came out of the cloudy hills of Arisaig; he had met many typical modern figures under circumstances which were sharply symbolic; and moreover he had absorbed the main modern atmosphere from the mere presence and chance phrases of Turnbull as such atmospheres can always be absorbed from the presence and the phrases of any man of great mental vitality. He had at last begun thoroughly to understand

[44] Ernest Haeckel (1834–1919) was a German naturalist and supporter of Darwinism.

[45] The massacre of St. Bartholomew's Eve was a plot hatched by Catherine de Medici, the Cardinal Duke of Guise, Charles IX and the Duke of Anjou (later Henry III) to destroy the power of the Huguenots by slaughtering the thousands of Huguenots gathered in Paris on 24 August 1572 to celebrate the marriage of the Huguenot Henri de Navarre (later Henry IV) to Marguerite de Valois, sister of Charles IX.

[46] John Kensit (1853–1902) was a political agitator and secretary of the Protestant Truth Society. He was fatally wounded in a religious riot in Liverpool.

what are the grounds upon which the mass of the modern world solidly disapproves of Catholicism; and he threw himself into replying to them with a hot intellectual enjoyment.

"I begin to understand one or two of your dogmas, Mr. Turnbull," he had said emphatically as they ploughed heavily up a wooded hill. "And every one that I understand I deny. Take any one of them you like. You hold that your heretics and sceptics have helped the world forward and handed on a lamp of progress. I deny it. Nothing is plainer from real history than that each of your heretics invented a complete cosmos of his own which the next heretic smashed entirely to pieces. Who knows now exactly what Nestorious[47] taught? Who cares? There are only two things that we know for certain about it. The first is that Nestorius was a heretic, taught something quite opposite to the teaching of Arius[48] the heretic who came before him, and something quite useless to John Turnbull the heretic who comes after. I defy you to go back to the Free Thinkers of the past and find any habitation for yourself at all. I defy you to read Godwin[49] or Shelley, or the deists of the eighteenth century,[50] or the nature-worshipping humanists of the Renaissance, without discovering that you differ from them twice as much as you differ from the Pope. You are a nineteenth century sceptic and you are always telling me that you ignore the cruelty of nature. If you had been an eighteenth century sceptic you would have told me that I ignore the kindness and benevolence of nature. You are an atheist and you

[47] Nestorius (died c. A.D. 451) was Archbishop of Constantinopole (A.D. 428–31). He taught that in Jesus Christ there were two separate persons, a divine one and a human one, a heresy condemned by the general Councils of Ephesus and Chalcedon.

[48] Arius (A.D. 256–336) was a priest of Alexandria who taught that Jesus was not co-eternal with God the Father but created by him and, therefore, inferior, a heresy condemned by the Council of Nicaea (A.D. 325), which gave rise to the Nicaean and Athenasian creeds.

[49] William Godwin (1756–1836) was an English novelist and romantic rationalist who influenced Shelley. His daughter by Mary Wollstonecraft became Shelley's second wife and wrote *Frankenstein* (1819).

[50] The deists of the eighteenth century believed that God created the universe and man but has since had nothing to do with them (a *Deus absconditus* point of view).

praise the deists of the eighteenth century. Read them instead of praising them, and you will find that their whole universe stands or falls with the deity. You are a materialist and you think Bruno[51] a scientific hero. See what he said and you will think him an insane mystic. No, the great Freethinker with his genuine ability and honesty does not in practice destroy Christianity. What he does destroy is the Freethinker who went before. Freethought may be suggestive, it may be inspiriting, it may have as much as you please of the merits that come from vivacity and variety. But there is one thing Freethought can never be by any possibility—Freethought can never be progressive. It can never be progressive because it will accept nothing from the past; it begins every time again from the beginning; and it goes every time in a different direction. All the rational philosophers have gone along different roads, so it is impossible to say which has gone furthest. Who can discuss whether Emerson was a better optimist than Schopenhouer[52] was pessimist; it is like asking if this corn is as yellow as that hill is steep. No! there are only two things that really progress; and they both accept accumulations of authority. They may be progressing up-hill or down; they may be growing steadily better or steadily worse; but they have steadily increased in certain definable matters; they have steadily advanced in a certain definable direction; they are the only two things it seems that ever *can* progress. The first is strictly physical science. The second is the Catholic Church."

"Physical science and the Catholic Church," said Turnbull sarcastically, "and no doubt the first owes a great deal to the second."

"If you pressed that point I might reply that it was very probable," answered MacIan calmly. "I often fancy that your historical generalisations rest frequently on random instances; I should not be surprised if your vague notions of the Church as the persecutor of science were a generalisation from Galileo. I should not be at

---

[51] Giordano Bruno (1550–1600), an Italian philosopher who taught in Paris, attempted to reconcile scholasticism with Aristotelianism. He was burned in Rome after becoming a Calvinist.

[52] Arthur Schopenhauer (1788–1860) was a German philosopher known for his theories and publications on the will and on pessimism.

all surprised if when you counted the scientific investigations and discoveries since the Fall of Rome you found that a great mass of them had been made by monks. But the matter is irrelevant to my meaning. I say that if you want an example of anything which has progressed in the moral world by the same method as science in the material world, by continually adding to without unsettling what was there before, then I say that there *is* only one example of it! And that is Us."

"With this enormous difference," said Turnbull, "that however elaborate be the calculations of physical science, their net result can be tested. Granted that it took millions of books I never read and millions of men I never heard of to discover the electric light. Still I can see the electric light. But I cannot see the supreme virtue which is the result of all your theologies and sacraments."

"Catholic virtue is often invisible because it is the normal," answered MacIan. "Christianity is always out of fashion because it is always sane; and all fashions are mild insanities. When Italy is mad on Art the Church seems too Puritanical; when England is mad on Puritanism the Church seems too artistic. When you quarrel with us now you class us with Kingship and despotism; but when you quarrelled with us first it was because we would not accept the divine despotism of Henry VIII. The Church always seems to be behind the times, when it is really beyond the times; it is waiting till the last fad shall have seen its last summer. It keeps the key of a permanent virtue."

"Oh I have heard all that," said Turnbull with genial contempt. "I have heard that Christianity keeps the key of virtue and that if you read Tom Paine[53] you will cut your throat at Monte Carlo. It is such rubbish that I am not even angry at it. You say that Christianity is the prop of morals; but what more do you do? When a doctor attends you and could poison you with a pinch of salt, do you ask whether he is a Christian? You ask whether he is a gentleman, whether he is an M.D., anything but that. When a soldier enlists to die for his country

[53] Tom Paine (1737–1809) was an Englishman who took French nationality and became a member of the Convention after defending the American and French revolutions in his *Rights of Man*. He died in New York.

or disgrace it, do you ask whether he is a Christian? You are more likely to ask whether he is Oxford or Cambridge at the Boat Race. If you think your creed essential to morals why do you not make it a test for these things?

"We once did make it a test for these things," said MacIan smiling, "and then you told us that we were imposing by force a faith unsupported by argument. It seems rather hard that having first been told that our creed must be false because we did use tests, we should now be told that it must be false because we don't. But I notice that most anti-Christian arguments are of the same logical calibre."

"That is all very well as a debating club answer," replied Turnbull good humouredly, "but the question still remains: Why don't you confine yourself more to Christians if Christians are the only really good men?"

"Who talked of such folly?" asked MacIan disdainfully. "Do you suppose that the Catholic Church ever held that Christians were the only good men? Why the Catholics of the Catholic Middle Ages talked about the virtues of all the virtuous Pagans until humanity was sick of the subject. No, if you really want to know what we mean when we say that Christianity has a special power of virtue, I will tell you. The Church is the only thing on earth that can perpetuate a type of virtue and make it something more than a fashion. The thing is so plain and historical that I hardly think you will ever deny it. You cannot deny that it is perfectly possible that to-morrow morning in Ireland or in Italy there might appear a man not only as good, but good in exactly the same way as St. Francis of Assisi. Very well, now take the other types of human virtue; many of them splendid. The English gentleman of Elizabeth was chivalrous and idealistic. But can you stand still here in this meadow and *be* an English gentleman of Elizabeth? The austere republican of the eighteenth century, with his stern patriotism and his simple life, was a fine fellow. But have you ever seen him? Have you ever seen an austere republican? Only a hundred years have passed and that volcano of revolutionary truth and valour is as cold as the mountains of the moon. And so it is and so it will be with the Ethics which are buzzing down Fleet Street at this instant as I speak. What phrase would inspire the London clerk or workman just now? Perhaps that he is a son of the British Empire on which the sun never sets; perhaps that he is a prop of his Trades Union, or a class-conscious proletarian something or other; perhaps merely that he is a gentleman when he obviously is not. Those names and notions are all honourable; but how long will they last? Empires break; industrial conditions change; the suburbs will not last for ever. What will remain? I will tell you. The Catholic Saint will remain."

"And suppose I don't like him," said Turnbull.

"On my theory the question is rather whether he will like you. Or more probably whether he will ever have heard of you. But I grant the reasonableness of your query. You have a right if you speak, as the ordinary man, to ask if you will like the saint. But as the ordinary man you do like him. You revel in him. If you dislike him it is not because you are a nice ordinary man, but because you are (if you will excuse me) a sophisticated prig of a Fleet Street editor. That is just the funny part of it. The human race has always admired the Catholic virtues however little it can practise them; and oddly enough it has admired most those of them that the modern world most sharply disputed. You complain of Catholicism for setting up an ideal of virginity; it did nothing of the kind. The whole human race set up an ideal of virginity; the Greeks in Athene, the Romans in the Vestal fire, set up an ideal of virginity. What then is your real quarrel with Catholicism? Your quarrel can only be, your quarrel really only is, that Catholicism has *achieved* an ideal of virginity; that it is no longer a mere piece of floating poetry. But if you, and a few feverish men, in top hats, running about in a street in London, choose to differ as to the ideal itself, not only from the Church, but from the Parthenon whose name means virginity, from the Roman Empire which went outwards from the virgin flame, from the whole legend and tradition of Europe, from the lion who would not touch virgins, from the unicorn who repects them, and who make up together the bearers of your own national shield, from the most living and lawless of your own poets, from Massinger[54] who wrote the

---

[54] Philip Massinger (1583–1640) was a dramatist best known as the author of *A New Way to Pay Old Debts*. He wrote *The Virgin Martyr* (1622) in collaboration with Thomas Dekker (1570–1632). It is the story of Dorothea, who dies a martyr rather than give up her love, Antonius, or her religion.

Virgin Martyr, from Shakespeare who wrote Measure for Measure; —
if you in Fleet Street differ from all this human experience, does it
never strike you that it may be Fleet Street that is wrong?"

"No," answered Turnbull. "I trust that I am sufficiently fair-
minded to canvas and consider the idea; but having considered it I
think Fleet Street is right, yes—even if the Parthenon is wrong. I
think that as the world goes on new psychological atmospheres are
generated, and in these atmospheres it is possible to find delicacies
and combinations which in other times would have to be represented
by some ruder symbol. Every man feels the need of some element of
purity in sex; perhaps they can only typify purity as the absence of sex.
You will laugh if I suggest that we may have made in Fleet Street an
atmosphere in which a man can be as passionate as Sir Lancelot and
as pure as Sir Galahad. But after all, we have in the modern world
erected many such atmospheres. We have for instance a new and
imaginative appreciation of children."

"Quite so," replied MacIan, with a singular smile. "It has been
very well put by one of the brightest of your young authors who
said: 'Unless you become as little children ye shall in no wise enter
the Kingdom of Heaven.' But you are quite right; there is a modern
worship of children. And what, I ask you, is this modern worship of
children? What in the name of all the angels and devils, is it except
the worship of virginity? Why should anyone worship a thing
merely because it is small or immature? No; you have tried to escape
from this thing and the very thing you point to as the goal of your
escape is only the thing again. Am I wrong in saying that these
things seem to be eternal?"

And it was with these words that they came in sight of the eternal
waters.

THE MAN WHO WAS THURSDAY

1907

FOREWORD

The Bolshevists have done a good many silly things; but the most strangely silly thing that ever I heard of was that they tried to turn this Anti-Anarchist romance into an Anarchist play. Heaven only knows what they really made of it; beyond apparently making it mean the opposite of everything it meant. Probably they thought that being able to see that a policeman is funny means thinking that a policeman is futile. Probably they would say that thinking Don Quixote funny means thinking chivalry futile; in other words, they are barbarians and have not learnt how to laugh. But in this case a certain consequence follows. Making fun of a policeman would always be fun enough for me. Treating this tale as a farce of balloons and escaped elephants would never trouble me; and I would never bore any body about the meaning of the allegory. But if somebody, even in Moscow or Vienna, starts making it mean something totally different, or flatly contrary, I cannot avoid a word about its real origin or outline. I do not want to take myself seriously; it is Bolshevism, among its other crimes, that is making me a serious person for a moment.

So many people have lately been occupied in turning good novels into bad plays, that the authors of this adaptation have conceived the bolder and more hopeful scheme of turning a bad novel into a good play. For though I know very little about "The Man Who Was Thursday," only a very casual acquaintance is needed to make sure that if it is a novel, it is a bad novel. To do it justice, by its own description, it is not a novel but a nightmare. And since that sub-title is perhaps the only true and reliable statement in the book, I may plead it as a sort of excuse for my share in the matter. Nightmares on the stage are not uncommon nowadays; and some of them are regarded as realistic studies, because they are examples of that very deep and bottomless sort of nightmare from which it happens to be difficult to wake up. Nevertheless a distinction between the dreams of to-day and those of that remoter day, or rather night, is essential to understanding whatever there may be to understand. To do them justice, the new nightmares do generally belong to a night: as day-dreams belong to a day. They are aspects; they are fragmentary and, to do them justice, they are frivolous. It was not so with a certain spirit that brooded for a certain time over the literature of my youth. I can remember the time when pessimism was dogmatic, when it was even orthodox. The people who had read Schopenhauer regarded themselves as having found out everything and found that it was nothing. Their system was a system, and therefore had a character of surrounding the mind. It therefore really resembled a nightmare, in the sense of being imprisoned or even bound hand and foot; of being none the less captive because it was rather in a lunatic asylum than a reasonable hell or place of punishment. There is a great deal in the modern world that I think evil and a great deal more that I think silly; but it does seem to me to have escaped from this mere prison of pessimism. Our civilisation may be breaking up; there are not wanting many exhilarating signs of it breaking down. But it is not merely closing in; and therefore it is not a nightmare, like the narrow despair of the 'nineties. In so far as it is breaking down, it seems to me more of a mental breakdown than a moral breakdown. In so far as it is breaking up, it may let in a certain amount of daylight as well as a great deal of wind. But it is not stifling like positive pessimism and materialism; and it was in the middle of a thick London fog of these things that I sat down and tried to write this story, nearly twenty years ago.

It is in relation to that particular heresy that much of its main suggestion must be understood. Perhaps it is not worth while to try to kill heresies which so rapidly kill themselves — and the cult of suicide committed suicide sometime ago. But I should not wish it supposed, as some I think have supposed, that in resisting the heresy of pessimism I implied the equally morbid and diseased insanity of optimism. I was not then considering whether anything is really evil, but whether everything is really evil; and in relation to the latter nightmare it does still seem to me relevant to say that nightmares are not true; and that in them even the faces of friends may appear as the faces of fiends. I tried to turn this notion of resistance to a nightmare into a topsy-turvey tale about a man who fancied himself alone among enemies, and found that each of the enemies was in fact on his own side and in his own solitude. That is the only thing that can be called a meaning in the story; all the rest of it was written for fun; and though it was great fun for me, I do not forget that sobering epigram which tells us that easy writing is dashed hard reading.

THE MAN WHO
WAS THURSDAY

G.K.Chesterton

TO EDMUND CLERIHEW BENTLEY[1]

A cloud was on the mind of men, and wailing went the weather,
Yea, a sick cloud upon the soul when we were boys together.
Science announced nonentity and art admired decay;
The world was old and ended: but you and I were gay;
Round us in antic order their crippled vices came—
Lust that had lost its laughter, fear that had lost its shame.
Like the white lock of Whistler, that lit our aimless gloom,
Men showed their own white feather[2] as proudly as a plume.
Life was a fly that faded, and death a drone that stung;
The world was very old indeed when you and I were young.
They twisted even decent sin to shapes not to be named;
Men were ashamed of honour; but we were not ashamed.
Weak if we were and foolish, not thus we failed, not thus;
When that black Baal[3] blocked the heavens he had no hymns from us.
Children we were—our forts of sand were even as weak as we,
High as they went we piled them up to break that bitter sea.
Fools as we were in motley, all jangling and absurd,
When all church bells were silent our cap and bells were heard.

Not all unhelped we held the fort, our tiny flags unfurled;
Some giants laboured in that cloud to lift it from the world.
I find again the book we found, I feel the hour that flings
Far out of fish-shaped Paumanok[4] some cry of cleaner things;

---

[1] Edmund Clerihew Bentley (1875–1956) was Chesterton's school friend at St. Paul's School on Hammersmith Road, and a member of that school's Junior Debating Club. He was the inventor of the comic verse form known as the clerihew and the author of several detective stories of which the best known is *Trent's Last Case*. From 1912 he was chief leader writer on the *Daily Telegraph*.

[2] White feather signifies cowardice. It was a practice to send a white feather to anyone thought to be a coward.

[3] Baal was the god of the Phoenician religion and type of all false gods.

[4] Paumanok is the name in Algonquian for Long Island, New York, where Walt Whitman was born. It can also mean "offering" and was the name given to shell beads used as a barter token.

And the Green Carnation[5] withered, as in forest fires that pass,
Roared in the wind of all the world ten million leaves of grass;
Or sane and sweet and sudden as a bird sings in the rain—
Truth out of Tusitala[6] spoke and pleasure out of pain.
Yea, cool and clear and sudden as a bird sings in the grey,
Dunedin[7] to Samoa spoke, and darkness unto day.
But we were young; we lived to see God break their bitter charms,
God and the good Republic come riding back in arms:
We have seen the City of Mansoul,[8] even as it rocked, relieved—
Blessed are they who did not see, but being blind, believed.

This is a tale of those old fears, even of those emptied hells,
And none but you shall understand[9] the true thing that it tells—

[5] The Green Carnation was the symbol of the decadent movement of the 1890s. Green flowers of various types can evolve as sports (chance mutations) alongside the normally colored varieties, but in most cases their lack of distinctive color and sometimes of scent leads to their being neglected by pollenating insects, and so they remain infertile; it was perhaps that very quality that attracted the "art for art's sake" devotees among the aesthetes and decadents.

[6] *Tusitala* means "the teller of tales" in Samoan. It was the name given to Robert Louis Stevenson (1850–94), the Scottish novelist, essayist and poet best known for *Treasure Island* and *Dr. Jekyll and Mr. Hyde*, when he went to Samoa to find purer air after contracting tuberculosis.

[7] Dunedin is the name of Edinburgh in Scottish Gaelic.

[8] The City of Mansoul was the capital of the universe in *The Holy War* (1682), an allegory by John Bunyan (1628–88). The image of Mansoul (Man's Soul) being relieved from siege was suggested to Chesterton by the sieges of Ladysmith and of Mafeking during the Boer War of 1899–1902.

[9] None but you shall understand is a reference to E. C. Bentley and Chesterton being fellow teenagers confronted by the 1800s when Chesterton at least was tormented by solipsism and doubt. In his *Autobiography* (1936) Chesterton wrote: "So far as the story had any sense in it, it was meant to begin with the picture of the world at its worst and to work towards the suggestion that the picture was not so black as it was already painted. I explained that the whole thing was thrown out in the nihilism of the Nineties in the dedicatory lines which I wrote to my friend Bentley, who had been through the same period and problems; asking rhetorically: 'Who shall understand but you?' In reply to which a book reviewer very sensibly remarked that if nobody understood the book except Mr. Bentley, it seemed unreasonable to ask other people to read it."

Of what colossal gods of shame[10] could cow men and yet crash,
Of what huge devils hid the stars, yet fell at a pistol flash.
The doubts that were so plain to chase, so dreadful to withstand—
Oh, who shall understand but you; yea, who shall understand?
The doubts that drove us through the night as we two talked amain,
And day had broken on the streets e'er it broke upon the brain.
Between us, by the peace of God, such truth can now be told;
Yea, there is strength in striking root, and good in growing old.
We have found common things at last, and marriage and a creed,
And I may safely write it now, and you may safely read.

G.K.C.

[10] Colossal gods of shame is a further reference to the aesthestes, decadents and nihilists of the 1890s.

I

THE TWO POETS OF SAFFRON PARK[11]

The suburb of Saffron Park lay on the sunset side of London, as red and ragged as a cloud of sunset. It was built of a bright brick throughout; its skyline was fantastic, and even its ground plan was wild. It had been the outburst of a speculative builder,[12] faintly tinged with art, who called its architecture sometimes Elizabethan and sometimes Queen Anne, apparently under the impression that the two sovereigns were identical. It was described with some justice as an artistic colony, though it never in any definable way produced any art. But although its pretensions to be an intellectual centre were a little vague, its pretensions to be a pleasant place were quite indisputable. The stranger who looked for the first time at the quaint red houses could only think how very oddly shaped the people must be who could fit in to them. Nor when he met the people was he disappointed in this respect. The place was not only pleasant, but perfect, if once he could regard it not as a deception but rather as a dream. Even if the people were not 'artists', the whole was nevertheless artistic.

[11] Saffron Park is a thinly disguised Bedford Park, which was the first of the so-called garden suburbs situated to the north of Chiswick and to the west of Kensington. The architect Norman Shaw produced a mixture of half-timbering and red brick twisted chimneys set along tree-lined roads that intersected at common lawns, with the whole district centered on the church of St. Michael and All Angels and a public house called The Tabard Inn. The area attracted such avant-garde figures as the painters Camille and Lucien Pissarro and the poet W. B. Yeats. At 8 Bath Road there lived Frances Blogg, who was later to be Chesterton's wife. There is little doubt that Chesterton is describing an amalgam of the many parties he attended in the area.

[12] A speculative builder refers to the builder of Bedford Park, Jonathan Comyns-Carr, who was bankrupted by the project and left to live in one of his own villas with, so it is said, a bailiff as his butler. A rhyme published in 1881 in the *St. James's Gazette* describes his achievement:

> This was a village builded
> For all who are aesthete
> Whose precious souls it fill did
> With utter joy complete.

That young man with the long, auburn hair and the impudent face—
that young man was not really a poet; but surely he was a poem. That
old gentleman with the wild, white beard and the wild, white hat—
that venerable humbug was not really a philosopher; but at least he was
the cause of philosophy in others. That scientific gentleman with the
bald, egg-like head and the bare, bird-like neck had no real right to the
airs of science that he assumed. He had not discovered anything new in
biology; but what biological creature could he have discovered more
singular than himself? Thus, and thus only, the whole place had
properly to be regarded; it had to be considered not so much as a
workshop for artists, but as a frail but finished work of art. A man
who stepped into its social atmosphere felt as if he had stepped into a
written comedy.

More especially this attractive unreality fell upon it about nightfall,
when the extravagant roofs were dark against the afterglow and the
whole insane village seemed as separate as a drifting cloud. This again was
more strongly true of the many nights of local festivity, when the little
gardens were often illuminated, and the big Chinese lanterns glowed in
the dwarfish trees like some fierce and monstrous fruit. And this was
strongest of all on one particular evening, still vaguely remembered in
the locality, of which the auburn-haired poet was the hero. It was not
by any means the only evening of which he was the hero. On many
nights those passing by his little back garden might hear his high, didactic
voice laying down the law to men and particularly to women. The attitude of women in such cases was indeed one of the paradoxes of the place.
Most of the women were of the kind vaguely called emancipated, and
professed some protest against male supremacy. Yet these new women
would always pay to a man the extravagant compliment which no ordinary woman ever pays to him, that of listening while he is talking.
And Mr. Lucian Gregory, the red-haired poet, was really (in some
sense) a man worth listening to, even if one only laughed at the end
of it. He put the old cant of the lawlessness of art and the art of lawlessness with a certain impudent freshness which gave at least a
momentary pleasure. He was helped in some degree by the arresting
oddity of his appearance, which he worked, as the phrase goes, for
all it was worth. His dark red hair parted in the middle was literally
like a woman's, and curved into the slow curls of a virgin in a

pre-Raphaelite[13] picture. From within this almost saintly oval, however, his face projected suddenly broad and brutal, the chin carried forward with a look of cockney contempt. This combination at once tickled and terrified the nerves of a neurotic population. He seemed like a walking blasphemy, a blend of the angel and the ape.

This particular evening, if it is remembered for nothing else, will be remembered in that place for its strange sunset. It looked like the end of the world. All the heaven seemed covered with a quite vivid and palpable plumage; you could only say that the sky was full of feathers, and of feathers that almost brushed the face. Across the great part of the dome they were grey, and with the strangest tints of violet and mauve and an unnatural pink or pale green; but towards the west the whole grew past description, transparent and passionate, and the last red-hot plumes of it covered up the sun like something too good to be seen. The whole was so close about the earth, as to express nothing but a violent secrecy. The very empyrean seemed to be a secret. It expressed that splendid smallness which is the soul of local patriotism. The very sky seemed small.

I say that there are some inhabitants who may remember the evening if only by that oppressive sky. There are others who may remember it because it marked the first appearance in the place of the second poet of Saffron Park. For a long time the red-haired revolutionary had reigned without a rival; it was upon the night of the sunset that his solitude suddenly ended. The new poet, who introduced himself by the name of Gabriel[14] Syme, was a very mild-looking mortal, with a fair, pointed beard and faint, yellow hair. But an impression grew that he was less meek than he looked. He signalized his entrance by differing with the established poet, Gregory, upon the whole nature of poetry. He said that he (Syme) was a poet of law, a poet of order; nay, he said he was a poet of respectability. So all the Saffron Parkers looked at him as if he had that moment fallen out of that impossible sky.

[13] The pre-Raphaelite Brotherhood was a group of English painters led by Rossetti, Millais and Holman Hunt, who in 1847–49 adopted a style in imitation of those painters who lived before Raphael (1483–1523). Their works, often illustrating moral themes, exhibited great attention to detail and the use of strikingly bright colors.

[14] Gabriel was not then as uncommon a name as it now is, but Chesterton intends it to contrast strongly with Lucian (Lucifer).

In fact, Mr. Lucian Gregory, the anarchic poet, connected the two events.

'It may well be,' he said, in his sudden lyrical manner, 'it may well be on such a night of clouds and cruel colours that there is brought forth upon the earth such a portent as a respectable poet. You say you are a poet of law; I say you are a contradiction in terms. I only wonder there were not comets and earthquakes on the night you appeared in this garden.'

The man with the meek blue eyes and the pale, pointed beard endured these thunders with a certain submissive solemnity. The third party of the group, Gregory's sister Rosamond, who had her brother's braids of red hair, but a kindlier face underneath them, laughed with such mixture of admiration and disapproval as she gave commonly to the family oracle.

Gregory resumed in high oratorical good humour.

'An artist is identical with an anarchist,' he cried. 'You might transpose the words anywhere. An anarchist is an artist. The man who throws a bomb is an artist, because he prefers a great moment to everything. He sees how much more valuable is one burst of blazing light, one peal of perfect thunder, than the mere common bodies of a few shapeless policemen. An artist disregards all governments, abolishes all conventions. The poet delights in disorder only. If it were not so, the most poetical thing in the world would be the Underground Railway.'

'So it is,' said Mr. Syme.

'Nonsense!' said Gregory, who was very rational when any one else attempted paradox. 'Why do all the clerks and navvies in the railway trains look so sad and tired, so very sad and tired? I will tell you. It is because they know that the train is going right. It is because they know that whatever place they have taken a ticket for that place they will reach. It is because after they have passed Sloane Square they know that the next station must be Victoria, and nothing but Victoria. Oh, their wild rapture! oh, their eyes like stars and their souls again in Eden, if the next station were unaccountably Baker Street!'

'It is you who are unpoetical,' replied the poet Syme. 'If what you say of clerks is true, they can only be as prosaic as your poetry.

The rare, strange thing is to hit the mark; the gross, obvious thing is to miss it. We feel it is epical when man with one wild arrow strikes a distant bird. Is it not also epical when man with one wild engine strikes a distant station? Chaos is dull; because in chaos the train might indeed go anywhere, to Baker Street or to Bagdad. But man is a magician, and his whole magic is in this, that he does say Victoria, and lo! it is Victoria. No, take your books of mere poetry and prose; let me read a time table, with tears of pride. Take your Byron, who commemorates the defeats of man; give me Bradshaw,[15] who commemorates his victories. Give me Bradshaw, I say!'

'Must you go?' inquired Gregory sarcastically.

'I tell you,' went on Syme with passion, 'that every time a train comes in I feel that it has broken past batteries of besiegers, and that man has won a battle against chaos. You say contemptuously that when one has left Sloane Square one must come to Victoria. I say that one might do a thousand things instead, and that whenever I really come there I have the sense of hair-breadth escape. And when I hear the guard shout out the word "Victoria", it is not an unmeaning word. It is to me the cry of a herald announcing conquest. It is to me indeed "Victoria"; it is the victory of Adam.'

Gregory wagged his heavy, red head with a slow and sad smile.

'And even then,' he said, 'we poets always ask the question, "And what is Victoria now that you have got there?" You think Victoria is like the new Jerusalem. We know that the New Jerusalem will only be like Victoria. Yes, the poet will be discontented even in the streets of heaven. The poet is always in revolt.'

'There again,' said Syme irritably, 'what is there poetical about being in revolt? You might as well say that it is poetical to be sea-sick. Being sick is a revolt. Both being sick and being rebellious may be the wholesome thing on certain desperate occasions; but I'm hanged if I can see why they are poetical. Revolt in the abract is—revolting. It is mere vomiting.'

The girl winced for a flash at the unpleasant word, but Syme was too hot to heed her.

[15] This is a reference to Bradshaw's Railway Guides, published by Henry Blacklock & Co. Ltd., Bradshaw House, Alms Hill Road, Manchester 8, England.

Say Victoria, and lo! it is Victoria.

'It is things going right,' he cried, 'that is poetical! Our digestions, for instance, going sacredly and silently right, that is the foundation of all poetry. Yes, the most poetical thing, more poetical than the flowers, more poetical than the stars—the most poetical thing in the world is not being sick.'

'Really,' said Gregory superciliously, 'the examples you choose—'

'I beg your pardon,' said Syme grimly, 'I forgot we had abolished all conventions.'

For the first time a red patch appeared on Gregory's forehead.

"You don't expect me,' he said, 'to revolutionize society on this lawn?'

Syme looked straight into his eyes and smiled sweetly.

'No, I don't,' he said; 'but I suppose that if you were serious about your anarchism, that is exactly what you would do.'

Gregory's big bull's eyes blinked suddenly like those of an angry lion, and one could almost fancy that his red mane rose.

'Don't you think, then,' he said in a dangerous voice, 'that I am serious about my anarchism?'

'I beg your pardon?' said Syme.

'Am I not serious about my anarchism?' cried Gregory, with knotted fists.

'My dear fellow!' said Syme, and strolled away.

With surprise, but with curious pleasure, he found Rosamond Gregory still in his company.

'Mr. Syme,' she said, 'do the people who talk like you and my brother often mean what they say? Do you mean what you say now?'

Syme smiled.

'Do you?' he asked.

'What do you mean?' asked the girl, with grave eyes.

'My dear Miss Gregory,' said Syme gently, 'there are many kinds of sincerity and insincerity. When you say "thank you" for the salt, do you mean what you say? No. When you say "the world is round", do you mean what you say? No. It is true, but you don't mean it. Now, sometimes a man like your brother really finds a thing he does mean. It may be only a half-truth, quarter-truth, tenth-truth; but then he says more than he means—from sheer force of meaning it.'

She was looking at him from under level brows; her face was grave and open, and there had fallen upon it the shadow of that unreasoning responsibility which is at the bottom of the most frivolous woman, the maternal watch which is as old as the world.

'Is he really an anarchist, then?' she asked.

'Only in that sense I speak of,' replied Syme; 'or if you prefer it, in that nonsense.'

She drew her broad brows together and said abruptly:

'He wouldn't really use—bombs or that sort of thing?'

Syme broke into a great laugh, that seemed too large for his slight and somewhat dandified figure.

'Good Lord, no!' he said, 'that has to be done anonymously.'

And at that the corners of her own mouth broke into a smile and she thought with a simultaneous pleasure of Gregory's absurdity and of his safety.

Syme strolled with her to a seat in the corner of the garden, and continued to pour out his opinions. For he was a sincere man and in spite of his superficial airs and graces, at root a humble one. And it is always the the humble man who talks too much; the proud man who watches himself too closely. He defended respectability with violence and exaggeration. He grew passionate in his praise of tidiness and propriety. All the time there was a smell of lilac all round him. Once he heard very faintly in some distant street a barrel-organ[16] begin to play, and it seemed to him that his heroic words were moving to a tiny tune from under or beyond the world.

He stared and talked at the girl's red hair and amused face for what seemed to be a few minutes; and then feeling that the groups in such a place should mix, rose to his feet. To his astonishment, he discovered the whole garden empty. Every one had gone long ago, and he went himself with a rather hurried apology. He left with a sense of champagne in his head which he could not afterwards explain. In the wild events which were to follow this girl had no part

[16] A barrel-organ will recur in the narrative where it seems to take on the function of a leitmotiv of normality.

at all; he never saw her again until all his tale was over. And yet, in some indescribable way, she kept recurring like a motive in music through all his mad adventures afterwards, and the glory of her strange hair ran like a red thread through those dark and ill-drawn tapestries of the night. For what followed was so improbable, that it might well have been a dream.

When Syme went out into the starlit street, he found it for the moment empty. Then he realized (in some odd way) that the silence was rather a living silence than a dead one. Directly outside the door stood a street lamp, whose gleam gilded the leaves of the tree that bent out over the fence behind him. About a foot from the lamp-post stood a figure almost as rigid and motionless as the lamp-post itself. The tall hat and long frock-coat were black; the face, in an abrupt shadow, was almost as dark. Only a fringe of fiery hair against the light, and also something aggressive in the attitude, proclaimed that it was the poet Gregory. He had something of the look of a masked bravo waiting sword in hand for his foe.

He made a sort of doubtful salute, which Syme somewhat more formally returned.

'I was waiting for you,' said Gregory. 'Might I have a moment's conversation?'

'Certainly. About what?' asked Syme in a sort of weak wonder.

Gregory struck out with his stick at the lamp-post, and then at the tree.

'About *this* and *this*,' he cried; 'about order and anarchy. There is your precious order, that lean, iron lamp, ugly and barren; and there is anarchy, rich, living, reproducing itself—there is anarchy, splendid in green and gold.'

'All the same,' replied Syme patiently, 'just at present you only see the tree by the light of the lamp. I wonder when you would ever see the lamp by the light of the tree.' Then after a pause he said, 'But may I ask if you have been standing out here in the dark only to resume our little argument?'

'No,' cried out Gregory, in a voice that rang down the street, 'I did not stand here to resume our argument, but to end it for ever.'

The silence fell again, and Syme, though he understood nothing, listened instinctively for something serious. Gregory began in a smooth voice and with a rather bewildering smile.

'Mr. Syme,' he said, 'this evening you succeeded in doing something rather remarkable. You did something to me that no man born of woman has ever succeeded in doing before.'

'Indeed!'

'Now I remember,' resumed Gregory reflectively, 'one other person succeeded in doing it. The captain of a penny steamer (if I remember correctly) at Southend.[17] You have irritated me.'

'I am very sorry,' replied Syme with gravity.

'I am afraid my fury and your insult are too shocking to be wiped out even with an apology,' said Gregory very calmly. 'No duel could wipe it out. If I struck you dead I could not wipe it out. There is only one way by which that insult can be erased, and that way I choose. I am going, at the possible sacrifice of my like and honour, to *prove* to you that you were wrong in what you said.'

'In what I said?'

'You said I was not serious about being an anarchist.'

'There are degrees of seriousness,' replied Syme. 'I have never doubted that you were perfectly sincere in this sense, that you thought what you said well worth saying, that you thought a paradox might wake men up to a neglected truth.'

Gregory stared at him steadily and painfully.

'And in no other sense,' he asked, 'you think me serious. You think me a *flâneur* who lets fall occasional truths. You do not think that in a deeper, a more deadly sense, I am serious.'

Syme struck his stick violently on the stones of the road.

'Serious!' he cried. 'Good Lord! is this street serious? Are these damned Chinese lanterns serious? Is the whole caboodle serious? One comes here and talks a pack of bosh, and perhaps some sense as well, but I should think very little of a man who didn't keep something in the background of his life that was more serious than all this talking—something more serious, whether it was religion or only drink.'

---

[17] Southend is a popular seaside resort on the Thames Estuary some thirty miles to the east of London.

'Very well,' said Gregory, his face darkening, 'you shall see something more serious than either drink or religion.'

Syme stood waiting with his usual air of mildness until Gregory again opened his lips.

'You spoke just now of having a religion. Is it really true that you have one?'

'Oh,' said Syme with a beaming smile, 'we are all Catholics[18] now.'

'Then may I ask you to swear by whatever gods or saints your religion involves that you will *not* reveal what I am now going to tell you to any son of Adam, and especially not to the police? Will you swear that! If you will take upon yourself this awful abnegation, if you will consent to burden your soul with a vow that you should never make and a knowledge you would never dream about, I will promise you in return —'

'You will promise me in return?' inquired Syme, as the other paused.

'I will promise you a very entertaining evening.'

Syme suddenly took off his hat.

'Your offer,' he said, 'is far too idiotic to be declined. You say that a poet is always an anarchist. I disagree; but I hope at least that he is always a sportsman. Permit me, here and now, to swear as a Christian, and promise as a good comrade and a fellow-artist, that I will not report anything of this, whatever it is, to the police. And now, in the name of Colney Hatch,[19] what is it?'

'I think,' said Gregory, with placid irrelevancy, 'that we will call a cab.'

[18] It should be remembered that when Chesterton wrote these words in 1907 or before, he was an Anglican and was not to be converted to Roman Catholicism for another fifteen years in 1922. He was very knowledgeable about and sympathetic to Roman Catholicism, and his theological position as outlined in *Orthodoxy* (1908) showed that he was not far removed doctrinally. However, he was at the time an Anglo-Catholic, may have intended Syme to be one, and was not above poking sly fun at the Roman Catholic position, as in his description of MacIan's dream in the 1909 version of *The Ball and the Cross*. We should also remember that some of the wishful thinking in Father Hugh Benson's utopian novels did countenance the revival of burning at the stake in a future ideal society, and Chesterton was always prepared to attack that sort of thing.

[19] Colney Hatch was the location of a lunatic asylum.

He gave two long whistles, and a hansom came rattling down the road. The two got into it in silence. Gregory gave through the trap the address of an obscure public-house on the Chiswick bank of the river.[20] The cab whisked itself away again, and in it these two fantastics quitted their fantastic town.

[20] An obscure public-house on the Chiswick bank of the river was only a couple of miles at most south of Saffron (Bedford) Park on the north bank of the Thames. The subsequent description of "a particularly dreary and greasy beershop" with a superb cuisine and wine list serving as a meeting place for anarchists is not as farfetched as it may seem. A group of anarchists led by Rudolf Rocker (1873–1958) did meet in a London public house where they maintained an armory and where the food was reputed to be very good. Jewish anarchists also met in a pub in Hanbury Street, Whitechapel, whereas teetotal Yiddish-speaking anarchists had a club on Jubilee Street, Stepney, in 1906.

II

THE SECRET OF GABRIEL SYME

The cab pulled up before a particularly dreary and greasy beershop, into which Gregory rapidly conducted his companion. They seated themselves in a close and dim sort of bar-parlour, at a stained wooden table with one wooden leg. The room was so small and dark, that very little could be seen of the attendant who was summoned, beyond a vague and dark impression of something bulky and bearded.

'Will you take a little supper?' asked Gregory politely. 'The *pâté de foie gras* is not good here, but I can recommend the game.'

Syme received the remark with stolidity, imagining it to be a joke. Accepting the vein of humour, he said, with a well-bred indifference:

'Oh, bring me some lobster mayonnaise.'

To his indescribable astonishment, the man only said, 'Certainly, sir!' and went away apparently to get it.

'What will you drink?' resumed Gregory, with the same careless yet apologetic air. 'I shall only have a *creme de menthe* myself: I have dined. But the champagne can really be trusted. Do let me start you with a half-bottle of Pommery at least?'

'Thank you!' said the motionless Syme. 'You are very good.'

His further attempts at conversation, somewhat disorganized in themselves, were cut short finally as by a thunderbolt by the actual appearance of the lobster. Syme tasted it, and found it particularly good. Then he suddenly began to eat with great rapidity and appetite.

'Excuse me if I enjoy myself rather obviously!' he said to Gregory, smiling. 'I don't often have the luck to have a dream like this. It is new to me for a nightmare to lead to a lobster. It is commonly the other way.'

'You are not asleep, I assure you,' said Gregory. 'You are, on the contrary, close to the most actual and rousing moment of your existence. Ah, here comes your champagne! I admit that there may be a slight disproportion, let us say, between the inner arrangements of this excellent hotel and its simple and unpretentious exterior. But that is all our modesty. We are the most modest men that ever lived on earth.'

'And who are *we*?' asked Syme, emptying his champagne glass.

'It is quite simple,' replied Gregory. '*We* are the serious anarchists, in whom you do not believe.'

'Oh!' said Syme shortly. 'You do yourselves well in drinks.'

'Yes, we are serious about everything,' answered Gregory.

Then after a pause he added:

'If in a few moments this table begins to turn round a little, don't put it down to your inroads into the champagne. I don't wish you to do yourself an injustice.'

'Well, if I am not drunk, I am mad,' replied Syme with perfect calm; 'but I trust I can behave like a gentleman in either condition. May I smoke?'

'Certainly!' said Gregory, producing a cigar-case. 'Try one of mine.'

Syme took the cigar, clipped the end off with a cigar-cutter out of his waistcoat pocket, put it in his mouth, lit it slowly, and let out a long cloud of smoke. It is not a little to his credit that he performed these rites with so much composure, for almost before he had begun them the table at which he sat had begun to revolve, first slowly and then rapidly, as if at an insane séance.

'You must not mind it,' said Gregory; 'it's a kind of screw.'

'Quite so,' said Syme placidly, 'a kind of screw! How simple that is!'

The next moment the smoke of his cigar, which had been wavering across the room in snaky twists, went straight up as if from a factory chimney, and the two, with their chairs and table, shot down through the floor as if the earth had swallowed them. They went rattling down a kind of roaring chimney as rapidly as a lift cut loose, and they came with an abrupt bump to the bottom. But when Gregory threw open a pair of doors and let in a red subterranean light, Syme was still smoking, with one leg thrown over the other, and had not turned a yellow hair.

Gregory led him down a low, vaulted passage, at the end of which was the red light. It was an enormous crimson lantern, nearly as big as a fireplace, fixed over a small but heavy iron door. In the door there was a sort of hatchway or grating, and on this Gregory struck five times. A heavy voice with a foreign accent asked him who he was. To this he gave the more or less unexpected reply, "Mr. Joseph Chamberlain".[21] The heavy hinges began to move; it was obviously some kind of password.

Inside the doorway the passage gleamed as if it were lined with a network of steel. On a second glance, Syme saw that the glittering pattern was really made up of ranks and ranks of rifles and revolvers, closely packed or interlocked.

'I must ask you to forgive me all these formalities,' said Gregory; 'we have to be very strict here.'

'Oh, don't apologize,' said Syme. 'I know your passion for law and order,' and he stepped into the passage lined with the steel weapons. With his long, fair hair and rather foppish frock-coat, he looked a singularly frail and fanciful figure as he walked down that shining avenue of death.

They passed through several such passages, and came out at last into a queer steel chamber with curved walls, almost spherical in shape, but presenting, with its tiers of benches, something of the appearance of a scientific lecture-theatre. There were no rifles or pistols in this apartment, but round the walls of it were hung more dubious and dreadful shapes, things that looked like the bulbs of iron plants, or the eggs of iron birds. They were bombs, and the very room itself seemed like the inside of a bomb. Syme knocked his cigar ash off against the wall, and went in.

'And now, my dear Mr. Syme,' said Gregory, throwing himself in an expansive manner on the bench under the largest bomb, 'now we are quite cosy, so let us talk properly. Now no human words can give you any notion of why I brought you here. It was one of those arbitrary emotions, like jumping off a cliff or falling in love. Suffice it to say that you were an inexpressibly irritating fellow, and, to do you justice, you are still. I would break twenty oaths of secrecy for the pleasure of taking you down a peg. That way you have of lighting a cigar would make a priest break the seal of confession. Well,

---

[21] "Mr. Joseph Chamberlain" is a somewhat incongruous password, as Joseph Chamberlain (1836–1914) was an English politician and leader of the Unionist Party, and an advocate of a strong imperialist policy.

you said that you were quite certain I was not a serious anarchist. Does this place strike you as being serious?'

'It does seem to have a moral under all its gaiety,' assented Syme; 'but may I ask you two questions? You need not fear to give me information, because, as you remember, you very wisely extorted from me a promise not to tell the police, a promise I shall certainly keep. So it is in mere curiosity that I make my queries. First of all, what is it really all about? What is it you object to? You want to abolish government?'

'To abolish God!' said Gregory, opening the eyes of a fanatic. 'We do not only want to upset a few despotisms and police regulations; that sort of anarchism does exist, but it is a mere branch of the Nonconformists. We dig deeper and we blow you higher. We wish to deny all those arbitrary distinctions of vice and virtue, honour and treachery, upon which mere rebels base themeselves. The silly sentimentalists of the French Revolution talked of the Rights of Man! We hate Rights as we hate Wrongs. We have abolished Right and Wrong.'

'And Right and Left,' said Syme with a simple eagerness, 'I hope you will abolish them too. They are much more troublesome to me.'

'You spoke of a second question,' snapped Gregory.

'With pleasure,' resumed Syme. 'In all your present acts and surroundings there is a scientific attempt at secrecy. I have an aunt who lived over a shop, but this is the first time I have found people living from preference under a public-house. You have a heavy iron door. You cannot pass it without submitting to the humiliation of calling yourself Mr. Chamberlain. You surround yourself with steel instruments which make the place, if I may say so, more impressive than homelike. May I ask why, after taking all this trouble to barricade yourselves in the bowels of the earth, you then parade your whole secret by talking about anarchism to every silly woman in Saffron Park?'

Gregory smiled.

'The answer is simple,' he said. 'I told you I was a serious anarchist, and you did not believe me. Nor do *they* believe me. Unless I took them into this infernal room they would not believe me.'

Syme smoked thoughtfully, and looked at him with interest. Gregory went on.

'The history of the thing might amuse you,' he said. 'When first I became one of the New Anarchists I tried all kinds of respectable disguises. I dressed up as a bishop. I read up all about bishops in our anarchist pamphlets, in *Superstition the Vampire* and *Priests of Prey*. I certainly understood from them that bishops are strange and terrible old men keeping a cruel secret from mankind. I was misinformed. When on my first appearing in episcopal gaiters in a drawing-room I cried out in a voice of thunder, "Down! down! presumptuous human reason!" they found out in some way that I was not a bishop at all. I was nabbed at once. Then I made up as a millionaire; but I defended Capital with so much intelligence that a fool could see I was quite poor. Then I tried being a major. Now I am a humanitarian myself, but I have, I hope, enough intellectual breadth to understand the position of those who, like Nietzsche, admire violence — the proud, mad war of Nature and all that, you know. I threw myself into the major. I drew my sword and waved it constantly. I called out "Blood!" abstractedly, like a man calling for wine. I often said, "Let the weak perish; it is the Law." Well, well, it seems majors don't do this. I was nabbed again. At last I went in despair to the President of the Central Anarchist Council, who is the greatest man in Europe.'

'What is his name?' asked Syme.

'You would not know it,' answered Gregory. 'That is his greatness. Caesar and Napoleon put all their genius into being heard of, and they *were* heard of. He puts all his genius into not being heard of, and he is not heard of. But you cannot be for five minutes in the room with him without feeling that Caesar and Napoleon would have been children in his hands.'

He was silent and even pale for a moment, and then resumed:

'But whenever he gives advice it is always something as startling as an epigram, and yet as practical as the Bank of England. I said to him, "What disguise will hide me from the world? What can I find more respectable than bishops and majors?" He looked at me with his large but indecipherable face. "You want a safe disguise, do you?

You want a dress which will guarantee you harmless; a dress in which no one would ever look for a bomb?" I nodded. He suddenly lifted his lion's voice. "Why, then, dress up as an *anarchist*, you fool!" he roared so that the room shook. "Nobody will ever expect you to do anything dangerous then." And he turned his broad back on me without another word. I took his advice, and have never regretted it. I preached blood and murder to those women day and night, and—by God!—they would let me wheel their perambulators.'

Syme sat watching him with some respect in his large, blue eyes.

'You took me in,' he said. 'It is really a smart dodge.'

Then after a pause he added:

'What do you call this tremendous President of yours?'

'We generally call him Sunday,' replied Gregory with simplicity. 'You see, there are seven members of the Central Anarchist Council, and they are named after days of the week. He is called Sunday, by some of his admirers Bloody Sunday. It is curious you should mention the matter, because the very night you have dropped in (if I may so express it) is the night on which our London branch, which assembles in this room, has to elect its own deputy to fill a vacancy in the Council. The gentleman who has for some time past played, with propriety and general applause, the difficult part of Thursday, has died quite suddenly. Consequently, we have called a meeting this very evening to elect a successor.'

He got to his feet and strolled across the room with a sort of smiling embarrassment.

'I feel somehow as if you were my mother, Syme,' he continued casually. 'I feel that I can confide anything to you, as you have promised to tell nobody. In fact, I will confide to you something that I would not say in so many words to the anarchists who will be coming to the room in about ten minutes. We shall, of course, go through a form of election; but I don't mind telling you that it is practically certain what the result will be.' He looked down for a moment modestly. 'It is almost a settled thing that I am to be Thursday.'

'My dear fellow,' said Syme heartily, 'I congratulate you. A great career!'

Gregory smiled in deprecation, and walked across the room, talking rapidly.

'As a matter of fact, everything is ready for me on this table,' he said, 'and the ceremony will probably be the shortest possible.'

Syme also strolled across the table, and found lying across it a walking-stick, which turned out on examination to be a swordstick, a large Colt's revolver, a sandwich case, and a formidable flask of brandy.[22] Over the chair, beside the table, was thrown a heavy-looking cape or cloak.

'I have only to get the form of election finished,' continued Gregory with animation, 'then I snatch up this cloak and stick, stuff these other things into my pocket, step out of a door in this cavern, which opens on the river, where there is a steam-tug already waiting for me, and then— then—oh, the wild joy of being Thursday!' And he clasped his hands.

Syme, who had sat down once more with his usual insolent languor, got to his feet with an unusual air of hesitation.

'Why is it,' he asked vaguely, 'that I think you are quite a decent fellow? Why do I positively like you, Gregory?' He paused a moment, and then added with a sort of fresh curiosity, 'Is it because you are such an ass?'

There was a thoughtful silence again, and then he cried out:

'Well, damn it all! This is the funniest situation I have ever been in in my life, and I am going to act accordingly. Gregory, I gave you a promise before I came into this place. That promise I would keep under red-hot pincers. Would you give me, for my own safety, a little promise of the same kind?'

'A promise?' asked Gregory wondering.

'Yes,' said Syme very seriously, 'A promise. I swore before God that I would not tell your secret to the police. Will you swear by Humanity, or whatever beastly thing you believe in, that you will not tell my secret to the anarchists?'

'Your secret?' asked the staring Gregory. 'Have you got a secret?'

'Yes,' said Syme, 'I have a secret.' Then after a pause, 'Will you swear?'

---

[22] These appurtenances, oddly enough, when taken together with the cloak seem to constitute the everyday paraphernalia that Chesterton carried around with him.

Gregory glared at him gravely for a few moments, and then said abruptly:

'You must have bewitched me, but I feel a furious curiosity about you. Yes, I will swear not to tell the anarchists anything you tell me. But look sharp for they will be here in a couple of minutes.'

Syme rose slowly to his feet and thrust his long, white hands into his long, grey trousers pockets. Almost as he did so there came five knocks on the outer grating, proclaiming the arrival of the first of the conspirators.

'Well,' said Syme slowly, 'I don't know how to tell you the truth more shortly than by saying that your expedient of dressing up as an aimless poet is not confined to you or your President. We have known the dodge for some time at Scotland Yard.'

Gregory tried to spring up straight, but he swayed thrice.

'What do you say?' he asked in an inhuman voice.

'Yes,' said Syme simply, 'I am a police detective. But I think I hear your friends coming.'

From the doorway there came a murmur of 'Mr. Joseph Chamberlain'. It was repeated twice and thrice, and then thirty times, and the crowd of Joseph Chamberlains (a solemn thought) could be heard trampling down the corridor.

III

THE MAN WHO WAS THURSDAY

Before one of the fresh faces could appear at the doorway, Gregory's stunned surprise had fallen from him. He was beside the table with a bound, and a noise in his throat like a wild beast. He caught up the Colt's revolver and took aim at Syme. Syme did not flinch, but he put up a pale and polite hand.

'Don't be such a silly man,' he said, with the effeminate dignity of a curate. 'Don't you see it's not necessary? Don't you see that we're both in the same boat? Yes, and jolly sea-sick.'

Gregory could not speak, but he could not fire either, and he looked his question.

'Don't you see we've checkmated each other?' cried Syme. 'I can't tell the police you are an anarchist. You can't tell the anarchists I'm a policeman. I can only watch you, knowing what you are; you can only watch me, knowing what I am. In short, it's a lonely, intellectual duel, my head against yours. I'm a policeman deprived of the help of the police. You, my poor fellow, are an anarchist deprived of the help of that law and organization which is so essential to anarchy. The one solitary difference is in your favour. You are not surrounded by inquisitive policemen; I am surrounded by inquisitive anarchists. I cannot betray you, but I might betray myself. Come, come! wait and see me betray myself. I shall do it so nicely.'

Gregory put the pistol slowly down, still staring at Syme as if he were a sea-monster.

'I don't believe in immortality,' he said at last, 'but if, after all this, you were to break your word, God would make a hell only for you, to howl in for ever.'

'I shall not break my word,' said Syme sternly, 'nor will you break yours. Here are your friends.'

The mass of the anarchists entered the room heavily, with a slouching and somewhat weary gait; but one little man, with a black beard and glasses—a man somewhat of the type of Mr. Tim

Healy[23] detached himself, and bustled forward with some papers in his hand.

'Comrade Gregory,' he said, 'I suppose this man is a delegate?'

Gregory, taken by surprise, looked down and muttered the name of Syme; but Syme replied almost pertly:

'I am glad to see that your gate is well enough guarded to make it hard for any one to be here who is not a delegate.'

The brow of the little man with the black beard was, however, still contracted with something like suspicion.

'What branch do you represent?' he asked sharply.

'I should hardly call it a branch,' said Syme, laughing; 'I should call it at the very least a root.'

'What do you mean?'

'The fact is,' said Syme serenely, 'the truth is I am a Sabbatarian. I have been specially sent here to see that you show a due observance of Sunday.'

The little man dropped one of his papers, and a flicker of fear went over all the faces of the group. Evidently the awful President, whose name was Sunday, did sometimes send down such irregular ambassadors to such branch meetings.

'Well, comrade,' said the man with the papers after a pause, 'I suppose we'd better give you a seat in the meeting?'

'If you ask my advice as a friend,' said Syme with severe benevolence, 'I think you'd better.'

When Gregory heard the dangerous dialogue end, with a sudden safety for his rival, he rose abruptly and paced the floor in painful thought. He was, indeed, in an agony of diplomacy. It was clear that Syme's inspired impudence was likely to bring him out of all merely accidental dilemmas. Little was to be hoped from them. He could not himself betray Syme, partly from honour, but partly also because, if he betrayed him and for some reason failed to destroy him, the Syme who escaped would be a Syme freed from all obligation of secrecy, a Syme who would simply walk to the nearest police

[23] Mr. Tim Healy was Timothy Michael Healy (1855–1951), M.P. for Wexford and elsewhere from 1880. He was later founder of the All for Ireland League in 1910 and became first Governor-General of the Irish Free State (1922–28).

station. After all, it was only one night's discussion, and only one detective who would know of it. He would let out as little as possible of their plans that night, and then let Syme go, and chance it.

He strode across to the group of anarchists, which was already distributing itself along the benches.

'I think it is time we began,' he said; 'the steam-tug is waiting on the river already. I move that Comrade Buttons takes the chair.'

This being approved by a show of hands, the little man with the papers slipped into the presidential seat.

'Comrades,' he began, as sharp as a pistol-shot, 'our meeting to-night is important, though it need not be long. This branch has always had the honour of electing Thursdays for the Central European Council. We have elected many and splendid Thursdays. We all lament the sad decease of the heroic worker who occupied the post until last week. As you know, his services to the cause were considerable. He organized the great dynamite coup of Brighton which, under happier circumstances, ought to have killed everybody on the pier. As you also know, his death was as self-denying as his life, for he died through his faith in a hygienic mixture of chalk and water as a substitute for milk, which beverage he regarded as barbaric, and as involving cruelty to the cow. Cruelty, or anything approaching to cruelty, revolted him always. But it is not to acclaim his virtues that we are met, but for a harder task. It is difficult properly to praise his qualities, but it is more difficult to replace them. Upon you, comrades, it devolves this evening to choose out of the company present the man who shall be Thursday. If any comrade suggests a name I will put it to the vote. If no comrade suggests a name, I can only tell myself that that dear dynamiter, who is gone from us, has carried into the unknowable abysses the last secret of his virtue and his innocence.'

There was a stir of almost inaudible applause, such as is sometimes heard in church. Then a large old man, with a long and venerable white beard, perhaps the only real working-man present, rose lumberingly and said:

'I move that Comrade Gregory be elected Thursday,' and sat lumberingly down again.

'Does any one second?' asked the chairman.

A little man with a velvet coat and pointed beard seconded.

'Before I put the matter to the vote,' said the chairman, 'I will call on Comrade Gregory to make a statement.'

Gregory rose amid a great rumble of applause. His face was deadly pale, so that by contrast his queer red hair looked almost scarlet. But he was smiling, and altogether at ease. He had made up his mind, and he saw his best policy quite plain in front of him like a white road. His best chance was to make a softened and ambiguous speech, such as would leave on the detective's mind the impression that the anarchist brotherhood was a very mild affair after all. He believed in his own literary power, his capacity for suggesting fine shades and picking perfect words. He thought that with care he could succeed, in spite of all the people around him, in conveying an impression of the institution, subtly and delicately false. Syme had once thought that anarchists, under all their bravado, were only playing the fool. Could he not now, in the hour of peril, make Syme think so again?

'Comrades,' began Gregory, in a low but penetrating voice, 'it is not necessary for me to tell you what is my policy, for it is your policy also. Our belief has been slandered, it has been disfigured, it has been utterly confused and concealed, but it has never been altered. Those who talk about anarchism and its dangers go everywhere and anywhere to get their information, except to us, except to the fountain head. They learn about anarchists from sixpenny novels; they learn about anarchists from tradesmen's newpapers; they learn about anarchists from *Ally Sloper's Half-Holiday*[24] and the *Sporting Times*.[25] They never learn about anarchists from anarchists. We have no chance of denying the mountainous slanders which are heaped upon our heads from one end of Europe to another. The man who has always heard that we are walking plagues has never heard our reply. I know that he will not hear it to-night, though my passion were to rend the roof. For it is deep, deep under the earth that the persecuted are permitted to assemble, as the Christians assembled in the Catacombs. But, if by some incredible

[24] *Ally Sloper's Half-Holiday* was a comic newspaper.
[25] The *Sporting Times* was and is a paper devoted to horse racing.

accident, there were here to-night a man who all his life had thus immensely misunderstood us, I would put this question to him: "When those Christians met in those Catacombs, what sort of moral reputation had they in the streets above? What tales were told of their atrocities by one educated Roman to another? Suppose" (I would say to him), "suppose that we are only repeating that still mysterious paradox of history. Suppose we seem as shocking as the Christians because we are really as harmless as the Christians. Suppose we seem as mad as the Christians because we are really as meek." '

The applause that had greeted the opening sentences had been gradually growing fainter, and at the last word it stopped suddenly. In the abrupt silence, the man with the velvet jacket said, in a high, squeaky voice:

'I'm not meek!'

'Comrade Witherspoon tells us,' resumed Gregory, 'that he is not meek. Ah, how little he knows himself! His words are, indeed, extravagant; his appearance is ferocious, and even (to an ordinary taste) unattractive. But only the eye of a friendship as deep and delicate as mine can perceive the deep foundation of solid meekness which lies at the base of him, too deep even for himself to see. I repeat, we are the true early Christians, only that we come too late. We are simple, as they were simple — look at Comrade Witherspoon. We are modest, as they were modest — look at me. We are merciful — '

'No, no!' called out Mr. Witherspoon with the velvet jacket.

'I say we are merciful,' repeated Gregory furiously, 'as the early Christians were merciful. Yet this did not prevent their being accused of eating human flesh. We do not eat human flesh — '

'Shame!' cried Witherspoon. 'Why not?'

'Comrade Witherspoon,' said Gregory, with a feverish gaiety, 'is anxious to know why nobody eats him (laughter). In our society, at any rate, which loves him sincerely, which is founded upon love — '

'No, no!' said Witherspoon, 'down with love.'

'Which is founded upon love,' repeated Gregory, grinding his teeth, 'there will be no difficulty about the aims which we shall pursue as a body, or which I should pursue were I chosen as the representative of that body. Superbly careless of the slanders that represent us as assassins and enemies of human society, we shall pursue, with moral courage and quiet, intellectual pressure, the permanent ideals of brotherhood and simplicity.'

Gregory resumed his seat and passed his hand across his forehead. The silence was sudden and awkward, but the chairman rose like an automaton, and said in a colourless voice:

'Does any one oppose the election of Comrade Gregory?'

The assembly seemed vague and subconsciously disappointed, and Comrade Witherspoon moved restlessly on his seat and muttered in his thick beard. By the sheer rush of routine, however, the motion would have been put and carried. But as the chairman was opening his mouth to put it, Syme sprang to his feet and said in a small and quiet voice:

'Yes, Mr. Chairman, I oppose.'

The most effective fact in oratory is an unexpected change in the voice. Mr. Gabriel Syme evidently understood oratory. Having said these first formal words in a moderated tone and with a brief simplicity, he made his next word ring and volley in the vault as if one of the guns had gone off.

'Comrades!' he cried, in a voice that made every man jump out of his boots, 'have we come here for this? Do we live underground like rats in order to listen to talk like this? This is talk we might listen to while eating buns at a Sunday School treat. Do we line these walls with weapons and bar that door with death lest any one should come and hear Comrade Gregory saying to us, "Be good, and you will be happy", "Honesty is the best policy", and "Virtue is its own reward"? There was not a word in Comrade Gregory's address to which a curate could not have listened with pleasure (hear, hear). But I am not a curate (loud cheers), and I did not listen to it with pleasure (renewed cheers). The man who is fitted to make a good curate is not fitted to make a resolute, forcible, and efficient Thursday (hear, hear).

'Comrade Gregory has told us, in only too apologetic a tone, that we are not the enemies of society. But I say that we are the enemies of society, and so much the worse for society. We are the enemies of society, for society is the enemy of humanity, its oldest and its most pitiless enemy (hear, hear). Comrade Gregory has told us (apologetically again) that we are not murderers. There I agree. We are not murderers, we are executioners (cheers).'

Ever since Syme had risen Gregory had sat staring at him, his face idiotic with astonishment. Now in the pause his lips of clay parted, and he said, with an automatic and lifeless distinctness:

'You damnable hypocrite!'

Syme looked straight into those frightful eyes with his own pale blue ones, and said with dignity:

'Comrade Gregory accuses me of hypocrisy. He knows as well as I do that I am keeping all my engagements and doing nothing but my duty. I do not mince words. I do not pretend to. I say that Comrade Gregory is unfit to be Thursday for all his amiable qualities. He is unfit to be Thursday because of his amiable qualities. We do not want the Supreme Council of Anarchy infected with a maudlin mercy (hear, hear). This is no time for ceremonial politeness, neither is it a time for ceremonial modesty. I set myself against comrade Gregory as I would set myself against all the Governments of Europe, because the anarchist who has given himself to anarchy has forgotten modesty as much as he has forgotten pride (cheers). I am not a man at all. I am a cause (renewed cheers). I set myself against Comrade Gregory as impersonally and as calmly as I should choose one pistol rather than another out of that rack upon the wall; and I say that rather than have Gregory and his milk-and-water methods on the Supreme Council, I would offer myself for election——'

His sentence was drowned in a deafening cataract of applause. The faces, that had grown fiercer and fiercer with approval as his tirade grew more and more uncompromising, were now distorted with grins of anticipation or cloven with delighted cries. At the moment when he announced himself as ready to stand for the post of Thursday, a roar of excitement and assent broke forth, and became uncontrollable, and at the same moment Gregory sprang to his feet, with foam upon his mouth, and shouted against the shouting.

'Stop, you blasted madmen!' he cried, at the top of a voice that tore his throat. 'Stop, you——'

But louder than Gregory's shouting and louder than the roar of the room came the voice of Syme, still speaking in a peal of pitiless thunder:

'I do not go to the Council to rebut that slander that calls us murderers; I go to earn it (loud and prolonged cheering). To the priest who says these men are the enemies of religion, to the judge who says these men are the enemies of law, to the fat parliamentarian who says these men are the enemies of order and public decency, to all these I will reply, "You are false kings, but you are true prophets. I am come to destroy you, and to fulfil your prophecies." '

The heavy clamour gradually died away, but before it had ceased Witherspoon had jumped to his feet, his hair and beard all on end, and had said:

'I move, as an amendment, that Comrade Syme be appointed to the post.'

'Stop all this, I tell you!' cried Gregory, with frantic face and hands. 'Stop it, it is all——'

The voice of the chairman clove his speech with a cold accent.

'Does any one second this amendment?' he said.

A tall, tired man, with melancholy eyes and an American chin beard, was observed on the back bench to be slowly rising to his feet. Gregory had been screaming for some time past; now there was a change in his accent, more shocking than any scream.

'I end all this!' he said, in a voice as heavy as stone. 'This man cannot be elected. He is a——'

'Yes,' said Syme, quite motionless, 'what is he?'

Gregory's mouth worked twice without sound; then slowly the blood began to crawl back into his dead face.

'He is a man quite inexperienced in our work,' he said, and sat down abruptly.

Before he had done so, the long, lean man with the American beard was again upon his feet, and was repeating in a high American monotone:

'I beg to second the election of Comrade Syme.'

'The amendment will, as usual, be put first,' said Mr. Buttons, the chairman, with mechanical rapidity. 'The question is that Comrade Syme——'

Gregory had again sprung to his feet, panting and passionate.

'Comrades,' he cried out, 'I am not a madman.'

'Oh, oh!' said Mr. Witherspoon.

'I am not a madman,' reiterated Gregory, with a frightful sincerity which for a moment staggered the room, 'but I give you a counsel which you can call mad if you like. No, I will not call it a counsel, for I can give you no reason for it. I will call it a command. Call it a mad command, but act upon it. Strike, but hear me! Kill me, but obey me! Do not elect this man.'

Truth is so terrible, even in fetters, that for a moment Syme's slender and insane victory swayed like a reed. But you could not have guessed it from Syme's bleak blue eys. He merely began:

'Comrade Gregory commands——'

Then the spell was snapped, and one anarchist called out to Gregory:

'Who are you? You are not Sunday'; and another anarchist added in a heavier tone, 'And you are not Thursday.'

'Comrades,' cried Gregory, in a voice like that of a martyr who in an ecstasy of pain has passed beyond pain, 'it is nothing to me whether you detest me as a tyrant or detest me as a slave. If you will not take my command, accept my degradation. I kneel to you. I throw myself at your feet. I implore you. Do not elect this man.'

'Comrade Gregory,' said the chairman after a painful pause, 'this is really not quite dignified.'

For the first time in the proceedings there was for a few seconds a real silence. Then Gregory fell back in his seat, a pale wreck of a man, and the chairman repeated, like a piece of clock-work suddenly started again:

'The question is that Comrade Syme be elected to the post of Thursday on the General Council.'

The roar rose like the sea, the hands rose like a forest, and three minutes afterwards Mr. Gabriel Syme, of the Secret Police Service, was elected to the post of Thursday on the General Council of the Anarchists of Europe.

Every one in the room seemed to feel the tug waiting on the river, the sword-stick and the revolver waiting on the table. The instant the election was ended and Syme had received the paper proving his election, they all sprang to their feet, and the fiery groups moved and mixed in the room. Syme found himself, somehow or other, face to face with Gregory, who still regarded him with a stare of stunned hatred. They were silent for many minutes.

'You are a devil!' said Gregory at last.

'And you are a gentleman,' said Syme with gravity.

'It was you that entrapped me,' began Gregory, shaking from head to foot, 'entrapped me into—'

'Talk sense,' said Syme shortly. 'Into what sort of devils' parliament have you entrapped me, if it comes to that? You made me swear before I made you. Perhaps we are both doing what we think right. But what we think right is so damned different that there can be nothing between us in the way of concession. There is nothing possible between us but honour and death,' and he pulled the great cloak about his shoulders and picked up the flask from the table.

'The boat is quite ready,' said Mr. Buttons, bustling up. 'Be good enough to step this way.'

With a gesture that revealed the shopwalker, he led Syme down a short, iron-bound passage, the still agonized Gregory following feverishly at their heels. At the end of the passage was a door, which Buttons opened sharply, showing a sudden blue and silver picture of the moonlit river, that looked like a scene in a theatre. Close to the opening lay a dark dwarfish steam-launch, like a baby dragon with one red eye.

Almost in the act of stepping on board, Gabriel Syme turned to the gaping Gregory.

'You have kept your word,' he said gently, with his face in shadow. 'You are a man of honour and I thank you. You have kept it even down to a small particular. There was one special thing you promised me at the beginning of the affair, and which you have certainly given me by the end of it.'

'What do you mean?' cried the chaotic Gregory. 'What did I promise you?'

'A very entertaining evening,' said Syme, and he made a military salute with the sword-stick as the steamboat slid away.

IV

THE TALE OF A DETECTIVE

Gabriel Syme was not merely a detective who pretended to be a poet; he was really a poet who had become a detective. Nor was his hatred of anarchy hypocritical. He was one of those who are driven early in life into too conservative an attitude by the bewildering folly of most revolutionists. He had not attained it by any tame tradition. His respectability was spontaneous and sudden, a rebellion against rebellion. He came of a family of cranks, in which all the oldest people had all the newest notions. One of his uncles always walked about without a hat, and another had made an unsuccessful attempt to walk about with a hat and nothing else. His father cultivated art and self-realization; his mother went in for simplicity and hygiene. Hence the child, during his tenderer years, was wholly unacquainted with any drink between the extremes of absinth and cocoa, of both of which he had a healthy dislike. The more his mother preached a more than Puritan abstinence the more did his father expand into a more than pagan latitude; and by the time the former had come to enforcing vegetarianism, the latter had pretty well reached the point of defending cannibalism.

Being surrounded with every conceivable kind of revolt from infancy, Gabriel had to revolt into something, so he revolted into the only thing left—sanity. But there was just enough in him of the blood of these fanatics to make even his protest for common sense a little too fierce to be sensible. His hatred of modern lawlessness had been crowned also by an accident. It happened that he was walking in a side-street at the instant of a dynamite outrage. He had been blind and deaf for a moment, and then seen, the smoke clearing, the broken windows and the bleeding faces. After that he went about as usual— quiet, courteous, rather gentle; but there was a spot on his mind that was not sane. He did not regard anarchists, as most of us do, as a handful of morbid men, combining ignorance with intellectualism. He regarded them as a huge and pitiless peril, like a Chinese invasion.[26]

[26] The Boxer uprising of 1899–1900 would have been very much in Chesterton's mind.

He poured perpetually into newspapers and their waste-paper baskets a torrent of tales, verses, and violent articles, warning men of this deluge of barbaric denial. But he seemed to be getting no nearer his enemy, and, what was worse, no nearer a living. As he paced the Thames Embankment, bitterly biting a cheap cigar and brooding on the advance of Anarchy, there was no anarchist with a bomb in his pocket so savage or so solitary as he. Indeed, he always felt that Government stood alone and desperate, with its back to the wall. He was too quixotic to have cared for it otherwise.

He walked on the Embankment once under a dark red sunset. The red river reflected the red sky, and they both reflected his anger. The sky, indeed, was so swarthy, and the light on the river relatively so lurid, that the water almost seemed of fiercer flame than the sunset it mirrored. It looked like a stream of literal fire winding under the vast caverns of a subterranean country.

Syme was shabby in those days. He wore an old-fashioned black chimney-pot hat; he was wrapped in a yet more old-fashioned cloak, black and ragged; and the combination gave him the look of the early villains in Dickens and Bulwer Lytton.[27] Also his yellow beard and hair were more unkempt and leonine than when they appeared long afterwards, cut and pointed, on the lawns of Saffron Park. A long, lean, black cigar, bought in Soho for two pence, stood out from between his tightened teeth, and altogether he looked a very satisfactory specimen of the anarchists upon whom he had vowed a holy war. Perhaps this was why a policeman on the Embankment spoke to him, and said, 'Good evening.'

Syme, at a crisis of his morbid fears for humanity, seemed stung by the mere stolidity of the automatic official, a mere bulk of blue in the twilight.

'A good evening is it?' he said sharply. 'You fellows would call the end of the world a good evening. Look at that bloody red sun and that bloody river! I tell you that if that were literally human blood, spilt and shining, you would still be standing here as solid as ever, looking out for some poor harmless tramp whom you could move on. You policemen are cruel to the poor, but I could forgive you even your cruelty if it were not for your calm.'

[27] Bulwer Lytton was Edward Bulwer (1803–73), Lord Lytton, English novelist (*The Last Days of Pompei*), poet, statesman and publisher.

'If we are calm,' replied the policeman, 'it is the calm of organized resistance.'

'Eh?' said Syme, staring.

'The soldier must be calm in the thick of the battle,' pursued the policeman. 'The composure of an army is the anger of a nation.'

'Good God, the Board Schools!'[28] said Syme. 'Is this undenominational education?'

'No,' said the policeman sadly, 'I never had any of those advantages. The Board Schools came after my time. What education I had was very rough and old-fashioned, I am afraid.'

'Where did you have it?' asked Syme, wondering.

'Oh, at Harrow,'[29] said the policeman.

The class sympathies which, false as they are, are the truest things in so many men, broke out of Syme before he could control them.

'But, good Lord, man,' he said, 'you oughtn't to be a policeman!'

The policeman sighed and shook his head.

'I know,' he said solemnly, 'I know I am not worthy.'

'But why did you join the police?' asked Syme with rude curiosity.

'For much the same reason that you abused the police,' replied the other. 'I found that there was a special opening in the service for those whose fears for humanity were concerned rather with the aberrations of the scientific intellect than with the normal and excusable, though excessive, outbreaks of the human will. I trust I make myself clear.'

'If you mean that you make your opinion clear,' said Syme, 'I suppose you do. But as for making yourself clear, it is the last thing you do. How comes a man like you to be talking philosophy in a blue helmet on the Thames Embankment?'

'You have evidently not heard of the latest development in our police system,' replied the other. 'I am not surprised at it. We are keeping

[28] The Board Schools were schools established under the terms of the 1870 Education Act which set up a Board of Education to implement free and universal elementary education. The terms of the 1870 Act remained in force until 1944.

[29] Harrow is a public school (in England a private fee-paying school) in north London. The term "public school" implies that it was originally open to the public as opposed to being restricted to religious postulants. The status of public school is now defined as belonging to the Headmaster's Conference.

it rather dark from the educated class, because that class contains most of our enemies. But you seem to be exactly in the right frame of mind. I think you might almost join us.'

'Join you in what?' asked Syme.

'I will tell you,' said the policeman slowly. 'This is the situation: the head of one of our departments, one of the most celebrated detectives in Europe, has long been of opinion that a purely intellectual conspiracy would soon threaten the very existence of civilization. He is certain that the scientific and artistic worlds are silently bound in a crusade against the Family and the State. He has, therefore, formed a special corps of policemen, policemen who are also philosophers. It is their business to watch the beginnings of this conspiracy, not merely in a criminal but in a controversial sense. I am a democrat myself, and I am fully aware of the value of the ordinary man in matters of ordinary valour or virtue. But it would obviously be undesirable to employ the common policeman in an investigation which is also a heresy hunt.'

Syme's eyes were bright with a sympathetic curiosity.

'What do you do, then?' he said.

'The work of the philosophical policeman,' replied the man in blue, 'is at once bolder and more subtle than that of the ordinary detective. The ordinary detective goes to pot-houses to arrest thieves; we go to artistic tea-parties to detect pessimists. The ordinary detective discovers from a ledger or a diary that a crime has been committed. We discover from a book of sonnets that a crime will be committed. We have to trace the origin of those dreadful thoughts that drive men on at last to intellectual fanaticism and intellectual crime. We were only just in time to prevent the assassination at Hartlepool,[30] and that was entirely due to the fact that our Mr. Wilks (a smart young fellow) thoroughly understood a triolet.'

'Do you mean,' asked Syme, 'that there is really as much connexion between crime and the modern intellect as all that?'

'You are not sufficiently democratic' answered the policeman,

[30] Hartlepool is a town in northeast England famous for hanging the sole survivor of a shipwreck, a monkey, as a French spy. It was inferred that he was French by the way he spoke.

'but you were right when you said just now that our ordinary treatment of the poor criminal was a pretty brutal business. I tell you I am sometimes sick of my trade when I see how perpetually it means merely a war upon the ignorant and the desperate. But this new movement of ours is a very different affair. We deny the snobbish English assumption that the uneducated are the dangerous criminals. We remember the Roman Emperors. We remember the great poisoning princes of the Renaissance. We say that the dangerous criminal is the educated criminal. We say that the most dangerous criminal now is the entirely lawless modern philosopher. Compared to him, burglars and bigamists are essentially moral men; my heart goes out to them. They accept the essential ideal of man; they merely seek it wrongly. Thieves respect property. They merely wish the property to become their property that they may more perfectly respect it. But philosophers dislike property as property; they wish to destroy the very idea of personal possession. Bigamists respect marriage, or they would not go through the highly ceremonial and even ritualistic formality of bigamy. But philosophers despise marriage as marriage. Murderers respect human life; they merely wish to attain a greater fullness of human life in themselves by the sacrifice of what seems to them to be lesser lives. But philosophers hate life itself, their own as much as other people's.'

Syme struck his hands together.

'How true that is,' he cried. 'I have felt it from my boyhood, but never could state the verbal antithesis. The common criminal is a bad man, but at least he is, as it were, a conditional good man. He says that if only a certain obstacle be removed — say a wealthy uncle — he is then prepared to accept the universe and to praise God. He is a reformer, but not an anarchist. He wishes to cleanse the edifice, but not to destroy it. But the evil philosopher is not trying to alter things, but to annihilate them. Yes, the modern world has retained all those parts of police work which are really oppressive and ignominious, the harrying of the poor, the spying upon the unfortunate. It has given up its more dignified work, the punishment of powerful traitors in the State and powerful heresiarchs in the Church. The moderns say we must not punish heretics. My only doubt is whether we have a right to punish anybody else.'

'But this is absurd!' cried the policeman, clasping his hands with an excitement uncommon in persons of his figure and costume, 'but it is intolerable! I don't know what you're doing, but you're wasting your life. You must, you shall, join our special army against anarchy. Their armies are on our frontiers. Their bolt is ready to fall. A moment more, and you may lose the glory of working with us, perhaps the glory of dying with the last heroes of the world.'

'It is a chance not to be missed, certainly,' assented Syme, 'but still I do not quite understand. I know as well as anybody that the modern world is full of lawless little men and mad little movements. But, beastly as they are, they generally have the one merit of disagreeing with each other. How can you talk of their leading one army or hurling one bolt. What is this anarchy?'

'Do not confuse it,' replied the constable, 'with those chance dynamite outbreaks from Russia or from Ireland, which are really the outbreaks of oppressed, if mistaken, men. This is a vast philosophic movement, consisting of an outer and an inner ring. You might even call the outer ring the laity and the inner ring the priesthood. I prefer to call the outer ring the innocent section, the inner ring the supremely guilty section. The outer ring — the main mass of their supporters — are merely anarchists; that is, men who believe that rules and formulas have destroyed human happiness. They believe that all the evil results of human crime are the results of the system that has called it crime. They do not believe that the crime creates the punishment. They believe that the punishment has created the crime. They believe that if a man seduced seven women he would naturally walk away as blameless as the flowers of spring. They believe that if a man picked a pocket he would naturally feel exquisitely good. These I call the innocent section.'

'Oh!' said Syme.

'Naturally, therefore, these people talk about "a happy time coming"; "the paradise of the future"; "mankind freed from the bondage of vice and the bondage of virtue", and so on. And so also the men of the inner circle speak — the sacred priesthood. They also speak to applauding crowds of the happiness of the future, and of mankind freed at last. But in their mouths' — and the policeman lowered his voice—'in their mouths these happy phrases have a horrible meaning. They are under no illusions; they are too intellectual to think that man upon this earth can ever be quite free of original sin and the struggle. And they mean death. When they say that mankind shall be free at last, they mean that mankind shall commit suicide. When they talk of a paradise without right or wrong, they mean the grave. They have but two objects, to destroy first humanity and then themselves. That is why they throw bombs instead of firing pistols. The innocent rank and file are disappointed because the bomb has not killed the king; but the high-priesthood are happy because it has killed somebody.'

'How can I join you?' asked Syme, with a sort of passion.

'I know for a fact that there is a vacancy at the moment,' said the policeman, 'as I have the honour to be somewhat in the confidence of the chief of whom I have spoken. You should really come and see him. Or, rather I should not say see him, nobody ever sees him; but you can talk to him if you like.'

'Telephone?' inquired Syme, with interest.

'No,' said the policeman placidly, 'he has a fancy for always sitting in a pitch-dark room. He says it makes his thoughts brighter. Do come along.'

Somewhat dazed and considerably excited, Syme allowed himself to be led to a side-door in the long row of buildings of Scotland Yard. Almost before he knew what he was doing, he had been passed through the hands of about four intermediate officials, and was suddenly shown into a room, the abrupt blackness of which startled him like a blaze of light. It was not the ordinary darkness, in which forms can be faintly traced; it was like going suddenly stone-blind.

'Are you the new recruit?' asked a heavy voice.

And in some strange way, though there was not the shadow of a shape in the gloom, Syme knew two things: first, that it came from a man of massive stature; and second, that the man had his back to him.

'Are you the new recruit?' said the invisible chief, who seemed to have heard all about it. 'All right. You are engaged.'

Syme, quite swept off his feet, made a feeble fight against this irrevocable phrase.

'I really have no experience,' he began.

'No one has any experience,' said the other, 'of the Battle of Armageddon.'

'But I am really unfit ——'

'You are willing, that is enough,' said the unknown.

'Well, really,' said Syme, 'I don't know any profession of which mere willingness is the final test.'

'I do,' said the other — 'martyrs. I am condemning you to death. Good day.'

Thus it was that when Gabriel Syme came out again into the crimson light of evening, in his shabby black hat and shabby, lawless cloak, he came out a member of the New Detective Corps for the frustration of the great conspiracy. Acting under the advice of his friend the policeman (who was professionally inclined to neatness), he trimmed his hair and beard, bought a good hat, clad himself in an exquisite summer suit of light blue-grey, with a pale yellow flower in the button-hole, and, in short, became that elegant and rather insupportable person whom Gregory had first encountered in the little garden of Saffron Park. Before he finally left the police premises his friend provided him with a small blue card, on which was written, 'The Last Crusade', and a number, the sign of his official authority. He put this carefully in his upper waistcoat pocket, lit a cigarette, and went forth to track and fight the enemy in all the drawing-rooms of London. Where his adventure ultimately led him we have already seen. At about half-past one on a February night he found himself steaming in a small tug up the silent Thames, armed with sword-stick and revolver, the duly elected Thursday of the Central Council of Anarchists.

When Syme stepped out on to the steam-tug he had a singular sensation of stepping out into something entirely new; not merely into the landscape of a new land, but even into the landscape of a new planet. This was mainly due to the insane yet solid decision of that evening, though partly also to an entire change in the weather and the sky since he entered the little tavern some two hours before. Every trace of the passionate plumage of the cloudy sunset had been swept away, and a naked moon stood in a naked sky. The moon was so strong and full, that (by a paradox often to be noticed) it seemed like a weaker sun. It gave, not the sense of bright moonshine, but rather of a dead daylight.

Over the whole landscape lay a luminous and unnatural discoloration, as of that disastrous twilight which Milton spoke of as shed by the sun in eclipse;[31] so that Syme fell easily into his first thought, that he was actually on some other and emptier planet, which circled round some sadder star. But the more he felt this glittering desolation in the moonlit land, the more his own chivalric folly glowed in the night like a great fire. Even the common things he carried with him—the food and the brandy and the loaded pistol—took on exactly that concrete and material poetry which a child feels when he takes a gun upon a journey or a bun with him to bed. The sword-stick and the brandy-flask, though in themselves only the tools of morbid conspirators, became the expressions of his own more healthy romance. The sword-stick became almost the sword of chivalry, and the brandy the wine of the stirrup-cup. For even the most dehumanized modern fantasies depend on some older and simpler figure; the adventures may be mad, but the adventurer must be sane. The dragon without St. George would not even be grotesque. So this inhuman landscape was only imaginative by the presence of a man really human. To Syme's exaggerative mind the bright, bleak houses and terraces by the Thames looked as empty as the mountains of the moon. But even the moon is only poetical because there is a man in the moon.

The tug was worked by two men, and with much toil went comparatively slowly. The clear moon that had lit up Chiswick had gone down by the time that they passed Battersea, and when they came under the enormous bulk of Westminster day had already begun to break. It broke like the splitting of great bars of lead, showing bars

[31] Milton's verse is:

> The sun . . .
> In dim eclipse disastrous twilight sheds
> On half the nations, and with fear of change
> Perplexes monarchs.
>
> *Paradise Lost*, I. 594.

of silver; and these had brightened like white fire when the tug, changing its onward course, turned inward to a large landing-stage rather beyond Charing Cross.

The great stones of the embankment seemed equally dark and gigantic as Syme looked up at them. They were big and black against the huge white dawn. They made him feel that he was landing on the colossal steps of some Egyptian palace;[32] and indeed the thing suited his mood, for he was, in his own mind, mounting to attack the solid thrones of horrible and heathen kings. He leapt out of the boat on to one slimy step, and stood, a dark and slender figure, amid the enormous masonry. The two men in the tug put her off again and turned up stream. They had never spoken a word.

[32] The colossal steps of some Egyptian palace is an apt description of the Victoria Embankment, as the obelisk known as Cleopatra's Needle is sited there.

V

THE FEAST OF FEAR

At first the large stone stair seemed to Syme as deserted as a pyramid; but before he reached the top he had realized that there was a man leaning over the parapet of the Embankment and looking out across the river. As a figure he was quite conventional, clad in a silk hat and frock-coat of the more formal type of fashion; he had a red flower in his button-hole. As Syme drew nearer to him step by step, he did not even move a hair; and Syme could come close enough to notice even in the dim, pale morning light that his face was long, pale, and intellectual and ended in a small triangular tuft of dark beard at the very point of the chin, all else being clean-shaven. This scrap of hair almost seemed a mere oversight; the rest of the face was of the type that is best shaven—clear-cut, ascetic, and in its way noble. Syme drew closer and closer, noting all this, and still the figure did not stir.

At first an instinct had told Syme that this was the man whom he was meant to meet. Then, seeing that the man made no sign, he had concluded that he was not. And now again he had come back to a certainty that the man had something to do with his mad adventure. For the man remained more still than would have been natural if a stranger had come so close. He was as motionless as a wax-work, and got on the nerves somewhat in the same way. Syme looked again and again at the pale, dignified, and delicate face, and the face still looked blankly across the river. Then he took out of his pocket the note from Buttons proving his election, and put it before the sad and beautiful face. Then the man smiled, and his smile was a shock, for it was all on one side, going up in the right cheek and down in the left.

There was nothing, rationally speaking, to scare any one about this. Many people have this nervous trick of a crooked smile, and in many it is even attractive. But in all Syme's circumstances, with the dark dawn and the deadly errand and the loneliness on the great dripping stones, there was something unnerving in it. There was the silent river and the silent man, a man of even classic face. And there was the last nightmare touch that his smile suddenly went wrong.

The spasm of smile was instantaneous, and the man's face dropped at once into its harmonious melancholy. He spoke without further explanation or inquiry, like a man speaking to an old colleague.

'If we walk up towards Leicester Square,' he said, 'we shall just be in time for breakfast. Sunday always insists on an early breakfast. Have you had any sleep?'

'No,' said Syme.

'Nor have I,' answered the man in an ordinary tone. 'I shall try to get to bed after breakfast.'

He spoke with casual civility, but in an utterly dead voice that contradicted the fanaticism of his face. It seemed almost as if all friendly words were to him lifeless conveniences, and that his only life was hate. After a pause the man spoke again.

'Of course, the Secretary of the branch told you everything that can be told. But the one thing that can never be told is the last notion of the President, for his notions grow like a tropical forest. So in case you don't know, I'd better tell you that he is carrying out his notion of concealing ourselves by not concealing ourselves to the most extraordinary lengths just now. Originally, of course, we met in a cell underground, just as your branch does. Then Sunday made us take a private room at an ordinary restaurant. He said that if you didn't seem to be hiding nobody hunted you out. Well, he is the only man on earth, I know; but sometimes I really think that his huge brain is going a little mad in its old age. For now we flaunt ourselves before the public. We have our breakfast on a balcony—on a balcony, if you please—overlooking Leicester Square.'

'And what do the people say?' asked Syme.

'It's quite simple what they say,' answered his guide. 'They say we are a lot of jolly gentlemen who pretend they are anarchists.'

'It seems to me a very clever idea,' said Syme.

'Clever! God blast your impudence! Clever!' cried out the other in a sudden, shrill voice which was as startling and discordant as his crooked smile. 'When you've seen Sunday for a split second you'll leave off calling him clever.'

Leicester Square from balcony height from the SW.

With this they emerged out of a narrow street, and saw the early sunlight filling Leicester Square. It will never be known, I suppose, why this square itself should look so alien and in some ways so Continental. It will never be known whether it was the foreign look that attracted the foreigners or the foreigners who gave it the foreign look. But on this particular morning the effect seemed singularly bright and clear. Between the open square and the sunlit leaves and the statue and the Saracenic outlines of the Alhambra,[33] it looked the replica of some French or even Spanish public place. And this effect increased in Syme the sensation, which in many shapes he had had through the whole adventure, the eerie sensation of having strayed into a new world. As a fact, he had bought bad cigars round Leiscester Square ever since he was a boy. But as he turned that corner, and saw the trees and the Moorish cupolas, he could have sworn that he was turning into an unknown Place de something or other in some foreign town.

At one corner of the square there projected a kind of angle of a prosperous but quiet hotel, the bulk of which belonged to a street behind. In the wall there was one large french window, probably the window of a large coffee-room; and outside this window, almost literally overhanging the square, was a formidably buttressed balcony, big enough to contain a dining-table. In fact, it did contain a dining-table, or more strictly a breakfast-table; and round the breakfast-table, glowing in the sunlight and evident to the street, were a group of noisy and talkative men, all dressed in the insolence of fashion with white waistcoats and expensive button-holes. Some of their jokes could almost be heard across the square. Then the grave Secretary gave his unnatural smile, and Syme knew that this boisterous breakfast party was the secret conclave of the European Dynamiters.

Then, as Syme continued to stare at them, he saw something that he had not seen before. He had not seen it literally because it was too large to see. At the nearest end of the balcony, blocking up a great part of the perspective, was the back of a great mountain of a man.

[33] The Alhambra was a theater in Leicester Square that has long since disappeared.

When Syme had seen him, his first thought was that the weight of him must break down the balcony of stone. His vastness did not lie only in the fact that he was abnormally tall and quite incredibly fat. This man was planned enormously in his original proportions, like a statue carved deliberately as colossal. His head, crowned with white hair, as seen from behind looked bigger than a head ought to be. The ears that stood out from it looked larger than human ears. He was enlarged terribly to scale; and this sense of size was so staggering, that when Syme saw him all the other figures seemed quite suddenly to dwindle and become dwarfish. They were still sitting there as before with their flowers and frock-coats, but now it looked as if the big man was entertaining five children to tea.

As Syme and the guide approached the side-door of the hotel, a waiter came out smiling with every tooth in his head.

'The gentlemen are up there, sare,' he said. 'They do talk and they do laugh at what they talk. They do say they will throw bombs at ze king.'

And the waiter hurried away with a napkin over his arm, much pleased with the singular frivolity of the gentlemen upstairs.

The two men mounted the stairs in silence.

Syme had never thought of asking whether the monstrous man who almost filled and broke the balcony was the great President of whom the others stood in awe. He knew it was so, with an unaccountable but instantaneous certainty. Syme, indeed, was one of those men who are open to all the more nameless psychological influences in a degree a little dangerous to mental health. Utterly devoid of fear in physical dangers, he was a great deal too sensitive to the smell of spiritual evil. Twice already that night little unmeaning things had peeped out at him almost pruriently, and given him a sense of drawing nearer and nearer to the headquarters of hell. And this sense became overpowering as he drew nearer to the great President.

The form it took was a childish and yet hateful fancy. As he walked across the inner room towards the balcony, the large face of Sunday grew larger and larger; and Syme was gripped with a fear that when he was quite close the face would be too big to be possible, and that he would scream aloud. He remembered that as a child he would not look at the mask of Memnon[34] in the British Museum, because it was a face, and so large.

By an effort braver than that of leaping over a cliff, he went to an empty seat at the breakfast-table and sat down. The men greeted him with good-humoured raillery as if they had always known him. He sobered himself a little by looking at their conventional coats and solid, shining coffee-pot; then he looked again at Sunday. His face was very large, but it was still possible to humanity.

In the presence of the President the whole company looked sufficiently commonplace; nothing about them caught the eye at first, except that by the President's caprice they had been dressed up with a festive respectability, which gave the meal the look of a wedding breakfast. One man indeed stood out at even a superficial glance. He at least was the common or garden Dynamiter. He wore, indeed, the high white collar and satin tie that were the uniform of the occasion; but out of this collar there sprang a head quite unmanageable and quite unmistakable, a bewildering bush of brown hair and beard that almost obscured the eyes like those of a Skye terrier. But the eyes did look out of the tangle, and they were the sad eyes of some Russian serf. The effect of this figure was not terrible like that of the President, but it had every diablerie that can come from the utterly grotesque. If out of that Stiff Tie and Collar there had come abruptly the head of a cat or a dog, it could not have been a more idiotic contrast.

The man's name, it seemed, was Gogol; he was a Pole, and in this circle of days he was called Tuesday. His soul and speech were incurably tragic; he could not force himself to play the prosperous and frivolous part demanded of him by President Sunday. And, indeed, when Syme came in the President, with that daring disregard of public suspicion which was his policy, was actually chaffing Gogol upon his inability to assume conventional graces.

'Our friend Tuesday,' said the President in a deep voice at once of

[34] Memnon in classical mythology was the son of Tithon and Aurora. He fought at the seige of Troy and was killed by Achilles. His statue from Thebes in Egypt was supposed to make musical sounds at daybreak when struck by the first rays of the sun at dawn (Aurora), but in fact the statue is in all probability that of Pharoah Amenhotpou III.

quietude and volume, 'our friend Tuesday doesn't seem to grasp the idea. He dresses up like a gentleman, but he seems to be too great a soul to behave like one. He insists on the ways of the stage conspirator. Now if a gentleman goes about London in a top hat and a frock-coat, no one need know that he is an anarchist. But if a gentleman puts on a top hat and a frock-coat, and then goes about on his hands and knees—well, he may attract attention. That's what Brother Gogol does. He goes about on his hands and knees with such inexhaustible diplomacy, that by this time he finds it quite difficult to walk upright.'

'I am not good at goncealment,' said Gogol sulkily, with a thick foreign accent; 'I am not ashamed of the cause.'

'Yes, you are, my boy, and so is the cause of you,' said the President good-naturedly. 'You hide as much as anybody; but you can't do it, you see, you're such an ass! You try to combine two inconsistent methods. When a householder finds a man under his bed, he will probably pause to note the circumstance. But if he finds a man under his bed in a top hat, you will agree with me, my dear Tuesday, that he is not likely even to forget it. Now when you were found under Admiral Biffin's bed—'

'I am not good at deception,' said Tuesday gloomily, flushing.

'Right, my boy, right,' said the President with a ponderous heartiness, 'you aren't good at anything.'

While this stream of conversation continued, Syme was looking more steadily at the men around him. As he did so, he gradually felt all his sense of something spiritually queer return.

He had thought at first that they were all of common stature and costume, with the evident exception of the hairy Gogol. But as he looked at the others, he began to see in each of them exactly what he had seen in the man by the river, a demoniac detail somewhere. That lop-sided laugh, which would suddenly disfigure the fine face of his original guide, was typical of all these types. Each man had something about him, perceived perhaps at the tenth or twentieth glance, which was not normal, and which seemed hardly human. The only metaphor he could think of was this, that they all looked as men of fashion and presence would look, with the additional twist given in a false and curved mirror.

Only the individual examples will express this half-concealed eccentricity. Syme's original cicerone bore the title of Monday; he was the Secretary of the Council, and his twisted smile was regarded with more terror than anything, except the President's horrible, happy laughter. But now that Syme had more space and light to observe him, there were other touches. His fine face was so emaciated, that Syme thought it must be wasted with some disease; yet somehow the very distress of his dark eyes denied this. It was no physical ill that troubled him. His eyes were alive with intellectual torture, as if pure thought was pain.

He was typical of each of the tribe; each man was subtly and differently wrong. Next to him sat Tuesday, the tousled-headed Gogol, a man more obviously mad. Next was Wednesday, a certain Marquis de St. Eustache, a sufficiently characteristic figure. The first few glances found nothing unusual about him, except that he was the only man at table who wore the fashionable clothes as if they were really his own. He had a black French beard cut square and a black English frock-coat cut even squarer. But Syme, sensitive to such things, felt somehow that the man carried a rich atmosphere with him, a rich atmosphere that suffocated. It reminded one irrationally of drowsy odours and of dying lamps in the darker poems of Byron and Poe. With this went a sense of his being clad, not in lighter colours, but in softer materials; his black seemed richer and warmer than the black shades about him, was if it were compounded of profound colour. His black coat looked as if it were only black by being too dense a purple. His black beard looked as if it were only black by being too deep a blue. And in the gloom and thickness of the beard his dark red mouth showed sensual and scornful. Whatever he was he was not a Frenchman; he might be a Jew; he might be something deeper yet in the dark heart of the East. In the bright-coloured Persian tiles and pictures showing tyrants hunting, you may see just those almond eyes, those blue-black beards, those cruel, crimson lips.

Then came Syme, and next a very old man, Professor de Worms, who still kept the chair of Friday, though every day it was expected that his death would leave it empty. Save for his intellect, he was in the last dissolution of senile decay. His face was as grey as his long grey beard, his forehead was lifted and fixed finally in a furrow of mild despair. In no other case, not even that of Gogol, did the bridegroom brilliancy of the morning-dress express a more painful contrast. For the red flower in his button-hole showed up against a face that was literally discoloured like lead; the whole hideous effect was as if some drunken dandies had put their clothes upon a corpse. When he rose or sat down, which was with long labour and peril, something worse was expressed than mere weakness, something indefinably connected with the horror of the whole scene. It did not express decrepitude merely, but corruption. Another hateful fancy crossed Syme's quivering mind. He could not help thinking that whenever the man moved a leg or arm might fall off.

Right at the end sat the man called Saturday, the simplest and the most baffling of all. He was a short, square man with a dark, square face clean-shaven, a medical practitioner going by the name of Bull. He had that combination of *savoir-faire* with a sort of well-groomed coarseness which is not uncommon in young doctors. He carried his fine clothes with confidence rather than ease, and he mostly wore a set smile. There was nothing whatever odd about him, except that he wore a pair of dark, almost opaque spectacles. It may have been merely a crescendo of nervous fancy that had gone before, but those black discs were dreadful to Syme; they reminded him of half-remembered ugly tales, of some story about pennies being put on the eyes of the dead. Syme's eye always caught the black glasses and the blind grin. Had the dying professor wore them, or even the pale Secretary, they would have been appropriate. But on the younger and grosser man they seemed only an enigma. They took away the key of the face. You could not tell what his smile or his gravity meant. Partly from this, and partly because he had a vulgar virility wanting in most of the others, it seemed to Syme that he might be the wickedest of all those wicked men. Syme even had the thought that his eyes might be covered up because they were too frightful to see.

VI

THE EXPOSURE

Such were the six men who had sworn to destroy the world. Again and again Syme strove to pull together his common sense in their presence. Sometimes he saw for an instant that these notions were subjective, that he was only looking at ordinary men, one of whom was old, another nervous, another short-sighted. The sense of an unnatural symbolism always settled back on him again. Each figure seemed to be, somehow, on the borderland of things, just as their theory was on the borderland of thought. He knew that each one of these men stood at the extreme end, so to speak, of some wild road of reasoning. He could only fancy, as in some old-world fable, that if a man went westward to the end of the world he would find something—say a tree—that was more or less than a tree, a tree possessed by a spirit; and that if he went east to the end of the world he would find something else that was not wholly itself—a tower, perhaps, of which the very shape was wicked. So these figures seemed to stand up, violent and unaccountable, against an ultimate horizon, visions from the verge. The ends of the earth were closing in.

Talk had been going on steadily as he took in the scene; and not the least of the contrasts of that bewildering breakfast-table was the contrast between the easy and unobtrusive tone of talk and its terrible purport. They were deep in the discussion of an actual and immediate plot. The waiter downstairs had spoken quite correctly when he said that they were talking about bombs and kings. Only three days afterwards the Tsar[35] was to meet the President of the French Republic[36] in Paris, and over their bacon and eggs upon their sunny balcony these beaming gentlemen had decided how both should die. Even the instrument was chosen; the black-bearded Marquis, it appeared, was to carry the bomb.

[35] The Tsar at the time was Nicolas II (1868–1918), Tsar of all the Russias (1894–1917).

[36] The President of the French Republic at the time was Armand Fallières, who held the office from 1906–1913.

Ordinarily speaking, the proximity of this positive and objective crime would have sobered Syme, and cured him of all his merely mystical tremors. He would have thought of nothing but the need of saving at least two human bodies from being ripped in pieces with iron and roaring gas. But the truth was that by this time he had begun to feel a third kind of fear, more piercing and practical than either his moral revulsion or his social responsibility. Very simply, he had no fear to spare for the French President or the Tsar; he had begun to fear for himself. Most of the talkers took little heed of him, debating now with their faces closer together, and almost uniformly grave, save when for an instant the smile of the Secretary ran aslant across his face as the jagged lightning runs aslant across the sky. But there was one persistent thing which first troubled Syme and at last terrified him. The President was always looking at him, steadily, and with a great and baffling interest. The enormous man was quite quiet, but his blue eyes stood out of his head. And they were always fixed on Syme.

Syme felt moved to spring up and leap over the balcony. When the President's eyes were on him he felt as if he were made of glass. He had hardly the shred of a doubt that in some silent and extraordinary way Sunday had found out that he was a spy. He looked over the edge of the balcony, and saw a policeman standing abstractedly just beneath, staring at the bright railings and the sunlit trees.

Then there fell upon him the great temptation that was to torment him for many days. In the presence of these powerful and repulsive men, who were the princes of anarchy, he had almost forgotten the frail and fanciful figure of the poet Gregory, the mere aesthete of anarchism. He even thought of him now with an old kindness, as if they had played together when children. But he remembered that he was still tied to Gregory by a great promise. He had promised never to do the very thing that he now felt himself almost in the act of doing. He had promised not to jump over that balcony and speak to that policeman. He took his cold hand off the cold stone balustrade. His soul swayed in a vertigo of moral indecision. He had only to snap the thread of a rash vow made to a villainous society, and all his life could be as open and sunny as the square beneath him. He had, on the other hand, only to keep his antiquated honour, and be delivered inch by inch into the power of this great enemy of mankind, whose very intellect was a torture-chamber. Whenever he looked down into the square he saw the comfortable policeman, a pillar of common sense and common order. Whenever he looked back at the breakfast-table he saw the President still quietly studying him with big, unbearable eyes.

In all the torrent of his thought there were two thoughts that never crossed his mind. First, it never occurred to him to doubt that the President and his Council could crush him if he continued to stand alone. The place might be public, the project might seem impossible. But Sunday was not the man who would carry himself thus easily without having, somehow or somewhere, set open his iron trap. Either by anonymous poison or sudden street accident, by hypnotism or by fire from hell, Sunday could certainly strike him. If he defied the man he was probably dead, either struck stiff there in his chair or long afterwards as by an innocent ailment. If he called in the police promptly, arrested every one, told all, and set against them the whole energy of England, he would probably escape; certainly not otherwise. They were a balconyful of gentlemen overlooking a bright and busy square; but he felt no more safe with them than if they had been a boatful of armed pirates overlooking an empty sea.

There was a second thought that never came to him. It never occurred to him to be spiritually won over to the enemy. Many moderns, inured to a weak worship of intellect and force, might have wavered in their allegiance under this oppression of a great personality. They might have called Sunday the superman.[37] If any such creature be conceivable, he looked, indeed, somewhat like it, with his earth-shaking abstraction, as of a stone statue walking. He might have been called something above man, with his large plans, which were too obvious to be detected, with his large face, which was too frank to be understood. But this was a kind of modern meanness to which Syme could not sink even in his extreme morbidity. Like any man, he was coward enough to fear great force; but he was not quite coward enough to admire it.

[37] The superman was the conception of George Bernard Shaw, who had derived it from Nietzsche's Ubermensch.

The men were eating as they talked, and even in this they were typical. Dr. Bull and the Marquis ate casually and conventionally of the best things on the table—cold pheasant or Strasbourg pie.[38] But the Secretary was a vegetarian, and he spoke earnestly of the projected murder over half a raw tomato and three-quarters of a glass of tepid water. The old Professor had such slops as suggested a sickening second childhood. And even in this President Sunday preserved his curious predominance of mere mass. For he ate like twenty men; he ate incredibly, with a frightful freshness of appetite, so that it was like watching a sausage factory. Yet continually, when he had swallowed a dozen crumpets or drunk a quart of coffee, he would be found with his great head on one side staring at Syme.

'I have often wondered,' said the Marquis, taking a great bite out of a slice of bread and jam, 'whether it wouldn't be better for me to do it with a knife. Most of the best things have been brought off with a knife. And it would be a new emotion to get a knife into a French President and wriggle it round.'

'You are wrong,' said the Secretary, drawing his black brows together. 'The knife was merely the expression of the old personal quarrel with a personal tyrant. Dynamite is not only our best tool, but our best symbol. It is as perfect a symbol of us as is incense of the prayers of the Christians. It expands; it only destroys because it broadens; even so, thought only destroys because it broadens. A man's brain is a bomb,' he cried out, loosening suddenly his strange passion and striking his own skull with violence. 'My brain feels like a bomb, night and day. It must expand! It must expand! A man's brain must expand, if it breaks up the universe.'

'I don't want the universe broken up just yet,' drawled the Marquis. 'I want to do a lot of beastly things before I die. I thought of one yesterday in bed.'

'No, if the only end of the thing is nothing,' said Dr. Bull with his sphinx-like smile, 'it hardly seems worth doing.'

The old Professor was staring at the ceiling with dull eyes.

'Every man knows in his heart,' he said, 'that nothing is worth doing.'

---

[38] Strasbourg pie is another name for pâté de foie gras.

There was a singular silence, and then the Secretary said:

'We are wandering, however, from the point. The only question is how Wednesday is to strike the blow. I take it we should all agree with the original notion of a bomb. As to the actual arrangements, I should suggest that to-morrow morning he should go first of all to—'

The speech was broken off short under a vast shadow. President Sunday had risen to his feet, seeming to fill the sky above them.

'Before we discuss that,' he said in a small, quiet voice, 'let us go into a private room. I have something very particular to say.'

Syme stood up before any of the others. The instant of choice had come at last, the pistol was at his head. On the pavement below he could hear the policeman idly stir and stamp, for the morning, though bright, was cold.

A barrel-organ in the street suddenly sprang with a jerk into a jovial tune. Syme stood up taut, as if it had been a bugle before the battle. He found himself filled with a supernatural courage that came from nowhere. That jingling music seemed full of the vivacity, the vulgarity, and the irrational valour of the poor, who in all those unclean streets were all clinging to the decencies and the charities of Christendom. His youthful prank of being a policeman had faded from his mind; he did not think of himself as the representative of the corps of gentlemen turned into fancy constables, or of the old eccentric who lived in the dark room. But he did feel himself as the ambassador of all these common and kindly people in the street, who every day marched into battle to the music of the barrel-organ. And this high pride in being human had lifted him unaccountably to an infinite height above the monstrous men around him. For an instant, at least, he looked down upon all their sprawling eccentricities from the starry pinnacle of the commonplace. He felt towards them all that unconscious and elementary superiority that a brave man feels over powerful beasts or a wise man over powerful errors. He knew that he had neither the intellectual nor the physical strength of President Sunday, but in that moment he minded it no more than the fact that he had not the muscles of a tiger or a horn on his nose like a rhinoceros. All was swallowed up in an ultimate certainty that the President was wrong and that the barrel-organ was right. There clanged in his mind that unanswerable and terrible truism in the song of Roland:

'Païens ont tort et Chrétiens ont droit,'[39]

which in the old nasal French[40] has the clang and groan of great iron. This liberation of his spirit from the load of his weakness went with a quite clear decision to embrace death. If the people of the barrel-organ could keep their old-world obligations, so could he. This very pride in keeping his word was that he was keeping it to miscreants. It was his last triumph over these lunatics to go down into their dark room and die for something that they could not even understand. The barrel-organ seemed to give the marching tune with the energy and the mingled noises of a whole orchestra; and he could hear deep and rolling, under all the trumpets and the pride of life, the drums of the pride of death.

The conspirators were already filing through the open window and into the rooms behind. Syme went last, outwardly calm, but with all his brain and body throbbing with romantic rhythm. The President led them down an irregular side stair, such as might be used by servants, and into a dim, cold, empty room, with a table and benches, like an abandoned board-room. When they were all in, he closed and locked the door.

The first to speak was Gogol, the irreconcilable, who seemed bursting with inarticulate grievance.

'Zso! Zso!' he cried, with an obscure excitement, his heavy Polish accent becoming almost impenetrable. 'You zay you nod 'ide. You zay you show himselves. It is all nuzzinks. Ven you vant talk importance you run yourselves in a dark box!'

The President seemed to take the foreigner's incoherent satire with entire good humour.

'You can't get hold of it yet, Gogol,' he said in a fatherly way.

[39] French for "The Pagans are wrong and the Christians are right".

[40] The old nasal French probably refers to the Anglo-Norman dialect spoken in England after the Conquest of 1066. The oldest manuscript of the *Song of Roland* is that in Oxford written in Anglo-Norman and known as Digby 23.

'When once they have heard us talking nonsense on that balcony they will not care where we go afterwards. If we had come here first, we should have had the whole staff at the keyhole. You don't seem to know anything about mankind.'

'I die for zem,' cried the Pole in thick excitement, 'and I slay zare oppressors. I care not for these games of gonzealment. I would zmite ze tyrant in ze open square.'

'I see, I see,' said the President, nodding kindly as he seated himself at the top of a long table. 'You die for mankind first, and then you get up and smite their oppressors. So that's all right. And now may I ask you to control your beautiful sentiments, and sit down with the other gentlemen at this table. For the first time this morning something intelligent is going to be said.'

Syme, with the perturbed promptitude he had shown since the original summons, sat down first. Gogol sat down last, grumbling in his brown beard about gombromise. No one except Syme seemed to have any notion of the blow that was about to fall. As for him, he had merely the feeling of a man mounting the scaffold with the intention, at any rate, of making a good speech.

'Comrades,' said the President, suddenly rising, 'we have spun out this farce long enough. I have called you down here to tell you something so simple and shocking that even the waiters upstairs (long inured to our levities) might hear some new seriousness in my voice. Comrades, we were discussing plans and naming places. I propose, before saying anything else, that those plans and places should not be voted by this meeting, but should be left wholly in the control of some one reliable member. I suggest Comrade Saturday, Dr. Bull.'

They all stared at him; then they all started in their seats, for the next words, though not loud, had a living and sensational emphasis. Sunday struck the table.

'Not one word more about the plans and places must be said at this meeting. Not one tiny detail more about what we mean to do must be mentioned in this company.'

Sunday had spent his life in astonishing his followers; but it seemed as if he had never really astonished them until now. They all moved feverishly in their seats, except Syme. He sat stiff in his, with his hand in his pocket, and on the handle of his loaded revolver. When the attack on him came he would sell his life dear. He would find out at least if the President was mortal.

Sunday went on smoothly:

'You will probably understand that there is only one possible motive for forbidding free speech at this festival of freedom. Strangers overhearing us matters nothing. They assume that we are joking. But what would matter, even unto death, is this, that there should be one actually among us who is not of us, who knows our grave purpose, but does not share it, who——'

The Secretary screamed out suddenly like a woman.

'It can't be!' he cried, leaping. 'There can't——'

The President flapped his large flat hand on the table like the fin of some huge fish.

'Yes,' he said slowly, 'there is a spy in this room. There is a traitor at this table. I will waste no more words. His name——'

Syme half rose from his seat, his finger firm on the trigger.

'His name is Gogol,' said the President. 'He is that hairy humbug over there who pretends to be a Pole.'

Gogol sprang to his feet, a pistol in each hand. With the same flash three men sprang at his throat. Even the Professor made an effort to rise. But Syme saw little of the scene, for he was blinded with a beneficent darkness; he had sunk down into his seat shuddering, in a palsy of passionate relief.

VII

THE UNACCOUNTABLE CONDUCT OF
PROFESSOR DE WORMS

'Sit down!' said Sunday in a voice that he used once or twice in his life, a voice that made men drop drawn swords.

The three who had risen fell away from Gogol, and that equivocal person himself resumed his seat.

'Well, my man,' said the President briskly, addressing him as one addresses a total stranger, 'will you oblige me by putting your hand in your upper waistcoat pocket and showing me what you have there?'

The alleged Pole was a little pale under his tangle of dark hair, but he put two fingers into the pocket with apparent coolness and pulled out a blue strip of card. When Syme saw it lying on the table, he woke up again to the world outside him. For although the card lay at the other extreme of the table, and he could read nothing of the inscription on it, it bore a startling resemblance to the blue card in his own pocket, the card which had been given to him when he joined the anti-anarchist constabulary.

'Pathetic Slav,' said the President, 'tragic child of Poland, are you prepared in the presence of that card to deny that you are in this company—shall we say *de trop*?'

'Right oh!' said the late Gogol. It made every one jump to hear a clear, commercial, and somewhat cockney voice coming out of that forest of foreign hair. It was irrational, as if a Chinaman had suddenly spoken with a Scotch accent.

'I gather that you fully understand your position,' said Sunday.

'You bet,' answered the Pole. 'I see it's a fair cop. All I say is, I don't believe any Pole could have imitated my accent like I did his.'

'I concede the point,' said Sunday. 'I believe your own accent to be inimitable, though I shall practise it in my bath. Do you mind leaving your beard with your card?'

'Not a bit,' answered Gogol; and with one finger he ripped off the whole of his shaggy head-covering, emerging with thin red hair and a pale, pert face. 'It was hot,' he added.

'I will do you the justice to say,' said Sunday, not without a sort of brutal admiration, 'that you seem to have kept pretty cool under it. Now listen to me. I like you. The consequence is that it would annoy me for just about two and a half minutes if I heard that you had died in torments. Well, if you ever tell the police or any human soul about us, I shall have that two and a half minutes of discomfort. On your discomfort I will not dwell. Good day. Mind the step.'

The red-haired detective who had masqueraded as Gogol rose to his feet without a word, and walked out of the room with an air of perfect nonchalance. Yet the astonished Syme was able to realize that this ease was suddenly assumed; for there was a slight stumble outside the door, which showed that the departing detective had not minded the step.

'Time is flying,' said the President in his gayest manner, after glancing at his watch, which like everything about him seemed bigger than it ought to be. 'I must be off at once; I have to take the chair at a Humanitarian meeting.'

The Secretary turned to him with working eyebrows.

'Would it not be better,' he said a little sharply, 'to discuss further the details of our project, now that the spy has left us?'

'No, I think not,' said the President with a yawn like an unobtrusive earthquake. 'Leave it as it is. Let Saturday settle it. I must be off. Breakfast here next Sunday.'

But the late loud scenes had whipped up the almost naked nerves of the Secretary. He was one of those men who are conscientious even in crime.

'I must protest, President, that the thing is irregular,' he said. 'It is a fundamental rule of our society that all plans shall be debated in full council. Of course, I fully appreciate your forethought when in the actual presence of a traitor——'

'Secretary,' said the President seriously, 'if you'd take your head home and boil it for a turnip it might be useful. I can't say. But it might.'

The Secretary reared back in a kind of equine anger.

'I really fail to understand——' he began in high offence.

'That's it, that's it,' said the President, nodding a great many times. 'That's where you fail right enough. You fail to understand. Why, you dancing donkey,' he roared, rising, 'you didn't want to be overheard by a spy, did you? How do you know you aren't overheard now?'

And with these words he shouldered his way out of the room, shaking with incomprehensible scorn.

Four of the men left behind gaped after him without any apparent glimmering of his meaning. Syme alone had even a glimmering, and such as it was it froze him to the bone. If the last words of the President meant anything, they meant that he had not after all passed unsuspected. They meant that while Sunday could not denounce him like Gogol, he still could not trust him like the others.

The other four got to their feet grumbling more or less, and betook themselves elsewhere to find lunch, for it was already well past midday. The Professor went last, very slowly and painfully. Syme sat long after the rest had gone, revolving his strange position. He had escaped a thunderbolt, but he was still under a cloud. At last he rose and made his way out of the hotel into Leicester Square. The bright, cold day had grown increasingly colder, and when he came out into the street he was surprised by a few flakes of snow. While he still carried the sword-stick and the rest of Gregory's portable luggage, he had thrown the cloak down and left it somewhere, perhaps on the steam-tug, perhaps on the balcony. Hoping, therefore, that the snow-shower might be slight, he stepped back out of the street for a moment and stood up under the doorway of a small and greasy hairdresser's shop, the front window of which was empty, except for a sickly wax lady in evening-dress.

Snow, however, began to thicken and fall fast; and Syme, having found one glance at the wax lady quite sufficient to depress his spirits, stared out instead into the white and empty street. He was considerably astonished to see, standing quite still outside the shop and staring into the window, a man. His top hat was loaded with snow like the hat of Father Christmas, the white drift was rising round his boots and ankles; but it seemed as if nothing could tear him away from the contemplation of the colourless wax doll in dirty evening-dress. That any human being should stand in such weather looking into such a shop was a matter of sufficient wonder to Syme; but his idle wonder turned suddenly into a personal shock; for he realized that the man standing there was the paralytic old Professor de Worms. It scarcely seemed the place for a person of his years and infirmities.

Syme was ready to believe anything about the perversions of this dehumanized brotherhood; but even he could not believe that the Professor had fallen in love with that particular wax lady. He could only suppose that the man's malady (whatever it was) involved some momentary fits of rigidity or trance. He was not inclined, however, to feel in this case any very compassionate concern. On the contrary, he rather congratulated himself that the Professor's stroke and his elaborate and limping walk would make it easy to escape from him and leave him miles behind. For Syme thirsted first and last to get clear of the whole poisonous atmosphere, if only for an hour. Then he could collect his thoughts, formulate his policy, and decide finally whether he should or should not keep faith with Gregory.

He strolled away through the dancing snow, turned up two or three streets, down through two or three others, and entered a small Soho[41] restaurant for lunch. He partook reflectively of four small and quaint courses, drank half a bottle of red wine, and ended up over black coffee and a black cigar, still thinking. He had taken his seat in the upper room of the restaurant, which was full of the chink of knives and the chatter of foreigners. He remembered that in old days he had imagined that all these harmless and kindly aliens were anarchists. He shuddered, remembering the real thing. But even the shudder had the delightful shame of escape. The wine, the common food, the familiar place, the faces of natural and talkative men, made

[41] Soho is situated between Shafesbury Avenue and Tottenham Court Road and is centered on Soho Square. The name is derived from a hunting call from the times when the area was open land outside the boundaries of the cities of London and Westminster. For most of this century Soho was a fairly cosmopolitan district noted for its foreign restaurants and interesting shops, but in recent years much of it has deteriorated into a locale of strip clubs, louche bookshops and blue cinemas.

him almost feel as if the Council of the Seven Days had been a bad dream; and although he knew it was nevertheless an objective reality, it was at least a distant one. Tall houses and populous streets lay between him and his last sight of the shameful seven; he was free in free London, and drinking wine among the free. With a somewhat easier action, he took his hat and stick and strolled down the stair into the shop below.

When he entered that lower room he stood stricken and rooted to the spot. At a small table, close up to the blank window and the white street of snow, sat the old anarchist Professor over a glass of milk, with his lifted livid face and pendent eyelids. For an instant Syme stood as rigid as the stick he leant upon. Then with a gesture as of blind hurry, he brushed past the Professor, dashing open the door and slamming it behind him, and stood outside in the snow.

'Can that old corpse be following me?' he asked himself, biting his yellow moustache. 'I stopped too long up in that room, so that even such leaden feet could catch me up. One comfort is, with a little brisk walking I can put a man like that as far away as Timbuctoo.[42] Or am I too fanciful? Was he really following me? Surely Sunday would not be such a fool as to send a lame man?'

He set off at a smart pace, twisting and whirling his stick, in the direction of Covent Garden. As he crossed the great market the snow increased, growing blinding and bewildering as the afternoon began to darken. The snow-flakes tormented him like a swarm of silver bees. Getting into his eyes and beard, they added their unremitting futility to his already irritated nerves; and by the time that he had come at a swinging pace to the beginning of Fleet Street,[43] he lost patience, and finding a Sunday teashop, turned into it to take shelter. He ordered another cup of black coffee as an excuse. Scarcely had he done so, when Professor de Worms hobbled heavily into the shop, sat down with difficulty and ordered a glass of milk.

Syme's walking-stick had fallen from his hand with a great clang,

[42] Timbuctoo or Timbuktu is on the River Niger in Mali and is the proverbial distant place across the Sahara Desert.

[43] Fleet Street is a continuation of the Strand running in the direction of St. Paul's and used to be the center of the newspaper industry.

which confessed the concealed steel. But the Professor did not look round. Syme, who was commonly a cool character, was literally gaping as a rustic gapes at a conjuring trick. He had seen no cab following; he had heard no wheels outside the shop; to all mortal appearances the man had come on foot. But the old man could only walk like a snail, and Syme had walked like the wind. He started up and snatched his stick, half crazy with the contradiction in mere arithmetic, and swung out of the swinging doors, leaving his coffee untasted. An omnibus going to the Bank went rattling by with an unusual rapidity. He had a violent run of a hundred yards to reach it; but he managed to spring, swaying upon the splashboard,[44] and pausing for an instant to pant, he climbed on to the top. When he had been seated for about half a minute, he heard behind him a sort of heavy and asthmatic breathing.

Turning sharply, he saw rising gradually higher and higher up the omnibus steps a top hat soiled and dripping with snow, and under the shadow of its brim the short-sighted face and shaky shoulders of Professor de Worms. He let himself into a seat with characteristic care, and wrapped himself up to the chin in the mackintosh rug.[45]

Every movement of the old man's tottering figure and vague hands, every uncertain gesture and panic-stricken pause, seemed to put it beyond question that he was helpless, that he was in the last imbecility of the body. He moved by inches, he let himself down with little gasps of caution. And yet, unless the philosophical entities called time and space have no vestige even of a practical existence, it appeared quite unquestionable that he had run after the omnibus.

Syme sprang erect upon the rocking car, and after staring wildly at the wintry sky, that grew gloomier every moment, he ran down the steps. He had repressed an elemental impulse to leap over the side.

Too bewildered to look back or to reason, he rushed into one of the little courts at the side of Fleet Street as a rabbit rushes into a hole. He had a vague idea, if this incomprehensible old Jack-in-the-box

[44] The splash-board was a screen at the front of a vehicle intended to screen passengers from being splashed with mud.

[45] The mackintosh rug was made from a rubber-coated waterproof fabric and was provided on the open top decks of public omnibuses to protect passengers from rain.

was really pursuing him, that in that labyrinth of little streets he could soon throw him off the scent. He dived in and out of those crooked lanes, which were more like cracks than thoroughfares; and by the time that he had completed about twenty alternate angles and described an unthinkable polygon, he paused to listen for any sound of pursuit. There was none; there could not in any case have been much, for the little streets were thick with the soundless snow. Somewhere behind Red Lion Court, however, he noticed a place where some energetic citizen had cleared away the snow for a space of about twenty yards, leaving the wet, glistening cobble-stones. He thought little of this as he passed it, only plunging into yet another arm of the maze. But when a few hundred yards farther on he stood still again to listen, his heart stood still also, for he heard from that space of rugged stones the clinking crutch and labouring feet of the infernal cripple.

The sky above was loaded with the clouds of snow, leaving London in a darkness and oppression premature for that hour of the evening. On each side of Syme the walls of the alley were blind and featureless; there was no little window or any kind of eye. He felt a new impulse to break out of this hive of houses, to get once more into the open and lamplit street. Yet he rambled and dodged for a long time before he struck the main thoroughfare. When he did so, he struck it much farther up than he had fancied. He came out into what seemed the vast and void of Ludgate Circus, and saw St. Paul's Cathedral sitting in the sky.

At first he was startled to find these great roads so empty, as if a pestilence had swept through the city. Then he told himself that some degree of emptiness was natural; first, because the snow-storm was even dangerously deep, and secondly, because it was Sunday. And at the very word Sunday he bit his lip; the word was henceforth for him like some indecent pun. Under the white fog of snow high up in the heaven the whole atmosphere of the city was turned to a very queer kind of green twilight, as of men under the sea. The sealed and sullen sunset behind the dark dome of St. Paul's had in it smoky and sinister colours—colours of sickly green, dead red or decaying bronze, that were just bright enough to emphasize the solid whiteness of the snow. But right up against these dreary colours rose the black bulk of the cathedral; and upon the top of the cathedral was a random splash and great stain of snow, still clinging as to an Alpine peak. It had fallen accidentally, but just so fallen as to half drape the dome from its very topmost point, and to pick out in perfect silver the great orb and the cross.[46] When Syme saw it he suddenly straightened himself, and made with his sword-stick an involuntary salute.

He knew that that evil figure, his shadow, was creeping quickly or slowly behind him, and he did not care. It seemed a symbol of human faith and valour that while the skies were darkening that high place of the earth was bright. The devils might have captured heaven, but they had not yet captured the cross. He had a new impulse to tear out the secret of this dancing, jumping, and pursuing paralytic; and at the entrance of the court as it opened upon the Circus he turned, stick in hand, to face his pursuer.

Professor de Worms came slowly round the corner of the irregular alley behind him, his unnatural form outlined against a lonely gaslamp, irresistibly recalling that very imaginative figure in the nursery rhymes, 'the crooked man who went a crooked mile'. He really looked as if he had been twisted out of shape by the tortuous streets he had been threading. He came nearer and nearer, the lamplight shining on his lifted spectacles, his lifted, patient face. Syme waited for him as St. George waited for the dragon, as a man waits for a final explanation or for death. And the old Professor came right up to him and passed him like a total stranger, without even a blink of his mournful eyelids.

There was something in this silent and unexpected innocence that left Syme in a final fury. The man's colourless face and manner seemed to assert that the whole following had been an accident. Syme was galvanized with an energy that was something between bitterness and a burst of boyish derision. He made a wild gesture as if to knock the old man's hat off, called out something like 'Catch me if you can', and went racing away across the white, open Circus.

[46] The great orb and the cross that surmount the dome of St. Paul's Cathedral refer to *The Ball and the Cross*.

Concealment was impossible now; and looking back over his shoulder, he could see the black figure of the old gentleman coming after him with long, swinging strides like a man winning a mile race. But the head upon that bounding body was still pale, grave, and professional, like the head of a lecturer upon the body of a harlequin.

This outrageous chase sped across Ludgate Circus, up Ludgate Hill, round St. Paul's Cathedral, along Cheapside, Syme remembering all the nightmares he had ever known. Then Syme broke away towards the river, and ended almost down by the docks. He saw the yellow panes of a low, lighted public-house, flung himself into it and ordered beer. It was a foul tavern, sprinkled with foreign sailors, a place where opium might be smoked or knives drawn.

A moment later Professor de Worms entered the place, sat down carefully, and asked for a glass of milk.

VIII

THE PROFESSOR EXPLAINS

When Gabriel Syme found himself finally established in a chair, and opposite to him, fixed and final also, the lifted eyebrows and leaden eyelids of the Professor, his fears fully returned. This incomprehensible man from the fierce council, after all, had certainly pursued him. If the man had one character as a paralytic and another character as a pursuer, the antithesis might make him more interesting, but scarcely more soothing. It would be a very small comfort that he could not find the Professor out, if by some serious accident the Professor should find him out. He emptied a whole pewter pot of ale before the Professor had touched his milk.

One possibility, however, kept him hopeful and yet helpless. It was just possible that this escapade signified something other than even a slight suspicion of him. Perhaps it was some regular form or sign. Perhaps the foolish scamper was some sort of friendly signal that he ought to have understood. Perhaps it was a ritual. Perhaps the new Thursday was always chased along Cheapside, as the new Lord Mayor is always escorted along it.[47] He was just selecting a tentative inquiry, when the old Professor opposite suddenly and simply cut him short. Before Syme could ask the first diplomatic question, the old anarchist had asked suddenly, without any sort of preparation:

'Are you a policeman?'

Whatever else Syme had expected, he had never expected anything so brutal and actual as this. Even his great presence of mind could only manage a reply with an air of rather blundering jocularity.

'A policeman?' he said, laughing vaguely. 'Whatever made you think of a policeman in connexion with me?'

'The process was simple enough,' answered the Professor patiently. 'I thought you looked like a policeman. I think so now.'

[47] The new Lord Mayor of the City of London (an area of about one square mile starting at Temple Bar) is driven in procession in a ceremonial coach in what is called the Lord Mayor's Show.

'Did I take a policeman's hat by mistake out of the restaurant?' asked Syme, smiling wildly. 'Have I by any chance got a number stuck on to me somewhere? Have my boots got that watchful look? Why must I be a policeman? Do, do let me be a postman.'

The old Professor shook his head with a gravity that gave no hope, but Syme ran on with a feverish irony.

"But perhaps I misunderstood the delicacies of your German philosophy. Perhaps policeman is a relative term. In an evolutionary sense, sir, the ape fades so gradually into the policeman, that I myself can never detect the shade. The monkey is only the policeman that may be. Perhaps a maiden lady on Clapham Common is only the policeman that might have been. I don't mind being the policeman that might have been. I don't mind being anything in German thought.'

'Are you in the police service?' said the old man, ignoring all Syme's improvised and desperate raillery. 'Are you a detective?'

Syme's heart turned to stone, but his face never changed.

'Your suggestion is ridiculous,' he began. 'Why on earth——'

The old man struck his palsied hand passionately on the rickety table, nearly breaking it.

'Did you hear me ask a plain question, you paltering spy?' he shrieked in a high, crazy voice. 'Are you, or are you not, a police detective?'

'No!' answered Syme, like a man standing on the hangman's drop.

'You swear it,' said the old man, leaning across to him, his dead face becoming as it were loathsomely alive. 'You swear it! You swear it! If you swear falsely, will you be damned? Will you be sure that the devil dances at your funeral? Will you see that the nightmare sits on your grave? Will there really be no mistake? You are an anarchist, you are a dynamiter! Above all, you are not in any sense a detective? You are not in the British police?'

He leant his angular elbow far across the table, and put up his large loose hand like a flap to his ear.

'I am not in the British police,' said Syme with insane calm.

Professor de Worms fell back in his chair with a curious air of kindly collapse.

'That's a pity,' he said, 'because I am.'

Syme sprang up straight, sending back the bench behind him with a crash.

'Because you are what?' he said thickly. 'You are what?'

'I am a policeman,' said the Professor with his first broad smile, and beaming through his spectacles. 'But as you think policeman only a relative term, of course I have nothing to do with you. I am in the British police force; but as you tell me you are not in the British police force, I can only say that I met you in a dynamiters' club. I suppose I ought to arrest you.' And with these words he laid on the table before Syme an exact facsimile of the blue card which Syme had in his own waistcoat pocket, the symbol of his power from the police.

Syme had for a flash the sensation that the cosmos had turned exactly upside down, that all trees were growing downwards and that all stars were under his feet. Then came slowly the opposite conviction. For the last twenty-four hours the cosmos had really been upside down, but now the capsized universe had come right side up again. This devil from whom he had been fleeing all day was only an elder brother of his own house, who on the other side of the table lay back and laughed at him. He did not for the moment ask any questions of detail; he only knew the happy and silly fact that this shadow, which had pursued him with an intolerable oppression of peril, was only the shadow of a friend trying to catch him up. He knew simultaneously that he was a fool and a free man. For with any recovery from morbidity there must go a certain healthy humiliation. There comes a certain point in such conditions when only three things are possible: first a perpetuation of Satanic pride, secondly tears, and third laughter. Syme's egotism held hard to the first course for a few seconds, and then suddenly adopted the third. Taking his own blue police ticket from his own waistcoat pocket, he tossed it on to the table; then he flung his head back until his spike of yellow beard almost pointed at the ceiling, and shouted with a barbaric laughter.

Even in that close den, perpetually filled with the din of knives, plates, cans, clamourous voices, sudden struggles and stampedes, there was something Homeric in Syme's mirth which made many half-drunken men look round.

'What yer laughing at, guv'nor?' asked one wondering labourer from the docks.

'At myself,' answered Syme, and went off again into the agony of his ecstatic reaction.

'Pull yourself together,' said the Professor, 'or you'll get hysterical. Have some more beer. I'll join you.'

'You haven't drunk your milk,' said Syme.

'My milk!' said the other, in tones of withering and unfathomable contempt, 'my milk! Do you think I'd look at that beastly stuff when I'm out of sight of the bloody anarchists? We're all Christians in this room, though perhaps,' he added, glancing around at the reeling crowd, 'not strict ones. Finish my milk! Great blazes! yes, I'll finish it right enough!' and he knocked the tumbler off the table, making a crash of glass and a splash of silver fluid.

Syme was staring at him with a happy curiosity.

'I understand now,' he cried; 'of course, you're not an old man at all.'

'I can't take my face off here,' replied Professor de Worms. 'It's rather an elaborate make-up. As to whether I'm an old man, that's not for me to say. I was thirty-eight last birthday.'

'Yes, but I mean,' said Syme impatiently, 'there's nothing the matter with you.'

'Yes,' answered the other dispassionately, 'I am subject to colds.'

Syme's laughter at all this had about it a wild weakness of relief. He laughed at the idea of the paralytic Professor being really a young actor dressed up as if for the foot-lights. But he felt that he would have laughed as loudly if a pepper-pot had fallen over.

The false Professor drank and wiped his false beard.

'Did you know,' he asked, 'that that man Gogol was one of us?'

'I? No, I didn't know it,' answered Syme in some surprise. 'But didn't you?'

'I knew no more than the dead,' replied the man who called himself de Worms. 'I thought the President was talking about me, and I rattled in my boots.'

'And I thought he was talking about me,' said Syme, with his rather reckless laughter. 'I had my hand on my revolver all the time.'

'So had I,' said the Profesor grimly; 'so had Gogol, evidently.'

Syme struck the table with an exclamation.

'Why, there were three of us there!' he cried. 'Three out of seven is a fighting number. If we had only known that we were three!'

The face of Professor de Worms darkened, and he did not look up.

'We were three,' he said. 'If we had been three hundred we could still have done nothing.'

'Not if we were three hundred against four?' asked Syme, jeering rather boisterously.

'No,' said the Professor with sobriety, 'not if we were three hundred against Sunday.'

And the mere name struck Syme cold and serious; his laughter had died in his heart before it could die on his lips. The face of the unforgettable President sprang into his mind as startling as a coloured photograph, and he remarked this difference between Sunday and all his satellites, that their faces, however fierce and sinister, became gradually blurred by memory like other human faces, whereas Sunday's seemed almost to grow more actual during absence, as if a man's painted portrait should slowly come alive.

They were both silent for a measure of moments, and then Syme's speech came with a rush, like the sudden foaming of champagne.

'Professor,' he cried, 'it is intolerable. Are you afraid of this man?'

The Professor lifted his heavy lids, and gazed at Syme with large, wide-open, blue eyes of an almost ethereal honesty.

'Yes, I am,' he said mildly. 'So are you.'

Syme was dumb for an instant. Then he rose to his feet erect, like an insulted man, and thrust the chair away from him.

'Yes,' he said in a voice indescribable, 'you are right. I am afraid of him. Therefore I swear by God that I will seek out this man whom I fear until I find him, and strike him on the mouth. If heaven were his throne and the earth his footstool, I swear that I would pull him down.'

'How?' asked the staring Professor. 'Why?'

'Because I am afraid of him,' said Syme; 'and no man should leave in the universe anything of which he is afraid.'

De Worms blinked at him with a sort of blind wonder. He made an effort to speak, but Syme went on in a low voice, but with an undercurrent of inhuman exaltation:

'Who would condescend to strike down the mere things that he does not fear? Who would debase himself to be merely brave, like any common prize-fighter? Who would stoop to be fearless—like a tree? Fight the thing that you fear. You remember the old tale of the English clergyman who gave the last rites to the brigand of Sicily, and how on his death-bed the great robber said, "I can give you no money, but I can give you advice for a lifetime: your thumb on the blade, and strike upwards." So I say to you, strike upwards, if you strike at the stars.'

The other looked at the ceiling, one of the tricks of his pose.

'Sunday is a fixed star,' he said.

'You shall see him a falling star,' said Syme, and put on his hat.

The decision of his gesture drew the Professor vaguely to his feet.

'Have you any idea,' he asked, with a sort of benevolent bewilderment, 'exactly where you are going?'

'Yes,' replied Syme shortly, 'I am going to prevent this bomb being thrown in Paris.'

'Have you any conception how?' inquired the other.

'No,' said Syme with equal decision.

'You remember, of course,' resumed the soi-disant de Worms, pulling his beard and looking out of the window, 'that when we broke up rather hurriedly the whole arrangements for the atrocity were left in the private hands of the Marquis and Dr. Bull. The Marquis is by this time probably crossing the Channel. But where he will go and what he will do it is doubtful whether even the President knows; certainly we don't. The only man who does know is Dr. Bull.'

'Confound it!' cried Syme. 'And we don't know where he is.'

'Yes,' said the other in his curious, absent-minded way, 'I know where he is myself.'

'Will you tell me?' asked Syme with eager eyes.

'I will take you there,' said the Professor, and took down his own hat from a peg.

Syme stood looking at him with a sort of rigid excitement.

'What do you mean?' he asked sharply. 'Will you join me? Will you take the risk?'

'Young man,' said the Professor pleasantly, 'I am amused to observe that you think I am a coward. As to that I will say only one word, and that shall be entirely in the manner of your own philosophical rhetoric. You think that it is possible to pull down the President. I know that it is impossible, and I am going to try it,' and opening the tavern door, which let in a blast of bitter air, they went out together into the dark streets by the docks.

Most of the snow was melted or trampled to mud, but here and there a clot of it still showed grey rather than white in the gloom. The small streets were sloppy and full of pools, which reflected the flaming lamps irregularly, and by accident, like fragments of some other and fallen world. Syme felt almost dazed as he stepped through this growing confusion of lights and shadows; but his companion walked on with a certain briskness towards where, at the end of the street, an inch or two of the lamplit river looked like a bar of flame.

'Where are you going?' Syme inquired.

'Just now,' answered the Professor, 'I am going just round the corner to see whether Dr. Bull has gone to bed. He is hygienic, and retires early.'

'Dr. Bull!' exclaimed Syme, 'Does he live round the corner?'

'No,' answered his friend. 'As a matter of fact he lives some way off, on the other side of the river, but we can tell from here whether he has gone to bed.'

Turning the corner as he spoke, and facing the dim river, flecked with flame, he pointed with his stick to the other bank. On the Surrey side[48] at this point there ran out into the Thames, seeming almost to overhang it, a bulk and cluster of those tall tenements, dotted with lighted windows, and rising like factory chimneys to an almost insane height. Their special poise and position made one block of buildings especially look like a Tower of Babel with a hundred eyes. Syme had never seen any of the sky-scraping buildings in America, so he could only think of the buildings in a dream.

Even as he stared, the highest light in this innumerably lighted turret abruptly went out, as if this black Argus[49] had winked at him with one of his innumerable eyes.

[48] This is a reference to the southern bank.

[49] Argus was a monster with a hundred eyes of which fifty always remained open. He was killed by Mercury whereupon Juno took his eyes and scattered them over the tail of the peacock.

Professor de Worms swung round on his heel, and struck his stick against his boot.

'We are too late,' he said, 'the hygienic Doctor has gone to bed.'

'What do you mean?' asked Syme. 'Does he live over there, then?'

'Yes,' said de Worms, 'behind that particular window which you can't see. Come along and get some dinner. We must call on him to-morrow morning.'

Without further parley, he led the way through several by-ways until they came out into the flare and clamour of the East India Dock Road. The Professor, who seemed to know his way about the neighbourhood, proceeded to a place where the line of lighted shops fell back into a sort of abrupt twilight and quiet, in which an old white inn, all out of repair, stood back some twenty feet from the road.

'You can find good English inns left by accident everywhere, like fossils,' explained the Professor. 'I once found a decent place in the West End.'

'I suppose,' said Syme, smiling, 'that this is the corresponding decent place in the East End?'

'It is,' said the Professor reverently, and went in.

In that place they dined and slept, both very thoroughly. The beans and bacon, which these unaccountable people cooked well, the astonishing emergence of Burgundy from their cellars, crowned Syme's sense of a new comradeship and comfort. Through all this ordeal his root horror had been isolation, and there are no words to express the abyss between isolation and having one ally. It may be conceded to the mathematicians that four is twice two. But two is not twice one; two is two thousand times one. That is why, in spite of a hundred disadvantages, the world will always return to monogamy.

Syme was able to pour out for the first time the whole of his outrageous tale, from the time when Gregory had taken him to the little tavern by the river. He did it idly and amply, in a luxuriant monologue, as a man speaks with very old friends. On his side, also, the man who had impersonated Professor de Worms was not less communicative. His own story was almost as silly as Syme's.

'That's a good get-up of yours,' said Syme, draining a glass of

Mâcon; 'a lot better than old Gogol's. Even at the start I thought he was a bit too hairy.'

'A difference of artistic theory,' replied the Professor pensively. 'Gogol was an idealist. He made up as the abstract or platonic ideal of an anarchist. But I am a realist. I am a portrait painter. But, indeed, to say that I am a portrait painter is an inadequate expression. I am a portrait.'

'I don't understand you,' said Syme.

'I am a portrait,' repeated the Professor. 'I am a portrait of the celebrated Professor de Worms, who is, I believe, in Naples.'

'You mean you are made up like him,' said Syme. 'But doesn't he know that you are taking his nose in vain?'

'He knows it right enough,' replied his friend cheerfully.

'Then why doesn't he denounce you?'

'I have denounced him,' answered the Professor.

'Do explain yourself,' said Syme.

'With pleasure, if you don't mind hearing my story,' replied the eminent foreign philosopher. 'I am by profession an actor and my name is Wilks. When I was on the stage I mixed with all sorts of Bohemian and blackguard company. Sometimes I touched the edge of the turf, sometimes the riff-raff of the arts, and occasionally the political refugee. In some den of exiled dreamers I was introduced to the great German Nihilist philosopher, Professor de Worms. I did not gather much about him beyond his appearance, which was very disgusting, and which I studied carefully. I understood that he had proved that the destructive principle in the universe was God; hence he insisted on the need for a furious and incessant energy, rending all things in pieces. Energy, he said, was the All. He was lame, short-sighted, and partially paralytic. When I met him I was in a frivolous mood, and I disliked him so much that I resolved to imitate him. If I had been a draughtsman I would have drawn a caricature. I was only an actor, I could only act a caricature. I made myself up into what was meant for a wild exaggeration of the old Professor's dirty old self. When I went into the room full of his supporters I expected to be received with a roar of laughter, or (if they were too far gone) with a roar of indignation at the insult. I cannot describe the surprise

I felt when my entrance was received with a respectful silence, followed (when I had first opened my lips) with a murmur of admiration. The curse of the perfect artist had fallen upon me. I had been too subtle, I had been too true. They thought I really was the great Nihilist Professor. I was a healthy minded young man at the time, and I confess that it was a blow. Before I could fully recover, however, two or three of these admirers ran up to me radiating indignation, and told me that a public insult had been put upon me in the next room. I inquired its nature. It seemed that an impertinent fellow had dressed himself up as a preposterous parody of myself. I had drunk more champagne than was good for me, and in a flash of folly I decided to see the situation through. Consequently it was to meet the glare of the company and my own lifted eyebrows and freezing eyes that the real Professor came into the room.

'I need hardly say there was a collision. The pessimists all round me looked anxiously from one Professor to the other Professor to see which was really the more feeble. But I won. An old man in poor health, like my rival, could not be expected to be so impressively feeble as a young actor in the prime of life. You see, he really had paralysis, and working within this definite limitation, he couldn't be so jolly paralytic as I was. Then he tried to blast my claims intellectually. I countered that by a very simple dodge. Whenever he said something that nobody but he could understand, I replied with something which I could not even understand myself. "I don't fancy," he said, "that you could have worked out the principle that evolution is only negation, since there inheres in it the introduction of lacunae, which are an essential of differentiation." I replied quite scornfully, "You read all that up in Pinckwerts; the notion that involution functioned eugenically was exposed long ago by Glumpe." It is unnecessary for me to say that there never were such people as Pinckwerts and Glumpe. But the people all round (rather to my surprise) seemed to remember them quite well, and the Professor, finding that the learned and mysterious method left him rather at the mercy of an enemy slightly deficient in scruples, fell back upon a more popular form of wit. "I see," he sneered, "you prevail like the false pig in Aesop." "And you fail," I answered, smiling, "like the hedgehog in Montaigne." Need I say that there is no hedgehog in Montaigne? "Your clap-trap comes off," he said; "so would your beard." I had no intelligent answer to this, which was quite true and rather witty. But I laughed heartily, answered, "Like the Pantheist's boots," at random, and turned on my heel with all the honours of victory. The real Professor was thrown out, but not with violence, though one man tried very patiently to pull off his nose. He is now, I believe, received everywhere in Europe as a delightful impostor. His apparent earnestness and anger, you see, make him all the more entertaining.'

'Well,' said Syme, 'I can understand your putting on his dirty old beard for a night's practical joke, but I don't understand your never taking it off again.'

'That is the rest of the story,' said the impersonator. 'When I myself left the company, followed by reverent applause, I went limping down the dark street, hoping that I should soon be far enough away to be able to walk like a human being. To my astonishment, as I was turning the corner, I felt a touch on the shoulder, and turning, found myself under the shadow of an enormous policeman. He told me I was wanted. I struck a sort of paralytic attitude, and cried in a high German accent, "Yes, I am wanted—by the oppressed of the world. You are arresting me on the charge of being the great anarchist, Professor de Worms." The policeman impassively consulted a paper in his hand, "No, sir," he said civilly, "at least not exactly, sir. I am arresting you on the charge of not being the celebrated anarchist, Professor de Worms." This charge, if it was criminal at all, was certainly the lighter of the two, and I went along with the man doubtful, but not greatly dismayed. I was shown into a number of rooms, and eventually into the presence of a police officer, who explained that a serious campaign had been opened against the centres of anarchy, and that this, my successful masquerade, might be of considerable value to the public safety. He offered me a good salary and this little blue card. Though our conversation was short, he struck me as a man of very massive common sense and humour. But I cannot tell you much about him personally, because——'

Syme laid down his knife and fork.

'I know,' he said, 'because you talked to him in a dark room.'

Professor de Worms nodded and drained his glass.

IX

THE MAN IN SPECTACLES

Burgundy is a jolly thing,' said the Professor sadly, as he set his glass down.

'You don't look as if it were,' said Syme, 'you drink it as if it were medicine.'

'You must excuse my manner,' said the Professor dismally, 'my position is rather a curious one. Inside I am really bursting with boyish merriment; but I acted the paralytic Professor so well, that now I can't leave off. So that when I am among friends, and have no need at all to diguise myself, I still can't help speaking slow and wrinkling my forehead—just as if it were my forehead. I can be quite happy, you understand, but only in a paralytic sort of way. The most buoyant exclamations leap up in my heart, but they come out of my mouth quite different. You should hear me say, "Buck up, old cock!" It would bring tears to your eyes.'

'It does,' said Syme; 'but I cannot help thinking that apart from all that you are really a bit worried.'

The Professor started a little and looked at him steadily.

'You are a very clever fellow,' he said; 'it is a pleasure to work with you. Yes, I have rather a heavy cloud in my head. There is a great problem to face,' and he sank his bald brow in his two hands.

Then he said in a low voice:

'Can you play the piano?'

'Yes,' said Syme in simple wonder, 'I'm supposed to have a good touch.'

Then, as the other did not speak, he added:

'I trust the great cloud is lifted.'

After a long silence, the professor said out of the cavernous shadow of his hands:

'It would have done just as well if you could work a typewriter.'

'Thank you,' said Syme, 'you flatter me.'

'Listen to me,' said the other, 'and remember whom we have to see to-morrow. You and I are going to-morrow to attempt something which is very much more dangerous than trying to steal the

Crown Jewels out of the Tower.[50] We are trying to steal a secret from a very sharp, very strong, and very wicked man. I believe there is no man, except the President, of course, who is so seriously startling and formidable as that little grinning fellow in goggles. He has not perhaps the white-hot enthusiasm unto death, the mad martyrdom for anarchy, which marks the Secretary. But then that very fanaticism in Secretary has a human pathos, and is almost a redeeming trait. But the little Doctor has a brutal sanity that is more shocking than the Secretary's disease. Don't you notice his detestable virility and vitality? He bounces like an india-rubber ball. Depend on it, Sunday was not asleep (I wonder if he ever sleeps?) when he locked up all the plans of this outrage in the round, black head of Dr. Bull.'

'And you think,' said Syme, 'that this unique monster will be soothed if I play the piano to him?'

'Don't be an ass,' said his mentor. 'I mentioned the piano because it gives one quick and independent fingers. Syme, if we are to go through this interview and come out sane or alive, we must have some code of signals between us that this brute will not see. I have made a rough alphabetical cipher corresponding to the five fingers—like this, see,' and he rippled with his fingers on the wooden table—'B A D, bad, a word we may frequently require.'

Syme poured himself out another glass of wine, and began to study the scheme. He was abnormally quick with his brains at puzzles, and with his hands at conjuring, and it did not take him long to learn how he might convey simple messages by what would seem to be idle taps upon a table or knee. But wine and companionship had always the effect of inspiring him to a farcical ingenuity, and the Professor soon found himself struggling with the too vast energy of the new language, as it passed through the heated brain of Syme.

'We must have several word-signs,' said Syme seriously—'words that we are likely to want, fine shades of meaning. My favourite word is "coeval". What's yours?'

[50] The Crown Jewels are kept in the Jewel Tower within the medieval fortress called the Tower of London. There have been various attempts to steal them but only one person, a Captain Blood, ever managed to get them outside the confines of the Tower. Even Captain Blood was captured and brought before King Charles II, who was so amused by his effrontery that he pardoned him.

'Do stop playing the goat,' said the Professor plaintively. 'You don't know how serious this is.'

' "Lush", too,' said Syme shaking his head sagaciously, 'we must have "lush". — Word applied to grass, don't you know?'

'Do you imagine,' asked the Professor furiously, 'that we are going to talk to Dr. Bull about grass?'

'There are several ways in which the subject could be approached,' said Syme reflectively, 'and the word introduced without appearing forced. We might say, "Dr. Bull, as a revolutionist, you remember that a tyrant once advised us to eat grass; and indeed many of us, looking on the fresh lush grass of summer——'

'Do you understand,' said the other, 'that this is a tragedy?'

'Perfectly,' replied Syme; 'always be comic in a tragedy. What the duce else can you do? I wish this language of yours had a wider scope. I suppose we could not extend it from the fingers to the toes? That would involve pulling off our boots and socks during the conversation, which however unobstrusively performed——'

'Syme,' said his friend with a stern simplicity, 'go to bed!'

Syme, however, sat up in bed for a considerable time mastering the new code. He was awakened next morning while the east was still sealed with darkness, and found his grey-bearded ally standing like a ghost beside his bed.

Syme sat up in bed blinking; then slowly collected his thoughts, threw off the bed-clothes, and stood up. It seemed to him in some curious way that all the safety and sociability of the night before fell with the bed-clothes off him, and he stood up in an air of cold danger. He still felt an entire trust and loyalty towards his companion; but it was the trust between two men going to the scaffold.

'Well,' said Syme with a forced cheerfulness as he pulled on his trousers, 'I dreamt of that alphabet of yours. Did it take you long to make it up?'

The Professor made no answer, but gazed in front of him with eyes the color of a wintry sea; so Syme repeated his question.

'I say, did it take you long to invent all this? I'm considered good at these things, and it was good hour's grind. Did you learn it all on the spot?'

The Professor was silent; his eyes were wide open, and he wore a fixed but very small smile.

'How long did it take you?'

The Professor did not move.

'Confound you, can't you answer?' called out Syme, in a sudden anger that had something like fear underneath. Whether or no the Professor could answer, he did not.

Syme stood staring back at the stiff face like parchment and the blank, blue eyes. His first thought was that the Professor had gone mad, but his second thought was more frightful. After all, what did he know about this queer creature whom he had heedlessly accepted as a friend? What did he know, except that the man had been at the anarchist breakfast and had told him a ridiculous tale? How improbable it was that there should be another friend there beside Gogol! Was this man's silence a sensational way of declaring war? Was this adamantine stare after all only the awful sneer of some threefold traitor, who had turned for the last time? He stood and strained his ears in this heartless silence. He almost fancied he could hear dynamiters come to capture him shifting softly in the corridor outside.

Then his eye strayed downwards, and he burst out laughing. Though the Professor himself stood there as voiceless as a statue, his five dumb fingers were dancing alive upon the dead table. Syme watched the twinkling movements of the talking hand, and read clearly the message:

'I will only talk like this. We must get used to it.'

He rapped out the answer with the impatience of relief:

'All right. Let's get out to breakfast.'

They took their hats and sticks in silence; but as Syme took his sword-stick, he held it hard.

They paused for a few minutes only to stuff down coffee and coarse thick sandwiches at a coffee-stall, and then made their way across the river, which under the grey and growing light looked as desolate as Acheron.[51] They reached the bottom of the huge block of buildings which they had seen from across the river, and began in

---

[51] Acheron was the river of Hell that nobody could cross a second time.

silence to mount the naked and numberless stone steps, only pausing now and then to make short remarks on the rail of the banisters. At about every other flight they passed a window; each window showed them a pale and tragic dawn lifting itself laboriously over London. From each the innumerable roofs of slate looked like the leaden surges of a grey, troubled sea after rain. Syme was increasingly conscious that his new adventure had somehow a quality of cold sanity worse than the wild adventures of the past. Last night, for instance, the tall tenements had seemed to him like a tower in a dream. As he now went up the weary and perpetual steps, he was daunted and bewildered by their almost infinite series. But it was not the hot horror of a dream or of anything that might be exaggeration or delusion. Their infinity was more like the empty infinity of arithmetic, something unthinkable, yet necessary to thought. Or it was like the stunning statements of astronomy about the distance of the fixed stars. He was ascending the house of reason, a thing more hideous than unreason itself.

By the time they reached Dr. Bull's landing, a last window showed them a harsh, white dawn edged with banks of a kind of coarse red, more like red clay than red cloud. And when they entered Dr. Bull's bare garret it was full of light.

Syme had been haunted by a half-historic memory in connexion with these empty rooms and that austere daybreak. The moment he saw the garret and Dr. Bull sitting writing at a table, he remembered what the memory was—the French Revolution. There should have been the black outline of a guillotine against that heavy red and white of the morning. Dr. Bull was in his white shirt and black breeches only; his cropped, dark head might well have just come out of its wig; he might have been Marat or a more slipshod Robespierre.

Yet when he was seen properly, the French fancy fell away. The Jacobins[52] were idealists; there was about this man a murderous

[52] Jacobins were members of a revolutionary political club that met in the *rue des Jacobins*. They were supporters of Robespierre and the Committee of Public Safety and were idealists in the sense that men could be made good by guillotining evil men until there were none left.

materialism. His position gave him a somewhat new appearance. The strong, white light of morning coming from one side creating sharp shadows, made him seem both more pale and more angular than he had looked at the breakfast on the balcony. Thus the two black glasses that encased his eyes might really have been black cavities in his skull, making him look like a death's-head. And indeed, if ever Death himself sat writing at a wooden table, it might have been he.

He looked up and smiled brightly enough as the men came in, and rose with the resilient rapidity of which the Professor had spoken. He set chairs for both of them, and going to a peg behind the door, proceeded to put on a coat and waistcoat of rough, dark tweed; he buttoned it up neatly, and came back to sit down at his table.

The quiet good humour of his manner left his two opponents helpless. It was with some momentary difficulty that the Professor broke silence and began, 'I'm sorry to disturb you so early, comrade,' said he, with a careful resumption of the slow de Worms manner. 'You have no doubt made all arrangements for the Paris affair?' Then he added with infinite slowness, 'We have information which renders intolerable anything in the nature of a moment's delay.'

Dr. Bull smiled again, but continued to gaze on them without speaking. The Professor resumed, a pause before each weary word:

'Please do not think me excessively abrupt; but I advise you to alter those plans, or if it is too late for that, to follow your agent with all the support you can get for him. Comrade Syme and I have had an experience which it would take more time to recount than we can afford, if we are to act on it. I will, however, relate the occurrence in detail, even at the risk of losing time, if you really feel that it is essential to the understanding of the problem we have to discuss.'

He was spinning out his sentences, making them intolerably long and lingering, in the hope of maddening the practical little Doctor into an explosion of impatience which might show his hand. But the little Doctor continued only to stare and smile, and the monologue was uphill work. Syme began to feel a new sickness and despair. The Doctor's smile and silence were not at all like the cataleptic stare and horrible silence which he had confronted in the Professor half an hour before. About the Professor's make-up and all his antics there was always something merely grotesque, like a gollywog.[53] Syme remembered those wild woes of yesterday as one remembers being afraid of Bogy in childhood. But there was daylight; here was a healthy, square-shouldered man in tweeds, not odd save for the accident of his ugly spectacles, not glaring or grinning at all, but smiling steadily and not saying a word. The whole had a sense of unbearable reality. Under the increasing sunlight the colours of the Doctor's complexion, the pattern of his tweeds, grew and expanded outrageously, as such things grow too important in a realistic novel. But his smile was quite slight, the pose of his head polite; the only uncanny thing was his silence.

'As I say,' resumed the Professor, like a man toiling through heavy sand, 'the incident that has occurred to us and has led us to ask for information about the Marquis, is one which you may think it better to have narrated; but as it came in the way of Comrade Syme rather than me——'

His words he seemed to be dragging out like words in an anthem; but Syme, who was watching, saw his long fingers rattle quickly on the edge of the crazy table. He read the message: 'You must go on. This devil has sucked me dry!'

Syme plunged into the breach with that bravado of improvisation which always came to him when he was alarmed.

'Yes, the thing really happened to me,' he said hastily. 'I had the good fortune to fall into conversation with a detective who took me, thanks to my hat, for a respectable person. Wishing to clinch my reputation for respectability, I took him and made him very drunk at the Savoy.[54] Under this influence he became friendly, and told me in so many words that within a day or two they hope to arrest the Marquis in France. So unless you or I can get on his track——

The Doctor was still smiling in the most friendly way, and his protected eyes were still impenetrable. The Professor signalled to Syme

[53] A gollywog is a black-faced doll with frizzy hair usually dressed in a brightly colored jacket with striped pants.

[54] The Savoy Hotel is situated on the Strand.

that he would resume his explanation, and he began again with the same elaborate calm.

'Syme immediately brought this information to me, and we came here together to see what use you would be inclined to make of it. It seems to me unquestionably urgent that——'

All this time Syme had been staring at the Doctor almost as steadily as the Doctor stared at the Professor, but quite without the smile. The nerves of both comrades-in-arms were near snapping under that strain of motionless amiability, when Syme suddenly leant forward and idly tapped the edge of the table. His message to his ally ran, 'I have an intuition.'

The Professor, with scarcely a pause in his monologue, signalled back, 'Then sit on it.'

Syme telegraphed, 'It is quite extraordinary.'

The other answered, 'Extraordinary rot!'

Syme said, 'I am a poet.'

The other retorted, 'You are a dead man.'

Syme had gone quite red up to his yellow hair, and his eyes were burning feverishly. As he said he had an intuition, and it had risen to a sort of light-headed certainty. Resuming his symbolic taps, he signalled to his friend, 'You scarcely realize how poetic my intuition is. It has that sudden quality we sometimes feel in the coming of spring.'

He then studied the answer on his friend's fingers. The answer was, 'Go to hell!'

The Professor then resumed his merely verbal monologue addressed to the Doctor.

'Perhaps I should rather say,' said Syme on his fingers, 'that it resembles that sudden smell of the sea which may be found in the heart of lush woods.'

His companion disdained to reply.

'Or yet again,' tapped Syme, 'it is positive, as is the passionate red hair of a beautiful woman.'

The Professor was continuing his speech, but in the middle of it Syme decided to act. He leant across the table, and said in a voice that could not be neglected:

'Dr. Bull!'

The Doctor's sleek and smiling head did not move, but they could have sworn that under his dark glasses his eyes darted towards Syme.

'Dr. Bull,' said Syme, in a voice peculiarly precise and courteous, 'would you do me a small favour? Would you be so kind as to take off your spectacles?'

The Professor swung round on his seat, and stared at Syme with a sort of frozen fury of astonishment. Syme, like a man who has thrown his life and fortune on the table, leaned forward with a fiery face. The Doctor did not move.

For a few seconds there was a silence in which one could hear a pin drop, split once by the single hoot of a distant steamer on the Thames. Then Dr. Bull rose slowly, still smiling, and took off his spectacles.

Syme sprang to his feet, stepping backwards a little, like a chemical lecturer from a successful explosion. His eyes were like stars, and for an instant he could only point without speaking.

The Professor had also started to his feet, forgetful of his supposed paralysis. He leant on the back of the chair and stared doubtfully at Dr. Bull, as if the Doctor had been turned into a toad before his eyes. And indeed it was almost as great a transformation scene.

The two detectives saw sitting in the chair before them a very boyish-looking young man, with a very frank and happy hazel eyes, an open expression, cockney clothes like those of a city clerk, and an unquestionable breath about him of being very good and rather commonplace. The smile was still there, but it might have been the first smile of a baby.

'I knew I was a poet,' cried Syme in a sort of ecstasy. 'I knew my intuition was as infallible as the Pope. It was the spectacles that did it! It was all the spectacles! Given those beastly black eyes, and all the rest of him, his health and his jolly looks, made him a live devil among dead ones.'

'It certainly does make a queer difference,' said the Professor shakily. 'But as regards the project of Dr. Bull——'

'Project be damned!' roared Syme, beside himself. 'Look at him! Look at his face, look at his collar, look at his blessed boots! You don't suppose, do you, that that thing's an anarchist?'

'Syme!' cried the other in an apprehensive agony.

'Why, by God!' said Syme, 'I'll take the risk of that myself! Dr. Bull, I am a police officer. There's my card,' and he flung down the blue card upon the table.

The Professor still feared that all was lost; but he was loyal. He pulled out his own official card and put it beside his friend's. Then the third man burst out laughing, and for the first time that morning they heard his voice.

'I'm awfully glad you chaps have come so early,' he said, with a sort of schoolboy flippancy, 'for we can all start for France together. Yes, I'm in the force right enough,' and he flicked a blue card towards them lightly as a matter of form.

Clapping a brisk bowler on his head and resuming his goblin glasses, the Doctor moved so quickly towards the door, that the others instinctively followed him. Syme seemed a little distrait, and as he passed under the doorway he suddenly struck his stick on the stone passage so that it rang.

'But Lord God Almighty,' he cried out, 'if this is all right, there were more damned detectives than there were damned dynamiters at the damned Council!'

'We might have fought easily,' said Bull; 'we were four against three.'

The Professor was descending the stairs, but his voice came up from below.

'No,' said the voice, 'we were not four against three — we were not so lucky. We were four against One.'

The others went down the stairs in silence.

The young man called Bull, with an innocent courtesy characteristic of him, insisted on going last until they reached the street; but there his own robust rapidity asserted itself unconsciously, and he walked quickly on ahead towards a railway inquiry office, talking to the others over his shoulder.

'It is jolly to get some pals,' he said. 'I've been half dead with the jumps, being quite alone. I nearly flung my arms round Gogol and embraced him, which would have been imprudent. I hope you won't despise me for having been in a blue funk.'

'All the blue devils in blue hell,' said Syme, 'contributed to my blue funk! But the worst devil was you and your infernal goggles.'

The young man laughed delightedly.

'Wasn't it a rag?' he said. 'Such a simple idea—not my own. I haven't got the brains. You see, I wanted to go into the detective service, especially the anti-dynamite business. But for that purpose they wanted some one to dress up as a dynamiter; and they all swore by blazes that I could never look like a dynamiter. They said my very walk was respectable, and that seen from behind I looked like the British Constitution. They said I looked too healthy and too optimistic, and too reliable and benevolent; they called me all sorts of names at Scotland Yard. They said that if I had been a criminal, I might have made my fortune by looking so like an honest man; but as I had the misfortune to be an honest man, there was not even the remotest chance of my assisting them by ever looking like a criminal. But at last I was brought before some old josser who was high up in the force, and who seemed to have no end of a head on his shoulders. And there the others all talked hopelessly. One asked whether a bushy beard would hide my nice smile; another said that if they blacked my face I might look like a negro anarchist; but this old chap chipped in with a most extraordinary remark. "A pair of smoked spectacles will do it," he said positively. "Look at him now; he looks like an angelic office boy. Put him on a pair of smoked spectacles, and children will scream at the sight of him." And so it was, by George! When once my eyes were covered all the rest, smile and big shoulders and short hair, made me look a perfect little devil. As I say, it was simple enough when it was done, like miracles; but that wasn't the really miraculous part of it. There was one really staggering thing about the business, and my head still turns at it.'

'What was that?' asked Syme.

'I'll tell you,' answered the man in spectacles. 'This big pot in the police who sized me up so that he knew how the goggles would go with my hair and socks—by God, he never saw me at all!'

Syme's eyes suddenly flashed on him.

'How was that?' he asked. 'I thought you talked to him.'

'So I did,' said Bull brightly; 'but we talked in a pitch-dark room like a coal-cellar. There, you would never have guessed that.'

'I could not have conceived it,' said Syme gravely.

'It is indeed a new idea,' said the Professor.

Their new ally was in practical matters a whirlwind. At the inquiry office he asked with business-like brevity about the trains for Dover. Having got his information, he bundled the company into a cab, and put them and himself inside a railway carriage before they had properly realized the breathless process. They were already on the Calais boat before conversation flowed freely.

'I had already arranged,' he explained, 'to go to France for my lunch; but I am delighted to have some one to lunch with me. You see, I had to send that beast, the Marquis, over with his bomb, because the President had his eye on me, though God knows how. I'll tell you the story some day. It was perfectly choking. Whenever I tried to slip out of it I saw the President somewhere, smiling out of the bow-window of a club or taking off his hat to me from the top of an omnibus. I tell you, you can say what you like, that fellow sold himself to the devil; he can be in six places at once.'

'So you sent the Marquis off, I understand,' asked the Professor. 'Was it long ago? Shall we be in time to catch him?'

'Yes,' answered the new guide, 'I've timed it all. He'll still be at Calais when we arrive.'

'But when we do catch him at Calais,' said the Professor, 'what are we going to do?'

At this question the countenance of Dr. Bull fell for the first time. He reflected a little, and then said:

'Theoretically, I suppose, we ought to call the police.'

'Not I,' said Syme. 'Theoretically I ought to drown myself first. I promised a poor fellow, who was a real modern pessimist, on my word of honour not to tell the police. I'm no hand at casuistry, but I can't break my word to a modern pessimist. It's like breaking one's word to a child.'

'I'm in the same boat,' said the Professor. 'I tried to tell the police and I couldn't, because of some silly oath I took. You see, when I was an actor I was a sort of all-round beast. Perjury or treason is the only crime I haven't committed. If I did that I shouldn't know the difference between right and wrong.'

'I've been through all that,' said Dr. Bull, 'and I've made up my mind. I gave my promise to the Secretary—you know him, man who smiles upside down. My friends, that man is the most utterly unhappy man that was ever human. It may be his digestion, or his conscience, or his nerves, or his philosophy of the universe, but he's damned, he's in hell! Well, I can't turn on a man like that, and hunt him down. It's like whipping a leper. I may be mad, but that's how I feel; and there's jolly well the end of it.'

'I don't think you're mad,' said Syme. 'I knew you would decide like that when first you——'

'Eh?' said Dr. Bull.

'When first you took off your spectacles.'

Dr. Bull smiled a little, and strolled across the deck to look at the sunlit sea. Then he strolled back again, kicking his heels carelessly, and a companionable silence fell between the three men.

'Well,' said Syme, 'it seems that we have all the same kind of morality or immorality, so we had better face the fact that comes of it.'

'Yes,' assented the Professor, 'you're quite right; and we must hurry up, for I can see the Grey Nose[55] standing out from France.'

'The fact that comes of it,' said Syme seriously, 'is this, that we three are alone on this planet. Gogol has gone, God knows where; perhaps the President has smashed him like a fly. On the Council we are three men against three, like the Romans who held the bridge.[56] But we are worse off than that, first because they can appeal to their organization and we cannot appeal to ours, and second because——'

'Because one of those other three men,' said the Professor, 'is not a man.'

Syme nodded and was silent for a second or two, then he said:

'My idea is this. We must do something to keep the Marquis in Calais till to-morrow midday. I have turned over twenty schemes in my head. We cannot denounce him as a dynamiter; that is agreed. We cannot get him detained on some trivial charge, for we should have to appear; he knows us, and he would smell a rat. We cannot pretend to keep him on anarchist business; he might swallow much

---

[55] The Grey Nose is *Cap Gris Nez*.

[56] Horatius and his two fellow Romans defended the Subicius bridge against the army of Lars Porsenna.

in that way, but not the notion of stopping in Calais while the Tsar went safely through Paris. We might try to kidnap him, and lock him up ourselves; but he is a well-known man here. He has a whole bodyguard of friends; he is very strong and brave, and the event is doubtful. The only thing I can see to do is actually to take advantage of the very things that are in the Marquis's favour. I am going to profit by the fact that he is a highly respected nobleman. I am going to profit by the fact that he has many friends and moves in the best society.'

'What the devil are you talking about?' asked the Professor.

'The Symes are first mentioned in the fourteenth century,' said Syme; 'but there is a tradition that one of them rode behind Bruce at Bannockburn.[57] Since 1350 the tree is quite clear.'

'He's gone off his head,' said the little Doctor, staring.

'Our bearings,' continued Syme calmly, 'are "argent a chevron gules charged with three cross crosslets of the field." The motto varies.'

The Professor seized Syme roughly by the waist-coat.

'We are just inshore,' he said. 'Are you sea-sick or joking in the wrong place?'

'My remarks are almost painfully practical,' answered Syme, in an unhurried manner. 'The house of St. Eustache also is very ancient. The Marquis cannot deny that he is a gentleman. He cannot deny that I am a gentleman. And in order to put the matter of my social position quite beyond a doubt, I propose at the earliest opportunity to knock his hat off. But here we are in the harbour.'

They went on shore under the strong sun in a sort of daze. Syme, who had now taken the lead as Bull had taken it in London, led them along a kind of marine parade until he came to some cafés, embowered in a bulk of greenery and overlooking the sea. As he went before them his step was slightly swaggering, and he swung his

[57] Robert the Bruce (1274–1329) was Robert I, King of Scotland. Bannockburn was a battle near Stirling in 1314 in which Robert the Bruce defeated the English army of King Edward II. The Scottish tactics could have been influenced by the advice of Knights Templar, who had fled from persecution in France in 1307 under Phillipe le Bel.

stick like a sword. He was making apparently for the extreme end of the line of cafés, but he stopped abruptly. With a sharp gesture he motioned them to silence, but he pointed with one gloved finger to a café table under a bank of flowering foliage at which sat the Marquis de St. Eustache, his teeth shining in his thick, black beard, and his bold, brown face shadowed by a light yellow straw hat and outlined against the violet sea.

X

THE DUEL

Syme sat down at a café table with his companions, his blue eyes sparkling like the bright sea below, and ordered a bottle of Saumur[58] with a pleased impatience. He was for some reason in a condition of curious hilarity. His spirits were already unnaturally high; they rose as the Saumur sank, and in half an hour his talk was a torrent of nonsense. He professed to be making out a plan of the conversation which was going to ensue between himself and the deadly Marquis. He jotted it down wildly with a pencil. It was arranged like a printed catechism, with questions and answers, and was delivered with an extraordinary rapidity of utterance.

'I shall approach. Before taking off his hat, I shall take off my own. I shall say, "The Marquis de Saint Eustach, I believe." He will say, "The celebrated Mr. Syme, I presume." He will say in the most exquisite French, "How are you?" I shall reply in the most exquisite cockney, "Oh, just the Syme——" '

'Oh, shut it,' said the man in spectacles. 'Pull yourself together, and chuck away that bit of paper. What are you really going to do?'

'But it was a lovely catechism,' said Syme pathetically. 'Do let me read it you. It has only forty-three questions and answers, and some of the Marquis's answers are wonderfully witty. I like to be just to my enemy.'

'But what's the good of it all?' asked Dr. Bull in exasperation.

'It leads up to my challenge, don't you see,' said Syme, beaming. 'When the Marquis has given the thirty-ninth reply, which runs——'

'Has it by any chance occurred to you,' asked the Professor, with a ponderous simplicity, 'that the Marquis may not say all the forty-three things you have put down for him? In that case, I understand, your own epigrams may appear somewhat more forced.'

Syme struck the table with a radiant face.

---

[58] Saumur is a sparkling white wine from the Loire valley.

'Why, how true that is,' he said, 'and I never thought of it. Sir, you have an intellect beyond the common. You will make a name.'

'Oh, you're as drunk as an owl!' said the Doctor.

'It only remains,' continued Syme, quite unperturbed, 'to adopt some other method of breaking the ice (if I may so express it) between myself and the man I wish to kill. And since the course of a dialogue cannot be predicted by one of its parties alone (as you have pointed out with such recondite acumen), the only thing to be done, I suppose, is for the one party, as far as possible, to do all the dialogue by himself. And so I will, by George!' And he stood up suddenly, his yellow hair blowing in the slight sea-breeze.

A band was playing in a *café chantant*[59] hidden somewhere among the trees, and a woman had just stopped singing. On Syme's heated head the bray of the brass band seemed like the jar and jingle of that barrel-organ in Leicester Square, to the tune of which he had once stood up to die. He looked across to the little table where the Marquis sat. The man had two companions now, solemn Frenchmen in frock-coats and silk hats, one of them with the red rosette of the Legion of Honour,[60] evidently people of a solid social position. Beside these black, cylindrical costumes, the Marquis, in his loose straw hat and light spring clothes, looked Bohemian and even barbaric; but he looked the Marquis. Indeed, one might say that he looked the king, with his animal elegance, his scornful eyes, and his proud head lifted against the purple sea. But he was no Christian king, at any rate; he was, rather some swarthy despot, half Greek, half Asiatic, who in the days when slavery seemed natural looked down on the Mediterranean, on his galley and his groaning slaves. Just so, Syme thought, would the brown-gold face of such a tyrant have shown against the dark green olives and the burning blue.

'Are you going to address the meeting?' asked the Professor peevishly, seeing that Syme still stood up without moving.

Syme drained his last glass of sparkling wine.

---

[59] A *café chantant* was a bar offering musical entertainment somewhat on the lines of a music hall or a vaudeville.

[60] The Legion of Honour is the *Légion d'Honneur*, a civil and military order instituted in 1802 by Napoleon Bonaparte as the highest level of decoration in France.

'I am,' he said, pointing across to the Marquis and his compan-ions, 'that meeting. That meeting displeases me. I am going to pull that meeting's great, ugly, mahogany-coloured nose.'

He stepped across swiftly, if not quite steadily. The Marquis, seeing him, arched his black Assyrian eyebrows in surprise, but smiled politely.

'You are Mr. Syme, I think,' he said.

Syme bowed.

'And you are the Marquis de Saint Eustache,' he said gracefully. 'Permit me to pull your nose.'

He leant over to do so, but the Marquis started backwards, upset-ting his chair, and the two men in top hats held Syme back by the shoulders.

'This man has insulted me!' said Syme, with gestures of explanation.

'Insulted you?' cried the gentleman with the red rosette, 'when?'

'Oh, just now,' said Syme recklessly. 'He insulted my mother.'

'Insulted your mother!' exclaimed the gentleman incredulously.

'Well, anyhow,' said Syme, conceding a point, 'my aunt.'

'But how can the Marquis have insulted your aunt just now?' said the second gentleman with some legitimate wonder. 'He has been sitting here all the time.'

'Ah, it was what he said!' said Syme darkly.

'I said nothing at all,' said the Marquis, 'except something about the band. I only said that I liked Wagner played well.'

'It was an allusion to my family,' said Syme firmly. 'My aunt played Wagner badly. It was a painful subject. We are always being insulted about it.'

'This seems most extraordinary,' said the gentleman who was *décoré*, looking thoughtfully at the Marquis.

'Oh, I assure you,' said Syme earnestly, 'the whole of your con-versation was simply packed with sinister allusions to my aunt's weaknesses.'

'This is nonsense!' said the second gentleman. 'I for one have said nothing for half an hour except that I liked the singing of that girl with black hair.'

'Well, there you are again!' said Syme indignantly. 'My aunt's was red!'

'It seems to me,' said the other, 'that you are simply seeking a pretext to insult the Marquis.'

'By George!' said Syme, facing round and looking at him, 'what a clever chap you are!'

The Marquis started up with eyes flaming like a tiger's.

'Seeking a quarrel with me!' he cried. 'Seeking a fight with me! By God! there was never a man who had to seek long. These gentlemen will perhaps act for me. There are still four hours of daylight. Let us fight this evening.'

Syme bowed with a quite beautiful graciousness.

'Marquis,' he said, 'your action is worthy of your fame and blood. Permit me to consult for a moment with the gentlemen in whose hands I shall place myself.'

In three long strides he rejoined his companions, and they, who had seen his champagne-inspired attack and listened to his idiotic explanations, were quite startled at the look of him. For now that he came back to them he was quite sober, a little pale, and he spoke in a low voice of passionate practicality.

'I have done it,' he said hoarsely. 'I have fixed a fight on the beast. But look here, and listen carefully. There is no time for talk. You are my seconds, and everything must come from you. Now you must insist, and insist absolutely, on the duel coming off after seven tomorrow, so as to give me the chance of preventing him from catching the 7.45 for Paris. If he misses that he misses his crime. He can't refuse to meet you on such a small point of time and place. But this is what he will do. He will choose a field somewhere near a wayside station, where he can pick up the train. He is a very good swordsman, and he will trust to killing me in time to catch it. But I can fence well too, and I think I can keep him in play, at any rate, until the train is lost. Then perhaps he may kill me to console his feelings. You understand? Very well then, let me introduce you to some charming friends of mine,' and leading them quickly across the parade, he presented them to the Marquis's seconds by two very aristocratic names of which they had not previously heard.

Syme was subject to spasms of singular common sense, not otherwise a part of his character. They were (as he said of his impulse

about the spectacles) poetic intuitions, and they sometimes rose to
the exaltation of prophecy.

He had correctly calculated in this case the policy of his opponent.
When the Marquis was informed by his seconds that Syme could only
fight in the morning, he must fully have realized that an obstacle
had suddenly arisen between him and his bomb-throwing business
in the capital. Naturally, he could not explain this objection to his
friends, so he chose the course which Syme had predicted. He induced
his seconds to settle on a small meadow not far from the railway, and
he trusted to the fatality of the first engagement.

When he came down very coolly to the field of honour, no one
could have guessed that he had any anxiety about a journey; his
hands were in his pockets, his straw hat on the back of his head, his
handsome face brazen in the sun. But it might have struck a stranger
as odd that there appeared in his train, not only his seconds carrying
the sword-case, but two of his servants carrying a portmanteau and a
luncheon basket.

Early as was the hour, the sun soaked everything in warmth, and
Syme was vaguely surprised to see so many spring flowers burning
gold and silver in the tall grass in which the whole company stood
almost knee-deep.

With the exception of the Marquis, all the men were in sombre
and solemn morning-dress, with hats like black chimney-pots; the
little Doctor especially, with the addition of his black spectacles,
looked like an undertaker in a farce. Syme could not help feeling a
comic contrast between this funereal church parade of apparel and
the rich and glistening meadow, growing wild flowers everywhere.
But, indeed, this comic contrast between the yellow blossoms and
the black hats was but a symbol of the tragic contrast between the
yellow blossoms and the black business. On his right was a little
wood; far away to his left lay the long curve of the railway line,
which he was, so to speak, guarding from the Marquis, whose goal
and escape it was. In front of him, behind the black group of his opponents, he could see, like a tinted cloud, a small almond-bush in
flower against the faint line of the sea.

The member of the Legion of Honour, whose name it seemed was

Colonel Ducroix, approached the Professor and Dr. Bull with great politeness, and suggested that the play should terminate with the first considerable hurt.

Dr. Bull, however, having been carefully coached by Syme upon this point of policy, insisted, with great dignity and in very bad French, that it should continue until one of the combatants was disabled. Syme had made up his mind that he could avoid disabling the Marquis and prevent the Marquis from disabling him for at least twenty minutes. In twenty minutes the Paris train would have gone by.

'To a man of the well-known skill and valour of Monsieur de St. Eustache,' said the Professor solemnly, 'it must be a matter of indifference which method is adopted, and our principal has strong reasons for demanding the longer encounter, reasons the delicacy of which prevent me from being explicit, but for the just and honourable nature of which I can——'

'*Peste!*'[61] broke from the Marquis behind, whose face had suddenly darkened, 'let us stop talking and begin,' and he slashed off the head of a tall flower with his stick.

Syme understood his rude impatience, and instinctively looked over his shoulder to see whether the train was coming in sight. But there was no smoke on the horizon.

Colonel Ducroix knelt down and unlocked the case, taking out a pair of twin swords, which took the sunlight and turned to two streaks of white fire. He offered one to the Marquis, who snatched it without ceremony, and another to Syme, who took it, bent it, and poised it with as much delay as was consistent with dignity. Then the Colonel took out another pair of blades, and taking one himself and giving another to Dr. Bull, proceeded to place the men.

Both combatants had thrown off their coats and waistcoats, and stood sword in hand. The seconds stood on each side of the line of fight with drawn swords also, but still sombre in their dark frock-coats and hats. The principals saluted. The Colonel said quietly, 'Engage!' and the two blades touched and tingled.

When the jar of the joined iron ran up Syme's arm, all the fantastic

---

[61] '*Peste!*' means 'a plague on you!'

fears that have been the subject of this story fell from him like dreams from a man waking up in bed. He remembered them clearly and in order as mere delusions of the nerves—how the fear of the Professor had been the fear of the tyrannic accidents of nightmare, and how the fear of the Doctor had been the fear of the airless vacuum of science. The first was the old fear that any miracle might happen, the second the more hopeless modern fear that no miracle can ever happen. But he saw that these fears were fancies, for he found himself in the presence of the great fact of the fear of death, with its coarse and pitiless common sense. He felt like a man who had dreamed all night of falling over precipices, and had woke up on the morning when he was to be hanged. For as soon as he had seen the sunlight run down the channel of his foe's foreshortened blade, and as soon as he had felt the two tongues of steel touch, vibrating like two living things, he knew that his enemy was a terrible fighter, and that probably his last hour had come.

He felt a strange and vivid value in all the earth around him, in the grass under his feet; he felt the love of life in all living things. He could almost fancy that he heard the grass growing; he could almost fancy that even as he stood fresh flowers were springing up and breaking into blossom in the meadow—flowers blood-red and burning gold and blue, fulfilling the whole pageant of the spring. And whenever his eyes strayed for a flash from the calm, staring, hypnotic eyes of the Marquis, they saw the little tuft of almond-tree against the skyline. He had the feeling that if by some miracle he escaped he would be ready to sit for ever before that almond-tree, desiring nothing else in the world.

But while earth and sky and everything had the living beauty of a thing lost, the other half of his head was as clear as glass, and he was parrying his enemy's point with a kind of clockwork skill of which he had hardly supposed himself capable. Once his enemy's point ran along his wrist, leaving a slight streak of blood, but it either was not noticed or was tacitly ignored. Every now and then he *riposted*, and once or twice he could almost fancy that he felt his point go home, but as there was no blood on blade or shirt he supposed he was mistaken. Then came an interruption and a change.

At the risk of losing all, the Marquis, interrupting his quiet stare, flashed one glance over his shoulder at the line of railway on his right. Then he turned on Syme a face transfigured to that of a fiend, and began to fight as if with twenty weapons. The attack came so fast and furious, that the one shining sword seemed a shower of shining arrows. Syme had no chance to look at the railway, but also he had no need. He could guess the reason of the Marquis's sudden madness of battle — the Paris train was in sight.

But the Marquis's morbid energy over-reached itself. Twice Syme, parrying, knocked his opponent's point far out of the fighting circle; and the third time his *riposte* was so rapid, that there was no doubt about the hit this time. Syme's sword actually bent under the weight of the Marquis's body, which it had pierced. Syme was as certain that he had stuck his blade into his enemy as a gardener that he has stuck his spade into the ground. Yet the Marquis sprang back from the stroke without a stagger, and Syme stood staring at his own sword-point like an idiot. There was no blood on it at all.

There was an instant of rigid silence, and then Syme in his turn fell furiously on the other, filled with a flaming curiosity. The Marquis was probably, in a general sense, a better fencer than he, as he had surmised at the beginning, but at the moment the Marquis seemed distraught and at a disadvantage. He fought wildly and even weakly, and he constantly looked away at the railway line, almost as if he feared the train more than the pointed steel. Syme, on the other hand, fought fiercely but still carefully, in an intellectual fury, eager to solve the riddle of his own bloodless sword. For this purpose, he aimed less at the Marquis's body, and more at his throat and head. A minute and a half afterwards he felt his point enter the man's neck below the jaw. It came out clean. Half mad, he thrust again, and made what should have been a bloody scar on the Marquis's cheek. But there was no scar.

For one moment the heaven of Syme again grew black with supernatural terrors. Surely the man had a charmed life. But this new spiritual dread was a more awful thing than had been the mere spiritual topsy-turvydom symbolized by the paralytic who pursued him. The Professor was only a goblin; this man was a devil — perhaps he was the Devil! Anyhow, this was certain, that three times had a human sword been driven into him and made no mark. When Syme had that thought he drew himself up, and all that was good in him sang high up in the air as a high wind sings in the trees. He thought of all the human things in his story—of the Chinese lanterns in Saffron Park, of the girl's red hair in the garden, of the honest, beer-swilling sailors down by the dock, of his loyal companions standing by. Perhaps he had been chosen as a champion of all these fresh and kindly things to cross swords with the enemy of all creation. 'After all,' he said to himself, 'I am more than a devil; I am a man. I can do the one thing which Satan himself cannot do—I can die', and as the word went through his head, he heard a faint and far-off hoot, which would soon be the roar of the Paris train.

He fell to fighting again with a supernatural levity, like a Moham-medan panting for Paradise. As the train came nearer and nearer he fancied he could see people putting up the floral arches in Paris; he joined in the growing noise and the glory of the great Republic whose gate he was guarding against Hell. His thoughts rose higher and higher with the rising roar of the train, which ended, as if proudly, in a long and piercing whistle. The train stopped.

Suddenly, to the astonishment of every one, the Marquis sprang back quite out of sword reach and threw down his sword. The leap was wonderful, and not the less wonderful because Syme had plunged his sword a moment before into the man's thigh.

'Stop!' said the Marquis in a voice that compelled a momentary obedience. 'I want to say something.'

'What is the matter?' asked Colonel Ducroix, staring. 'Has there been foul play?'

'There has been foul play somewhere,' said Dr. Bull, who was a little pale. 'Our principal has wounded the Marquis four times at least, and he is none the worse.'

The Marquis put up his hand with a curious air of ghastly patience.

'Please let me speak,' he said. 'It is rather important. Mr. Syme,' he continued turning to his opponent, 'we are fighting to-day, if I remember right, because you expressed a wish (which I thought ir-rational) to pull my nose. Would you oblige me by pulling my nose now as quickly as possible? I have to catch a train.'

'I protest that this is most irregular,' said Dr. Bull indignantly.

'It is certainly somewhat opposed to precedent,' said Colonel Ducroix, looking wistfully at his principal. 'There is, I think, one case on record (Captain Bellegarde and the Baron Zumpt) in which the weapons were changed in the middle of the encounter at the request of one of the combatants. But one can hardly call one's nose a weapon.'

'Will you or will you not pull my nose?' said the Marquis in exasperation. 'Come, come, Mr. Syme! You wanted to do it, do it! You can have no conception of how important it is to me. Don't be so selfish! Pull my nose at once, when I ask you!' and he bent slightly forward with a fascinating smile. The Paris train, panting and groaning, had grated into a little station behind the neighbouring hill.

Syme had the feeling he had more than once had in these adventures—the sense that a horrible and sublime wave lifted to heaven was just toppling over. Walking in a world he half understood, he took two paces forward and seized the Roman nose of this remarkable nobleman. He pulled it hard, and it came off in his hand.

He stood for some seconds with a foolish solemnity, with the pasteboard proboscis still between his fingers, looking at it, while the sun and the clouds and the wooded hills looked down upon this imbecile scene.

The Marquis broke the silence in a loud and cheerful voice.

'If any one has any use for my left eyebrow,' he said, 'he can have it. Colonel Ducroix, do accept my left eyebrow! It's the kind of thing that might come in useful any day,' and he gravely tore off one of his swarthy Assyrian brows, bringing about half his brown forehead with it and politely offered it to the Colonel, who stood crimson and speechless with rage.

'If I had known,' he spluttered, 'that I was acting for a poltroon[62] who pads himself to fight—'

'Oh, I know, I know!' said the Marquis, recklessly throwing various parts of himself right and left about the field. 'You are making a mistake; but it can't be explained just now. I tell you the train has come into the station!'

---

[62] A poltroon is a coward.

'Yes,' said Dr. Bull fiercely, 'and the train shall go out of the station. It shall go out without you. We know well enough for what devil's work——'

The mysterious Marquis lifted his hands with a desperate gesture. He was a strange scarecrow, standing there in the sun with half his old face peeled off, and half another face glaring and grinning from underneath.

'Will you drive me mad?' he cried. 'The train——'

'You shall not go by the train,' said Syme firmly, and grasped his sword.

The wild figure turned towards Syme, and seemed to be gathering itself for a sublime effort before speaking.

'You great fat, blasted, blear-eyed, blundering thundering, brainless, God-forsaken, doddering, damned fool!' he said without taking breath. 'You great silly, pink-faced, towheaded turnip! You——'

'You shall not go by this train,' repeated Syme.

'And why the infernal blazes,' roared the other, 'should I want to go by the train?'

'We know all,' said the Professor sternly. 'You are going to Paris to throw a bomb!'

'Going to Jericho[63] to throw a Jabberwock!'[64] cried the other, tearing his hair, which came off easily.

'Have you all got softening of the brain, that you don't realize what I am? Did you really think I wanted to catch that train? Twenty Paris trains might go by for me. Damn Paris trains!'

'Then what did you care about?' began the Professor.

'What did I care about? I didn't care about catching the train; I cared about whether the train caught me, and now, by God! it has caught me.'

[63] Going to Jericho is the equivalent of "going to blazes" or "going to Hell". Jericho in this case is not the city to the north of the Dead Sea in Palestine but a country estate of that name where Henry VIII had assignations with young ladies, no doubt in order to "play Old Harry".

[64] Jabberwock was a fabulous monster mentioned in *Jabberwocky*, a poem from Lewis Carroll's *Alice through the Looking Glass*. Lewis Carroll was the pseudonym of Charles Dodgson (1832–98).

'I regret to inform you,' said Syme with restraint, 'that your remarks convey no impression to my mind. Perhaps if you were to remove the remains of your original forehead and some portion of what was once your chin, your meaning would become clearer. Mental lucidity fulfils itself in many ways. What do you mean by saying that the train has caught you? It may be my literary fancy, but somehow I feel that it ought to mean something.'

'It means everything,' said the other, 'and the end of everything. Sunday has us now in the hollow of his hand.'

'Us!' repeated the Professor, as if stupefied. 'What do you mean by "us"?'

'The police, of course!' said the Marquis, and tore off his scalp and half his face.

The head which emerged was the blond, well brushed, smooth-haired head which is common in the English constabulary, but the face was terribly pale.

'I am Inspector Ratcliffe,' he said, with a sort of haste that verged on harshness. 'My name is pretty well known to the police, and I can see well enough that you belong to them. But if there is any doubt about my position, I have a card——' and he began to pull a blue card from his pocket.

The Professor gave a tired gesture.

'Oh, don't show it us,' he said wearily; 'we've got enough of them to equip a paper-chase.'

The little man named Bull had, like many men who seem to be of a mere vivacious vulgarity, sudden movements of good taste. Here he certainly saved the situation. In the midst of this staggering transformation scene he stepped forward with all the gravity and responsibility of a second, and addressed the two seconds of the Marquis.

'Gentlemen,' he said, 'we all owe you a serious apology; but I assure you that you have not been made the victims of such a low joke as you imagine, or indeed of anything undignified in a man of honour. You have not wasted your time; you have helped to save the world. We are not buffoons, but very desperate men at war with a vast conspiracy. A secret society of anarchists is hunting us like hares; not such unfortunate madmen as may here or there throw a bomb through starvation or German philosophy, but a rich and powerful and fanatical church, a church of eastern pessimism, which holds it holy to destroy mankind like vermin. How hard they hunt us you can gather from the fact that we are driven to such disguises as those for which I apologize, and to such pranks as this one by which you suffer.'

The younger second of the Marquis, a short man with a black moustache, bowed politely, and said:

'Of course, I accept the apology; but you will in your turn forgive me if I decline to follow you further into your difficulties, and permit myself to say good morning! The sight of an acquaintance and distinguished fellow-townsman coming to pieces in the open air is unusual, and, upon the whole, sufficient for one day. Colonel Ducroix, I would in no way influence your actions, but if you feel with me that our present society is a little abnormal, I am now going to walk back to the town.'

Colonel Ducroix moved mechanically, but then tugged abruptly at his white moustache and broke out:

'No, by George! I won't! If these gentlemen are really in a mess with a lot of low wreckers like that, I'll see them through it. I have fought for France, and it is hard if I can't fight for civilization.'

Dr. Bull took off his hat and waved it, cheering as at a public meeting.

'Don't make too much noise,' said Inspector Ratcliffe, 'Sunday may hear you.'

'Sunday!' cried Bull, and dropped his hat.

'Yes,' retorted Ratcliffe, 'he may be with them.'

'With whom?' asked Syme.

'With the people out of that train,' said the other.

'What you say seems utterly wild,' began Syme. 'Why, as a matter of fact —— But, my God,' he cried out suddenly, like a man who sees an explosion a long way off, 'by God! If this is true the whole bally lot of us on the Anarchist Council were against anarchy! Every born man was a detective except the President and his personal Secretary. What can it mean?'

'Mean!' said the new policeman with incredible violence. 'It means that we are struck dead! Don't you know Sunday? Don't you know that his jokes are always so big and simple that one has never thought of them? Can you think of anything more like Sunday than this, that he should put all his powerful enemies on the Supreme Council, and then take care that it was not supreme? I tell you he has bought every trust, he has captured every cable, he has control of every railway line—especially of *that* railway line!' and he pointed a shaking finger towards the small wayside station. 'The whole movement was controlled by him; half the world was ready to rise for him. But there were just five people, perhaps, who would have reisisted him . . . and the old devil put them on the Supreme Council, to waste their time in watching each other. Idiots that we are, he planned the whole of our idiocies! Sunday knew that the Professor would chase Syme through London, and that Syme would fight me in France. And he was combining great masses of capital, and seizing great lines of telegraphy, while we five idiots were running after each other like a lot of confounded babies playing blind man's buff.'

'Well?' asked Syme with a sort of steadiness.

'Well,' replied the other with sudden serenity, 'he has found us playing blind man's buff to-day in a field of great rustic beauty and extreme solitude. He has probably captured the world; it only remains to him to capture this field and all the fools in it. And since you really want to know what was my objection to the arrival of that train, I will tell you. My objection was that Sunday or his Secretary has just this moment got out of it.'

Syme uttered an involuntary cry, and they all turned their eyes towards the far-off station. It was quite true that a considerable bulk of people seemed to be moving in their direction. But they were too distant to be distinguished in any way.

'It was a habit of the late Marquis de St. Eustache,' said the new policeman, producing a leather case, 'always to carry a pair of opera-glasses. Either the President or the Secretary is coming after us with that mob. They have caught us in a nice quiet place where we are under no temptations to break our oaths by calling the police. Dr. Bull, I have a suspicion that you will see better through these than through your own highly decorative spectacles.'

He handed the field-glasses to the Doctor who immediately took off his spectacles and put the apparatus to his eyes.

'It cannot be as bad as you say,' said the Professor, somewhat shaken. 'There are a good number of them certainly, but they may easily be ordinary tourists.'

'Do ordinary tourists,' asked Bull, with the field-glasses to his eyes, 'wear black masks half-way down the face?'

Syme almost tore the glasses out of his hands, and looked through them. Most men in the advancing mob really looked ordinary enough; but it was quite true that two or three of the leaders in front wore black half-masks almost down to their mouths. This disguise is very complete, especially at such a distance, and Syme found it impossible to conclude anything from the clean-shaven jaws and chins of the men talking in the front. But presently as they talked they all smiled, and one of them smiled on one side.

XI

THE CRIMINALS CHASE THE POLICE

Syme put the field-glasses from his eyes with an almost ghastly relief.

'The President is not with them, anyhow,' he said and wiped his forehead.

'But surely they are right away on the horizon,' said the bewildered Colonel, blinking and but half recovered from Bull's hasty though polite explanation. 'Could you possibly know your President among all those people?'

'Could I know a white elephant among all those people!' answered Syme somewhat irritably. 'As you very truly say, they are on the horizon; but if he were walking with them . . . by God! I believe this ground would shake.'

After an instant's pause the new man called Ratcliffe said with gloomy decision:

'Of course the President isn't with them. I wish to Gemini he were. Much more likely the President is riding in triumph through Paris, or sitting on the ruins of St. Paul's Cathedral.'

'This is absurd!' said Syme. 'Something may have happened in our absence; but he cannot have carried the world with a rush like that. It is quite true,' he added, frowning dubiously at the distant fields that lay towards the little station, 'it is certainly true that there seems to be a crowd coming this way; but they are not all the army that you make out.'

'Oh, they,' said the new detective contemptuously; 'no, they are not a very valuable force. But let me tell you frankly that they are precisely calculated to our value — we are not much, my boy, in Sunday's universe. He has got hold of all the cables and telegraphs himself. But to kill the Supreme Council he regards as a trivial matter, like a post card; it may be left to his private Secretary,' and he spat on the grass.

Then he turned to the others and said somewhat austerely:

'There is a great deal to be said for death; but if any one has any preference for the other alternative, I strongly advise him to walk after me.'

With these words, he turned his broad back and strode with silent energy towards the wood. The others gave one glance over their shoulders, and saw that the dark cloud of men had detached itself from the station and was moving with a mysterious discipline across the plain. They saw already, even with the naked eye, black blots on the foremost faces, which marked the masks they wore. They turned and followed their leader, who had already struck the wood, and disappeared among the twinkling trees.

The sun on the grass was dry and hot. So in plunging into the wood they had a cool shock of shadow, as of divers who plunge into a dim pool. The inside of the wood was full of shattered sunlight and shaken shadows. They made a sort of shuddering veil, almost recalling the dizziness of a cinematograph. Even the solid figures walking with him Syme could hardly see for the patterns of sun and shade that danced upon them. Now a man's head was lit as with a light of Rembrandt, leaving all else obliterated; now again he had strong and staring white hands with the face of a negro. The ex-Marquis had pulled the old straw hat over his eyes, and the black shade of the brim cut his face so squarely in two that it seemed to be wearing one of the black half-masks of their pursuers. The fancy tinted Syme's overwhelming sense of wonder. Was he wearing a mask? Was any one wearing a mask? Was any one anything? This wood of witchery, in which men's faces turned black and white by turns, in which their figures first swelled into sunlight and then faded into formless night, this mere chaos of chiaroscuro (after the clear daylight outside), seemed to Syme a perfect symbol of the world in which he had been moving for three days, this world where men took off their beards and their spectacles and their noses, and turned into other people. That tragic self-confidence which he had felt when he believed that the Marquis was a devil had strangely disappeared now that he knew that the Marquis was a friend. He felt almost inclined to ask after all these bewilderments what was a friend and what an enemy. Was there anything that was apart from what it seemed? The Marquis had taken off his nose and turned out to be a detective. Might he not just as well take off his head and turn out to be a hobgoblin? Was not everything, after all, like this bewildering woodland, this dance of dark and light? Everything only a glimpse, the glimpse always unforeseen, and always forgotten. For Gabriel Syme had found in the heart of that sun-splashed wood what many modern painters had found there. He had found the thing which the modern people call Impressionism, which is another name for that final scepticism which can find no floor to the universe.

As a man in an evil dream strains himself to scream and wake, Syme strove with a sudden effort to fling off this last and worst of his fancies. With two impatient strides he overtook the man in the Marquis's straw hat, the man whom he had come to address as Ratcliffe. In a voice exaggeratively loud and cheerful, he broke the bottomless silence and made conversation.

'May I ask,' he said, 'where on earth we are all going to?'

So genuine had been the doubts of his soul, that he was quite glad to hear his companion speak in an easy, human voice.

'We must get down through the town of Lancy to the sea,' he said. 'I think that part of the country is least likely to be with them.'

'What can you mean by all this?' cried Syme. 'They can't be running the real world in that way. Surely not many working men are anarchists, and surely if they were, mere mobs could not beat modern armies and police.'

'Mere mobs!' repeated his new friend with a snort of scorn. 'So you talk about mobs and the working classes as if they were the question. You've got that eternal idiotic idea that if anarchy came it would come from the poor. Why should it? The poor have been rebels, but they have never been anarchists; they have more interest than any one else in there being some decent government. The poor man really has a stake in the country. The rich man hasn't; he can go away to New Guinea in a yacht. The poor have sometimes objected to being governed badly; the rich have always objected to being governed at all. Aristocrats were always anarchists, as you can see from the barons' wars.'

'As a lecture on English history for the little ones,' said Syme, 'this is all very nice; but I have not yet grasped its application.'

'Its application is,' said his informant, 'that most of old Sunday's right-hand men are South African and American millionaires. That is why he has got hold of all the communications; and that is why the last four champions of the anti-anarchist police force are running through a wood like rabbits.'

'Millionaires I can understand,' said Syme thoughtfully, 'they are nearly all mad. But getting hold of a few wicked old gentlemen with hobbies is one thing; getting hold of great Christian nations is another. I would bet the nose off my face (forgive the allusion) that Sunday would stand perfectly helpless before the task of converting any ordinary healthy person anywhere.'

'Well,' said the other, 'it rather depends what sort of person you mean.'

'Well, for instance,' said Syme, 'we could never convert that person,' and he pointed straight in front of him.

They had come to an open space of sunlight, which seemed to express to Syme the final return of his own good sense; and in the middle of this forest clearing was a figure that might well stand for that common sense in an almost awful actuality. Burnt by the sun and stained with perspiration, and grave with the bottomless gravity of small necessary toils, a heavy French peasant was cutting wood with a hatchet. His cart stood a few yards off, already half full of timber; and the horse that cropped the grass was, like his master, valorous but not desperate; like his master, he was even prosperous, but yet was almost sad. The man was a Norman, taller than the average of the French and very angular; and his swarthy figure stood dark against a square of sunlight, almost like some allegoric figure of labour frescoed on a ground of gold.

'Mr. Syme is saying,' called out Ratcliffe to the French Colonel, 'that this man, at least, will never be an anarchist.'

'Mr. Syme is right enough there,' answered Colonel Ducroix, laughing, 'if only for the reason that he has plenty of property to defend. But I forgot that in your country you are not used to peasants being wealthy.'

'He looks poor,' said Dr. Bull doubtfully.

'Quite so,' said the Colonel; 'that is why he is rich.'

'I have an idea,' called out Dr. Bull suddenly; 'how much would he take to give us a lift in his cart? Those dogs are all on foot, and we could soon leave them behind.'

'Oh, give him anything!' said Syme eagerly. 'I have piles of money on me.'

'That will never do,' said the Colonel; 'he will never have any respect for you unless you drive a bargain.'

'Oh, if he haggles!' began Bull impatiently.

'He haggles because he is a free man,' said the other. 'You do not understand; he would not see the meaning of generosity. He is not being tipped.'

And even while they seemed to hear the heavy feet of their strange pursuers behind them, they had to stand and stamp while the French Colonel talked to the French wood-cutter with all the leisurely badinage and bickering of market-day. At the end of the four minutes, however, they saw that the Colonel was right, for the wood-cutter entered into their plans, not with the vague servility of a tout too-well paid, but with the seriousness of a solicitor who had been paid the proper fee. He told them that the best thing they could do was to make their way down to the little inn on the hills above Lancy, where the innkeeper, an old soldier who had become *dévot* in his latter years, would be certain to sympathize with them, and even to take risks in their support. The whole company, therefore, piled themselves on top of the stacks of wood, and went rocking in the rude cart down the other and steeper side of the woodland. Heavy and ramshackle as was the vehicle, it was driven quickly enough, and they soon had the exhilarating impression of distancing altogether those, whoever they were, who were hunting them. For, after all, the riddle as to where the anarchists had got all these followers was still unsolved. One man's presence had sufficed for them; they had fled at the first sight of the deformed smile of the Secretary. Syme every now and then looked back over his shoulder at the army on their track.

As the wood grew first thinner and then smaller with distance, he could see the sunlit slopes beyond it and above it; and across these was still moving the square black mob like one monstrous beetle. In the very strong sunlight and with his own very strong eyes, which were almost telescopic, Syme could see this mass of men quite plainly. He could see them as separate human figures; but he was increasingly surprised by the way in which they moved as one man. They seemed to be dressed in dark clothes and plain hats, like any common crowd out of the streets; but they did not spread and sprawl and trail by various lines to the attack, as would be natural in an ordinary mob. They moved with a sort of dreadful and wicked woodenness, like a staring army of automatons.

Syme pointed this out to Ratcliffe.

'Yes,' replied the policeman, 'that's discipline. That's Sunday. He is perhaps five hundred miles off, but the fear of him is on all of them, like the finger of God. Yes, they are walking regularly; and you bet your boots that they are talking regularly, yes, and thinking regularly. But the one important thing for us is that they are disappearing regularly.'

Syme nodded. It was true that the black patch of the pursuing men was growing smaller and smaller as the peasant belaboured his horse.

The level of the sunlit landscape, though flat as a whole, fell away on the farther side of the wood in billows of heavy slope towards the sea, in a way not unlike the lower slopes of the Sussex downs. The only difference was that in Sussex the road would have been broken and angular like a little brook, but here the white French road fell sheer in front of them like a waterfall. Down this direct descent the cart clattered at a considerable angle, and in a few minutes, the road growing yet steeper, they saw below them the little harbour of Lancy and a great blue arc of the sea. The travelling cloud of their enemies had wholly disappeared from the horizon.

The horse and cart took a sharp turn round a clump of elms, and the horse's nose nearly struck the face of an old gentleman who was sitting on the benches outside the little café of 'Le Soleil d'Or'. The peasant grunted an apology, and got down from his seat. The others also descended one by one, and spoke to the old gentleman with fragmentary phrases of courtesy, for it was quite evident from his expansive manner that he was the owner of the little tavern.

He was a white-haired, apple-faced old boy, with sleepy eyes and a grey moustache; stout, sedentary, and very innocent, of a type that may often be found in France, but is still commoner in Catholic Germany. Everything about him, his pipe, his pot of beer, his flowers, and his beehive, suggested an ancestral peace; only when his visitors looked up as they entered the inn-parlour, they saw the sword upon the wall.

The Colonel, who greeted the innkeeper as an old friend, passed rapidly into the inn-parlour, and sat down ordering some ritual refreshment. The military decision of his action interested Syme, who sat next to him, and he took the opportunity when the old innkeeper had gone out of satisfying his curiosity.

'May I ask you, Colonel,' he said in a low voice, 'why we have come here?'

Colonel Ducroix smiled behind his bristly white moustache.

'For two reasons, sir,' he said; 'and I will give first, not the most important, but the most utilitarian. We came here because this is the only place within twenty miles in which we can get horses.'

'Horses!' repeated Syme, looking up quickly.

'Yes,' replied the other; 'if you people are really to distance your enemies it is horses or nothing for you, unless of course you have bicycles and motor-cars in your pocket.'

'And where do you advise us to make for?' asked Syme doubtfully.

'Beyond question,' replied the Colonel, 'you had better make all haste to the police station beyond the town. My friend, whom I seconded under somewhat deceptive circumstances, seems to me to exaggerate very much the possibilities of a general rising; but even he would hardly maintain, I suppose, that you were not safe with the gendarmes.'

Syme nodded gravely; then he said abruptly:

'And your other reason for coming here?'

'My other reason for coming here,' said Ducroix soberly, 'is that it is just as well to see a good man or two when one is possibly near to death.'

Syme looked up at the wall, and saw a crudely painted and pathetic religious picture. Then he said:

'You are right,' and then almost immediately afterwards; 'has any one seen about the horses?'

'Yes,' answered Ducroix, 'you may be quite certain that I gave orders the moment I came in. Those enemies of yours gave no impression of hurry, but they were really moving wonderfully fast, like a well-trained army. I had no idea that the anarchists had so much discipline. You have not a moment to waste.'

Almost as he spoke, the old innkeeper with the blue eyes and white hair came ambling into the room, and announced that six horses were saddled outside.

By Ducroix's advice the five others equipped themselves with some portable form of food and wine, and keeping their duelling swords as the only weapons available, they clattered away down the steep, white road. The two servants, who had carried the Marquis's luggage when he was a marquis, were left behind to drink at the café by common consent, and not at all against their own inclination.

By this time the afternoon sun was slanting westward, and by its rays Syme could see the sturdy figure of the old innkeeper growing smaller and smaller, but still standing and looking after them quite silently, the sunshine in his silver hair. Syme had a fixed, superstitious fancy, left in his mind by the chance phrase of the Colonel, that this was indeed, perhaps, the last honest stranger whom he should ever see upon the earth.

He was still looking at this dwindling figure, which stood as a mere grey blot touched with a white flame against the great green wall of the steep down behind him. And as he stared, over the top of the down behind the innkeeper, there appeared an army of black-clad and marching men. They seemed to hang above the good man and his house like a black cloud of locusts. The horses had been saddled none too soon.

XII

THE EARTH IN ANARCHY

Urging the horses to a gallop, without respect to the rather rugged descent of the road, the horsemen soon regained their advantage over the men on the march, and at last the bulk of the first buildings of Lancy cut off the sight of their pursuers. Nevertheless, the ride had been a long one, and by the time they reached the real town the west was warming with the colour and quality of sunset. The Colonel suggested that, before making finally for the police station, they should make the effort, in passing, to attach to themselves one more individual who might be useful.

'Four out of the five rich men in this town,' he said, 'are common swindlers. I suppose the proportion is pretty equal all over the world. The fifth is a friend of mine, and a very fine fellow; and what is even more important from our point of view, he owns a motor-car.'

'I am afraid,' said the Professor in his mirthful way, looking back along the white road on which the black, crawling patch might appear at any moment, 'I am afraid we have hardly time for afternoon calls.'

'Doctor Renard's house is only three minutes off,' said the Colonel.

'Our danger,' said Dr. Bull, 'is not two minutes off.'

'Yes,' said Syme, 'if we ride on fast we must leave them behind, for they are on foot.'

'He has a motor-car,' said the Colonel.

'But we may not get it,' said Bull.

'Yes, he is quite on your side.'

'But he might be out.'

'Hold your tongue,' said Syme suddenly. 'What is that noise?'

For a second they all sat as still as equestrian statues, and for a second—for two or three or four seconds—heaven and earth seemed equally still. Then all their ears, in an agony of attention, heard along the road that indescribable thrill and throb that means only one thing—horses!

The Colonel's face had an instantaneous change as if lightning had struck it, and yet left it scatheless.

'They have done us,' he said, with brief military irony. 'Prepare to receive calvalry!'

'Where can they have got the horses?' asked Syme, as he mechanically urged his steed to a canter.

The Colonel was silent for a little, then he said in a strained voice:

'I was speaking with strict accuracy when I said that the "Soleil d'Or" was the only place where one can get horses within twenty miles.'

'No!' said Syme violently, 'I don't believe he'd do it. Not with all that white hair.'

'He may have been forced,' said the Colonel gently. 'They must be at least a hundred strong, for which reason we are all going to see my friend Renard, who has a motor-car.'

With these words he swung his horse suddenly round a street corner, and went down the street with such thundering speed, that the others, though already well at the gallop, had difficulty in following the flying tail of his horse.

Dr. Renard inhabited a high and comfortable house at the top of a steep street, so that when the riders alighted at his door they could once more see the solid green ridge of the hill, and the white road across it, standing up above all the roofs of the town. They breathed again to see that the road as yet was clear, and they rang the bell.

Dr. Renard was a beaming, brown-bearded man, a good example of that silent but very busy professional class which France has preserved even more perfectly than England. When the matter was explained to him he pooh-poohed the panic of the ex-Marquis altogether; he said, with the solid French scepticism, that there was no conceivable probability of a general anarchist rising. 'Anarchy,' he said, shrugging his shoulders, 'it is childishness!'

'Et ça,' cried out the Colonel suddenly, pointing over the other's shoulder, 'and that is childishness isn't it?'

They all looked round, and saw a curve of black cavalry come sweeping over the top of the hill with all the energy of Attila. Swiftly as they rode, however, the whole rank still kept well together, and they could see the black vizards of the first line as level as a line of uniforms. But although the main black square was the same, though travelling faster, there was now one sensational difference which they could see clearly upon the slope of the hill, as if upon a slanted map. The bulk of the riders were in one block; but one rider flew far ahead of the column, and with frantic movements of hand and heel urged his horse faster and faster, so that one might have fancied that he was not the pursuer but the pursued. But even at that great distance they could see something so fanatical, so unquestionable in his figure, that they knew it was the Secretary himself.

'I am sorry to cut short a cultured discussion,' said the Colonel, 'but can you lend me your motor-car now, in two minutes?'

'I have a suspicion that you are all mad,' said Dr. Renard, smiling sociably; 'but God forbid that madness should in any way interrupt friendship. Let us go round to the garage.'

Dr. Renard was a mild man with monstrous wealth; his rooms were like the Musée de Cluny,[65] and he had three motor-cars. These, however, he seemed to use very sparingly, having the simple tastes of the French middle class, and when his impatient friends came to examine them, it took them some time to assure themselves that one of them even could be made to work. This with some difficulty they brought round into the street before the Doctor's house. When they came out of the dim garage they were startled to find that twilight had already fallen with the abruptness of night in the tropics. Either they had been longer in the place than they imagined, or some unusual canopy of cloud had gathered over the town. They looked down the steep streets, and seemed to see a slight mist coming up from the sea.

'It is now or never,' said Dr. Bull. 'I hear horses.'

'No,' corrected the Professor, 'a horse.'

And as they listened, it was evident that the noise rapidly coming nearer on the rattling stones, was not the noise of the whole cavalcade but that of the one horseman, who had left it far behind—the insane Secretary.

Syme's family, like most of those who end in the simple life, had once owned a motor-car, and he knew all about them. He had

---

[65] Musée de Cluny is a museum on the rue Du Sommerard in Paris that houses a collection of thousands of objets d' art from the fourteenth, fifteenth and sixteenth centuries, plus the ruins of a palace known as the Thermes de Julien.

leapt at once into the chauffeur's seat, and with flushed face was wrenching and tugging at the disused machinery. He bent his strength upon one handle, and then said quite quietly:

'I am afraid it's no go.'

As he spoke, there swept round the corner a man rigid on his rushing horse, with the rush and rigidity of an arrow. He had a smile that thrust out his chin as if it were dislocated. He swept alongside of the stationary car, into which its company had crowded, and laid his hand on the front. It was the Secretary, and his mouth went quite straight in the solemnity of triumph.

Syme was leaning hard upon the steering-wheel, and there was no sound but the rumble of the other pursuers riding into the town. Then there came quite suddenly a scream of scraping iron, and the car leapt forward. It plucked the Secretary clean out of his saddle, as a knife is whipped out of its sheath, trailed him kicking terribly for twenty yards, and left him flung flat upon the road far in front of his frightened horse. As the car took the corner of the street with a splendid curve, they could just see the other anarchists filling the street and raising their fallen leader.

'I can't understand why it has grown so dark,'[66] said the Professor at last in a low voice.

'Going to be a storm, I think,' said Dr. Bull. 'I say, it's a pity we haven't got a light on this car, if only to see by.'

'We have,' said the Colonel, and from the floor of the car he fished up a heavy, old-fashioned, carved iron lantern with a light inside it. It was obviously an antique, and it would seem as if its original use had been in some way semi-religious, for there was a rude moulding of a cross upon one of its sides.

'Where on earth did you get that?' asked the Professor.

'I got it where I got the car,' answered the Colonel, chuckling, 'from my best friend. While our friend here was fighting with the steering-wheel, I ran up the front steps of the house and spoke to Renard, who was standing in his own porch, you will remember. "I

---

[66] The Secretary who has just been flung flat in the road is Monday, the first day of the week when God said: "Let there be light!"

suppose," I said, "there's no time to get a lamp." He looked up, blinking amiably at the beautiful arched ceiling of his own front hall. From this was suspended, by chains of exquisite ironwork, this lantern, one of the hundred treasures of his treasure-house. By sheer force he tore the lamp out of his own ceiling, shattering the painted panels, and bringing down two blue vases with his violence. Then he handed me the iron lantern, and I put it in the car. Was I not right when I said that Dr. Renard was worth knowing?'

'You were,' said Syme seriously, and hung the heavy lantern over the front. There was a certain allegory of their whole position in the contrast between the modern automobile and its strange, ecclesiastical lamp.

Hitherto they had passed through the quietest part of the town, meeting at most one or two pedestrians, who could give them no hint of the peace or the hostility of the place. Now, however, the windows in the houses began one by one to be lit up, giving a greater sense of habitation and humanity. Dr. Bull turned to the new detective who had led their flight, and permitted himself one of his natural and friendly smiles.

'These lights make one feel more cheerful.'

Inspector Ratcliffe drew his brows together.

'There is only one set of lights that make me more cheerful,' he said, 'and they are those lights of the police station which I can see beyond the town. Please God we may be there in ten minutes.'

Then all Bull's boiling good sense and optimism broke suddenly out of him.

'Oh, this is all raving nonsense!' he cried. 'If you really think that ordinary people in ordinary houses are anarchists, you must be madder than an anarchist yourself. If we turned and fought these fellows, the whole town would fight for us.'

'No,' said the other with an immovable simplicity, 'the whole town would fight for them. We shall see.'

While they were speaking the Professor had leant forward with sudden excitement.

'What is that noise?' he said.

'Oh, the horses behind us, I suppose,' said the Colonel. 'I thought we had got clear of them.'

'The horses behind us! No,' said the Professor, 'it is not horses, and it is not behind us.'

Almost as he spoke, across the end of the street before them two shining and rattling shapes shot past. They were gone almost in a flash, but every one could see that they were motor-cars, and the Professor stood up with a pale face and swore that they were the other two motor-cars from Dr. Renard's garage.

'I tell you they were his,' he repeated, with wild eyes, 'and they were full of men in masks!'

'Absurd!' said the Colonel angrily. 'Dr. Renard would never give them his cars.'

'He may have been forced,' said Ratcliffe quietly. 'The whole town is on their side.'

'You still believe that?' asked the Colonel incredulously.

'You will all believe it soon,' said the other with a hopeless calm.

There was a puzzled pause for some little time, and then the Colonel began again abruptly:

'No, I can't believe it. The thing is nonsense. The plain people of a peaceable French town——'

He was cut short by a bang and a blaze of light, which seemed close to his eyes. As the car sped on it left a floating patch of white smoke behind it, and Syme had heard a shot shriek past his ear.

'My God!' said the Colonel, 'some one has shot at us.'

'It need not interrupt conversation,' said the gloomy Ratcliffe. 'Pray resume your remarks, Colonel. You were talking, I think, about the plain people of a peaceable French town.'

The staring Colonel was long past minding satire. He rolled his eyes all round the street.

'It is extraordinary,' he said, 'most extraordinary.'

'A fastidious person,' said Syme, 'might even call it unpleasant. However, I suppose those lights out in the field beyond this street are the Gendarmerie. We shall soon get there.'

'No,' said Inspector Ratcliffe, 'we shall never get there.'

He had been standing up and looking keenly ahead of him. Now he sat down and smoothed his sleek hair with a weary gesture.

'What do you mean?' asked Bull sharply.

'I mean that we shall never get there,' said the pessimist placidly. 'They have two rows of armed men across the road already; I can see them from here. The town is in arms, as I said it was. I can only wallow in the exquisite comfort of my own exactitude.'

And Ratcliffe sat down comfortably in the car and lit a cigarette, but the others rose excitedly and stared down the road. Syme had slowed down the car as their plans became doubtful, and he brought it finally to a standstill just at the corner of a side-street that ran down very steeply to the sea.

The town was mostly in shadow, but the sun had not sunk; wherever its level light could break through, it painted everything a burning gold. Up this side-street the last sunset light shone as sharp and narrow as the shaft of artificial light at the theatre. It struck the car of the five friends, and lit it like a burning chariot. But the rest of the street, especially the two ends of it, was in the deepest twilight, and for some seconds they could see nothing. Then Syme, whose eyes were the keenest, broke into a little bitter whistle, and said:

'It is quite true. There is a crowd or an army or some such thing across the end of that street.'

'Well, if there is,' said Bull impatiently, 'it must be something else—a sham fight or the mayor's birthday or something. I cannot and will not believe that plain, jolly people in a place like this walk about with dynamite in their pockets. Get on a bit, Syme, and let us look at them.'

The car crawled about a hundred yards farther, and then they were all startled by Dr. Bull breaking into a high crow of laughter.

'Why, you silly mugs!' he cried, 'What did I tell you. That crowd's as law-abiding as a cow, and if it weren't, it's on our side.'

'How do you know?' asked the Professor, staring.

'You blind bat,' cried Bull, 'Don't you see who is leading them?'

They peered again, and then the Colonel, with a catch in his voice, cried out:

'Why, it's Renard!'

There was, indeed, a rank of dim figures running across the road, and they could not be clearly seen; but far enough in front to catch the accident of the evening light was stalking up and down the unmistakable

Dr. Renard, in a white hat, stroking his long brown beard, and holding a revolver in his left hand.

'What a fool I've been!' exclaimed the Colonel. 'Of course, the dear old boy has turned out to help us.'

Dr. Bull was bubbling over with laughter, swinging the sword in his hand as carelessly as a cane. He jumped out of the car and ran across the intervening space, calling out:

'Dr. Renard! Dr. Renard!'

An instant after Syme thought his own eyes had gone mad in his head. For the philanthropic Dr. Renard had deliberately raised his revolver and fired twice at Bull, so that the shots rang down the road.

Almost at the same second as the puff of white cloud went up from this atrocious explosion a long puff of white cloud went up also from the cigarette of the cynical Ratcliffe. Like all the rest he turned a little pale, but he smiled. Dr. Bull, at whom the bullets had been fired, just missing his scalp, stood quite still in the middle of the road without a sign of fear, and then turned very slowly and crawled back to the car, and climbed in with two holes through his hat.

'Well,' said the cigarette-smoker slowly, 'what do you think now?'

'I think,' said Dr. Bull with precision, 'that I am lying in bed at No. 217 Peabody Buildings,[67] and that I shall soon wake up with a jump; or, if that's not it, I think that I am sitting in a small cushioned cell in Hanwell,[68] and that the doctor can't make much of my case. But if you want to know what I don't think, I'll tell you. I don't think what you think. I don't think, and I never shall think, that the mass of ordinary men are a pack of dirty modern thinkers. No, sir, I'm a democrat, and I still don't believe that Sunday could convert

[67] This is obviously Dr. Bull's address but it is nonetheless an odd one, because Peabody Buildings were austere factory-like housing blocks for "the artisan and labouring poor of London" built under the terms of a housing trust established by American philanthropist, George Peabody (1795–1869). By 1890 the Peabody Donation Fund had provided over 5,000 dwellings for the London poor. Dr. Bull would seem to have lived in the Bermondsey block.

[68] Hanwell is a district in the west of London synonymous with the lunatic asylum located there.

one average navvy or counter-jumper.[69] No, I may be mad, but humanity isn't.'

Syme turned his bright blue eyes on Bull with an earnestness which he did not commonly make clear.

'You are a very fine fellow,' he said. 'You can believe in a sanity which is not merely your sanity. And you're right enough about humanity, about peasants and people like that jolly old innkeeper. But you're not right about Renard. I suspected him from the first. He's rationalistic, and, what's worse, he's rich. When duty and religion are really destroyed, it will be by the rich.'

'They are really destroyed now,' said the man with a cigarette, and rose with his hands in his pockets. 'The devils are coming on!'

The men in the motor-car looked anxiously in the direction of his dreamy gaze, and they saw that the whole regiment at the end of the road was advancing upon them, Dr. Renard marching furiously in front, his beard flying in the breeze.

The Colonel sprang out of the car with an intolerant exclamation.

'Gentlemen,' he cried, 'the thing is incredible. It must be a practical joke. If you knew Renard as I do — it's like calling Queen Victoria a dynamiter. If you had got the man's character into your head — '

'Dr. Bull,' said Syme sardonically, 'has at least got it into his hat.'

'I tell you it can't be!' cried the Colonel, stamping. 'Renard shall explain it. He shall explain it to me,' and he strode forward.

'Don't be in such a hurry,' drawled the smoker. 'He will very soon explain it to all of us.'

But the impatient Colonel was already out of earshot, advancing towards the advancing enemy. The excited Dr. Renard lifted his pistol again, but perceiving his opponent, hesitated, and the Colonel came face to face with him with frantic gestures of remonstrance.

'It is no good,' said Syme. 'He will never get anything out of that old heathen. I vote we drive bang through the thick of them, bang

---

[69] Navvy, originally "navigator", was a manual laborer employed in the construction of canals, but the meaning has extended to include those employed on railway or road construction. Counter-jumper is a now-obsolete term for a shop assistant in Britain and a clerk in the United States.

as the bullets went through Bull's hat. We may be all killed, but we must kill a tidy number of them.'

'I won't 'ave it,' said Dr. Bull, growing more vulgar in the sincerity of his virtue. 'The poor chaps may be making a mistake. Give the Colonel a chance.'

'Shall we go back, then?' asked the Professor.

'No,' said Ratcliffe in a cold voice, 'the street behind us is held too. In fact, I seem to see there another friend of yours, Syme.'

Syme spun round smartly, and stared backwards at the track which they had travelled. He saw an irregular body of horsemen gathering and galloping towards them in the gloom. He saw above the foremost saddle the silver gleam of a sword, and then as it grew nearer the silver gleam of an old man's hair. The next moment, with shattering violence, he had swung the motor round and sent it dashing down the steep side-street to the sea, like a man that desired only to die.

'What the devil is up?' cried the Professor, seizing his arm.

'The morning star has fallen!' said Syme as his own car went down the darkness like a falling star. The others did not understand his words, but when they looked back at the street above they saw the hostile cavalry coming round the corner and down the slopes after them; and foremost of all rode the good innkeeper, flushed with the fiery innocence of the evening light.

'The world is insane!' said the Professor, and buried his face in his hands.

'No,' said Dr. Bull in adamantine humility, 'it is I.'

'What are we going to do?' asked the Professor.

'At this moment,' said Syme, with a scientific detachment, 'I think we are going to smash into a lamp-post.'

The next instant the automobile had come with a catastrophic jar against an iron object. The instant after that four men had crawled out from under a chaos of metal, and a tall lean lamp-post that had stood up straight on the edge of the marine parade stood out, bent and twisted, like the branch of a broken tree.

'Well, we smashed something,' said the Professor, with a faint smile. 'That's some comfort.'

'You're becoming an anarchist,' said Syme, dusting his clothes with his instinct of daintiness.

'Every one is,' said Ratcliffe.

As they spoke, the white-haired horseman and his followers came thundering from above, and almost at the same moment a dark string of men ran shouting along the sea-front. Syme snatched a sword, and took it in his teeth; he stuck two others under his arm-pits, took a fourth in his left hand and the lantern in his right, and leapt off the high parade on to the beach below.

The others leapt after him, with a common acceptance of such decisive action, leaving the *débris* and the gathering mob above them.

'We have one more chance,' said Syme, taking the steel out of his mouth. 'Whatever all this pandemonium means, I suppose the police station will help us. We can't get there, for they hold the way. But there's a pier or breakwater runs out into the sea just here, which we could defend longer than anything else, like Horatius and his bridge.[70] We must defend it till the Gendarmerie turn out. Keep after me.'

They followed him as he went crunching down the beach, and in a second or two their boots broke not on the sea gravel, but on broad, flat stones. They marched down a long, low jetty, running out in one arm into the dim, boiling sea, and when they came to the end of it they felt that they had come to the end of their story. They turned and faced the town.

That town was transfigured with uproar. All along the high parade from which they had just descended was a dark and roaring stream of humanity, with tossing arms and fiery faces, groping and glaring towards them. The long dark line was dotted with torches and lanterns; but even where no flame lit up a furious face, they could see in the farthest figure, in the most shadowy gesture, an organized hate. It was clear that they were the accursed of all men, and they knew not why.

Two or three men, looking little and black like monkeys, leapt over the edge as they had done and dropped on to the beach. These

[70] See n. 56.

came ploughing down the deep sand, shouting horribly, and strove to wade into the sea at random. The example was followed, and the whole black mass of men began to run and drip over the edge like black treacle.

Foremost among the men on the beach Syme saw the peasant who had driven their cart. He splashed into the surf on a huge cart-horse, and shook his axe at them.

'The peasant!' cried Syme. 'They have not risen since the Middle Ages.'

'Even if the police do come now,' said the Professor mournfully, 'they can do nothing with this mob.'

'Nonsense!' said Bull desperately; 'there must be some people left in the town who are human.'

'No,' said the hopeless Inspector, 'the human being will soon be extinct. We are the last of mankind.'

'It may be,' said the Professor absently. Then he added in his dreamy voice, 'What is all that at the end of the *Dunciad*?[71]

> Nor public flame, nor private, dares to shine;
> Nor human light is left, nor glimpse divine!
> Lo! thy dread Empire, Chaos, is restored;
> Light dies before thine uncreating word:
> Thy hand, great Anarch, lets the curtain fall;
> And universal darkness buries all.

'Stop!' cried Bull suddenly, 'the gendarmes are out.'

The low lights of the police station were indeed blotted and broken with hurrying figures, and they heard through the darkness the clash and jingle of a disciplined cavalry.

'They are charging the mob!' cried Bull in ecstasy or alarm.

'No,' said Syme, 'they are formed along the parade.'

'They have unslung their carbines,' cried Bull, dancing with excitement.

---

[71] The Dunciad is a scathing attack on the poets of his day by Alexander Pope (1688–1744). Chesterton is quoting from *The New Dunciad* of 1742, which in 1743 was incorporated in *The Dunciad* as "Book the Fourth". He quotes vv. 651–56, as usual from memory and equally as usual almost correctly, but v. 652 should begin: "Nor human spark is left".

'Yes,' said Ratcliffe, 'and they are going to fire on us.'

As he spoke there came a long crackle of musketry, and bullets seemed to hop like hailstones on the stones in front of them.

'The gendarmes have joined them!' cried the Professor, and struck his forehead.

'I am in the padded cell,' said Bull solidly.

There was a long silence, and then Ratcliffe said, looking out over the swollen sea, all a sort of grey purple:

'What does it matter who is mad or who is sane? We shall all be dead soon.'

Syme turned to him and said:

'You are quite hopeless then?'

Mr. Ratcliffe kept a stony silence; then at last he said quietly:

'No; oddly enough I am not quite hopeless. There is one insane little hope that I cannot get out of my mind. The power of this whole planet is against us, yet I cannot help wondering whether this one silly little hope is hopeless yet.'

'In what or whom is your hope?' asked Syme with curiosity.

'In a man I never saw,' said the other, looking at the leaden sea.

'I know what you mean,' said Syme in a low voice, 'the man in the dark room. But Sunday must have killed him by now.'

'Perhaps,' said the other steadily; 'but if so, he was the only man whom Sunday found it hard to kill.'

'I heard what you said,' said the Professor, with his back turned. 'I am also holding hard on to the thing I never saw.'

All of a sudden, Syme who was standing as if blind with introspective thought, swung round and cried out, like a man waking from sleep:

'Where is the Colonel? I thought he was with us!'

'The Colonel! Yes,' cried Bull, 'where on earth is the Colonel?'

'He went to speak to Renard,' said the Professor.

'We cannot leave him among all those beasts,' cried Syme. 'Let us die like gentlemen if——'

'Do not pity the Colonel,' said Ratcliffe, with a pale sneer. 'He is extremely comfortable. He is——'

'No! no! no!' cried Syme in a kind of frenzy, 'not the Colonel too! I will never believe it!'

'Will you believe your eyes?' asked the other, and pointed to the beach.

Many of their pursuers had waded into the water shaking their fists, but the sea was rough, and they could not reach the pier. Two or three figures, however, stood on the beginning of the stone footway, and seemed to be cautiously advancing down it. The glare of a chance lantern lit up the faces of the two foremost. One face wore a black half-mask, and under it the mouth was twisting about in such a madness of nerves that the black tuft of beard wriggled round and round like a restless, living thing. The other was the red face and white moustache of Colonel Ducroix. They were in earnest consultation.

'Yes, he is gone too,' said the Professor, and sat down on a stone. 'Everything's gone. I'm gone! I can't trust my own bodily machinery. I feel as if my own hand might fly up and strike me.'

'When my hand flies up,' said Syme, 'it will strike somebody else', and he strode along the pier towards the Colonel, the sword in one hand and the lantern in the other.

As if to destroy the last hope or doubt, the Colonel, who saw him coming, pointed his revolver at him and fired. The shot missed Syme, but struck his sword, breaking it short at the hilt. Syme rushed on, and swung the iron lantern above his head.

'Judas before Herod!' he said, and struck the Colonel down upon the stones. Then he turned to the Secretary, whose frightful mouth was almost foaming now, and held the lamp high with so rigid and arresting a gesture, that the man was, as it were, frozen for a moment, and forced to hear.

'Do you see this lantern?' cried Syme in a terrible voice. 'Do you see the cross carved on it, and the flame inside? You did not make it. You did not light it. Better men than you, men who could believe and obey, twisted the entrails of iron and preserved the legend of fire. There is not a street you walk on, there is not a thread you wear, that was not made as this lantern was, by denying your philosophy of dirt and rats. You can make nothing. You can only destroy. You will destroy mankind; you will destroy the world. Let that suffice you. Yet this one old Christian lantern you shall not destroy. It shall go where your empire of apes will never have the wit to find it.'

He struck the Secretary once with the lantern so that he staggered; and then, whirling it twice round his head, sent it flying far
out to sea, where it flared like a roaring rocket and fell.

'Swords!' shouted Syme, turning his flaming face to the three behind him. 'Let us charge these logs, for our time has come to die.'

His three companions came after him sword in hand. Syme's
sword was broken, but he rent a bludgeon from the fist of a fisher-
man, flinging him down. In a moment they would have flung themselves upon the face of the mob and perished, when an interruption
came. The Secretary, ever since Syme's speech, had stood with his
hand to his stricken head as if dazed; now he suddenly pulled off his
black mask.

The pale face thus peeled in the lamplight revealed not so much
rage as astonishment. He put up his hand with an anxious authority.

'There is some mistake,' he said. 'Mr. Syme, I hardly think you
understand your position. I arrest you in the name of the law.'

'Of the law?' said Syme, and dropped his stick.

'Certainly!' said the Secretary. 'I am a detective from Scotland
Yard,' and he took a small blue card from his pocket.

'And what do you suppose we are?' asked the Professor, and
threw up his arms.

'You,' said the Secretary stiffly, 'are, as I know for a fact,
members of the Supreme Anarchist Council. Disguised as one of
you, I——'

Dr. Bull tossed his sword into the sea.

'There never was any Supreme Anarchist Council,' he said. 'We
were all a lot of silly policemen looking at each other. And all these
nice people who have been peppering us with shot thought we were
the dynamiters. I knew I couldn't be wrong about the mob,' he said,
beaming over the enormous multitude, which stretched away to the
distance on both sides. 'Vulgar people are never mad. I'm vulgar
myself, and I know. I am now going on shore to stand a drink to
everybody here.'

XIII

THE PURSUIT OF THE PRESIDENT

Next morning five bewildered but hilarious people took the boat for Dover. The poor old Colonel might have had some cause to complain, having first been forced to fight for two factions that didn't exist, and then knocked down with an iron lantern. But he was a magnanimous old gentleman, and being much relieved that neither party had anything to do with dynamite, he saw them off on the pier with great geniality.

The five reconciled detectives had a hundred details to explain to each other. The Secretary had to tell Syme how they had come to wear masks originally in order to approach the supposed enemy as fellow-conspirators; Syme had to explain how they had fled with such swiftness through a civilized country. But above all these matters of detail which could be explained, rose the central mountain of the matter that they could not explain. What did it all mean? If they were all harmless officers, what was Sunday? If he had not seized the world, what on earth had he been up to? Inspector Ratcliffe was still gloomy about this.

'I can't make head or tail of old Sunday's little game any more than you can,' he said. 'But whatever else Sunday is, he isn't a blameless citizen. Damn it! do you remember his face?'

'I grant you,' answered Syme, 'that I have never been able to forget it.'

'Well,' said the Secretary, 'I suppose we can find out soon, for to-morrow we have our next general meeting. You will excuse me,' he said, with a rather ghastly smile, 'for being well acquainted with my secretarial duties.'

'I suppose you are right,' said the Professor reflectively. 'I suppose we might find it out from him; but I confess that I should feel a bit afraid of asking Sunday who he really is.'

'Why?' asked the Secretary, 'for fear of bombs?'

'No,' said the Professor, 'for fear he might tell me.'

'Let us have some drinks,' said Dr. Bull, after a silence.

Throughout their whole journey by boat and train they were highly convivial, but they instinctively kept together. Dr. Bull, who had always been the optimist of the party, endeavoured to persuade the other four that the whole company could take the same hansom cab from Victoria; but this was overruled, and they went in a four-wheeler, with Dr. Bull on the box, singing. They finished their journey at an hotel in Piccadilly Circus, so as to be close to the early breakfast next morning in Leicester Square. Yet even then the adventures of the day were not entirely over. Dr. Bull, discontented with the general proposal to go to bed, had strolled out of the hotel at about eleven to see and taste some of the beauties of London. Twenty minutes afterwards, however, he came back and made quite a clamour in the hall. Syme, who tried at first to soothe him, was forced at last to listen to his communication with quite new attention.

'I tell you I've seen him!' said Dr. Bull, with thick emphasis.

'Whom?' asked Syme quickly. 'Not the President?'

'Not so bad as that,' said Dr. Bull, with unnecessary laughter, 'not so bad as that. I've got him here.'

'Got whom here?' asked Syme impatiently.

'Hairy man,' said the other lucidly, 'man that used to be hairy man—Gogol. Here he is,' and he pulled forward by a reluctant elbow the identical young man who five days before had marched out of the Council, with thin red hair and a pale face, the first of all the sham anarchists who had been exposed.

'Why do you worry with me?' he cried. 'You have expelled me as a spy.'

'We are all spies!' whispered Syme.

'We're all spies!' shouted Dr. Bull. 'Come and have a drink.'

Next morning the battalion of the reunited six marched stolidly towards the hotel in Leicester Square.

'This is more cheerful,' said Dr. Bull; 'we are six men going to ask one man what he means.'

'I think it is a bit queerer than that,' said Syme. 'I think it is six men going to ask one man what they mean.'

They turned in silence into the Square, and though the hotel was in the opposite corner, they saw at once the little balcony and a figure that looked too big for it. He was sitting alone with bent head, poring over a newspaper. But all his councillors, who had come to vote him down, crossed that Square as if they were watched out of heaven by a hundred eyes.

They had disputed much upon their policy, about whether they should leave the unmasked Gogol without and begin diplomatically, or whether they should bring him in and blow up the gunpowder at once. The influence of Syme and Bull prevailed for the latter course, though the Secretary to the last asked them why they attacked Sunday so rashly.

'My reason is quite simple,' said Syme. 'I attack him rashly because I am afraid of him.'

They followed Syme up the dark stair in silence, and they all came out simultaneously into the broad sunlight of the morning and the broad sunlight of Sunday's smile.

'Delightful!' he said. 'So pleased to see you all. What an exquisite day it is. Is the Tsar dead?'

The Secretary, who happened to be the foremost, drew himself together for a dignified outburst.

'No, sir,' he said sternly, 'there has been no massacre. I bring you news of no such disgusting spectacles.'

'Disgusting spectacles?' repeated the President, with a bright, inquiring smile. 'You mean Dr. Bull's spectacles?'

The Secretary choked for a moment, and the President went on with a sort of smooth appeal:

'Of course, we all have our opinions and even our eyes, but really to call them disgusting before the man himself——'

Dr. Bull tore off his spectacles and broke them on the table.

'My spectacles are blackguardly,' he said, 'but I'm not. Look at my face.'

'I dare say it's the sort of face that grows on one,' said the President, 'in fact, it grows on you; and who am I to quarrel with the wild fruits upon the Tree of Life? I dare say it will grow on me some day.'

'We have no time for tomfoolery,' said the Secretary, breaking in savagely. 'We have come to know what all this means. Who are you? What are you? Why did you get us all here? Do you know who and what we are? Are you a half-witted man playing the conspirator, or are you a clever man playing the fool? Answer me, I tell you.'

'Candidates,' murmured Sunday, 'are only required to answer eight out of the seventeen questions on the paper. As far as I can make out, you want me to tell you what I am, and what you are, and what this table is, and what this Council is, and what this world is for all I know. Well, I will go so far as to rend the veil of one mystery. If you want to know what you are, you are a set of highly well-intentioned young jackasses.'

'And you,' said Syme, leaning forward, 'what are you?'

'I? What am I?' roared the President, and he rose slowly to an incredible height, like some enormous wave about to arch above them and break. 'You want to know what I am, do you? Bull, you are a man of science. Grub in the roots of those trees and find out the truth about them. Syme, you are a poet. Stare at those morning clouds. But I tell you this, that you will have found out the truth of the last tree and the topmost cloud before the truth about me. You will understand the sea, and I shall be still a riddle; you shall know what the stars are, and not know what I am. Since the beginning of the world all men have hunted me like a wolf—kings and sages, and poets and law-givers, all the churches, and all the philosophies. But I have never been caught yet, and the skies will fall in the time I turn to bay. I have given them a good run for their money, and I will now.'

Before one of them could move, the monstrous man had swung himself like some huge ourang-outang over the balustrade of the balcony. Yet before he dropped he pulled himself up again as on a horizontal bar, and thrusting his great chin over the edge of the balcony, said solemnly:

'There's one thing I'll tell you though about who I am. I am the man in the dark room, who made you all policemen.'

With that he fell from the balcony, bouncing on the stones below like a great ball of india-rubber, and went bounding off towards the corner of the Alhambra, where he hailed a hansom cab and sprang inside it. The six detectives had been standing thunderstruck and livid in the light of his last assertion; but when he disappeared into the cab, Syme's practical senses returned to him, and leaping over the balcony so recklessly as almost to break his legs, he called another cab.

He and Bull sprang into the cab together, the Professor and the Inspector into another, while the Secretary and the late Gogol scrambled into a third just in time to pursue the flying Syme, who was pursuing the flying President. Sunday led them a wild chase towards the north-west, his cabman, evidently under the influence of more than common inducements, urging the horse at breakneck speed. But Syme was in no mood for delicacies, and he stood up in his own cab shouting, 'Stop thief!' until crowds ran along beside his cab, and policemen began to stop and ask questions. All this had its influence upon the President's cabman, who began to look dubious, and to slow down to a trot. He opened the trap to talk reasonably to his fare, and in so doing let the long whip droop over the front of the cab. Sunday leant forward, seized it, and jerked it violently out the man's hand. Then standing up in front of the cab himself, he lashed the horse and roared aloud, so that they went down the streets like a flying storm. Through street after street and square after square went whirling this preposterous vehicle, in which the fare was urging the horse and the driver trying desperately to stop it. The other three cabs came after it (if the phrase be permissible of a cab) like panting hounds. Shops and streets shot by like rattling arrows.

At the highest ecstasy of speed, Sunday turned round on the splashboard where he stood, and sticking his great grinning head out of the cab, with white hair whistling in the wind, he made a horrible face at his pursuers, like some colossal urchin. Then raising his right hand swiftly, he flung a ball of paper in Syme's face and vanished. Syme caught the thing while instinctively warding it off, and discovered that it consisted of two crumpled papers. One was addressed to himself, and the other to Dr. Bull, with a very long, and it is to be feared partly ironical, string of letters after his name. Dr. Bull's address was, at any rate, considerably longer than his communication, for the communication consisted entirely of the words:

'What about Martin Tupper[72] *now*?'

'What does the old maniac mean?' asked Bull, staring at the words. 'What does yours say, Syme?'

Syme's message was at any rate, longer, and ran as follows:

> 'No one would regret anything in the nature of an interference by the Archdeacon more than I. I trust it will not come to that. But, for the last time, where are your goloshes? The thing is too bad, especially after what uncle said.'

The President's cabman seemed to be regaining some control over his horse, and the pursuers gained a little as they swept round into the Edgware Road. And here there occurred what seemed to the allies a providential stoppage. Traffic of every kind was swerving to right or left or stopping, for down the long road was coming the unmistakable roar announcing the fire-engine, which in a few seconds went by like a brazen thunder-bolt. But quick as it went by, Sunday had bounded out of his cab, sprung at the fire-engine, caught it, slung himself on to it, and was seen as he disappeared in the noisy distance talking to the astonished fireman with explanatory gestures.

'After him!' howled Syme. 'He can't go astray now. There's no mistaking a fire-engine.'

The three cabmen, who had been stunned for a moment, whipped up their horses and slightly decreased the distance between themselves and their disappearing prey. The President acknowledged this proximity by coming to the back of the car, bowing repeatedly, kissing his hand, and finally flinging a neatly folded note into the bosom of Inspector Ratcliffe. When that gentleman opened it, not without impatience, he found it contained the words:

> 'Fly at once. The truth about your trouser-stretchers is known. — A FRIEND.'

The fire-engine had struck still farther to the north, into a region that they did not recognize; and as it ran by a line of high railings shadowed with trees, the six friends were startled, but somewhat relieved, to see the President leap from the fire-engine, though

---

[72] Martin Tupper (1810–89) was the author of *Proverbial Philosophy* (1838–42) and of poems collected as *The Crock of Gold* (1844).

whether through another whim or the increasing protest of his entertainers they could not see. Before the three cabs, however, could reach up to the spot, he had gone up the high railings like a huge grey cat, tossed himself over, and vanished in a darkness of leaves.

Syme, with a furious gesture, stopped his cab, jumped out, and sprang also to the escalade. When he had one leg over the fence and his friends were following, he turned a face on them which shone quite pale in the shadow.

'What place can this be?' he asked. 'Can it be the old devil's house? I've heard he has a house in North London.'

'All the better,' said the Secretary grimly, planting a foot in a foothold, 'we shall find him at home.'

'No, but it isn't that,' said Syme, knitting his brows. 'I hear the most horrible noises, like devils laughing and sneezing and blowing their devilish noses!'

'His dogs barking, of course,' said the Secretary.

'Why not say his black-beetles barking!' said Syme furiously, 'snails barking! geraniums barking! Did you ever hear a dog bark like that?'

He held up his hand, and there came out of the thicket a long growling roar that seemed to get under the skin and freeze the flesh—a low thrilling roar that made a throbbing in the air all about them.

'The dogs of Sunday would be no ordinary dogs,' said Gogol, and shuddered.

Syme had jumped down on the other side, but he still stood listening impatiently.

'Well, listen to that,' he said, 'is that a dog—anybody's dog?'

There broke upon their ears a hoarse screaming as of things protesting and clamouring in sudden pain; and then, far off like an echo, what sounded like a long nasal trumpet.

'Well, his house ought to be hell!' said the Secretary; 'and if it is hell, I'm going in!' and he sprang over the tall railings almost with one swing.

The others followed. They broke through a tangle of plants and shrubs, and came out on an open path. Nothing was in sight, but Dr. Bull suddenly struck his hands together.

'Why, you asses,' he cried, 'it's the Zoo!'

As they were looking round wildly for any trace of their wild quarry, a keeper in uniform came running along the path with a man in plain clothes.

'Has it come this way?' gasped the keeper.

'Has what?' asked Syme.

'The elephant!' cried the keeper. 'An elephant has gone mad and run away!'

'He has run away with an old gentleman,' said the other stranger breathlessly, 'a poor old gentleman with white hair!'

'What sort of old gentleman?' asked Syme, with great curiosity.

'A very large and fat old gentleman in light grey clothes,' said the keeper eagerly.

'Well,' said Syme, 'if he's that particular kind of old gentleman, if you're quite sure that he's a large and fat old gentleman in grey clothes, you may take my word for it that the elephant has not run away with him. He has run away with the elephant. The elephant is not made by God that could run away with him if he did not consent to the elopement. And, by thunder, there he is!'

There was no doubt about it this time. Clean across the space of grass, about two hundred yards away, with a crowd screaming and scampering vainly at his heels, went a huge grey elephant at an awful stride, with his trunk thrown out as rigid as a ship's bowsprit, and trumpeting like the trumpet of doom. On the back of the bellowing and plunging animal sat President Sunday with all the placidity of a sultan, but goading the animal to a furious speed with some sharp object in his hand.

'Stop him!' screamed the populace. 'He'll be out of the gate!'

'Stop a landslide!' said the keeper. 'He is out of the gate!'

And even as he spoke, a final crash and roar of terror announced that the great grey elephant had broken out of the gates of the Zoological Gardens, and was careering down Albany Street like a new and swift sort of omnibus.

'Great Lord!' cried Bull, 'I never knew an elephant could go so fast. Well, it must be hansom cabs again if we are to keep him in sight.'

As they raced along to the gate out of which the elephant had vanished, Syme felt a glaring panorama of the strange animals in the cages which they passed. Afterwards he thought it queer that he should have seen them so clearly. He remembered especially seeing pelicans, with their preposterous, pendent throats. He wondered why the pelican was the symbol of charity, except it was that it wanted a good deal of charity to admire a pelican. He remembered a hornbill, which was simply a huge yellow beak with a small bird tied on behind it. The whole gave him a sensation, the vividness of which he could not explain, that Nature was always making quite mysterious jokes. Sunday had told them that they would understand him when they had understood the stars. He wondered whether even the archangels understood the hornbill.

The six unhappy detectives flung themselves into cabs and followed the elephant, sharing the terror which he spread through the long stretch of the streets. This time Sunday did not turn round, but offered them the solid stretch of his unconscious back, which maddened them, if possible, more than his previous mockeries. Just before they came to Baker Street, however, he was seen to throw something far up into the air, as a boy does a ball meaning to catch it again. But at their rate of racing it fell far behind, just by the cab containing Gogol; and in faint hope of a clue or for some impulse unexplainable, he stopped his cab so as to pick it up. It was addressed to himself, and was quite a bulky parcel. On examination, however, its bulk was found to consist of thirty-three pieces of paper of no value wrapped one round the other. When the last covering was torn away it reduced itself to a small slip of paper, on which was written:

'The word, I fancy, should be "pink".'[73]

The man once known as Gogol said nothing, but the movements of his hands and feet were like those of a man urging a horse to renewed efforts.

Through street after street, through district after district, went the prodigy of the flying elephant, calling crowds to every window,

[73] "Pink" may be a reference to a pink elephant, implying that Syme and his companions were drunk.

and driving the traffic left and right. And still through all this insane publicity the three cabs toiled after it, until they came to be regarded as part of a procession, and perhaps the advertisement of a circus. They went at such a rate that distances were shortened beyond belief, and Syme saw the Albert Hall [74] in Kensington when he thought that he was still in Paddington. The animal's pace was even more fast and free through the empty, aristocratic streets of South Kensington, and he finally headed towards that part of the skyline where the enormous Wheel of Earl's Court[75] stood up in the sky. The wheel grew larger and larger, till it filled heaven like the wheel of stars.

The beast outstripped the cabs. They lost him round several corners, and when they came to one of the gates of the Earl's Court Exhibition[76] they found themselves finally blocked. In front of them was an enormous crowd; in the midst of it was an enormous elephant, heaving and shuddering as such shapeless creatures do. But the President had disappeared.

'Where has he gone to?' asked Syme, slipping to the ground.

'Gentleman rushed into the Exhibition, sir!' said an official in a dazed manner. The he added in an injured voice: 'Funny gentleman, sir. Asked me to hold his horse, and gave me this.'

He held out with distaste a piece of folded paper, addressed: 'To the Secretary of the Central Anarchist Council.'

The Secretary, raging, rent it open, and found written inside it:

> 'When the herring runs a mile,
> Let the Secretary smile;
> When the herring tries to *fly*
> Let the Secretary die.
>   Rustic Proverb'

[74] The Albert Hall is a great rotunda built in 1871 to the design of Captain Folke and General Scott. It is 240 feet in diameter and 155 feet high and is used for public events ranging from wrestling bouts to symphony concerts.

[75] The enormous Wheel of Earl's Court was a Ferris wheel that towered 300 feet over Warwick Road. Carriages the size of railway cars revolved on the 284-foot-diameter Great Wheel, which had been designed by Lieutenant Walter B. Bassett, AMICE, USN (d. 1907). The wheel was a popular attraction from 1893 until 1906, when it was demolished.

[76] The Earl's Court Exhibition site is on Warwick Road. It now consists of a large exhibition hall where various shows are held.

The enormous Wheel of Earl's Court . . . filled heaven like the wheel of stars.

'Why the eternal crikey,'[77] began the Secretary, 'did you let the man in? Do people commonly come to your Exhibition riding on mad elephants? Do——'

'Look!' shouted Syme suddenly. 'Look over there!'

'Look at what?' asked the Secretary savagely.

'Look at the captive balloon!' said Syme, and pointed in a frenzy.

'Why the blazes should I look at a captive balloon?' demanded the Secretary. 'What is there queer about a captive balloon?'

'Nothing,' said Syme, 'except that it isn't captive!'

They all turned their eyes to where the balloon swung and swelled above the Exhibition on a string, like a child's balloon. A second afterwards the string came in two just under the car, and the balloon, broken loose, floated away with the freedom of a soap bubble.

'Ten thousand devils!' shrieked the Secretary. 'He's got into it!' and he shook his fists at the sky.

The balloon, borne by some chance wind, came right above them, and they could see the great white head of the President peering over the side and looking benevolently down on them.

'God bless my soul!' said the Professor with the elderly manner that he could never disconnect from his bleached beard and parchment face. 'God bless my soul! I seemed to fancy that something fell on the top of my hat!'

He put up a trembling hand and took from that shelf a piece of twisted paper, which he opened absently, only to find it inscribed with a true lover's knot and the words:

'Your beauty has not left me indifferent.—From LITTLE SNOW-DROP.'

There was a short silence, and then Syme said, biting his beard:

'I'm not beaten yet. The blasted thing must come down somewhere. Let's follow it!'

---

[77] Crikey is an exclamation of astonishment and was originally a euphemism for "Christ!"

XIV

THE SIX PHILOSOPHERS

Across green fields, and breaking through blooming hedges, toiled six draggled detectives, about five miles out of London. The optimist of the party had at first proposed that they should follow the balloon across South England in hansom cabs. But he was ultimately convinced of the persistent refusal of the balloon to follow the roads, and the still more persistent refusal of the cabmen to follow the balloon. Consequently the tireless though exasperated travellers broke through black thickets and ploughed through ploughed fields till each was turned into a figure too outrageous to be mistaken for a tramp. Those green hills of Surrey saw the final collapse and tragedy of the admirable light grey suit in which Syme had set out from Saffron Park. His silk hat was broken over his nose by a swinging bough, his coat-tails were torn to the shoulder by arresting thorns, the clay of England was splashed up to his collar; but he still carried his yellow beard forward with a silent and furious determination, and his eyes were still fixed on that floating ball of gas, which in the full flush of sunset seemed coloured like a sunset cloud.

'After all,' he said, 'it is very beautiful!'

'It is singularly and strangely beautiful!' said the Professor. 'I wish the beastly gas-bag would burst!'

'No,' said Dr. Bull, 'I hope it won't. It might hurt the old boy.'

'Hurt him!' said the vindictive Professor, 'hurt him! Not as much as I'd hurt him if I could get up with him. Little Snowdrop!'

'I don't want him hurt, somehow,' said Dr. Bull.

'What!' cried the Secretary bitterly. 'Do you believe all that tale about his being our man in the dark room? Sunday would say he was anybody.'

'I don't know whether I believe it or not,' said Dr. Bull. 'But it isn't that that I mean. I can't wish old Sunday's balloon to burst because——'

'Well,' said Syme impatiently, 'because?'

'Well, because he's so jolly like a balloon himself,' said Dr. Bull desperately. 'I don't understand a word of all that idea of his being the same man who gave us all our blue cards. It seems to make everything nonsense. But I don't care who knows it, I always had a sympathy for old Sunday himself, wicked as he was. Just as if he was a great bouncing baby. How can I explain what my queer sympathy was? It didn't prevent my fighting him like hell! Shall I make it clear if I say that I liked him because he was so fat?'

'You will not,' said the Secretary.

'I've got it now,' cried Bull, 'it was because he was so fat and so light. Just like a balloon. We always think of fat people as heavy, but he could have danced against a sylph. I see now what I mean. Moderate strength is shown in violence, supreme strength is shown in levity. It was like the old speculations—what would happen if an elephant could leap up in the sky like a grasshopper?'

'Our elephant,' said Syme, looking upwards, 'has leapt into the sky like a grasshopper.'

'And somehow,' concluded Bull, 'that's why I can't help liking old Sunday. No, it's not an admiration of force, or any silly thing like that. There is a kind of gaiety in the thing, as if he were bursting with some good news. Haven't you sometimes felt it on a spring day? You know Nature plays tricks, but somehow that day proves they are good-natured tricks. I never read the Bible myself, but that part they laugh at is literal truth, "Why leap ye, ye high hills?" The hills do leap—at least, they try to. . . . why do I like Sunday? . . . how can I tell you? . . . because he's such a Bounder.'

There was a long silence, and then the Secretary said in a curious, strained voice:

'You do not know Sunday at all. Perhaps it is because you are better than I, and do not know hell. I was a fierce fellow, and a trifle morbid from the first. The man who sits in darkness, and who chose us all, chose me because I had all the crazy look of a conspirator—because my smile went crooked, and my eyes were gloomy, even when I smiled. But there must have been something in me that answered to the nerves in all these anarchic men. For when I first saw Sunday he expressed to me, not your airy vitality, but something both gross and sad in the Nature of Things. I found him smoking in a twilight room, a room with brown blind down, infinitely more depressing than the genial darkness in which our master lives. He sat there on a bench, a huge heap of a man, dark and out of shape. He listened to all my words without speaking or even stirring. I poured out my most passionate appeals, and asked my most eloquent questions. Then, after a long silence, the Thing began to shake, and I thought it was shaken by some secret malady. It shook like a loathsome and living jelly. It reminded me of everything I had ever read about the base bodies that are the origin of life—the deep sea lumps and protoplasm. It seemed like the final form of matter, the most shapeless and the most shameful. I could only tell myself, from its shudderings, that it was something at least that such a monster could be miserable. And then it broke upon me that the bestial mountain was shaking with a lonely laughter, and the laughter was at me. Do you ask me to forgive him that? It is no small thing to be laughed at by something at once lower and stronger than oneself.'

'Surely you fellows are exaggerating wildly,' cut in the clear voice of Inspector Ratcliffe. 'President Sunday is a terrible fellow for one's intellect, but he is not such a Barnum's freak physically as you make out. He received me in an ordinary office, in a grey check coat, in broad daylight. He talked to me in an ordinary way. But I'll tell you what is a trifle creepy about Sunday. His room is neat, his clothes are neat, everything seems in order; but he's absent-minded. Sometimes his great bright eyes go quite blind. For hours he forgets that you are there. Now absentmindedness is just a bit too awful in a bad man. We think of a wicked man as vigilant. We can't think of a wicked man who is honestly and sincerely dreamy, because we daren't think of a wicked man alone with himself. An absent-minded man means a good-natured man. It means a man who, if he happens to see you, will apologize. But how will you bear an absent-minded man who, if he happens to see you, will kill you? That is what tries the nerves, abstraction combined with cruelty. Men have felt it sometimes when they went through wild forests, and felt that the animals there were at once innocent and pitiless. They might ignore or slay. How would you like to pass ten mortal hours in a parlour with an absent-minded tiger?'

'And what do you think of Sunday, Gogol?' asked Syme.

'I don't think of Sunday on principle,' said Gogol simply, 'any more than I stare at the sun at noonday.'

'Well, that is a point of view,' said Syme thoughtfully. 'What do you say, Professor?'

The Professor was walking with bent head and trailing stick, and he did not answer at all.

'Wake up, Professor!' said Syme genially. 'Tell us what you think of Sunday.'

The Professor spoke at last very slowly.

'I think something,' he said, 'that I cannot say clearly. Or, rather, I think something that I cannot even think clearly. But it is something like this. My early life, as you know, was a bit too large and loose. Well, when I saw Sunday's face I thought it was too large —everybody does, but I also thought it was too loose. The face was so big, that one couldn't focus it or make it a face at all. The eye was so far away from the nose, that it wasn't an eye. The mouth was so much by itself, that one had to think of it by itself. The whole thing is too hard to explain.'

He paused for a little, still trailing his stick, and then went on:

'But put it this way. Walking up a road at night, I have seen a lamp and a lighted window and a cloud make together a most complete and unmistakable face. If any one in heaven has that face I shall know him again. Yet when I walked a little farther I found that there was no face, that the window was ten yards away, the lamp ten hundred yards, and the cloud beyond the world. Well, Sunday's face escaped me; it ran away to right and left, as such chance pictures run away. And so his face has made me, somehow, doubt whether there are any faces. I don't know whether your face, Bull, is a face or a combination in perspective. Perhaps one black disk of your beastly glasses is quite close and another fifty miles away. Oh, the doubts of a materialist are not worth a dump. Sunday has taught me the last and the worst doubts, the doubts of a spiritualist. I am a Buddhist, I suppose; and Buddhism is not a creed, it is a doubt. My poor dear Bull, I do not believe that you really have a face. I have not faith enough to believe in matter.'

Syme's eyes were still fixed upon the errant orb, which, reddened in the evening light, looked like some rosier and more innocent world.

'Have you noticed an odd thing,' he said, 'about all your descriptions? Each man of you finds Sunday quite different, yet each man of you can only find one thing to compare him to—the universe itself. Bull finds him like the earth in spring, Gogol like the sun at noonday. The Secretary is reminded of the shapeless protoplasm, and the Inspector of the carelessness of virgin forests. The Professor says he is like a changing landscape. This is queer, but it is queerer still that I also have had my odd notion about the President, and I also find that I think of Sunday as I think of the whole world.'

'Get on a little faster, Syme,' said Bull; 'never mind the balloon.'

'When I first saw Sunday,' said Syme slowly, 'I only saw his back; and when I saw his back, I knew he was the worst man in the world. His neck and shoulders were brutal, like those of some apish god. His head had a stoop that was hardly human, like the stoop of an ox. In fact, I had at once the revolting fancy that this was not a man at all, but a beast dressed up in men's clothes.'

'Get on,' said Dr. Bull.

'And then the queer thing happened. I had seen his back from the street, as he sat in the balcony. Then I entered the hotel, and coming round the other side of him, saw his face in the sunlight. His face frightened me, as it did every one; but not because it was brutal, not because it was evil. On the contrary, it frightened me because it was so beautiful, because it was so good.'

'Syme,' exclaimed the Secretary, 'are you ill?'

'It was like the face of some ancient archangel, judging justly after heroic wars. There was laughter in the eyes, and in the mouth honour and sorrow. There was the same white hair, the same great, grey-clad shoulders that I had seen from behind. But when I saw him from behind I was certain he was an animal, and when I saw him in front I knew he was a god.'

'Pan,' said the Professor dreamily, 'was a god and an animal.'

'Then, and again and always,' went on Syme like a man talking to himself, 'that has been for me the mystery of Sunday, and it is also the mystery of the world. When I see the horrible back, I am sure the noble face is but a mask. When I see the face but for an instant, I know the back is only a jest. Bad is so bad, that we cannot but think good an accident; good is so good, that we feel certain that evil could be explained. But the whole came to a kind of crest yesterday when I raced Sunday for the cab, and was just behind him all the way.'

'Had you time for thinking then?' asked Ratcliffe.

'Time,' replied Syme, 'for one outrageous thought. I was suddenly possessed with the idea that the blind, blank back of his head really was his face—an awful, eyeless face staring at me! And I fancied that the figure running in front of me was really a figure running backwards, and dancing as he ran.'

'Horrible!' said Dr. Bull, and shuddered.

'Horrible is not the word,' said Syme. 'It was exactly the worst instant of my life. And yet ten minutes afterwards, when he put his head out of the cab and made a grimace like a gargoyle, I knew that he was only like a father playing hide-and-seek with his children.'

'It is a long game,' said the Secretary, and frowned at his broken boots.

'Listen to me,' cried Syme with extraordinary emphasis. 'Shall I tell you the secret of the whole world? It is that we have only known the back of the world. We see everything from behind, and it looks brutal. That is not a tree, but the back of a tree. That is not a cloud, but the back of a cloud. Cannot you see that everything is stooping and hiding a face? If we could only get round in front—'

'Look!' cried out Bull clamorously, 'the balloon is coming down!'

There was no need to cry out to Syme, who had never taken his eyes off it. He saw the great luminous globe suddenly stagger in the sky, right itself, and then sink slowly behind the trees like a setting sun.

The man called Gogol, who had hardly spoken through all their weary travels, suddenly threw up his hands like a lost spirit.

'He is dead!' he cried. 'And now I know he was my friend—my friend in the dark!'

'Dead!' snorted the Secretary. 'You will not find him dead easily. If he has been tipped out of the car, we shall find him rolling as a colt rolls in a field, kicking his legs for fun.'

'Clashing his hoofs,' said the Professor. 'The colts do, and so did Pan.'

'Pan again!' said Dr. Bull irritably. 'You seem to think Pan is everything.'

'So he is,' said the Professor, 'in Greek. He means everything.'

'Don't forget,' said the Secretary, looking down, 'that he also means Panic.'

Syme had stood without hearing any of the exclamations.

'It fell over there,' he said shortly. 'Let us follow it!'

Then he added with an indescribable gesture:

'Oh, if he has cheated us all by getting killed! It would be like one of his larks.'

He strode off towards the distant trees with a new energy, his rags and ribbons fluttering in the wind. The others followed him in a more footsore and dubious manner. And almost at the same moment all six men realized that they were not alone in the little field.

Across the square of turf a tall man was advancing towards them, leaning on a strange long staff like a sceptre. He was clad in a fine but old-fashioned suit with knee-breeches; its colour was that shade between blue, violet, and grey which can be seen in certain shadows of the woodland. His hair was whitish grey, and at the first glance, taken along with his knee-breeches, looked as if it was powdered. His advance was very quiet; but for the silver frost upon his head, he might have been one of the shadows of the wood.

'Gentlemen,' he said, 'my master has a carriage waiting for you in the road just by.'

'Who is your master?' asked Syme, standing quite still.

'I was told you knew his name,' said the man respectfully.

There was a silence, and then the Secretary said:

'Where is this carriage?'

'It has been waiting only a few moments,' said the stranger. 'My master has only just come home.'

Syme looked left and right upon the patch of green field in which he found himself. The hedges were ordinary hedges, the trees seemed ordinary trees; yet he felt like a man entrapped in fairy-land.

He looked the mysterious ambassador up and down, but he could discover nothing except that the man's coat was the exact colour of the purple shadows, and that the man's face was the exact colour of the red and brown and golden sky.

'Show us the place,' Syme said briefly, and without a word the man in the violet coat turned his back and walked towards a gap in the hedge, which let in suddenly the light of a white road.

As the six wanderers broke out upon this thoroughfare, they saw the white road blocked by what looked like a long row of carriages, such a row of carriages as might close the approach to some house in Park Lane. Along the side of these carriages stood a rank of splendid servants, all dressed in the grey-blue uniform, and all having a certain quality of stateliness and freedom which would not commonly belong to the servants of a gentleman, but rather to the officials and ambassadors of a great king. There were no less than six carriages waiting, one for each of the tattered and miserable band. All the attendants (as if in court-dress) wore swords, and as each man crawled into his carriage they drew them, and saluted with a sudden blaze of steel.

'What can it all mean?' asked Bull of Syme as they separated. 'Is this another joke of Sunday's?'

'I don't know,' said Syme as he sank wearily back in the cushions of his carriage; 'but if it is, it's one of the jokes you talk about. It's a good-natured one.'

The six adventurers had passed through many adventures, but not one had carried them so utterly off their feet as this last adventure of comfort. They had all become inured to things going roughly; but things suddenly going smoothly swamped them. They could not even feebly imagine what the carriages were; it was enough for them to know that they were carriages, and carriages with cushions. They could not conceive who the old man was who had led them; but it was quite enough that he had certainly led them to the carriages.

Syme drove through a drifting darkness of trees in utter abandonment. It was typical of him that while he had carried his bearded chin forward fiercely so long as anything could be done, when the whole business was taken out of his hands he fell back on the cushions in a frank collapse.

Very gradually and very vaguely he realized into what rich roads the carriage was carrying him. He saw that they passed the stone gates of what might have been a park, that they began gradually to climb a hill which, while wooded on both sides, was somewhat more orderly than a forest. Then there began to grow upon him, as upon a man slowly waking from a healthy sleep, a pleasure in everything. He felt that the hedges were what hedges should be, living walls; that a hedge is like a human army, disciplined, but all the more alive. He saw high elms behind the hedges, and vaguely thought how happy boys would be climbing there. Then his carriage took a turn of the path, and he saw suddenly and quietly, like a long, low, sunset cloud, a long, low house, mellow in the mild light of sunset. All the six friends compared notes afterwards and quarrelled; but they all agreed that in some unaccountable way the place reminded them of their boyhood. It was either this elm-top or that crooked path, it was either this scrap of orchard or that shape of a window; but each man of them declared that he could remember this place before he could remember his mother.

When the carriages eventually rolled up to a large, low, cavernous gateway, another man in the same uniform, but wearing a silver star on the grey breast of his coat, came out to meet them. This impressive person said to the bewildered Syme:

'Refreshments are provided for you in your room.'

Syme, under the influence of the same mesmeric sleep of amazement, went up the large oaken stairs after the respectful attendant. He entered a splendid suite of apartments that seemed to be designed specially for him. He walked up to a long mirror with the ordinary instinct of his class, to pull his tie straight or to smooth his hair; and there he saw the frightful figure that he was—blood running down his face from where the bough had struck him, his hair standing out like yellow rags of rank grass, his clothes torn into long, wavering tatters. At once the whole enigma sprang up, simply as the question of how he had got there, and how he was to get out again. Exactly at the same moment a man in blue, who had been appointed as his valet, said very solemnly:

'I have put out your clothes, sir.'

'Clothes!' said Syme sardonically. 'I have no clothes except these', and he lifted two long strips of his frock-coat in fascinating festoons, and made a movement as if to twirl like a ballet girl.

'My master asks me to say,' said the attendant, 'that there is a fancy dress ball to-night, and that he desires you to put on the costume that I have laid out. Meanwhile, sir, there is a bottle of Burgundy and some cold pheasant, which he hopes you will not refuse, as it is some hours before supper.'

'Cold pheasant is a good thing,' said Syme reflectively, 'and Burgundy is a spanking good thing. But really I do not want either of them so much as I want to know what the devil all this means, and what sort of costume you have got laid out for me. Where is it?'

The servant lifted off a kind of ottoman a long peacock-blue drapery, rather of the nature of a domino,[78] on the front of which was emblazoned a large golden sun, and which was splashed here and there with flaming stars and crescents.

'You're to be dressed as Thursday, sir,' said the valet somewhat affably.

'Dressed as Thursday!' said Syme in meditation. 'It doesn't sound a warm costume.'

'Oh, yes, sir,' said the other eagerly, 'the Thursday costume is quite warm, sir. It fastens up to the chin.'

'Well, I don't understand anything,' said Syme, sighing. 'I have been used so long to uncomfortable adventures that comfortable adventures knock me out. Still, I may be allowed to ask why I should be particularly like Thursday in a green frock spotted all over with the sun and moon. Those orbs, I think, shine on other days. I once saw the moon on Tuesday, I remember.'

'Beg pardon, sir,' said the valet, 'Bible also provided for you', and with a respectful and rigid finger he pointed out a passage in the first chapter of Genesis. Syme read it wondering. It was that in which the fourth day of the week is associated with the creation of the sun and moon. Here, however, they reckoned from a Christian Sunday.

'This is getting wilder and wilder,' said Syme as he sat down in a chair. 'Who are these people who provide cold pheasant and Burgundy, and green clothes and Bibles? Do they provide everything?'

[78] A domino is a long, loose, hooded robe often worn with a mask at carnivals.

'Yes, sir, everything,' said the attendant gravely. 'Shall I help you on with your costume?'

'Oh, hitch the bally thing on!' said Syme impatiently.

But though he affected to despise the mummery, he felt a curious freedom and naturalness in his movements as the blue and gold garment fell about him; and when he found that he had to wear a sword, it stirred a boyish dream. As he passed out of the room he flung the folds across his shoulder with a gesture, his sword stood out at an angle, and he had all the swagger of a troubadour. For these disguises did not disguise, but reveal.

XV

THE ACCUSER

As Syme strode along the corridor he saw the Secretary standing at the top of a great flight of stairs. The man had never looked so noble. He was draped in a long robe of starless black, down the centre of which fell a band or broad stripe of pure white, like a single shaft of light. The whole looked like some very severe ecclesiastical vestment. There was no need for Syme to search his memory or the Bible in order to remember that the first day of creation marked the mere creation of light out of darkness. The vestment itself would alone have suggested the symbol; and Syme felt also how perfectly this pattern of pure white and black expressed the soul of the pale and austere Secretary, with his inhuman veracity and his cold frenzy, which made him so easily make war on the anarchists, and yet so easily pass for one of them. Syme was scarcely surprised to notice that, amid all the ease and hospitality of their new surroundings, this man's eyes were still stern. No smell of ale or orchards could make the Secretary cease to ask a reasonable question.

If Syme had been able to see himself, he would have realized that he, too, seemed to be for the first time himself and no one else. For if the Secretary stood for that philosopher who loves the original and formless light, Syme was a type of the poet who seeks always to make the light in special shapes, to split it up into sun and star. The philosopher may sometimes love the infinite; the poet always loves the finite. For him the great moment is not the creation of light, but the creation of the sun and moon.

As they descended the broad stairs together they overtook Ratcliffe, who was clad in spring green like a huntsman, and the pattern upon whose garment was a green tangle of trees. For he stood for that third day on which the earth and green things were made, and his square, sensible face, with its not unfriendly cynicism, seemed appropriate enough to it.

They were led out of another broad and low gateway into a very

large old English garden, full of torches and bonfires, by the broken
light of which a vast carnival of people were dancing in motley
dress. Syme seemed to see every shape in Nature imitated in some
crazy costume. There was a man dressed as a windmill with enormous sails, a man dressed as an elephant, a man dressed as a balloon;
the two last, together, seemed to keep the thread of their farcical
adventures. Syme even saw, with a queer thrill, one dancer dressed
like an enormous hornbill, with a beak twice as big as himself—the
queer bird which had fixed itself on his fancy like a living question
while he was rushing down the long road at the Zoological Gardens.
There were a thousand other such objects, however. There was a
dancing lamp-post, a dancing apple-tree, a dancing ship. One would
have thought that the untamable tune of some mad musician had set
all the common objects of field and street dancing an eternal jig. And
long afterwards, when Syme was middle-aged and at rest, he could
never see one of those particular objects—a lamp-post, or an apple-
tree, or a windmill—without thinking that it was a strayed reveller
from that revel of masquerade.

On one side of this lawn, alive with dancers, was a sort of green
bank, like the terrace in such old-fashioned gardens.

Along this, in a kind of crescent, stood seven great chairs, the
thrones of the seven days. Gogol and Dr. Bull were already in their
seats; the Professor was just mounting to his. Gogol, or Tuesday,
had his simplicity well symbolized by a dress designed upon the division of the waters, a dress that separated upon his forehead and fell
to his feet, grey and silver, like a sheet of rain. The Professor, whose
day was that on which the birds and fishes—the ruder forms of
life—were created, had a dress of dim purple, over which sprawled
goggle-eyed fishes and outrageous tropical birds, the union in him
of unfathomable fancy and of doubt. Dr. Bull, the last day of Creation, wore a coat covered with heraldic animals in red and gold, and
on his crest a man rampant. He lay back in his chair with a broad
smile, the picture of an optimist in his element.

One by one the wanderers ascended the bank and sat in their
strange seats. As each of them sat down a roar of enthusiasm rose
from the carnival, such as that with which crowds receive kings.

Cups were clashed and torches shaken, and feathered hats flung in the air. The men for whom these thrones were reserved were men crowned with some extraordinary laurels. But the central chair was empty.

Syme was on the left hand of it and the Secretary on the right. The Secretary looked across the empty throne at Syme, and said, compressing his lips:

'We do not know yet that he is not dead in a field.'

Almost as Syme heard the words, he saw on the sea of human faces in front of him a frightful and beautiful alteration, as if heaven had opened behind his head. But Sunday had only passed silently along the front like a shadow, and had sat in the central seat. He was draped plainly, in a pure and terrible white, and his hair was like a silver flame on his forehead.

For a long time—it seemed for hours—that huge masquerade of mankind swayed and stamped in front of them to marching and exultant music. Every couple dancing seemed a separate romance; it might be a fairy dancing with a pillar-box, or a peasant girl dancing with the moon; but in each case it was, somehow, as absurd as Alice in Wonderland, yet as grave and kind as a love-story. At last, however, the thick crowd began to thin itself. Couples strolled away into the garden-walks, or began to drift towards that end of the building where stood smoking, in huge pots like fish-kettles, some hot and scented mixtures of old ale or wine. Above all these, upon a sort of black framework on the roof of the house, roared in its iron basket a gigantic bonfire, which lit up the land for miles. It flung the homely effect of firelight over the face of vast forests of grey or brown, and it seemed to fill with warmth even the emptiness of upper night. Yet this also, after a time, was allowed to grow fainter; the dim groups gathered more and more round the great cauldrons, or passed, laughing and clattering, into the inner passages of that ancient house. Soon there were only some ten loiterers in the garden; soon only four. Finally the last stray merry-maker ran into the house whooping to his companions. The fire faded, and the slow, strong stars came out. And the seven strange men were left alone, like seven stone statues on their chairs of stone. Not one of them had spoken a word.

They seemed in no haste to do so, but heard in silence the hum of insects and the distant song of one bird. Then Sunday spoke, but so dreamily that he might have been continuing a conversation rather than beginning one.

'We will eat and drink later,' he said. 'Let us remain together a little, we who have loved each other so sadly, and have fought so long. I seem to remember only centuries of heroic war, in which you were always heroes—epic on epic, iliad on iliad, and you always brothers in arms. Whether it was but recently (for time is nothing), or at the beginning of the world, I sent you out to war. I sat in the darkness, where there is not any created thing, and to you I was only a voice commanding valour and an unnatural virtue. You heard the voice in the dark, and you never heard it again. The sun in heaven denied it, the earth and sky denied it, all human wisdom denied it. And when I met you in the daylight I denied it myself.'

Syme stirred sharply in his seat, but otherwise there was silence, and the incomprehensible went on.

'But you were men. You did not forget your secret honour, though the whole cosmos turned an engine of torture to tear it out of you. I knew how near you were to hell. I know how you, Thursday, crossed swords with King Satan, and how you, Wednesday, named me in the hour without hope.'

There was complete silence in the starlit garden, and then the black-browed Secretary, implacable, turned in his chair towards Sunday, and said in a harsh voice:

'Who and what are you?'

'I am the Sabbath,' said the other without moving. 'I am the peace of God.'

The Secretary started up, and stood crushing his costly robe in his hand.

'I know what you mean,' he cried, 'and it is exactly that that I cannot forgive you. I know you are contentment, optimism, what do they call the thing?—an ultimate reconciliation. Well, I am not reconciled. If you were the man in the dark room, why were you also Sunday, an offence to the sunlight? If you were from the first our father and our friend, why were you also our greatest enemy?

We wept, we fled in terror; the iron entered into our souls — and you are the peace of God! Oh, I can forgive God His anger, though it destroyed nations; but I cannot forgive Him His peace.'

Sunday answered not a word, but very slowly he turned his face of stone upon Syme as if asking a question.

'No,' said Syme, 'I do not feel fierce like that. I am grateful to you, not only for wine and hospitality here, but for many a fine scamper and free fight. But I should like to know. My soul and heart are as happy and quiet here as this old garden, but my reason is still crying out. I should like to know.'

Sunday looked at Ratcliffe, whose clear voice said:

'It seems so *silly* that you should have been on both sides and fought yourself.'

Bull said:

'I understand nothing, but I am happy. In fact, I am going to sleep.'

'I am not happy,' said the Professor with his head in his hands, 'because I do not understand. You let me stray a little too near to hell.'

And then Gogol said, with the absolute simplicity of a child:

'I wish I knew why I was hurt so much.'

Still Sunday said nothing, but only sat with his mighty chin upon his hand, and gazed at the distance. Then at last he said:

'I have heard your complaints, in order. And here I think, comes another to complain, and we will hear him also.'

The falling fire in the great cresset threw a last long gleam, like a bar of burning gold, across the dim grass. Against this fiery band were outlined in utter black the advancing legs of a black-clad figure. He seemed to have a fine close suit with knee-breeches such as that which was worn by the servants of the house, only that it was not blue, but of this absolute sable. He had, like the servants, a kind of sword by his side. It was only when he had come quite close to the crescent of the seven and flung up his face to look at them, that Syme saw, with thunder-struck clearness, that the face was the broad, almost ape-like face of his old friend Gregory, with its rank red hair and its insulting smile.

'Gregory!' gasped Syme, half-rising from his seat. 'Why, this is the real anarchist.'

'Yes,' said Gregory, with a great and dangerous restraint, 'I am the real anarchist.'

' "Now there was a day," ' murmured Bull, who seemed really to have fallen asleep, ' "when the sons of God came to present themselves before the Lord, and Satan came also among them." '

'You are right,' said Gregory, and gazed all round. 'I am a destroyer. I would destroy the world if I could.'

A sense of a pathos far under the earth stirred up in Syme, and he spoke brokenly and without sequence.

'Oh, most unhappy man,' he cried, 'try to be happy! You have red hair like your sister.'

'My red hair, like red flames, shall burn up the world,' said Gregory. 'I thought I hated everything more than common men can hate anything; but I find that I do not hate everything so much as I hate you!'

'I never hated you,' said Syme very sadly.

Then out of this unintelligible creature the last thunders broke.

'You!' he cried. 'You never hated because you never lived. I know what you are all of you, from first to last—you are the people in power! You are the police—the great fat, smiling men in blue and buttons! You are the Law, and you have never been broken. But is there a free soul alive that does not long to break you, only because you have never been broken? We in revolt talk all kind of nonsense doubtless about this crime or that crime of the Government. It is all folly! The only crime of the Government is that it governs. The unpardonable sin of the supreme power is that it is supreme. I do not curse you for being cruel. I do not curse you (though I might) for being kind. I curse you for being safe! You sit in your chairs of stone, and have never come down from them. You are the seven angels of heaven, and you have had no troubles. Oh, I could forgive you everything, you that rule all mankind, if I could feel for once that you had suffered for one hour a real agony such as I——'

Syme sprang to his feet, shaking from head to foot.

'I see everything,' he cried, 'everything that there is. Why does each thing on the earth war against each other thing? Why does each small thing in the world have to fight against the world itself?

Why does a fly have to fight the whole universe? Why does a dandelion have to fight the whole universe? For the same reason that I had to be alone in the dreadful Council of the Days. So that each thing that obeys law may have the glory and isolation of the anarchist. So that each man fighting for order may be as brave and good a man as the dynamiter. So that the real lie of Satan may be flung back in the face of this blasphemer, so that by tears and torture we may earn the right to say to this man, "You lie!" No agonies can be too great to buy the right to say to this accuser, "We also have suffered."

'It is not true that we have never been broken. We have been broken upon the wheel. It is not true that we have never descended from these thrones. We have decended into hell. We were complaining of unforgettable miseries even at the very moment when this man entered insolently to accuse us of happiness. I repel the slander; we have not been happy. I can answer for every one of the great guards of Law whom he has accused. At least——'

He had turned his eyes so as to see suddenly the great face of Sunday, which wore a strange smile.

'Have you,' he cried in a dreadful voice, 'have you ever suffered?'

As he gazed, the great face grew to an awful size, grew larger than the colossal mask of Memnon, which had made him scream as a child. It grew larger and larger, filling the whole sky; then everything went black. Only in the blackness before it entirely destroyed his brain he seemed to hear a distant voice saying a commonplace text that he had heard somewhere, 'Can ye drink of the cup that I drink of?'

*　　*　　*

When men in books awake from a vision, they commonly find themselves in some place in which they might have fallen asleep; they yawn in a chair, or lift themselves with bruised limbs from a field. Syme's experience was something much more psychologically strange if there was indeed anything unreal, in the earthly sense, about the things he had gone through. For while he could always remember afterwards that he had swooned before the face of Sunday, he could not remember having ever come to at all. He could only remember that gradually and naturally he knew that he was and had been walking along a country lane with an easy and conversational companion. That companion had been a part of his recent drama; it was the red-haired poet Gregory. They were walking like old friends, and were in the middle of a conversation about some triviality. But Syme could only feel an unnatural buoyancy in his body and a crystal simplicity in his mind that seemed to be superior to everything that he said or did. He felt he was in possession of some impossible good news, which made every other thing a triviality, but an adorable triviality.

Dawn was breaking over everything in colours at once clear and timid; as if Nature made a first attempt at yellow and a first attempt at rose. A breeze blew so clean and sweet, that one could not think that it blew from the sky; it blew rather through some hole in the sky. Syme felt a simple surprise when he saw rising all round him on both sides of the road the red, irregular buildings of Saffron Park. He had no idea that he had walked so near London. He walked by instinct along one white road, on which early birds hopped and sang, and found himself outside a fenced garden. There he saw the sister of Gregory, the girl with the gold-red hair, cutting lilac before breakfast, with the great unconscious gravity of a girl.

The text of this book has been set in Bembo by the Neumann Press of Long Prairie, Minnesota. Printed on Sebago paper by Thomson Shore, Dexter, Michigan. Bound in Kennet cloth by John H. Dekker & Sons. Cover and jacket design by Darlene Lawless O'Rourke.